Life

ITS FORMS AND CHANGES

Second Edition

Concepts in Science

Life
ITS FORMS AND CHANGES

Second Edition

Paul F. Brandwein
Robert Stollberg
Arthur W. Greenstone
Warren E. Yasso
Daniel J. Brovey

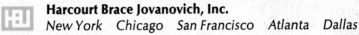

Harcourt Brace Jovanovich, Inc.
New York   Chicago   San Francisco   Atlanta   Dallas

THE AUTHORS

Paul F. Brandwein, Adjunct Professor, Conservation and Education, University of Pittsburgh; President, Center for the Study of Instruction; Director, School Department, Harcourt Brace Jovanovich, Inc.; formerly Director, The Pinchot Institute for Conservation Studies, Milford, Pennsylvania; formerly chairman of department and teacher, now consultant to elementary, junior, and senior high schools.

Robert Stollberg, Professor of Physical Science, San Francisco State College, San Francisco, California; past-President, National Science Teachers Association; formerly Science Teaching Consultant in California and Pacific Coast states, India, and Africa.

Arthur W. Greenstone, formerly Chairman, Physical Science Department, Bayside High School, New York, New York.

Warren E. Yasso, Associate Professor of Science Education, Teachers College, Columbia University, New York, N. Y.; formerly Assistant Professor, Department of Geology, Virginia Polytechnic Institute, Blacksburg, Virginia.

Daniel J. Brovey, Assistant Professor of Education, Queens College, City University of New York, New York, New York.

WITH THE ASSISTANCE OF

Albert Gordon, Professor of Biology, Graduate School of Arts and Science, New York University, New York, New York.

Hy Ruchlis, designer, Laboratory Experiences; Adjunct Professor, Fairleigh Dickinson University, Rutherford, New Jersey.

Acknowledgments: For permission to reprint copyrighted material, acknowledgment is made to the following:

The quotation appearing on page 158 is taken from "Miss T" from *Peacock Pie* by Walter de la Mare. Reprinted by permission of the Literary Trustees of Walter de la Mare and The Society of Authors as their representative.

Academic Press: from *Atlas of Bacterial Flagellation* by Einar Leifson, © 1960 by Academic Press.

Cornell University Press: from *Ancient Plants and the World They Lived In* by Henry N. Andrews, Jr., copyright 1947 by Comstock Publishing Company, Inc. Used by permission of Cornell University Press.

Dodd, Mead & Co.: from *Biology in Action* by N. J. Berrill, © 1966 by Dodd, Mead & Co., reprinted by permission of Mr. W. Gordon Whaley.

Harcourt Brace Jovanovich, Inc.: for Body Charts, pp. 103, 106, 108, 111, 115, 117, 124, 125, 195, reproduced from *Your Biology,* Second Edition, by Smith and Lisonbee, research and copyright © 1957 by Harcourt Brace Jovanovich, Inc. Drawn by Caru Studios, N. Y.

Harper & Row, Inc.: from *Bacteriology* by Einar Leifson, © 1942 by Hoeber Medical Division, Harper & Row, Publishers, Incorporated; from *Atlas of Descriptive Histology* by Edward J. Reith and Michael H. Ross, © 1965 by Hoeber Medical Division, Harper & Row, Publishers, Incorporated.

J. B. Lippincott Company: from *Histology* by Ham and Leeson, © 1965 by J. B. Lippincott Company.

Ella Thea Smith: for Frog Charts, pp. 98, 101, 102, from "The Leopard Frog," © 1959, 1960, by Harcourt Brace Jovanovich, Inc.; for Corn Chart, p. 151, from "Seed Plants," © 1959 by Harcourt Brace Jovanovich, Inc.; reproduced from *Exploring Biology,* Sixth Edition by Ella Thea Smith, by permission of the author.

Cover Photograph: Harbrace by Jim Theologos.

Copyright © 1972, 1968 by Harcourt Brace Jovanovich, Inc.

PRINTED IN THE UNITED STATES OF AMERICA

ISBN 0-15-366330-8

CONTENTS

UNIT ONE

UNIT FOUR

UNIT FIVE

UNIT SIX

UNIT SEVEN

Introduction

You are alive; and, of course, that is of great importance. It seems as if everything that makes up the life around us moves, feeds, breathes, and grows, among other things. There are elephants, cows, oaks, bread mold, fish, penguins, bacteria — all alive. Is there anything about living things that makes an elephant and an oak like each other and like a tiny, invisible bacterium? Are there, in short, any hidden likenesses we cannot see or touch?

To be alive — this is of tremendous importance. But *no* living thing can remain alive unless it has an *environment* in which it can live. A fish dies on land. An eagle dies in water. In studying living things, we study them in their environment. Destroy the environment, and the living things in it die.

You — as you study living things — have the privilege of using two powerful tools. The first of these is *verified and organized knowledge.* This is reliable knowledge. The second of these tools is a way of acquiring, verifying, and organizing *new knowledge.* Therefore we have a way of adding to the knowledge of the world in which we live. As you shall see, neither is more important than the other.

There is a great meaning behind the phrase *verified and organized knowledge*; it is also *cumulative knowledge.* When Newton, the great English scientist, said "I stood on the shoulders of giants," he meant that he could go further in his work because of the verified knowledge gathered by others. He could, in short, rely on that knowledge.

We know more today about forces than did Newton or Galileo, more about heat than Boyle, more about inheritance than Mendel, more about the nature of disease than Pasteur, and more about the atom than John Dalton. Why?

Each scientist depends upon the accuracy of the work of those who went before him; he does indeed "stand on the shoulders" of others. In other words, scientific work is cumulative; it builds one discovery on another and another. For example, in the field of biology, men first thought diseases were caused by evil spirits, then by

bad air (malaria means "bad air"). Then Pasteur and Koch discovered that germs cause disease. These scientists, of course, had the work of others who went before them to build upon.

In building upon others' work, scientists use certain processes of investigation which a great scientist, the physicist Percy Bridgman, called "the methods of intelligence." These methods include reading what other scientists have done, accurate observation, careful design of an investigation (including an experiment), developing theories, and the like. This book will give you a great number of opportunities to use the processes of the scientist in your own investigating.

As well as an opportunity to investigate, this book also brings you *some* of the cumulative work of scientists who have investigated the vast field of life. Notice we say "some." It would, of course, be impossible, and not necessary at this point in your studies, to try to bring you all the knowledge accumulated over the centuries. Ninety percent of all scientists who have ever lived are alive and at work today; every hour they produce enough knowledge to fill a book the size of a volume in an encyclopedia.

Thus we have selected highlights from this great collection of knowledge, and we have organized the knowledge in such a way that it falls into patterns. There are such patterns of knowledge—or *concepts,* as we shall call them. Let's illustrate how the organization of knowledge into concepts can be of use to you.

Examine the structure shown above. ❶ Does it belong to a fish? a reptile? You would say, "Obviously it belongs to a bird." From one simple structure, a feather, you can construct an image in your mind of an entire animal. Thus, we would say you have a concept of "birdness." Furthermore, possession of the concept of a bird enables you to recognize as a bird any of the millions of animals with feathers.

Look at the photograph of the object above. ❶ Surely you recognize it as a leaf. What image does this bring to your mind? Certainly a plant of some kind—perhaps a tree or a bush. In any event, you have a concept of "plantness"; you recognize any object with leaves as being a plant.

A book organized around concepts, therefore, is able to organize a great deal of knowledge simply and effectively. This is exactly what we have done in this book. Because the book is organized around concepts, you will find it easier to organize your own work and learning.

Science, however, is not learned only through reading; concepts are attained, after all, through experience, through investigation, through constant exploration. The scientist has indeed developed an art of investigation that enables him to add to knowledge. And so, even as you begin to make your own concepts of science, you begin to inquire into the ways the living world works.

Life
ITS FORMS AND CHANGES
Second Edition

LIVING THINGS IN THEIR ENVIRONMENT

A Study in Interdependence

Compare the environments of the two sets of animals.

Here is a hummingbird feeding its young. Who built the nest? Who gathers the food? Who protects the group?

Here is a man feeding his cattle. Who gathers the food? Who protects the cattle?

What is the difference in the two environments?

Fresh-Water Communities

1. LIFE IN A POND

What is the meaning of the *green* you see on the surface of this pond? ❶ Of course you know that the green is due to green plants. But do you know that you would not be alive if green plants disappeared from this earth? What is your explanation for your dependence on green plants? Let us probe this question further.

"Producers" in a Pond

If you examined some of the greenish water under a microscope, you would find it full of floating, tiny green plants. These green plants,

called algae (al′jē), are of many shapes and sizes. However, all are greenish and all are manufacturing food.

Let's get acquainted with some common algae. For a start, you might investigate the green film that grows on the sides of an aquarium. Suppose you scrape some of this material into a drop of aquarium water and examine it under a microscope. What you see may resemble some of the plants pictured on pages 5 and 6. (If you have not had experience using a microscope, you will probably want to study the special section **The Microscope: An Aid to Observation** on pages 533–38.)

Several kinds of small green plants may be present in your aquarium water, but a wider variety of microscopic and small plants can be found in ponds, gently running streams, outdoor fish pools, and other damp or wet places. If it is possible to collect these plants, bring them into the schoolroom in glass jars and examine them under the microscope. The photographs here and on the following page illustrate some of the smaller plants you are likely to find. These photomicrographs, photographs taken through a microscope, will help you in identifying some of these plants.

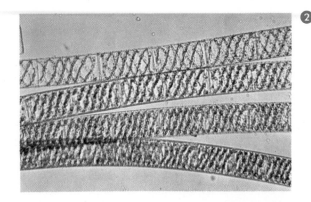

❷ Pondscum [*Spirogyra* (spī′rə·jī′rə)] is usually bright green and is slippery to touch. It forms long strings in the water, and its floating masses sometimes almost cover ponds. Notice the green spiral band within each cell. Notice, too, that the cells of *Spirogyra* are shaped like cylinders that are joined to each other end to end to make up the long strings.

❸ Stonewort [*Chara* (ka′rə)] is branched and has needlelike branches arranged in whorls spaced along the main stem. Stiff and limy, these plants grow only in ponds with a large amount of dissolved limestone in the water.

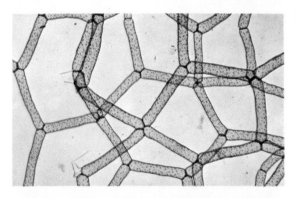

❹ Water net [*Hydrodictyon* (hī′drə·dik′tē·ən)] forms green nets that float in sunny, still ponds. Notice how the long cells of *Hydrodictyon* join together to form meshes in the net. Each of these cells appears to be tubelike in shape.

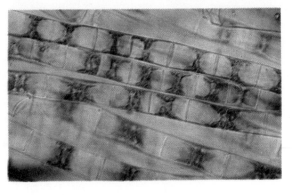

❺ *Ulothrix* (yo͞ol′ə·thriks), like *Spirogyra*, forms unbranched strings of green cells. It often forms a green, fuzzy covering on rocks and sticks in pond water. The cells of *Ulothrix* are short and somewhat like cubes with rounded corners. They contain beltlike, green

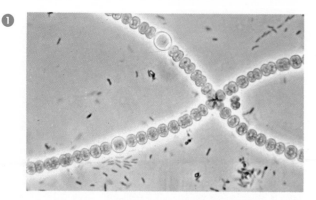

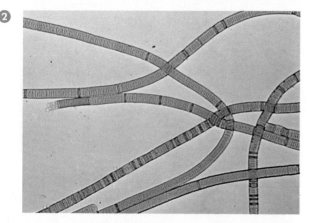

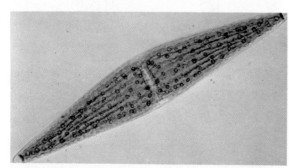

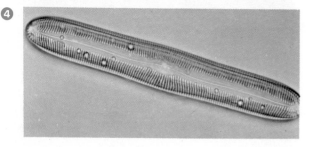

structures, giving a banded appearance to each strand.

Ulothrix forms long strings somewhat like those of *Spirogyra*. But as you examine these two algae, you will notice at least one striking difference between them. What is it?

❶ *Nostoc* (nos′tok) forms a slippery mass on ponds, rocks, and sticks. Some forms float in the water and look like muddy masses of jelly. Under the microscope, *Nostoc* looks like necklaces of round beads. Each "bead" is actually a cell that appears green in color. The cells, which remain attached, are surrounded by a slippery jelly.

❷ *Oscillatoria* (os′ə·lə·tō′rēə) forms blue-green strings that move (oscillate) slowly back and forth in shallow water. Each string is composed of many disk-shaped cells attached end to end.

❸ Desmids (des′midz) are beautifully formed green cells found in many shapes and patterns. They are sometimes boat-shaped, crescent-shaped, or cross-shaped. Many of the little plants are covered with spines, knobs, grooves, or markings of various kinds. Desmids are pinched-in (constricted) in the middle so that each one appears to be composed of two identical half-cells.

❹ Diatoms (dī′ə·tomz) are usually a beautiful golden color and have intricate designs on their cell walls. They are often found clustered on leaves lying in stagnant pools. They add a golden color to the leaves. Like the desmids, the diatoms come in a great variety of shapes and designs, only one of which is shown here. The glassy walls of diatoms consist of two overlapping halves that fit together somewhat like a box and its cover. How are diatoms different from all the other algae pictured here?

All these tiny plants are sometimes called the "grass" of the water. Grasses on the land are a basic food for many kinds of animals. These tiny algae are the basic food for many kinds of animal life in a pond. So we say they are the basic food producers in water, just as land grasses are the basic food producers on land.

There are other pond plants, of course. The bottoms and sides of the pond may be covered with other, large green plants. If the water is clear enough for you to see the bottom, you may watch these long strands weaving back and forth with, perhaps, a tiny fish or two swimming just above them.

Several kinds of water weeds may be found rooted in the mud or sand two to five feet under the surface of the water. *Elodea* (elō·dē′ə) and *Vallisneria* (val′is·nē′rēə), common water weeds, are good examples. Some of these water plants grow entirely under the water, while others have leaves that float on the surface, such as this water lily.  Fish and other aquatic animals find shelter among such plants. Ducks like to eat

the roots and fruits that some of these plants produce. ❻

At the edges of the pond a variety of plants may grow partially in the water, with their stems and leaves rising above the water surface. Swamp potato plants, cattails, and rushes are common examples of plants growing along the water's edge.

The leaves of these and almost all other plants are the factories for making food. Examine some of them for yourself. ■ Turn the page to see the meaning of this black square.

■ A Note on the Art of Investigation

One learns to investigate by investigating, just as one learns to paint by painting, or to do anything by doing it. Of course, learning certain aspects of the art of investigation may be made easier by instruction. The goal is to make it possible for you to do simple investigations, then more difficult ones, with the objective of enabling you to investigate on your own.

The investigations that you will have the opportunity to do will be of three kinds.

a. The first kind, which we will call **An Apprentice Investigation** will be found throughout the book. The symbol ■ indicates that you should go to the investigation before reading on. Here you will have the opportunity to engage in gathering specimens, studying structures and functions, and performing simple tests designed to illustrate these functions. These investigations are illustrated with photographs and drawings so that you may see how the investigations are done, even as you do them. You will find an example of this kind of investigation on page 9.

b. Having "seen," by means of the Apprentice Investigation, how an investigation may be done, you are then given an opportunity to do **An Investigation On Your Own.** A question may be asked, and few directions (if any) are given. The solution to the on-your-own problem is generally not to be found in this book. It is an invitation to investigate in your own way, perhaps in the classroom laboratory or at home. You will find the on-your-own investigations appearing at the end of the Apprentice Investigations.

c. A third kind of investigation appears in the last section of each chapter, the section entitled Relating the Concepts, under the heading Extending the Concepts. These are research investigations. Some may be completed within a hour or so. Some may take weeks or even months to complete. Again, you are on your own. Your ability to complete the investigation depends somewhat upon your understanding of the methods and processes of investigating used in the Apprentice Investigations. You will find an example of this kind of investigation on page 23.

Throughout you will find an enormous number of observations that will interest you. Some of them will surely arouse your curiosity. No doubt you will want to probe further on your own.

■ AN APPRENTICE INVESTIGATION into Making a Blueprint of Water-Plant Leaves

Did you ever make a blueprint? Blueprints are commonly used for building plans, but you can use them to make "shadow" prints of leaves or parts of plants. You will need two pieces of glass about 4 inches square, a sheet of blueprint paper (from an artist's supply store or stationery store), and a water plant.

First, place a water-plant leaf on a paper towel to remove the water. Then darken the room as much as possible and place a piece of blueprint paper about 4 inches square on one piece of glass. (Be sure the chemically treated side of the paper is turned *away* from the glass.) Now lay the water-plant leaf on the blueprint paper and place the second piece of glass over it. ❶ Hold this "glass sandwich" firmly with your fingers in direct sunlight or close to an electric light for one or two minutes. You can try different lengths of time to find the best exposure.

Remove the blueprint paper and rinse it thoroughly in a pan of water for several minutes. ❷ Now observe your blueprint. ❸ It can

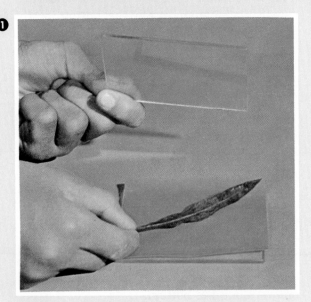

be dried by placing it between layers of newspaper for several hours with a heavy book placed on top to keep it from curling up while drying.

You may wish to make a collection of blueprints of leaves of water plants. If you do, label each blueprint, giving the name of the plant and where you collected it. Later on, while you are studying other kinds of plants, you may want to add other leaf prints to your collection.

An Investigation On Your Own

What are some differences between the leaves of grasses and the leaves of shrubs? Compare their blueprints. What are your observations? From an analysis of your observations, can you make a statement about the differences that is generally true?

"Consumers" in a Pond

When you think of animal life in a pond, you probably think of large animals such as fish, frogs, and turtles. All of these are probably there, but there may be hundreds of other different kinds of animals as well. Depending upon the part of the country you live in, you may find muskrat, beaver, marten, otter, and mink. Since these animals breathe with lungs, they must hold their breath when they swim under the water, just as you must. Marten, otter, and mink feed chiefly on fish. Muskrat and beaver eat parts of plants, mainly bark and tender plant shoots. Muskrats may also eat small water animals.

Ducks and herons feed at the water's edge, the ducks on plant material and the herons on fish, frogs, and other animals. Other birds, such as the redwing blackbird, live near the water but do not feed on its plant life.

Several kinds of reptiles, turtles for example, live in ponds. Some turtles eat pond plants; some eat pond animals such as fish, frogs, and insects. There may also be water snakes, which eat fish and frogs.

Of course, frogs, toads, and salamanders live in ponds. These animals lay their eggs in the water. The eggs hatch into tadpoles (in the case of frogs and toads) or into tiny salamanders, both of which breathe through gills like a fish. They finally change into adults with lungs. As adults, they feed on insects and other small animals.

Then, of course, there are the fish. Large fish, such as pike and the bass pictured above move around hunting other fish to eat. ❶ These predatory fish also eat frogs and other small water animals. On the bottom of the pond may be catfish and carp. They like to eat dead and decaying animals that sink to the bottom. Most of the smaller fish live in or near the weed beds where they are protected. Here they can get the food they prefer. Many smaller fish, such as pumpkinseed fish and crappies, eat water insects, worms, crayfish, and even small, young fish. The small, young fish are also eaten in large numbers by larger fish, snakes, frogs, and turtles.

You will, of course, find still other kinds of animals. Water snails live on the water plants and scrape off pieces of plants with their file-like tongues. Mussels may be found in the mud. Different kinds of worms and insects move along the bottom.

Many kinds of insects live in the water their entire lives. Others spend only their early stages in the water, such as the nymph of the dragonfly. Water bugs and beetles, such as these whirligig beetles, may be found in the water. But the most numerous forms of insect life you are likely to find are the **larvae** [(lär′vē); singular, *larva*] of insects such as mosquitoes, May flies, dragonflies, midgets, and caddis flies. Here are some mosquito larvae. The word *larva* is the name given to the young, immature form of some insects. (For example, the larva of a butterfly is a caterpillar.) The aquatic larvae eat a variety of tiny water plants and animals. The mosquito larvae live on algae and tiny water animals such as water fleas and fairy shrimps.

Water fleas, fairy shrimps, and cyclops are all small animals that are related to crayfish and lobsters. They live on plant life in the water and, in turn, serve as food for insect larvae and other very small animals in the water, especially tiny, young fish.

Other small animals found in ponds include the hydra (related to the jellyfish of the ocean waters), the fresh-water sponge, the crayfish, and different kinds of leeches.

Finally, any pond is likely to have billions upon billions of single-celled organisms—organisms composed of but a single cell. You have already seen some of the single-celled plant organisms.

These, then, are the kinds of plants and animals commonly found in fresh-water ponds. They all affect each other and are affected by each other. They form what we call a *community*. A community of living things is interdependent. That is, one living thing depends upon the others in the community. Why not study an interdependent living community in your own home—a homemade "pond" for example. It will have to be a micropond, of course. ∎

■ AN APPRENTICE INVESTIGATION into Making a Micropond

It is not difficult to make a micropond or an aquarium. The aquarium shown here contains several kinds of water plants, some tropical fish, and a snail. ❶ Pond snails, pond or stream minnows (*minnows* refers to the young of several varieties of fish), and small sunfish can be used.

Be sure to have at least a gallon of water to each inch of fish size. For example, a five-gallon tank should not have more than two fish, each about 2½ inches long, or five fish, each about 1 inch long.

You should have plenty of water plants already established in the aquarium before you add the animals. You can either buy the plants or you can use water plants that you have collected yourself, such as *Elodea*.

An Investigation On Your Own

You can make a very useful study of the community in your micropond. For instance, which algae do you find? Select *one* for your study. How long does it remain? Does it increase in population? If it does not increase in number, why not?

Perhaps you can develop a hypothesis on the nature of the rise and fall of the algae in your micropond. Do you have enough evidence to support your hypothesis?

REVIEW

1. Why do biologists speak of the plants and animals that live in a pond as forming a "pond community"?

2. Is there any relationship between mosquito larvae living in a pond and the algae living there? What evidence do you have for your statement?

3. Is there any relationship between mosquito larvae in a pond and small fish that live there?

4. Is there any relationship between small fish in a pond and herons? Explain your answer.

5. Is there any relationship between a heron and the algae in a pond? (Keep in mind that herons do not eat algae.) Explain your answer.

6. In the pond community, what roles do the larger plants such as water lilies, swamp potatoes, and cattails play?

NEW VIEW

1. Is there any relationship between the energy that you get from food and the energy from sunlight locked up by the algae in manufacturing their food? Explain your answer.

2. Why is it that the glass walls of an aquarium will sometimes become covered with green algae if the aquarium is in direct sunlight? What has the sunlight to do with it?

3. A properly stocked aquarium, with a proper balance of fish and plants, will last indefinitely without much attention. What would happen if such an aquarium were placed in a dark closet? Explain your answer.

4. Would you expect the life in a swiftly flowing, cold mountain stream to be the same as that in a pond community? Why?

2. LIFE IN A SWIFTLY FLOWING STREAM

Mountain streams and ponds both contain fresh water, but that is about as far as the similarities go. If we compare them with land environments, a pond and a mountain stream are about as different as a forest is from a desert. Why is this so?

Pond water is warm for most of the year. A mountain stream is fed by melting snows and is usually ice cold. A pond is usually stagnant, that is, the water is not mixed and churned. Most ponds are fed new water only by creeks or by seepage of ground water from the surrounding land. A mountain stream rushes toward the valleys below and is mixed violently, thrown into the air, and churned by its swift flow, usually over rocks. Thus the water becomes mixed with a great amount of air. A mountain stream is usually crystal clear, whereas a pond is generally muddy.

Animals in Mountain Streams

What do you suppose would happen if we took all the living creatures from a pond and put them in a swiftly flowing mountain stream? For one thing, the swiftness of the stream would simply wash them away. But obviously, some creatures are able to live in mountain streams. Why?

We say that the organisms in a pond are adapted to the pond environment; they are not adapted to life in the kind of environment found in a mountain stream. At this point in your study, what hypothesis would you offer to explain the difference? Is the difference, for example, inherited? Is it learned?

The insect larvae in a mountain stream are usually streamlined or flattened. Many simply hang onto stones and rocks as the water rushes over them—an effective adaptation.

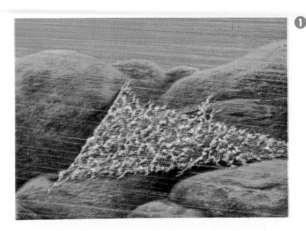

One kind of interesting insect, the caddis fly, has a larva that makes a case in which it lives. There are over 400 different kinds of caddis flies in the United States, and the larvae of many kinds of caddis flies live in ponds. However, only the water-net caddis fly lives in swiftly flowing streams. It builds its net, or case, in the shape of a funnel. The wide end of the net points upstream, and the narrow end, downstream. At the narrow end it builds a silk den to which it cements tiny pebbles. The larva lives in the den. As water rushes downstream, the funnel net catches smaller insect larvae and other tiny animals, which the water-net caddis fly larva eats.

Scientists study organisms in their environment in order to investigate the interdependence of the organisms and their environment. These scientists are known as **ecologists** (i·kol′ə·jist) and their science is, of course, **ecology.** In studying the adaptation of the caddis fly to its environment, you have been studying its ecology. Why would ecologists study pollution of the water, air, or land?

The water-net caddis fly is adapted to life in the environment we call a mountain stream with its rushing water—not to the environment we know as the pond.

Some fish and tadpoles have sucking mouths by which they hang onto rocks to keep from being swept away by the current when they are resting. Trout, the major kind of fish in swiftly flowing streams, keep from being swept downstream by swimming hard upstream. ❶ Pond fish would be dashed against rocks in a very few minutes in a mountain stream.

The differences between animal life in ponds and swiftly flowing streams are even greater than their outward appearances, however. The way the body uses the substances in water is also different.

Comparatively little oxygen is dissolved in pond water, compared with the amount dissolved in the water of mountain streams. Pond fish and other pond animals have become adapted to a poor supply of oxygen and therefore survive well in that environment. However, if you put a mountain trout in a pond, it would suffocate in just a few minutes. A trout requires a great deal more oxygen than a catfish or a pumpkinseed fish. Put in other words, a trout is adapted to an environment different from that of a catfish.

Plants in Mountain Streams

The plants in mountain streams are also different. That is, they have different adaptations to the special environment of the mountain stream. The algae that are adapted to living in ponds are not generally found in the clear, swift mountain streams, except perhaps around rocks in a quiet pocket. Any floating plant life in the swiftly moving stream would be quickly washed away.

The main plants that are adapted to life in mountain streams are those that root themselves firmly into the gravel bottoms. Even these plants are found usually only at the edges or in pools of relatively quiet water. ❷

Some kinds of plants commonly found in ponds have also adapted to life in mountain streams. An alga called *Cladophora* (klad·of'ə·rə) lives both in ponds and mountain streams. These plants have structures to attach themselves to the bottoms of streams, even in swiftly flowing water. Certain algae also have similar structures. However, the plant life of mountain streams is limited when compared with that of a pond.

Interdependence in Living Communities

In a mountain stream, as in a pond or anywhere else, there is an interdependent community. Insect larvae and other tiny animals live on the plants (usually rooted) that have manufactured food. The tiny animals are eaten by slightly larger animals. These, in turn, are eaten by still larger animals such as the trout. The trout are often caught and eaten by otter, bears, and other land animals.

As animals and plants die in the water, their bodies decay. *Decay* simply means that the complex substances of the body are changed by bacteria into simpler substances. These simpler substances are used again by green plants to manufacture food. Then the same chain of life starts over again: plants make food, small animals eat plants, larger animals eat small animals, and so on.

REVIEW

1. Is the following sentence true or false? Fish are fish; any fish that can live in a mountain stream can live in a pond. Explain your answer.

2. What are some important differences between the water in a mountain stream and the water in a pond?

3. What are some of the adaptations of animals in a swiftly flowing stream?

4. What is meant by these terms: *interdependent community, ecologist, ecology?*

NEW VIEW

1. A student made the following statement: "A trout cannot live in a pond, partly because of the lack of oxygen in a pond as compared with the larger amounts of oxygen in a mountain stream. Therefore, a sunfish, which does well in a pond, ought to do even better in a mountain stream where there is more oxygen." Would you consider this assumption on the ecology of the sunfish true or false? Explain your answer.

2. The total plant life growing in a mountain stream is generally much less than you would find growing in a pond, for equal volumes of water. Would you expect a cubic yard of mountain stream to have on the average, more than, less than, or the same amount of animal life as an equal volume of pond water? Explain.

3. Would you expect life at the bottom of a deep lake (say 150 feet deep) to be the same as life near the surface of a lake? Explain your answer as fully as you can.

3. LIFE IN A DEEP LAKE

You might expect that life in a lake would be just the same as life in a pond. Both ponds and lakes may be fed by streams or springs. Often the water in ponds and lakes is stagnant in the sense that it is not flowing swiftly, as in mountain streams. However, there are great differences in the kinds of life in both environments. These differences result mainly from the fact that ponds are usually shallow and lakes are generally quite deep. In deep lakes the differences in water temperature between top and bottom layers cause patterns of water movement. See for yourself. ■

"Climates" in a Lake

When water warms up, it expands. When it cools down, it contracts. When a volume of water contracts, its molecules become packed more closely together than they were before. Therefore, a glassful of cool water could contain more molecules than a glassful of warm water, and thus a glassful of cool water is heavier than a glassful of warm water. Does this help to explain the results of the previous investigation?

When the sun shines on a lake, it warms the water as far down as sunlight penetrates. Also, the light is absorbed as it penetrates the water. Therefore the deeper the water, the less light there is left to warm the deeper water. This means that the surface water is heated the most. Because this water is heated, it expands and becomes lighter. Thus it remains at the surface.

The warm, lighted water near the surface to about 45 feet below the surface is an excellent environment for algae of all sorts. Here these tiny green plants manufacture food. Green plants are the first link in what we call a **food chain**. In a food chain one kind of organism provides food for a second; the second provides food for a third, and so on. In talking about food chains, the word *link* is often used to designate the living organisms that occupy a certain position or *niche* * (nich). The algae provide abundant food for a variety of tiny animals including the microscopic one-celled organisms, fairy shrimp, the larvae of insects, and other animals. These, in turn, form an abundant supply of food for small fish and other animals. And these, in turn, are food for larger fish, turtles, frogs, and so on. Thus the food chain is established.

So many algae thrive in the upper water of lakes (although they are seldom as dense as in a pond), that the layer of algae may cut down on the amount of sunlight reaching deeper water. Therefore, at the deeper levels, there is less light for plants to use in manufacturing their food. There is also less light to warm the water.

For example, when the surface water is about 72 degrees Fahrenheit (72°F) on a midsummer day, the water 50 feet below may be about 50°F. If the bottom is 130 feet below the surface, the temperature there may well be about 41°F. ❶

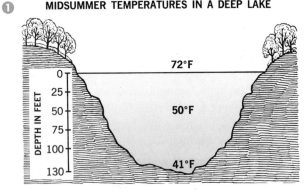

MIDSUMMER TEMPERATURES IN A DEEP LAKE

DEPTH IN FEET

0 — 25 — 50 — 75 — 100 — 130

72°F

50°F

41°F

* Some scientists prefer to use the word *niche* instead of *link* to indicate a certain position in a food chain.

You will need two small battery jars, two small bottles with caps (such as pill bottles or vials), and some ink or dye.

a. Fill one battery jar with cold water.

b. Fill one small bottle with cold water. Add a drop or two of ink or dye to this bottle and cap it.

c. Fill the second battery jar with hot water.

d. Fill the second small bottle with hot water. Add dye or ink to the bottle and cap it.

e. Moving as slowly as possible so as not to disturb the water, place the small bottle of *hot* water at the bottom of the battery jar of *cold* water.❶ Carefully remove the cap and take your hand out slowly. Observe what happens.❷

f. Now place the small bottle of *cold* water into the battery jar of *hot* water, and remove the cap. Does anything happen?❸ How do you explain your observation? How does the movement of the water affect life in a pond or a lake?

An Investigation On Your Own

What do you predict would happen if you were to place a bottle of *cold* fresh water in a jar of *cold* salt water? Prepare the salt water by dissolving ten teaspoons of salt in a pint of water. Do your observations confirm your prediction?

It is clear, then, that there is a considerable difference in temperature at different levels in a deep lake. There are other differences, too. For one thing, winds blow the surface of the water into waves. This motion of waves and winds mixes air into the water. The waves cause the water itself to turn over and to mix down to a depth of 30 feet or so. Below this depth there is very little mixing of the water. So the deeper water has but little air mixed with it and is quiet water.

Life at the Bottom

Would you expect to find life at the bottom of a deep lake? Very few or no green plants grow there, so the first link in the food chain does not seem to be available.

There will be fish and other animals there, however. How can this be? In the upper regions of the water, green plants die, their bodies sink slowly through the water, and finally they may come to rest on the bottom. Tiny plant-eating animals can, therefore, eat this falling "rain" of green plants either while they are drifting down or after they reach the bottom. Also, animals in the surface region of the lake die. As their bodies or body parts sink down, they too may be eaten by fish and other animals in deeper parts of the lake. And finally, the several kinds of meat-eating lake fish living in the cold, still, deep waters hunt and eat the living fish and other kinds of animals that eat the dead animals. These deep-water fish will sometimes rise to higher levels to hunt fish at the bottom of the warmer, lighted regions above.

Seasons in a Lake

When autumn comes, an interesting change begins to occur in the lake water. The air becomes colder because the sun's radiation is much less intense. Therefore, the surface water cools down, contracts, and becomes heavier. Then the cooler, heavier surface water begins to sink. As the weather becomes colder, the surface water continues to cool and to sink. ❶ As you can see in the diagram, this cooling and sinking of the surface water acts like a giant spoon that mixes the water thoroughly.

What happens next is interesting and extremely important to life in a lake. You will recall that as water cools, it keeps contracting and becoming heavier. As the temperature of water drops down to 39°F, something unusual happens. If you cool it just a bit more, it expands somewhat and becomes lighter. From now on, the cooler it becomes, the more it expands until it becomes solid ice. Water is unusual in this respect. See for yourself. ■

Winter in a Deep Lake

If water behaved like most other substances, it would become heavier and heavier as it cooled until it finally froze. This, then, means that the coldest water would settle to the bottom, where it would freeze. If this were so, during a long, cold winter the lake would freeze completely solid from the bottom to the top. This would kill all or almost all of the life in the water. What do you think does happen?

❶ WATER MIXING IN A DEEP LAKE IN AUTUMN

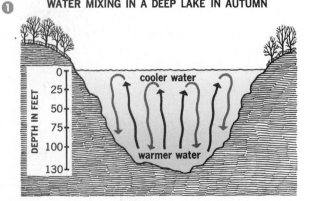

■ AN APPRENTICE INVESTIGATION into the Contraction and Expansion of Water

It is simple to test the contraction of water as it cools and its expansion as it nears the freezing point and freezes.

Your teacher will show you how to insert a glass tube, about 8 inches long, through a one-holed stopper. Carefully fill a Pyrex flask to the top with very hot water. Insert the stopper containing the tube. If the flask is full enough, this will force water up into the tube. ❶ Mark the water level with paint or a wax pencil. As the water cools, what happens to the water level? ❷

Fill a small plastic bottle with cold water. ❸ Place it in the freezing compartment of a refrigerator. After the water is solidly frozen, remove the bottle and check the level of the top of the ice. ❹ Let the ice melt. What happens to the level of the melted ice?

An Investigation On Your Own

What is the difference in the behavior of salt water and fresh water as quantities are cooled? Can you freeze salt water? Try it.

What actually happens is that the water cools to 39°F and sinks to the bottom. Warm water from below rises up to the surface, is cooled to 39°F, and then it sinks. This keeps going on until the entire lake from top to bottom is 39°F.

When the temperature of the entire lake from top to bottom is 39°F, what happens next? Exposed to the cold winter air, the surface water cools below 39°F and, as you will recall, it expands slightly. As it becomes colder and continues to expand, it becomes lighter. Therefore it remains floating on top of the warmer water below. The surface water keeps cooling and expanding until finally, at about 32°F, it freezes to solid ice.

As the weather gets colder, the ice gets thicker, but it always stays at the surface. So a deep lake still has much unfrozen water even in a very cold, long winter.

The diagram shows you what the lake-water temperatures are in winter.❶ The heaviest water is at the bottom at 39°F. Nearer the surface, at a depth of about 25 feet, it is slightly cooler, 37°F. Finally, on the surface, there is ice at 32°F.

Look at the table of summer and winter lake temperatures. In what part of the lake would you expect life to be more active in the winter? As you can see, the warmest water is near the bottom of the lake. In the summer, as you know, life is more abundant and active near the surface of the lake.

SUMMER AND WINTER LAKE TEMPERATURES

Depth of water	Approximate summer temperatures (°F)	Approximate winter temperatures (°F)
surface	72°	32°
25 feet	60°	37°
50 feet	50°	38°
130 feet	41°	39°

What happens to life in the lake during the cold winter months when the lake's surface is covered with ice and snow? As you would expect, the cover over the lake in winter prevents air from mixing with the water. This results in less dissolved oxygen in the winter water. The snow and ice also protect the water below from the cold winter air. Thus, the changes in air temperature have less effect on water temperature below the ice covering. Because the temperature of the water in winter remains fairly constant, vertical movement of the water is limited.

Finally—and very importantly—the sheet of surface ice does not let light pass through it as easily as liquid water does. Thus less light reaches the water in winter than reaches it in summer. And when a layer of snow covers the ice, as often happens, very little light penetrates to the water below.

The result of the environmental changes of winter is that life in a lake goes on at a slower pace. Digestion, respiration, indeed all activities for living, take place much more slowly when it is cold. Plants manufacture less food in winter, and they need less food, since their

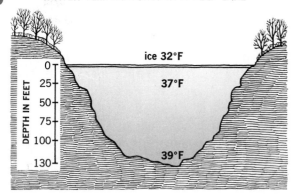

❶ WINTER TEMPERATURES IN A DEEP LAKE

ice 32°F

37°F

39°F

DEPTH IN FEET
0
25
50
75
100
130

bodies are living at a slower rate of speed. Many plants die during the winter, and only a few reproduce themselves. Animals, as well, are sluggish. Those that do move about, move more slowly than in summer. They eat little and live mainly on food (usually fat) that they stored in their bodies during the long summer months. Also, because there is less light in a lake in winter than there is in summer, the "food factories" of life are slowed down or are destroyed. Consequently, many water animals die in the winter from lack of food.

One animal that lives the year-round in some American lakes is the muskrat. In this unusual photograph, made under water beneath an ice-covered surface, you see a muskrat surfacing for air through a small hole in the ice. ❷

Finally, as we stated earlier, there is also much less oxygen available in winter for respiration. Besides less oxygen mixed into the water by winds, less oxygen is given off into the water by plants. There are, of course, fewer plants to manufacture food, a process in which oxygen is given off. And the fewer plants are manufacturing less food.

Some kinds of animals **hibernate**. While in this state of hibernation, their body chemistry slows down until it almost ceases entirely. Hibernating lake animals go through the winter in a kind of deep sleep while lying buried in the mud or sand at the bottom of the lake.

Spring in a Deep Lake

When spring comes, the sun's radiation finally melts the ice. The surface water is warmed until it reaches 39°F again. At this temperature it is slightly heavier than the water 25 to 30 feet below the surface, which is about 37°F. Remember that water is

heaviest at about 39°F. Therefore, the 39°F surface water sinks and the deeper, cooler, lighter water below it rises. This starts the mixing of the water again until finally the region down to about 45 feet has been mixed with the air from the surface.

Algae start manufacturing more food and reproduce themselves again as they are swept down and up with the currents of the sinking and rising water. Food manufacturing again goes on at a faster rate in the warming water. The water animals, most of which have eaten very little in winter, once again start a more active life.

On the basis of your study up to this point, would you accept this statement: The ecology of an environment must be maintained if the plants and animals in it are to survive. Why? Why not?

REVIEW

1. Why is it that the difference in the depth of a pond and a large lake makes so great a difference in the nature of the living communities?

2. Explain why it is that a deep lake never freezes completely from top to bottom in winter.

3. Why is it that sunlight does not penetrate to the bottom of a deep lake?

4. How do fish living at the bottom of a deep lake get food when green plants do not grow that far down?

NEW VIEW

1. Sometimes Eskimos make igloos out of blocks of ice or snow. How do you think they stay warm in such a shelter?

2. One of the best times to fish in either lakes or ponds is in the spring after the water has warmed up somewhat. Can you think of reasons why fish seem to bite better in the spring in terms of facts you have learned in this chapter?

3. Now you know about life at the bottom of a lake—say 100 feet down. Would you guess that there are or are not living things at the bottom of the deeper parts of the oceans—say three miles down? Explain your answer.

4. RELATING THE CONCEPTS

Life in a pond, a river, or a lake seems to have some order after all. Animals and plants are not just thrown together. They live together in a community, depending each on the other. Clearly, *all living things are dependent on one another and on their environment.*

This statement is one of our basic views or *concepts* about living things. A concept helps us to organize our thoughts about a certain aspect of the universe. You have just begun your study of this concept, and of the other concepts presented in this chapter.

Reviewing the Concepts

▶ *Animals and plants are adapted to different environments.* The environments of freshwater ponds, mountain streams, and deep lakes are clearly different. Animals and plants, securing materials and energy in these different environments are, therefore, also different from each other in some ways. They have become adapted to their individual environments in ways in which they can be successful in securing and using the materials and energy present in these environments.

▶ *Plants and animals within a given environment are interdependent.* The organisms in a given environment depend on each other for food and shelter. They interchange matter and energy.

▶ *Interdependent living things are joined in a community.* Biologists speak of the community of living things in a pond as a "pond community." They use similar terms for the life in a lake or a mountain stream. They are speaking of the life that is found typically in such places. However, the term *community* means more than this. A community includes not only the living things adapted to it, but the physical environment as well. The physical environment includes conditions such as heat and moisture. The community includes the interdependence that exists among its living members.

▶ *In any living community there are food chains typical of that community.* For example, insect larvae feed on algae. The insect larvae are eaten by a variety of small animals, including tiny fish. These, in turn, are eaten by yet larger fish. Finally, the larger fish may be eaten by other kinds of animals. When plants and animals die in the water, their bodies decay, and the complex materials of which they are composed are changed to simpler materials by decay bacteria. These simpler materials are then used again by green plants as raw materials. And thus the food chain starts all over again.

Testing Yourself

1. Account for the fact that pond water is relatively clear in the winter but turns a greenish color in the middle of summer. Why does this color develop only in the middle or late summer?

2. What part do algae play in the living communities of fresh water?

3. How does the ecology of a pond differ from that of an equal area of land? Analyze at least three factors: temperature, moisture, and oxygen supply.

4. In what ways does a pond environment differ from that of a swiftly flowing mountain stream? How do these differences affect the kinds of living communities in each?

5. What part do decay bacteria play in the living communities of fresh waters?

6. Explain why green plant life does not live at the bottom of deep lakes.

7. Explain what is meant by a food chain, and give an example. What is always the first link in any food chain? Explain why this is so.

8. What are the sources of food for fish and other animals that live at the bottom of deep lakes? Explain your answer.

9. Explain why deep lakes do not freeze solidly in the cold winter weather.

10. Account for the fact that living things become more numerous and more active in the spring and summer in lakes. Consider all the reasons you can think of.

Extending the Concepts

Investigation. What is the relationship of the speed of reproduction of pond organisms to the temperature of pond water?

Collect three pints of pond water from the same place near the shore of a pond. Bring them to the classroom and place the water in three clear glass jars of the same size. Be certain to keep the glass jars covered during this investigation.

Add a pea-size bit of hard-boiled egg yolk to each jar and let the jars stand overnight at room temperature.

Now place one jar in the refrigerator. Keep another jar at room temperature. Place the remaining jar on a window sill, either near a radiator or in the path of direct sunlight. Keep records of the temperature of each jar.

How does the number of organisms in each jar compare with the others? Are you sure your method of counting is fairly accurate? Might there be another environmental factor influencing your results? If so, how would you eliminate it?

Suggested Reading

Barnett, L., and the Editors of LIFE, *The World We Live In*, New York, Time, Inc., 1955. Beautiful illustrations and excellent descriptions of the world's communities.

Morgan, A. H., *Field Book of Ponds and Streams*, New York, G. P. Putnam's Sons, 1939. A good beginning reference.

Buchsbaum, R. M., *Animals Without Backbones*, Chicago, University of Chicago Press, 1948. Although a college text, this is one of the best invertebrate zoology texts for simple explanations.

Needham, J., and P. Needham, *A Guide to the Study of Freshwater Biology*, New York, Holden-Day, 1962. There are sections on growing and maintaining plants and animals.

2 | Marine Communities

Man inhabits the land. Although his various underwater activities make the aquatic environment more and more familiar to him, he still carries out his life activities on land.

Yet, the oceans cover more than 70 percent of the earth and there are more plants and animals in the waters of the earth than on the land. One estimate is that all the trees, grass, and other green plants of the land manufacture only about one tenth of the food used by all organisms on this earth, whereas the green plants of the oceans manufacture nine tenths.

As you can well imagine, there are enough plants in the oceans to feed great numbers of plant-eating animals. This being so, it follows that there are enough plant-eaters in the oceans to feed a tremendous number of flesh-eaters as well. This is also true.

1. FRESH–WATER AND MARINE ENVIRONMENTS

There are great differences between marine (salt-water) communities and fresh-water communities. The differences are even greater than those between communities in ponds and communities in mountain streams that you read about in Chapter 1.

Both fresh and ocean waters vary from place to place in the amount of substances that are dissolved in them. Ocean water contains, on the average, about 3,500 parts of dissolved salts to each 100,000 parts of water. In other words, 100,000 pounds of sea water contains, on the average, 3,500 pounds of different salts. By contrast, the Mississippi River contains only 20 pounds of dissolved salts in 100,000 pounds of water. The Missouri River has about 40 pounds of salts in 100,000 pounds of water. Lake Superior has only 6 pounds in 100,000 pounds of water.

Sodium chloride—common table salt—accounts for over three fourths of the dissolved salts in sea water. Calcium chloride, potassium sulfate, sodium sulfate, and magnesium chloride are other common salts found in sea water. There are also traces of elements such as iodine, bromine, aluminum, copper, and even gold. (A ton of sea water contains about one grain—five cents worth—of gold.) However, common table salt mainly makes the great difference between the environments of ocean water and of fresh water.

Any fresh-water animal or plant would soon die in sea water because of the salt it contains. Why? See for yourself. ■

■ AN APPRENTICE INVESTIGATION into the Effects of Salt Water on Fresh-Water Life

Gather together the following: a microscope, microscope slides with cover slips, four quart jars, common teaspoon, eye dropper, forceps, absorbent tissue or paper towel, table salt, and some *Spirogyra.*

You will need to make up four bottles of different salt solutions. Use tap water that has stood in an open jar for at least 24 hours. (This lets the chlorine, if any is present, escape into the air.) Make your four solutions as follows: (1) 1 teaspoon salt for the first pint of water; (2) 4 level teaspoons for the second pint; (3) 8 level teaspoons for the third pint; and (4) 16 level teaspoons for the last pint.

Now you are ready to begin. With a medicine dropper, place a small drop of fresh water on a microscope slide. With a forceps, place part of a strand of *Spirogyra* in the water on the slide. Place a cover slip over the drop and study the cells carefully under the microscope. Do you see the green, spiral chloroplast in each cell? ❶

Now place a drop of your weakest salt solution on another microscope slide, add a bit of *Spirogyra,* and place a cover slip over it. *Observe carefully* any changes in the cells' contents and appearance. Now repeat the procedure with your second solution. Continue observing the slide for several minutes. ❷

Repeat the same procedure, using each of the other salt solutions. Each time, use a fresh drop of salt solution on a clean slide. Here is what happened with the last solution in one trial. ❸ Make a note of the time it takes before you see any changes in the appearance of the *Spirogyra* cells for each of the solutions.

You might like to repeat the same procedure using protozoans, one-celled algae, or a small section from a larger water plant such as *Elodea.*

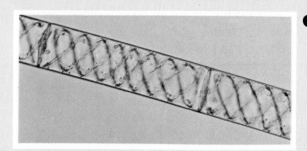

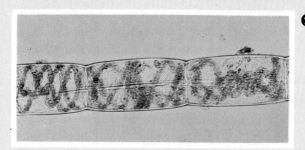

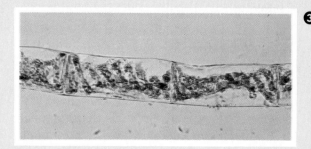

An Investigation On Your Own

Now that you know how to do an investigation of this sort, you may wish to try further investigations on your own. Set up your own materials to answer the following questions.

Will a plant recover its original condition and movement if the salt water is drawn out and replaced by pond water or aquarium water again? Will a plant finally adapt itself to salt water of high concentration if it is given time to adjust to increasing amounts a little at a time? You might try this procedure especially for *Elodea.*

Clearly, just as there are differences between the environments we call fresh-water communities, so are there differences among marine communities. You know that fresh-water organisms cannot live long in sea water. However, organisms in one kind of ocean environment would also die if suddenly moved to a different ocean environment.

The cold northern parts of the oceans, for example, make a different environment than the warm tropical parts of the oceans. However, with regard to their dissolved substances, the environments in cold northern waters and in the warm tropical waters may be quite similar. But the differences in temperature alone result in populations of living things that are quite different. In tropical waters there are vast schools of small, gaily colored fish, but no seals. In northern waters you will find seals, of course, as well as kinds of fish not found in tropical waters.

There are also differences between the kinds of life that live in the shallow waters along the shores and the kinds that live near the surface farther out to sea. There are differences in the kinds of life that live, say, down to 50 feet, and the kinds that live near or at the ocean bottoms, which are sometimes several miles deep. This will become clearer as we study tidal pools next.

REVIEW

1. Using the information given on page 24, determine how many times more concentrated dissolved salts are in sea water than in the water of Lake Superior.

2. What, from your investigations, are the effects of salt water on fresh-water organisms?

NEW VIEW

1. In the library, find out how the sea became so much saltier than fresh waters.

2. Sometimes, heavy rains cause rivers to rise. This fresh water then flows into the seas in great amounts and dilutes the sea water near the river's mouth. Certain animals and plants are often killed when this happens. Why?

2. LIFE IN THE SHALLOW AND THE DEEP

You undoubtedly know that there are tides in the oceans. The ocean water rises twice a day along most shores to produce high tides. When this occurs, the sea water floods over low-lying rocks. Then, twice a day, the ocean level drops, often several feet. This leaves the low-lying rocks standing above the water. There are often hollow areas in and around the rocks, and sea water remains in these pockets as small pools. If you have ever played along such tidal pools, you know that they are rich in a variety of organisms.

Life in the Tidal Pools

Unless you know the kinds of life that live in tidal pools, you may not be certain whether some of these living things are animals or plants. Some animals seem rooted to the rocks and even look like plants.

Look at the animal shown in the photograph. ❶ It is called a sea anemone (ə·nem′ ə·nē). (An anemone is a kind of flower. Someone probably thought this animal looked like the flower and gave it its name.) The sea anemone is related to the fresh-water hydra and also to the jellyfish. The anemone lives with its base attached to a rock and its many tentacles spread out. The tentacles contain large numbers of stinging cells. Whenever a small fish or another sea animal touches one of these tentacles, a part of the stinging cell shoots out. This paralyzes the prey. Then the tentacles bend and guide the tiny animal into the "mouth" opening that lies at the center

of the tentacles. If you should touch the tentacles with your finger, you might get a slight tingling or prickly sensation from the stinging cells.

Sometimes sea anemones attach themselves to old sea shells. Hermit crabs can often be found living inside the same sea shells.  By sticking its legs and claws out of the shell, the crab walks around carrying its shell and the anemone with it. As the crab tears up the food it catches to eat, some of this food is picked up by the anemone's tentacles. So the anemone gets a free lunch. The crab may also find this relationship rewarding because the anemone helps disguise the crab and its sea shell. Also, the stinging cells of the anemone may help protect the crab from some of its enemies.

If you look carefully in a tidal pool, you may find a relative of the sea anemone, called *Obelia* (ō·bēl′ē·ə). *Obelia* is a colony of many small anemonelike animals attached together. These inch-high, branching strands of animals look like branched plants, and most people mistake them for plants. However,

they have tentacles with stinging cells that catch tiny animals. They guide this food into their "mouths" just as anemones do.

The very rock that forms the base of the tidal pool may have been built by other colony animals similar to the anemone. These are called the corals. Each tiny coral is like an anemone, but it secretes a limey substance that forms a rocky case in which it lives. Millions upon millions of these tiny coral animals live on top of the rocky cases of other corals that have died. In time, they can build the foundations of great rocky reefs and islands. Many of the Pacific islands upon which people live started as reef formations built by the corals.

For example, the well-known Bikini Atoll, in the Marshall Islands, is a ring-shaped coral island. Another famous coral formation is the Great Barrier Reef, which lies from 15 to 100 miles off the northeastern coast of Australia.

Many other animals also may be found in tidal pools. Occasionally there may be small jellyfish swimming around, catching tiny animals with their tentacles and stinging cells.

27

There are almost certain to be some sea urchins and starfish. ❶ There may be sand dollars, sponges, sea cucumbers, moss animals (so called because they look almost exactly like mats or branching fans), and a variety of tiny snails and clams each with its own peculiar and interesting shell protecting its soft body. There are probably several kinds of worms and, of course, small fish darting back and forth in the water.

You may well ask which are the real plants when so many of the animals look like plants. The real plants here would include a wide variety of seaweeds that are relatives of the fresh-water algae. Some of these marine algae are green, some are red, and some are brown. ❷ Some are too small to be seen without a microscope and some are many feet long. Some look like long straps or ribbons, some are branched. Some have floats that

keep the branches at or near the surface. But whatever their size, shape, or color, all are manufacturing food.

The main plant food for the plant-eating animals of the tidal pools, however, are the microscopic algae. ❸ By *microscopic*, we mean, of course, something so small that it can be seen only with the help of the microscope. These microscopic marine algae are swept in from the ocean with the tides. They are the "grass" of the seas, just as the fresh-water algae are the "grass" of the fresh waters of the world. Algae account for most of the food manufactured in the seas, and they are the chief source of plant food for sea animals. The numbers of these tiny plants vary from place to place in the ocean. However, one study made in England showed that each cubic foot of sea water contained over twelve million plants.

These algae, along with millions of microscopic protozoans, are swept into the tidal pools at each high tide. Protozoans and a wide variety of other small animals, such as tiny shrimplike animals, use the algae for food. Larger animals eat the smaller animals. And even larger animals feed on these animals. So food chains are set up just as they are in fresh-water communities. Recall that the first link in the food chain always connects the green plants that manufacture food to the animals that eat the plants. The other links connect a series of larger and ever-larger flesh-eating animals.

From Shore to Deep

Sea water is often quite clear in spite of the millions of algae and protozoans that are floating in it. These floating microscopic algae, protozoans, and other microscopic organisms together are called **plankton** (plangk′ tən). When the water is clear, a good way

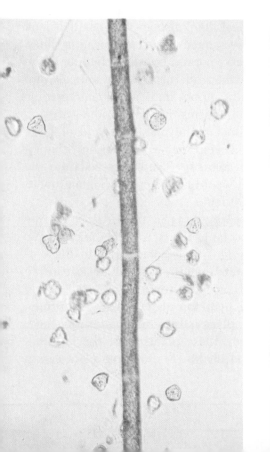

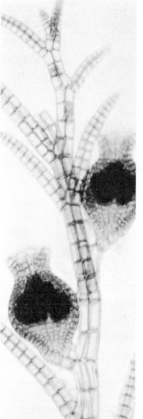

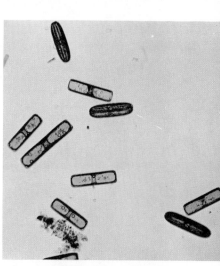

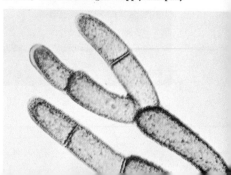

to examine life in the shallow bottoms is to take a boat ride just off the shore in southern Florida or along other shallow places of the ocean. Your view may include corals, such as those you see here. ❶

While looking at the ocean bottom you may see an amazing number and variety of animals moving about. Sometimes the entire bottom itself seems to be quivering and moving. It may be almost completely covered with tiny snails and clams and oyster drills, each moving about in search of food.

Groups or schools of fish, many brightly colored, may swim by the reefs or shelves of rock on the bottom. You may see a skate or ray lying flat on the bottom if your eyes are sharp. Their coloration makes them difficult to see. Suddenly one may swim away, raising a great cloud of silt from the bottom.

Large shellfish such as conches and whelks may move slowly about, dragging their limey homes with them as they go. And as you might expect, here also are animals that look like plants: anemones, sea fans, sea lilies, sponges, and corals. Invisible, but far more numerous than all these larger animals, are the millions upon millions of microscopic plankton organisms that float in the water.

Here also are the plants. A kind of large alga called kelp comes in various shapes, sizes, and colors. ❷ These seaweeds are the plants you would notice easily. Some grow as long as 200 feet.

Here, however, as in the tidal pools, the most important plants are the microscopic algae. Sunlight easily penetrates to the bottom of these shallow parts of the ocean. So these floating microscopic algae (collectively called the plankton algae) grow plentifully. Each tiny plant is busy manufacturing food. Here, again, these plants form the first link in the food chains. Microscopic plant-eating

animals and many shellfish, such as clams, feed on these plants. Starfish and other animals, such as the beaked parrot fish, feed on the shellfish. Larger fish and mammals, such as dolphins, feed on these shellfish and other animals, and so the chain continues. Each plant and animal seems to have a definite function in the living community of the shallow ocean bottom.

The "Blue Water"

The color of ocean water over the shallow bottoms usually looks greenish. This is caused by the reflection of light from sand, rocks, and plant life on the bottom itself. If you ride in a boat away from the shore over and beyond the shallow water, you will come to a place where the water appears to change color. The green color disappears suddenly, and the water becomes blue—usually a deep, rich blue. ❸ This color change marks the place where the ocean bottom suddenly drops away in a steep, sloping shelf or a cliff. You are now at the edge of the open sea; you are over water that is very deep.

This "blue water" extends over most of the ocean until you reach the shallow waters near land on the other side—or around islands.

The average depth of the oceans is about 12,000 feet—more than two miles. However, the bottom of the ocean is very like the surface of dry land in that there are mountains, valleys, hills, cliffs, trenches, and plains.

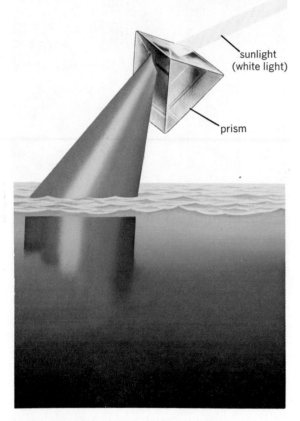

sunlight (white light)

prism

Some of the mountains rise completely out of the sea. These form islands. The deepest trench in the sea—the Marianas Trench—is 35,600 feet deep. The highest mountain on earth is Mt. Everest. It is a little over 29,000 feet high. So the Marianas Trench is much farther below sea level than Mt. Everest is above sea level.

There is, then, a tremendous variation in the depths at which living things may inhabit the sea. What does this lead you to expect about the *kinds* of life in the sea?

You would expect, from what you already know about life in deep lakes, that there would be great differences in life near the surface of the blue water and life in its depths. You would be right in this view.

Light and Life

You probably know that the sunlight we see, called "white light," is composed of many colors. A prism, like that shown in the drawing, separates the white light into its many colors. ① As you can see in the diagram, the colors in the spectrum range from red to violet, encompassing all the colors visible to the naked eye. Infrared and ultraviolet rays are not visible and, thus, are not considered part of the spectrum.

Sunlight penetrates the water and is absorbed as it travels downward. Notice in the drawing that the red rays travel only a short distance and that the blue and green rays penetrate to the greatest depths. In the deeper levels of water, so little light penetrates that the human eye cannot detect it. Here it seems completely dark.

How deeply the light penetrates depends upon many things. It varies according to the cloudiness of the water, the number of plants growing in the water, the time of day, the season of the year. However, it is convenient for us to think of the oceans as being divided into two main horizontal layers: a lighted layer and an unlighted layer. The lighted layer may be any depth having enough light for plants to live. The unlighted layer is, of course, the remainder of the ocean. So you see, the depth of these horizontal layers may vary greatly from time to time and from place to place. You would expect, would you not, that the surface of the ocean would generally be warmer than the deepest levels. Why?

We usually think of plants as absorbing and using only the red-orange and blue-violet parts of sunlight to manufacture food. This is often true of many plants. ② As the light is absorbed by the plant, the light energy is converted to chemical energy by the plant as it manufactures its food. However,

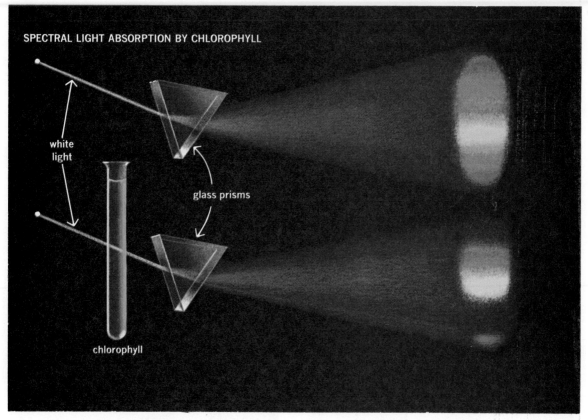

SPECTRAL LIGHT ABSORPTION BY CHLOROPHYLL

white light

glass prisms

chlorophyll

many plants living in the ocean are able to use almost all the different rays of the spectrum to manufacture their food. For example, the diatoms (which were shown earlier on page 6) can capture the light energy they need from any of the rays of the spectrum, from red through violet. As we stated before, red through violet contains all the light we can see with our eyes.

The strength of the light is also important to plants in capturing light energy. We call this strength *intensity,* and we measure it in **foot-candles.** A foot-candle is the amount of light that a certain sized candle will give at a distance of 1 foot. Ten foot-candles is the amount of light that 10 candles will give if they are 1 foot away.

Some plants of the ocean are able to capture the energy from light as dim as 10 foot-candles. Other ocean plants need more light, and some require the brightness of 6,000 foot-candles. The requirement of light of different strength varies, of course, with different kinds of plants. Where would you think a plant needing strong light might usually be located in the water, near the surface or deeper down? Where do you think a land plant needing strong light would grow best?

Like water plants, land plants differ in their light requirements. For each kind of plant there is a certain intensity of light that is best. In the investigation on the next page, you can see for yourself the reactions of some plants to light. ■

■ AN APPRENTICE INVESTIGATION into the Reactions of Different Plants to Light

You will need four plants: two plants of one kind and two plants of another kind. Geranium plants and fern plants should react well. One of these plants grows best in strong light, the other grows best in shade. Your investigation should enable you to find out which is which. You will also need a room with sunny windows on one side and a dark area on the opposite side to investigate the amount of light that these types of plants need.

Place one of each kind of plant on the window sill or very near the window. ❶ A south window is best. Here they should get direct sunlight or at least strong light. Place the other two plants as far away from the window as possible, where the light is dim. ❷ Make certain that no strong sunlight reaches these other two plants.

Water all four plants each time one becomes dry. Give them enough water so that you are sure all of the soil is moist. Leave the plants in these same locations for many weeks. Observe them carefully each week.

Which kind of plant grows better in strong light? ❸ Which kind of plant grows better in dim light? ❹

How will you decide what the phrase "growing better" means? Will the number of leaves the plant produces be an indication? Will the color of the leaves? The height of the stem? Think about these things.

And don't forget that during a period of several months the geranium plant will bloom and then the flowers will fall off. Will this mean that the geranium plant is not "growing well"? Might light intensity affect flowering?

If you can locate a light meter used in photography, you can actually measure the difference in light intensity of the locations of each plant. Notice the different positions of the needle on the light meter in different locations in the room. Do you think the light meter is more sensitive than your eyes to different light intensities?

❶

❷

An Investigation On Your Own

At what intensity of light does a geranium grow best?

Be careful in designing your experiment. Will you want a *control* experiment? Search out the meaning of a *control.*

REVIEW

1. What is the main kind of plant food eaten by the animal life in the tidal pools? How do these plants get in the tidal pools?

2. Someone estimated that it takes 10 pounds of food to make 1 pound of the animal that eats it. Suppose that, in a tidal pool, algae are eaten by tiny shrimplike animals. These are, in turn, eaten by small fish, and the small fish are eaten by larger fish. Suppose one of these larger fish darts out of the tidal pool during high tide and is eaten by a large tuna fish that weighs 400 pounds. How many pounds of algae were required to add a single pound to the weight of the tuna?

NEW VIEW

1. Below 800 feet in the ocean there is generally no variation at all in the temperature in winter and summer. In the shallow tidal pools, however, the water temperature varies greatly because of contact with the air above it. How well do you think a fish accustomed to living 800 feet below the surface would do if you forced it to live in a tidal pool? Why? (Ignore pressure differences in answering this question.)

2. In the tropics, the temperature of the water in tidal pools rises to about 85°F. In the polar regions, tidal water is barely above freezing (and sometimes below it) during the winter months. Would you expect differences in the kind and amount of tidal-pool life in the two regions? Explain your answer.

3. FOOD CHAINS AND THEIR LINKS

Floating throughout the oceans of the world are countless billions upon billions of microscopic algae. Mainly, these algae are the kind called diatoms. Here and there in the ocean are floating masses of much larger algae that we have mentioned before, commonly called seaweed.

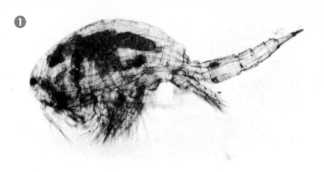

As in the shallow waters, the microscopic algae form the "grass" that is the first link in most of the food chains of the open sea. Each individual alga plant manufactures food. Here, as in the shallow waters, the microscopic protozoans and tiny shrimplike animals eat the algae, and larger animals eat the smaller animals.

One of the shrimplike animals is particularly interesting. It is called a copepod (kō′ pə·pod). ❶ Copepods are all quite small. Some are microscopic, and many are so small you would need a magnifying glass to see them well. But these tiny plant-eating animals are so numerous that they are the chief second link, or niche, in the food chains of the open oceans. That is, they eat the plants that make up the first niche. A wide variety of small animals eat the copepods. However —and here is a surprise—these tiny copepods are also one of the chief foods of the largest animal that ever lived: the whalebone whale.

Whalebone whales weigh over 100 tons and may be over 100 feet long. They swim through the water with their mouths open, thereby forcing in sea water. Then they close their mouths and force the water out through sievelike structures in their mouths. These structures are called "whalebone." In this way the copepods and other tiny animals are strained out and are then swallowed.

Other kinds of whales (the toothed whales), sharks, squid, and a great variety of fish, live in the open sea. Each is a part of some food chain or chains in which they eat certain animals and, in turn, are eaten by other animals.

Life in the Ocean Depths

As you will recall, no light reaches the ocean depths. Thus no green plants are found growing in this unlighted layer.

Would you expect to find animal life in the ocean depths when there is no plant life to form the first link of the food chains? Offhand, you might think not. After all, there must be food-manufacturing plants for there to be animal life. But keep in mind that the food-manufacturing plants do grow above in the lighted layer, just as they do in the deep lakes.

As plants and animals from the upper layers die, their bodies drift downward in the water. Furthermore, fish and other animals that feed near the surface swim down into deeper water from time to time and are there preyed upon by other sea animals.

Each animal has its own depth range. That is, it normally swims, say, from 200 feet to 300 feet below the surface. Then other fish may have a depth range of from 250 feet to 350 feet. This overlap in depth ranges keeps going down and down so that there are fish and a few other animals down far below the lighted levels of the sea. Even though the first niche of the food chains, the green plants, are fairly near the surface, some of the chains extend, niche by niche, down even to the deep ocean bottoms, miles below the surface.

There are some deep-sea fish that have been observed and photographed from special underwater devices men have taken deep below the ocean's surface. One of these de-

vices, called a bathysphere, was made in 1930 by William Beebe. Beebe descended to an ocean depth of more than 3,000 feet (slightly over half a mile).

A more recent diving craft, the bathyscaph, invented by Auguste Piccard, can go over 6 miles below the ocean's surface. At this depth the pressures against the bathyscaph are tremendous. Sea water weighs about 64 pounds per cubic foot. The pressure of water means the weight of the water that presses in on anything below its surface. The pressure, then, on the bathyscaph at 6 miles below the surface is 14,080 pounds per square inch.

In 1963 important undersea explorations and investigations were made by the Frenchman, Jacques-Yves Cousteau. Cousteau established a colony of scientists, whom he called "oceanauts," on Roman Reef, 36 feet below the surface of the water of the Red Sea. Here, in a specially designed undersea house, called Starfish House, and in the surrounding water, the oceanauts lived and worked for a month without returning to the surface. At a depth of 85 feet, another structure, called Deep Cabin, was anchored on a ledge. Here the reactions of the men to living at an even deeper level in the sea were investigated.

In addition to the investigations into the reactions of living and working beneath the sea, explorations down to a depth of 1,000 feet were made in an undersea craft. The self-powered undersea craft, appropriately named the Diving Saucer, was equipped with floodlights, metal claws for picking up objects, and still and movie cameras for recording the explorations. ❷

In 1965 Scott Carpenter, one of the original seven astronauts, became an "aquanaut." He led two teams of men who lived and worked 205 feet beneath the Pacific Ocean in Sealab II. For thirty days these aquanauts, wearing SCUBA (Self Contained Underwater Breathing Apparatus), investigated the sea directly from their underwater home.

Typical deep-sea fish seen from undersea explorations live under enormous water pressures—nearly 14,000 pounds per square inch at the depth of 6 miles, as you may recall. They would burst if brought quickly to the surface. Can you figure out why they are not mashed by the water pressures down in the depths where they live? (Keep in mind that even you live under pressure in the "ocean of air." The air around you has a pressure of nearly 15 pounds per square inch.)

What do these fish of the deep eat? They have pointed, long teeth and some produce peculiar luminous lights. ❶ These animals eat each other; they are flesh-eaters. Some of course, eat fish that occasionally swim down from above, and some eat the bodies of dead animals that sink from above.

The purpose of the luminous structures of these deep-sea fish is not understood. What purpose do you think they might serve? Although there is no light where they live, except that which they produce themselves, they do have eyes, as you can see from the drawing. The eyes of most seem to work very well, too, since some of the fish were quite curious about diving vessels and their lights. They would look in through the windows of the vessel while the scientists were looking out at them. Perhaps their luminous structures attract other fish.

Life on the Dark Bottoms

Scientists once believed that there was no life on the deep ocean bottoms. They were wrong. Like a slow rain falling from the lighted regions above, dead animals and plants slowly settle to the bottom of the ocean. All of this material that is not caught and eaten on the way down comes to rest on the bottom.

Now it is known that there is a surprising variety of life living near the bottom that feeds off this bottom material. In fact, the animals that live on the bottom may be mainly scavengers, animals that eat dead plants and animals rather than kill live ones for food. As you will remember, tiny plants called **decay bacteria** finish the job by breaking down the complex body substances of dead organisms. The simpler substances that they then make are released back into the water for use again by plants.

REVIEW

1. What is the most common first niche in shallow-ocean-bottom food chains? Does this differ from that in the tidal pools?

2. What do the protozoans in the water use for food?

3. If you flew in an airplane above the shoreline of the ocean, you would see a change in color of the water. It would appear green near the shore, but it would suddenly turn a deep blue farther out. Here and there you might see green patches even in the blue water. How would you account for these green patches?

4. How would you describe the general appearance of the ocean floor? Is it generally flat like a plain?

5. How far down in the ocean would you usually expect to find green plants? Why? What is the first niche in the food chains of the open ocean waters? What is a common second niche?

6. About how many niches are in the food chain of which the giant whalebone whale is the final niche? What are the other niches?

7. What do animals living below the green-plant level in the ocean use for food?

8. What are scavengers?

9. What do decay bacteria do that is important for other living things?

NEW VIEW

1. What is a typical food chain that exists in the shallow ocean bottoms? Use at least three or four organisms in the chain. You may need to consult an encyclopedia or one of the references at the end of this chapter to get your answer. (See *Suggested Reading* on p. 41.)

2. If you looked through a glass-bottomed boat and saw the shallow bottom of the ocean "crawling" with animal life of many kinds, what could you say about the plant life in that area? What kind of plant life could you most likely assume to be there?

3. If, in another region, you found almost no animal life on the bottom, what could you say about the plant life? (Think carefully. Might things other than the lack of plant life be involved?)

4. Shellfish such as oysters and conches have heavy shells made of lime (calcium salts). Where do you think the animals get the calcium to make their shells?

5. Scientists believe that life began in the sea. Which would you guess came first, plants or animals? Why?

6. From what you know now about the different colored rays that make up light, can you explain why many plant leaves are green? (Assume that the red-orange and the blue-violet parts of sunlight are being absorbed. What colors are being reflected?)

7. Surface water has a large amount of oxygen dissolved in it. Some of it is dissolved from the air. Part of this supply of oxygen also results from the fact that the plants give off oxygen. How do the deeper waters get enough oxygen to keep animals alive? There are no green plants growing there to give off oxygen, and the water is far from the air above. Biologists do not know the complete answer to this question, but a partial answer lies in the fact that cold water sinks. (Remember the situation in lakes.) How would this fact account for oxygen in the deep water? When would the greatest mixing of water occur, in the summer or in the winter? Would there be more sinking of cold surface water in the tropical seas where the air temperature does not change much or in the oceans with great seasonal changes in air temperature?

8. Since Cousteau's French "oceanauts" pioneered in living and working deep in the sea, American "aquanauts" have performed similar feats. Read about the work of both the oceanauts and the aquanauts. What discoveries have they made about life in the deeps?

4. RELATING THE CONCEPTS

In the oceans of the world, as in the fresh waters, each kind of living thing appears to fill a particular niche. It eats (or makes food) and is eaten by some other living thing. Thus the flow of materials and energy between living things and their environment goes on endlessly.

The statements of the concepts that follow are meant to focus your attention on the oceans of the world as environments for life.

Reviewing the Concepts

▶ *The green plants of the oceans capture light energy and use it to make food.* More food is manufactured by ocean plants than by all land plants together.

▶ *There is an interdependence among the organisms inhabiting the oceans.* The "grass" of the oceans is composed of microscopic, single-celled green plants, the plankton algae. They form the first link in a food chain.

A wide variety of life in abundance is found in the tidal pools and the surface waters of the ocean. The abundance of life occurs because the plankton algae are numerous in these lighted waters and thus are a rich source of food for animal life.

In the oceans, food chains exist in which green plants are eaten by small animals, and these, in turn, are eaten by larger animals. These chains are sometimes short, as in the case of the giant whalebone whales. Algae are eaten by copepods, and copepods are eaten by the whales.

Animals that live in the unlighted depths of this ocean may obtain food in various ways. They may live on animals that swim down from above. They may eat each other. They may depend on the "rain" of the dead organisms and their parts that slowly settle down from the upper layers of water.

Many of the animals that live on the ocean bottoms are scavengers; they live on dead organisms that settle to the bottom.

Testing Yourself

1. Why are the plankton algae often called the "grass" of the sea?

2. Give an example of an ocean food chain.

3. What kind of living thing is always the first link in any food chain? Why must this be so?

4. What is the basic reason that there is a wider variety of life in tidal pools and surface waters than elsewhere in ocean waters?

5. Why is it that few or no green plants are found in the unlighted depths of ocean waters?

6. What portion of sunlight is absorbed and used for energy by ocean plants? What portion of sunlight is reflected by the green plants? Explain your answer fully.

7. Considering the earth as a whole, in what environment would you say that the greatest amount of food manufacturing by green plants is carried on? Give several reasons for your choice.

8. How is life able to exist at the bottom of deep oceans when green plants cannot live there?

9. Work out some food chains that would have their final niches at the bottom of deep oceans. Consider fish that eat other fish and also consider the scavengers that live on dead organisms. Be sure to explain what the first niches in these chains are and where these living things are found.

10. What did each of these sea-explorers achieve?

    Beebe   Piccard   Cousteau

Extending the Concepts

Investigation 1. If you live near the ocean, your teacher or parents may help you collect organisms in tidal pools. (CAUTION: Do not attempt to collect living things in the ocean unless an adult accompanies you.) Try the shallow tidal pools for collecting, where the water has sandy or rocky, plant-covered bottoms. Use a net to collect the organisms, and place them in jars of ocean water.

Each jar with the water (and organisms) you have collected should be labeled with the place and approximate depth at which the water was collected. Examine samples from each jar under a microscope.

Use the books at the end of this unit to help you identify the organisms you collected.

Investigation 2. Take a field trip to study the plant and animal life washed up on the shore. Keep a careful record. The books suggested at the end of this unit will help you identify them.

Suggested Reading

Hausman, L., *Beginner's Guide to Seashore Life*, New York, G. P. Putnam's Sons, 1949. A good beginner's guide.

Miner, R. W., *Fieldbook of Seashore Life*, New York, G. P. Putnam's Sons, 1950. Another book useful in identifying organisms living near the seashore.

Zim, H., and L. Ingle, *Seashores*, New York, Golden Press, 1955.

3 Land Communities

Environmental conditions on land vary far more than they vary in the waters of the earth. Water heats up slowly and cools down more slowly than does land. Therefore, differences between winter and summer temperatures in the water are never as great as they are at many places on the land. The water far below the surface of a deep lake or ocean never gets colder than about 39°F. That temperature, after all, is still above freezing. Most parts of the United States have long periods of winter during which the temperature stays well below freezing.

1. LAND MASSES, CLIMATES, AND LIFE

The location of a land mass on the earth helps determine its climate—both the altitude (height above sea level) and the latitude (distance from the equator). Mount Kenya in Africa is exactly on the equator.❶ Yet it is so high that snow often covers its peak. You would expect the lands closer to the equator to be much hotter, and those farther north and south, nearer the poles, to be much colder. Why is this so? See for yourself. ■

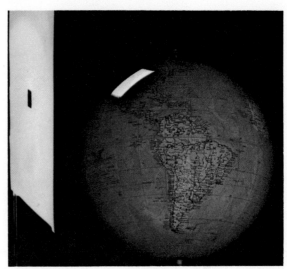

You will need a flashlight, a globe of the earth, and a piece of cardboard in which you have cut a one-inch-square hole.

Hold the cardboard exactly one foot from the globe, with the hole over the equator. Hold the flashlight two feet away from the globe so that its light shines through the hole in the cardboard and directly onto the globe. ❶ Notice that the light hits the equator region on the globe in the form of a square. The flashlight should be directly over the equator on your globe, just as the sun at times is directly over the equator on the earth.

Now repeat the steps above, but this time move the cardboard vertically upward so that the hole is over an area several inches above the equator, as shown in the photograph. ❷ Be sure the cardboard is still one foot away from the globe and the flashlight is not moved. Now the beam of light hits the globe on a slant. This is essentially what the sun's rays do in the northern latitudes and southern latitudes of the earth.

Now examine the patch of light falling onto the globe. You will notice that it is a *rectangle* instead of a *square* as it was at the equator. The same amount of light comes through the square in the cardboard. However, it is spread out over a larger surface area of the earth farther away from the equator. This means that the light is less intense at any point. Here in the northern latitudes, the sun's rays hit the earth at a slant and with less intensity. Thus the earth warms up less at these latitudes than at the equator and in the tropical zones.

An Investigation On Your Own

This may need to be a long-term investigation. What is the difference in intensity in the sunlight coming into your classroom on or around May 20 and December 20? Plan your investigation carefully.

Altitude as well as latitude helps to determine climate. As you probably learned from your earlier studies, climate is also influenced by large bodies of water nearby. Because water cools off and warms up more slowly than land does, large bodies of water become an important influence on the climates of shore communities. Climate, in turn, helps to determine the kind of life that is found in any area. In this chapter we will examine typical environments from the arctic to the equator and from high mountain tops to low valleys and deserts.

Life from North to South

Imagine that you are flying in a jet airplane to a place in Greenland north of the Arctic Circle. Suppose that you then fly southwest from Greenland to Canada, just northwest of Hudson Bay, and there turn south. You enter the United States just west of the Great Lakes and continue south into Illinois. You keep going south to New Orleans and from there southeastward into South America. You end your journey directly on the equator just north of the Amazon River in Brazil. Your plane has stayed at about the

same altitude throughout your trip from Greenland. What changes in climate and in living communities would you expect to find?

Greenland—An Arctic Biome

We use the word **biome** (bī′ōm) to group the animal life and plant life that is typical of any given climate. For example, scientists speak about desert biomes and tropical rain forest biomes. The climate of Greenland, together with the plants and animals found there, make up what we may call an arctic biome.

Although the Norsemen who discovered the island of Greenland gave it its name for its coasts of green, it is only the rim of the land at the edge of the sea that ever becomes green. More than three fourths of Greenland's surface is covered by permanent ice that is up to 10,000 feet thick.

In the summer in northern Greenland, when the sun shines without setting for four long months, a few plants grow in the thin, rocky soil along the coast. ❶ Mosses and **lichens** (lī′kənz), especially the lichens sometimes called "reindeer moss," cover much

of the ground where there is no ice. Further south along the coast, scrubby willow trees, alder trees, and birch trees grow. This is about the extent of the natural vegetation in this arctic biome. Even in July the temperatures in Greenland average only about 40°F. In winter the temperatures average from about 30° below zero in the north to about 20° above zero in the south. Only along the coastal areas is the temperature higher.

In winter there are many weeks in which the sun scarcely shines at all on parts of Greenland. Even when the sun becomes brighter in summer, it lies far to the south and its rays are not very strong or intense. So not much plant life grows in this arctic climate.

As there is so little plant life, there is, as you would expect, very little animal life. Birds include a few sea birds and the ptarmigan (tär′mə·gən).❷ Reindeer [caribou (kar′ə·bōō)], polar bears, rabbits, and foxes are the main animals. Of course, the people who live in Greenland have brought in their own animals, but the naturally occurring wildlife are chiefly the ones mentioned above.

How do these animals live? Rabbits eat the lichens and mosses, the first link in the food chain. The rabbits, of course, form the second link. The foxes become the third link when they eat the rabbits. ❸ In another food chain, the reindeer also eat reindeer moss (actually a lichen) and, in turn, are often eaten by the Eskimos who live in Greenland. So man makes the third link in this food chain. Polar bears live chiefly on seals, walruses, and fish. So the polar bear is really one link in the food chains of the sea. This is also true of the sea birds that eat fish. Ptarmigans eat the leaves and buds of birch and willow trees and may be eaten by foxes and, of course, by people. The food chains in arctic biomes are short and simple.

SIMPLE FOOD CHAIN OF THE ARCTIC ❸

What happens in the winter when the temperature drops and stays well below zero for long periods? Most birds migrate to warmer climates farther south. The ptarmigans, the foxes, and the rabbits (actually, arctic hares) stay in Greenland, but they change their brownish summer coats to coats of white. This causes them to blend with the snow and makes them difficult to see.

A Canadian Arctic Biome

As you move into northern Canada you are still in an arctic biome, but it is getting warmer and conditions are changing somewhat. In summer, in northern Canada, you will find many more animals than in Greenland. The ptarmigan, arctic fox, arctic wolf, and arctic hare are here, but there are also many water birds and shore birds. Lemmings, ground squirrels, and other rodents are usually numerous. These are eaten by snowy owls, foxes, weasels, and wolves. The largest animals are the muskox and the caribou. The caribou migrate north in the short summer when food becomes more available there.

For two or three months a year the land turns green on these generally flat lands,

commonly called **tundra.** ❶ There are no trees except for patches of dwarf willows, alders, and birch. Most of the ground remains frozen the year round, but the top few inches thaw in summer and provide water for mosses, lichens, and a wide variety of small, hardy grasses and shrubs.

As the long winter approaches, the ground squirrels and other rodents burrow into the ground or find other safe places to *hibernate.* In land animals, hibernation is a kind of deep sleep in which the heart beats very, very slowly and breathing almost stops.

During the winter the caribou travel south in search of plant life, and the hares eat what lichens and mosses they can dig out from under the mantle of snow. As in Greenland, the foxes and wolves live on the hares, usually becoming quite thin by the time summer returns with its increase in active animals that can be caught for food.

A Spruce and Fir Biome

As you move farther south in Canada you begin to find scattered clumps of trees. Go a little farther south and you enter great forests of spruce and fir trees that seem to

stretch endlessly in all directions. These trees grow so densely that very little light gets through them to the ground. Therefore, there is very little plant life under such trees. The needlelike leaves of these trees fall and make a deep layer on the ground. Only a few bushes appear here and there. Where there are breaks in the forest, wild grasses grow.

Typical animals of the fir and spruce forests of Canada are seed-eating birds, moose, bobcats (lynxes), ground squirrels and other rodents, and wolverines.

A Temperate Hardwood Forest Biome

As you travel south over the Canadian border into the United States you are still in great fir and spruce forests. However, just west of the Great Lakes you begin to find another definite change. The evergreen forest becomes sprinkled more and more with hardwood trees such as oak and hickory. If you continue southward below Lake Michigan, you will be in what were, before the white man, almost endless hardwood forests. This is all changed now, but there are still patches of woodland left. Farther east of here are large areas that must look much as always.

These regions are, of course, much warmer than the arctic and even warmer than the fir and spruce biomes. The summers here are quite hot, although the winters may be well below freezing for many days.

In the spring the hardwood trees grow a new crop of leaves. Beneath them are a wide variety of bushes and grasses. Just what plants grow in such biomes depends a great deal on the amount of rainfall. For example, in the Midwest, which is comparatively dry, the trees are mainly oaks and hickories. Farther east and north, where it is wetter and cooler, the trees may be mainly maples and beeches.

Just as there are many kinds of plants growing in a hardwood forest biome, so are there many kinds of animals. Plant-eaters include birds, mice, ground squirrels, muskrats, squirrels and other rodents, rabbits, and deer. Meat-eating animals include foxes, skunks (which also eat fruit and berries), shrews, snakes, owls, and hawks.

Food chains in these hardwood forests are complex and interdependent. Food chains that are interdependent and spread over the biome are more nearly **food webs.**

47

A Tropical Rain Forest

Now, from New Orleans you will fly across the Gulf of Mexico and the Caribbean Sea to South America. Soon you will be just over the equator in Brazil. Here you will have to parachute to earth because you are over a tropical rain forest and there is no way to land your airplane in this jungle. ❶

You probably will have to cut your parachute cords because you are almost certain to have landed in a giant tree, perhaps 125 feet high. However, there are probably long vines stretching through the branches, so you should have no trouble swinging down.

Coming in at tree-top level is, as a matter of fact, an excellent way to learn about rain forests. If you came in on the ground, you might never realize that a tropical rain for-est is made up of layers. The giant trees towering up to 125 feet and higher form one layer. Under them grow several layers of trees. Those of the second layer grow, perhaps, 100 feet tall. A third group of trees forms yet another layer with their tops about 50 feet above the ground. Still another layer may reach only 20 or 30 feet in height. So even if you slipped from your vine you could probably catch yourself on one or another of the layers of trees on your way to the ground.

As you might imagine, environments differ in the different layers in a tropical forest. The top trees, of course, get full sunlight. Each layer below it gets less light than the layer just above it. One scientist, Dr. W. C. Allee, made a study of the amount of the light that filtered through the layers of trees and vines in a rain forest in Panama. He found that the jungle floor received only $\frac{1}{500}$ of the light that hit the highest trees.

The plants at or near the ground in a tropical rain forest must, therefore, be able to live in dense shade.

You will find temperature differences, too, resulting from differing amounts of sunlight at the various levels. There can also be extremes of temperature within one level. For example, the tops of the highest trees be-

come very hot during the day but cool down a great deal at night. The lower trees and the ground stay almost at the same temperature day and night.

Many kinds of plants, such as these orchids, are able to grow on the trees in rain forests. ❷ These aerial plants are supported by the trees and vines, and their roots are in the air. The bromeliads are aerial plants that collect and hold rain water in specially formed leaves. ❸ The roots may grow into cracks and furrows in the trunk of the tree or vine that supports them and here they catch dust, leaves that fall, and other materials. These collected materials act like a sponge to hold water, also providing a source of minerals that the roots can absorb.

The tropical rain forest has a bewildering variety of plant life, including hundreds of different kinds of trees. The animal life is also varied. Here, for example, is a tapir guarding its young. ❹ Climbing the tree is a two-toed sloth. ❺ Many kinds of birds, such as this toucan, fly through the forests. ❻ Among the tremendous numbers of insects is this leopard moth. ❼ And there are anteaters, monkeys, pigs, small and giant snakes, lizards, frogs, salamanders, deer, jaguars, parrots, and so on.

You can imagine how complicated the food webs are in a tropical rain forest. Year-round warmth, sunlight, and a tremendous amount of rain make conditions ideal for green plants to grow and make food. This, in turn, provides an ideal feeding ground for a great variety of animals.

Keep in mind, however, that plants and animals must be adapted to the environments they live in. A tropical rain forest would be no place for a cherry tree or an oak tree. The wide-leaved evergreen trees of the tropical rain forest would crowd them out. They would die from the lack of sunlight in the dense shade cast by the towering rain forest trees. Even in the northern forests young trees often become weak and die when they are too densely shaded by the mature trees around them.

A polar bear would probably die of the heat and humidity. A few of the northern plants and animals might adapt satisfactorily to a rain forest. However, *none* of the animals or plants of the tropical rain forest could be expected to live in an arctic biome, a fir and spruce biome, or even a temperate hardwood forest. If nothing else killed them, the winter cold would kill them all. Also, the lack of moisture would destroy many of them, even in the warm summertime.

REVIEW

1. Why does the location of a place in relation to the equator affect its climate?

2. Explain why temperatures of land masses vary much more than the temperatures of lakes and oceans.

3. Why are the food chains of an arctic biome shorter than those of a hardwood or tropical rain forest biome?

4. Keeping in mind that the basic link in a food chain is between green plants and an ani-mal that eats them, explain why there are many more animals in a forest biome than in an arctic biome.

5. What are three important differences in environmental conditions at the top layer and at the ground level of a tropical rain forest? What differences in plant life would you expect at these two levels?

NEW VIEW

1. A biologist was asked to collect plants and animals for a museum. He was told to collect them from both the ocean and the land and from the Arctic Circle to the equator. Which group of plants and animals would you expect to vary more among themselves, those from the sea or those from the land? Explain your answer.

2. A tropical rain forest is to be cut away to make room for a village. The lower-level plants are to be left to beautify the town. Do you think these lower-level plants will live after the taller trees are cut away? Explain your answer.

3. The air is warmed or cooled by contact with the ground or with the water surface beneath it. Reasoning from what you know about the difference in time it takes for water and land to warm or cool, explain why only the land at the edge of the sea becomes green in Greenland.

2. LIFE FROM HIGH TO LOW

It is often necessary to know something of one science to understand another science. You need to know a bit about the physics of air expansion and compression in order to understand why there are deserts. On our continent, deserts are usually found to the east of high mountain ranges. Why is this so?

You probably know that as air expands, it cools, and as air is compressed, it becomes warm. If not, pump air into a bicycle tire and feel the base of the pump. When air is compressed it gets hot very quickly as the result of *molecular bombardment* (that is, molecules hitting against each other and against other obstacles). When you compress air, you force the molecules closer together. When the molecules are closer together, they hit each other and the walls of their container more often. The more often the molecules collide, the more heat there is.

Expansion is the opposite of compression. When a gas expands, the molecules move farther apart; they hit each other less often. The less often they collide, the less heat there is. Expanding gases automatically become cooler.

Cooling and Heating on a Mountain

The prevailing winds that blow across our continent blow from the west. We call them the prevailing westerlies. Some of the air moving in off the Pacific Ocean goes inland at California. This air has picked up a large amount of moisture from its trip over the ocean.

When this air arrives at the western base of the Sierra Nevada range in California, it is forced to climb the mountainside. More air pushing in behind it forces it up. As the air is pushed up the mountainside, it expands. This happens simply because the higher up the air goes, the less air there is piled up above it in the atmosphere. What we call air pressure is simply the air's own weight. The higher up you go, the less air there is above you, so the less pressure the atmosphere has.

For every 1,000 feet the air rises up the western slope of the Sierra Nevada, it cools about $5\frac{1}{2}°$F, if we consider only *expansion* of the air. So 2,000 feet up the side of a mountain, the air would be about 11° cooler than it would be in the western valley below.

Study the diagram at the bottom of the page. ❶ It shows air traveling up the west slope of the Sierra Nevada and down the other side. The air temperature is about 80°F in the western valley. One thousand feet high it cools, as it expands, to $74\frac{1}{2}°$F. For every additional thousand feet it rises, it becomes another $5\frac{1}{2}°$ cooler because it expands. If the Sierra Nevada peaks are 10,000 feet high at this point, the air as it slips over the peaks should be at a temperature of 25°F.

❶ THE EFFECT OF EXPANSION AND CONTRACTION ON AIR TEMPERATURE

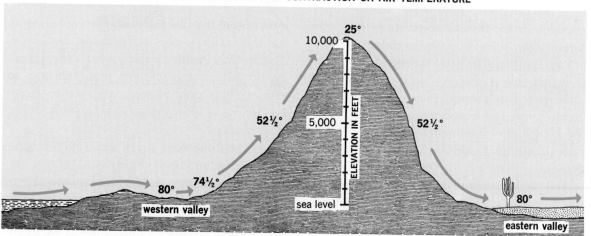

As the air sinks down the eastern slope of the mountains it becomes compressed because there is more air above it pressing down. Therefore, it is warmed $5\frac{1}{2}°$ for every 1,000 feet it drops. If the eastern valley is exactly the same height as the western valley, the air will warm up again to 80°F. If the eastern valley is 1,000 feet lower than the western valley, the air in the eastern valley then, of course, would be warmer. It would be $85\frac{1}{2}°$F.

This much we know. Mountain tops are bound to be cooler than the valleys below because air moves up over the mountains and becomes cooler as it rises. The higher up on the mountain you are, the cooler the air is.

Condensation on a Mountainside

Something else besides expansion and contraction is also important. As you know, all matter has three forms: solid, liquid, and gas. *Liquid* water is of course very familiar, and water in its *solid* form of ice is also familiar. But water in the form of a *gas,* called "water vapor," is often not so noticeable. The water vapor in the air is usually not visible, just as air itself is not visible. How do we know it is there? As long as the water vapor in the air is in the form of a gas, we do not directly detect its presence. But when water vapor changes from the gaseous state into the liquid state, then it is easy to detect.

You are familiar with the beads of moisture that collect like dew on a cold bottle of soda pop. This moisture has come from the air and has condensed against the sides of the cold bottle. Remember how you can see your breath on a cold day? What happens is that the air you exhale (your breath) is saturated with moisture and is cooled by the cold outside air. At the lower temperature of the outside air it can no longer hold its moisture. The moisture from your breath then condenses out in the form of a cloud of tiny water particles. This cloud of tiny water particles floating in the air is what you see.

What do we actually mean by *condense?* When something changes from a gas form to a liquid form, the change is called **condensation.** When water vapor (gas) changes to liquid droplets, as on the cold bottle of soda pop, we say it condenses. As the moisture from the warm air condenses against the outside of the cold bottle of soda pop, it also gives off heat to the bottle. This is one way a bottle of soda pop gradually becomes warmer and warmer. Whenever any gas condenses, it gives off heat to its surroundings.

Warm air can hold more water vapor, or gas, than can cold air. In fact, when warm, moist air becomes cold enough, some of its water vapor will condense out in the form of droplets. If these droplets are small enough to remain floating in the air, clouds of moisture appear. These actually are the clouds that you see in the sky. As the droplets in the clouds collect and become large enough, they fall to earth as rain or, if it is cold enough, as ice.

Now let's get back to the air that is rising up the western side of the mountain range and that is expanding and cooling. As the air goes higher it will finally become cool enough for the water vapor to condense and form clouds. The water droplets will collect and finally fall on the western mountainside as rain. If it is cold enough, the water vapor condenses as snow crystals and a snow storm may result.

Let's assume that the water vapor begins to condense and form clouds at 4,000 feet. As the diagram shows, air starting in the western valley at 80°F cools by expansion $5\frac{1}{2}°$ for every 1,000 feet it rises. ❶ So at 4,000 feet up the mountainside its temperature is 58°F.

However, now condensation of water vapor begins. The amount of heat given off by the condensing water vapor is not as great as the amount of cooling of the expanding air. In fact, after condensation begins, the air still cools $3\frac{1}{5}°$ for each 1,000 feet the air rises. Suppose the air goes up an additional 6,000 feet (from 4,000 feet to 10,000 feet) before it arrives at the top of the mountain. It cools only $19\frac{1}{5}°$ ($6 \times 3\frac{1}{5}$) more by the time it has reached the top. This adds up to a total drop in air temperature of $41\frac{1}{5}°$ ($4 \times 5\frac{1}{2}$ plus $6 \times 3\frac{1}{5}$) since it left the valley. So the 80°F valley air cooled to $38\frac{4}{5}°F$ by the time it reached the top of the Sierra Nevada.

Compressed Air and Desert Conditions

Now, let's follow the air down the eastern slope. As the air sinks down it becomes compressed, therefore it heats up. Since hot air can hold more water vapor than cold air can, there will be no more condensation of water vapor. The air will warm up at a consistent rate of $5\frac{1}{2}°$ for each 1,000 feet it drops. Since the valley below is a drop of 10,000 feet, the total amount of warming will be $5\frac{1}{2} \times 10$, or

55°F. Recall that the air at the top of the mountain was $38\frac{4}{5}°F$. The air will have reached a temperature of $93\frac{4}{5}°F$ by the time it sinks to the eastern valley below. The same air that started up the western slope of the mountains, moist and at a temperature of 80°, has been dried by loosing its moisture and has been warmed to almost 94°F.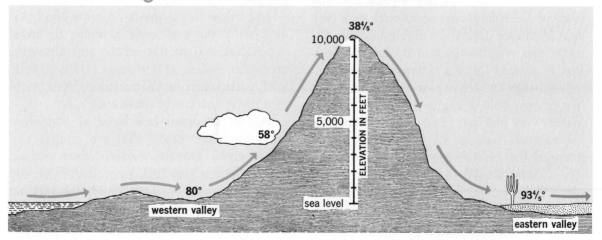

Can you now see why deserts lie to the east of high mountain ranges on our continent? Because clouds form on the *western* slopes of the mountains, the heavy rainfalls occur there. As the air sinks down the *eastern* slopes, it does so as dry air. The air becomes even drier as it sinks and heats up from compression. So the moist, relatively cool air of the western valley has changed to dry, hot air in the eastern valley. Desert conditions are thus created.

What is your guess as to how often rain falls in a desert area? At what seasons do you think rain occurs? It is not difficult to find the answers.

You can study the weather maps to determine how often rain falls in a known desert area. Do you know a better way to find out?

❶ THE EFFECT OF CONDENSATION ON AIR TEMPERATURE

Mountain Peaks and Living Things

The highest peak in the Sierra Nevada range is Mount Whitney, 14,495 feet above sea level. It is so high that air at its top is usually below the freezing point the year round. Therefore, condensation of the moisture in the air results in snow, and the peak is snowcapped at all times of the year.

On such snow-capped peaks there is little or no life. ❶ The snow packs down deeper and deeper, year after year, until its own weight changes it into a kind of ice pack that is very like the permanent ice pack covering most of Greenland. An occasional bird may fly over this ice pack and a mountain goat may sometimes wander up into its lower edges. But, in general, this is a region of little life.

Just below the ice cap of a high mountain is a narrow belt or region in which the climate is very like that of an arctic biome (like the narrow coastline of Greenland). Even many of the animals are similar. The snowshoe rabbit (similar to the arctic hare) lives here. Only a few, low-growing plants such as mosses and lichens are generally found. Occasionally a patch of cold-resistant grass or a gnarled shrub sticks up out of the thin soil. Here, as in the arctic, the temperatures are very cold during the greater part of the year. As you can see, then, similar environments have resulted in similar living things and in similar communities.

Below the high arctic zone of mountains is another narrow band that is very like the spruce and fir biome of northern Canada. Spruce and alpine fir trees grow in this region, and again the animals are similar to those in the spruce and fir biome of northern Canada.

Just below this is another narrow band that is heavily covered with Douglas fir trees, much larger than the spruce and alpine fir trees above them. It is warmer at this altitude and, particularly on the western slopes, there is a great amount of moisture.

Below this band is a band of ponderosa pine trees and below that are juniper and scrub trees. On the eastern lower slopes, where there is very little rainfall and the only source of water is usually from the melting snows at the peaks, even the scrub trees soon cease and the landscape is that of a desert.

Desert Life

Of all the land of the world, about one fifth is desert. Deserts vary in many ways from each other, but all share in common a severe lack of rainfall and surface water. Therefore, they have much less plant life than most other areas of the world. Would you expect much animal life?

Air that sweeps over the American deserts east of the Sierra Nevada is hot and dry. Any moisture that may exist in the sandy, rocky soil quickly evaporates into the air. The occasional rains either evaporate as fast as they fall or quickly sink far below the surface of the land. Therefore, plants that live in the desert must be adapted to a life of little moisture. Cactus plants, mesquite (mes·kēt′), yucca (yuk′ə), agaves (ə·gä′vēz) (century plants), sagebrush, and a few specialized kinds of grasses are some typical plants that are able to exist there.

It does rain occasionally on the desert. When it does, a surprising variety of short-lived plants grow, bloom, and then die, leaving their seeds to repeat the performance when the next brief rain comes.

Plants that live but one season or one year in any climate are called **annuals.** However, the desert annuals have seeds that are able to absorb water rapidly and to **germinate** (start producing a young plant) swiftly. They are capable of flowering and producing seeds before the swift return of the desert dryness robs them of all moisture. Many of these annuals live out their entire life span in six to eight weeks.

Other desert plants live for years but have special structures adapted to desert conditions. The Mariposa lily stores food and moisture in an underground bulb, as other lilies do. Growing rapidly after a rain, this desert lily produces beautiful flame-colored blooms. Then the foliage dies, leaving the bulb buried underneath the ground. In still other plants, such as the brittle-bush, all the branches die during the long dry season. The living underground parts then send up new shoots when the rain returns. The ocotillo always keeps its branches, but grows leaves only during heavy rains which thoroughly soak the ground with water. The leaves remain only as long as ground moisture is available.

55

Many desert plants are adapted to their environment by means of specialized structures for acquiring and conserving moisture. Some of these plants, such as the familiar cactuses, have thick, waxy green stems that both store water and manufacture food. The leaves have become modified until they remain only as protective spines. The huge saguaro cactus grows to 50 feet and may weigh 12 tons. ❶ A small variety of cactus is the Teddy Bear cholla. ❷

Some of the desert plants have shallow roots that spread out for great distances so that they can absorb water from the sudden, short-lived rains. A few plants have solved the water problem by sending their roots as far down as 100 feet. At this depth they often run into a permanent supply of underground water.

Except for the sudden appearance of carpets of flowering annuals during the brief, heavy rainfalls, desert plants are usually widely spaced. In many climates there is sufficient moisture for plants to grow close together. However, a desert plant that tried to grow close to another plant that had already sent out its shallow but extensive root system might simply die from lack of water. The established plant would absorb most of the water from its network of roots before the young plant could secure enough water to last it over the long dry season.

Were you to walk over a desert during the middle of the day, it would seem to be deserted except for the widely spaced plants. You might not see a single animal. You might even assume that there were so few edible plants that animals could not exist. However, if you were to find a shady spot under a giant cactus and wait silently until evening, you would be astonished. Out of burrows in the ground, out from under brush, from

❷

cracks in rocks, and from a myriad of other protected places would spring a surprising variety of animal life. They, like you, require shade from the intense heat of the day and the glare of the burning sun. Like you, the desert animals, with few exceptions, would have rested quietly in a shady spot during the hot day.

The white-footed mouse, the badger, the tiny kit fox, the pocket mouse, and the kangaroo rat spend the hot day in holes and burrows in the ground. In summer, the surface of many American deserts have burning temperatures of over 150°F. However, soil and sand make good insulators. A foot and a half under the surface of the earth the temperature may be only 60°F. So the burrowing animals such as this kangaroo rat sleep and rest during the day in cool comfort.❸

The pack rat makes a tiny cave in old cactus pads and other plant debris that he mounds up. The spotted skunk, the jack rabbit, and the coyote crawl into shade under bushes or cactuses. The cold-blooded reptiles (whose body temperature remains close to that of their surroundings, however hot) usually find some rocky crevice to crawl into. However, the lizards, more than any other desert animal, remain active both day and night. Some birds, the turkey vulture and the road runner, also remain active during the hot desert day. With evening, more birds become active. Quail and thrashers move about eating insects, spiders, and seeds. Among the desert's daytime animals are the ground squirrels, iguanas, and tortoises, such as this one.❹ These animals retire in the evening in burrows or in other protected spots. However, the animals that slept during the day spend the night hunting and avoiding being eaten by other animals.

The food chains on the desert are fairly

57

simple just as they are in the arctic biomes, and for basically the same reason: there are relatively few kinds of plants and animals found there.

As in other biomes, green plants are the first link in the food chains. In the desert, the green cactus is the common first link. The mice, kangaroo rats, and other rodents form a basic second link. They eat plant life and sometimes insects and spiders, and, in turn, they are eaten by horned owls, hawks, badgers, coyotes, bobcats, skunks, snakes, and kit foxes. ❶ The spotted skunk also eats insects and cactus fruits, and, in turn, he may be eaten by various other desert hunters. The coyote eats almost any smaller animal he can catch or can dig out. However, jack rabbits are one of his main fares.

Desert animals, no less than desert plants, must conserve what little water they can get. As an adaptation to desert life, many animals sleep during the hot day. Rarely is there water to drink. The plant-eating animals get their water from the tissues of the desert plants they eat, and the meat-eating animals get water from the tissues of the animals they eat.

An animal extraordinary in its ability to survive in the desert is the tiny kangaroo rat. (See page 57, ❸) This animal usually eats nothing but dry seeds, which are only about $\frac{1}{20}$ water. (Cactus tissue eaten by other animals may have as much as $\frac{9}{10}$ free water.) The kangaroo rat gains some water through his **cellular respiration** (part of which is the oxidizing of food for energy), just as all other animals do. However, this could not begin to take care of his water needs. His body, more than that of any other animal we know, has become adapted in special ways for retaining water. Most animals lose much water in body excrements and by evaporation of water from the lungs, exhaled while breathing. The kangaroo rat loses an incredibly small amount of moisture in these ways.

The kangaroo rat remains healthy on a few dry seeds. Could a coyote? Of course not. The kangaroo rat and the coyote are different animals; they eat different foods; they are adapted to different environments. If we want to keep kangaroo rats alive, we need to keep them in their environment. Or we could say, to keep kangaroo rats alive, we need to conserve their environment. To keep sequoia trees or oak trees alive, we need to conserve their environment. To keep ourselves alive—and healthy—we need to conserve our environment. When people say that *the environment must be conserved,* what do they mean?

REVIEW

1. Explain why air expands as it rises.

2. What causes air to contract as it flows down a mountainside?

3. If you are familiar with the concept of the molecular nature of matter, explain why expansion cools air and contraction heats it.

4. Why are deserts found on the eastern side of high mountain ranges on our continent?

5. Are there good reasons to explain the fact that plants and animals living near the tops of high mountains are so similar to those in arctic biomes? Explain your answer.

6. In what ways are desert plants different from those that grow in more moist climates? Give several examples.

7. How do desert animals get water?

8. How do some desert animals keep cool?

NEW VIEW

1. In general, in South America the prevailing wind direction is opposite to that of our continent. The prevailing winds there blow from east to west. Where would you expect to find deserts in relation to high mountain ranges in South America? You can check your hypothesis with an atlas or map that shows mountain ranges and general topography. Can you predict prevailing wind directions by studying the locations of deserts and mountains in other areas of the world?

2. Death Valley is in eastern California and is just east of the high Panamint Mountains. The valley is nearly 300 feet below sea level. The highest temperature ever recorded in the United States was in Death Valley, 134°F. The Panamint Mountains rise to 11,000 feet. Assume that the land west of the Panamint Mountains is about 700 feet high. Assume, also, that air rising over the Panamints begins condensing water vapor at 4,000 feet. With these facts in mind, determine the air temperature on the flat land *west* of the Panamints the day the temperature reached 134°F in Death Valley. You will find the basic facts you need below.

3. THE CONSERVATION OF MATTER AND INTERDEPENDENCE

By now you have examined a wide variety of living communities. You have studied life in the water and on the land. Wherever you have looked, you have found that living things depend upon other living things for their existence. You have found that green plants and plant-eating animals form the first links in food chains that may be short and simple or long and quite complex.

Perhaps several questions have occurred to you by now. Plants and animals have lived on the earth for many millions of years. Each organism takes in the materials it needs in order to live and "locks up" that material in its body. Can this go on forever or are the materials that living things need likely to be completely used up some day? There is a limited amount of matter in the world. Do living things use up this matter—destroy it— or can it be used again?

It is impossible to destroy matter except in a special way. You may already know that matter is changed into energy during nuclear reactions (as in nuclear, or atomic, bombs). When the bomb is exploded, some of its matter is converted into energy. Although a certain amount of matter is changed into energy during a nuclear reaction, the *total* amount of matter and energy remains the same.

land level west of the Panamints	700 feet
height of Panamints	11,000 feet
land level of Death Valley	*minus* 300 feet (300 feet below sea level)
condensation level on Panamints	4,000 feet
cooling rate of rising air	$5\frac{1}{2}$°F for each 1,000 feet
warming rate of falling air	$5\frac{1}{2}$°F for each 1,000 feet
cooling rate of condensing, rising air	$3\frac{1}{5}$°F for each 1,000 feet

■ AN APPRENTICE INVESTIGATION into a System

Is matter created or destroyed in this system? What is your hypothesis? How will you know whether your hypothesis is supported?

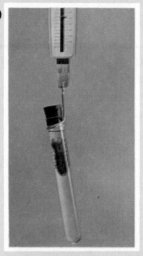

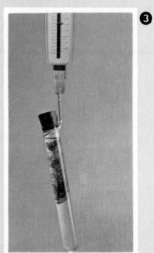

Take a sprig of *Elodea.* Be sure it has a bud on it. Try to get a sprig about two inches long. Measure it carefully and record your measurements. ❶ Place the sprig in a large test tube of pond or aquarium water. Close the tube with a rubber stopper so no air enters. Now hang the tube from a spring scale. ❷ Place the whole set-up in medium light.

Your test tube encloses an environment. In it you find water, dissolved air, and dissolved minerals. There are undoubtedly microscopic animals and plants in the water. So too there is the sprig of *Elodea.* It gets energy from the sun and is at room temperature. The sprig of Elodea has a "home" as it were. It has the physical conditions necessary for life: water, air, light, warmth. Its home is a kind of *system.* The system supplies the *Elodea* with all its needs.

Does the whole set-up gain weight, lose weight or remain the same? ❸ After two weeks of growth, how long is the sprig of Elodea? ❹ Does it increase in size?

An Investigation On Your Own

Demonstrate convincingly that the substances did not come from the test tube. What controls will you use?

However, we can safely say that nuclear reactions do not occur in living things. Even under ordinary conditions in chemical laboratories, nuclear reactions do not occur. For instance, you can take an iron nail and put it into an acid that will dissolve the iron. You can combine the iron nail in thousands of different ways with other elements, but you *cannot* destroy the quantity of iron that was in the nail. All you can do is convert the pure iron to other forms of iron and combine it with other substances. Scientists call this the *conservation of matter.* It is usually put this way: *In ordinary chemical change, mat-*

ter is neither created nor destroyed. Is this true of living matter? See for yourself. ■

What has happened in the investigation is this. The "home" of the *Eleodea* supplies it with all its needs for life. In Greek, the term for home is **oikos** (ē′kōs). Ecologists call a *system* which supplies living things with all their needs for life an **ecosystem** (ek′ō·sis′-təm). For a fish, the pond is its ecosystem. The forest is the ecosystem for a deer. For man, is not the entire earth his ecosystem? Is not man interdependent with living things all over the earth? Does not man get the matter he needs for life from all over the earth?

Combining Atoms

All the matter, all the atoms of any element present on earth today were probably in existence millions upon millions of years ago. Excluding nuclear change, they will still be here millions upon millions of years from now.

By recombining the atoms of elements, different compounds can be made. If you combine hydrogen, oxygen, and carbon in certain proportions, you will get a sugar. ❶ If you combine them again in different proportions, you will get a different sugar. ❷ If you combine them in still different proportions, you will get a starch. If you combine them once again in still different proportions, you will get cellulose. ❸ If you burn cellulose (for example, the wood of a match), the carbon atoms (C) in cellulose combine with the oxygen (O) and the hydrogen (H) from the air to produce water (H_2O) and carbon dioxide (CO_2). And, if burning is not complete, some carbon remains.

In this kind of chemical change matter is not lost and matter is not created. If you change the proportions of carbon, hydrogen, and oxygen, and the positions of attachment of the atoms, you will get fats. If you remove

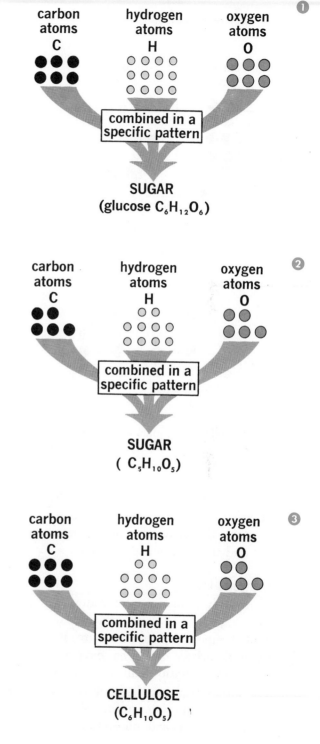

❶

carbon atoms
C

hydrogen atoms
H

oxygen atoms
O

combined in a specific pattern

SUGAR
(glucose $C_6H_{12}O_6$)

❷

carbon atoms
C

hydrogen atoms
H

oxygen atoms
O

combined in a specific pattern

SUGAR
($C_5H_{10}O_5$)

❸

carbon atoms
C

hydrogen atoms
H

oxygen atoms
O

combined in a specific pattern

CELLULOSE
($C_6H_{10}O_5$)

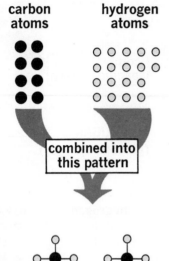

carbon atoms   hydrogen atoms

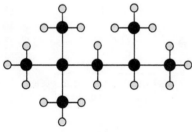

combined into this pattern

a model of a molecule of gasoline

the oxygen and recombine the hydrogen and carbon, you will get waxes and gasoline. ❶ The atoms themselves are not changed, however, and they are not destroyed.

Borrowed Atoms

Your body is made up of water, fats, proteins, sugars, and some other compounds. These compounds, in turn, are made up largely of carbon, hydrogen, oxygen, and nitrogen atoms, with small amounts of some other atoms such as those of the elements copper, calcium, iron, sulfur, sodium, chlorine, magnesium, and phosphorus.

Where do you get these substances? You get them from the food you eat, the liquids you drink, and the air you breathe. However, most come from the food you eat. How do these substances get into the food you eat? If you eat beef, for instance, these substances get into the meat from the air the cow breathes, the water it drinks, and the food it eats. The cow, of course, eats plants.

How do plants get the atoms? You know the answer. The plants take in water (hydrogen and oxygen) from the ground. Along with the water, they take in a variety of minerals containing elements such as iron, phosphorus, and calcium. They also take in nitrogen from compounds dissolved in the ground water, and they take in carbon in the form of carbon dioxide from the air.

How do these substances get into the ground water and into the air? This is a part of the story you may not have thought about yet. Why are these materials finally not all used up? After all, plants and animals have lived on the earth for many millions of years. Each living thing requires these substances for its own life. Shouldn't they all be used up by now?

You probably know the answer or you can think it out in a short time. The answer actually has three parts. One part is that plants and animals do not live forever. If they did, each would permanently lock up a certain number of these atoms. After a time there would be few atoms left for other plants and animals. But all plants and animals die. And you know that although plants and animals die, the atoms of which they are made cannot be destroyed. Now for the second part of the answer.

When plants and animals die, their bodies are decayed by bacteria. *Decaying* means only that the atoms are released in different and simpler compounds. These different compounds are able to be used by other plants and animals. Or, and here is the third part of the answer, the plants and animals are eaten by other animals, and the atoms are recombined within these new animal bodies and are used over again.

The actual fact is that the plants and animals of the world keep using and reusing the same old atoms. The atoms are indestructible and are used again and again in a wide variety of compounds that living things need and make.

It is interesting and startling to realize that atoms now in your body were used by other animals and by plants many hundreds or thousands of times before you made use of them. Atoms in your body (actual parts of what you now are) might have been, at different times, a part of a rose petal, a wolf, shale in the sea, a tall pine tree, a paramecium, or a bacterium. However, you, as an individual living thing, are quite new. But you, as a mass of elements and compounds, are much older than the hills.

You are now the owner of these elements and compounds, but someday other animals and plants will make use of the very same substances. In a sense, you have just borrowed some of the substances from the earth's great store. You will use them for a while, as other living things have before you. Then you will give them up and other forms of life will borrow them for a time.

REVIEW

1. In Chapter 2 the statement was made that it takes, on the average, 10 pounds of food to make 1 pound of the animal that eats the food. How do you account for this if the conservation of matter is really true? Has something been lost? How do you explain what has happened?

2. It is possible to stock an aquarium with a balance of plants and animals. If it is balanced correctly, you can place a glass cover on the aquarium and not touch it for months or years. This sealed microworld will get along fine without attention. How do you account for this in terms of the conservation of matter and what you now know about the interrelations of plants and animals? Is your aquarium an ecosystem?

NEW VIEW

It is easy to burn sugar until nothing is left but gases. The gases are carbon dioxide and water vapor. Try it by heating the sugar in a crucible to a high heat if you do not believe it will all burn away. The chemical equation for the reaction (using a simple sugar such as corn syrup) is as follows:

$$C_6H_{12}O_6 + 6O_2 \longrightarrow 6H_2O + 6CO_2$$

sugar　　oxygen　　　water　　carbon
　　　　from the　　　　　　dioxide
　　　　air

Here is an explanation of the equation. One molecule of sugar is composed of 6 atoms of carbon, 12 atoms of hydrogen, and 6 atoms of oxygen. When sugar burns, it combines with 6 molecules of oxygen, each molecule containing 2 atoms. This burning process recombines the atoms to make 6 molecules of water, each molecule containing 2 atoms of hydrogen and 1 atom of oxygen. It also recombines the atoms to make 6 molecules of carbon dioxide, each of which contains 1 atom of carbon and 2 atoms of oxygen.

Now count the total number of atoms of each element on each side of the arrow. You will find that no atoms are gained and no atoms are lost. Therefore, we say that the equation *balances*. Matter is conserved.

Now explain the following chemical equation for the burning of hydrogen in oxygen.

$$2H_2 + O_2 \longrightarrow 2H_2O$$

4. THE CONSERVATION OF ENERGY AND INTERDEPENDENCE

What about the energy you use in living and moving? Energy can no more be created nor destroyed than can matter. You cannot destroy energy. However, you can change one kind of energy into another kind of energy. For example, light energy can be changed into thermal energy, which can make generators turn (mechanical energy). Thermal energy includes what was once referred to as "heat" energy. A generator changes mechanical energy to electrical energy. The electrical energy can be changed by an electric light bulb back to thermal energy and light energy. So you see, you can change the *form* of energy, but you cannot destroy it.

Often, as far as *useful* purposes are concerned, a considerable amount of energy is lost as heat into the atmosphere and elsewhere. But as far as scientists have been able to discover, you *cannot* destroy energy. *Energy cannot be created or destroyed; it can be changed from one form to another.*

Your body uses chemical energy to make energy of motion or thermal energy. Of course, without thermal energy you could not survive. Where do you get this energy?

You probably know the answer. You get this energy from the foods you eat. Chemical energy is locked up in these foods. But where does your food get the chemical energy? You know the answer to this, too. The chemical energy of food is really trapped energy of the sun. Green plants, by means of light energy from the sun, are able to change water and carbon dioxide into sugars. These sugars may then be changed into starches, fats, and proteins. However, the sun's energy, converted to chemical energy, is still locked up in these foods.

Animals may then eat the plants. When that occurs, the sugars, starches, fats, and proteins may either be made into parts of the animal's own body or they may be broken down to release the energy. When you eat beef, you take in not just elements and compounds, but also their stored energy. When you eat vegetables, or sugars and starches, you also take in the energy stored in the molecules. Your body uses this energy as it is needed for living, for bodily functions such as keeping warm, moving, and thinking.

But the concept of the conservation of energy is a little different from the conservation of matter. This needs explaining. The atoms of your body will someday be released and will be available to other living things, as you know. The energy *you are now using* will *not*, however, be available to other living things. Your body is giving off heat. This is not lost immediately. It is warming your surroundings slightly. Eventually, however, it will radiate out into space and be gone from the earth. Or, perhaps, you will soon pound a nail with a hammer. Energy from your food will be changed into energy of the motion of your arm. This energy will cause the hammer to move and the moving hammer will drive the nail into a piece of wood. The energy of your moving arm will thus be changed to heat of friction as the nail goes through the wood. This heat of friction will be conducted or radiated away from the wood, eventually into outer space.

Most of the energy released for living activities, and for everything else for that matter, is chiefly lost as far as useful purposes are concerned. Only a small amount of the energy released from the food you eat is channeled into activities. Much of the energy released is in the form of thermal energy. It is eventually lost from the earth. It is not destroyed, but eventually most of it radiates into the atmosphere and then out into space. Thus, the energy needed for living things must be constantly renewed. This can only be accomplished by green plants trapping more sunlight to be changed into chemical energy for all living things. So, although energy is never destroyed, it is constantly being lost for use here on earth and must be replaced continually by the energy of sunlight. This is the world ecosystem; in it living things are interdependent with each other and with their environment. Generally, man is found distributed over the entire world ecosystem.

We can now clearly begin to understand three major concepts:

In chemical change, matter is neither created nor destroyed.

Energy may be transformed from one form to another, but it is neither created nor destroyed.

The total amount of matter and energy is conserved.

It is interesting to determine how many changes or transfers of energy you find around you. How many examples of the change of one form of energy to another can you think of? For example, into how many different forms of energy is electricity transformed in your home? Can you think of other examples of the change of chemical energy into energy of motion or electrical energy? Living things change the chemical energy of foods into the energy of motion and into the electrical-chemical energy that travels along nerves.

REVIEW

1. A pile of wood was completely burned. The wood weighed 200 pounds before it was burned. All the gases that escaped in the burning were collected and weighed along with the ashes that remained. The gases and ashes, altogether, weighed 215 pounds. Where did the additional 15 pounds come from? Was matter created?

2. A boy had a bird in a cage. He weighed the food and water he gave it, the bird itself, and the bird's droppings. He found that, over a few weeks' time, the bird had not gained at all in weight although he had fed it 7 ounces of food and nearly a pound of water. The droppings over this period of time weighed a total of 4 ounces. How would you account for this apparent loss of matter?

NEW VIEW

A farmer reported that he had developed a new chicken feed. He said that it was so concentrated and good that for every 10 pounds of food he fed the chickens they gained at least 12 pounds of weight. What do you think of this statement and why?

5. RELATING THE CONCEPTS

In your earlier work (Chapters 1 and 2) you learned that organisms adapted to water environments are dependent upon one another and upon their environment. There is a continuing exchange or flow of materials and energy between living things. For instance, the food chains, which are made up of living things, show how green plants are basic to the capture of energy from the sun and how animals depend on the green plants.

On the other hand, each organism—whether a diatom, or a protozoan, or a whale—is adapted to the physical conditions found in the environment. These include oxygen content, concentration of salts, temperature, pressure, and the like. All organisms are part of their ecosystem, depending on it, giving to it, and taking from it.

Reviewing the Concepts

▶ *Environmental conditions on land vary to a greater degree than they do in water.* On land, temperatures range from the cold temperatures of the frozen arctic and of high mountain tops to the hot temperatures of the tropics and of the low valleys alongside great mountain ranges. Rainfall and humidity vary from the humid, tropical rain forests to the dry deserts.

▶ *The types and numbers of living things vary with the environmental conditions.* Few plants are able to live in the arctic biomes or on cold mountain tops. Consequently, there are few animals found in these places. As the first link in the food chain always connects a green plant and an animal that eats it, there can be few animals when there are few plants. Furthermore, the food chains in arctic biomes and on high mountain tops are usually short. This, too, is a result of so little plant life that long, elaborate food chains cannot be supported.

▶ *On land, as in the water, living things have developed that are adapted to the environmental conditions of a particular region.* Desert plants, for example, are quite different from those found in tropical rain forests or in temperate hardwood forests.

▶ *Green plants must have light, water, and warmth to live and manufacture food.* Because of the increase in light, water, and warmth, the number and variety of green plants increase as one goes from the Arctic Circle to the tropics. As the number and variety of plants increase, so do the number and variety of animals, for they are bound through food chains ultimately to green plants for their material and energy.

The increase in number and variety of plants and animals from the arctic to the tropics is roughly similar to the increase in number and variety of plants and animals from the frozen mountain tops to the green valleys. The organisms live in an ecosystem.

▶ *The effect of mountains on the temperature and humidity of air creates desert conditions.* Highly specialized plants and animals capable of enduring extreme dryness have developed as a result of these conditions. Their ecosystems are special.

▶ Where living things are concerned, neither matter nor energy are created nor destroyed. In fact, the major concept, *the totality of matter and energy is conserved,* governs the behavior of matter and energy generally. This concept is known as the Law of Conservation of Matter and Energy.

Testing Yourself

1. Why is it that there is such a similarity between arctic plants and animals and plants and animals of cold mountain tops?

2. Explain why the environmental conditions in a tropical rain forest biome result in living communities greatly different from those communities found in a temperate hardwood forest biome.

3. Why are the North American deserts found to the east of high mountain ranges?

4. Describe some of the ways in which plants and animals have become adapted to the dry conditions of desert life. Give examples showing how animals and plants can live with so little water.

5. Would you say that animals are physically adapted to their physical environments in terms of structure and the workings of their bodies or adapted by their habits (ways of living)? Might it be both? In considering

your answer to this problem, think of life in a particular biome, say a desert.

6. A green water plant, *Cabomba*, is placed in a plastic bag. Nothing can diffuse into or out of the bag.

After a month, the students notice that the plant stem is definitely longer; it has grown. Nevertheless, the weight of the bag has not changed. Explain the results.

7. The total amount of heat given off by a small mouse is measured. It is found that a given amount of matter has been changed to form this heat. What concept applies to the example cited?

Extending the Concepts

Investigation 1. Over the next few weeks or months, make a continuing study of the land communities near your home. Although man has greatly changed the natural environment of any region he has inhabited by his modern ways of living, you can still find out about the natural communities of plants and animals typical of the climate in which you live.

If this work can be shared with others in your class, you can, over a period of time, develop an excellent and worthwhile report on the living community or communities of your region. Library references will help you to identify plants and animals as well as to determine the food chains. (Units 4 and 5 will also help you in identifying plants and animals at the large group, or phylum, level.)

Investigation 2. Create specific artificial climates and determine what plants will live and thrive in them. An aquarium or a wide-mouthed gallon jar will do for such a terrarium in which you create an artificial environment.

To create a woodland terrarium, cover the bottom of your jar or aquarium with about 1 inch of pebbles or coarse gravel. Spread about ½ inch of sand over this and then add a layer of garden soil mixed with peat moss to a depth of about 1 inch. First, plant patches of mosses and small ferns in the soil. Then add water slowly until it comes about halfway up to the top of the bottom layer of pebbles or gravel. A glass cover should be placed on the top of the jar or aquarium. Your terrarium should be situated in a place out of direct sunlight but where it will get strong light.

Try other small plants in your woodland terrarium to see how well they do.

A desert-type terrarium can be made by following the procedure described above for a woodland terrarium, except do not add soil and peat moss. Instead, place a 2-inch layer of sand on top of the gravel. You can plant small cactuses and cactuslike plants. Add a very small amount of water (a cupful or two) once every two weeks or so. The amount of water required will depend upon the number of plants, the size of your terrarium, and the dryness of the air. Do not place a cover on the desert terrarium. The air will remain drier if you leave it open for moisture to escape.

Investigation 3. Smog, pollution (in lakes and oceans), and pesticides are found wherever man lives. Is he destroying his ecosystem? Will he adapt to the new ecosystem he is developing? Investigate this problem in the library and the daily newspaper. Perhaps you should suspend your final response and wait for more evidence.

THE
ORGANIZATION
OF
LIVING
THINGS

Compare these two plants—both molds. Both are plants in the genus *Penicillium*.

Which one depends on man? How?

Which one grows in the environment— in the wild, as it were?

How does man make an environment for organisms? Is it possible for organisms to survive without man? How?

4 Cells as Building Blocks

1. BASIC UNITS OF LIFE

A hen's egg is easy to get and easy to examine. You can do this at home.

When you crack the egg open and place its contents in a saucer, notice at least two things: the yellow and the white. You may be surprised to learn that the yellow (the **yolk**) is only a huge supply of proteins, fats, minerals, and vitamins in the hen's egg. It serves only as food for the tiny spot of living stuff that appears as a whitish speck on the yolk. ❶ This whitish speck contains both the **nucleus** of the egg and the living material, known as **cytoplasm** (sī′tə·plaz′əm), that you will learn more about later. The white substance, the **albumen** (al·byoō′mən), is protein and protects the delicate living parts.

If the nucleus is fertilized by a sperm, the egg could develop into a chick. However, most eggs, like the ones you eat, are not fertilized. Nevertheless, the hen's egg is a huge *cell*, with a nucleus and cytoplasm. It also has a great store of food to be used by a developing chick over the 21 days it remains in the egg. What has the hen's egg to do with the structure of living things? Let's look into this.

Study the photomicrographs (photographs taken with a microscope) at the right. One shows a cell that was part of the sheet of cells from the inner lining of the cheek of a person. ❷ Another shows the cells that make up the skin of a frog. ❸The last are cells that make up the covering layer of an onion bulb. ❹ All the cells have a nucleus, cytoplasm, and a cell membrane. The top cell is labeled. See if you can identify the structures in the lower two photographs.

In both animal cells and plant cells the nucleus and cytoplasm (as well as the surrounding cell membrane) are part of the living material of the cell. Together they comprise the basic living stuff of which all life is made. This basic material is called **protoplasm** (prō′tə·plaz′əm). It is typically a grayish, jellylike material that contains tiny particles.

You may have noticed at least one difference between the animal and plant cells you examined. The plant cells are rectangular. This is, in part, due to the presence of a tough **cell wall** that keeps the cell a certain shape.

Most plant cells, then, have at least one structure different from those of an animal cell, namely, a rather stiff cell wall. It is stiff because in most plant cells it is made up of strands of a substance called **cellulose** (sel′yə· lōs). Cellulose makes up cotton and much of wood. Often you will hear the cell wall of plants called "a woody cell wall." In addition to this tough cell wall, the plant and animal cells all have a nucleus, cytoplasm, and cell membrane.

An Old Theory and New Ideas

How common is the cell in the structure of living things? We must go back at least 300 years for part of the answer.

In 1665, to be exact, an Englishman named Robert Hooke examined a plant tissue called

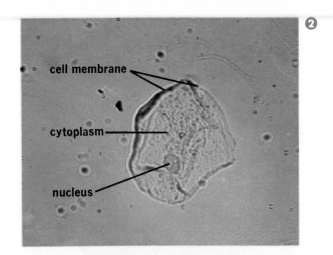

cell membrane

cytoplasm

nucleus

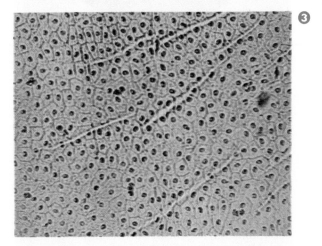

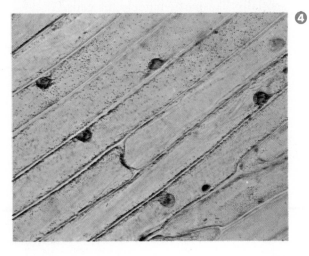

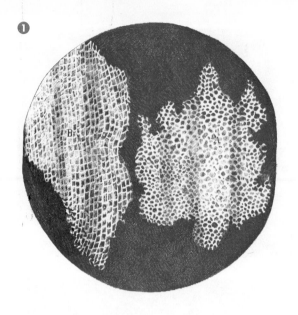

cork with a crude microscope. He reported that this tissue all seemed to be made up of compartments, or *cells*, surrounded by walls. In fact, he made a drawing of what he saw.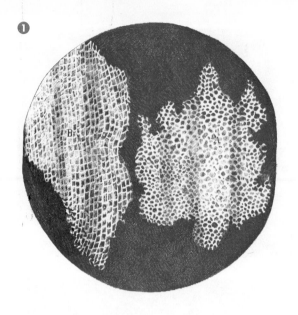

One hundred and seventy-four years later, in 1839, a German biologist named Theodor Schwann published a book that reported the investigations that he and another German named Matthias Schleiden had been carrying out. In his book Schwann said: "We have seen that all organisms are composed of essentially like parts, namely, of cells."

Schleiden and Schwann had stated the *cell theory*. As you may already know, a **theory** is a statement that explains the facts—the confirmed observations—as far as they are known.

The tremendous importance of this theory, the explanation that all living things are made of cells, can hardly be felt today. But in their day the view that *every* living thing, plant or animal, simple or complex, was made up of from one to several billions of the *same things*—cells—was astounding. Of course, Schleiden and Schwann depended upon the work of many other biologists who had studied cells, the French botanist Dutrochet (dōō·trō·shā′) being the foremost.

Does this cell theory still hold today, after more than 120 years of continuous investigation by scientists?

What Hooke saw was just the woody cell walls of dead plant cells. His microscope was not powerful enough for him to have seen the contents of living cells. Also, Hooke probably had no idea that all living organisms, animal and plant, were made of cells. Recall that it took almost 175 years before it was recognized by Schleiden and Schwann that cells were the building blocks of living things. Between Hooke and Schleiden and Schwann, a host of scientists of all nations studied the structure of living things.

In other words, Schleiden and Schwann brought together the observations of many scientists to form an *explanation* of the way living things were built. You will recall that an explanation of facts (*confirmed observations*) is known as a theory. To repeat, a theory is an explanation of the facts. Schleiden and Schwann's cell theory of the structure of living things still lives. However, is this theory completely true? Let's go further into a study of the cell.

Inside the Cell

Wouldn't it be convenient if we could simply climb into a cell to study it firsthand? However, since this is not possible, let's study the photograph of a cell magnified thousands of times by a high-powered electron microscope. Under this high magnification we would see what is shown in the photograph. ❷ Notice that this cell does not seem to be as simple as the ones shown on page 71. The nucleus and cytoplasm have other structures within them.

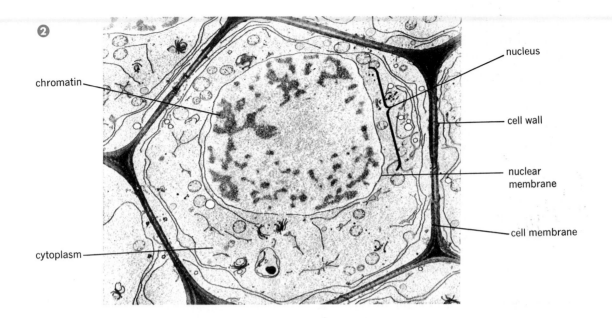

❷

chromatin

cytoplasm

nucleus

cell wall

nuclear membrane

cell membrane

THE NUCLEUS. Notice the dark-colored material labeled *chromatin* in the nucleus of the cell. This material makes up the **chromosomes** that form during cell division, as you shall see in Chapter 18. Chromosomes are made up of complex molecules. The molecules are extremely important because they carry a kind of chemical "blue print" that determines what the living organism will be like.

You started as a fertilized egg. The egg cell in your mother's body was fertilized when a sperm cell from your father joined and merged with the egg cell. From that original fertilized egg cell have come all of the billions of cells that now make up your body. The original egg cell divided and divided, again and again, thousands of times. Each time a division occurred, equal parts of the chromosome material went to each of the two new cells that were produced. Somehow the "blue print," or "code," of what you were to be like was in that original set of chromosomes in that original fertilized egg.

The nucleus has another important function, too. For the moment, let's say that it governs the life of the cell. If the nucleus is removed from a cell, the cell soon dies. Somehow the nucleus controls the life functions of the cell. Some of the ways in which this is done are known, whereas other ways have not been discovered.

THE CYTOPLASM. The cytoplasm is usually considered to be all the living material outside the nucleus, excluding, of course, the cell membrane. Both the physical and chemical structure of cytoplasm vary with the type of cell. The cytoplasm of nerve cells produces and carries the nerve message. The cytoplasm of muscle cells is capable of great contraction. The difference in the cytoplasm makes these cells different in structure and in chemical activity.

However, the nucleus governs the activity of the cytoplasm. The nucleus produces chemicals that move out into the cytoplasm and cause it to perform its particular tasks.

THE CELL MEMBRANE. Each cell is covered with a *living membrane*. The membrane keeps the liquid cell contents together. It also helps to control the flow of water and dissolved materials in and out of the cell. A living cell membrane permits certain dissolved substances such as simple sugars and salts to **diffuse** (di·fyōoz′) through, but keeps other dissolved substances from doing so. You might say that a living animal or plant membrane operates much like a control gate, permitting diffusion on a *selective* basis. Sometimes a large amount of one substance will be allowed to enter a cell. At another time the same cell membrane may admit little or none of the very same substance. You will learn more about this later in this unit.

THE CELL WALL. Plant cells, you will recall, have rather stiff cellulose walls outside the cell membranes. The cellulose walls of the cells give strength and support to the larger many-celled plants such as trees. Cell walls have nothing to do with controlling the flow of dissolved materials in and out of cells. Their entire function seems to be that of giving support and strength.

THE SIZES OF CELLS. Most cells are microscopic in size. However, there are some nerve cells up to three feet or more in length. You could not see such a cell without a microscope, though, for its width is of microscopic dimensions.

Recall that in a chicken egg the living parts of the cell are only the cell membrane and a tiny spot on the surface of the yolk. This spot contains the cytoplasm and the nucleus with its chromosomes. The cell membrane surrounds both this part and the yolk.

A chicken egg is much larger than even an elephant egg. (Elephants do not *lay* eggs, of course, but all higher animals including elephants and man develop from fertilized eggs.) All birds have relatively large eggs, due to the fact that they are *laid* and that the young develop *outside* of the bird's body. So there must be space in all bird eggs to have a great amount of stored food ready for the baby bird. There must also be room for the bird to develop and grow inside the shell.

Egg cells, in general, are the largest of living cells. The human egg cell, for example, is about the size of a small dot and can be seen without a magnifying glass.

Suppose you were to measure the cells of an animal's body and average their size. Which do you think would have larger cells, an elephant or a cat? In other words, do you think it likely that cells in different animals are about the same size? If this is so, it would mean that an elephant is larger than a cat because it has *more* cells. Or do you think it more likely that an elephant has just about the same number of cells as a cat, but that the cells are, on the average, much larger in an elephant? And how do you think the cells in a baby animal compare in size with the cells of an adult animal of the same kind? As a project, you might like to find the answers to these questions, using a microscope and prepared slides of tissues from various kinds of animals.

By now you know that a single cell can be quite complicated and can really do everything necessary for living that a many-celled animal can do. You also know that it is the chemistry of the protoplasm, that is, the behavior of the substances in the chromosomes of the nucleus and in the cytoplasm, that makes the life and activity of a cell possible.

What if these same cell substances were organized some other way, without a nucleus, without cytoplasm, and without a cell membrane? Would life be possible without an organization into cells?

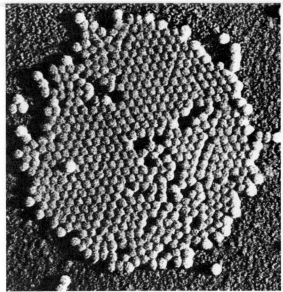

Viruses—a Partial Answer

Do you know what happens when you have a common cold? The viruses that cause many of the common colds have found their way into your body. In fact, many of man's diseases and those of other animals and even of plants are caused by the things called viruses. Influenza and poliomyelitis are among the diseases.

What is a virus? Here is a photomicrograph of a virus that causes influenza. ❶ And here is the virus that causes poliomyelitis. ❷ If either of these viruses found its way into your body, under the right conditions it would multiply until millions of them existed. Viruses multiply in number just as all living things do. The viruses must have energy to do this, of course. They seem to use food and oxygen to produce energy and materials for their growth in just the same way as living cells do.

Then, are viruses cells? *No, they are not.* The photographs above are magnified many thousands of times. They actually show the *molecules* of which viruses are made. Viruses are considerably smaller than the smallest known cells. Scientists have not been able to find a cellular structure to them.

Are viruses alive, then? That depends on your point of view. One of the most basic characteristics of life is that it can reproduce itself. Single-celled organisms can reproduce themselves simply by dividing to make two organisms like themselves. Viruses do the same thing. Each virus duplicates itself to form two identical viruses. Each duplicate, in turn, forms two more viruses. Soon there are thousands, then millions, then billions.

Many scientists believe that viruses are certainly alive. Other scientists are more cautious. They point out that viruses can exist and reproduce only when they are inside living cells. They also believe that the living cells that the viruses invade are what keep them growing and dividing. They believe that the living cell somehow affects the protein molecules of the virus to keep them existing and reproducing.

Any living cell, as you know, takes raw materials and changes them into materials it can use. Perhaps, say some scientists, when the virus is inside a living cell its protein molecules are affected in some way that makes them grow and duplicate themselves. The strongest point to this argument is that no one has ever been able to induce a virus to reproduce itself outside living cells.

Perhaps the viruses are bridges between the nonliving and the living world. Perhaps something like viruses were among the first living things on the earth. Someday scientists may have an answer to the question of whether viruses are alive.

At this point, then, we modify slightly the cell theory which came down to us from the year 1839 when Schleiden and Schwann stated it. We can say only that living things are generally made up of cells. The only possible exception we know are the viruses. However, Schleiden and Schwann's theory does hold for living things like you, dogs, trees, grass, and bees. But how does this theory hold true for things such as bacteria, yeasts, and all the living things in a drop of water?

REVIEW

1. All cells are said to be similar in structure. How true is this? Illustrate your answer.

2. In 1839, was it truer to call Schleiden and Schwann's statements about cells a theory or a fact? Which is truer now? Why is it still called a theory?

3. Could a cell reproduce without a nucleus? What is the reason for your answer?

4. Are viruses organisms? What are the reasons for your answer?

NEW VIEW

1. When and if a living thing is created in the laboratory, will it more likely be a cell like a cheek cell, a plant cell, or a viruslike organism? Why?

2. Of these structures, which would you say is basic to life: cell membrane, cytoplasm, cell wall, chromosomes? Why?

3. Of these two, an animal cell and a green plant cell, which is more basic to the life of other organisms. Why?

2. "FREE–LIVING CELLS"

You have probably begun to suspect that whenever a word or a phrase is put into quotation marks, it does not mean exactly what it usually means. The heading of this section is one such phrase.

You know by now that no living thing is really free-living. For instance, all living things depend on their ecosystems for the energy they use. Surely it would seem to you that a cell—your cheek cell, for instance—could not actually be free-living.

There are, however, living things, made up of a single cell, that do live singly and freely in their environment. It is appropriate to study one of these free-living, single-celled organisms to learn what we can about the work of a single cell as part of an organism.

The free-living cell we shall study is the *Paramecium*, one of a group of single-celled, aquatic animals known as **protozoans** (prō·tə·zō'ənz).

Structure and Function
in the Paramecium Cell

Look at the two pictures. The first is an enlarged photomicrograph.❶ The second is a drawing of a paramecium and shows, even more clearly, the parts of this single-celled animal.❷ Study the two pictures carefully. How many of the parts labeled on the drawing can you find in the photograph?

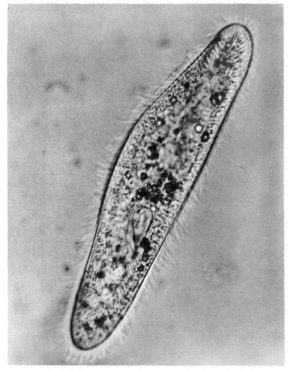

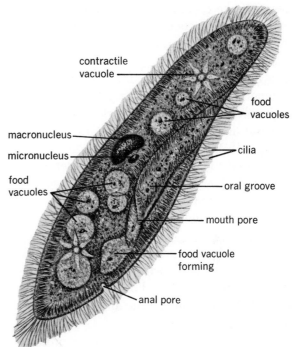

contractile vacuole

food vacuoles

macronucleus

micronucleus

cilia

food vacuoles

oral groove

mouth pore

food vacuole forming

anal pore

As you read on in your study of the paramecium, refer back often to the pictures.

GETTING FOOD. In their natural environment, paramecia move about in what seems to be an aimless fashion. When they hit something, they simply back up a bit and then start off again in a different direction. They continue to move in this apparent trial-and-error fashion until they happen upon some bacteria or other particles of food.

Look again at the drawing of a paramecium. ❷ Do you see the **oral groove,** the **mouth pore,** and the several **food vacuoles** (vak′yōō·ōlz)? When a paramecium bumps into bacteria, the bacteria are swept into the oral groove by tiny hairlike structures called **cilia** (sil′ē·ə). The oral groove is a sunken place in the wall of the animal. It leads to a tiny opening and a funnel-like tube that

extends from the mouth pore into the interior of the cell. Cilia in the oral groove sweep bacteria through the mouth pore and into the animal.

As more and more bacteria are carried into the cell, a small clump of bacteria forms. This mass of bacteria, surrounded by a small bit of fluid, forms a food vacuole, which flows away from the mouth pore and circulates inside the cell. A paramecium feeding on a mass of bacteria is soon filled with food vacuoles packed with bacteria.

If a red dye, powdered carmine, is placed in the water surrounding the paramecia, they will collect this dye into their food vacuoles as well. This will stain the food vacuoles red.

The bacteria are digested by **enzymes** (en′zīmz) that are secreted into the food vacuoles. Each food vacuole becomes smaller

77

and smaller as the digested food is absorbed by the body cell. Finally the vacuole disappears. If there are any indigestible particles, they are slowly moved to the **anal pore,** where they are literally pushed out of the animal's body.

GETTING OXYGEN. This, for a paramecium, is much simpler than getting food. Oxygen is dissolved in the water in which the paramecium lives. It diffuses into the animal, along with the water, through the cell membrane. Once inside the cell, the oxygen combines with the food. This releases energy and produces carbon dioxide and water, as is done in all living things.

GETTING RID OF WASTE PRODUCTS. Carbon dioxide is a waste product that occurs when oxygen is combined with food. In the paramecium, the carbon dioxide diffuses out through the cell membrane and into the surrounding water.

In all living organisms, whenever proteins (either food or cell materials) are broken down, waste products are produced. These are poisonous to the living cell and, of course, must be removed before they harm the cell. More complex animals have complicated mechanisms (kidneys and bladders) for removing the wastes. These wastes are usually in the form of urea, which, when dissolved in water, forms urine.

It is believed that the paramecium also produces a waste product called ammonia. The ammonia then, like carbon dioxide, diffuses through the cell membrane and into the surrounding water, a simple way to excrete wastes.

MAINTAINING A WATER BALANCE. All organisms must maintain a proper amount of water within their cells. If the amount of water drops too low, the concentration of salts and other dissolved substances within the cell becomes too great, and the cell may die. And, if too much water enters the cells, the concentration of substances within the cell becomes too low, and the cell may die. It is also possible with too much water inside the cell that the cell membrane could actually split from internal pressure.

Thus a paramecium, like any animal, must maintain its water balance. The contents of its cytoplasm are more concentrated in salts and other materials than is the surrounding water. If nothing were done to balance this, water would flow through the cell membrane into the cell until the cell swelled up and the thin cell membrane burst.

The **contractile vacuole** is the paramecium's mechanism for getting rid of excess water. The radiating canals slowly fill with water. They then contract and force the water into the round central vacuole. This vacuole then contracts and forces the water through the cell membrane.

MOVEMENT. You already know that paramecia move. But how do they move? Look again at the drawing of a paramecium on page 77. Do you see the tiny hairlike cilia that cover the animal's body? You know that these cilia beat back and forth and sweep food particles into the animal's mouth pore.

Cilia also move the animal about. They move like many tiny oars, beating swiftly in one direction, then moving back limply and more slowly to their original position. In this way the animal moves ahead. When a paramecium backs up or turns around, it does so by changing the direction of the beating motion of the cilia.

Study the drawing.❶ It illustrates how the cilia move—not all at once, but one after another in a rhythmic motion. As the animal moves forward, the cilia at the front end beat backward first. Then cilia just behind the first cilia beat, then the next cilia, and so on. This wavelike pattern of beating cilia thus moves the animal.

RESPONSIVENESS. Paramecia do not have to bump into bacteria to discover that they are there. Bacteria cause the decay of materials dissolved in the water. Decaying materials usually produce a small amount of acid and other substances.

Paramecia are sensitive to acids and respond to very small amounts by moving toward them, much in the same way that you might detect the smell of food cooking in your kitchen and move in that direction. Of course, the paramecium has no brain and is not conscious of the presence of acids in the water. It probably moves almost automatically as molecules of acid hit the cell membrane.

Such an automatic response is called a "tactic (tak'tik) response," or a "taxis" [(tak'sis); plural, *taxes*]. That is, the animal moves toward or away from stimuli in an unconscious and seemingly automatic fashion. Have you ever seen a moth attracted to light? It is a kind of tactic response.

RESPONSE TO GRAVITY. Most protozoans, but not all, are apparently negatively **geotactic.** In other words, they move *up* in water, *away* from the pull of gravity. If you found any protozoans in pond water while studying Chapter 1, you probably found some forms only at the bottom of your jar of pond water and other forms concentrated mainly at the top. Of course they could be reacting to stimuli other than gravity. Can you think of stimuli that would differ at the top and bottom of the jar? Would there be the same amount of oxygen at the surface and at the bottom? Would the light be the same? Would food particles, bacteria, and chemicals be evenly distributed throughout the jar?

① HOW A PARAMECIUM MOVES

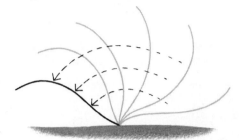

beating movement of a cilium, moving animal forward

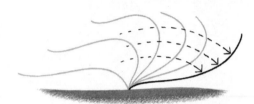

movement of a cilium back to original position

wavelike pattern of cilia

RESPONSE TO LIGHT. Most protozoans are positively **phototactic,** that is, they will move *toward* the light if it is not too intense. This is generally true of most protozoans that are capable of motion. However, if the light is too intense or suddenly and sharply increased, they may move to regions of less light.

RESPONSE TO TEMPERATURE. Although paramecia can withstand a wide temperature range, most seem to prefer a moderate temperature of about 75–85°F. If the temperature is raised or lowered sufficiently, they will move and collect in an area of a more moderate temperature. This reaction to temperature is called **thermotaxis.** If you added heat to one end of a test tube of paramecia at 80°F, would you say that they would have a *positive* or a *negative* thermotactic response?

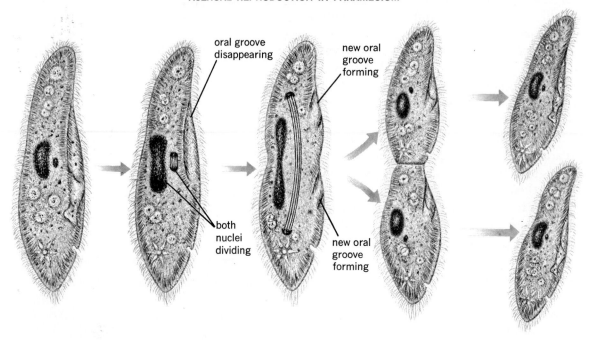

oral groove
disappearing

new oral
groove
forming

both
nuclei
dividing

new oral
groove
forming

What sort of response, positive or negative, would they have if you added heat to a test tube of paramecia that had a temperature of 50°F?

RESPONSE TO FOREIGN SUBSTANCES OR ENE-MIES. Paramecia, like many other organisms, also respond to the action of foreign substances or enemies. Some biologists consider the action you are about to investigate a protective device. What do you think? ■

REPRODUCTION. Paramecia and other protozoans reproduce themselves by dividing in two. The drawings show several stages of a dividing paramecium. **1** The paramecia and some other protozoans have two nuclei: a large one, the *macronucleus*, and a small one, the *micronucleus*. Both of these nuclei divide when the animal divides. Thus the two new paramecia that result are part of the original cell and have the characteristics of the original cell. This kind of reproduction, in which there is only one parent, is one type of **asexual reproduction.** *Asexual* means "without sex." The particular form of asexual reproduction that occurs in paramecia is called **fission** (fish′ən). It is the most common way protozoans reproduce.

There is also another method of reproduction called **conjugation** (kon′jŏŏ·gā′shən) that sometimes occurs, and involves two paramecia. Since two animals are necessary, conjugation is a form of **sexual reproduction.**

When conjugation occurs, two paramecia join at their oral grooves. Then the small nucleus in each animal divides several times. One part of each small nucleus moves to the other paramecium, where it joins with the remaining part of the small nucleus there. So conjugation exchanges materials from the nuclei of both animals. You will recall that the nuclei contain the chromosomes, which make an organism what it is. This exchange

■ AN APPRENTICE INVESTIGATION into a Response of Paramecium

Place a drop or so of your culture of paramecia on a slide. Put a cover slip on the drop.

Now place a drop of ink on one edge of the cover slip. Draw the ink under the cover slip by placing a blotter on the other side. You will notice that as the blotter draws the water from under the cover slip, the ink is drawn in. Now examine the paramecia. What has happened?

Look at the photomicrograph. ❶ Notice the many long threads in the water beside the paramecium. These are called **trichocysts** (trik'ə·sists). When a paramecium is attacked by an enemy or irritated by strong chemicals, it shoots out these threads. Is the trichocyst reaction a protective device?

The trichocysts are also probably used to anchor the animal when it is feeding. Then the threads are shot only part way out of the body.

An Investigation On Your Own

Under what different conditions will a paramecium shoot out its trichocysts?

---

of nuclear material seems to strengthen or to vitalize the cells. Finally, the cells separate.

A healthy and well-fed paramecium may divide by fission several times a day. Conjugation occurs only occasionally.

Single-Celled Animals and Single Animal Cells

Clearly, *Paramecium* is a free-living animal. That is, within its own body it has the structures that enable it to move about freely in its environment. True, like all living things, a paramecium depends on its environment for food and oxygen. One of your cheek cells, on the other hand, is not free-living; it depends on other cells for the requirements of life. For example, a cheek cell depends upon the blood stream for food and oxygen. It also depends upon the blood stream to carry away

its wastes, such as urea and carbon dioxide. A cheek cell is, after all, a unit of structure and function in a many-celled organism.

Paramecium has within it all the structures necessary to perform its life functions.

Let's list the functions that keep an organism alive: getting food, respiration, responsiveness, reproduction, and excretion. What structures does the paramecium have that enables it to perform each of these functions?

The animal has cilia, a macronucleus and a micronucleus, a cell membrane, an oral groove, food vacuoles, a mouth pore, contractile vacuoles, and an anal pore. In this section you have studied how the paramecium uses these structures to perform its life activities. These functions, structures, and responses of *Paramecium* are summarized in the table on the next page.

Life function	Structure and response
GETTING FOOD	cilia, oral groove, and food vacuoles. (Also moves about to collect food.)
RESPIRATION	cell membrane, through which oxygen diffuses into the cell, and carbon dioxide out of the cell.
RESPONSIVENESS	cilia; the entire animal responds to changes in the environment by moving toward or away from stimuli.
REPRODUCTION	entire animal divides by fission (asexual reproduction). During sexual reproduction, chromosomes (from nuclei) are exchanged through oral groove and mouth pore.
EXCRETION	cell membrane, through which ammonia diffuses. Water is removed by means of the contractile vacuole. Anal pore.

Apparently, *Paramecium* is able to carry on, within its single cell, all the activities that characterize a living thing. It has the structures—cilia, food vacuoles, contractile vacuoles, and the like—that enable it to carry out its life functions. Within a single-celled animal these structures, such as cilia and food vacuoles, are called **organelles** (ôr′gan·elz′). Put in another way, a paramecium has organelles that enable it to carry on its life functions. Put still another way, a paramecium— a single-celled animal—is *organized* to carry on its life functions. We say that a paramecium is an *organism*. On the other hand, a

cheek cell or a muscle cell, such as is part of our bodies, is a *part* of an organism.

There is, then, an important difference between a *single-celled animal* (*Paramecium*) and a *single animal cell* (a cheek cell). The single-celled animal is an organism, able to fend for itself—organized to carry on life functions. Indeed, that is the meaning of *organism:* a living thing organized to carry on life activities.

A single animal cell, such as a nerve cell or an onion cell, is only a part of an organism—a many-celled organism. Nevertheless, whether we think of single-celled animals or plants, or single animal or plant cells, the cell is still the basic unit of structure and function.

REVIEW

1. What are the differences and similarities between a single animal cell and a single-celled animal? Compare function as well as structure, using *Paramecium* as an example of a single-celled animal and a human cheek cell as an example of a single animal cell.

2. Choose a single-celled animal that you have studied and describe how it carries on these functions: locomotion, respiration, reproduction, excretion, responsiveness.

3. Identify the structures in the following diagram of the single-celled organism, *Paramecium*. Explain the function of each structure.

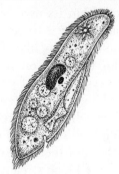

NEW VIEW

1. Sometimes paramecia have small green dots in them. What do you suppose these are? In the library, check your hypothesis.

2. The graph below shows the rise and fall of a population (the total number of organisms) of *Paramecium* in a liter of pond water.

What might be an explanation for the rise and fall of the population of *Paramecium*?

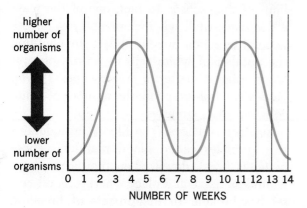

NUMBER OF WEEKS

3. CELLS AS PART OF MULTICELLULAR ORGANISMS

It is well to look back for a moment. We recognize that wherever we see a living thing we find cells. With the exception of the viruses, this seems to be true of animals and plants. We also have come to realize that single-celled animals such as *Paramecium* (and other kinds of protozoans you may have studied, such as *Amoeba*) carry on within a single cell all the functions of life. That is, a single-celled animal is an *organism,* a complete living thing.

However, as you will recall, a cheek cell is not an organism, it is a part of an organism —you. The skin cells that covered the frog were not organisms; they were part of an organism. These organisms are known as *multicellular* (many-celled) *organisms*.

How do cells come to be part of a multicellular organism? Let's study the multicellular organism in which we have the most interest—man. However, it is well to emphasize at this time that we study ourselves as organisms only as a case for understanding how cells make up a multicellular organism.

A First Combination

Take a good look at your hand. Of what is it made? Cells, of course. Feel your hand. Surely, you feel some bone. You feel flesh, which is made up mainly of muscle. Notice the blood vessels and feel your pulse. Blood is being pumped into your hand.

There are many kinds of cells bound together into the many kinds of **tissues** that make up the human hand. One, of course, is *skin tissue.* Scientists call it **epithelial** (ep′ə·thē′lē·əl) **tissue.** Another is **muscle tissue,** the kind that makes up all of your voluntary muscles (muscles you can contract voluntarily, that is, when you want to). A third kind is **connective tissue,** the kind that straps the bones firmly together and that joins tendons by which muscles are attached to bones. A fourth is **nerve tissue.** A fifth is **bone tissue.**

What is a tissue? A study of your own tissues will furnish us with some observations.

Blood Tissue

Blood is a good example of a tissue that is made of both cells and nonliving material. This nonliving material is called "extracellular material." Blood consists of several kinds of cells floating in a fluid. The fluid is a complex, soupy material, the **plasma.** When plasma diffuses out of a capillary into spaces between cells, it becomes part of the **lymph** (limf).

The plasma contains two kinds of blood cells. The **red blood cells** carry oxygen from the lungs to the body cells and some carbon

83

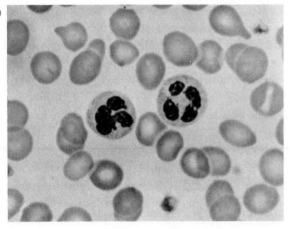

dioxide away from the cells. Notice that red blood cells, shown here as they appear in the blood stream, have no nuclei. Consequently they cannot reproduce, nor do they live very long. **White blood cells** have large, darkly staining nuclei. They live and act almost as if they were independent single-celled animals in your body. But they are a part of you. Their function is to get rid of the disease bacteria that find their way into your body.

Suppose that you ran a splinter into your finger. Some bacteria are almost certain to get into the wound. It is possible that they might multiply and make you ill, or even kill you, since they throw off poisonous waste materials as they destroy your tissues. However, soon the white cells in your blood stream move toward the wound. Here they collect in such numbers that there may be thousands of them in a tiny wound. Because they have the ability to change their shapes, the white cells can literally *flow around* the offending bacteria and digest and destroy them. As this occurs, the wound soon fills with a mass of bacteria, tissue cells, lymph, and dead and dying white cells. This mass, called "pus," is a sign that the white cells are at work.

Bacteria may also enter your body through natural body openings, such as your mouth. If the bacteria are the kind that cause disease, your entire body may become ill. The white cells, of course, work on these bacteria, as well. As the bacteria reproduce themselves by dividing in your body, the white cells also reproduce. By dividing and redividing, the white cells can increase in number to millions of themselves. In fact, one of the ways a doctor can tell whether or not you have a general infection in your body is by counting the number of white cells in a drop of your blood placed under a microscope. If you have a general infection, the number of white cells increases greatly.

BLOOD PLATELETS. The blood also contains tiny particles called blood **platelets.** These platelets break down when they arrive at a wound or arrive at a place where a blood vessel has broken. In the process of breaking down, they release an enzyme. (An enzyme causes or speeds up a chemical reaction.) The platelet enzyme causes a chemical change to occur in the blood so that fibers are formed and the blood clots. You can judge how important they are. What do you suppose would happen if you cut yourself and there were no blood platelets?

PLASMA. The fluid part of the blood, plasma, is also very important. It carries the red cells, white cells, platelets, and many other things as well.

Although the red blood cells carry away much of the carbon dioxide produced by cells, the plasma also carries some away in a dissolved form. The plasma, as well, carries to the cells all of the dissolved foods that they need. Most of the waste materials produced by the cells or by bacteria are carried away by the plasma to the **kidneys** (or kidneylike tubes in many other animals). In the kidneys, the wastes are removed from the blood stream and become part of the urine, which is then excreted from the body.

A variety of important chemicals called **hormones** (hôr′mōnz) are circulated throughout the body by the plasma. These hormones, produced by various glands in the body, control and regulate the growth and function of the entire body.

BLOOD TISSUE AND REPAIRS. One important difference between a living machine like you and a nonliving machine like an automobile is that the living machine constantly repairs itself. As you know, parts wear out in both. This is true of the blood as well as all other tissues. An adult human being has about 25 million million (25,000,000,000,000) red blood cells in his body. *Every second about 10 million of these die* and are literally digested by white blood cells that remain in the liver and in an organ called the **spleen** (splēn). *Also every second, 10 million new blood cells are produced* to replace the ones that have died. These new red blood cells are produced by the division of special red blood cells that have nuclei. These reproducing blood cells always remain in the marrow of your bones. They are never found in the blood stream. (Marrow, as you probably know, is the soft substance in the center of bones. You may have seen it often in a ham bone or in the bone of a round steak.)

Bone and Cartilage—
Connective and Supportive Tissues

Next time your mother has chicken for dinner, ask her for the lower part of the leg and the foot. When you remove the skin, you will notice some strong fiberlike structures. Pull them. Notice how the fibers are attached to the bones and how they move the lower parts of the foot.

The fibers connecting bone to bone are called **ligaments**. Those connecting muscle to bone are the **tendons**. Can you find a tendon? a ligament? Ligaments and tendons, because they connect tissues, are known as **connective tissues. Bones** and **cartilage**, because they support and shape the body, are known as **supportive tissues.**

Connective and supportive tissues, like blood tissue, also contain much nonliving material. Bone cells secrete the hard, rocklike substance that we call bone. However, a living bone is far more than just this nonliving substance. The bone tissue is just as alive as any other tissue in your body. Living cells lie in regular patterns throughout the nonliving bone material. And if the bone is broken, the living cells go to work to secrete new bony material to repair the break.

The dead, hard material of a bone is mainly calcium phosphate, a compound containing the minerals calcium and phosphorus, combined with oxygen. If you take a leg bone of a chicken (or any other small bone) and leave it in a jar of weak acid (such as vinegar) for several weeks you will find that you can bend it easily. ❷ Most of the cal-

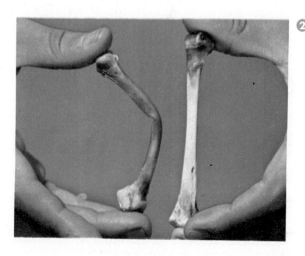

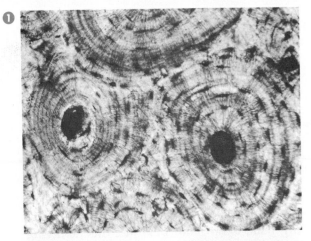

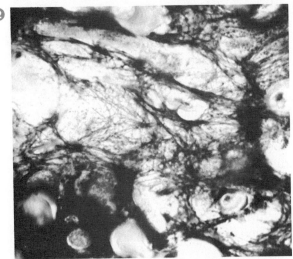

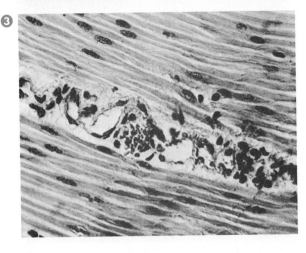

cium phosphate, the extracellular material, has dissolved out of the bone and into the acid. What is left is the softer material—dead cells, connective tissue such as cartilage, and some fibers.

The photomicrograph reveals that individual bone cells are arranged in a series of circles around a central tube, or canal. ❶ The nonliving bony material is secreted by these bone cells. Observe that this bony material (shown in white) is also laid down in regular patterns around the canals through which blood vessels run. Bone cells, like any other living cell, must have food and oxygen and must give off wastes. The blood supplies and carries away the soluble substances these cells use or produce. Notice also the threadlike extensions of the bone cells. The necessary food, oxygen, and other substances diffuse from cell to cell through these extensions.

Tendons, ligaments, and some cartilage are similar to bone except that they contain fibers instead of calcium phosphate. Here is a photomicrograph of one kind of cartilage. ❷ These cartilage cells secrete fibrous materials that are strong but flexible. Your ears and the tip of your nose are cartilage. Feel your ears and bend them around. The cartilage bends without breaking then springs back into shape. This is possible because the flexible fibers in cartilage run in all directions and give strength to the cartilage whichever way you bend it. Cartilage is often called "gristle."

Tendons and ligaments resemble cartilage except that the fibers all lie in one direction. This gives great strength when they are pulled. Tendons, you recall, fasten muscles to bones. When a muscle contracts, a tendon is put under great strain. However, the tendon fibers, like the strands of a strong rope, keep the tendon from breaking. Ligaments are sheets of connective tissue that connect

■ AN APPRENTICE INVESTIGATION into the Structure of a Muscle Cell

Next time you have meat for dinner, ask for a bit of the raw meat. In class, tease it apart in a drop of water on a glass slide until you have only a few fibers. Place these fibers in a drop of water on a clean slide and stain them with a drop of dilute iodine. Place a cover slip on top.

Perhaps your slide is similar to the photomicrograph shown here. 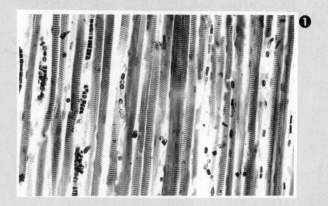 Notice the stripes in the very long cells. These are *striated* (strī′āt·əd) muscle cells.

Now feel the upper part of your arm. The muscle that bends your arm is made up of millions of striated muscle cells in bundles. Of course, the muscle is also made up of blood and connective and nerve tissues, but it is mainly striated muscle.

An Investigation On Your Own

Are the striated muscle fibers of the same length? The same thickness? You will need to find a way of measuring objects being examined with the microscope.

bones at joints. They, too, are extremely tough. However, while tendons are not elastic, ligaments are elastic. This elasticity permits the joints to move.

There is, finally, one other kind of connective tissue that binds things together in your body. This loose connective tissue has fibers running in all directions, but the tissue is not as dense and full of fibers as are cartilage, tendons, and ligaments. The loose connective tissue holds together muscle cells that make up muscles, and surrounds groups of nerve cells that make up nerves.

Muscle Tissue

Animals are generally distinguished from plants by their ability to move. Therefore the movement of animals must be clearly dependent on a special kind of tissue. Examine for yourself some parts of this special tissue, muscle tissue. ■

There are three kinds of muscle tissue. The tissue you just examined is **voluntary muscle tissue,** or striated tissue. These striped, or striated cells are typical of all voluntary muscle cells. They make up the muscles that are fastened to the bones and that move the bones. They are under your voluntary control.

A second kind of muscle tissue is found in your heart, and only there. The **heart muscle tissue** is striped similarly to voluntary muscle tissue, but it is branched. This tissue has the ability to contract rapidly and then relax for a split second of rest, then contract again and relax, continuing for a lifetime.

The third kind of muscle tissue in your body is called **smooth muscle tissue.** As you notice in the photomicrograph, it has no stripes. ❸ Smooth muscle can only contract and relax slowly. However, smooth muscle tissue can stay contracted for a much longer time than can voluntary muscle tissue.

Smooth muscle is found in the walls of your digestive tract, where its contractions and relaxations move the food along. It is also found in the walls of your veins and arteries. In general, smooth muscle tissue is responsible for the movements of many of your internal organs. This muscle tissue is not under your voluntary control, nor is the heart muscle tissue. You can do nothing voluntarily to speed up or slow down your internal organs. Neither can you control blushing nor keep your nose from getting red on a cold day. The responsibility for these events rests with the tiny, smooth muscles in the small blood vessels of your face or in your nose. When the smooth muscles in these vessels relax, it allows the blood (under pressure) to fill the vessels. This results in a red coloration and you blush or your nose gets red.

The action of your intestines is slow and rhythmic, much like the motions of an earthworm, and from much the same basic kind of muscle structure. Your intestines, like an earthworm, have two main layers of muscles, one running lengthwise and the other running crosswise, or in circles, around the intestines. Neither has bones to which the muscles attach. Watch an earthworm move.

Its body stretches out and then contracts, usually in sections. When the circular muscles contract, they make the earthworm smaller around and longer as the muscles squeeze in. When the circular muscles relax and the lengthwise muscles contract, the earthworm becomes thicker and shorter.

Your intestinal muscles work this way continuously. In one section of intestine, the ringlike smooth muscles will contract, the lengthwise muscles relax. As in the earthworm, this section becomes thin and lengthens a bit. A few moments later the lengthwise muscles in this section contract and the ringlike muscles relax. Then, this section becomes thicker and a little shorter. By the alternating pattern of relaxing and contracting, these muscles cause food to be mixed and slowly moved through the digestive system.

Nerve Tissue

If you were to design muscle cells that needed to contract, you would obviously make them rather long. Suppose you had to design nerve cells. Keep in mind that they must carry messages from one part of the body to another. You would probably design them much as they actually are, long and thin.

Here is a photomicrograph of a nerve cell. ❶ Compare it with the drawing of different kinds of nerve cells, called **neurons** (nŏŏr′onz). ❷ As you see, they are made up of cell-like parts and long fibers. Nerve messages, called **impulses,** travel from neuron to neuron throughout the nerve tissue. Impulses from the long neuron fiber enter the tiny frayed-looking ends near the cell body. Once in the cell body, the impulses can go out any path and over to other nerve cells.

The many connection points between neurons permit messages to go in a variety of directions. It works something like the central switchboard of a telephone system. If you dial the telephone number of a friend, the automatic switchboard connects your wire to the particular wire of your friend—among the tens of thousands of possible connections. The electrical message (impulse) then travels to his telephone. In a roughly similar fashion (which is not understood fully), nerve messages, or nerve impulses as they are called in your body, travel specific paths and bypass many connection points (or "switchboards") in order to make the right connection.

Decide to move the little finger of your right hand. An impulse goes from your brain down your spinal cord and out to precisely the right muscles for moving the correct finger. To do this, the impulse had to bypass many wrong connections. Yet it was accomplished easily.

Somehow, learning is tied up with the way impulses move over the neurons, which in turn must make the right connection with other neurons. If you throw a ball to a small child and ask him to catch it, he will hold out his hands in the general direction from which the ball is coming. However, the chances are good that the ball will go right between his hands. The nerve impulses did not go to the right muscles at the right time.

You will recall that most cells of the body are microscopically small. You can only see them with a microscope. This is true of the nerve cells, too. However, although they are microscopically thin, some are amazingly long. There are neurons, for example, that run from the base of your spinal cord down your leg to your foot and toes. In an adult these can be three or more feet long.

When we use the word *nerve,* we mean a whole bundle of individual neurons in which

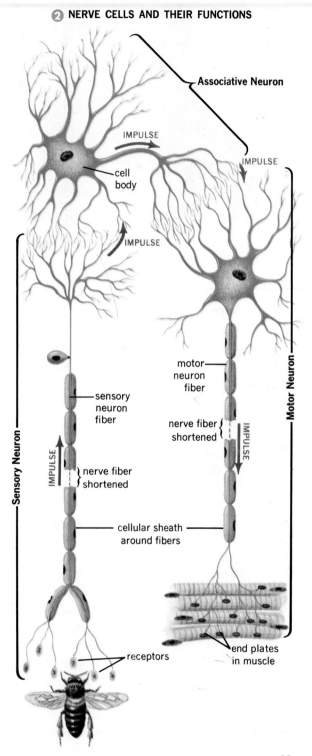

Associative Neuron

IMPULSE

IMPULSE

cell body

IMPULSE

IMPULSE

Sensory Neuron

Motor Neuron

sensory neuron fiber

motor neuron fiber

nerve fiber shortened

IMPULSE

IMPULSE

nerve fiber shortened

cellular sheath around fibers

receptors

end plates in muscle

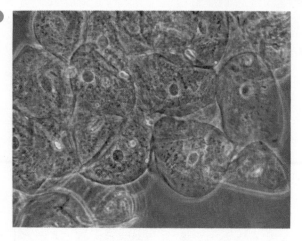

the long wirelike strands are held together by a connective-tissue sheath. Each bundle of neurons (or each nerve) has blood vessels that supply the cells with food and oxygen. As in other tissues, the blood also removes waste products that result as neurons carry on their activities. At present, scientists believe that nerve impulses are transmitted as the result of both chemical and electrical changes.

Protective and Gland Tissues

You have already begun a study of these tissues. You have examined skin cells, or covering cells, from your cheek and from the skin of a frog. Your own skin cells are exceedingly important to you.

You are approximately seven tenths water. If you did not have a skin, seven tenths of you would evaporate rather quickly. Luckily for you, you are covered with skin—a tough, elastic sheet that prevents evaporation. But evaporation of perspiration, which is secreted by sweat glands in the skin, does take place.

Your skin has other functions, of course. It protects the soft, underlying tissues from blows and injuries. It acts as a barrier against disease germs entering the body.

Look at your lips in a mirror. The skin becomes thin but it does not end there. Epithelial cells line your cheek. ❶ If you have not done so before, examine your cheek cells now. These cells interlock to form a thin membrane, called a **mucous membrane,** that continues right into your mouth and down your esophagus. This mucous membrane lines your entire digestive tract.

Recall that these cells are broad and flat. Epithelial cells (whether skin or mucous membrane or whatever else) are basically protective and covering cells. Fastened tightly together and often many cells deep, they form a tough, elastic sheet.

THE SKIN. The human skin contains a number of different structures in the epithelial tissue. Study the drawing of the skin. ❷ The outside layer of the skin is made up of layers of dead cells. These keep peeling off as new cells to replace them are produced in the lower layer of living cells. Oil from the glands in your scalp often mats these dead cells together so that they scale off in tiny patches called "dandruff." You might like to dust off a bit of dandruff from your scalp and stain and examine it under the microscope.

The outside layer of your skin is called the **epidermis** (ep′ə·dûr′mis). It includes both the dead outer layer and a living inner layer of cells. The inner layer of the epidermis is also well supplied with nerve endings. These nerve endings detect heat, cold, pressure, and pain. When you become too warm, your skin flushes, or becomes a redder color. Remember that this is caused by the relaxation of the smooth muscles of the blood vessels in your skin, permitting more blood to enter the skin. When this occurs, more blood lies nearer the outside air and the heat radiates away. The same thing happens if your skin becomes too cold. Your nose and ears are thin and could freeze on a very cold day. However, the muscles of the small blood vessels relax and a great deal of blood circulates through the skin, keeping it warm.

The **dermis** (dûr′mis) lies underneath the epidermis. The dermis, the inner layer of your skin, is entirely alive. It contains many blood vessels and nerves. Several other things are embedded in the dermis; for one thing, a great amount of fat is stored here. As you can see from the drawing, the fat is stored in special storage cells that become full and round from the fat they contain. Even a thin person has some fat stored in his dermis. A fat person may have an almost solid layer of it. Have you ever noticed the layer of fat on a ham or on a leg of lamb? It lies just under the outer skin and forms a thick layer.

The skin of a human being has many sweat glands. These glands are coiled tubes that secrete a watery, salty substance that flows out of the ends of the tubes (the pores) at the surface of the epidermis. When it is hot, of course, the sweat glands increase the amount of sweat. As the sweat evaporates, it cools the body. On a cold day very little sweat is secreted. So there are two ways in which your body cools itself and maintains its constant temperature of about 98.6°F: by changing the amount of blood in the skin and by sweating. Did you know that it is a good idea to eat more salt during hot weather when you are sweating a lot?

STRUCTURES MADE OF SKIN. Your hair is made of epithelial tissue; hair is a kind of *modified* skin. Again, look back at the drawing of the skin. You will notice that hairs have their living roots in the dermis and grow up through the epidermis. The base of each hair is a mass of actively dividing cells that produce layer after layer of hair cells that keep pushing upward and out of the skin.

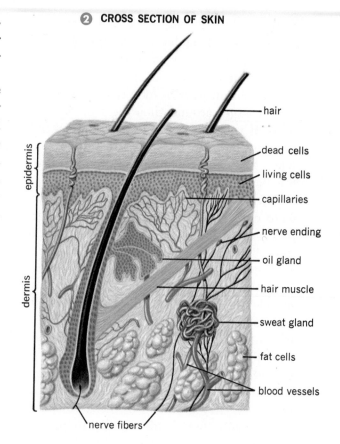

2 CROSS SECTION OF SKIN

epidermis
dermis

hair
dead cells
living cells
capillaries
nerve ending
oil gland
hair muscle
sweat gland
fat cells
blood vessels
nerve fibers

Only the base of the hair shaft is alive. The cells above soon die, so that most of the hair is just dead cells. That is why it does not hurt to cut your hair.

It does hurt, just a bit, to pull a hair out, however. That is because nerve endings lie in the living base of a hair. Capillaries are also found here since they supply the hair cells with the food and oxygen for living, growing, and dividing.

Pull out a single hair from your head. Examine the root carefully. Do you see the whitish mass around the root? Examine it more closely under a magnifying glass. You will discover that it is a sheath and at least part of an oil gland. Next to each hair lies an oil gland. The oil gland secretes oil into a sheath that surrounds the hair shaft. This keeps the hair from becoming dry and brittle. The oil also seeps out onto the skin, keeping it pliable too.

The hair on your head is thicker and each hair is larger around than the hair on other parts of your body. But if you will carefully examine the skin on your arm or skin anywhere else, you will find that it, too, has many fine hairs.

Did you ever get goose pimples when you were chilly? Do you know what goose pimples are? When you become chilly, tiny smooth muscles connected to the sheath of each hair automatically contract. This action pulls the hairs up straighter. The contracted muscle and the push of the hair against the skin causes a tiny bump to appear. These tiny muscles are not under your voluntary control. They work automatically, as do all the smooth muscles of your body.

Your finger nails are also a kind of modified skin. They grow out of the dermis from special cells that divide rapidly to produce new finger nail cells. These, like hair cells, die very quickly, and the dead cells form the tough plates of nail material.

Your teeth are made of specialized epithelial cells, as are the feathers of birds, the scales of snakes and other reptiles, the scales on birds' legs, as well as fish scales. Even hooves of cows and horses and the antlers of deer are made of specialized skin cells. The oil glands and sweat glands of your skin are also made of epithelial tissue.

Many of the glands in your body are considered part of the epithelial system. You will study these glands more thoroughly later. But for the moment, think about such glands as the salivary glands and the digestive glands. Each gland produces a different kind of secretion.

Your salivary glands secrete a fluid which contains an enzyme that digests starch. Your stomach glands secrete an acid fluid with an enzyme that digests proteins. Your intestinal glands and your pancreas secrete fluids with enzymes that can digest starches, fats, and proteins. The endocrine glands, which secrete their products into the blood, make a variety of complex substances that we call *hormones*. Each of these hormones has a powerful influence on the control, regulation, and growth of your body.

Tissues Into ?

Clearly, you are made up of five tissues: blood, connective and supportive, muscle, nerve, and epithelial tissues. All animals with backbones (sometimes called **vertebrates**), such as the mammals, birds, reptiles, and fishes, contain these same tissues. The multicellular but less complex animals (sometimes called **invertebrates**) are also made up of tissues, except that they may lack certain ones. For instance, sponges lack blood tissue.

Obviously, tissues seem to work together. You probably know why. The body systems of an animal are made up of organs. Your heart is an organ, and so is your brain. Your lungs, stomach, and intestines are all organs. Consider your heart, for instance. This organ is also made up of a variety of materials and structures. It, too, is designed for a particular task. The heart is covered with a thin, sheetlike membrane that secretes a slick fluid (*mucus*). This fluid permits the heart to beat inside the membrane sac with little friction. Attached to the heart is some fat that serves as food storage. The walls of the heart are mainly muscle (cardiac muscle), found nowhere else in the body. The chambers inside the heart are lined with another smooth membrane that prevents friction as blood flows through them. Just underneath the membrane is a fibrous sheet that is extremely tough. The heart, as you know, has valves. There are valves between the auricles and the ventricles. There are valves between the ventricles and the great arteries that leave the heart. There are nerves and even a collection of nerve cells that form a group, or node, that regulates the heart so that it beats with regularity.

An **organ,** then, is a group of tissues that work together to perform particular tasks.

Organs Into ?

By now it should be very clear that cells in a multicellular organism do not wander about loose. They are grouped with other similar cells into tissues. Tissues have similar functions. All muscle tissue contracts. Nerve tissue carries nerve impulses. Epithelial tissue covers and protects.

Clearly, the cell is not only the unit of structure in living things. It is also the unit of *function.* That is, cells carry out the work of the living things. Cells, in multicellular organisms, carry out their functions within groups of similar cells, the tissues. And, of course, the tissues do not function separately. They are grouped together into organs: the heart, the kidneys, the lungs. Even the organs do not float about. They are grouped into **organ systems.** It is these organ systems that make up the organism.

Do you see once more the meaning of the word *organism?* It is well to dwell on this: an organism is organized. Through its organization, it is adapted to carry on its life functions. Thus, one important clue to the makeup of a living thing is its organization.

Study the drawing showing how one organism—a human being—is adapted for movement by its organization. ❶ Do you see once

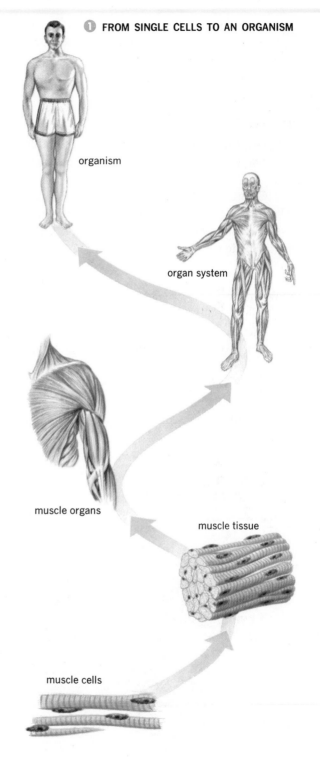

❶ FROM SINGLE CELLS TO AN ORGANISM

organism

organ system

muscle organs

muscle tissue

muscle cells

again why the cell is considered to be the unit of structure and function? Do you see why the term *organism* actually means an organization to carry on the function of living things?

REVIEW

1. Regroup these in order of their ascending organization: cell, organism, organ system, organ, tissue.

2. Compare and contrast three types of muscle cells with regard to their structure and function.

3. Describe at least one type of cell in each of the following tissues: epithelial, nerve, blood, connective.

NEW VIEW

1. Can you name any organ that is not made up of each of the five tissues?

2. When does the red blood cell lose its nucleus? (The library will help.)

3. Which cells, if any, have more than one nucleus? How do you account for this?

4. Identify the following cells, according to tissue.

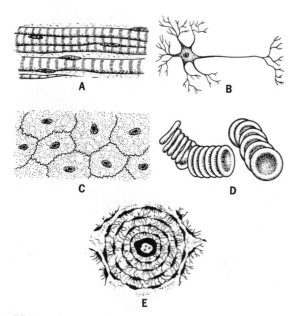

4. RELATING THE CONCEPTS

The words *organism* and *organized* obviously have a common origin. Our studies show clearly that organisms are organized— cells into tissues, tissues into organs, organs into organ systems, and organ systems into the organism.

Break a rock apart and you will have bits of rock. Tear an organism apart, that is, destroy its structure, and it dies. The structure of an organism enables it to carry out its functions. If it cannot function, it is no longer an organism.

In the study of multicellular organisms the following concepts were emphasized.

Reviewing the Concepts

▶ *The cell is the unit of structure and function.* Whenever we examine multicellular plants or animals, we find they are composed of cells. The cells have particular structures and functions. Like cells are formed into tissues. Tissues in turn make up the organs of the organisms.

▶ *Tissues are adapted by the structure of their cells to carry on particular functions.* For example, muscle cells, long and spindle-shaped, are adapted for contraction. Epithelial cells, flat or box shaped, are adapted for covering and protecting.

▶ *Single-celled organisms are to be differentiated from single cells that are part of an organism.* A single-celled organism such as *Paramecium* has all the structures (organelles) to carry on all its life functions. Cells that are part of an organism have special adaptations for special functions. For example, the neuron fibers of nerve cells are adapted for carrying impulses.

Testing Yourself

1. Relate these scientists in terms of their field of study: Hooke, Dutrochet.

2. What is a theory?

3. State the cell theory. To what kind of organisms doesn't it apply?

4. What is the function of the cell membrane? The chromosomes?

5. Which cellular structures are common to plants and animals? Which are found in plants only?

6. What is the difference between a single-celled animal and a single animal cell?

7. In a paramecium, what is the function of the

   a. contractile vacuole?   d. oral groove?

   b. food vacuole?   e. anal pore?

   c. trichocysts?

8. Distinguish between tissue and organ, organ and organelle, organ and organ system.

9. What is the function of each of these tissues?

   a. epithelial tissue   d. muscle tissue

   b. connective tissue   e. blood tissue

   c. nerve tissue

10. Is a virus an organism? If so, why? If not, why not?

Extending the Concepts

Investigation 1. Begin a careful study of single-celled animals. If you continue your study, you will soon become quite expert in identification of at least the common proto-zoans. For this study, you may wish to turn now to **The Microscope: An Aid to Observation** (p. 533) which gives many suggestions for investigations with the microscope.

Investigation 2. The culture of *Amoeba* is quite different from the culture of organisms such as *Paramecium*. Try to cultivate *Amoeba*. To culture an organism is, in a sense, to develop an ecosystem in which it survives and reproduces. True?

A useful reference is *A Sourcebook for the Biological Sciences*, by Morholt, Brandwein, and Joseph (New York, Harcourt Brace Jovanovich, 1966).

Investigation 3. Some interesting, beautifully formed organisms are the single-celled plants, called desmids and diatoms. They belong to a group of plants commonly called algae.

The culture of diatoms is fairly easy in pond water or in a special solution you can prepare. Again see *A Sourcebook for the Biological Sciences*, by Morholt and others.

Suggested Reading

Schneider, Leo, *You and Your Cells*, New York, Harcourt Brace Jovanovich, 1964.

Stanley, W. M., and E. G. Valens, *Viruses and the Nature of Life*, New York, Dutton, 1961.

Swanson, C. P., *The Cell* (2nd ed.), Englewood Cliffs, N. J., Prentice-Hall, 1964.

5 | Multicellular Animals as Organisms

Suppose that you made a pile of the following: a tank of oxygen, two smaller tanks of hydrogen and nitrogen, cans of carbon, calcium, phosphorus, potassium, sulfur, sodium, and a bit of iodine. Add an iron nail and tiny pieces of zinc, copper, cobalt, manganese, and magnesium. Now add a little of the poisonous gas chlorine. Finally, mix up just a touch of several other elements and stir everything together. You would now have all the ingredients of a human being.

But would you have a human being? Of course not. You would have the basic substances, but you would be far from having any sort of living material. Something is missing—for one thing, a proper organization. In an organism cells are organized into tissues, tissues into organs, organs into organ systems, and organ systems into the organism. The organism is then organized—but for what?

A Word About Adaptation

A hand is obviously suited for grasping. The eyes are obviously suited for seeing. The biologist prefers to say that parts of an organism are *adapted* for their functions. So the heart is adapted for pumping blood, muscles for contracting, skin cells for covering.

Now this does not mean that the organs *know* that this is their function. As you shall see, adaptation of an organ for a certain function depends upon many factors. One factor is the environment. Indeed, in Unit One you examined the concept that organisms are interdependent with each other and with their environment. That is to say, organisms are adapted to their environment. Another factor in adaptation is the heredity of the organism; this is the subject of Unit Six. Still another factor is to be found in the evolution of the organism in relation to the environment, the subject of Unit Seven. In order to study the evolution of organisms one needs to know something of the nature of organisms and of their environment. One needs to know how the body systems of animals are adapted to their functions.

1. BODY SYSTEMS OF AN ORGANISM— THE FROG

Before you begin dissecting the frog, examine the guides to dissection in the Reference Charts, pages 98–102. Even a casual glance will show how these drawings will help in identifying the organs of the frog. ■

■ AN APPRENTICE STUDY IN ANATOMY: The Frog

External Anatomy

Examine your preserved frog or a frog that has just been killed. Notice that the skin is loose and moist. As you examine the skin, notice the blood vessels on the underside. A frog breathes partly through its moist skin. This is why a frog, even though it can live on land, must live in a damp place.

As you examine the animal further, notice the difference between the sizes of the front and hind legs.  The front legs help the frog land after leaping. They are also used to stuff food into the mouth. How are the hind legs adapted for leaping and swimming? The hind legs have powerful muscles. Notice the membrane between the toes of the hind feet. This makes them excellent swimming organs.

Look at the eyes. Notice their position on the head. Because of their location, the frog can lie nearly submerged in water with eyes (and nostrils) remaining above the surface. The frog has upper and lower eyelids just as you have. However, it has a third eyelid as well. This eyelid comes up over the eye from beneath the lower eyelid and is transparent. It protects the eye when the frog is swimming. Later, you will learn how a fish's eye is protected.

Notice the large eardrums just behind the eyes. They are quite similar to your eardrums even though they are located on the outside of the body. Sound vibrations cause them to vibrate back and forth. The vibrations are carried through a small chamber underneath each eardrum and to the inner ear where nerves carry the message to the brain.

Next, open the mouth and pull out the tongue. Notice it is attached at the front of the mouth. Its free end is forked. A frog uses its tongue to catch insects for food. As the frog flicks its tongue at an insect, the sticky end

traps the insect. Then the tongue with the food is instantly rolled back into the mouth.

Notice that the frog has small teeth lining the upper jaw. These help hold the animals the frog catches for food. Two larger teeth can also be seen or felt in the roof of the mouth.

Internal Anatomy

Examine your dissected frog.  Locate all the organ systems shown in the guides to dis-

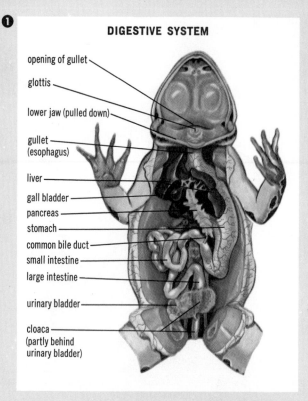

DIGESTIVE SYSTEM

- opening of gullet
- glottis
- lower jaw (pulled down)
- gullet (esophagus)
- liver
- gall bladder
- pancreas
- stomach
- common bile duct
- small intestine
- large intestine
- urinary bladder
- cloaca (partly behind urinary bladder)

these? Do you have any digestive organs the frog does not have?

The *liver* is easy to find since it is the largest organ in the frog. It is also the largest organ in your body. The *pancreas* is harder to find. The liver and pancreas both secrete important digestive juices containing enzymes that digest specific foods. If you cut into the liver slightly, you may be able to locate the *gall bladder*. The gall bladder stores the bile from the liver and then releases the bile into the intestine as needed.

The Circulatory System. The circulatory system in the frog consists of a heart with three chambers and arteries and veins to carry the blood throughout the body. 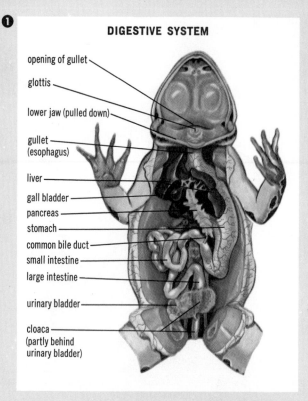 The three chambers of the heart include *two auricles* and *one ventricle*. Perhaps you know that your heart has four chambers, two auricles and two ventricles. You can examine the frog's heart more easily if you remove it by cutting it away from the body. Now look for the two auricles and the single ventricle. Blood coming through the *veins* from the body (except from the lungs) collects in the *right* auricle. Blood coming from the lungs collects in the *left* auricle. Both auricles contract and the blood is forced into the ventricle. Then the ventricle contracts and blood is pumped through the *arteries* to all parts of the body. Find at least one vein leading to the heart. Find at least one artery leading from the heart. Can you find other veins or arteries in the body? Which organs do the arteries supply? Perhaps you can find the arteries supplying the muscles of both legs.

The Respiratory System. The respiratory system includes the frogs' moist skin, with its very heavy supply of blood vessels, and the *lungs.*

You breathe by raising and lowering your ribs and by contracting your diaphragm (dī′ə·fram). A frog does not have a diaphragm. All of the

section. As you dissect the animal, refer constantly to them. By the end of your dissection, you should be able to identify the major organs of the frog's body. Try to determine how the organs and tissues in the animal you are dissecting compare with the Anatomy Charts. You should learn the functions of the various organs. You would expect the functions of the organs of the frog often to be similar to the functions of the organs in your body. Study the following systems especially.

The Digestive System. The digestive system includes the mouth, short *gullet* (or esophagus), *stomach,* looped *small intestine, large intestine,* and *cloaca* (klō·ā′kə). 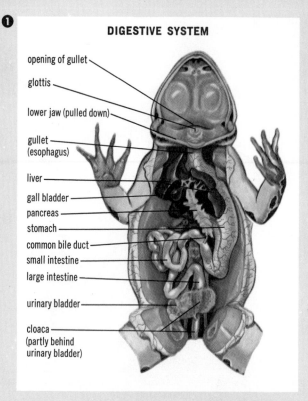 Undigested foods, urine, and sperms or eggs all leave the body through an opening, the *anus,* at the end of the cloaca of the frog. Have you found these organs? Do you have any organs similar to

RESPIRATORY SYSTEM

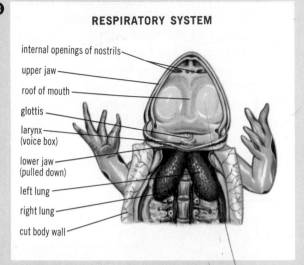

internal openings of nostrils
upper jaw
roof of mouth
glottis
larynx (voice box)
lower jaw (pulled down)
left lung
right lung
cut body wall

CIRCULATORY SYSTEM

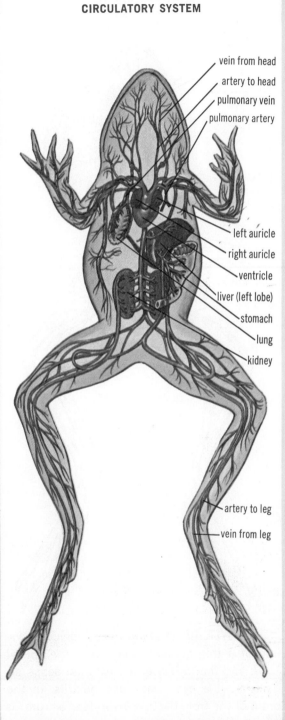

vein from head
artery to head
pulmonary vein
pulmonary artery
left auricle
right auricle
ventricle
liver (left lobe)
stomach
lung
kidney
artery to leg
vein from leg

internal organs of the frog are in one large cavity. The frog breathes air into its lungs by swallowing movements; the floor of the mouth moves up and down as if the frog were swallowing. Actually, a frog that is sitting quietly will breathe air into and out of its mouth for long periods of time without much of the air going down into the lungs. Because the mouth lining is moist and full of blood vessels, considerable exchange of oxygen and carbon dioxide from the blood stream occurs within the mouth. However, an active frog needs more oxygen than it can get from its skin and mouth alone. Therefore, every so often it closes its *nostrils* by means of tiny valves of skin, and in this way air is forced down into the lungs when it swallows.

A frog's lungs are quite small in relation to its size. Your lungs are proportionately much larger. Furthermore, a frog's lungs are simple sacs, whereas yours are masses of branching tubes and blood vessels ending in spongy masses of air sacs and capillaries. Since the frog also breathes through its skin and the lining of its mouth, its respiratory system can be considered rather more primitive than yours.

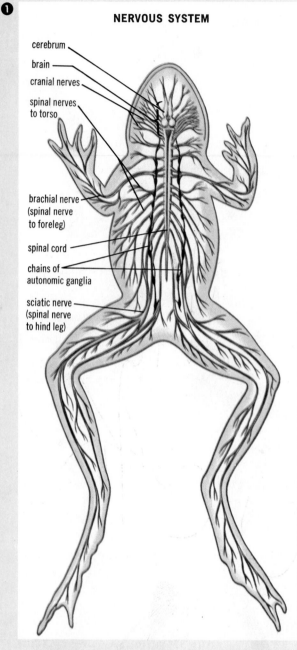

NERVOUS SYSTEM

cerebrum

brain

cranial nerves

spinal nerves to torso

brachial nerve (spinal nerve to foreleg)

spinal cord

chains of autonomic ganglia

sciatic nerve (spinal nerve to hind leg)

considerably larger in relation to other parts of the brain than it is in a fish, for example. Chip away the top of the skull with your forceps. Uncover the brain and find the cerebrum. How does it connect to the spinal cord? Try to find the nerves leading to the eyes and the ears.

In man, the cerebrum is the center of all conscious activities, decisions, and learning—

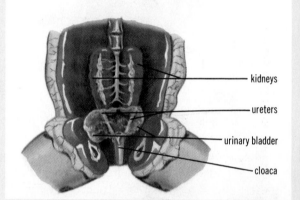

EXCRETORY SYSTEM

kidneys

ureters

urinary bladder

cloaca

the center of intelligence. If this is so, then we might guess that a frog is more intelligent than a fish. However, the frog's cerebrum is still primitive when compared with your cerebrum or even when compared with that of a cat or dog. Therefore, you can assume that the frog must not be as intelligent as a cat or a dog.

Carefully push aside the digestive organs and locate the backbone, which contains the spinal cord.

Nerve impulses from the limbs and other parts of the body travel up through the spinal cord to the brain. And impulses from the brain travel down through the spinal cord to the various parts of the body. Find at least one nerve leading to each of the front limbs and the main nerve in each of the hind limbs.

The Excretory System. Carbon dioxide is excreted chiefly through the skin although a considerable amount is excreted through the

The Nervous System. The nervous system of a frog contains the *brain*, the *spinal cord*, and the *nerves*. ❶ Its external sense organs are the eyes, ears, and nostrils. In the brain of the frog, the *cerebrum* (ser′ə·brum) is

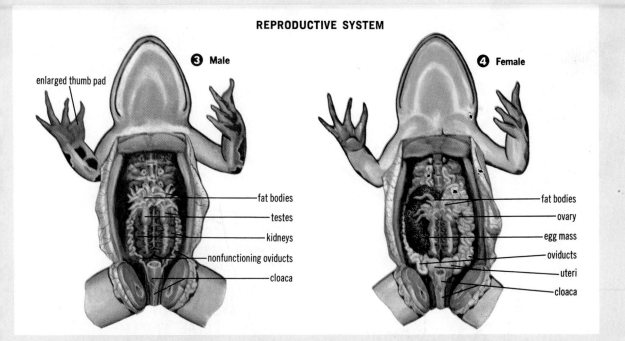

REPRODUCTIVE SYSTEM

❸ Male

enlarged thumb pad

fat bodies
testes
kidneys
nonfunctioning oviducts
cloaca

❹ Female

fat bodies
ovary
egg mass
oviducts
uteri
cloaca

lungs and mouth. The main organs of the excretory (eks′krə·tôr′ē) system are the *kidneys.* ❷

Carefully remove the digestive organs and find two of these dark red organs, one at either side of the backbone. These are the kidneys specialized to remove nitrogen wastes from the blood stream. These wastes dissolved in water become urine. From the kidneys, the urine goes through tubes into the *urinary bladder* and from there into the *cloaca.* From here it passes through the anus to the outside of the body.

The Reproductive System. The reproductive system in the male includes the *testes* (tes′tēz) and its ducts. ❸ These are organs in which the male reproductive cells, sperms, are formed. The two testes are small, oval, and yellow or yellowish white in color and are located just above the *kidneys,* nearer the head end of the animal. A good guide in locating them is to look for the *fat bodies* that are often attached both to them and to the kidneys. You will see these fat bodies as fingerlike branches projecting out

from behind the testes. These fat bodies store food that is used by the frog, particularly during its winter hibernation.

The *ovaries* (ō′və·rēz) of the female are approximately in the same location as the testes of the male. ❹ In the spring, when eggs are to be laid, these ovaries become large with eggs. At other times of the year, the ovaries may be small and difficult to find.

Both sperms and eggs travel through tubes that empty into the *cloaca.* In the spring of the year, the female lays her eggs in the water. The male deposits sperms over them as they are being laid. After a short time, the fertilized eggs hatch into tadpoles which eventually become adult frogs.

The Skeletal System. The skeletal system is the last system we shall study in the frog. This system consists of the skull, the backbone, the front limbs and hind limbs, and the shoulder and hip bones to which they are connected. Notice how the separate bones fit to-

101

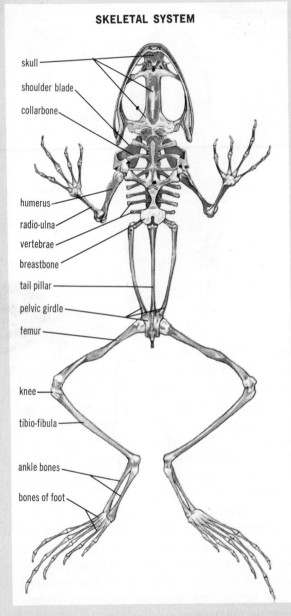

SKELETAL SYSTEM

skull
shoulder blade
collarbone
humerus
radio-ulna
vertebrae
breastbone
tail pillar
pelvic girdle
femur
knee
tibio-fibula
ankle bones
bones of foot

gether. ❶ The frog's backbone consists of a few separate bones called *vertebrae* [(vûr′tə·brā), singular, *vertebra*.] They, like the other bones, are fastened together by ligaments. The ligaments between the movable joints of the limbs are essential to the frog's leaping motion—its special method of locomotion.

REVIEW

1. The frog is obviously an organism. Why?
2. How is the frog adapted for life on land? in water?
3. How is the frog adapted for
   a. locomotion?
   b. respiration?
   c. responsiveness to the environment?
   d. reproduction?
   e. using food?

NEW VIEW

What adaptations would a frog need to develop in order to survive completely in water? on land?

2. BODY SYSTEMS OF MAN— THE SKELETAL SYSTEM

Perhaps your school has a human skeleton. Direct examination is, of course, the best way to study any structure. But if this is not possible, study the Reference Chart of the Human Skeletal System at the right. ■

Your backbone supports your entire body and must stand up against all kinds of shocks when you play or run. In addition, it contains the **spinal cord**, a thick rope of nerves running from the brain down through a hollow canal in the center of the backbone. Nerve tissue is extremely soft and delicate and therefore easily damaged. The spinal cord of nerve tissue controls many of your activities. It carries nerve impulses from the brain to all parts of the body, and it carries other impulses (of pain, heat, and cold, for example) from the body to the brain. Therefore the backbone, which consists of many separate vertebrae, is of great service to you, not only by being the chief supporting structure for your body, but also by protecting the delicate spinal cord.

■ AN APPRENTICE STUDY IN ANATOMY: The Human Skeletal System

You should know your own skeleton, should you not?

Look at the Reference Chart of the Human Skeleton.❶ Study it carefully. Or even better, if your school has a skeleton, study it. You should be able to answer these questions.

a. How is the upper arm bone, the **humerus** (hyoo′mər·əs), similar to the upper thigh bone, the **femur** (fē′mər)?

b. How is the lower arm similar in bone structure to the lower leg?

c. Why is the knee considered to be a hinge joint? Move your own knee to help you understand why.

d. Why is the shoulder joint called a ball-and-socket joint?

e. Where else is there another hinge joint in the body skeleton? Another ball-and-socket joint?

f. To what parts of the skeleton are the collarbones attached?

g. Is there a bone in the front of the nose?

The skeletal system of your body performs three main functions.

h. How does it provide form and support for the entire body?

i. How do some of the bones—the skull, the ribs, and the vertebrae, in particular—provide protection for soft body parts?

j. How do the long bones of the body (hands, feet, arms, and legs, particularly) act as levers that are worked by a system of muscles connected to the bones?

An Investigation On Your Own

Next time your family has turkey, chicken, duck, or any whole animal (like rabbit) for dinner, ask the members of your family to save the bones. Can you put some of them together to make up the arm bones? the leg bones?

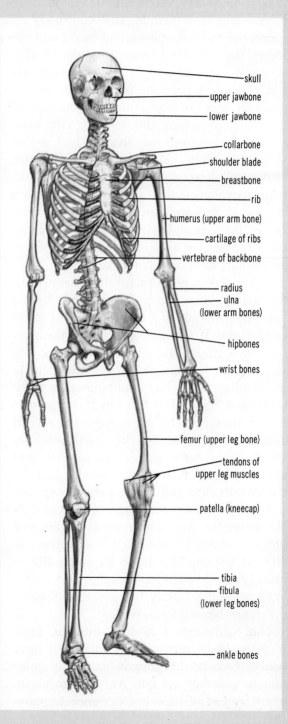

❶

skull
upper jawbone
lower jawbone
collarbone
shoulder blade
breastbone
rib
humerus (upper arm bone)
cartilage of ribs
vertebrae of backbone
radius
ulna
(lower arm bones)
hipbones
wrist bones
femur (upper leg bone)
tendons of upper leg muscles
patella (kneecap)
tibia
fibula
(lower leg bones)
ankle bones

Are Bones Necessary?

Is it necessary for living things to have bones? You need them because your body requires the strong framework of bones and the levers that the long bones provide, so that you can move about. However, bones are just one solution to the problem of support and movement in living things. Thousands of other organisms have also developed the same solution. The frog you studied had a fine skeletal system. Dogs, cats, fish, birds, snakes, all have skeletal systems much like your own. Recall that all animals with such an inside skeleton are often called vertebrates, because all have a backbone made up of vertebrae. Are all animals vertebrates? Do all animals have bones and skeletons?

Did you ever go fishing, using earthworms for bait? (Some people call them fishing worms.) How are the bones arranged in an earthworm? If you dig up some earthworms from rich garden soil and dissect them, you will find no bones. Yet earthworms seem to get along quite well without bones or a skeletal system. Why? How fast can an earthworm move? How quickly can it avoid danger? If you were to place a living earthworm on moist paper toweling or newspapers and study its movements, you would find its movements slow and helpless compared, say, with your movements or those of a cat or dog. However, the earthworm seems to be well fitted or adapted to the life it lives in the soil. How suited would it be to an active life of running along on the top of the ground, catching food and avoiding being eaten? What a difference bones can make!

The earthworm is a tiny creature. How large could an earthworm be and not have bones? Perhaps that sounds like a silly question to you, but it's not. An average earthworm weighs perhaps $\frac{1}{6}$ of an ounce. Suppose that you invent an earthworm that weighs 50 pounds. How do you think it would manage? Would it get along as well? If so, why? If not, why not?

The force of gravity, of course, pulls everything down toward the ground (more accurately, toward the center of the earth). If it were not for your skeletal system, you would flow down onto the floor in a shapeless heap. The force of gravity has little effect in forcing the tiny earthworm out of shape. But if an earthworm weighed 50 or 100 pounds, it would probably be unable to move. At best, it could barely pull itself along, an inch or so in an hour.

There are many other animals without a skeletal system, but the ordinary earthworm is a giant among them. Only a few animals without skeletons are larger than the earthworm, and these animals live in the sea. Can you figure out why an animal without a skeletal system would get along better in water than on dry land? (*Clue:* How much do you seem to weigh in water?)

If you do not know what happens to weight when it is put in water, it is easy to find out. You can fasten a string or cord to a brick or a rock and suspend it from a spring scale and read the weight. ❶ If you then lower the brick or rock into a pail of water, you will discover that it seems to weigh less. ❷

Outside Skeletons

Did you ever eat a lobster or a crab? Did they have any bones?

Insects belong to the same large group of animals as lobsters and crabs. Do insects have bones? If you tried to dissect a grasshopper, you would find it harder to cut into than an earthworm. The outside of the body is covered with a tough substance. Would you find any bones in an insect?

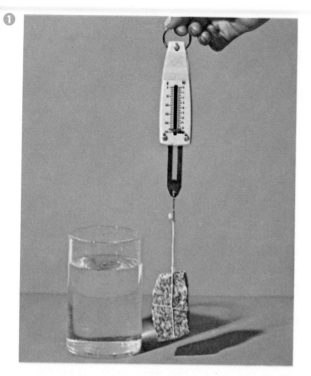

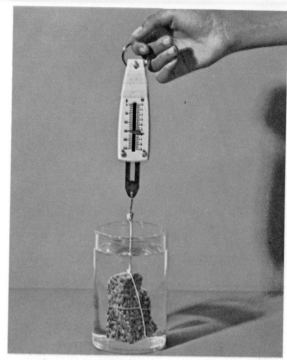

There are no bones in insects, spiders, crabs, lobsters, or similar animals. However, you have seen many insects crawling and flying around. They can move rapidly. Did you ever try to catch a fly? It is faster than you are. How can this be if an insect has no bones? How can the wings of a fly move so rapidly and how can it fly so accurately if it has no bones? The earthworm can move only sluggishly. Examine a grasshopper carefully to see if you can determine for yourself why it can fly so rapidly.

An insect's body is covered with a hard, fingernail-like covering. Scientists call this an **exoskeleton** (ek′sō·skel′ə·tən). *Exo–* means "outside." An insect and its relatives (spiders, crabs, lobsters, and crayfish) have an outside skeletal system even though they have no bones. Muscles are attached to various sections of the exoskeleton.

When a fly moves or flies, its muscles contract just as your own do when you move. But instead of these muscles moving bones, they move sections of the exoskeleton. So these sections are levers just as your bones are. And, of course, the exoskeleton also protects the soft insides of the animal.

As you now have discovered, there are animals with no skeletons, animals with inside skeletons, and animals with outside skeletons. Do all seem to be well fitted or adapted for living? Because skeletons provide levers upon which muscles can act quickly and accurately, animals with skeletal systems can move much faster than animals without them. Because strong support is needed to hold up the weight of large animals, animals without skeletal systems are generally very small. Many are so small they can only be seen with a microscope.

REVIEW

1. How is each of the following especially adapted by structure for its function: the knee joint, shoulder joint, hip joint? Which two are similar?

2. Locate each of the following bones and give its function: humerus, femur, radius, fibula, clavicle.

NEW VIEW

1. Compare the skeleton of man and the frog. What are their similarities? differences?

2. Could an organism the size of a whale develop with an exoskeleton and without an internal skeleton? Support your answer.

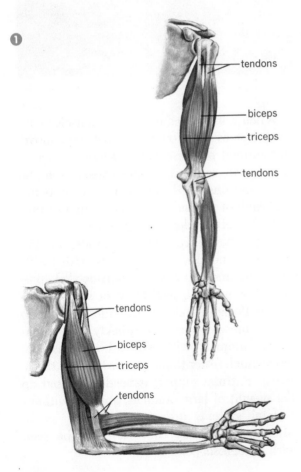

tendons

biceps

triceps

tendons

tendons

biceps

triceps

tendons

3. BODY SYSTEMS OF MAN— THE MUSCULAR SYSTEM

Bend your arm and flex your muscle. Feel the muscle in your upper arm. It is the **biceps** (bī′seps).❶ It is the muscle that pulls up your lower arm. It is a lifting muscle. The more powerful it is, the more weight you can lift.

Now straighten your arm. Where do you think the muscle is that straightened your arm? Would it be on the top of the upper arm bone along with the biceps? Or would you expect to find it underneath the upper arm bone? The biceps bends or flexes your arm. So it is called a **flexor** muscle. The muscle that extends or straightens your arm is located on the opposite side of the upper arm bone. It is called an **extensor** muscle because it extends your arm. It is the **triceps.** Study the drawings of the arm again; they show how the biceps and triceps work the bones like levers to bend and extend your arm.

Most of the muscles in your body are arranged in pairs. One of each pair bends a joint and the other moves the bones the opposite way. These pairs of flexors and extensors are fastened to the bones by strong *tendons*. The tendons at one end of a muscle are fastened to one bone, and the tendons at the other end of the muscle are usually fastened to another bone. The two bones are usually joined at the joint.

Animals with exoskeletons also have their muscles arranged in pairs. These muscles are arranged very like those of your own arm. But, of course, the muscles are fastened to the exoskeleton rather than to bones.

Recall that muscles of the type we have been studying, flexors and extensors, are kinds of muscles known as *voluntary muscles*. That is, they are controlled by conscious will, at least in part. Most voluntary muscles consist of striated (striped) muscle cells (see page 87).

MUSCLES UNATTACHED TO BONES. Not all of your muscles are arranged in pairs or are attached to bones. Did you ever watch your tongue in a mirror? The tongue is made up of many muscles, marvelously arranged so that it can stretch out, contract, turn in almost any direction, or become pointed or rounded.

Stand in front of a mirror and move your lips in various ways. Speak a sentence. Then pucker your lips as if to kiss the mirror. Your lips are chiefly muscles. They have no bones, and, like your tongue, they can be placed in an almost endless series of positions. The largest of the lip muscles are arranged in a circular fashion. Lying under these outside lip muscles are many more muscles. They are arranged in many different positions to permit you to move your lips in a variety of ways.

These muscles, like the other muscles over which you have control, are voluntary muscles.

INVOLUNTARY MUSCLES. Did you ever try swallowing while standing on your head? It is not at all difficult. You can even swallow water while standing on your head. How do you think that food and water can go from your mouth to your stomach when you are upside down? Obviously it does not just fall up to your stomach. Muscles push it up. Your mouth is connected to your stomach by a muscular tube called the **esophagus** (i·sof′ə·gəs). Can you figure out how the muscles might be arranged to squeeze food and water along so that, even when you are upside down, they go to your stomach?

Look at a garden hose (or better, a soft, rubber tube) and see if you can invent in your mind some muscular arrangement that would force food or water to move along in such a tube. Would the muscles be arranged lengthwise or in a circular pattern in the tube?

In your esophagus and throughout your digestive tract, including your intestines, food and water are pushed along by circular muscles that contract one after another. When one of the circular muscles contracts just behind a bit of food or water, it closes off the tube tightly as if you had tied a string around the tube. Therefore the food or water cannot move back up the tube. Then the next circular muscle contracts and this forces the food or water a bit farther along.

All of this, of course, occurs quite automatically. You decide to swallow something, but once you have done so, you no longer have voluntary control of it. The circular muscles take over automatically. Recall that muscles of the intestine are known as *involuntary muscles*. They are not under control of the conscious will.

In your body there are several valves that are powerful circular muscles. Some digestive glands, for example, pass their fluids through tubes. The flow of these fluids is controlled by circular muscle valves. One interesting circular valve lies between your stomach and your intestine. As long as the food in your stomach is mixed mainly with *saliva* [secreted in your mouth by **salivary** (sal′ə·ver′ē) **glands**], the food stays in your stomach. However, your stomach also secretes a digestive juice which is acid in nature. When the food is sufficiently mixed with this acidic juice, the valve opens and the food passes into the intestines.

Now in the same way you studied your skeletal system, investigate a portion of your voluntary muscle system. ■

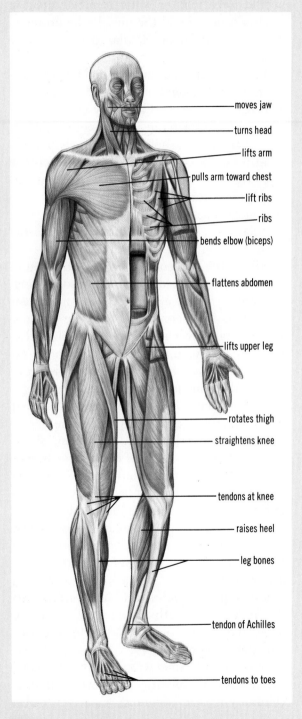

moves jaw

turns head

lifts arm

pulls arm toward chest

lift ribs

ribs

bends elbow (biceps)

flattens abdomen

lifts upper leg

rotates thigh

straightens knee

tendons at knee

raises heel

leg bones

tendon of Achilles

tendons to toes

Study the Reference Chart. ❶ It shows where the voluntary muscles that do the following are located:

a. lifts the upper leg (another extensor muscle)

b. bends, or flexes, the elbow (a flexor muscle)

c. flattens the abdomen

d. pulls the arm toward the chest

e. turns the head

f. moves the jaw

Once you have identified these muscles, can you find on your own

g. a muscle or muscles that bend the knee?

h. the calf muscle? What does it do?

i. a muscle that rotates the right arm?

Now that you have done this by means of the muscle chart, try to locate these same muscles in your own body. Feel for them. What seems to happen when a muscle contracts? When it relaxes? How does a muscle do its work?

An Investigation On Your Own

How fast can you run the hundred-yard dash? Consider all the muscles involved in your running and the tremendous number of muscle contractions and relaxations that occur. The oxygen required by your muscles in the few seconds of such a race is about seven quarts; yet your blood can supply only about one quart. How is it possible for muscles to contract without a full supply of oxygen? A textbook in physiology may be helpful in your research.

REVIEW

1. How do flexors and extensors adapt the body for motion?

2. What functions would be impossible without tendons? without ligaments?

3. How does voluntary (striated) muscle compare or contrast with involuntary muscle (smooth or cardiac) in structure? in function?

NEW VIEW

1. Compare the musculature of frog and man. How are they similar? How are they different?

2. Investigate the effect of exercise on development of muscle. You would need a book on the physiology of the body.

3. Muscles, of course, all have names to distinguish them from each other. If you are interested in knowing the special names of muscles, refer to a textbook on human anatomy.

4. BODY SYSTEMS OF MAN— THE NERVOUS SYSTEM

Your nervous system is the communication system of the billions of cells that make up your body. Most kinds of animals have nervous systems which coordinate the activities of the cells that make up their bodies. Certain exceptions are the single-celled organisms. Even they are thought by some to have kinds of fibers that ease communication between different parts of the body, and thus coordinate their activities.

Your cells are highly specialized. Muscle cells specialize in contracting. They cannot get food or digest it or get rid of wastes all by themselves. They must depend on other cells, equally specialized to carry on these functions for them. Gland cells secrete juices. They can do little else. Some organ system must exist to conduct messages (impulses) from cell to cell, to coordinate the activities of the cells so that they work together smoothly and in harmony.

The individual cells of your body can be compared to the individual persons of a great city. Each cell has a specialized part to play in the life of your body just as each person in a city has a part to play in the life of a city. Each person in a city depends upon many other persons for what he needs. Each cell in your body depends upon all the other cells and their specialized work to keep you alive and in good health.

Functions of a Nervous System

Your nervous system does three things to make possible many simple and complex reactions. First, your nervous system enables you to *detect,* or become aware of things around you. You have a variety of specialized nerve endings that are sensitive to stimuli such as light, sound, heat, cold, and pressure. You detect these environmental surroundings through sense organs of sight, hearing, smell, and taste, and sensations such as cold, heat, pressure, pain.

Second, your nervous system carries impulses from your sense organs to your brain where the stimulus received by your sense organs is interpreted. This system operates something like a telephone system in a city through which individuals can report a fire, the need for food, or the fact that a furnace has broken down and needs repairing. Not only are impulses carried to your brain from the sense organs, but in turn, your brain sends impulses out through nerves to the parts of your body that should take action. Your stomach sends a message to your brain that lets it know you need food. Your brain may send an impulse that causes you to ask when dinner will be ready. Or it may send an impulse to thousands of different muscle cells which cause you to walk into the kitchen, open the refrigerator, and take out some food and eat it.

Suppose you were stung by a bee. If this or something similar has happened to you, then you must recall that you reacted quickly. It is perhaps more accurate to say that your body reacted before you were actually aware of what happened. How did this occur? First, the sting of the bee was sensed by nerve endings in your skin. This *stimulus* caused a *response*, the quick withdrawal of your body from the painful stimulus. The stimulus caused an impulse to move up the sensory nerve to the spinal cord (p. 89). When the impulse reached the spinal cord, another impulse traveled immediately back to the muscles through a motor nerve. This caused the muscle to contract; you jumped or moved away. A fraction of a second later the original impulse still traveling up your spinal cord reached your brain. Perhaps you said "Ouch," swatted at the bee, or did several other complicated things. But you had already reacted.

This kind of action, involving a few nerve connections—sensory nerve, spinal cord, and motor nerve—is known as a **reflex act.** Reflex acts can occur without thinking, without involving the brain. Blinking is a reflex act; so is swallowing or withdrawing a part of your body from a painful stimulus. What other reflexes do you know of?

Your nervous system sends impulses continuously over hundreds of different paths by means of nerves that branch throughout your entire body. In this way, *communication* is provided between cells.

In brief, your body responds to a change, or a stimulus, in the environment. A stimulus such as touching a hot object causes a *re-sponse* (moving away); that is, whenever there is a response, there has been some stimulus.

A stimulus reaches the spinal cord and the brain by means of *sensory* nerves. The nerve impulse traveling back to a muscle (which contracts) or to a gland (which secretes) is carried by *motor* nerves.

The nervous system also has a third function. It *coordinates* your activities. You, a cat, a fly, or any other multicellular animal moves smoothly and in a coordinated fashion. The cells and body parts work beautifully together. This coordination exists because the incredibly efficient nervous system makes it possible for each part of the body to do just what it should do at exactly the right moment. Of course, sometimes mistakes do occur. You try to catch a ball and, instead, it hits you. Or, you occasionally startle and embarrass yourself by saying something you did not intend to say. But, by and large, the human nervous system, and that of all the vertebrates, carries on activities far beyond the capacity of the most complicated electronic brain that man has ever invented or is ever likely to invent. Let's study it more closely. ■

REVIEW

1. Distinguish between sensory nerves and motor nerves.

2. What is the function of the cerebrum? the cerebellum? the medulla? the spinal cord?

3. Define a reflex act. Give an example and describe the pathway of the impulses.

4. What are the general functions of the nervous system?

NEW VIEW

Compare the brains of man and the frog. What parts are similar? What parts are different? Which brain is more complex? Why?

■ AN APPRENTICE STUDY IN ANATOMY: The Human Nervous System

By studying the Reference Chart, you will notice that there are several parts of the human nervous system: the brain, the spinal cord, and the nerves. ❶

Notice the brain and its three parts.

The Cerebrum. This largest part of the brain governs thinking, judgment, and movement of all voluntary muscles.

The Cerebellum. This portion controls coordination of the body muscles.

The Medulla. This area controls certain vital functions, such as breathing.

Also notice the *spinal cord,* which is a center to which all the body nerves run. The spinal cord, as you can see, connects with the brain.

Try to trace the path of these messages, or nerve impulses, through the nervous system.

a. Someone steps on your toe. You withdraw your toe. (Apparently your brain is involved because you say, "Oh!")

b. You walk along and you see a can. You kick it.

c. You ate too much. What is the path of the nerve impulses from the stomach?

d. You plan an investigation. You write it down.

e. You decide to take a deep breath.

f. You are asleep. Which nerves are in control of the function of your internal organs?

An Investigation On Your Own

Ask your mother to purchase a sheep's brain. Identify the major parts of the brain. Can you find other parts? You will need a laboratory manual with directions for dissecting vertebrates, particularly the mammals.

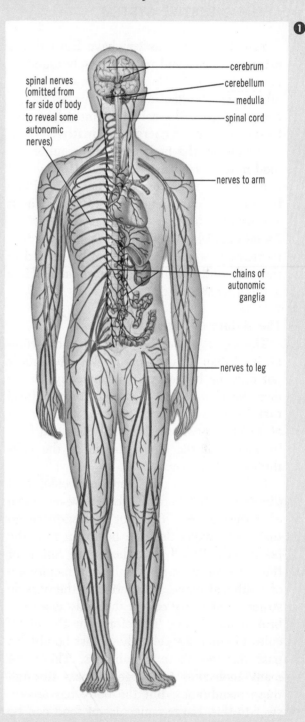

❶

spinal nerves (omitted from far side of body to reveal some autonomic nerves)

cerebrum
cerebellum
medulla
spinal cord

nerves to arm

chains of autonomic ganglia

nerves to leg

5. BODY SYSTEMS OF MAN— THE DIGESTIVE SYSTEM

Your body cells, as you have learned, are extremely small and packed closely together. However, the foods we eat—meats, vegetables, and the like—are mountainous in size compared with the cells that must have the food as sources of energy and matter.

Obviously, the body generally cannot use food in the form it is swallowed. However, it is possible that glucose and similar food can be used without digestion. All other foods are broken down by the digestive system. Large chunks of food are broken down into particles so small that they can be carried to the cells and can be taken into them. How is this accomplished?

The Nature of Digestion

The digestion of food is much more complicated than it may seem at first. Food must not only be broken up mechanically, but it must be changed to a *soluble* form, a form that dissolves in water. The body fluids (most of which are water) carry the dissolved food by means of the blood stream to the cells throughout the body.

Food is broken down into molecules that dissolve in the body fluids. However, even after this occurs, it does not necessarily mean that these molecules can be taken into the body cells. Recall that the entire lining of the digestive tract is an unbroken membrane of epithelial tissue. Furthermore, the outside structure of every cell in the body is an unbroken membrane. Therefore, for the molecules to enter the cells, they must be able to pass through these membranes. There are many molecules too large to pass through these membranes. But the body has an answer to this. Large molecules of food can be broken down into small molecules that are able to pass through the membranes.

There is also an interesting complication with membranes. At one time, a membrane will allow a specific kind of molecule to pass through it, whereas at another time it may not allow the very same kind of molecule to pass through. The reasons for this reaction of membranes are not yet known. However, this reaction has been given a name, the *selectivity of membranes.*

In summary, then, digestion does three main things: (1) it breaks up food into tiny particles; (2) it breaks the tiny particles into molecules that will dissolve in the body fluids; (3) it changes large molecules into molecules small enough to pass through the membranes of the body.

The Process of Digestion

Digestion takes place in two different ways: *mechanical* and *chemical*. The mechanical work is that of tearing, cutting, grinding, and mashing large chunks of food into a fine mush. It is accomplished by the teeth and tongue, contractions of the stomach, and movements of the intestines.

The chemical work of digestion is done by *enzymes*, substances found in digestive juices in the body. These enzymes regulate the chemical changes that break down the large molecules into smaller ones.

STARCH DIGESTION. It is simple to investigate the digestion of starch and thus learn about enzyme action on starches. A cracker is largely starch. If you chew a cracker for a long time, you will discover that the taste changes. After chewing a while, you will detect a sweet taste. As it is being chewed, the cracker mixes with your saliva. Can you figure out what happens? The following investigation will make it clear. ■

■ AN APPRENTICE INVESTIGATION into the Importance of Starch Digestion

Part 1. In order to learn what happened to the cracker, you will need at least three test tubes, two crackers, and either Benedict's solution or Fehling's solution. Either of these can be used to test for sugar. Your teacher will show you how.

Chew one cracker until you detect a sweet taste. Then place this chewed-up cracker into one test tube. Test for sugar by adding Benedict's solution and heating the tube until the contents boil. If an orange-red color appears, sugar is present.❶

Crush a second cracker with your fingers and place it into a test tube. Add a little water. Test this cracker for sugar. Did an orange-red color appear?❷

Now put some pure saliva into the third test tube. Make the test for sugar. Is there any sugar present in saliva?❸

Is this what you found?

a. A cracker does not show evidence of having sugar in it.
b. Saliva does not show evidence of having sugar in it.
c. When saliva is mixed with a cracker, sugar seems to appear.

How do you account for these findings? Remember that a cracker consists largely of flour and that flour is mainly a starch.

Do you find similar results when you repeat the investigation? Why is it necessary to repeat an investigation?

An Investigation On Your Own

Which acts faster, cold saliva, saliva at body temperature, or saliva boiled for ten minutes? Set up an investigation to determine this. How do you explain your results?

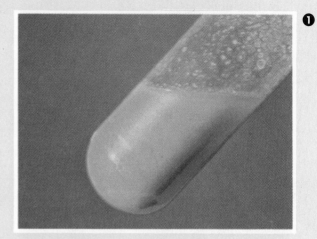

Turn each test tube upside down in a beaker so that the membrane is under the water.  Label one beaker "starch"; label the other "sugar." Place the beakers in a warm place and leave them until the next day.

Remove the test tube from the beaker labeled "starch." Pour some water from the beaker into a test tube and add a drop or two of dilute iodine solution. If starch is present, the water will turn blue-black. If not, it will remain a pale yellow color. Did starch pass through the membrane and into the water?

Next, test the water from the beaker labeled "sugar." Pour some water from this beaker into a test tube, add Benedict's solution, and heat the test tube. If sugar is present, a brick-red color appears.  Did sugar go through the membrane?

Is this what you found?

a. Starch did not go through the membrane.

b. Sugar did go through the membrane.

Why were sugar molecules able to pass through (*diffuse* through) the membrane and into the test tube but starch molecules were not able to?

A membrane is not really solid. Like anything else, it is made of molecules, and there are always spaces between molecules. One theory of diffusion indicates that although these spaces are much too small to be seen, they are large enough for the small molecules of simple sugar to pass through. However, they are not large enough for the much larger starch molecules to pass through.

An Investigation On Your Own

If simple sugars pass through membranes and if starch does not, which would be the substance most easily stored by a plant? Set up an investigation to illustrate this. (*Clue:* Bean seeds that have soaked overnight could be used.) How would you set up your control?

Part 2. To help you understand the importance of starch digestion, you will need two test tubes, rubber bands, two pieces of cellophane or animal membrane (Goldbeater's membrane), two beakers, dilute iodine solution, Benedict's solution, a soluble starch solution, and corn syrup.

Pour a small amount of starch solution into one test tube and an equal amount of corn syrup into the second test tube. Place a piece of cellophane, or Goldbeater's membrane, over the mouth of each test tube and secure it with a rubber band so the tube cannot leak. Fill each beaker about one-fourth full of water.

Now you can see why starch digestion is important since starch molecules cannot pass through the cell membranes. When digestion occurs, enzymes change the large molecules of starch into the smaller molecules of sugar. Sugar molecules, as you have seen, can pass through the membranes and into the cells that need them. The enzymes that digest starch to sugar are found in saliva and in the intestines. Actually, the second enzyme that digests starch is produced by the pancreas, but this enzyme acts in the intestines.

PROTEIN AND FAT DIGESTION. Protein and fat molecules are even larger than starch molecules. Therefore, proteins and fats must also be broken down and changed into smaller molecules. Proteins are digested by enzymes in your stomach and intestines, as well as by an enzyme from the pancreas. Fats are digested only in the intestines by an enzyme produced by the pancreas.

SUGAR DIGESTION. Not all the sugar we eat is the type into which starch is changed. Some sugars, for example, table sugar, are made up of molecules that must be broken down into small molecules before they can be used by the cells. Several enzymes produced by the small intestine break down these complex sugars into simple sugars.

A Study of Your Digestive System

If your school has a mannikin model or torso of the human body, you will certainly want to take apart the torso. But if none is available, study carefully the drawing of the human digestive system. ❶ Your digestive system consists of a food tube and three organs that lie outside the food tube. The food tube consists of the **mouth, esophagus, stomach, small intestine,** and **large intestine.** The large intestine opens to the outside through the anus. The three organs lying outside the

❶ HUMAN DIGESTIVE SYSTEM

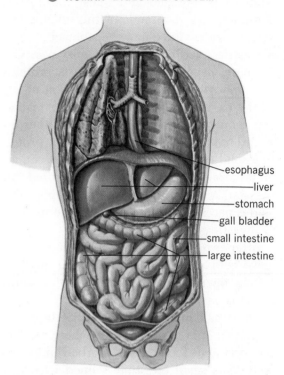

esophagus
liver
stomach
gall bladder
small intestine
large intestine

food tube are the **liver,** the **gall bladder,** and the **pancreas** (pan′krē·əs). The pancreas, which lies behind the stomach, is not shown in the drawing.

As food is taken into the mouth and ground up by the teeth, it is mixed with saliva from three pairs of salivary glands. The enzymes in saliva begin the digestion of starches. Saliva also contains *mucus* (myo͞o′kəs), which lubricates the food so that it will pass down the food tube easily.

The esophagus is a tube, about a foot long, that connects the mouth with the stomach. Food is pushed down the esophagus and into the stomach by circular muscles.

The stomach has three layers of muscle arranged in three different ways. These contract in different directions, turning, squeezing, and mixing the food. The lining of the

115

stomach is wrinkled and thick. Throughout the lining are thousands of tiny glands that secrete **gastric juice** into the stomach.

Gastric juice contains two enzymes. One of these, *pepsin* (pep′sin), digests proteins. You may wish to study the digestion of egg white (a protein) by pepsin. Your teacher can show you how to do this. The other enzyme, *rennin* (ren′in), changes milk protein to a solid curd so that other enzymes can act on it more easily. An acid is also secreted into the stomach from glands in the lining. This acid is necessary for the pepsin to do its work of digesting proteins.

After two or three hours, a circular muscle valve between the stomach and the small intestine opens and the food (now a soupy mass) is pushed into the intestines.

The small intestine is the chief organ of digestion. It is also the place where most of the digested foods are absorbed into the body. The small intestine is lined with tiny glands that secrete enzymes. These intestinal enzymes digest proteins and complex sugars.

The pancreas is a digestive gland. It secretes **pancreatic juice** into a tube that empties into the small intestine just below the stomach. These pancreatic enzymes digest all three basic foods—proteins, starches, and fats. Proteins, for example, are partly broken down by the pancreatic enzymes. Then intestinal enzymes complete the job.

The liver, also a digestive gland, is the largest gland in your body. It may weigh up to five or six pounds. This gland has several functions, one of which is to secrete **bile**. The bile passes down a tube and is stored in a small pouch called the gall bladder. From there the bile is passed, as it is needed, into the small intestine. Bile helps break up large drops of fat into small droplets. An enzyme from the pancreas then digests the fat.

Within the small intestine, the digested foods diffuse through the lining and into the blood stream. Undigested materials pass from the small intestine into the large intestine. These materials are very watery. The main function of the large intestine is to absorb the water from the undigestible materials. These materials then become more solid and are passed through the anus as waste.

Now can you trace what happens to a sandwich you have eaten at lunch?

a. Through what part of the digestive system does it first pass? The mouth. Name the parts of the digestive system, in order, through which it passes?

b. What does the gall bladder do?

c. Of what importance is the liver?

d. What gland (that produces important enzymes) is not shown in the drawing of the human digestive system?

REVIEW

1. What are the functions of the digestive system?

2. What are the functions of digestive enzymes?

3. Diffusion is sometimes defined as the movement of molecules from the region of their greatest concentration to the region of their lowest concentration. How true is this of diffusion from the small intestine into the blood stream? Give examples.

NEW VIEW

1. Compare the digestive systems of the frog (page 98) and of man (page 115).

a. How are they similar?

b. How are they different?

c. Which system is the most complex? Why?

2. Which organ of the digestive system produces the greatest variety of enzymes? Which organs do not produce enzymes?

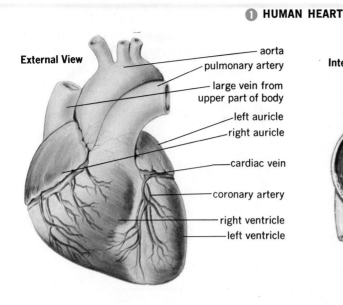

External View

aorta

pulmonary artery

large vein from
upper part of body

left auricle

right auricle

cardiac vein

coronary artery

right ventricle

left ventricle

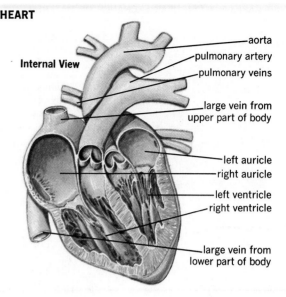

Internal View

aorta

pulmonary artery

pulmonary veins

large vein from
upper part of body

left auricle

right auricle

left ventricle

right ventricle

large vein from
lower part of body

6. BODY SYSTEMS OF MAN— THE CIRCULATORY SYSTEM

The whole point of taking matter and energy (in the form of food substances) into your body is to supply the substances to each cell. True, the digestive system breaks the substances down into small molecules. But in the end, the molecules must be transported to each cell. This is the function of your circulatory system.

Circulation of the Blood

The transportation system of your body consists chiefly of but one organ system: the circulatory system. The main parts of this system are shown in the reference chart of the human circulatory system (page 122).

Perhaps the most familiar organ of this system is your heart. Your heart has four chambers or cavities. It has pumped blood through your body since before you were born. It will continue to do so, never stopping and never tiring, until the moment you die.

Your heart is, of course, made up of muscle. Cardiac muscle, the muscle that makes up your heart, is involuntary muscle; but cardiac muscle is modified in structure from all other involuntary muscle. After all, your heart beats an average of 72 times per minute every minute of your life. How many times does it beat in an hour? a day? a year?

The chamber of your heart that contracts most powerfully is the lower left chamber. This chamber is known as the **left ventricle.** When the muscles of the left ventricle contract, blood is forced in a mighty surge, or *pulse,* out of a great artery that branches into all parts of your body. **Arteries** are the blood vessels that carry blood away from the heart. Study carefully the two drawings of the heart. ❶ As you read on, refer to the drawings of the external and internal views of the heart as often as you need to.

The arteries divide and redivide like the branches of a tree until, finally, the tubes become microscopically thin blood vessels. The large arteries are heavy, strong tubes with

117

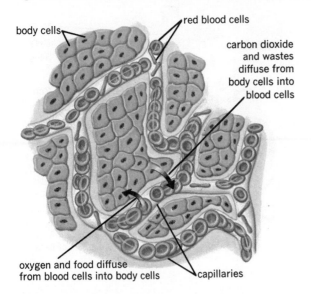

body cells

red blood cells

carbon dioxide and wastes diffuse from body cells into blood cells

oxygen and food diffuse from blood cells into body cells

capillaries

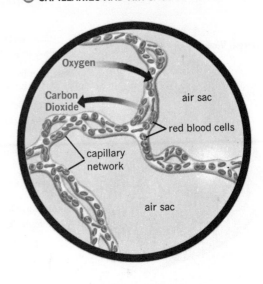

Oxygen

Carbon Dioxide

air sac

red blood cells

capillary network

air sac

muscular, elastic walls. Each time the heart beats, blood rushes through them. You can actually feel the pushing of blood in an artery that comes close to the surface of the skin (at the wrist or at the neck, for example). In contrast, as the arteries branch and rebranch, they become microscopically thin until the walls are but a single cell thick.

These thin, delicate tubes only one cell thick are not called arteries. They are called **capillaries** (kap′ə·ler′ez). The capillaries are so thin, in fact, that ten of them placed side by side are no wider than a hair. No cell in your body is very far from a capillary. The small molecules dissolved in the blood easily pass through the membranes of the capillary walls and from here diffuse into nearby cells. Recall how sugar passes through a piece of cellophane or Goldbeater's membrane.

Look at the drawing showing blood flowing through capillaries next to the body cells. ❶ Oxygen and foods in solution (dissolved) diffuse through the capillary wall

and the cell membranes into the cells. Waste materials including carbon dioxide diffuse out of the body cells and into the capillary. Since the capillaries are the locations in the body where the blood and the other body cells exchange materials, capillaries must occur in every part of the body.

Let's observe the circulation of blood in a capillary. ∎

As the capillaries continue on, the walls become thick again. They now are called **veins.** Veins are the blood vessels that carry blood back to the heart. The small veins merge to form larger veins. These larger veins then merge to form yet larger veins. Eventually, all the blood from the entire body is carried by two large veins back into the heart.

As the blood arrives back at the heart, it empties into the upper right chamber. This is a thin-walled collecting chamber called the **right auricle.** When the right auricle is full, it suddenly contracts, a valve closes between it and the vein bringing blood in. This forces

■ AN APPRENTICE INVESTIGATION of Circulation of Blood in a Capillary

If you have a small goldfish or other small fish, you can observe the circulation of blood. The photograph shows you how to keep the fish moist and alive without harming it. ❶ The arteries and tiny capillaries in the tail of a fish are visible with the aid of the microscope. You can see the blood moving in pulses through small arteries. Notice that it flows more steadily in the capillaries and small veins. ❷

Be sure to keep the cotton moist throughout your investigation and to spread the tail of the fish over the hole in the thin piece of cork on which the fish is placed. A thin microscope slide placed over the fish's tail helps hold it in place. The hole in the cork must, of course, be directly above the hole in the microscope stage.

The webs between the toes of a frog's hind legs are another place in which you can investigate the circulation of blood. If you can secure a live frog, you might like to observe circulation in the web between two toes.

An Investigation On Your Own

Can you build a working model of a circulatory system that would include a small artery (an arteriole), capillaries, and a small vein (a venule)?

❷

the blood down into the **right ventricle.** Now the right ventricle contracts and a valve closes, keeping the blood from flowing back up into the right auricle. This insures that the blood flows out a great artery and to the lungs. In the lungs, the artery divides and redivides until, again, the tubes become thin-walled capillaries.

The drawing shown here shows a microscopic view of the **air sacs** and the capillaries of the lungs. ❷ Now you will notice something interesting. The capillaries form a kind of loose network surrounding an air sac.

There are millions of tiny air sacs in your lungs. Air is inhaled from outside your body and eventually enters these air sacs. Oxygen

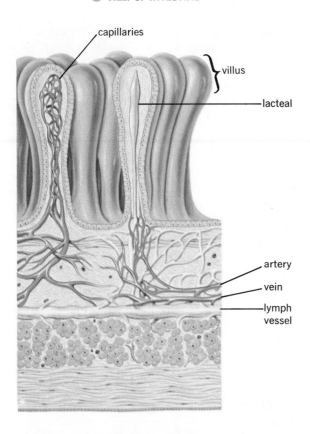

① VILLI OF INTESTINE

capillaries

villus

lacteal

artery

vein

lymph vessel

from the inhaled air diffuses through the air-sac walls into the capillaries that surround each sac. In return, carbon dioxide diffuses through the capillary walls and out into the air sacs. Each time you *exhale*, you exhale air containing this carbon dioxide. The carbon dioxide is produced and given off into the blood by the cells of your body. Each time you *inhale*, you take air into the air sacs where the oxygen from this air diffuses into the blood. The oxygen now dissolved in the blood is then distributed to all the cells of your body.

The capillaries leaving the lungs merge again and again becoming large and thick vessels carrying the oxygen-fresh blood back

into the **left auricle** of the heart. When full, the left auricle contracts, forcing the blood into the left ventricle. Valves, of course, close to keep the blood from flowing backwards. Now the blood is ready again to be pumped from the left ventricle out through the arteries to the body cells.

How does the food that you have digested get into the blood stream? Study the drawing showing a section of the wall of the small intestine. ① Notice that the inner wall is covered with fingerlike projections [**villi** (vil′ī); singular, *villus*]. The villi increase the amount of surface through which digested foods can be absorbed. Inside each villus are capillaries. Small molecules of digested proteins and digested starches and sugars diffuse into the capillaries and are carried away by the blood. Some of these materials go directly into the cells for immediate use. However, extra sugars that the body does not need immediately are carried to your liver. Here the sugars are stored in a form called *glycogen* (glī′kə·jen), or animal starch.

Look again at a villus and notice that it contains another small tube (shown in yellow on the drawing). This small tube, or vessel, called a **lacteal** (lak′tē′əl) absorbs digested fats. [When fats are digested, they are broken up into small molecules of *glycerin* (glis′ər·in) and small molecules of fatty acids.] As the lacteals merge, they form larger and larger vessels until one large vessel results. The fatty acids and glycerin from this vessel empty into the blood stream in a large vein near the heart.

The Lymphatic System

The lacteals are part of a somewhat separate transportation system of your body called the **lymphatic** (lim·fat′ik) **system.** The fluid inside the tubes of the lymphatic system

120

is called lymph. Much of the waste products of your cells is picked up by the lymphatic system and is finally poured back into the blood stream in the same way as the fatty acids are.

Not all of the lymph is in the *lymphatics* (lymph vessels). Every living cell of your body is bathed in lymph. If you have ever had a blister, you have seen lymph. It is the clear, watery substance that fills up a blister.

Lymph is actually just the liquid part of the blood. When food and oxygen diffuse out of the capillaries and into the cells, they become dissolved materials in this liquid part of the blood. And, once out of the blood stream, the liquid is called lymph. But, as you now know, not all of the lymph diffuses back into the capillaries again. A considerable amount of it, filled with waste materials, diffuses into the lymphatic system and is carried back to the blood stream later.

Exercise and Circulation

The heart is helped in its work of pumping blood through the body by the valves in your veins. The valves are constructed so that blood can flow up the veins toward the heart, but not backwards away from the heart. Study the diagram to see how the valves work. ②

How does all this help move blood along? It would not help at all except for the action of your muscles. When the large muscles of your body contract, they squeeze against the veins. This helps push the blood along the veins. The valves close if the blood starts to move backwards, away from your heart. Therefore, the blood can only be squeezed in one direction, toward the heart.

This is one reason why exercise is so important. It helps move the blood along. It also moves lymph in the lymphatic system. The

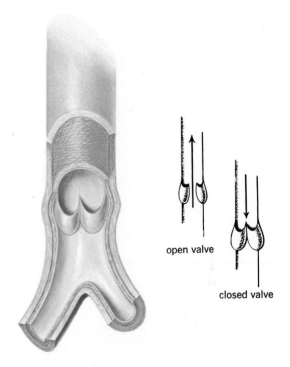

② SECTION OF VEIN WITH VALVE

open valve

closed valve

lymphatics, which carry away a great amount of the poisonous waste products from the cells, are not a direct part of the circulatory system. The heart is not directly connected to the lymphatics and does not pump lymph. However, the lymph vessels have many more valves than the veins of the circulatory system. There are approximately ten or more to every inch of lymphatics. The *only* thing that pumps lymph through the lymphatics is the squeezing action of your large muscles as they contract.

Did you know that when people are hospitalized for a long time and cannot move about, they are massaged? It is not difficult to see why this is necessary from what you now know about lymphatics, valves, and veins.

You are now ready to trace a drop of blood through your circulatory system. ■

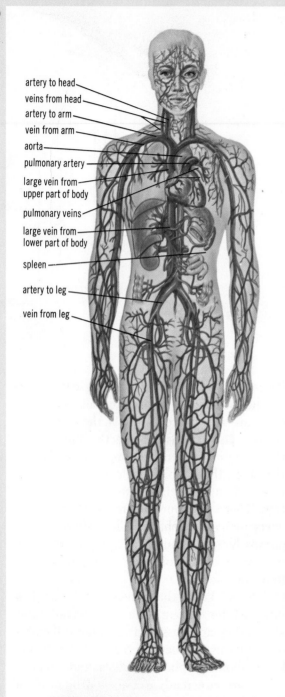

artery to head

veins from head

artery to arm

vein from arm

aorta

pulmonary artery

large vein from
upper part of body

pulmonary veins

large vein from
lower part of body

spleen

artery to leg

vein from leg

Study the Reference Chart. In it you will find drawings of your heart, its blood vessels, and the blood vessels of the entire body. The maroon color indicates blood that has given up a great amount of its oxygen (deoxygenated blood) to the cells. The bright red color indicates oxygenated blood. When the substance **hemoglobin** (hē′mə·glō′bin) in the red blood cells combines with oxygen in the lungs, the hemoglobin tends to become a redder color; when the oxygen leaves the hemoglobin and enters the body cells, the hemoglobin tends to be a maroon color.

a. Trace a drop of venous (deoxygenated) blood from the right arm back to the heart. Which are the main blood vessels through which the deoxygenated blood travels?

b. Trace a drop of arterial (oxygenated) blood from the aorta down to the right toe. Which are the main blood vessels through which the oxygenated blood travels?

c. Trace a drop of blood in its travels from the right auricle to the lungs.

d. Trace a drop of blood from the left ventricle to the front of the head.

e. Place a finger on an artery in which you can feel a pulse at the wrist; at the throat; at the temple.

An Investigation On Your Own

Locate the portal vein. What is its function? How does it differ from any other vein in the body?

Determine how the temporary tying of the portal vein would affect the blood's supply of glucose, amino acids, fatty acids.

1. What is the function of
   a. the heart?
   b. arteries?
   c. veins?

2. What part do each of the following play in the function of the heart?
   a. the left auricle
   b. the right auricle
   c. the left ventricle
   d. the right ventricle

3. What kind of blood—deoxygenated or oxygenated—do each of the following blood vessels carry?
   a. the pulmonary vein
   b. the pulmonary artery
   c. the vein entering the right auricle
   d. the artery leaving the left ventricle

4. Describe the role of the lymphatic system.

NEW VIEW

Compare the hearts of the frog and of man. How are they similar? How are they different?

7. BODY SYSTEMS OF MAN—THE RESPIRATORY AND EXCRETORY SYSTEMS

Every living thing, as you know, must have a constant supply of materials in order to live. Some foods can be stored in an animal or a plant body. However, no living thing has ever developed a means of storing much oxygen. And every living cell must be provided *constantly* with a supply of oxygen so that life will not cease. Thus, a continuous supply of oxygen must always be available.

You have never quit breathing since you were born. You can hold your breath for a short while, of course. But during this time, oxygen, already in the air in your lungs, continues diffusing into the blood stream. And carbon dioxide continues diffusing from the blood into the lungs. Finally, you must breathe again. Your respiratory system must steadily provide oxygen for your blood stream. It must steadily release the carbon dioxide from your blood.

The word *respiration* does not refer solely to breathing. Recall that breathing means getting air into your lungs (inhaling) and removing the air containing excess carbon dioxide that has been returned from your body to the lungs (exhaling). Respiration also includes the oxidation of food by living cells as well as the transportation of oxygen to the cells and the removal of carbon dioxide, the result of cellular respiration, from the cells. So respiration includes what goes on inside the cells, the transporting of oxygen and carbon dioxide between the cells and the lungs, the exchange of gases between the blood and the lungs, and the breathing process.

Nevertheless, the respiratory system is considered a body system designed for the exchange of gases. Oxygen from the air is brought into contact with the capillaries of the lungs, and carbon dioxide from the capillaries is given off to the air from the lungs.

But the lungs are also part of another system—the excretory system. This system removes cell wastes from the blood stream and eliminates them from the body. Among the wastes removed from the blood stream are carbon dioxide, water, certain nitrogen compounds, such as urea, and inorganic salts, mainly sodium chloride. The lungs excrete the carbon dioxide and much of the water. Some water, salts, and a little urea are also given off by the sweat glands. The principal organs of the excretory system, however, are the kidneys. The kidneys excrete urine, composed mainly of nitrogenous wastes and various inorganic salts dissolved in water.

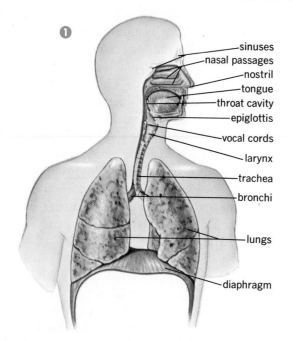

- sinuses
- nasal passages
- nostril
- tongue
- throat cavity
- epiglottis
- vocal cords
- larynx
- trachea
- bronchi
- lungs
- diaphragm

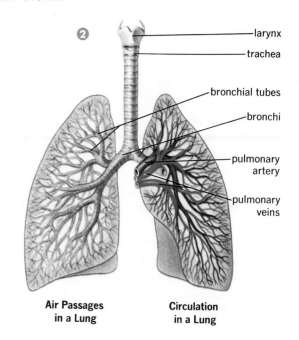

- larynx
- trachea
- bronchial tubes
- bronchi
- pulmonary artery
- pulmonary veins

Air Passages in a Lung   **Circulation in a Lung**

A Study of Your Respiratory System

Can you trace a breath of inhaled air into the lungs? Can you trace a bubble of exhaled air from a tip of the right lung and out through the nose?

You are already familiar with the main features of your own respiratory system.  Air enters the lungs when your chest cavity is enlarged as you inhale. Your lungs are composed of air tubes with many branches. Recall that each air tube ends in an air sac which is surrounded by tiny capillaries.

The outside of the lungs is covered with a smooth, slick membrane. The chest cavity itself is lined with another slick membrane. There is almost no space between these membranes. The outer surface of the lungs touches the inner surface of the chest wall. When you breathe in, by lifting your ribs and contracting your **diaphragm** (the muscle that separates your chest cavity from your abdominal cavity), the chest cavity becomes larger. This

immediately reduces the pressure inside the lungs, causing the outside air to rush into your nose or mouth, down the **trachea** (trā′kē·ə) and its branches, and into the air sacs. When you breathe out, you simply relax the muscles between the ribs and the muscular diaphragm. Then the ribs swing down and the organs in your abdomen push the relaxed diaphragm up, domelike, into the chest cavity. This creates a pressure inside the lungs that is greater than the pressure of the outside air. Therefore, the air rushes out of your nose and mouth once again.

A Study of Your Excretory System

Just as every living cell must have oxygen, every living cell must give off its waste products. You know how the lungs expel carbon dioxide and water. Now consider the kidneys, the chief organs of the excretory system.

The blood entering the kidneys contains large amounts of nitrogen wastes in the form of urea and other salts dissolved in water. Since urea, which comes from the breakdown of amino acids by the cells, is a *poisonous* waste, it must be removed promptly from the blood. Inside the kidneys some two million "filters" remove most of the urea and some of the water and dissolved salts. This fluid, which is now known as urine, flows from the kidneys, down the ureters to the bladder. There the urine is stored until it is excreted from the body through the urethra. ❸

The sweat glands, which also remove water, dissolved salt, and a little urea from the blood stream, are located in the dermis layer of the skin (see page 91). Even on a cool day, these glands excrete over a pint of water. Each pore of your skin is actually the opening of a sweat gland.

In Summary

Now, having studied your own body's systems and having compared it with those of other animals, you have a fair idea of the meaning of organization in living things. A living thing is not a jumble, like a pile of dust, or a rock. It is organized. A living thing shows more than the organization of a wooden board that is now perhaps part of a house. The wooden board shows its plant origin but it is no longer alive. Break it apart, and it is still wood, still showing a kind of structure. But break a living thing apart and it is no longer a living thing. That is, it is no longer organized to carry on its life functions. Put another way, it is no longer adapted—as is a living thing—for getting energy from its environment.

REVIEW

1. About one fifth of inhaled air is oxygen; exhaled air is about one sixth oxygen. How do you account for this difference?

❸ **EXCRETORY SYSTEM**

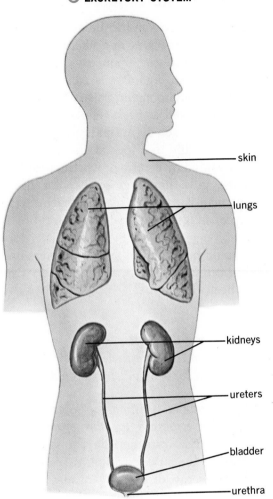

- skin
- lungs
- kidneys
- ureters
- bladder
- urethra

2. Distinguish between the meaning of the words *breathing* and *respiration*.

3. How is each of these cell wastes excreted: water, carbon dioxide, urea, sodium chloride?

NEW VIEW

1. Compare the respiratory systems of the frog and man. How are they similar? How are they different?

2. Which respiratory system is the most complex? Which excretory system? Explain.

8. RELATING THE CONCEPTS

As we study one multicellular living thing after another, there is one characteristic of life that is impressed upon us: *organization for function.* An organism is adapted to live in a certain environment; this is true of simple-celled as well as multicellular organisms. Furthermore, each organism is adapted by its structure for life in a special environment. A fish is adapted by certain of its structures (for instance, gills, fins, and scales) for life in water; man is adapted by his structure (for instance, lungs, legs, and skin) for life on land.

It would be useful for you to examine once again (and in other forms) the concepts you have been developing.

Reviewing the Concepts

▶ *Organisms are adapted by their structure and function for life in a special environment.*

▶ *An epithelial system of organisms is adapted by structure for the protection of organisms.* For instance, the flat shinglelike structure of the outer covering tissue protects the body against disease organisms.

▶ *A skeletal system is adapted by its structure to give form and support to the organism.* The hard, strong, and sometimes flexible material (ligament, cartilage, and bone) formed by connective tissue cells is useful for the attachment of muscle, and to give form to the body.

▶ *The muscular system is adapted by its structure to facilitate movement of the organism.* By their connection to bones, the shapes of the cells, their ability to contract and expand, muscles are adapted to move the body.

▶ *A nervous system is adapted by structure for the coordination of the different organ systems of the organisms.* The structure and interconnection of the neurons, their connections to muscles and glands, coordinate the responses of the body to stimuli.

▶ *A digestive system is adapted by its structure for the function of breaking down food substances.* Through the function of its digestive glands which secrete enzymes, food substances are broken down from large (generally nondiffusible) molecules into diffusible, generally smaller molecules.

▶ *A respiratory system is adapted by its structure for the interchange of the gases in air with the gases in blood.* The thin walls of the cells in the respiratory system are adapted for easy gas exchange.

▶ *A circulatory system is adapted by its structure for the circulation of materials to the cells of the body.* The heart of multicellular organisms (especially the large vertebrate organisms we have been studying) is adapted for pumping the circulating blood. Arteries, veins, and capillaries are adapted by their structure to maintain circulation and exchange with the cells.

▶ *A reproductive system is adapted by structure for reproduction of the organism.* Sperms produced by the testes and eggs produced by the ovaries are the cells generally taking part in reproduction of multicellular organisms.

▶ *An excretory system is adapted by structure for the excretion of waste substances.* The kidneys are specially adapted for excretion of nitrogenous wastes, the skin for partial excretion of salts, the lungs for excretion of carbon dioxide.

Testing Yourself

1. Describe one important difference between the epithelial system of the frog and of man that adapts each to life in a different environment.

2. Describe one important difference between the skeletal system of the frog and of man that adapts each to life in a different environment.

3. Describe one important difference between the respiratory system of the frog and of man that adapts each to life in a different environment

4. Describe at least 5 structures in the frog and in man that show a relationship in structure between these organisms.

5. Describe 5 life functions that show a relationship between the frog and man.

6. How does the nervous system in man function in
    a. recognition of the environment?
    b. interpretation of the environment?
    c. response to the environment?

7. How does the digestive system in man function in
    a. breaking down food substances?
    b. absorbing food substances?

8. How does the circulatory system in man function in
    a. exchanging gases with the lungs?
    b. exchanging food substances with the intestine? the cells?

9. Do all functions of the nervous system in man require the action of the brain? Explain your answer.

10. How does the excretory system of man function in the excretion of
    a. carbon dioxide?
    b. salts?

Extending the Concepts

Investigation 1. If you can, get a bone of a chicken (perhaps a leg bone) and compare it with the leg bone of a mammal (such as a lamb). How is a bird's bone adapted for flight?

Study a grasshopper's legs and a frog's legs. How are the hind legs of a grasshopper or frog adapted for jumping?

Examine a chicken's foot. How is a bird's foot adapted for perching?

Observe a squirrel. How is a squirrel adapted for climbing?

Examine a beetle (like the Japanese beetle). How is the outer wing different from the inner wing? How are they adapted for different functions?

Investigation 2. Invent a way to determine how far apart nerve endings are in the skin on the inner part of your lower arm. (*Clue:* If the skin is touched with a hair or the point of a pin, you will feel it. Can you feel two hairs or the points of two pins?)

You may need to invent an instrument that can separate the hairs or pins just far enough so you can feel two points rather than one. Is this necessary? Do you have a better way?

Try to develop a hypothesis upon which the investigation is based.

Suggested Reading
Best, C. H., and N. B. Taylor, *The Living Body* (5th ed.), New York, Holt, Rinehart and Winston, 1970.

Biological Sciences Curriculum Study, *Biological Science: An Inquiry into Life* (2nd ed.), New York, Harcourt Brace Jovanovich, 1968.

6 Multicellular Plants as Organisms

There is a difference between the body structure of animals and plants. An animal has cells that make up tissues. The tissues make up organs. The organs make up organ systems such as the nervous system and the digestive system which you have just studied.

The organization is not quite the same in plants. There are cells, of course, and in higher plants there are tissues. We can even call the roots, the stems, and the leaves of a tree organs because these structures are made up of different tissues that work together to do special jobs for the tree. However, there are no organ systems comparable to those of animals.

Many botanists would consider the higher green plant to be organized into two main systems: the roots make up a **root system** below the ground, and the stems and leaves make up a **shoot system** above the ground.

Plant Tissues

Clearly, plants do not have the great variety of tissues and organ systems that animals have. However, we can separate the tissues in a plant according to their functions.

Some plant cells specialize in producing new tissues, that is, the cells divide, each cell becoming two new cells. Thus, dividing cells build up new tissues. These reproducing cells lie in definite layers and regions in a plant and make up what we call the *growth tissue*. One kind of growth tissue is found at the *tips* of roots and stems. The growth tissue at the tips of roots and stems is called the **meristematic** (mer′ə·stə·mat′ik) **tissue.** ❶ Meristematic tissue is responsible for growth in length. Thus, the tip of a moss or a fern, as well as a seed plant, will grow in length because of the division of the cells of the meristematic tissue. Another growth tissue is found in rings or strands in roots and stems. This growth tissue is known as **cambium** (kam′bē·əm) **tissue.** The photograph shows the cells of cambium in the stem of a tree. ❷ Growth tissue produces all the other kinds of plant tissues.

The second kind of plant tissue is *protective tissue*. Bark is a protective tissue. So are the outer cell layers on leaves, stems, and roots. Protective tissue forms sheets of cells that protect the underlying tissues. The protective covering tissue of a plant is called the **epidermis,** as is your own. In many cases, as in the bark of trees, there are many layers of dead cells, just as there are many layers of

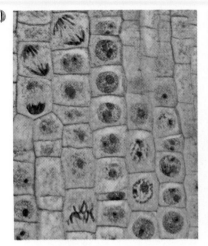

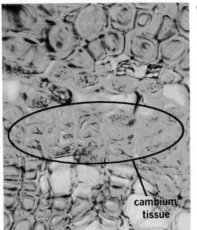

cambium tissue

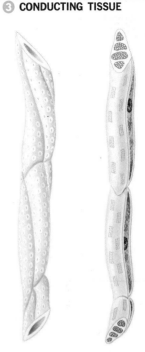
xylem cells   phloem cells

dead cells in the epidermis or outer skin of the palms of your hands. The bark of a tree is only masses of dead epidermal cells.

The third kind of plant tissue is called *supporting tissue.* There are many kinds of supporting tissue. The most prominent kind is found chiefly in the stems and roots. This tissue is made up of thick-walled, woody strengthening cells. These kinds of cells give a tree its strength and form, and serve the same purpose as the skeleton of an animal.

The fourth kind of plant tissue is *conducting tissue.* There are two sorts. Water and dissolved minerals are conducted from the roots to the leaves and other parts of the plant by **xylem** (zī′ləm) **tissue.** Food, manufactured in the leaves, is conducted to other parts of the plant by **phloem** (flō′em) **tissue.** As shown in the drawing, the cells of conducting tissues form what amounts to long tubes. These tubes are often found grouped together into bundles called **fibrovascular** (fī′brō·vas′kyə·lar) **bundles.**

A fifth kind, found especially in green plants, may be called *food-producing tissue.* Look at the photomicrograph. As you can see, this tissue is made up of cells that contain

the green coloring matter chlorophyll. Chlorophyll is the substance that carries on food manufacturing in plants. The chlorophyll-containing tissue is located mainly in the leaves of green plants, although it is sometimes found in the stems.

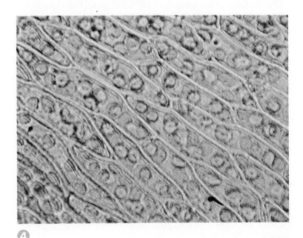

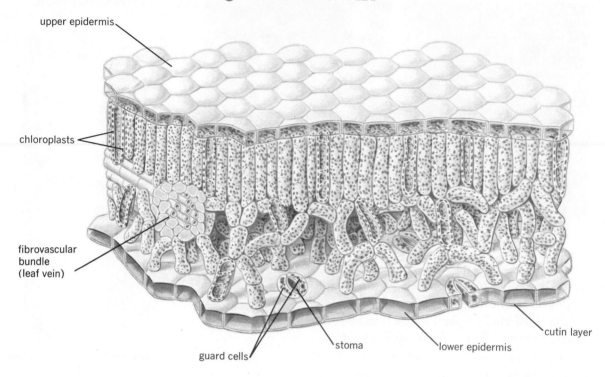

upper epidermis

chloroplasts

fibrovascular
bundle
(leaf vein)

guard cells

stoma

lower epidermis

cutin layer

1. THE STRUCTURE AND FUNCTION OF THE LEAF

If it is fall or spring, you might make a collection of leaves. How many different shapes can you collect? As you collect leaves, notice their position on a branch. Notice how the branches lie so that light easily reaches the leaves.

Study the drawing of a cross section of a green leaf.**❶** Now, look at the photograph of a leaf showing the branching veins.**❷**

The Anatomy of a Leaf

Notice again the main tissues that you have already studied in the leaf. The top and the undersurface of the leaf are covered by a layer of protective tissue, the epidermis. The cells of the epidermis are somewhat flat and

fit snugly together. The outer surfaces of these cells are covered with a layer of a waxy substance called **cutin** (kyoo'tin). Cutin is secreted by the epidermal cells and insures that the leaf is waterproof. What do you think would happen if the leaf were not waterproof?

Between the top and the bottom layers of epidermis are cells that have small, green, capsulelike structures in them. Each of these capsules is called a **chloroplast** and contains chlorophyll. It is in the chloroplast that photosynthesis (the manufacture of sugar) takes place. Also notice that the inner cells toward the top of the leaf are long and thin and rather close together. Beneath this layer, the remaining cells are farther apart.

Look at the fibrovascular bundle (leaf vein) shown in the drawing.**❶** The word *vascular* comes from Latin and means "little vessel," a small vein. *Fibro–* refers to the long fiber-like structure of the vessels. (Study the charts of the corn plant on page 152 and find the fibrovascular bundles.) The fibrovascular bundle is a bundle of tiny conducting tubes, the conducting tissues of the leaf. Each fibrovascular bundle contains both xylem and phloem cells. The xylem cells begin near the tips of the roots of a plant and form continuous tubes and other structures that carry water and minerals up through the trunk, through the branching stems, up the stem of the leaf [called a **petiole** (pet′ē·ōl)], and out into the flattened *blade* of the leaf. In the blade of the leaf, the conducting tissue branches to supply all parts with water and minerals. The other major type of cells in the conducting tissue, the phloem cells, carry manufactured food out of the leaf blade, down the petiole, and, by branching, to all parts of the tree including the roots.

Next time you eat celery, tear the stalk down its length. You cannot help but notice the long strands that curl up. These are the fibrovascular bundles. And you can easily tease out the fibrovascular bundles in spinach.

You will recall that in photosynthesis the green plant cell combines carbon dioxide and

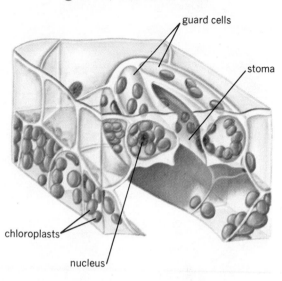

guard cells

stoma

chloroplasts

nucleus

water to form sugar. How does carbon dioxide get into the leaf where it is used for food manufacture? Gases, such as carbon dioxide, are not supplied from the soil water, so they do not come up through the xylem tubes. Also, like all living things, the plant uses oxygen for respiration. How does oxygen get into the plant?

Notice the hole, or pore, in the drawing of the lower epidermis.❸ Notice the special **guard cells** that surround each pore [called a **stoma** (stō′mə) from a Greek word meaning "mouth"]. The stomata [(stō′mə′tə), plural of *stoma*] let air enter the leaf. The spaces that you saw between the lower layer of cells inside the leaf allow the air to come into contact with the cell wall of each cell. Carbon dioxide from the air dissolves in the film of moisture that covers each cell. From the cell surface it diffuses through the cell membrane and into the cell. Once inside the cell, the carbon dioxide can be used in photosynthesis. As the supply becomes used up, more carbon dioxide diffuses into the leaf

There are thousands of stomata in the undersurface of a leaf. A single square inch of an oak leaf has over 100,000 stomata.

Water is precious to a plant. All of the cellular processes of plants and animals require that chemicals be dissolved in water. But a plant, in addition, must have water as a raw material for food manufacture. So it is important to a plant that not too much water be lost.

Look at the photographs of the two geranium leaves removed from a plant. ❶ The petioles of each leaf were wrapped in plastic, and the leaf on the right was covered with vaseline to prevent the loss of water from its stomata. The lower photograph shows the condition of the leaves after several days. ❷

A tremendous amount of water *is* lost from a green plant. For example, over 1,800 gallons of water may evaporate into the air from a single apple tree during its six-month growing period. This great loss of water is not wholly wasted, however, as it helps pull more water into the roots and up the stems as you will see later.

Nonetheless, if the hundreds of thousands of stomata on a single leaf were to remain open at night when the plant was not making food and was not needing carbon dioxide, there would be an even greater loss of water. The guard cells regulate the opening and closing of the stomata, widening them in the daylight and narrowing or closing them at night. By this ability to open and close the stomata, guard cells regulate both the amount of carbon dioxide that enters the leaf and the amount of water (and oxygen) that escapes from it.

Look back to the drawing on page 131 and notice that the walls of the guard cells next to the stoma are very thick, while the walls elsewhere are thin. This difference in

from the outside air. Do all leaves have stomata?

It is known that the leaves of some kinds of underwater plants do not have stomata and guard cells. Can you explain how they might get carbon dioxide for the process of photosynthesis?

If you examined the leaves of a moss, would you expect them to have stomata? Investigate for yourself to see if they do have stomata.

The stomata carry on one of the most important functions of the land plant. While stomata permit air to enter, they also permit water to leave. Yet if too much water evaporates, the plant wilts.

■ AN APPRENTICE INVESTIGATION into Diffusion

Pour some corn syrup or molasses into the  top of a thistle tube. (Hold your finger over the stem of the tube as you fill it.) Cover the larger end of the thistle tube with a Goldbeater's membrane or another animal membrane. (Even cellophane will do.) Fasten the membrane with a rubber band. Place the thistle tube, upside down, in a beaker of water and mark the level of the syrup in the thistle tube with paint or a wax pencil.❶ Observe what is happening after a half hour, and again after several hours have passed.❷ Does the level of the syrup remain the same? How does this investigation apply to the functioning of guard cells?

An Investigation On Your Own

Instead of corn syrup, use a 1 percent solution of corn starch. What do you observe? How do you account for it? Compare your results with those obtained with the sugar solution.

the thickness of the guard cell walls is an important fact in the functioning of these cells. How is this so? As the morning sunlight hits the leaf, the chlorophyll in the guard cells start making sugar. Soon, the concentration of sugar inside the guard cells is much greater than the concentration of sugar in the other epidermal cells surrounding them. How important is this concentration of sugar to the guard cells?

In the investigation above, you can see for yourself what happens when there are different concentrations of a substance on opposite sides of an animal or plant membrane. ■

What has happened is this. There are more water molecules (a greater concentration) in the glass of water than there are in the syrup inside the thistle tube. Therefore, simple diffusion occurs. Simple diffusion is the process of movement of molecules from a place of greater concentration to a place of lesser concentration. Any substance that can pass through a membrane will diffuse from the side of its greatest concentration to the side of its least concentration. Of course some of the sugar in the thistle tube diffuses out into the water in the glass as well, since there was a high concentration of sugar inside the thistle tube and no sugar in the glass of water. However, the water diffuses in more easily and rapidly since its molecules are much smaller than are sugar molecules. Because of their small size, the water molecules pass through the membrane more easily. Now, back to the guard cells.

When the guard cells contain more sugar in solution than do the surrounding epidermal cells, diffusion of water occurs just as it did in the investigation. Water begins to diffuse from the neighboring epidermal cells, through the cell membranes, and into the guard cells. This, of course, swells up the guard cells. But the inner walls of the guard cells next to the stomata are very thick and do not swell out easily. Instead, the thinner walls along the other sides of the guard cells swell out. As these thinner walls swell out, they actually pull the thick inner walls of the two guard cells farther apart. So the opening between the guard cells becomes larger.

Most of the day the stomata stay open. When night comes, the guard cells stop making sugar; there is no more light to provide the needed energy. The sugar that remains in the guard cells continues to diffuse into the cells surrounding them (as it has been doing all day). Also some of the sugar is changed to starch within the cells. Soon the concentration of sugar inside the guard cells has become equal to that in the surrounding epidermal cells. At this time, excess water diffuses out of the guard cells and the guard cells begin to shrink, causing the thick inner walls to come together again. The stomata between them are now narrowed or closed and they remain that way until the next day when light again hits the leaf.

This, of course, is a simplified explanation of the process. There are other factors involved, but we will leave these for later study.

Leaves have other functions as well. You have eaten celery. When you have, you have enjoyed eating the petioles of the leaves. Lettuce and cabbage leaves serve as food. In short, some leaves store so much food that they serve as food sources for some animals. Of course, the leaves of grasses are the fundamental food sources for most of the grazing animals of the world.

Some leaves are specially adapted for storing food. The bulb leaves of the onion are such specially adapted leaves. Brussels sprouts are eaten for the food value in their leaves.

Look at the onion and amaryllis bulbs in the photograph and notice the thick leaves. ❶ The stored food serves as energy for the growth of the plant. Yet the fundamental function of the green leaf is to make food. Only because the green leaf captures energy from the sun is life possible for us and other animals. We are going to study the structure of the plant before we study the chemistry of photosynthesis in Chapter 9. (But you may, if you wish, read Chapter 9 now.)

REVIEW

1. What is the major function of the leaf? What structures in the leaf are mainly involved in carrying out this function?

2. How are food substances and water carried throughout the leaf?

3. What is the function of the guard cells? What is the explanation of their function?

NEW VIEW

1. A bag made of a membrane that allows only water to pass through is filled with a mild solution of salt. The bag is placed into a stronger solution of salt in water.

What do you predict will happen?

2. The evaporation of water from the parts of a plant exposed to the air is known as **transpiration**. As you have read, the amounts of water lost by transpiration through the leaves of plants are surprisingly great. Design and carry out an investigation of just how much water is lost by a plant (such as a geranium) in one day. Read about transpiration in an advanced textbook. What problems about transpiration are yet to be understood by botanists?

2. THE STRUCTURE AND FUNCTION OF THE STEM

The stem (that is, the trunk, branches, and twigs) of a tree does several things. By rising above the ground and branching, a widespread attachment for the leaves is provided.

The arrangement of the leaves on the stem is of great significance. If you are able to examine many stems, you will notice that the leaves are not arranged at random along the stem. Rather, they are arranged around the stem in definite locations. The patterns of leaf arrangement vary according to the kind of plant. In one kind of plant, the leaves may be positioned alternately by the stem, first on one side and then on the opposite side. Or they may form a spiral pattern up the stem, or be located exactly opposite each other. But whatever the arrangement, you can be certain that they are located in the very best position to catch sunlight. In fact, the primary function of a stem is to hold the leaves up into the sunlight and to support them there.

As well as being in a position to catch sunlight, leaves must also have a supply of water and minerals from the soil. Furthermore, the food that the leaves manufacture must be made available to all the cells of the plant. Thus, a second function of a stem is to transport materials.

A third function of stems is storage of food. Many stems store food until it is needed by the cells of the plant.

Did you ever look closely at the new, smaller twigs of a tree in the summertime? They are green. They contain chlorophyll. You can guess, therefore, that a fourth function of at least some stems is to assist the leaves in manufacturing food for the entire plant.

Now let's take a closer look at one kind of stem, the stem of a tree.

The Outer Structure of a Tree Stem

If it is possible, cut a small twig from a tree. Examine it as you read on.

There are several interesting structures you can see without cutting into the twig. Does your twig look something like the one shown in the drawing on the next page? If it is necessary, refer to the drawing (as well as to your twig, if you have one) as you read on.

One of the first things to notice is that there are swellings at the tip of the twig. As you examine them closely, you will notice that they seem to be covered with overlapping, tiny scales. These swellings are the buds and they are covered with *bud scales* which protect them.

Pull the bud scales away from the buds on your twigs. Notice the soft, greenish tissue underneath. This tissue is the growth tissue,

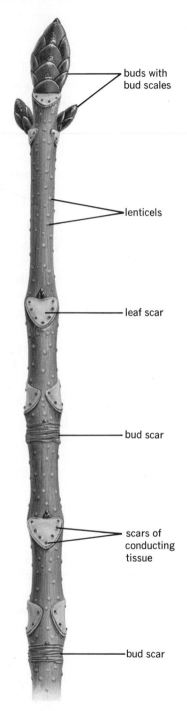

buds with
bud scales

lenticels

leaf scar

bud scar

scars of
conducting
tissue

bud scar

ready to start active cell division when stimulated by the warmth of spring. Now, the buds are resting, or are dormant, and are protected by the bud scales from dying out. Next spring, watch for the opening of the buds on trees and bushes. If it is possible, cut twigs from a variety of trees and bushes while studying this chapter and place them in jars of water. Examine the buds every day. After several days you may find some of the buds swelling. In time, some of these will develop into leaves. If you have twigs cut from flowering bushes, such as the forsythia or willow, you may even get a few flowers. Do all the buds burst into leaf at the same time? How do you explain your observation?

Recall that plants grow in length only at their tips. Some of these buds are *stem buds*. In the spring, when they start growing, they will produce new stem material and new leaves. Other buds are *flower buds*. They will develop into flowers for the tree. Flowers, of course, are the reproductive structures of flowering plants. You will learn more about them in Unit Four.

Study your stem carefully once again. Do you find a number of ringlike marks close together and surrounding the twig not far back from the tip? Two sets of bud scars are shown in the drawing. ❶ The scars closest to the tip are the scars left when the bud scales dropped off from the stem bud last spring as the bud developed and grew, producing the new twig length.

That part of the twig from these scars to the tip is the growth of the twig during the last summer's growing season. How many years old is that part of the twig in the picture between the two sets of bud scars? How many sets of bud scars can you find on your twig? How old is the entire twig that you cut from the tree?

As the stem bud starts growing, it produces a thin skin (epidermis) that protects the underlying tissues from drying out. You can see the epidermis on your twig just back from the bud at the end. This epidermis becomes thicker as time goes on. A thick, corky material finally is built up. This bark is excellent protection against drying and injury.

Look carefully at the epidermis and bark on your twig. Do you find scars shaped much like a half-moon? These are **leaf scars,** where the leaves were attached to the twig. If you look closely (a magnifying glass will help), you will notice tiny dots or spots arranged in a pattern inside the leaf scar in the drawing of the twig. Can you guess what these spots are? Remember that a leaf must obtain water from the stem and must send food materials back into the stem. If you guessed that the spots are the ends or scars of the conducting tissue, you are right. They are the ends of bundles of xylem tubes and phloem tubes, together with basic supporting tissue for strength. In the fall, when a tree drops its leaves, a protective layer of cells grows across the scar where the leaf was attached.

As you examine the bark again, notice the raised, oval or circular spots. These spots are tiny breaks in the bark called **lenticels** (len′ tə·səlz). Lenticels are pores that let air enter the twig. On green twigs that have an epidermis but not yet a thick bark, these pores serve as stomata do in a leaf. However, in an older twig covered with bark, no photosynthesis takes place. If you took careful measurements of the gases surrounding a twig, you would find that the air diffusing into the lenticels has more oxygen and less carbon dioxide than the air diffusing out of the lenticels. In a younger, green twig, on the other hand, the flow of gases would be just the opposite.

The living cells of a twig are as active as all living cells. They need energy and must get it by oxidizing sugars or other food materials. In the process of oxidation within the cells, oxygen is used and carbon dioxide is given off. You might say that the lenticels are the "breathing pores" of the plant, although this is not actually so since there is no respiratory system or pump such as lungs, trachea, or gills. The exchange of gases in plants occurs by slow diffusion. But, after all, a tree is by no means as active as a dog, or an insect, or a fish. A tree must oxidize food, but it need do so only very slowly as compared with most animals. Therefore, diffusion through stomata and lenticels supplies sufficient oxygen to meet the plant's needs.

You have probably seen a cork stopper. Cork comes from the bark of a cork tree. The brown streaks in the cork are the lenticels, deep holes running from the outside to the inner surface of the very thick bark.

The Inner Structure of a Tree Stem

Peel back a piece of the bark from the cut end of your twig. The part of the twig that is only a year or two old will probably be rather green underneath the outer bark.

Feel the material just under the bark you have peeled off. Is it damp? You have torn tender cells apart in removing the bark. The cells are filled with fluid. Protoplasm itself, you will recall, is a thick semiliquid. Remember also that cells have huge vacuoles containing a rather clear liquid. The dampness you felt was chiefly this liquid, often called "sap." It is the same liquid that moves up and down a stem through the conducting tubes. Sap is mostly water containing dissolved minerals from the soil and sugars from the leaves. However, sap also includes many substances made by the cells themselves.

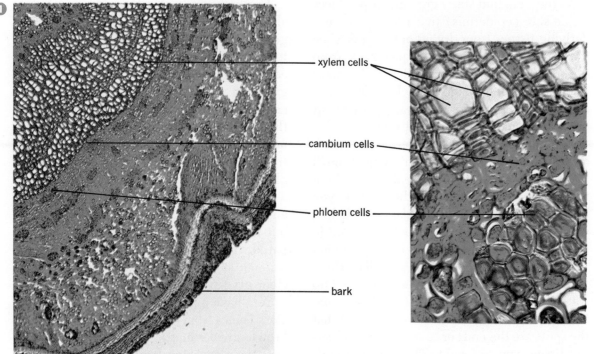

xylem cells

cambium cells

phloem cells

bark

Look at the photomicrograph of a cross section of part of an oak stem. ❶ Notice that the bark on the stem is quite thick. Some distance inside the bark lies the very thin layer of the growth tissue, the cambium layer. Inside this cambium, or growth, layer is wood tissue. In older stems the center part of the wood tissue, the **heartwood**, is darker in color, and the outer part, the **sapwood**, is lighter. Let's study these parts more closely to see what their function is.

Look carefully at the cells shown in the photomicrograph. ❷ The cambium layer, as you already know, is a thin layer of growth tissue. During the warm growing season, the cambium cells divide rapidly. The cells that they produce toward the outside, or the bark side, of the tree become phloem cells. The new cells produced on the inside of the cambium layer become xylem cells, or new wood.

In the spring and early summer there is usually a great amount of water in the ground. The leaves manufacture food rapidly, and much of it moves into the cambium layer. With plenty of food and water available, the cambium cells divide rapidly, producing large cells. In late summer and early fall, the division of the cambium cells slows down. The cells they produce at this time of year are much smaller. In the photograph at the left above, notice how the xylem cells in the upper left corner vary in size.

The old xylem (the heartwood) mainly gives strength to the tree and is no longer used to conduct materials. It also serves as a storage area for a variety of waste materials from the tree. The living part of the xylem tissue is the sapwood. Through the xylem tissue of the sapwood, soil water and minerals are conducted upward.

Suppose that you cut a four-inch-wide ring around a tree and removed all the tissue from that ring down to the cambium layer. Would the cambium layer replace the outer layers? Here is a photograph of a tree from which just such a ring of tissue has been removed.  Removing this outer ring of tissue is a good way to kill unwanted trees. This process, called **girdling,** is often used to clear a land of unwanted trees. Sometimes rabbits, deer, or other animals kill young trees by eating a complete ring of bark from around the tree.

Why do girdled trees die? Why doesn't the cambium heal the wound? If you were to examine a tree periodically that had been girdled, you would discover something interesting: the roots die first, then the stems and leaves die. This may seem surprising since the injury was only to the stem. How can you account for this? If you were to make a chemical analysis, you would find that the roots had run out of food. They died of starvation. It would seem to mean that girdling a tree cuts off the food supply to the roots.

In a girdled tree, this is precisely what happens. The phloem tissue, which conducts foods and other materials downward from the leaves, is found inside the inner bark, between the bark and the cambium layer. The phloem cells, as we said earlier, are produced by the dividing cambium layer. The phloem cells lying end to end make up what amount to extremely long, branched tubes extending from the leaves to the roots. Only those phloem tissues made in the past two years or so conduct the food material. The older phloem tissue becomes crushed as the cambium divides to form new phloem cells. The new cells push outward and crush the older cells against the outside bark.

The outer, corky layers of bark are formed by a thin ring of another growth tissue called cork cambium. The cells produced by the cork cambium are spongy, waxy, waterproof cells that prevent the evaporation of moisture from the tree. Soon after the bark cells are produced by the cork cambium they die. New cells continue to be produced. This continuous production of new cells creates pressure, causing the dead cells to split into furrows and ridges. This splitting of dead cells accounts for the roughness of bark.

Look back at the photomicrograph showing a cross section of wood from an oak tree on page 138. You are looking into the ends of long lines of cells that form tubes. Wood is made up of xylem tissue which conducts water from the roots to the leaves, as well as to the rest of the plant. Xylem tissue is composed of strings of long cells with hollow cavities, lying end to end. Try to locate the xylem tissue in two kinds of stems—one from a woody plant and one from a nonwoody plant—by means of the investigation on the following page. ■

■ AN APPRENTICE INVESTIGATION into Xylem Tissue

Place a twig of a tree or bush and a stalk of celery in a beaker of water to which you have added some food coloring. ❶ After twenty-four hours, observe the twig and celery. You will probably find some of the coloring in the leaves of the celery. Remove the twig and celery stalk from the water and examine them. Cut off and discard the portions of the twig and stalk that were under the surface of the colored water. Then cut a small section across the bottom of both the twig and celery stalk. ❷ Do your cross sections reveal that the colored area forms a continuous circle in the twig, while there are individual colored areas in the celery stalk?

Next cut a long slant diagonally through the twig; then make a shallow cut across the celery stalk about an inch and a half from the bottom and gently strip down the loosened portion of the stem. ❸ Now you can see the food coloring inside and along the length of both the twig and the stalk. The colored material, along with the water, has been carried up in the xylem tubes. Observe that in the longitudinal sections you have just prepared, as in the cross sections, the xylem forms a continuous circle in the twig while the xylem tubes are in individual bundles in the celery.

An Investigation On Your Own

Is the rate at which water rises in the xylem affected by the outside temperature? In designing your investigation, be certain to exclude such variables as light. Are there other variables you should control?

The celery stalk is actually a leafstalk rather than a stem of the celery plant. Repeat the apprentice investigation with the stems of several different herbaceous plants. Predict whether or not the results will be the same. Was your prediction correct?

Look at the photograph of the pine trunk shown here.  The xylem tissue is arranged in alternating bands of light and dark. The light bands of xylem were produced in the spring when the cambium was particularly active. These xylem cells are large. The dark bands of xylem were made in the late summer and fall when the cambium was less active. These cells are smaller and have thicker walls.

Ordinarily, a tree will produce only one layer of light wood and one layer of dark wood each year. These yearly layers form the rings or bands seen in a cross section of a trunk or a branch. They are the **annual rings** (*annual* means "yearly"). Therefore, by counting the annual rings of a tree trunk, you can determine with fair accuracy the age of the tree.

Count the rings in the tree trunk shown in the photograph. How old was the tree when it was cut? If you can find any tree stumps in your neighborhood or any trunks or branches cut for firewood, try counting the annual rings.

Many of the giant redwood trees in California have been alive more than 2,000 years. In fact, scientists can often tell something about the weather hundreds, or even thousands, of years ago by examining the annual rings. How is this possible? In a very dry year, the annual ring would be narrow and the cells would be relatively small. In a year that was very wet, the annual ring would be wider than in a dry year because larger cells would be made.

Variations such as this are commonly found in pine trees. And since pines grow rather close together, a young pine might spend some ten to twenty years before it becomes tall enough to get its needles (leaves) into the open sunlight. While the tree is young and densely shaded by the older trees around it, the cambium produces fewer and smaller cells. After the tree reaches up into the direct sunlight, more food can be made and the cambium cells can produce more and larger xylem cells during a growing season.

The environment of a plant or an animal can, and often does, stunt its growth and development. Most plants and animals have to compete with other plants and animals for light, air, food, and water. The amounts of these materials that are available definitely affect growth and development.

Stems of Nonwoody Plants

Suppose you make a cross section of the stem of a corn plant or a bean plant. Both plants are nonwoody plants, known as **herbaceous** (hûr·bā′shəs) plants. This group of plants also includes many other familiar garden vegetables and flowers. In the stems of these plants you would not see any annual rings of growth. And, as you have no doubt observed, there is no bark on the stem of corn, beans, or other herbaceous plants.

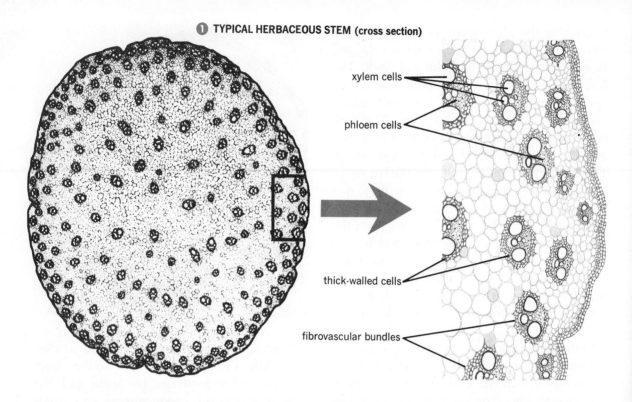

xylem cells

phloem cells

thick-walled cells

fibrovascular bundles

The drawing shown here is a cross section of a typical herbaceous, or nonwoody, plant. ① As you can see, there are no annual rings. There is no bark. Where, then, are the conducting tissues?

Recall the fibrovascular bundles that you studied in the leaf (p. 130) and their function as supply lines for water, minerals, and food for all the cells of the leaf. Fibrovascular bundles similar to those of the leaf are found throughout the stems of many herbaceous plants. Here, as in the leaf, they are the conducting tissue. Notice the xylem and phloem cells. Notice also the thick-walled cells, surrounding the bundles, which give the plant some support. It is easy to understand why herbaceous plants with their scattered bundles containing only a few xylem cells certainly could never have the strength of a tree with its layer after layer of xylem cells.

The main support of herbaceous plants is largely due to a ring of layers of thick-walled cells lying near the outside of the stem. You will usually find no layer of cambium cells. Once an herbaceous stem has developed its fibrovascular bundles, it usually has attained its maximum size in thickness. There is no growth outward, no new xylem or phloem cells are formed. After all, there is no cambium present to divide and form new conducting tissue.

Many cells fill in the spaces around the bundles of conducting tissue. The area around the conducting tissue is known as **pith,** and the cells making up the pith are generally storage cells. Some of our commonly eaten foods are the stems of herbaceous plants that have become adapted for food storage.

The stems of herbaceous plants are easily obtained and dissected. Collect a number of

■ AN APPRENTICE INVESTIGATION into a Root System

Take a potted geranium. Choose a plant that has been growing for some time. Tap the sides of the pot in order to loosen the soil, and lift out the plant. ❶ What do you see as one of the functions of the roots?

Of course, roots anchor the plant in the soil. What else do they do?

An Investigation On Your Own

Are root systems of plants alike? Plant different seeds in good soil in flower pots: carrots, beets, corn, wheat, petunia, or zinnia. After a week or so, examine the roots. How do the roots appear after three weeks?

In early spring, dig up a few roadside weed plants. How do their root systems compare with those you have studied?

❶

these plants and see if you can locate the different tissues with the aid of a magnifying glass or a microscope.

REVIEW

1. What are the various functions of the stems of plants?

2. Draw and identify the structures of a twig. Check your drawing against the one shown on page 136. How old is the twig you drew?

3. The outside of a tree is cut so that all the cambium and phloem are removed. What will happen? Why?

NEW VIEW

1. Explain how the rings in a tree trunk enable you to determine its age?

2. What uses does man make of different trees? Don't ignore uses in the past. For example, certain tribes of Indians used tree trunks to make canoes.

3. THE STRUCTURE AND FUNCTION OF THE ROOT

In your study of living organisms, you have by now seen that the various structures function to keep living organisms living. A major function of the leaves of plants, for example, is food-making. You have also seen that, because sunlight is the source of energy for photosynthesis, the leaves are shaped to expose the maximum of surface to the sun. A major function of the stems of plants is the conducting of materials from the leaves and the roots. Another function of many stems is to support the plant as it grows. You will recall that both of these functions are performed by special tissues.

These relationships between function and structure become more fascinating as you learn more about them. From what you already know, can you think of functions that roots might perform? Let's investigate. ■

The Intricate Root System

Roots divide and subdivide as do the branches above them. Finally, they divide down into myriads of small rootlets. Certain areas of the rootlets are covered by **root hairs.** Root hairs are so fine and of such delicate construction that they are easily damaged.

When you think of a tree's roots, you probably think only of the large roots that often partly show along the top of the ground. However, these visible roots are something like the large trunk and main branches of the tree. Both the large roots and the large branches simply support the really actively functioning plant parts. As you know, the leaves are the most important structures on the branches. The root hairs are the really important parts of the root system of a plant. Through them absorption takes place.

Most plants have a diffuse root system similar to that of the corn plant you will study on page 151—several roots originating at the base of the stem. However, some plants, such as radishes, carrots, dandelions, and some trees, have a single, enlarged main root from which smaller rootlets grow.

The total amount of roots on a plant might surprise you. Did you ever see squashes growing in a garden? The root system of a single squash plant was once carefully measured. It was found that the total length of all its roots together was about 16 miles. Other plants have even larger root systems. The spreading root system of a single rye plant was once measured and found to be 380 miles long!

The root system of a tree is more compact, as a rule, than that of a squash or rye plant. The general shape of an entire tree is, in fact, very like a dumbbell. The roots usually spread out to form a circular area under the ground that is about as wide as the circular area covered by the branches above the ground.

Roots and the Soil

Soils are made up of mineral particles in the form of sand, clay, or silt; of **humus** (hyoo′məs), or organic matter (decayed and partially decayed plant and animal materials); of water; and of air. Soil also contains bacteria, protozoans, and other organisms such as worms and insect larvae.

The Table of Soil Composition below shows the approximate composition of a typical, rich, farm soil in the Midwestern United States.

TABLE OF SOIL COMPOSITION

air	25%
mineral particles	40%
water	25%
organic matter	10%

Let's examine the composition of a sample of soil. ■

Clay particles form the major part of most good soils. Clay helps soils hold water. Sand particles, on the other hand, are hard and solid and hold water poorly. Clay soils hold so much water that there is little space left for air to penetrate. But sandy soils have plenty of air spaces into which roots can grow and get oxygen.

Humus (organic matter) is extremely important as a part of good soil. Humus is spongy and absorbent and holds a tremendous amount of moisture. It actually creates air spaces in the soil and makes the soil loose and crumbly. Excess water drains easily from humus soil and air filters through it readily.

Roots are not like so many soda straws stuck into the ground, sucking up the dissolved minerals in the soil. Roots, instead, are extremely active.

A plant must have nitrates, phosphates, sulfates, potassium, calcium, magnesium, iron, boron, manganese, and probably other

■ AN APPRENTICE INVESTIGATION into Soil Composition

Take a handful of garden soil and put it into  a battery jar half full of water. Stir it vigorously and then let it settle for about ten minutes. The heavier mineral particles will settle on the bottom of the jar; the organic matter will float on the surface of the water.❶

Now tip the battery jar slowly and carefully as you filter most of the water and the organic matter through a piece of filter paper. (Be sure *not* to upset any of the heavier matter from the bottom of the battery jar.) The material that remains on the filter paper is organic matter.❷  Place some mineral matter from the battery jar in a watch glass; place the organic matter from the filter paper in another watch glass. Let the contents of each watch glass dry thoroughly.

Feel both the mineral particles and the organic matter with your fingers, and examine both samples with a magnifying glass, or observe them under a microscope. You can easily see the difference between the materials in the two samples. The mineral particles are hard and gritty.❸  The organic matter is soft, spongy, and mushy.❹

The mineral matter was originally rocky material—sandstone, limestone, granite—that wore down into the sand, silt, and even smaller particles called clay. Good soils have a mixture of all these particles, as well as a good supply of organic matter.

An Investigation On Your Own

Can you make a good garden soil? Start with washed sand. Then add the other materials in sufficient amounts to make the sand a good garden soil. How can you find out if it is good? In designing your investigation, be sure to include a control experiment as part of your experimental procedure.

minerals. These dissolved substances come chiefly from the decay of organic materials and from the chemical action of plant roots on soil particles.

Plant roots actually release compounds that act on soil substances. In turn, soil substances act on the roots. The chemical relationship between soil and roots is extremely complex and there is much yet to be learned. It is important to remember, however, that plant roots change and help make the soil what it is, just as the soil and its substances help make the plants what they are. Each affects the other.

The Structure of a Root

You have almost certainly eaten many roots. Beets, carrots, radishes, turnips, and sweet potatoes are all roots. More accurately, the parts of these roots that you eat are the large, fleshy, storage parts of the plant's root system.

Examine the photograph of the cross section of a carrot. ❶ Notice the thickness of the outer layer of epidermis. Underneath the epidermis is a wide layer of phloem tissue. As you will remember, sugars and other food materials travel down from the leaves and stems through the tubelike cells of this tissue. The carrot that we eat is the root where the food materials of the carrot plant are stored.

Look carefully at the inside edge of the phloem tissue. Do you see a ring of darker-colored tissue? This is the cambium or growth tissue. It forms an entire ring just as it does in the stem of a tree. As in a stem, the cambium in the root will divide rapidly, producing phloem tissue toward the outside and xylem tissue toward the inside.

The roots of a tree, unlike a carrot root, have far more xylem tissue or wood than they have phloem tissue. Furthermore, a tree develops a barklike corky layer on the outside of its older roots. The phloem tissue of a carrot root is thick because it also serves as a storage place for sugars and other foods.

If you eat a bite of a raw carrot, you have no trouble detecting the sweet taste of the sugar stored there. You might like to cut out a piece of phloem tissue and a piece of xylem tissue (which forms the core of the carrot) and eat them separately. Is sugar stored only in the phloem tissue?

Notice the lighter colored rays of material that radiate out something like the spokes of a wheel throughout the xylem tissue. These are called **vascular rays** and are made up of conducting cells. Water and minerals move outward from the xylem tissue to the other parts of the roots through these vascular rays. Food material moves from the phloem tissue inward to the cambium and xylem through the conducting cells of these same vascular rays. So the function of vascular rays is to permit the movement of fluids sideways, or horizontally, in roots just as phloem and xylem permit the movement of fluids up and down the length of a root. (Vascular rays are also found in some stems.)

■ AN APPRENTICE INVESTIGATION of Root Hairs

Place a moist piece of blotting paper in a saucer or in a small, shallow dish. Sprinkle a few radish seeds on the blotting paper. Then cover the saucer or dish with another saucer or dish, placed upside down. If necessary, you may stick a piece of cellophane tape over the edges at two places to hold the dishes in place.

Keep the dish in a warm room for several days. Each day, lift the top dish and look at the seeds. Do not keep this "pocket garden" open for more than a minute or so at a time. Be certain the blotting paper is always moist, but do not let water stand in the dish.

After a few days you will find that the seeds have germinated and that each is developing a tiny root and a stem.

Carefully examine the root of one of the radish seedlings. You will find it covered with a thick, fuzzy growth of white, hairlike structures. ❶ These are root hairs. If you wish, use a magnifying glass to see them more clearly.

Let your radish seedlings grow for four or five days. On what part of the growing root are the root hairs found? Are new ones being formed? Are older ones dying?

An Investigation On Your Own

In what direction do roots grow? Design a procedure to determine this.

Will roots grow up toward water? This investigation is not as easy to do as it sounds. In designing your experimental procedure, try to develop a valid control.

The roots of a tree also show annual rings just as its stems do. Thus you can tell the age of a root by counting its annual rings. As in the trunks of trees, the annual rings in the roots are also composed of woody xylem tissue.

Root Hairs and Roots

As we stated earlier, root hairs are the most important, actively functioning parts of the root system. Study the drawing of the epidermis of a root showing the structure of a root hair. ❷ Notice that the root hair is an extension of an individual epidermal cell.

Some of these extremely fine root hairs can be seen without a magnifying glass. Suppose you see for yourself. ■

❷ **STRUCTURE OF A ROOT HAIR**

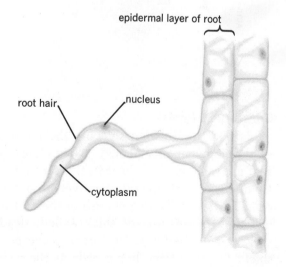

epidermal layer of root

root hair

nucleus

cytoplasm

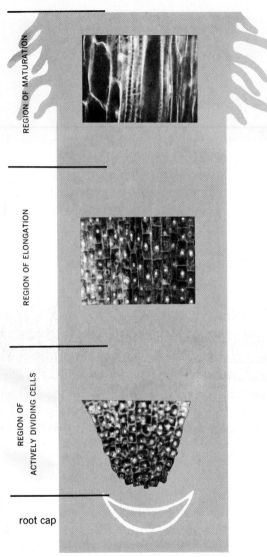

REGION OF MATURATION

REGION OF ELONGATION

REGION OF ACTIVELY DIVIDING CELLS

root cap

Growth and Roots

Look at the drawing showing the regions of development of a root.❶ As in stems, a root grows in length only at its tip. The *living* tip of a root is composed of actively dividing cells. However, the extreme tip of the root is made up of an area of thick-walled, dead cells, called a **root cap.** This root cap acts as a shield to protect the living cells as the root grows and pushes its way through the soil. As the outer cells of the root cap are worn away, new cells are produced by the actively dividing cells that lie just behind the root cap. This area of cells, whose function is to divide and produce new root cells, pushes the growing root through the soil. Like the actively dividing tissue at the tip of the stem and the tips of the branches, this dividing tissue is also called meristematic tissue.

The actively dividing cells also leave cells behind themselves. Each time a layer of these cells divides, the dividing layer is pushed further into the soil by the added length of the root tip. As this occurs, the cells left behind do not keep on dividing. These cells do, however, expand and become longer. So, just behind the region of actively dividing cells is a **region of elongation.** Here, the cells change in length, but not in diameter. Study these regions in the drawing.

Behind the region of elongation is a region where the cells mature, a **region of maturation.** This is the region where root hairs start to develop from the epidermal cells.

Root hairs do not live very long. They develop rapidly, live for a few days to a few weeks, and then die. However, as the root tip grows forward, new root hairs keep developing in the maturation region behind the root tip. They take the place of the hairs further back that are dying.

Absorption of water, with its dissolved minerals, occurs chiefly through the root hairs. As you can see, then, the absorption of water in a plant occurs mainly near the root tips. Throughout the growing season, a tree's root system is pushing millions upon millions of tiny root tips through the soil. The roots branch and rebranch so that these root tips thread through almost every inch of soil within the root system.

Diffusion and Root Hairs

Do you remember your investigation of diffusion on page 133? Any time a plant or an animal membrane lies between solutions of different concentrations, diffusion through the membrane occurs. *Water* actually diffuses *both ways* but it goes faster from the side with the least dissolved substances in it to the side with the most dissolved substances in it.

The cell membrane of a root hair lies between the water of the soil, with its dissolved materials, and the cell fluids themselves. Normally, the cell fluids have more dissolved materials in them than does the water outside the cell. The cell fluids contain sugars as well as many other materials. Therefore, water diffuses from the soil and through the cell membrane, carrying its dissolved materials with it. Once inside the root-hair cell, the water diffuses from cell to cell until it reaches the xylem tissue. In this tissue it is carried up the root and stem to the leaves.

Diffusion, however, by no means accounts fully for the absorption of substances dissolved in the soil water. Scientists do not yet know how to account for some of their observations. For instance, root hairs sometimes absorb minerals *selectively*. In other words, minerals sometimes diffuse into the root-hair cell when the concentration of the mineral is greater inside the cell than it is outside in the soil water. No one yet knows the explanation of this *active* absorption that apparently defies the principle of diffusion.

In any event, the important thing to remember is that root hairs take an *active* part in selecting and absorbing materials from the soil. It is a selective process by which the root hairs absorb, for the most part, just what the plant needs and in the amounts that it needs.

The root hairs thread out between soil particles. They even secrete a gluelike substance that holds them firmly to the particles. This is why you are unlikely to find root hairs on the roots of a plant that you pull out of the ground. The tiniest rootlets and their root hairs usually break off and remain attached to the soil.

Diffusion does, however, account for most of the flow of *water* into a plant from the soil. As we said earlier, living plant cells normally have a higher concentration of dissolved substances within them than does the water in the surrounding soil. So there is a more or less steady flow of water by diffusion through the membranes of the root hairs and from cell to cell throughout the roots.

Were the situation reversed—if, for example, you poured a salt solution onto a plot of grass—the direction of the flow of water by diffusion would also be reversed. The grass would die. You can easily see this for yourself by growing grass in several pots of soil. If you water some of the pots with ordinary water, and others with a strong salt solution, you can watch the grass that you watered with the salt solution wilt and die. The direction of the flow of water by diffusion is reversed in the plants watered with the salt solution.

Root Pressure and Imbibition

You will recall from an earlier investigation with diffusion that the solution rose in the tube against the force of gravity. *Because of diffusion of a liquid*, there seemed to be a *pressure* created against gravity. This pressure in plants is called **root pressure.** If bushes or vines are cut or pruned during the growing season, the stumps will "bleed" as root pressure continues to force solutions up the xylem tissue.

■ AN APPRENTICE INVESTIGATION of Imbibition

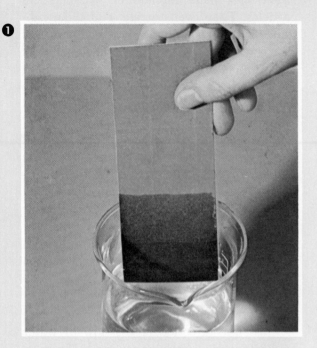

Hold a piece of cloth or a paper towel over a glass of water and let just a tip of it touch the water. Water rises in the cloth or paper. ❶ You have made a wick. If you left the cloth or paper in the water, it would continue to pick up, or **imbibe** (im·bīb′), water until the water was gone. This process is called imbibition (im′bi·bish′ən). The water would rise in the cloth or paper and then evaporate from it. As it evaporated, more water would rise to take its place.

An Investigation On Your Own

Are there any other theories to account for the rise of water in plants? Books on botany will help you with additional information on various theories accounting for the rise of water in plants. Begin your study with a college textbook.

Root pressure accounts, in part, for the rise of sap (a general term that applies to all plant fluids) through the xylem, from the roots to the leaves. However, root pressure created by diffusion of water from the soil cannot account for this entirely.

A tremendous amount of water evaporates from the leaves of a plant. It diffuses out through the stomata of the leaves and into the air. Most botanists believe that this evaporation, or *transpiration,* of water from leaves is the most important factor in pulling water up from the roots to the tops of plants. How does this work? Try the investigation above. ■

Imbibition probably accounts for a great deal of the rise of water in a tree or other plant. Water evaporates from the leaves. Like wicks, the cells in the leaf imbibe, or pull up,

more water from the cells just below them. These cells, in turn, pull up more water from the cells below them. Water in the xylem tissue is imbibed by the cells that lie alongside them in the leaves. Because the xylem tissue is continuous from the stem down into the roots, imbibition occurs, cell to cell, continuously from the leaves to the roots and their root hairs. According to this theory, then, a plant is like a great wick, evaporating from the top and drawing water up from the bottom.

The Corn Plant

Now that you have studied the structures and functions of some of the main tissues and organs of plants, let's look at the anatomy of a multicellular plant. ■

■ AN APPRENTICE STUDY IN ANATOMY: The Corn Plant

On the next two pages a plant is, in a sense, dissected for you. We have chosen the corn plant mainly because it is familiar.

First, plant several corn seeds in good garden soil. Examine one of the seedlings when it reaches a stage comparable to that in the drawing below.❶ On your seedling, identify the young roots and shoot.

If you can, continue growing some of your corn seedlings and watch the development of the roots into the adult root system and of the shoot into stem, leaves, and flowers. Compare an adult corn plant with the drawing.❷

Both the *brace roots* and the *fibrous roots* take up water from the soil, as well as hold the plant firmly in the ground. The stem supports the plant, holding the leaves in a position favorable for exposure to light. Another main function of the stem is to conduct food from the leaves to the roots. The leaves are, of course, its food-making organs.

The corn's tassels are its male flowers. The female flowers consist of young ears with silks. Within the young ear are structures that contain the egg cells of the corn. Pollen is blown by the wind to the silks, usually those of a

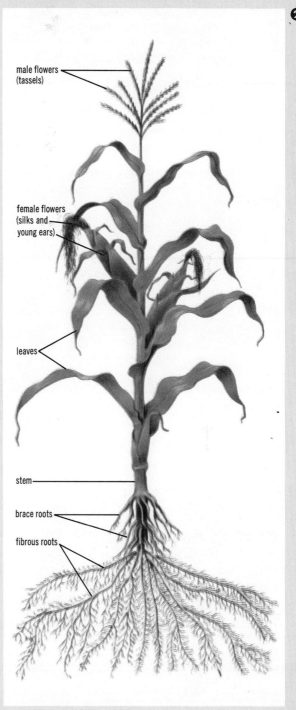

male flowers (tassels)

female flowers (silks and young ears)

leaves

stem

brace roots

fibrous roots

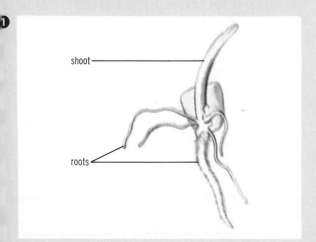

shoot

roots

❶

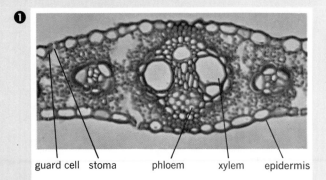

guard cell   stoma   phloem   xylem   epidermis

❷

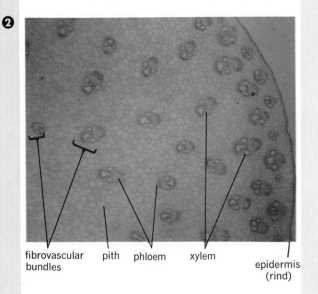

fibrovascular   pith   phloem   xylem   epidermis
bundles   (rind)

cortex   central cylinder   epidermis

❸

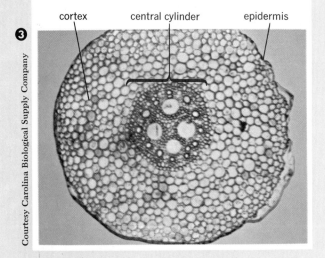

neighboring corn plant, carrying the sperm cells to the egg cells. Fertilization then takes place, and a mature ear of corn develops. (In Chapter 12, you'll study the reproduction of flowering plants in detail. Turn there now for a preview, if you wish.)

If you made a cross-section slide of a corn leaf, stained it, and examined it under the microscope, you would see something like this.❶ It is easy to identify the parts: *xylem* cells are large (almost like two eyes) and the smaller *phloem* cells lie below and between the xylem. What materials are carried by the xylem cells? by the phloem? Notice that these two kinds of cells seem to be bound together in a bundle: all the tissue within that bundle makes up the *vein*—that is, a *fibro-vascular bundle.* In this photomicrograph there is a large vein in the center flanked by a small vein on either side.

Find the parts labeled *guard cell* and *stoma,* located in the *epidermis.* Can you identify other stomata and guard cells in the photomicrograph? How do the stomata and guard cells function to permit passage of gases in and out of the leaf?

Now examine the cross section of the stem of the corn.❷ Notice again the *fibrovascular bundles:* they contain xylem and phloem cells just as do the veins in the leaf. In the stem of corn, the bundles are scattered throughout the *pith,* a food storage tissue. And the outside layer of cells in the stem is the epidermis.

Now study the cross section of the root.❸ Try to identify these parts: the *central cylinder,* within which the xylem and phloem tissues are contained; the *cortex,* with its loosely packed cells; and the root's *epidermis.* What is the function of each part?

Now that you have studied examples of animal organisms and plant organisms, how would you state the major differences between an animal and a plant? What are the major similarities?

An Investigation On Your Own

It is fine to study a book, but the book is merely a preparation for studying the actual organism. By studying the book along with the organism, you will have a more complete idea of the plant as an organism.

How are seeds of different plants alike in structure? different in structure? (*Clue:* Soak seeds in water overnight before dissecting them.) Begin by making a comparison of corn seeds with the seeds of limas or other beans. Use references to help you identify the parts of these seeds. (You may, if you wish, also read ahead in this book in Chapter 12, where you will find pictures of bean seeds.)

Now make a study of the seeds of several other plants. Try these: pea, squash, radish, beet, oat, wheat, rye, zinnia, sunflower, millet, watermelon, orange, apple, walnut, pecan, or other common fruits, nuts, grains, garden flowers, and vegetables. Which of these resemble the corn in structure? Which resemble the bean? Can you account for the likenesses and differences you observe?

Next, allow some seeds of the corn, bean, and others you have examined to germinate. Compare the structures of the young seedlings with that of the corn seedling illustrated on page 150. Examine the root hairs of the seedlings. Are the root hairs distinctive for each plant? Or are they similar?

Where does the energy for growth of the seedlings come from? Separate into halves several soaked seeds, and several others of the same kind after they have germinated. Place a drop of iodine solution on each. What color do you predict the seed will turn? the germinated seed? What is the basis for your prediction?

REVIEW

1. What are the various functions of roots?
2. Which roots do we use as food?
3. How is the structure of the root similar to the structure of the stem?
4. Compare and contrast the functions of the root and the root hair.
5. Why would salt poured on roots destroy the plant?

NEW VIEW

1. Willow trees generally need a great amount of water. Should they not grow well in the sand on the seashore? Explain your answer.
2. How can we determine the age of a root?

4. RELATING THE CONCEPTS

As you expected, plants—as organisms—are adapted to their environment. Certainly plants have a structure different from that of animals, but like animals they are successful organisms. To be successful as an organism, that is, to survive, means at least two things: the first is to be adapted to your environment, the second is to reproduce.

For the moment, we have emphasized the study of plants and animals with special attention to the structure and functions which adapt them to their environment. Furthermore, in the great variety of multicellular animals and plants, we have seen that there is a basic pattern in structure. Plant and animal organisms are composed of cells; these cells in turn comprise the tissues; tissues are organized in organ systems; in turn, these make up the organism.

Reviewing the Concepts

▶ To reemphasize: *The basic unit of structure and function in plants, as in animals, is the cell.*

▶ *Plants are adapted to survival on land by means of root and shoot systems.* The root system anchors the plant and absorbs substances from the soil. The shoot system extends the leafy structure to where it can capture the sun's energy.

▶ *Green plants are adapted by structure for the manufacture of sugar.* Green plants have photosynthetic tissue, composed of plant cells containing chloroplasts.

▶ *Plant organisms are adapted by structure for survival in a dry land environment.* Epidermal layers and the substances they secrete protect the leaf and some stems against loss of water by evaporation, and bark protects woody stems against evaporation. Conducting tissue deep in the stem, in turn, transmits water to all parts of the plant. The guard cells are adapted by structure to protect the plant from wilting. Also, they permit the necessary gases to be taken into and released from the plant. (In Unit Three, when you examine photosynthesis in greater detail, you will have an opportunity to study this exchange of gases.)

▶ *Plant organisms are specially adapted for absorption of water and minerals.* Root hairs present a vast surface for the absorption of vast quantities of water and minerals.

▶ *Woody plant organisms are specially adapted for growth in length and thickness.* The divisions of meristematic cells provide for growth at the tip of stem and branches and at the tips of roots. Cambium cells provide for growth in width.

▶ *Green plants are specially adapted by structure for reproduction.* Reproduction of plants and animals is to be studied in greater detail later in Chapter 12.

Testing Yourself

1. Compare or contrast green plants and animals with regard to the ways in which they get food.
2. Compare or contrast green plants and animals with regard to the following functions:
    a. respiration
    b. locomotion
    c. growth
3. How are green plants adapted for life on land?
4. How are the leaves of green plants adapted for photosynthesis?
5. How are the following types of cells adapted for their function?
    a. xylem
    b. root hairs
    c. bark cells
6. Where are the major points of growth in trees? Why are the points of growth located there?
7. How does the concentration of salts in a cell affect the flow of water into it? The flow of water out of it?

Extending the Concepts

Investigation. You have been studying the structure of organisms. By this time you have a good idea of what is meant by the concept, *organisms are adapted by structure to perform the functions necessary to life within the special environment in which they live.*

Probably no structure of plants illustrates this better than the structure of the reproductive organs of flowering plants, the flowers.

Conduct an investigation into the adaptation of several flowers for reproduction of the plant organism. First, choose a large flower in order to be able to identify its structures. A tulip is a good flower for such a purpose, so is a gladiola, or a garden pea. Now use the descriptions in Chapter 12 to help you understand the functions of each structure of a flower.

The following questions will help you in your study.

1. Sometimes insects carry the pollen grains from one plant to another. How are the flowering structures of plants adapted to attract insects?

2. The top of the pistil (the stigma) is adapted for holding pollen. How?

3. Before the flower opens, how is it protected? By which structures?

4. How is the flower adapted to protect the developing seeds?

5. How is the pollen grain adapted for penetrating to the ovule?

You will want to use reference books in addition to this book. Books that may be useful to you can be found among high school biology or botany texts or college biology or botany texts. If you haven't already done so, this is a good time to become fully acquainted with your library. A scientist uses the library as often as he does the laboratory.

Suggested Reading

Went, Fritz W., and the Editors of LIFE, *The Plants* (Life Nature Library), New York, Time, Inc., 1963.

Farb, and the Editors of LIFE, *The Forest* (Life Nature Library), New York, Time, Inc., 1962.

Weisz and Fuller, *The Science of Botany*, New York, McGraw-Hill, 1962.

Milne and Milne, *Plant Life*, Englewood Cliffs, Prentice-Hall, 1959.

Galston, *The Life of the Green Plant* (2nd ed.) Foundations of Modern Biology Series, Englewood Cliffs, Prentice-Hall, 1964).

Van Overbeek, *The Lore of Living Plants* (Vistas of Science Series), New York, McGraw-Hill, 1964.

Kurtz and Allen, *Adventures in Living Plants*, Tucson, University of Arizona Press, 1965.

THE
WORK
OF
CELLS

Both kinds of corn are grown by man.

What is the difference between the two? How did the difference come to be?

Which form is not found normally in the field? How has man been able to develop this form?

Which corn is used as food by man? Does this corn need man's attention? How?

7 | Cells as Chemists

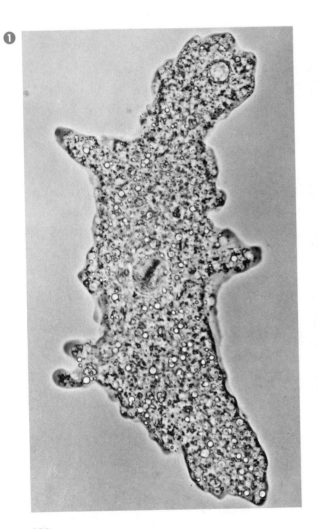

Have you ever heard the old rhyme:

> It's a very odd thing—
> As odd as can be—
> That whatever Miss T. eats
> Turns into Miss T.

You may at some time have noticed a curious thing. Let's suppose that you are eating a meal. At the same time, you are feeding your pet dog scraps of the meal under the table. Isn't it strange that the food you eat makes more of *you*, while the same food makes more of your dog?

Let's turn now to the work of cells, to find out how it is that cells make more of you, more of a dog, and more of Miss T.

1. THE CELL AND ITS LIVING STUFF

You studied *Paramecium* in Chapter 4 and found it to contain many different structures. But of what are the cell's structures made? The "stuff" of which they are made has been named *protoplasm*, meaning "living stuff." Recall, too, that in any cell the protoplasm is identified as having at least three main structures: a cell membrane, cytoplasm, and a nucleus. Collectively, these structures make up protoplasm, the living part of the cell.

What if you could get a good look at protoplasm. You might find that it assumes different forms in different cells. Generally, however, you could make a good model of protoplasm if you were to take a bit of raw egg white and mix it thoroughly with a sprinkling of black pepper. Look at the photomicrograph, on the opposite page, of an amoeba (ə·mē′bə) and you will quickly see the resemblance.❶

Sometimes protoplasm flows much like a liquid, while at other times it seems to be more solid and even rigid, like a gelatin.

In short, protoplasm may be more rigid in some cells and more flowing in others, and may even vary within the same cell at different times. For example, when an amoeba moves, parts of its protoplasm flow; when an amoeba is resting, its protoplasm seems more rigid.

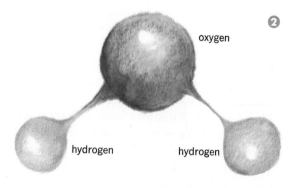

or another way of showing the structure

O = oxygen   H = hydrogen

APPROXIMATE CHEMICAL COMPOSITION OF PROTOPLASM

oxygen	76.0%
carbon	10.5%
hydrogen	10.0%
nitrogen	2.5%
phosphorus	0.3%
potassium	0.3%
sulfur	0.2%
chlorine	0.1%
sodium calcium magnesium iron	less than 0.1%
copper zinc cobalt	traces

A Closer Look at Protoplasm

Study the table of the approximate chemical composition of protoplasm. This table is based upon hundreds of studies of different kinds of plant and animal protoplasm. You will notice that it reveals an interesting fact. About 99 percent of protoplasm is made up of just four elements: carbon, oxygen, nitrogen, and hydrogen.

A very large part of all protoplasm is simply water. Your body, for example, is about 70 percent water. A water molecule is very simple. You may recall from your earlier work that it is made up only of hydrogen and oxygen. Two atoms of hydrogen are joined to one atom of oxygen as shown in the model.❷

Water is important to all living organisms, since it is the solvent that dissolves the many substances that living protoplasm needs. As you shall see, many of the substances needed for life could not be used by the cell if they were not dissolved in water.

Substances in Protoplasm

Suppose you filled a glass with water. If it is drinkable, it is usually clear. Nevertheless, you probably know that even drinking water is not pure water chemically.

For instance, if you took ten drops of your drinking water and dropped them on a clean glass plate and let them evaporate, what would be left behind?

If, instead of drinking water, you used ten drops of sea water or pond water, what would be left behind?

You would find that the substances dissolved in the water were left behind after the water evaporated in both instances.

You are aware, no doubt, that water dissolves minerals from the soil. It will also, in time, dissolve rocks with which it comes in contact. The word *mineral* simply means "a substance in the earth." Salt (sodium chloride, chemically abbreviated as NaCl) is a mineral substance.

Compare the mineral substances in the drinking water supplied to a city with those substances in a pond and with those in sea water as shown in the table below.

AMOUNTS OF SOME SUBSTANCES DISSOLVED IN WATER

(parts of a substance in a million parts of water)

Element	Drinking water	River water	Sea water
chlorine	6	13	18,980
sodium	65	65	10,561
magnesium	14	23	1,272
sulfur			884
calcium	35	74	400
potassium	6	6.40	380
bromine			65
boron	0.11	0.13	4.60
fluorine	0.40	0.60	1.40
iodine			0.05
iron	0.01	0.01	0.02

Notice that certain substances are common in all. The most common are the substances sodium and chlorine, which you are familiar with in table salt.

The water you drink, then, is a solution of substances. Drinking water is a very dilute solution of these substances. Sea water is a more concentrated solution of somewhat similar substances. It is important for you to know that you supply your protoplasm not only with water but also with the substances dissolved in the water.

Thus, the water you eat is a solution of substances. Is it strange to say "the water you eat"? See for yourself. ■

Table salt, sodium chloride (NaCl), is made up of two elements, sodium (Na) and chlorine (Cl).

A very common type of sugar, **glucose** ($C_6H_{12}O_6$), is made up of carbon (C), hydrogen (H), and oxygen (O).

Glucose belongs to a group of compounds called **organic compounds.** Organic compounds are mainly those which have carbon in them. Organic compounds were once thought to be made only by living things, but we now know this is not so. Nevertheless, the name stuck. On the other hand, **inorganic compounds** generally are those which have no carbon in them. Sodium chloride, potassium chloride, magnesium sulfate, and water are examples of inorganic compounds.

The point is that protoplasm is made up of both inorganic and organic compounds. But it is the organic compounds mainly that give protoplasm its unique characteristics.

Study once again the table showing the amounts of some substances dissolved in water. Each one of the elements listed in the table is of the greatest importance, even those that are found in extremely small amounts. Chiefly, these elements are found

■ AN APPRENTICE INVESTIGATION into the Water in Protoplasm

Take an apple and cut it into eight equal parts. Slowly dry out four parts by heating them in a water bath for several hours.  You can prepare a water bath by placing four parts of the apple in a dry beaker, and then placing this beaker inside a larger beaker containing a moderate amount of water.

Compare the dried sections of the apple with the fresh sections. Are the dried sections larger or smaller than the fresh sections? ❷ Can you explain why?

An Investigation On Your Own

Compare dried apricots with a fresh apricot, or compare raisins with a fresh grape.

What is the amount of water in dried vegetables as compared with that in fresh vegetables? How would you determine this?

In designing your experimental procedures, be careful how you set up your control experiment. How will you measure the amount of water for a given weight?

Recall, too, that an apple is sweet. The water in a juicy apple dissolves sugar as well as other substances. What is the difference between substances such as sugar and table salt?

in living protoplasm as parts of four classes of organic compounds, in addition to being found in water and inorganic compounds. These major classes of organic compounds found in protoplasm are *carbohydrates, fats, proteins*, and *nucleic acids*.

REVIEW

1. Distinguish between cytoplasm and protoplasm.

2. Distinguish between water as a compound and the water you drink.

3. What are the differences between inorganic and organic compounds? Give examples of both kinds.

4. If it were possible to make protoplasm in a test tube, what kinds of substances would you put into it?

NEW VIEW

1. What might be some possible differences between plant and animal protoplasm?

2. Can you think of any organism that can live without water? Which one?

2. ORGANIC COMPOUNDS IN PROTOPLASM

Now let's look at some of the organic compounds more closely. Let's try to understand how protoplasm is able to make some of these compounds.

We will begin with a simple investigation into an organic compound with which you are familiar—albumen, a protein. Albumen is fairly easy to get if you can get the white of an egg. You may have already used it to make a model of protoplasm.

Suppose you were to take the white of an egg and place a bit of it in boiling water. It becomes solid. You know this solid as the white of an egg.

This simple investigation is of the utmost importance. It teaches us the effect of heat on some substances in protoplasm. Can you change the egg white back as it was before you placed it in the boiling water? No, you cannot. Can a baby chicken hatch from a fertilized egg that has been boiled? No, it cannot. Boiling somehow kills protoplasm.

The point to remember, then, is that the activities of protoplasm take place at a temperature lower than boiling—lower than most chemical reactions in a laboratory. For instance, your body is maintained at a temperature of 98.6°F (37°C).*

How is it that cells (that is, the protoplasm of cells) carry out their activities at temperatures lower than the temperatures in the test tube of the chemist?

You may already be familiar with enzymes. However, if you are not, try this investigation for yourself. ■

Protoplasm, then, is able to carry on its life activities because of one kind of organic substance, *enzymes*. You have already studied one type of enzyme, the digestive enzyme diastase. Recall that you also studied the digestive function of saliva (which has a kind of starch-splitting enzyme in it). But the enzymes in protoplasm do a wide variety of things, as you will see. Some enzymes *synthesize* (build up) many complex organic compounds, while other enzymes break them down.

Enzymes are necessary in the synthesis of the important organic compounds found in protoplasm—the familiar compounds we mentioned before: carbohydrates, fats, proteins, and nucleic acids.

Let's examine the class of organic compounds known as carbohydrates.

Carbohydrates

Suppose you took some potato starch, corn starch, and a piece of bread and added a drop of a very weak iodine solution to each. Each would turn a blue-black color. This is a well-known test for starches. You are already familiar with the test for sugar that uses Benedict's solution.

Sugars, starches, and woody materials, such as cellulose, are some of the common carbohydrates.

As you may know, there are a number of different sugars. The kind of sugar you eat at the table is called *sucrose*. Most sugar that we buy is sucrose and much of it comes from sugar cane plants. In fact, we often call it cane sugar. Sugar beets produce sucrose, too, and quite a bit of sugar sold in stores is beet sugar. You might find it interesting to read the labels of sugar sacks at a grocery store to discover whether the sugar is cane sugar or beet sugar. The chances are that you will find both kinds for sale. There is really no difference between cane sugar and beet sugar. Both are pure sucrose.

* 212°F (or 100°C) is the boiling point of water.

■ AN APPRENTICE INVESTIGATION into the Action of Enzymes

Take six test tubes and place in each one about 1 teaspoon of a 1 percent starch solution. Into two of the tubes add about ½ teaspoon of saliva. Into two others, add a pinch of *diastase* (dī'ə·stāz), an enzyme that breaks down starch. Leave the last two test tubes with only the starch solution.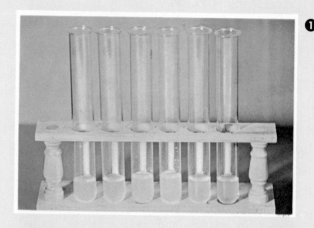

Place all the tubes in warm (not hot) water for about five minutes. Then add to each tube about ½ teaspoon of Benedict's solution. Now place all the tubes in a beaker of hot water. 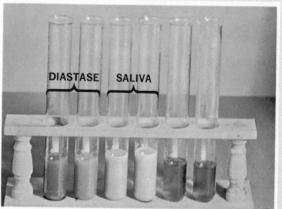 You can keep the water hot by placing the beaker on an electric hot plate, but do not boil it. Why? What results do you find?

As you have seen, the tubes containing diastase and saliva became green to orange-red. This color change shows that sugar is present. Benedict's solution, as you may know, is changed from blue to green or orange-red in the presence of sugar. Hence the diastase and the saliva both changed the starch to sugar. Saliva contains an enzyme that acts much like diastase. Why are the other two tubes still blue?

An Investigation On Your Own

The enzyme *urease* (yōōr'ē·āz) functions to break up urea, a waste substance produced by cells, into ammonia and carbon dioxide. You can test for the presence of ammonia by using the indicator phenolphthalein (fē'nōl·thāl'ēn). Three or four drops of a 1 percent solution of phenolphthalein in alcohol turn a solution containing ammonia a pink color.

Determine first how fast urease acts. Can you slow down the action of urease?

Be certain to include a careful control experiment in your design of experimental procedure. How will you measure the slowing action of the enzyme?

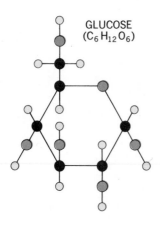

GLUCOSE
($C_6H_{12}O_6$)

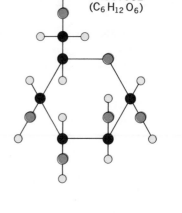

FRUCTOSE
($C_6H_{12}O_6$)

Another sugar you may know about is found in grapes and is sometimes called grape sugar. This is the same as the sugar found in corn syrup, *glucose*. A molecule of glucose is made up of 6 atoms of carbon, 6 atoms of oxygen, and 12 atoms of hydrogen. Chemists often write the formula for glucose like this:

$$C_6H_{12}O_6$$

Now look at the model of a molecule of glucose. ❶ A model is simply a structure that enables chemists to explain to each other how they think a molecule is put together. A model, of course, is based on scientific evidence, although sometimes scientists start with a model and then experiment to find out how true the model is.

Another common sugar called *fructose* is the sugar found in fruits such as apples and oranges. It, too, is made up of 6 atoms of carbon, 6 atoms of oxygen, and 12 atoms of hydrogen. The formula for fructose is written exactly the same as the formula for glucose.

$$C_6H_{12}O_6$$

What, then, is the difference between glucose and fructose? The difference lies only in the positions of the atoms, as you can see by examining its model. ❷ The model shows where chemists believe the atoms of the fructose molecule lie in relation to each other.

You have just learned about one of the most important ideas in chemistry. This idea is that the *arrangement* of atoms in a molecule makes a great difference in the kind of substance you have. If the atoms are arranged one way, you have one substance. However, if the same atoms are arranged in a slightly different way, a different substance is formed. The arrangement of the atoms also makes a difference in the way a substance behaves.

The Synthesis of Large Molecules

A molecule of glucose and a molecule of fructose combine to make sucrose. This is important for your study of the way protoplasm acts to synthesize larger molecules. In combining two smaller molecules to make the larger one, *water is split off*. As this happens, the two smaller molecules become linked to each other. The new molecule is then really a linking, or bonding, of two similar molecules. The action of linking two similar molecules is known as **polymerization** (pə·lim′ər·ə·zā′shən). As you will soon see, specific enzymes are involved in the numerous examples of polymerization.

GLUCOSE

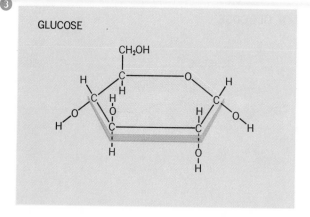

GLUCOSE

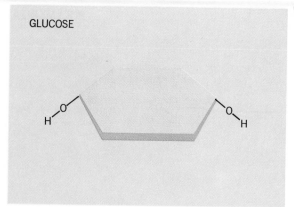

Green plants especially carry on this process of polymerization. Plants *polymerize* (pə·lim′ə·rīz) molecules of glucose and fructose to form molecules of sucrose by means of enzymes.

The "living test tubes," that is, the protoplasm in cells, carry on this important job of polymerization, which can be shown by the following chemical equation.

$$C_6H_{12}O_6 + C_6H_{12}O_6 \longrightarrow C_{12}H_{22}O_{11} + H_2O$$

glucose   fructose   sucrose   water

In the equation, notice how two molecules of simple sugars, each with the formula $C_6H_{12}O_6$, combine to form one molecule of a more complex sugar, sucrose, with the formula $C_{12}H_{22}O_{11}$, and one molecule of water, H_2O. This is what happens in the polymerization of just two simple sugar molecules to form sucrose.

In a similar way, plant cells also carry on polymerization of more than two simple sugar molecules. When, for instance, large numbers of glucose molecules are polymerized, the complex carbohydrates we know as starches are formed. Like the sugars, the starches are familiar substances. A potato contains a considerable amount of starch, and grains such as wheat, corn, and rice, and many food products made from them are rich in starch.

A plant can polymerize an even larger number of glucose molecules to produce **cellulose,** the woody material that forms the walls of plant cells. Cotton, wood, and similar plant materials are chiefly cellulose.

This process of building giant molecules from small molecules (polymerization) goes on constantly in living plant cells. Also, many animal cells can carry on the process of polymerizing large molecules of carbohydrates from small molecules of sugars. Sugars, for example, are stored in your liver in the form of glycogen, commonly called animal starch. Glycogen is the result, therefore, of the combination of many glucose molecules. That is to say, your liver cells can polymerize glucose to form glycogen. Just as enzymes are necessary to polymerize starch, so enzymes are necessary to polymerize glucose into glycogen.

Before studying the process of polymerization in detail, let us consider another model of glucose. ❸ In this model, letters represent each of the twenty-four atoms. In the final model the shape of the molecule is the same, but only those letters representing the part of the molecule concerned with polymerization are shown. ❹ Now let's use this model to

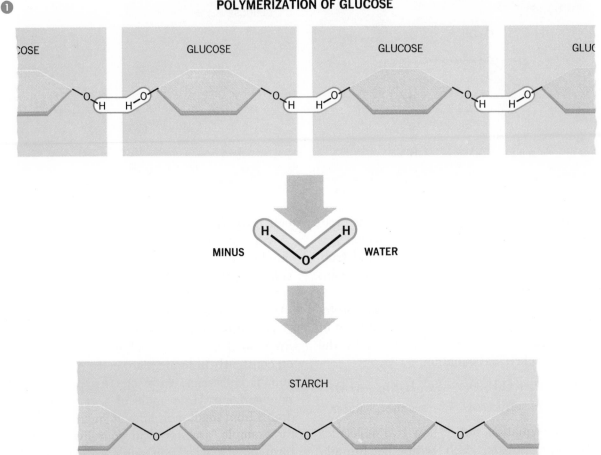

look more closely at the process of polymerization.

The diagram shows what happens when molecules of glucose, in a plant cell, combine to make a starch molecule. ① Each time one glucose molecule is added to another, a molecule of water is split off. After the plant cell has, with the aid of enzymes, combined many, many molecules of glucose, it has produced a giant molecule of starch. Chemists aren't sure just *how many* glucose molecules are combined, so they use an x to represent this number. The formula for starch, then, becomes $(C_6H_{10}O_5)_x$, which indicates that x molecules of glucose have polymerized. In the process, x molecules of water are split off, as you can see in the equation

$$x C_6H_{12}O_6 \longrightarrow (C_6H_{10}O_5)_x + x H_2O$$

| x molecules of glucose | 1 molecule of starch | x molecules of water |

REVERSING THE PROCESS. Both plants and animals polymerize simple sugars to starch in order to store them. Recall that when this happens molecules of water are split off. But what does a plant or animal do in order to move the starch out of the cells where it is

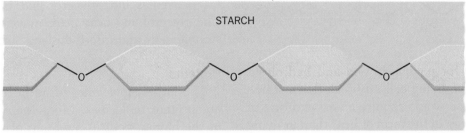

STARCH

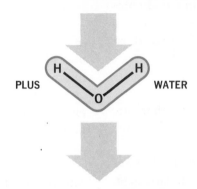

PLUS   WATER

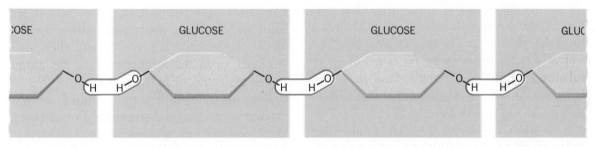

GLUCOSE   GLUCOSE   GLUCOSE   GLUC

stored? The polymerization process is simply reversed. The large molecules are broken down into small molecules by enzymes. Recall that your saliva, for instance, contains an enzyme that breaks down the starch you eat.

On a chemical level, what happens as complex molecules are broken down? Perhaps you will be willing to make an educated guess. When molecules of glucose are polymerized to form starch, recall that *water molecules are split off*. Now when starch is broken down to form glucose, *water molecules are added* at each point in the break.

Study the diagram to fix this in your mind.

The breaking down of complex organic molecules, such as starch and glycogen, is, in a way, just the opposite of polymerization. The breaking down of complex organic molecules *with the addition of water* is called **hydrolysis** (hī·drol'ə·sis). Therefore, in hydrolysis in protoplasm, water is added, and large molecules are broken down into smaller molecules. In polymerization, water is taken away, or split off, and larger molecules are built up from small molecules. It is necessary to emphasize that in living cells enzymes are

167

necessary for polymerization and hydrolysis. Outside the living cell, to break down starch into glucose would require an expenditure of more energy in the form of heat than in living protoplasm. Even the cellulose in wood chips can be hydrolyzed into simple sugars, but only at much higher temperatures than those taking place in the body (98.6°F).

Fats

Fats are even larger molecules than are sugar molecules. Yet both plant and animal cells are able to synthesize fats.

Fats, like carbohydrates, are made of atoms of carbon, hydrogen, and oxygen. However, the atoms are arranged differently. One portion of the large molecule of fat is always a substance known as *glycerol* (glis′ər·ōl). The rest of a large molecule of fat is made up of substances called *fatty acids*. One part of a fatty acid molecule is a long chain of carbon and hydrogen atoms. ①

Now study the diagram of the common fat *palmitin*. ② At the right is the glycerol portion; the three chains at the left each represent a fatty acid portion.

As you can see, fats are very large molecules. The fat molecule we have diagramed here is one of the smaller ones. When you eat fats they must be digested or changed into small molecules. Then they can go through the intestinal membrane or through cell membranes anywhere. Digestive juices break down the fat molecules into glycerol and fatty acids. Later, if these are to be stored, the glycerol and fatty acids are recombined again to form fat in storage cells. Then, as fats are needed by the body, the storage cells break down the fat molecules into glycerol and fatty acids. The glycerol and fatty acids move out of the storage cells and into the blood stream.

Proteins

The largest molecules of all in protoplasm are protein molecules. More than one sixth of the human body is made up of giant protein molecules.

A protein molecule consists of thousands of atoms, chiefly hydrogen, oxygen, carbon, and nitrogen. Other elements such as phosphorus, sulfur, and magnesium also may be attached to the molecule. However, it is the element *nitrogen* that mainly makes the composition of a protein different from that of a carbohydrate or fat.

There is a tremendous variety of proteins. The human body, for example, has perhaps over 100,000 different kinds of proteins. Each kind differs from the others either in the kinds of elements it contains and their proportions, or in the arrangement of the atoms in the molecule, or in both.

Proteins differ in function as much as they do in composition and structure. For instance, the blood protein *hemoglobin* is able to combine chemically with oxygen in order to carry oxygen to the cells. The muscle protein *myosin* (mī′ō·sin) enables the muscle cells to do their work.

The size of a protein molecule can be judged by its formula. Hemoglobin from human blood, for example, has the following formula:

$$C_{3032}H_{4816}O_{872}N_{780}S_8Fe_4$$

This formula means that in one molecule of hemoglobin there are 3,032 atoms of carbon, 4,816 atoms of hydrogen, 872 atoms of ox-

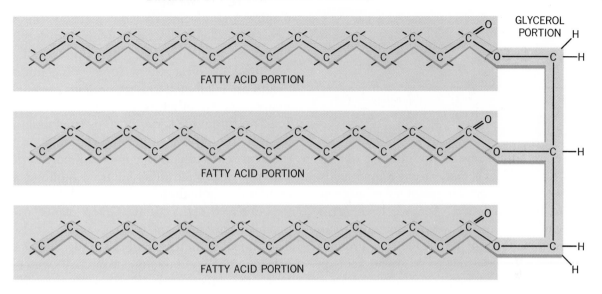

GLYCEROL PORTION

FATTY ACID PORTION

FATTY ACID PORTION

FATTY ACID PORTION

ygen, 780 atoms of nitrogen, 8 atoms of sulfur, and 4 atoms of iron. (Page 184 contains a diagram of part of a hemoglobin molecule.)

However, again, it is the *arrangement* of the atoms that is important. The almost endless varieties of proteins are the result, in large part, of the almost endless ways in which these giant molecules can be arranged.

You can understand why proteins are outstanding and are of particular importance to living things.

Amino Acids—The Alphabet of Proteins

There are twenty-six letters in our alphabet. By arranging these letters in different ways, we form all the thousands upon thousands of different words by which we communicate with each other. Change one letter in the word *house* and you get something totally different: *mouse*. By changing the order of letters, you change *pin* to *nip; last* to *salt* to *slat,* and so on with many other words. The numbers of ideas and thoughts that can be developed simply by changing the num-

ber, order, and position of twenty-six letters is really amazing.

It is even more amazing that all of the thousands upon thousands of proteins, each greatly different from the others, are made up of only twenty-four or so **amino** (ə·mēn′ō) **acids** that can be compared to the letters of our alphabet. These amino acids are the building blocks from which proteins are made, just as the letters of our alphabet are the building blocks from which all words are made.

You have already seen how large-molecule carbohydrates such as starch are built by adding more and more of only one building block, glucose, in the process of polymerization. In polymerization, recall, molecules of water are split off as the smaller molecules are linked.

In much the same way, the twenty-four or so amino acids provide for an almost infinite number of different varieties of proteins. Recall that there are approximately 100,000 different kinds of proteins in your own body.

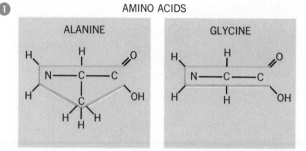

AMINO ACIDS

ALANINE

GLYCINE

These are only a few of the millions of proteins that could be made from amino acids.

Most words in our language have but from two to fourteen letters. Yet, we have many thousands of different words. Imagine a single word made up of 100,000 letters. Proteins can use the twenty-four or so amino acids in any combination, and can combine over 100,000 of these in a single protein. Thus, you can see that the possible number of proteins is infinitely greater than the possible number of words in the English language.

The diagram shows two simple amino acids, alanine and glycine. ❶ Now see how these two amino acids can be built up into large molecules or chains called **polypeptides** (pol′i-pep′tīdz). ❷ Next these long polypeptide chains are combined to form proteins of enormous size. In other words, any protein is built up through a series of steps from amino acids by the process of polymerization. Study the figure carefully. Is the process of polymerization of a protein different from building a complex carbohydrate such as starch?

FOODS AND AMINO ACIDS. Green plants, especially, can make *all* of the amino acids. They make them from carbohydrates and the substances they take up from soil water. Using the amino acids that they have made, they can make all of the proteins they need.

Animals cannot make all of the amino acids they need. Your body, for example, is capable of making only fifteen amino acids. There are

❷

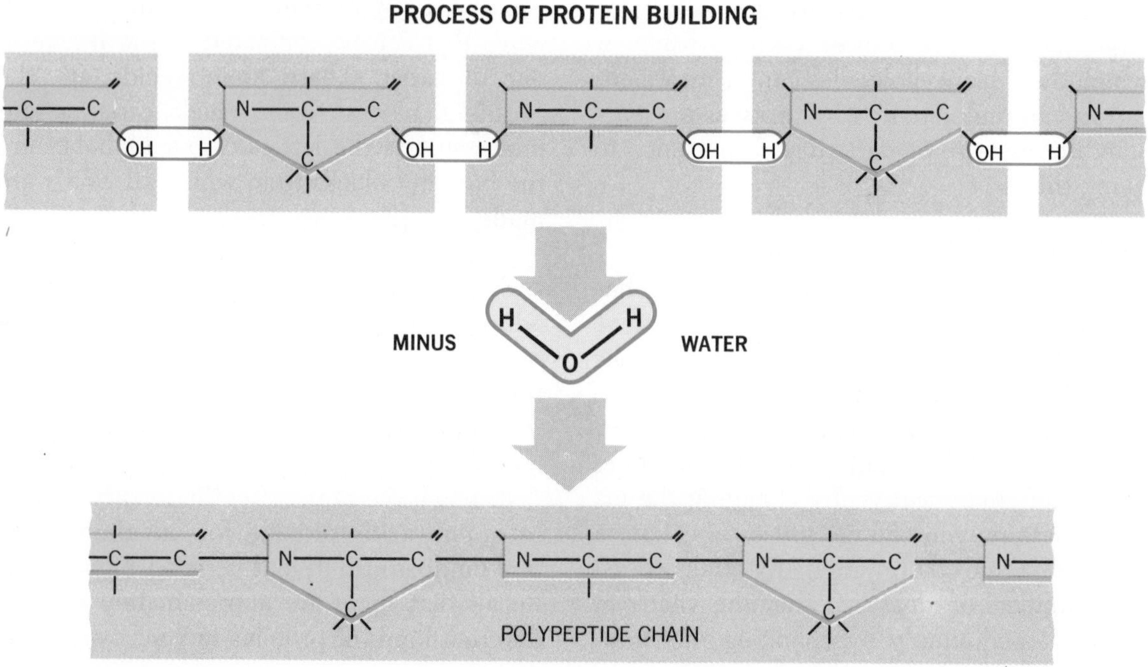

PROCESS OF PROTEIN BUILDING

MINUS   WATER

POLYPEPTIDE CHAIN

nine others that your body must have. These nine can be obtained by eating plants or by eating meat from animals that ate plants containing these other amino acids.

CELL SPECIALISTS. A single-celled organism makes all of the kinds of proteins it needs. Therefore, this single cell (that is, its protoplasm) must be a complete chemical factory. This is not true of the individual cells in a many-celled organism. Muscle cells make certain proteins from amino acids taken from the blood stream (and from amino acids that the muscle cells manufacture). Nerve cells make other proteins. Bone cells make still different ones, and so it goes. Each type of cell makes the proteins it needs, both from the amino acids it manufactures and from the common pool of amino acids circulating in the blood stream.

Nucleic Acids

In a later unit, you will be studying how organisms pass on their characteristics to their offspring. For the moment, it is enough to know simply that this occurs and that the characteristics are carried in a kind of code, or blueprint, in the nucleus of the cells. Specifically, the *chromosomes* in the cell nucleus carry the blueprints that determine heredity.

One of the present mysteries of life is what these blueprints in the chromosomes really are and how they work. We know that the chromosomes contain very complex substances called **nucleic** (noō·klā′ik) **acids.** Nucleic acids are giant molecules, much larger than carbohydrate or fat molecules, and they are built up of smaller molecules by polymerization. Nucleic acids also occur in almost endless varieties. The difference between one arrangement of atoms and another in nucleic acids is of great significance in biology. The

arrangement may determine, for example, whether you inherit brown eyes or blue eyes.

One type of nucleic acid is found in all chromosomes. It is almost *never* found anywhere else except in chromosomes. This important nucleic acid is called **DNA** [for **deoxyribonucleic** (dē·ok′sē·rī′bō·noō·klā′ik) **acid**]. There is evidence that DNA may be the main carrier of heredity. It is an extremely long chain in which one kind of small molecule alternates with another kind. ❸ These small molecules keep alternating thousands of times throughout the DNA molecule so that it is about a thousand times as long as it is thick. Hanging from this molecular chain, like clothes from a clothesline, are other groups of atoms and molecules.

Chromosomes also contain another nucleic acid called **RNA** [for **ribonucleic** (rī'bō·nōo·klā'ik) **acid**], which you will study in some detail in Chapter 17.

However, it is sufficient for the present study to know that DNA is the substance in the chromosomes and is a kind of master builder. The master molecule DNA dictates what kind of protein, or carbohydrate, or fat that the cell shall make. For instance, the wheat plant makes the protein called *gluten* (glōot'n). Corn cells form the protein called *zein* (zē'in). It is the DNA that determines how different molecules will combine and what they will form. How DNA does this is given over to later study (Chapter 17).

We now come to the main concept with which we have been dealing. Protoplasm within the cell is a kind of chemical laboratory. The master molecule, or code, or director, within the cell—whatever you wish to call it—is DNA. DNA, through its tremendously complex structure, dictates what substances will be built, how, and even when.

REVIEW

1. What kind of process is indicated in the following chemical reaction?

$$x\,C_6H_{12}O_6 \longrightarrow (C_6H_{10}O_5)_x + x\,H_2O$$
$$\text{glucose} \qquad \text{starch} \qquad \text{water}$$

2. What kind of process is indicated in the following chemical reaction?

$$(C_6H_{10}O_5)_x + x\,H_2O \longrightarrow x\,C_6H_{12}O_6$$
$$\text{starch} \qquad \text{water} \qquad \text{glucose}$$

3. What is the relationship between these two chemical processes?

NEW VIEW

Assume that a scientist has discovered how a green plant makes glucose. He can reproduce this process cheaply, the way the plant does. Now he wishes to proceed further with duplicating some of the other plant processes—producing starch, cellulose, fats, and complex proteins.

What would he need to learn to duplicate these processes?

3. RELEASE OF ENERGY IN THE CELL

Suppose that you owned a large factory. Suppose, too, that you manufactured thousands of different products in that factory. To make glass in your factory, you would require a tremendous amount of heat to melt sand, lime, and other materials and to keep the glass in a molten state.

To make different products, you might need different fuels as sources of heat. You might need the energy in different amounts (some in bursts, some being released slowly over a long period of time) for the different processes occurring in your factory.

Now, if you could imagine a factory in which you would also need to make your own sources of energy (heat would be only one source), you would have some idea of what a living cell is like. Every living cell carries on thousands of energy transformations. Many of these transformations store up energy and many release energy. Also, different cellular reactions store up and release different amounts of energy.

Some of the cell's functions require a fast but small release of energy comparable, say, to the flame of a match. Some of the work requires a great amount of energy released over a long period of time. And finally, the cell must retain a large store of fuel (that is, chemical energy) in reserve for use as needed.

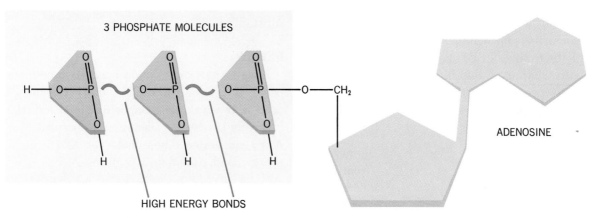

3 PHOSPHATE MOLECULES

ADENOSINE

HIGH ENERGY BONDS

Cells store their fuel—their chemical energy—mainly in the form of starches and fats. As needed, these stores of energy are changed to other substances such as glucose and other simple sugars from which the energy can be released more easily. These energy changes, called *the cell's energy process,* are used for the many cell functions of living, for example, rebuilding parts of the cell and cell division. Or, if you wish to think of it in another way, the cell's energy process is behind the work of the cell.

Research over the past half century has yielded information that places certain organic compounds containing phosphorus at the center of the cell's energy process. These substances are known by the abbreviations **ATP** and **ADP**. These are the abbreviations that chemists use.

ATP and ADP in the Cell's Energy Process

As we mentioned above, these two sets of letters stand for two important organic compounds containing phosphorus in living cells.

ATP stands for **adenosine triphosphate.**
ADP stands for **adenosine diphosphate.**

Adenosine (ad'ə·nō'sēn) is a very complicated substance. Triphosphate (trī·fəs'fāt) means "three phosphate groups." Diphosphate means "two phosphate groups."

The general structure of a molecule of adenosine triphosphate is represented in the diagram shown above.❶ If you were to analyze adenosine, you would find that it is a proteinlike substance.

For ease in writing adenosine triphosphate, we shall use the biologist's way of referring to it, simply as ATP (T for *tri–*). And adenosine diphosphate, ADP (D for *di–*).

ATP might also be written APPP
and
ADP might also be written APP.

The main point is that ATP changes into ADP and is accompanied by a release, or burst, of energy in the cell.

$$APPP \longrightarrow APP + P + energy$$

Notice, however, that one phosphate group (P) splits off ATP (APPP) when this happens. Now, if this were the only process occurring, soon all of the ATP (APPP) would be used up. The cell's energy process would run down, and soon the cell would not have energy for its work.

The ATP–ADP Cycle

As we just stated, when ATP breaks down, it yields a burst of energy. In your later work in science, you will learn how the three phosphate groups (PPP) are *bonded* to each other with what are called **high-energy bonds**, usually represented with this symbol $\sim$. When a phosphate bond is broken, energy is released. To review,

$$A—P\sim P\sim P \longrightarrow A—P\sim P + P + \text{energy}$$
$$\text{(from a high-energy bond)}$$

To renew the ATP (APPP), the opposite reaction must occur. That is, a synthesis of ATP (APPP) from ADP (APP) must occur.

$$\text{energy} + P + A—P\sim P \longrightarrow A—P\sim P\sim P$$

Where does the energy for the synthesis of ATP (APPP) come from? It comes from the oxidation of glucose. When glucose is oxidized (combined with oxygen), it yields the energy that converts ADP into ATP.

Thus, there are *three* main reactions that take place as the cell releases its energy. ❶

The energy from the oxidation of glucose is the energy used to synthesize ATP from ADP. Other substances, such as proteins and fats, can also be broken down to yield energy if necessary. This energy can also be used to make ATP from ADP. It is clear, however, that the substance ATP is the center of the cell's energy process.

Now sit perfectly still. Stay as quiet as you can be. Hold your breath as you read this paragraph. You are apparently still, but your circulatory system is carrying substances to all your cells. In each cell, ATP is being broken down to ADP, and, in turn, ADP is being built up into ATP.

You are alive. And in good part you are alive because of the action of that singular substance ATP.

REVIEW

In as many words as you need (two or three pages if necessary), explain the cell's energy process. In your discussion, be sure to include the following key terms: adenosine triphosphate (or ATP), adenosine diphosphate (or ADP), high-energy bond, oxidation, and glucose.

NEW VIEW

Yeasts, oaks, insects, frogs, rabbits, horses, men, and all the main groups of living things that have been investigated have ATP as central to their cell energy process. What does this tell you about the relationships of living things? What major substance found in the cell might act in the inheritance of the cell energy process?

4. RELATING THE CONCEPTS

Schleiden and Schwann developed the cell theory more than a hundred years ago in 1839. They stated that the cell is the unit of structure and function for all living things. They based their work on the investigations of many scientists of many nations—Leeuwenhoek, Hooke, Dutrochet, Malpighi.

Today, the cell theory is still true (except for such organisms as the viruses). But it has been extended greatly. The work on protoplasm, which you have begun to study—the nucleus (chromosomes, DNA), the function of the cytoplasm (ATP, ADP), and oxidation —had not been done in the time of Schleiden and Schwann. However, their theory, as all theories do, helped to direct further work. A host of scientists brought the following concepts to the point where they are fruitful for you to study.

CELL ENERGY PROCESS

Breakdown of ATP releasing energy

1 $APPP \longrightarrow APP + P +$ energy for cell activities

Rebuilding ATP from ADP storing energy

2 energy $+ P + APP \longrightarrow APPP$

Oxidation of glucose for synthesizing ATP releasing energy

3 $C_6H_{12}O_6 + 6O_2 \longrightarrow 6CO_2 + 6H_2O +$ energy for synthesizing ATP

glucose   oxygen   carbon dioxide   water

The cell energy process is often simplified as a cycle called the ATP-ADP cycle.

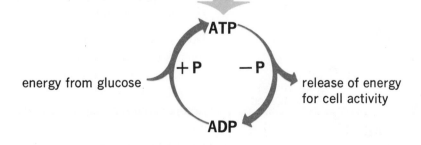

ATP

$+P$ $-P$

energy from glucose   release of energy for cell activity

ADP

Reviewing the Concepts

▶ A fundamental concept still apparent in your studies of this chapter is this: *The cell is the unit of structure and function of all living organisms.*

▶ *The cell's chemical activity is based on the action of enzymes.* Enzymes such as diastase, urease, and those that break down ATP and oxidize glucose are basic to the cell's chemical activity.

▶ *The cell's activity in building up compounds is based on two general chemical processes: polymerization and hydrolysis.* In a way, polymerization in the cell is the opposite of hydrolysis. In polymerization, water is split off when compounds are combined. The splitting off of water results in linking two or more compounds. For example, sugars are linked to form starch, amino acids are linked to form proteins. In hydrolysis, complex compounds are broken down into simpler compounds, such as starch into sugars, proteins into amino acids, as water is added.

▶ *A process of yielding energy (the cell's energy process) is central to all the cell's activities.* By now, the cycle representing the cell energy process should have impressed itself on you because of its central importance to all cell functions. When a phosphate group (P) is added to ADP, energy is built up; when a phosphate group is taken away from ATP, energy is released.

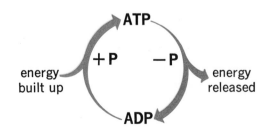

Testing Yourself

1. What is the significance of the class of substances known as enzymes?
2. What is the significance of these classes of substances: carbohydrates, proteins, fats?
3. What is the significance of the class of substances known as nucleic acids?
4. What is the significance of polymerization in the activity of the cell? Give an example.
5. What is the significance of hydrolysis in the activity of the cell? Give an example.
6. What is the function of the oxidation of glucose in the cell energy cycle?
7. What activities would stop if phosphates were excluded from the diet?

Extending the Concepts

Investigation 1. If you have patience and good technique, you may want to isolate a small amount of adenosine triphosphate. Perhaps you will use a common single-celled plant as the source of ATP.

What method will you use?

Many experiments of scientists are based on the isolation of pure substances. Otherwise, how could the functions of ATP or DNA be determined? Of course, we are aware that the apparatus for isolating pure ATP is probably not available to you. But you will get some idea of the problems of isolating a pure substance from some investigations.

One method is given in *A Sourcebook for the Biological Sciences,* Morholt and others.

Investigation 2. In the body, glycogen in the liver is hydrolyzed to glucose. Can you duplicate this procedure in the laboratory?

Probably you should start with some powdered glycogen. Add about 0.5 gram of glycogen to 100 milliliters of distilled water. How can you test for glucose?

Now add five drops of hydrochloric acid to your mixture of glycogen and water, and heat the mixture in a glass double boiler. The temperature of the mixture must not exceed $212°F$ ($100°C$).

Test for the presence of glucose every half hour. Suppose the formula of glycogen is $(C_6H_{10}O_5)_x$. What is your explanation of the formation of glucose? Write a formula.

Investigation 3. Who were some of the scientists who did the work on DNA (deoxyribonucleic acid)? Who were some of the scientists who did the work on ATP (adenosine triphosphate)?

Where might you find some of the descriptions of the work? In the *Scientific American,* perhaps? In *Science World,* perhaps?

One of the skills most important in all kinds of study is the ability to use the library. Library research often precedes research in the laboratory.

Suggested Reading

Asimov, Isaac, *The World of Carbon,* New York, Macmillan, 1966.

Berman, William, *Beginning Biochemistry,* New York, Sentinel, 1968.

8 | Cells in Balance

An automobile, even your automobile, will eventually break down and change into junk. The paint will finally flake or peel off. The chromium will scale away. The upholstery will rot or break down chemically. Finally, the entire car will become a pile of junk *unless it is constantly maintained and repaired.*

One of the most extraordinary things about an organism is that, given a proper environment, it maintains itself. A muscle cell is much the same thing today, tomorrow, or ten years from now. A muscle cell is constantly oxidizing food to replace its worn out parts. As fast as the cell oxidizes food, it absorbs more food to replace that which has been used. Its ATP must also be constantly replenished.

As fast as the protoplasm of a cell breaks down, it builds new protoplasm from the materials flowing in the blood stream. Unlike a nonliving machine, an organism or a living cell is constantly at work maintaining itself. Bathed in a fluid that supplies the raw materials it needs, a living cell continues taking in what it needs, synthesizing more of itself, throwing out materials from broken down protoplasm and from the oxidation of foods, and maintaining a constant but ever-changing balance between itself and the outside environment.

The total activity of a cell or organism in maintaining itself is called its **metabolism** (mə·tab′ə·liz′əm). Metabolism in the body, in short, takes in *all* the chemical changes in *all* the cells of the body. At any given moment, thousands of complex chemical changes, metabolic changes, are occurring in the cells of your body as they carry on their functions and maintain the chemical balance that makes them what they are.

1. MAINTAINING BALANCE IN FOOD SUBSTANCES

Let's again compare an organism to a factory. An automobile factory must use a tremendous amount of materials in a variety of forms, from glass and steel bars and plates to woven fabrics, copper wire, and tiny bolts and screws. These basic materials must be available in the proper amounts and at the proper times to keep finished automobiles rolling off the assembly line.

If even one essential basic material were suddenly not available, the finished automobiles could not be produced. If a few of the basic materials were not available, it might be possible to use substitutes. The automobiles might not be as good as they should be, but perhaps they could be produced. However, if a crucial basic material, such as steel, were not available, the entire factory would soon shut down.

An organism is comparable. It takes in a wide variety of materials in the form of food, water, and air. As long as all the basic materials are available in the proper amounts, the organism is healthy. If certain materials are not available, the organism may get by for some time. However, if the crucial basic materials are not available, the organism will become ill and perhaps die.

To remain healthy, the human body needs a variety of *nutrients* in its diet: proteins, carbohydrates, fats, minerals, water, and vitamins.

Can a human being stay alive and healthy if he eats nothing but meats? Many Eskimos eat mainly meats and they seem to remain relatively healthy. The meats they eat contain proteins and fats. Both vitamins and minerals are also found in these meats. The cells of the Eskimo break down the proteins and fats into simpler compounds and build carbohydrates as they are needed.

Can a person eat nothing but carbohydrates and remain healthy? Probably not. Carbohydrates do not contain certain minerals, vitamins, and certain other raw materials needed by the body. You need nitrogen compounds, for example. Recall that proteins are nitrogen compounds, but carbohydrates are not. Carbohydrates contain nothing but carbon, hydrogen, and oxygen. So if you tried to live on nothing but starches and sugars, you would become ill.

Look at the results of an experiment with young rats. One was fed on a diet of insuf-

ficient protein. At the age of 11 weeks, this rat weighed only 70 grams.

Another rat from the same litter was fed a diet that furnished plenty of protein. At 11 weeks, this rat weighed 193 grams—more than twice as much as its undernourished litter-mate.  A rat, like most mammals, needs pretty much the same materials that you need.

You can, however, live and remain healthy on a *well-balanced* diet of vegetables and fruits. They do not contain as much protein as meats, but if you ate a large enough variety, you would obtain a sufficient amount of the amino acids you need, as well as vitamins, fats, minerals, and carbohydrates. Your body could make the protein it needs from the amino acids. However, you could not stay alive and healthy if you ate, say, nothing but potatoes and beans. Not all of the amino acids, vitamins, and other raw materials your body needs are found in these two foods.

Look at the tables, on the next page, of basic materials your body needs and of a diet plan that supplies your cells with the substances needed for functioning well. Check your diet against the diet plan. Do you have a well-balanced diet?

BASIC MATERIALS FOR GROWTH AND REPAIR OF THE HUMAN BODY

	Carbohydrates	Fats	Proteins	Minerals	Vitamins
Major elements in each group of substances	carbon hydrogen oxygen	carbon hydrogen oxygen	carbon hydrogen oxygen nitrogen sulfur phosphorus (some)	sodium potassium magnesium phosphorus calcium iron iodine cobalt (trace) zinc (trace) manganese (trace) copper (trace) fluorine (trace)	carbon hydrogen oxygen
Main food substances in each group	grains potatoes vegetables (starchy) fruits	meats butter cream cheese egg yolk	meats dairy products egg white vegetables grains	salt grains vegetables milk meats sea foods	fish-liver oils milk butter cream egg yolk green and yellow vegetables wheat germ fruits tomatoes potatoes meats

A DAILY DIET PLAN*

Food needed	Amount needed
milk	$\frac{3}{4}$ to 1 quart
tomatoes, oranges, grapefruit, green cabbage, raw salad greens	1 or more servings
leafy green or yellow vegetables	1 or more servings
potatoes, other vegetables, and fruits	2 or more servings
eggs	1 a day (or at least 3 or 4 a week)
lean meat, poultry, fish	1 or more servings
cereals	2 servings of whole-grain products or enriched bread
fats	some butter or margarine

* Developed by the U.S. Government.

Carbohydrate Balance

You will recall from the last chapter how giant molecules of carbohydrates are polymerized from glucose. Carbohydrates are the so-called energy food, and carbohydrates in the bodies of living things are the main substances oxidized to release energy.

However, not all of the carbohydrates in your body are flowing around in your blood stream ready to be oxidized. Most are stored at various places, chiefly in the liver.

When food is taken into the body, all of the carbohydrates are digested into molecules of glucose. The glucose is able to pass through your intestinal walls and into your blood stream. This glucose-rich blood is carried by a special vein (the *portal vein*) directly to the liver. There, most of the glucose is absorbed by the liver cells, where it is changed into glycogen. However, some glucose circulates into all cells.

Suppose that you suddenly start running. The glucose in your muscle cells is quickly oxidized and energy is released. Recall that energy is used to change ADP molecules to ATP molecules. The ATP gives off energy as fast as your muscle cells need the energy.

As the muscle cells use up their glucose, more glucose is taken from the blood stream. Human blood normally contains about 0.1 percent glucose. As the muscle cells take glucose from the blood, this percentage begins to drop. Immediately, the liver changes some of its stored glycogen to glucose, which then diffuses out of the liver cells into the blood. The liver is, then, both a storehouse for carbohydrates and a regulator of blood sugar.

Plants also store carbohydrates in the form of starch. A white potato is a *tuber*—that is, a specialized underground stem that takes glucose from the plant fluids and changes it into starch for storage.

Eat a piece of raw potato. It tastes starchy. But if you chew a piece of the yellowish sprout that often grows out of potatoes when they have been kept too long, you will find that the sprout tastes sweet. As the sprout grows, the starch in the tuber is hydrolyzed into glucose. The glucose is then oxidized to supply energy for the growth of the sprout. Plants, as well as animals, maintain a balance of sugar in their fluids and also store surplus carbohydrates in the form of starches.

Fats as Stored Foods

Starches are not the only kind of foods stored in organisms. Although fats are found in some form in all living cells, some cells are especially designed for fat storage. A fat cell may swell up with stored fat until it is scarcely more than a cell membrane surrounding a large drop of oil. ❶

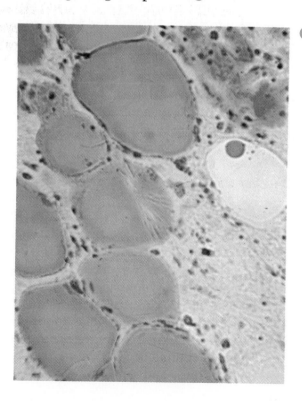

Fats are concentrated in some seeds and fruits to such an extent that they are distinctly oily. If you rub a piece of nut across a piece of paper or crush it on paper, it will leave a greasy spot.

Fats are stored in animal bodies in various tissues. Remember the fatty layer in the dermis, for example (Chapter 4). When people overeat and become "fat," this fatty layer may become quite thickened with stored fat.

Fats, you will recall from your studies in Chapter 7, are made up of glycerol and fatty acids. When you eat fats, they are broken down in the intestines into these two substances. These two substances are carried by the blood to fat storage cells where they are recombined again into fat.

Sugars and starches may also be changed into fat in the body. If you eat more carbohydrates than your body needs for energy, some of the surplus sugar in the blood may be changed into fat and stored for future use. Then, if the liver's supply of glycogen becomes low, some of the stored fat is broken down into glycerol and fatty acids. These two substances can be oxidized, by a complex chemical process, with a release of energy. So the body maintains a balance in the amount of fatty acids and glycerol in the blood stream just as it maintains a balance in the amount of sugar contained in the blood stream.

Protein Balance

Proteins, as you know, are the most complex molecules contained in living cells. Remember that proteins are made up of a variety of some twenty-four amino acids, and that these amino acids make up perhaps 100,000 different kinds of proteins found in your body.

When you eat proteins (lean meat, cheese, eggs, milk, beans, and peas, for example),

they are hydrolyzed into amino acids by your body cells. These amino acids are then reassembled (polymerized) into the different kinds of proteins needed by your cells and tissues.

Remember that your body can manufacture only fifteen of the twenty-four amino acids it needs to build its proteins. The nine other amino acids must come from the food you eat. If you ate nothing but beans, you would not get all of these nine amino acids. Meat, cheese, eggs, and milk are much better sources. And if you ate only beef, you still might not get all the nine amino acids you need. This again illustrates the necessity of having a well-balanced diet.

Who do you think should have more protein in his diet: a child or an adult? A child should, of course. Although both must have protein to repair body cells, a child is growing fast and needs additional protein to build new cells. As you can see, then, it is even more important that children and young people have well-balanced diets containing a variety of proteins.

Some amino acids from the food you eat cannot be used by your cells. Each cell takes out of the blood stream only the amino acids it needs. Those that are not needed by any cells are oxidized for energy. Carbon dioxide and water are also produced when amino acids are oxidized.

You will remember that amino acids contain nitrogen (Chapter 7). Thus, proteins also contain nitrogen. As special cells in the liver break down surplus amino acids, the nitrogen is released in the form of *urea*. Urea is carried by means of the blood stream to the kidneys, which remove it in the form of urine.

Have you ever seen photographs of persons who have starved for a long time? They

■ AN APPRENTICE INVESTIGATION into Minerals in the Body

Soak a piece of cotton in distilled water. Now wipe the palms of your hands and your face with the cotton. Try not to lose any of the water in it. Then squeeze the water into a test tube. Repeat this procedure until you have about a fifth of a test tube of the distilled water containing some of the substances from your face and hands.

Now add a few drops of silver nitrate ($AgNO_3$) to the test tube. Does a white cloud form in the water? ❶ We call this a white **precipitate**. The white precipitate shows that salt (a chloride) is present. How can you be sure the chloride was not present in the distilled water?

An Investigation On Your Own

Which part of your hand (palm or back) excretes more salt in perspiration?

How would you determine this? How would you measure the amount of salt excreted?

This investigation may introduce difficulties in technique. How will you minimize the error in measurement?

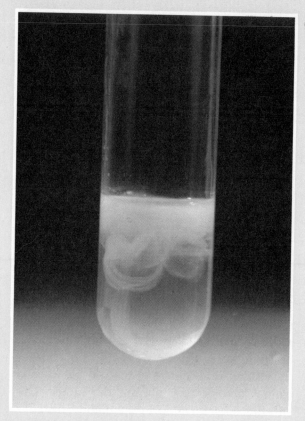

appear to be only skin and bones. When this occurs, the glycogen (animal starch) in the liver is used up first, then the stored fat. After both the glycogen and stored fat are used up, the body starts literally using up *itself*. The proteins that are the actual parts of cells are then broken down into their amino acids, which are then oxidized for energy in place of the missing glycogen and fat.

Even the cells of healthy persons (and all animals) break down (wear out) in time, and the nitrogen from the cellular proteins is released. The body must constantly maintain its health by building new cells to replace the worn out ones. Often, only parts of cells break

down, and the proteins you eat provide the amino acids to build up new cell proteins to replace these cell parts. The nitrogen balance in the body is, perhaps, even more precisely regulated than is the sugar or fat balance.

Mineral Balance

Without certain substances, commonly known as minerals, cells could not function. Minerals, which are inorganic substances not usually containing carbon (C), must be taken into and maintained in the body. It is a simple matter to locate one of the minerals in your body. To see for yourself, try the investigation above. ■

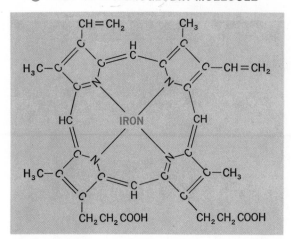

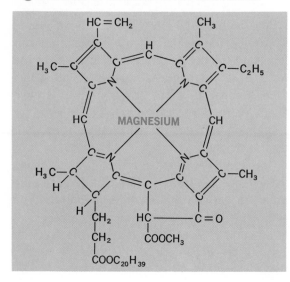

No doubt the results of this simple investigation have not surprised you. You know that your perspiration is salty, and so are tears. The salt in perspiration and tears is mainly sodium chloride (NaCl). Without sufficient sodium chloride, the cells of your body cannot function.

Without sufficient iron, the red blood cells cannot absorb oxygen from the lungs. The substance *hemoglobin* in the blood cells contains iron as part of its molecule. ①

Strangely enough, without sufficient iodine, your body cells might not grow properly. Iodine is necessary for building the hormone *thyroxin* (thī·rok′sin), a substance necessary for growth.

Almost all organisms need generally the same minerals in order to maintain life. Without magnesium, plant cells could not photosynthesize. In the chlorophyll molecule, magnesium is one of the atoms. ②

The soil, of course, must constantly be replenished with minerals: nitrates, phosphates, and certain quantities of potassium, calcium, copper, iron, boron, magnesium, as well as a few other mineral salts. Otherwise, plants could not thrive. You too depend, in the last

analysis, upon the soil for most of your inorganic substances.

Vitamins as Regulators

At about the turn of this century, it was discovered that animals could not be kept alive if they were fed only pure proteins, fats, and carbohydrates, even if all the necessary minerals were contained in the diet. It was later found that a number of substances that we now call vitamins were absolutely necessary for health and even for life itself. The vitamins were given letters instead of names. So we have vitamins A, B, C, D, E, and K. Vitamin B was later found to be composed of several vitamins, so they were called B_1, B_2, and so forth, up to B_{15}.

Vitamins A, D, E, and K dissolve in oils and fats, so they are often called the fat-soluble vitamins. One of the chief reasons that you should have fats in your diet is so you will have enough of these vitamins. Vitamins B_1 through B_{15} and vitamin C are water-soluble vitamins and are found chiefly in grains and vegetables.

VITAMIN A. This vitamin is found in fish-liver oils, butter, cream, egg yolk, and in carrots and other green and yellow vegetables. Actually, plants do not contain vitamin A. However, they have a yellow substance, called *carotene* (kar′ə·tēn′), which, when eaten by animals, is changed by animal cells into vitamin A. You get vitamin A from cream and butter because cows eat green plants which contain the carotene from which the cows make vitamin A.

Recall your study of the microscopic plants called algae? Most algae contain good quantities of carotene. Small sea animals, such as copepods, eat the algae and change the yellow carotene into vitamin A. Small fish then eat the copepods and larger fish eat the small fish. The larger fish store the vitamin A in their livers. So, if you ever need to take cod-liver oil (a rich source of vitamin A), you can remember that the marine algae and copepods made it possible for you to stay in good health.

If a person does not have enough vitamin A, peculiar changes occur in the membrane linings of the digestive and respiratory passages. These membranes may become infected and serious trouble can result. In addition to this, a severe lack of vitamin A may cause the transparent covering of the eyeball (the cornea) to soften and become irritated. Ulcers of the cornea and even permanent blindness may result. A common symptom of vitamin A deficiency is that a person can see well in bright light but not at night, a condition called *night blindness.* Do you know that pilots who have to fly airplanes at night during wartime are often given food especially rich in vitamin A?

VITAMIN B COMPLEX. All the B vitamins are generally found in the same foods, so it is easier to think of them as a group, or complex.

There are at least fifteen of these vitamins, and they are usually found in meats, whole-grained and enriched cereals and flours, milk, eggs, and a variety of vegetables.

Each of these B vitamins that has been studied seems to have a special regulatory job in the body. Without enough B_1, also called *thiamin* (thī′ə·min), a disease of the nervous system called beriberi develops. Without B_2 [now called *riboflavin* (rī′bō·flā′vin)], the skin and tissues beneath it cannot maintain themselves. Sores develop at the corners of the mouth and elsewhere. As you will see later, this vitamin as well as others in the B complex are converted in the body into special kinds of enzymes, the respiratory enzymes. Respiratory enzymes are used in the cell's energy process. Many of them enable the cells to oxidize glucose and other carbohydrates.

Another of the B vitamins, called *niacin* (nī′ə·sin), is also useful in the body as a regulator. Niacin acts in conjunction with riboflavin to maintain the growth of the body.

The other vitamins in this group also have particular functions in the body. Just what some B vitamins do is still not clear, and scientists are still investigating their functions.

VITAMIN C. Inadequate amounts of this vitamin, now known as *ascorbic* (ə·skôr′bik) *acid,* produce a variety of symptoms. The gums become sore and tiny blood vessels break under the skin and produce hemorrhages. A person deficient in this vitamin is always tired. If there is a severe lack of vitamin C, the disease called scurvy results. A person who has scurvy can be cured by eating citrus fruits, tomatoes, raw cabbage, and certain other fruits and vegetables that are rich in vitamin C. Unfortunately, the body does not store vitamin C. So it is a good idea to include such fruits and vegetables in the diet daily.

VITAMIN D. This, like vitamin B, is really a group of vitamins. About ten are now known Lack of vitamin D causes rickets, a disease in which the bones do not develop properly. Sunlight, particularly the ultraviolet light from the sun, causes the skin to change certain substances that it contains into vitamin D. Milk is often irradiated, that is, it is treated with ultraviolet light to stimulate the production of vitamin D in the milk. Fish-liver oils are a good source of vitamin D as well as vitamin A.

VITAMIN K. This vitamin is also actually a group of vitamins. They are necessary for the proper clotting of blood. A deficiency of vitamin K may result in hemorrhages in which bleeding cannot be stopped. Fortunately, the K vitamins are found in most foods, so it is rare for a person in the United States to suffer from a vitamin K deficiency.

VITAMIN E. This vitamin may be necessary for reproduction, but we do not yet know very much about vitamin E.

Exactly how the vitamins work is not clearly understood. However, it is possible that they work something like enzymes, which you will study more closely later in this chapter.

REVIEW

1. Explain why a person cannot remain healthy if he eats nothing but carbohydrates. Why can a person stay healthy if he has a well-balanced diet of vegetables and fruits? Where will he get proteins?

2. Describe the way in which the amount of glucose in the blood stream is regulated.

3. What vitamins are water-soluble and, therefore, found chiefly in grains and vegetables?

4. What vitamins are fat-soluble and, therefore, found chiefly in such oil-rich foods as butter, cream, egg yolk, and fish and meat oils?

5. What is meant by the phrase "vitamin B complex"?

6. Why is vitamin D often called the sunshine vitamin? What is vitamin D enriched milk?

NEW VIEW

1. If the blood sugar drops much below 0.1 percent, the liver converts its glycogen into glucose, which then diffuses into the blood stream. You may wish to use library references to find out what causes the liver to do this. In other words, what is the mechanism by which a drop in the blood-sugar concentration causes the liver to start converting starch to sugar?

2. Explain how it is possible to get vitamin A from eating green and yellow vegetables when these vegetables actually do not contain vitamin A. Explain why fish liver contains vitamin A.

3. What is enriched flour and bread? Use library references to help you answer this question.

4. You may find it interesting to study just how foods are irradiated. Use library references.

2. THE CELL IN BALANCE

You must have seen wilted lettuce at sometime in your life. Why does lettuce wilt? Putting the question another way, how would you make the lettuce crisp again? You would put it in water, wouldn't you?

Clearly you are acting on the assumption that it is a loss of water that made the lettuce limp. Further, you are making the assumption that the water somehow can get back into the lettuce. Let's look into this, for losing water and regaining it is a matter of life and death.

We need first to study the movement of substances as they are mixed with water. ∎

Do gases diffuse? How do you detect the odor of perfume coming from an open bottle? Obviously molecules of gases also diffuse in the air.

■ AN APPRENTICE INVESTIGATION into Simple Diffusion

Take a crystal or so of potassium permanganate (a purple crystal) and drop it into a jar of water. The crystal is easy to follow as it sinks into the water. As it sinks, it dissolves, leaving a purple trail behind it.❶ Even as you watch, the color spreads throughout the water.❷❸

The spreading of one substance in another substance we call **simple diffusion.** The dissolved particles of potassium permanganate *diffused* throughout the molecules of water until they were evenly distributed.

An Investigation On Your Own

If you take a jar of water (1 liter of water will do) and add to each 10 grams of salt (NaCl), what will happen? How can you find out? After all, you cannot see salt diffusing as you saw the potassium permanganate.

How soon does the salt become equally distributed?

Here again, you will need to be careful with your technique. Perhaps the technique suggested is not useful. Can you invent another?

❶

❷

❸

Now let's review what you have learned about diffusion and carry it a bit further. Substances obviously diffuse. For the moment, we may assume that it is the smallest particles of substances, usually the molecules, that diffuse. You have probably learned from your earlier studies in science that molecules of all substances are in some kind of motion. The movement of the molecules of gases is fastest, those of solids is slowest. Perhaps you have learned that all molecules have what we call *kinetic* (ki·net′ik) *energy*, the energy of

movement. It is this kinetic energy of molecules that causes their motion.

The Cell Membrane and Diffusion

As we have stated, molecules of substances diffuse. Do *all* substances diffuse through cell membranes? Diffusion becomes a bit more complicated in living things. For instance, analysis of bone cells shows that they have more calcium than other cells. Red blood cells have more iron than other blood cells. Cells of the thyroid gland have more iodine than other cells. Fat cells have more fat than other cells. Clearly, if substances diffuse, they do not seem to diffuse equally into all cells. Somehow the cells are selective.

Why do different kinds of cells take different amounts of particular substances into themselves? There seem to be several factors involved. But we may see one possible explanation for diffusion if we examine molecules of starch and sugar.

Large and Small Molecules

A starch molecule, as you know, is very large. A glucose molecule is quite small. When you compare the weights of the two different molecules (the molecular weights), which range from 10,000 to 50,000 for starch and only 180 for glucose, you find quite a difference in these two molecules. Such a great difference in the molecular weights of the two molecules gives you a general idea of how much larger the starch molecule is than the glucose molecule.

Perhaps starch molecules are so large that they cannot pass through living cell membranes. However, when they are broken down into the smaller glucose molecules they *can* go through cell membranes. It is believed that the size of molecules has some effect on the ability of a substance to diffuse through a membrane. However, some large molecules do indeed diffuse through living membranes. Diffusion through living membranes cannot be explained solely on the basis of *size* of molecules alone. But for now, let's assume that the size of a molecule generally determines whether or not it will pass through a membrane.

You will recall that fat molecules and protein molecules are much, much larger even than starch molecules. The molecular weights of proteins are estimated to range from 35,000 to 20,000,000. Such giant molecules are broken down into smaller molecules that do pass through the cell membranes. Digestive enzymes hydrolyze the giant molecules into thousands of amino acid molecules, each small enough to slip through the membrane that lines the digestive tract and, later, through cell membranes into different cells of the body.

One explanation, then, of the movement of molecules through membranes is that cell membranes somehow generally keep out large molecules and let small ones through. Membranes themselves, of course, are composed of molecules, just as are all other structures in cells. The molecules of membranes, however, are not packed tightly together. There are spaces between them.

Water, a very small molecule containing only three atoms (H_2O, or HOH), easily passes through the spaces between the molecules making up the membranes of plants or animals. Salts and minerals are usually small enough so they also are able to pass through membranes. Glucose and amino acids are also relatively small molecules, so they, too, can pass through cell membranes. However, as we mentioned earlier, the explanation of size does not totally account for the passage of all substances into cells.

Diffusion and Living Organisms

There is more to diffusion than substances merely passing into the cells. Let's look further into this. ■

The fluids (cell sap) of a tree or any other plant generally have far more sugar, salts, and other minerals in solution inside their cells than does the soil water that surrounds their roots. Therefore, most of the water that a plant uses enters the plant by diffusion through the membranes of the root hairs. In

■ AN APPRENTICE INVESTIGATION
into the Effect of Concentration on Diffusion Through a Membrane

Take some inner "skin" from one of the scales of a red onion (or a leaf of *Elodea* will also do), and place it in a 10 percent glucose solution on a slide. Place the slide under the microscope and examine it. Continue to observe the protoplasm. It seems to be shrinking slowly, as in the photographs from top to bottom. ❶ ❷ ❸

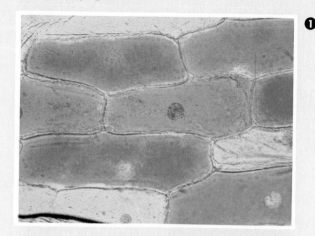

From your earlier work, you know that water is the main substance in protoplasm. Water leaving the cell would account for the remainder of the cell's contents decreasing in size. Moreover, the molecules of any substance in a solution tend to diffuse independently of all other substances.

A 10 percent sugar solution is a very *concentrated* solution. There is proportionately less water in this solution than in most protoplasm. In other words, there are more water molecules in a certain amount of protoplasm than in the same amount of sugar solution. As there are more water molecules (a higher *concentration*) in the protoplasm, they diffuse out into the sugar solution. Diffusion continues until the solutions on both sides of the membrane are equally concentrated.

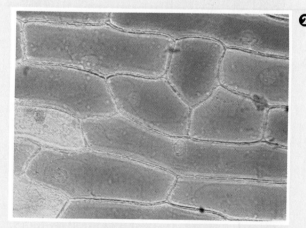

Glucose molecules are, of course, distributed among the water molecules both inside and outside the plant cell. But, since glucose molecules are larger than water molecules, they diffuse through the cell membrane more slowly. Therefore, the faster-diffusing water molecules pass out of the cell faster than sugar molecules diffuse into the cell. Thus, the protoplasm in the cell decreases in size from the loss of much of its water.

An Investigation On Your Own

What happens if you put onion skin in distilled water on a slide? Explain what you see.

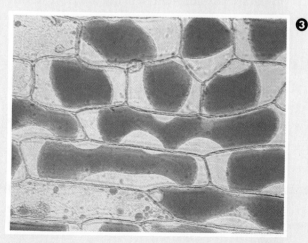

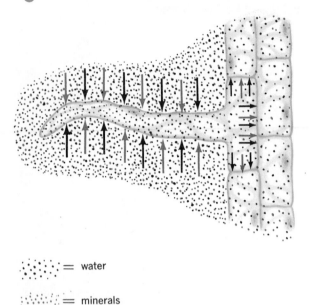

:·.·.·: = water

:·.·.·: = minerals

➡ = direction of diffusion

this way, a green plant steadily absorbs water from the soil.

Minerals, of course, diffuse into plants along with the water. As you know, plants use the minerals they absorb in making protoplasm and other materials. Because the minerals are constantly being used in building new substances, there are usually fewer free minerals in solution inside the plant than there are in the soil water. And so diffusion through the plant membranes of molecules from their regions of greatest concentration to regions of less concentration constantly continues. Fix this in mind by studying the drawing. ❶

Suppose, however, that you poured strong salt water around the roots of green plants. This would mean that the concentration of salt in the water around the roots is greater than the concentration of the salts and other

materials inside the plant cells. That is, the water molecules are now more concentrated in the cells of the roots than they are in the soil water. So diffusion of water proceeds faster in the opposite direction. Therefore, water diffuses out of the roots faster than it diffuses in. Because of the water loss, the plants quickly wilt and probably will die. Pouring salt water around the plants is an effective way to kill weeds in driveways and walks.

Can you determine why a shipwrecked sailor might die if he drank sea water? Sea water does not poison him, but the concentration of salts in sea water is greater than the concentration of salts in the blood. Or you might say, the concentration of water molecules in the blood is greater than the water molecules in the sea water in his digestive tract. On the basis of what you know about the diffusion of substances, determine, in terms of the body organ systems, what might happen if the sailor drank a great quantity of sea water.

Inside the bodies of both plants and animals, diffusion has an important role. Many different kinds of substances are continuously diffused from regions of greater concentration to regions of lesser concentration. Let's follow glucose around the body.

After a meal, glucose diffuses into the blood stream through the intestinal membrane. The glucose in the blood then diffuses through cell membranes into the cells of the body. The cells, as you have learned, oxidize the glucose to release its energy. Because of the continuing oxidation of glucose, its concentration in the cells always remains low.

The liver cells, as you know, change glucose molecules into the giant starch molecules called glycogen. Molecules of glycogen are so large they cannot diffuse through the cell membranes again in this form. As rapidly as new glucose molecules enter the liver cells, they are combined to make glycogen. Thus the concentration of glucose in the liver cells is kept low, and this low concentration causes glucose to continue diffusing into them.

As the body becomes active, the cells throughout the body oxidize more of their glucose. Thus the concentration of glucose is lowered in these cells and, in turn, causes new glucose molecules to diffuse into the cells from the blood stream. The diffusion of glucose out of the blood stream and into the body cell results in a drop in the concentration of glucose in the blood. As the amount of glucose in the blood decreases, enzymes cause the liver cells to change some of the stored glycogen back into glucose. As this process continues, the concentration of glucose in the liver cells builds up until it is greater than the concentration in the blood stream. Then the glucose diffuses out through the membranes of the liver cells and into the blood stream. Soon the blood stream contains more glucose than the muscle cells. Therefore, the glucose diffuses from the blood stream into the muscle cells through the cell membranes. Here it is once again oxidized for its energy. Remember from Chapter 7 that the energy from the oxidation of glucose is the energy used to build ATP molecules from ADP molecules as fast as the ATP molecules are broken down.

Selectivity of Membranes

Recall that living membranes, such as those in body cells, can regulate, to a degree, the amount of materials that diffuse through them, *regardless of the concentration of such materials.*

Sometimes the membranes of plant root hairs will allow a mineral that is dissolved in soil water to diffuse through for a short time and then stop it from diffusing, although the concentration of that mineral is still much greater in the soil water than in the root-hair cells.

All living membranes seem to be able to regulate their **permeability** (pûr′mē·ə·bil′ə·tē) to some extent. By permeability we mean the quality of membranes that allows substances to diffuse through them.

All membranes are usually what we call **semipermeable.** That is, they allow some substances to diffuse through and do not allow others.

If *you* cannot drink sea water, how can plants and animals that live in the sea keep water inside their bodies? As you might guess, the cell fluids of many sea plants, and some simple sea animals, have salt and water concentrations about equal to that of the sea water around them. If the water concentration in their body cells becomes a little lower than that in the sea, additional water diffuses into the cells until the concentration of water in the cells becomes normal again. If the concentration of water in the cells becomes a little greater, the cells lose water by diffusion until the water balance is corrected again.

Other more complicated marine animals, such as fish, have a constant problem maintaining their water balances. Marine fish have cell fluids with *lower* concentrations of salts than the surrounding sea water. Therefore, fish that live in a salt-water environment steadily lose water by diffusion through the cell membranes of their gills, which are in contact with the salt water. From this continuous diffusion process they would quickly die of a lack of water were they not also able to release great quantities of salt from their gill cells.

In addition to losing water constantly by diffusion, marine fish also take in additional salt by drinking great quantities of sea water. The salt from the sea water diffuses through the cell membranes of the intestines despite the fact that the sea water contains a higher concentration of salt than the intestinal cells. This additional salt eventually reaches the gills and then diffuses from the cells of the gills out into the sea water again, even though the water around the gills has a greater concentration of salt. Here is a good example of living membranes regulating diffusion regardless of the concentrations of substances on either side of it.

Again, this action can only be accomplished by living cell membranes. Why or how this happens is not yet understood. All we can say is that it is one of the thousands of examples of the way in which living things are adapted to their environment.

The Living Membrane

Obviously, a membrane in a living cell is not like just any other membrane, such as the Goldbeater's membrane that you used in some of the investigations. A living cell membrane is *selective*. You have seen how it allows some substances to enter while it keeps others out. Simply saying that the cell membrane is alive does not explain how the cell membrane selects the substances that are allowed to pass through it and/or how it rejects others that are not needed or might be harmful.

The explanation that large molecules cannot pass through the membrane whereas smaller molecules· can is to some extent true many times. But it is not always true. Molecules of some small proteins and molecules of some fats, which are much larger than glucose molecules and which may even approach the size of a starch molecule, sometimes do pass through certain cell membranes.

We also know that the make-up of the cell membrane itself often changes. This might explain why it is sometimes permeable to certain molecules and other times not.

Imagine the structure of the cell membrane as constantly changing and you will have a better concept of a living cell membrane than if you were to think of it as a membrane with holes in it and one that never changes.

How is it, then, that certain cells collect, or take in, certain substances? For instance, the red blood cells collect iron; certain cells of the thyroid gland collect iodine. It is more accurate to say that *the cell membrane is selective*. One explanation of this is that certain cells have special substances in them that hold onto substances that enter the cell. These special substances cannot diffuse out of the cell.

For instance, you know that red blood cells contain hemoglobin. Hemoglobin is a huge molecule containing iron that does not diffuse out of the blood cell. However, there are substances containing iron that are in solution in the blood or lymph. These substances can release the iron. Once the iron is released, it diffuses into the red blood cell through the cell membrane. Once inside the blood cell, the hemoglobin combines with the iron and firmly holds it. In a similar way, other body cells hold on to certain substances that diffuse in through their cell membranes.

When we say then that cells are in balance, we mean they are in balance with their environment. That is, they take in the substances they need to maintain their life activities. Thus, for example, a red blood cell is in balance with its environment (the blood plasma) when it takes in iron and other substances it needs to carry on its functions. To maintain this balance, a healthy cell membrane is needed.

If a cell membrane loses its ability to select the substances to diffuse into it, the cell dies. Boil a lettuce leaf. This will kill the cells and, of course, the cell membrane. The lettuce leaf will be limp. No matter how much you soak the boiled (dead) lettuce leaf in water, it will not become crisp again. The cells of the leaf are dead. The cell membranes are dead and are no longer semipermeable. All substances can now diffuse through the membranes into the cells and diffuse out again. Now the cell membranes cannot keep the cells in balance with their environment. When this occurs, the organism containing these cells is no longer alive.

REVIEW

1. What is the relationship of kinetic energy of molecules to diffusion?

2. What is the function of the cell membrane in regard to diffusion of substances into the cell?

3. How do you explain the selective nature of the membrane?

4. Suppose the cell membrane were impermeable. What might happen? State at least two consequences of total impermeability.

5. Suppose the cell membrane were completely permeable. State at least two consequences of total permeability.

6. Discuss the role of diffusion in (a) the movement of water into the roots, (b) the delivery of glucose to the cells.

NEW VIEW

1. How would you relate the kinetic energy of molecules to the rate of diffusion? Can you develop a theoretical statement that compares the speed of motion of particles with the rate of diffusion?

2. Can you develop a model that coincides with the constantly changing character of the cell membranes?

3. What will happen if you add distilled water to *Elodea* cells that have been soaked in sugar solution until they have begun to shrink?

3. REGULATION OF THE BODY BY CELLS

Apparently the man shown in the photograph is a giant; he is 9 feet 3 inches tall and twenty-six years old. ❶ But what made him so? His parents were of normal size. Would you be surprised to know that the secretion of certain cells is responsible for the giant size of the man in the picture? The cells responsible

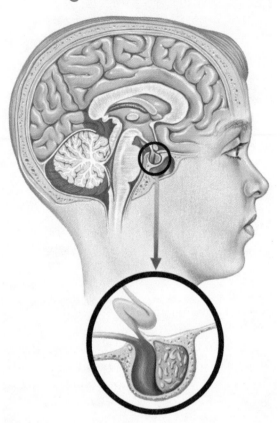

① PITUITARY GLAND

Hormones as Chemical Messengers

Early in this century a Canadian physician, Dr. F. G. Banting, and his co-worker C. H. Best did a remarkable series of experiments. Later they were joined by the chemist C. M. MacLeod. The results of these experiments have saved many lives.

You may already know of the disease known as diabetes. A person with diabetes does not oxidize glucose efficiently. The result is that glucose that would ordinarily be oxidized to build up ATP from ADP remains in the blood stream. The glucose, in turn, is excreted in the urine. Obviously, one test for diabetes is to determine whether the urine contains glucose. In moments of high excitement, all of us may excrete glucose in the urine, but the diabetic does it regularly.

Banting and Best made use of some clues left by the French scientist Claude Bernard. Bernard suggested that the pancreas, a gland lying near the stomach, had a substance in it that governed the oxidation of glucose. Banting and his co-workers decided to produce diabetes in animals. How could they do it? Based on Bernard's theory, they removed the pancreases from their experimental animals. Bernard was correct. These animals then developed diabetes. When they injected an extract of the pancreas into an animal whose pancreas had been removed and who, therefore, had diabetes, the animal recovered. It was a simple but brilliant piece of work. After many years of experimenting, the scientists developed a pure extract of *insulin*. Today different kinds of insulin are used in the treatment of diabetes, but the effect is the same. The insulin introduced into the blood stream enables the cells to oxidize glucose.

Actually the pancreas is a double gland. It is a **duct gland** as well as a **ductless gland.** A duct gland transports its substances by

for the secretion compose the **pituitary gland,** a small gland the size of a small walnut, found at the base of the brain, or just over the roof of the mouth. **①** These cells secrete a substance that affects the growth of the long bones of the body. Recall that a substance that is secreted by a gland directly into the *blood stream* and that has an effect elsewhere in the body is known as a *hormone.*

Hormones are being secreted by glandular cells in your body right now. You have come to expect that your body is never at rest; its cells are constantly at work. Now to the picture you already have of the cell's activities— oxidation, selection of substances by the membrane, the work of enzymes, the work of ATP, cell division—we add the work of hormones.

means of *ducts*. Thus the liver sends bile through a duct into the intestine. ❷ The bile, you will recall, helps in the digestion of fats. By means of a duct into the upper intestine, the pancreas sends digestive enzymes that digest proteins, fats, and carbohydrates. As such, the pancreas is a duct gland.

The pancreas also has groups of cells, or islands of cells, that secrete insulin directly into the blood stream. The insulin diffuses into the blood capillaries surrounding these cells. These islands of cells, called the *islets of Langerhans*, make the pancreas a *ductless* gland as well.

Insulin is a hormone, as we have indicated. It is a so-called chemical messenger. Although it is produced in the islets of Langerhans, it affects every cell of the body. You will sometimes see the word *endocrine* used for *hormone,* and the glands which secrete the endocrine are then called endocrine glands. An entire science called *endocrinology* is given over to their study.

One way to get a bird's-eye-view of hormones is to combine them into a table. Study the table on the following page of Some Endocrine Glands and Their Functions. Notice that an oversecretion of a hormone may produce one effect, while an undersecretion will produce another effect. For your body to be at the peak of health, the amount of hormones must be regulated. How this is done is not known, but we have several clues.

A Master Gland

As many different investigators continued their work into the function of the endocrine glands, the evidence seemed to point to the fact that in the normal body the glands worked together. Soon it became clear that when there was a failure of the pituitary gland, other glands also broke down.

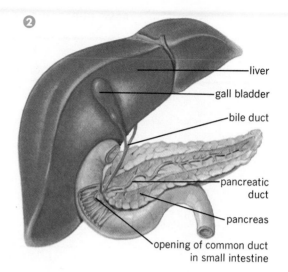

❷

liver
gall bladder
bile duct
pancreatic duct
pancreas
opening of common duct in small intestine

Over the years, it was finally worked out in the laboratory that the pituitary produced hormones that controlled the secretion of hormones by other glands. Thus secretions of the pituitary gland cause the sex glands (ovaries in the female, testes in the male) to produce their hormones. Still another secretion of the pituitary gland causes the mammary glands to secrete milk. And again, another pituitary secretion affects the islets of Langerhans, and still another the thyroid.

More and more evidence points to the concept that the many substances produced by the body cells affect each other. Further, many different substances may affect a single cell function. You know that the cell has its energy process. You have begun to know, further, that

a. the breakdown of ATP to ADP releases energy.

b. the breakdown (oxidation) of glucose is needed to build up ATP from ADP.

c. the oxidation of glucose is controlled by enzymes (respiratory enzymes).

d. the oxidation of glucose is also controlled by insulin, a hormone.

Gland	Hormone secreted	Role in the body	Effect of too much hormone	Effect of too little hormone
pancreas	insulin	sugar balance in blood	weakness, trembling, shock, coma, frequent hunger	diabetes
pituitary	(many)	control of other gland secretions	(many symptoms affected, depending upon gland)	
		growth	giantism	midget
		kidney function	excessive water in body	excessive loss of water
thyroid	thyroxin	oxidation rate of cells	irritability, nervous activity	lack of energy, poor development of tissues and growth when severe in infancy
parathyroid	parathormone	calcium and phosphorus balance	bone deformation	spasms or death if severe
adrenal medulla	adrenalin	stimulation to meet emergencies	increased blood pressure, pulse rate, glucose in blood	unknown
adrenal cortex	(several, including cortisone)	salt balance, carbohydrate metabolism	excessive maleness	Addison's disease
ovary	estrogen	development of female sex characteristics		interference with development of female sex characteristics
	progesterone	control of ovary and uterus during pregnancy		sterility or miscarriage
testis	testosterone	development of male sex characteristics		interference with development of male sex characteristics

Somehow all of these substances produced by cells act together to affect the work of the cells. How this is done is not yet known. But we are beginning to learn through the work of cell physiologists and biological chemists.

Plant Hormones

Do all organisms have hormones that regulate cellular activities? Do plants have hormones? Suppose you were to do the following investigation. ■

■ AN APPRENTICE INVESTIGATION into Plant Hormones and Phototropism

Fill 5 flower pots three quarters with sand. Then plant 5 oat seeds in each pot and add water so that the sand is moist but not wet. It must be kept moist and the pots kept away from direct heat. Label 2 pots A, 2 pots B, and 1 pot C.

As soon as the oat seedlings begin to push through the soil, place a box (a cardboard box), with a window cut out in one side, over two of the pots (labeled A). Place the pots against the side away from the cut-out window.❶ Let the oats in the remaining three pots grow for an additional day in complete darkness.

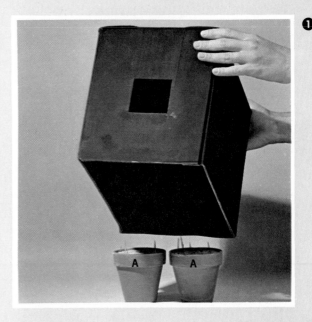

After the oats have grown at least a half inch tall, remove the two pots labeled B from the dark. With a sharp razor blade, cut about $\frac{1}{8}$ inch off the tip of each seedling.❷ What purpose does the remaining pot C serve?

Place the seedlings from which you have cut the tips in another box like the one you prepared before. Place the remaining pot of uncut seedlings (labeled C) in full sunlight. Turn the pot several times so that it gets the sun from all sides. After two days, compare all the seedlings. Were your results like those here?❸

An Investigation On Your Own

Devise a procedure to determine if plant hormones can reverse the results in pot B?

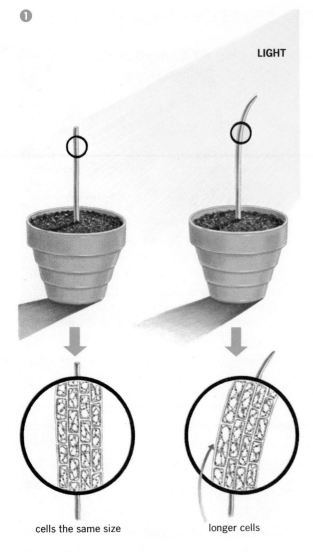

LIGHT

cells the same size   longer cells

How can you explain the observation that the seedlings with tips cut off did not bend toward the light? Or if they did bend, the bending could be very slight.

Suppose you assume that hormones were involved in making the plant bend. We call the response of a plant to a stimulus a **tropism** (trō′piz·əm). There are different kinds of tropisms, depending upon the stimulus. A **geotropism** is a response to gravity (*geo–*). A **phototropism** is a response to light

(*photo–*). In addition, the response can be either toward or away from the stimulus. If the response is growth *toward* the stimulus, it is called a *positive* tropism; growth away from the stimulus, a *negative* tropism. The response that you observed in the oat plant is a positive phototropism (a bending or growth toward light). Where would you say the hormones were produced? It would seem that the cells in the tips of the plants produced the hormones that caused the positive phototropism. Plant physiologists from the Netherlands, Fritz Went and Kenneth Thimann, did the early work showing that the tips of plants produce growth hormones. These plant hormones were named **auxins** (ôk′sinz).

How does an auxin act? Compare the cells of a seedling whose tip has been removed and those of one whose tip is intact.❶ You cannot help but notice that the cells on the side away from the light are longer than those on the side near the light. For reasons we do not yet understand, light causes the hormone to diffuse to the darker side of the plant. Once on the dark side, the hormone causes the elongation of the cells. Thus the plant bends as it grows longer on one side.

Balance as a Result of Cellular Action

The evidence is now overwhelming, is it not? Cells produce a great variety of substances, among which are enzymes and hormones. The enzymes affect all manner of body activities: digestion of carbohydrates, digestion of proteins, digestion of fats. The growth hormone of the pituitary affects growth of the bones, the sex hormones affect body form, insulin affects oxidation of glucose in the cells. An increase or a decrease of a single hormone can change the body's functions. Hormones obviously affect the way the body works. They keep it in balance.

Everywhere we look, it becomes clear that living things are made of cells. The cell is the unit of structure of the organism. Everywhere we look at an organism, we see the cell's activities affecting the body's function. Clearly, the cell is the unit of function as well. Put the two concepts together: *The cell is the unit of both structure and function in an organism.*

REVIEW

1. Distinguish between hormones and enzymes.

2. What is the function of the master gland?

3. Compare or contrast the functions of the adrenal medulla and the adrenal cortex.

4. What are certain of the functions of estrogen, progesterone, and testosterone?

5. How do plant hormones differ in their action from animal hormones?

NEW VIEW

1. How does an auxin act to cause a *positive* geotropism of the tip of the root? a *negative* geotropism of the tip of the stem?

2. What might be done to isolate an auxin? What might be done to isolate a hormone such as cortisone? The library will help.

4. RELATING THE CONCEPTS

As you grow in experience, the concepts you have begun to develop grow in depth. Through the study of living things, you come to know the beauty of the organization of living things. Their organization seems so simple, so economical in design. Yet there is unity. The unit of organization of the multicellular organism is the cell. The cell is also the unit of function. Now you can add to your large concept of organisms: *Cells, through their chemical functions, that is, through their secretion of substances, coordinate the functions of organisms.*

The study of the chemical function of cells in balancing the body discloses these following concepts.

Reviewing the Concepts

▶ *To maintain their functions, the cells in an organism require a balanced intake of matter and energy.* Food substances—carbohydrates, fats, proteins, minerals, vitamins, and water—furnish the matter and energy intake of the body. In the main, carbohydrates and fats are used by cells to derive energy for movement, growth, and repair. Proteins, also used as a source of energy, furnish substances (matter) for the repair of the body, as do minerals—calcium carbonate for bone structure, iron for hemoglobin in the red blood cells, and the like. Vitamins are often the source of substances that coordinate the body, such as respirative enzymes.

▶ *Cells secrete substances that coordinate body activities.* Recall that digestive enzymes secreted by cells break down food substances so that they are fit for absorption by the body. Cells produce digestive enzymes to oxidize the food.

Moreover, cells produce hormones that coordinate central activities of the body, such as growth (thyroxin and the growth hormone from the pituitary) and utilization of sugar (insulin).

▶ *Through the function of its cell membrane, the cell regulates intake and exit of substances.* The cell membrane has the singular property of selectivity. Through its activity (not yet fully understood) the cell membrane regulates the diffusion of substances useful in its metabolism.

► *In multicellular organisms the cell is specialized in its structure and function.* In the multicellular organism, cells are specialists. Thyroid cells do *not* produce insulin; they produce thyroxin. The thyroid cell is a specialist.

Similarly, a nerve cell does not contract to move bones. It specializes in carrying impulses.

In a multicellular organism, when a cell becomes a specialist, it performs one special function and generally loses other functions.

Thus a muscle cell that is specialized for contraction doesn't secrete substances to form bones; bone cells take care of their special function.

How beautifully an organism is coordinated through the activities of its cells.

Testing Yourself

1. An organism exchanges matter and energy with the environment. Support this statement with specific examples.

2. What do we mean when we say an organism is organized for specific life activities. Give specific examples.

3. The cells of an organism are the units of structure. Use specific examples to support this statement.

4. Cells within a multicellular organism are specialized for their function. Support this statement with specific examples.

5. Through their action, cells coordinate the body functions. Name some specific examples.

6. Why don't all substances enter or leave the body with equal ease? Support your answer with examples.

7. How do cells regulate the function of growth?

8. How do cells regulate the function of oxidation of sugar?

9. What would happen if the body did not have a sufficient intake of
   a. proteins?
   b. minerals?
   c. glucose?
   d. vitamin A?
   e. riboflavin?

10. What would happen if the body secreted
   a. insufficient thyroxin?
   b. insufficient insulin?
   c. excessive pituitary growth hormone?
   d. excessive thyroxin?

Extending the Concepts

Investigation 1. Make a study into the historic collaboration that produced insulin. Your study should disclose how Banting arrived at his problem, what Best and MacLeod each contributed, what effect the discovery of insulin has had on other research.

Investigation 2. The substance *gibberellin* has an effect on the growth of plants. Does it have an effect on the reproduction of a protozoan, such as *Paramecium?* Set up an investigation to help you determine this.

In your experimental procedure, be certain to set up your control experiments to isolate the following factors.

Concentration of Gibberellin. In many cases, too much of a substance inhibits growth. It may even be poisonous. Too little of the substance may have no effect. To determine the *optimum* (the best) concentration is often difficult.

Concentration of the Organisms. How will you count your paramecia?

Theoretically speaking, is gibberellin a hormonelike substance or an enzymelike substance? (Recall that a theory is an explanation of facts or observations.)

Certain substances (particularly antibiotics) have been used to accelerate the growth of young animals, especially pigs. Do these substances accelerate the growth of insects, such as grasshoppers or crickets?

One reason for the choice of crickets is that these animals undergo *incomplete metamorphosis*, that is, the young are recognizable because they have somewhat the form of the adult. Nevertheless, they molt as they grow from young to adult. You have, therefore, a way of recognizing growth by counting the number of molts.

Perhaps these substances will increase the growth of young to adult by speeding up molting, without a great increase in size.

Suggested Reading

Tanner, J. M., G. R. Taylor, and the Editors of LIFE, *Growth*, New York, Time, Inc., 1965.

Ames, Gerald, and Rose Wyler, *Food and Life*, Mankato, Minnesota, Creative Educational Society, 1966.

Cannon, Walter B., *The Wisdom of the Body*, New York, Norton, 1963.

Gerard, Ralph W., editor, *Food for Life* (Phoenix Science Series), Chicago, University of Chicago Press, 1965.

Ravielli, Anthony, *Wonders of the Human Body*, New York, Viking Press, 1954.

9 | The Capture of Energy by Cells

To be alive requires energy. When hearts beat, when muscles contract, when food is digested, or when cells change starch to glucose, energy is being used. No physical or chemical change in any living organism occurs without some change in energy. Where do we get the energy for our hearts to beat, for our muscles to lift books or to bicycle? "From food substances," you would say. But food substances (such as carbohydrates, fats, and proteins) are made up of matter that is converted into energy. For matter (such as carbohydrates) to be converted into energy, the carbohydrates must have energy stored in them. Where do carbohydrates get their store of energy? You probably suspect the answer from your earlier work in science. You probably know that green plants make carbohydrates. Today we know much more about the way in which green plants make food than did van Helmont, Priestley, Jan Ingenhousz and other early investigators of photosynthesis. Today we also know more about how plants capture energy.

First, we shall look at what seems plainly obvious as we examine the capture of energy by a plant. This was not at all obvious, however, several hundred years ago. Then secondly, we shall look inside the process from the viewpoint of what scientists are discovering about the capture of energy even as you read this.

1. A BASIC PROCESS

Early in the 17th century, the scientist Jean-Baptiste van Helmont planned a most important experiment. It seemed simple. First he filled a large tub with 200 pounds of soil that had been dried in a furnace. He then moistened the soil thoroughly with rainwater and planted a young willow tree that weighed 5 pounds.❶

During the five-year growing period, van Helmont moistened the soil with rainwater when there was need. He devised a cover for the vessel to keep out additional dirt. The tree grew and grew.

After five years, van Helmont removed the tree, roots and all, and found that it weighed 169 pounds and 3 ounces.❷ He again dried the soil and found the original weight of the soil, which was 200 pounds, lacking only two ounces. He then concluded that 164 pounds of wood, bark, and roots came from the *water* only.

Was he right? It would be more nearly correct to say that he was partly right. Remember that he worked early in the 17th century, when little was known about the growth of plants. Today we know that plants take in much more than water. Many years after van Helmont's experiment, Joseph Priestley, working in the late 1700's, discovered that, in addition to water, a plant takes in *carbon dioxide* (CO_2) from the air. He found, too, that green plants release oxygen (O_2).

Seven years after Priestley's discovery, Jan Ingenhousz showed that plants could restore oxygen to the air when there was sufficient sunlight. In short, light was necessary for the production of oxygen.

Thus, on the basis of such experiments 150 years ago, the first general outlines of how a green plant restored oxygen to the air were beginning to be understood. We know more about the process today, but not nearly enough.

Why is this process important? Simply this: If green plants were to halt the process of producing oxygen, life on earth would cease. It would cease not only because oxygen was not being produced, but also because food was not being produced. To gain further insight into the process, first review carefully the structure of the green plant (Chapter 6).

Recall that in water there are dissolved minerals and the dissolved gases, oxygen and carbon dioxide. Recall, too, that air is made up mainly of nitrogen, oxygen, carbon dioxide, water vapor, and some other gases, mainly argon and helium.

Which of the elements and compounds in water and air does the plant use for its growth? Of course, you already know which of these elements are useful from your knowledge of the work of van Helmont, Priestley, and Jan Ingenhousz. You are also now aware

VAN HELMONT'S WILLOW TREE

❶ original tree

soil = 200 pounds
tree =   5 pounds
TOTAL = 205 pounds

❷ after 5 years growth

soil = 199 pounds 14 ounces
tree = 169 pounds 3 ounces
       368 pounds 17 ounces
TOTAL = 369 pounds 1 ounce

■ AN APPRENTICE INVESTIGATION into Growth in a Green Plant

How tall was it after two weeks of growth? ❸ One class found that their plants grew about an inch and a half in two weeks.

Since the coleus was sealed in the plastic bag, it must have taken certain substances for growth from the substances in the bag. Obviously they came from the air and water in the bag. Did any come from the soil? Which?

An Investigation On Your Own

Determine whether seeds, say radish or marigold seeds, will grow into young plants in a similar environment. How much do the young plants grow between the first and second week? How will you measure the plants without opening the bag? This may be difficult, but you are equal to the task.

Take a young coleus plant in a small pot of garden soil. Water the soil thoroughly. Place a large plastic bag over the plant. You may have to use sticks to keep the bag from touching the leaves. ❶ Tie the bag so that no air gets into it and place it where it gets good light but not direct sunlight, which would heat it. Do this if only to convince yourself that a green plant such as coleus grows even when imprisoned.

How tall was the plant when you started? ❷

of the elements contained in the molecules of the substances that sustain life. See for yourself the importance of the process of food-making in plants by doing the investigation above. Let's examine a little closer the environment that is necessary for the green plant to capture energy. ■

Green plants appear to be green only when grown in light. From your work in Chapter 7, you know that the green leaf contains chlorophyll. It is this substance which requires light in order to develop. If no light is available, the chloroplasts, the bodies that make the chlorophyll, do not manufacture chlorophyll. In fact, if any green plant is permitted to develop without light, they grow more spindly and white. We say they are **etiolated** (ē′tē·ə·lāt′əd). Look at the photographs of two potato plants: Pot A has been grown on a window sill. ❶ Pot B has been grown in a dark closet. ❷ Apparently in some way *chlorophyll* (in the chloroplast) and the presence of *light* are connected.

Look at the photograph of the geranium plant growing in light. ❸ Half of one of its leaves has been covered with dark paper to keep the light from hitting it. The leaf was removed later from the plant and tested for starch by placing it in a weak iodine solution. Notice the results. ❹ The half of the leaf that was exposed to the light turned a blueblack color. This shows that starch was present. The half of the leaf covered with black paper remained the color of the iodine solution, showing that no starch was present. What does this mean?

The geranium seems to make starch only in light. Actually, it makes the sugar glucose. The glucose is then changed into starch. Let's analyze sugar and starch for a moment to see whether or not the structure of these com-

pounds gives us a clue to what happens as plants use light in the presence of chlorophyll.

Turn back to Chapter 7, page 164, and study again the model of a glucose molecule. The model shows that glucose contains carbon, hydrogen, and oxygen. From carbon, hydrogen, and oxygen, then, green plants must make the glucose. The plants then polymerize the glucose molecules into starch.

However green plants make glucose *only in light* as a result of the capture of light by chlorophyll. Light, as energy, is basic to the world ecosystem.

What is the plant's source of carbon for making glucose? Remember the sealed plastic bag with the green plant? A brief analysis was made of what composed the plant's environment: air and water. To go a step further, you know that air contains the gases nitrogen, oxygen, water vapor, carbon dioxide, and argon. The only source of carbon for the plant seems to be the carbon dioxide. Do you know of any other possible source? Is it true that the plant gets its carbon from the carbon dioxide? See for yourself. ■

On the basis of many experiments done by scientists over the world, it is clear that green plants absorb carbon dioxide (CO_2). This carbon dioxide is the source of the carbon and oxygen that plants use in making glucose. Water (H_2O) is the source of the hydrogen—the remaining substance needed for making a molecule of glucose.

Furthermore, these experiments indicate that carbon dioxide is taken in *in the presence of light,* not in the absence of light. In most green plants, such as the geranium or oak or corn plant, the carbon dioxide in the air enters the plant through the *stomata.*

To summarize for a moment, you now know the following about green plants.

a. Green plants have chlorophyll.

b. As a result of the capture of light by chlorophyll, green plants make sugar and starch.

c. Green plants use carbon dioxide (CO_2) and water (H_2O) as their sources of carbon, hydrogen, and oxygen.

On the basis of many experiments done by many scientists, it seems clear that somehow, in the presence of light, green plants use chlorophyll to combine atoms of hydrogen, carbon, and oxygen into glucose. (As you shall see later, some oxygen is released by the plant when this happens.) This process is known as **photosynthesis.** The word *photosynthesis* literally means a *putting together* (synthesis) in the presence of *light* (photo). It must be obvious to you that without photosynthesis, life as we know it could not go on.

Photosynthesis is the basic process by which the green plant captures the sun's energy. It uses this energy to make glucose and, in turn, other substances upon which all animals and even some other nongreen plants [**fungi** (fun′jī)] are completely dependent. Photosynthesis is basic to the health of any ecosystem. True?

REVIEW

1. A fungus plant cannot photosynthesize. Why not?

2. If a corn plant is grown in deep shade, it becomes pale green, and soon topples over. How do you explain this?

3. What is the source of the green plant's carbon? hydrogen? oxygen? Describe an investigation which supports your statement on the absorption of one of these three elements.

NEW VIEW

1. We are dependent upon green plants, but green plants are not dependent upon us. How true is this statement?

2. Chlorophyll has sometimes been called the most important substance in the world. Why?

3. Carry out your own investigation of the relation of starch production and light, using a procedure similar to that on page 205. But in your investigation, use a different kind of plant, such as a potato. How do your results compare with those in the photographs on page 205?

■ AN APPRENTICE INVESTIGATION into the Use of Carbon Dioxide by Plants

You will need six test tubes with stoppers, sprigs of green water plants such as *Elodea*, aquarium water, and about 25 ml of 0.1 percent bromthymol (brōm'thī'mol) blue solution. Pour the bromthymol blue solution into a beaker and add enough aquarium water to fill the six test tubes. Then, with a straw, blow your breath into the bromthymol solution in the beaker. The carbon dioxide in your exhaled breath will turn the bromthymol blue solution a *yellow color*. The yellow color indicates the presence of carbon dioxide. Place a sprig of water plant into each of four test tubes. Fill all six test tubes with the yellow solution and stopper them. The test tubes without plants are the controls.❶

Place all the test tubes in medium sunlight. In an hour or so, the water in the test tubes containing the green plants will turn blue.❷ The yellow bromthymol blue has turned blue again. The carbon dioxide which originally changed the bromthymol blue to yellow has apparently left the test tube. Where has it gone?

The two test tubes without plants tell us the answer. Since the aquarium water in these test tubes is still yellow, carbon dioxide must still be present in the water. It did not escape into the air. Therefore, in the other four test tubes the plants probably absorbed the carbon dioxide. It seems, then, that *the Elodea has taken in carbon dioxide.*

An Investigation On Your Own

In what kind of light does photosynthesis occur at its *optimum*? (*Clue:* Try test tubes wrapped in cellophane of different colors. Also, the growth of *Elodea* can be measured by increase in length, so why not an increase in width?)

2. PHOTOSYNTHESIS— A DIFFERENT VIEW

You have now begun a study of the process of photosynthesis. You have some idea of what raw materials are taken into the plant and how they are used. You know that light energy is required, and you are now somewhat acquainted with chlorophyll.

However, photosynthesis is, as you can imagine, a very complex process. What really takes place in the green plant? The way in which the photosynthetic process occurs is much the same in all green plants, from the smallest alga to the giant redwood tree.

What you have learned up to now has been known for quite some time. But scientists have been investigating the process of photosynthesis much more thoroughly for many years now. As you might expect, today much is known about the process.

Scientists now believe the process of photosynthesis occurs in two main steps. One of these steps can occur in the dark, and thus is known as the **dark reaction** and the other, called the **light reaction,** can occur *only* in the light. It was believed not long ago that the dark reaction could occur only in the dark, but it is now known that this reaction also occurs in the light.

The Light Reaction

The light reaction always occurs first. Light energy is captured by the chlorophyll of the plant. The light energy is then transformed into chemical energy bound up in the chlorophyll molecules in the plant. The energy now is available for splitting the water molecules taken in by the plant. Refer to the diagram on the opposite page as you read on about the different steps in photosynthesis. ❶

Notice that a molecule of oxygen (O_2) is released during this reaction. Recent investigations have shown that the oxygen given off by green plants during photosynthesis is given off as the water molecules are split. Notice that hydrogen (H_2) is also produced as the water molecules are split.

The Dark Reaction

Once the water molecule is split, the hydrogen now quickly combines with the carbon dioxide, CO_2, to form water and another simple substance. This substance eventually forms the sugar glucose, as shown in the diagram. ❶ This simple substance is given the general formula CH_2O. It is easy to see how six molecules of this substance might be combined into glucose ($C_6H_{12}O_6$). However, all of the precise steps leading to the formation of the glucose in the green leaf are still not fully understood. But as research continues, the facts will accumulate and theories will develop to explain the evidence.

When we write the complete chemical reaction for photosynthesis, the light and dark reactions are combined into one reaction. ❷ This simple chemical equation summarizes all the intermediate reactions. However, it is enough to understand this equation for the

❷   PHOTOSYNTHESIS EQUATION

$$12\,H_2O + 6\,CO_2 + \text{light energy} \xrightarrow{\text{chlorophyll}} C_6H_{12}O_6 + 6\,O_2 + 6\,H_2O$$

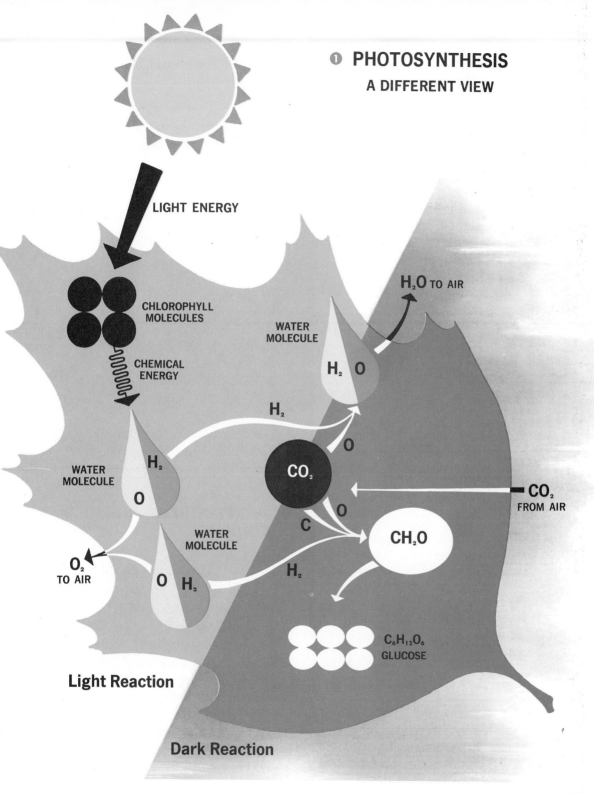

● PHOTOSYNTHESIS
A DIFFERENT VIEW

LIGHT ENERGY

CHLOROPHYLL
MOLECULES

CHEMICAL
ENERGY

WATER
MOLECULE

H_2 O

H_2O TO AIR

H_2

O

CO_2

CO_2
FROM AIR

WATER
MOLECULE

H_2

O

C

O

CH_2O

WATER
MOLECULE

O H_2

H_2

O_2
TO AIR

$C_6H_{12}O_6$
GLUCOSE

Light Reaction

Dark Reaction

present. As you go on in your study of science, you will have an opportunity to examine new evidence as it is discovered. The study of photosynthesis will continue until it is fully understood, since it is the basic energy process in the world of living things.

The highlights of photosynthesis are summarized in the following table.

As you learned in Chapter 7, the main product of photosynthesis, glucose, is soon polymerized into starch. From the carbohydrates (glucose and starch) the green plant can synthesize fats and proteins.

SUMMARY OF PHOTOSYNTHESIS

Location	in plant cells containing chlorophyll
Necessary materials	water, carbon dioxide
Time of occurrence	first step occurs when light shines on plant cells. The remaining steps occur with or without light.
Changes in energy	light energy changed to, and stored as, chemical energy
Changes in substances	CO_2 and H_2O used to form glucose, and then later, starch and other substances. This results in growth of plant and, therefore, in an increase in size and weight of plant.
Products	oxygen released into surrounding environment, water released, and glucose made available for the processes of living

REVIEW

1. Develop your own table (in your notebook) of the steps occurring in photosynthesis, like this.

Photosynthesis

Parts of organisms in which it takes place
The materials necessary
When it occurs
Changes in energy
Changes in matter
Products made

2. What is the source of the oxygen that green plants release?

NEW VIEW

It is possible to "tag" an atom by using radioactive atoms. Thus, it is possible to form water from hydrogen and a special radioactive form of oxygen. Let's call this oxygen O^x.

A green plant is watered with H_2O^x. It is given CO_2 as well. The oxygen in the carbon dioxide is not O^x. It is regular oxygen (O).

You know oxygen is given off by the green plant as it photosynthesizes. Which type of oxygen will be given off?

3. PHOTOSYNTHESIS AND OTHER SYNTHESES

Plant cells

a. carry on photosynthesis.
b. synthesize all of their needed carbohydrates, proteins, and fats.
c. synthesize many other substances, for example, vitamins.

However, before plant cells can synthesize other substances, the plant must first engage in photosynthesis. Photosynthesis and its production of glucose is the first step to all other plant activities. For instance, recall that molecules of glucose may be polymerized to make starch. Recall, too, that plants and animals store much of their food supply as starch. But some plants store part of their food as proteins or as fats. For instance, the seeds of the bean plant have a high protein content. Other seeds, for example, nuts, have a high fat content. You may know, for instance, that the cotton seed has a great store of oil. The corn that we eat, a seed, is also high in fat content.

Just as chlorophyll was necessary for the process of photosynthesis, other special substances are necessary to synthesize fats, proteins, and vitamins. These specific substances, you will recall, are the enzymes (Chapter 8). Enzymes not only function in the synthesis of carbohydrates, fats, proteins, and vitamins, they also function in breaking them down. In the dark reaction in photosynthesis, enzymes are necessary for putting the CH_2O molecules together into glucose with six carbon atoms, $C_6H_{12}O_6$.

Plants and animals have many enzyme systems in common, but only green plants are able to use the radiant energy of light by means of photosynthesis. Animals must get their energy by eating plants or other animals that have eaten plants.

There are exceptions, however, to the general rule that all living organisms except green plants must depend directly or indirectly upon green plants for their food. There is a group of plants able to make food without light. The energy they use for making food substances comes from sources other than light and the process of photosynthesis.

In the discussions of photosynthesis and all other kinds of synthesis, you should not lose sight of the main point: It is the *energy* that is important. The products made are important only in terms of their ability to store and release the energy that is needed to carry on the activities of living.

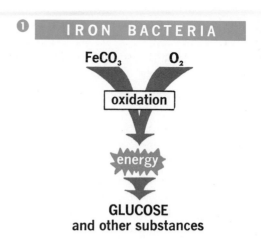

❶ IRON BACTERIA

$FeCO_3$ O_2

oxidation

energy

GLUCOSE and other substances

Energy, of course, must be obtained in order to synthesize substances such as glucose, protein, fat, or vitamins. And green plants are able to capture this energy from light. If green plants got this energy from some other source, *it would be just as useful.* In fact, as we stated before, there are such plants. These plants are called **chemosynthetic** (kēm′ō·sin·thet′ik) plants. *Photosyn*thetic plants get their energy from light. *Chemo*synthetic plants get their energy from chemicals. (It is better to say *substances* or *chemical energy* than it is to say *chemicals.*) In the correct terms, photosynthetic plants use radiant energy, while chemosynthetic plants use chemical energy.

Chemosynthetic Plants

One group of these chemosynthetic plants uses *iron* rather than light as its source of basic energy for manufacturing food substances. These are the so-called **iron bacteria.** The iron bacteria live in water that contains large amounts of dissolved iron compounds, such as iron carbonate ($FeCO_3$). The bacteria absorb the iron compounds and combine them with oxygen (oxidation).❶ In short, they oxidize iron carbonate. This oxidation

process releases energy that is then used to synthesize substances such as sugars, fats, and proteins.

There are also other chemosynthetic bacteria. One kind lives in water, soils, and sewage containing large amounts of hydrogen sulfide (H_2S). (Hydrogen sulfide gives spoiled eggs their odor.) These chemosynthetic bacteria are known as **sulfur bacteria.** They are able to use hydrogen sulfide as a source of energy to make their glucose.**❶** The sulfur bacteria then use the energy in glucose (as any green plant does) to carry on the processes of living. Other chemosynthetic bacteria, the **hydrogen bacteria,** oxidize hydrogen to get energy.

Where does the energy come from that these bacteria are able to use from iron, hydrogen sulfide, and hydrogen? It is easy to show sunlight is a source of energy, so it is not difficult to believe that green plants can use the sun's energy to manufacture food. However, it is more difficult to understand how the oxidation of iron, hydrogen sulfide, and hydrogen releases energy.

Have you ever seen hydrogen produced? It can be produced by breaking apart water molecules (H_2O) with an electric current.

This process is called **electrolysis** (i·lek′trol′ ə·sis) and is easily done. ▉

Where did the hydrogen get its energy? The energy released in the tiny explosion did not come just from the hydrogen. It actually came from the *chemical reaction* as the hydrogen combined with oxygen from the air. Remember that *electrical energy* was necessary to separate the hydrogen from the oxygen in the water molecules. Therefore, breaking water molecules into hydrogen and oxygen *consumes energy.* Combining hydrogen and oxygen to make molecules of water *releases energy.* These reactions can be written like this:

$$2H_2O + \text{electrical } \textbf{energy} \xrightarrow{\text{acid}} 2H_2 + O_2$$

and

$$2H_2 + O_2 \xrightarrow[\text{match}]{\text{lighted}} 2H_2O + \textbf{energy}$$

Think about winding a watch. The parts of the watch themselves do not have energy. But if you wind the watch, the energy from the movement of your fingers winds up a spring in the watch. Now the watch contains *energy,* and it will slowly release that energy in turning the hands of the watch.

Some chemical reactions are similar to locking up energy in the spring of a watch. If you put energy into causing a chemical reaction to occur, that same energy can usually be taken out again by reversing the chemical reaction. As you just saw, it takes energy to break up a water molecule into hydrogen and oxygen. You can get that energy back again by oxidizing hydrogen (combining it again with oxygen). This is what the hydrogen bacteria do. They simply trigger off a chemical reaction (in which hydrogen takes part) that releases energy. The other chemosynthetic

■ AN APPRENTICE INVESTIGATION into Breaking Apart Water Molecules

Carefully add a few drops of sulfuric acid to water in a Hoffman apparatus, and connect the wires from the electrodes to a 6-volt or a 12-volt battery. Some of the water breaks up into hydrogen and oxygen. Hydrogen collects in one tube of the apparatus, oxygen collects in the other tube.

By inverting a small, dry test tube over each tube of the apparatus and opening the clamps, you can collect one test tube of hydrogen and another test tube of oxygen.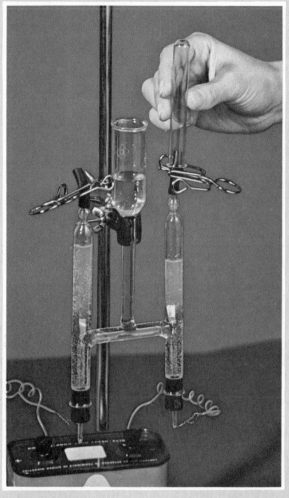

When a lighted match is brought to the mouth of the test tube of hydrogen, the gas explodes with a loud pop. Energy has been released. The hydrogen has combined suddenly with oxygen in the air to form water again. You can see the tiny drops of water on the walls of the test tube.

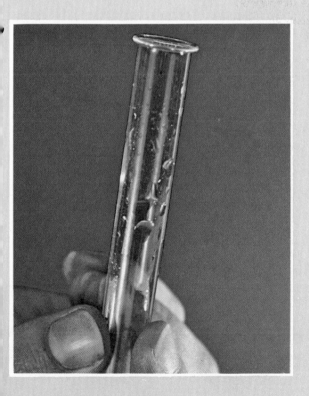

An Investigation On Your Own

On the basis of the volumes of gas collected, predict which tube of the Hoffman apparatus contains the hydrogen, the oxygen. Verify your prediction.

You probably know that a battery has both a positive and a negative terminal. Determine the relationship that exists between the gas collected in each tube and the terminal of the battery to which the electrode in that tube is connected. Plan your procedure carefully.

213

$$12\,H_2O + 6\,CO_2 + \text{light energy} \xrightarrow{\text{chlorophyll}} C_6H_{12}O_6 + 6\,O_2 + 6\,H_2O$$

bacteria also release energy by their chemical reactions. The iron bacteria oxidize iron. The sulfur bacteria oxidize sulfur. Both reactions release energy.

What, then, is an essential difference between photosynthesis and chemosynthesis? The photosynthetic process is different, at least in one way, from the process by which the chemosynthetic bacteria get energy. The bacteria obtain energy to produce glucose by oxidizing hydrogen or other substances.

Look again at the equation for photosynthesis. ❶ In a way, what the green plant does may be compared to winding a watch or coiling a spring. The green plant takes two substances (CO_2 and H_2O) each without energy available to the plant, and combines them into a new substance (sugar) that contains energy. However, the green plant must use energy to combine these substances. The energy used in combining the two substances comes from the sunlight trapped by the chlorophyll molecules. Thus the process of photosynthesis is, in a sense, one of trapping and storing the energy from sunlight, just as winding a watch is, in a sense, one of capturing the energy from your muscles and storing it in the coiled watch spring.

Photosynthesis and Respiration

In green plants the trapping of energy—the coiling of the "energy spring"—is photosynthesis. In both plants and animals the releasing of energy—the uncoiling of the energy spring—is a kind of burning process that occurs within living cells, called *respiration,* or *cellular oxidation,* or just plain *oxidation.*

Read again the equation for the process of photosynthesis. Notice that light energy is an essential ingredient for the chemical reaction to take place. Keep in mind that it is this light energy that is finally locked up in the glucose.

Respiration (cellular oxidation) is essentially the reverse of photosynthesis. Here is the usual way chemists show this process of cellular oxidation. ❷ The arrow beside the word *energy* indicates that energy is released by cellular oxidation. Why is there no similar arrow in the equation for photosynthesis?

This release of energy by an oxidation process in the cells is not so different from the oxidation of chemosynthetic bacteria. Only the substance used is different. The release of energy in our body cells results from the oxidation of glucose. The release of energy in chemosynthetic bacteria results from the

$$6\,O_2 + C_6H_{12}O_6 \longrightarrow 6\,H_2O + 6\,CO_2 + \text{energy} \uparrow$$

oxygen   glucose   water   carbon dioxide

oxidation of hydrogen and other substances.

Now you can see how chemosynthesis in bacteria is related to photosynthesis in green plants. If you again compare the process to the winding of a watch, green plants use the energy of sunlight to coil the energy spring, while chemosynthetic bacteria themselves release the energy needed to coil the energy spring. In both instances the energy is stored in glucose. Then as either green plants or chemosynthetic bacteria need energy to manufacture other foods or to carry on the processes of growing and living, they uncoil the spring by oxidizing the glucose.

The Cell's Energy Process and Photosynthesis

Let's place the cell's energy process, which you studied in Chapter 7, page 172, in a very practical everyday situation in the human body, for example, in a gland cell producing saliva. To produce saliva, the cell requires energy.

1. Remember the changes of ATP to ADP.

$$ATP \longrightarrow ADP + P + \textbf{energy}$$

2. The gland cell resynthesizes ATP in the following way:

$$\textbf{energy} + ADP + P \longrightarrow ATP$$

3. The cell gets the energy it needs to resynthesize ATP by oxidizing the glucose it has synthesized:

$$C_6H_{12}O_6 + 6O_2 \longrightarrow 6CO_2 + 6H_2O + \textbf{energy}$$
glucose

In your body, the salivary gland cells, as well as all the cells of your body, get their energy from glucose either directly or indirectly from plants. *Therefore, the basic source of all energy for all animal cells is the process of photosynthesis with its resulting glucose.*

In a sense, then, even the energy released when ATP breaks down was put there from the glucose made as chlorophyll captured the sun's radiant energy.

REVIEW

1. Give a detailed account of your understanding of the reason why green plants are called "energy producers."

2. How do chemosynthetic plants such as iron bacteria secure their energy?

3. What chemical reaction do you know that can be compared to the energy released by the spring of a watch? Where did each substance get the energy that is released?

4. What process carried on by green plants is comparable to the winding of a watch? Explain your answer.

5. Show how respiration is the opposite of photosynthesis both chemically and in terms of energy locked up or released.

NEW VIEW

1. Are chemosynthetic bacteria energy producers or energy consumers? Explain your answer.

2. Are chemosynthetic bacteria more like green plants or more like animals in the manner in which they secure energy? Explain your answer.

3. Certain chemosynthetic bacteria secure energy by oxidizing hydrogen. Do you think it possible for bacteria to secure energy by oxidizing water? Explain. (In answering, keep in mind that it takes energy to separate a water molecule into hydrogen and oxygen.)

4. Why are animals often called "energy consumers"?

5. Now that you know more about photosynthesis and chemosynthesis, what would your answer be to these questions? Could animals live without green plants? Could green plants live without animals?

4. RELATING THE CONCEPTS

A botanist once said that if he were to choose the single most terrible disease in the world, he would choose a disease that would destroy chlorophyll. Do you agree? Why?

Perhaps the reasoning that led the botanist to insist that the loss of chlorophyll would be disastrous to the world followed the concepts of this chapter. Think about this as you review the following concepts.

Reviewing the Concepts

▶ *The basic source of energy for life processes is light energy.* Without light energy, the process of photosynthesis does not occur. Without the food-making by photosynthesis, all organisms would die; they simply would lack the chemical energy (food substances) necessary for their metabolism, or life activities. Although part of the process of making carbohydrates (sugar and starch) can occur in the dark (the dark reaction), the initial process, the combination of CO_2 and H_2O in the presence of chlorophyll, requires light energy.

▶ *The photosynthetic process is basic to the metabolic processes in all living things.* The basic reaction in photosynthesis

$$\text{energy} + 6\,CO_2 + 6\,H_2O \longrightarrow C_6H_{12}O_6 + 6\,O_2$$

locks up chemical energy in the form of food. Respiration (oxidation), releasing the stored energy in food, is opposite to photosynthesis.

$$6\,O_2 + C_6H_{12}O_6 \longrightarrow 6\,CO_2 + 6\,H_2O + \text{energy}$$

Furthermore, carbohydrates, such as glucose, produced in photosynthesis are needed for polymerization of starches, proteins, and fats.

▶ *Organisms interchange matter and energy with the environment.* Naturally, this concept is no longer new to you. Whenever and wherever you have studied organisms, you have found them taking matter (CO_2, H_2O, carbohydrates, fats, protein) and its stored energy from the environment and returning matter (CO_2, H_2O, and in the case of green plants, O_2) and its stored energy to the environment.

The activities of chemosynthetic organisms (that is, organisms other than photosynthetic ones) certainly fit into this concept.

▶ *Organisms are interdependent with each other and with the environment.* This is a vast and major concept (or as it is sometimes called, a conceptual scheme). A conceptual scheme is a major organizing idea through which we view the world around us.

For instance, do you find *any organism* that is not interdependent with its environment? You would certainly become a famous scientist if you ever did.

Testing Yourself

1. Complete the following reaction:

$$\text{energy} + \ ? \ + H_2O \xrightarrow[\text{chlorophyll}]{\text{sunlight}} C_6H_{12}O_6 + O_2$$

2. Complete the following reaction:

$$C_6H_{12}O_6 + \ ? \ \longrightarrow CO_2 + H_2O + \text{energy}$$

3. Which of these following substances is the source of the oxygen (O_2) for the production of glucose: H_2O or CO_2?

What evidence indicates this?

4. How is photosynthesis a chemosynthetic activity?

How is the photosynthesis of green plants more important to the activity of animals than the chemosynthetic activity of bacteria?

5. Describe the release of energy in a chemosynthetic organism. How is the process different from, and similar to, photosynthesis?

6. We understand now what was wrong with van Helmont's conclusion. After all, he was a brilliant scientist. Why didn't he see what was wrong?

7. The sun is the original source of energy for *all life*. Do you find any exception to this? Perhaps chemosynthetic bacteria are an exception. Are they? Explain.

Extending the Concepts

Investigation 1. In order to survive, men who will live for long periods of time in their spaceships will require food and oxygen, of course. They will also need to get rid of wastes such as CO_2 and H_2O.

One of the methods of survival being considered is the use of a green algae, such as *Chlorella* (klor·el′ə). *Chlorella* is a single-celled green plant which, as a green plant, photosynthesizes.

Can you develop a system whereby the algae can be used to furnish O_2 and food, and remove CO_2 and H_2O, from the spaceship? (It is said that *Chlorella* makes a satisfying cake to eat, a kind of plant hamburger.)

Try to draw a diagram of the scheme you have invented. Of course, such schemes and blueprints are already in existence. Try to find one or several.

Investigation 2. Are all chloroplasts the same shape? You have already studied *Elodea* and geranium plants and have some idea of the shape of chloroplasts. What was the shape of those that you saw?

Study several plants to begin with, plants in different plant groups—algae, mosses, ferns, seed plants.

Is there any similarity in the shape of chloroplasts in a given group of plants, say, the mosses?

Compare these two organisms.

What is the difference in their environment? Which organism is dependent on man for the maintenance of its environment? Could the organism survive without man's aid?

How is the environment of the oak different from that of the orange? How does the oak survive?

10 | The Thallophytes — Chained to the Waters

1. THE GRASS OF THE WATERS

If you keep an aquarium of tropical fish or goldfish, you may have been faced with a typical problem. At one time or another the aquarium may have become quite green. If you were curious enough to examine some of the green water under a microscope, you probably were surprised to find that the green coloring consisted of organisms of many interesting shapes. These were probably all algae. Or you may have examined some aquarium water or pond water and observed algae like those illustrated on pages 5 and 6.

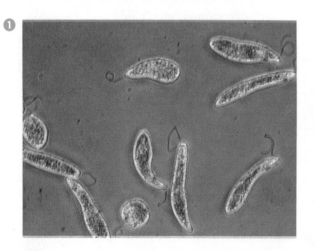

❶

The Algae—Single-Celled to Many-Celled

Compare for a moment, in your mind, a moss plant or a fern, or even a seed plant, with several types of algae. Clearly, the algae do not have roots, stems, or leaves. Some algae such as the huge seaweeds have structures called **holdfasts,** which attach them to rocks or the sea bottom. But holdfasts are not roots. Roots function to hold land plants in the soil and to absorb nutrients and water from the soil, as you know. The holdfasts of the large seaweeds do anchor the plant in the earth, but they do not usually absorb water and nutrients.

In spite of the fact that algae have no roots, stems, or leaves, algae do have many forms—from a single cell to many cells. See for yourself by examining two quite different kinds of algae. ■

Like *Protococcus* and *Spirogyra, Euglena* is a simple green organism you may have seen. ❶ If you are able to collect pond or aquarium water, try to find a *Euglena* that is dividing and watch it carefully. You are observing an asexual form of reproduction called fission. When *Euglena* or any other single-celled organism divides, each daughter cell is exactly like the parent cell.

■ AN APPRENTICE INVESTIGATION into Algae

You have probably seen a green cast to bark on the side of a tree. If this green material can be found where you live, remove some of it from the tree (with a bit of the bark) and bring it to class. Keep it for a few days in a dish in which a half inch of water has been added. Cover the dish to keep the bark moist.

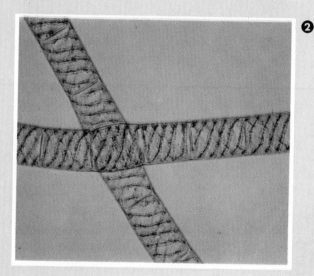

After a few days, scrape off some of the green material and examine it under a microscope. Much of it should be composed of the single-celled (unicellular) alga *Protococcus*. It is a very tiny alga living either as single cells or in clumps of cells. ❶ Since it does not move about, reproduction by cell division often keeps the daughter cells clumped together.

Let's compare *Protococcus* with *Spirogyra*. *Spirogyra* may be collected in ponds. Look for a slimy, bright green mass. To some it looks like fine, green hair.

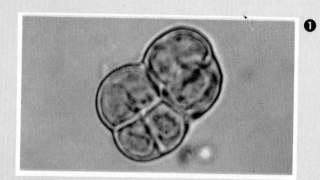

Place a tiny strand in a drop of its own water on a microscope slide. Notice the long filament of many cells, each with a characteristic chloroplast of an unusual shape. ❷ *Spirogyra* is a filamentous alga unlike *Protococcus*. What shape is the chloroplast?

You may stain the *Spirogyra* with a drop of iodine solution. As the *Spirogyra* absorbs the iodine, notice that blue-black spots appear along the chloroplast. ❸ These are called pyrenoids (pī′rə·noidz). Pyrenoids are centers for starch formation. Why did the pyrenoids turn blue-black when iodine was added?

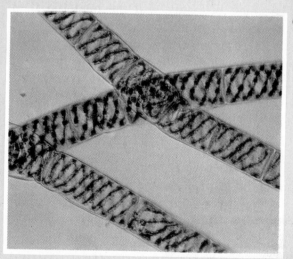

Notice the differences between *Protococcus* and *Spirogyra*. *Spirogyra* is a filament of many cells, all alike and joined together end to end.

An Investigation On Your Own

Collect and study other filamentous algae. Do you find any pyrenoids? Or is *Spirogyra* the only alga with pyrenoids?

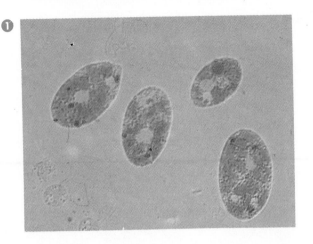

Another single-celled organism that is commonly found in pond or aquarium water is *Chlamydomonas*. ❶

Both *Euglena* and *Chlamydomonas* move about and seem to act like animals. However, some biologists (but not all) are beginning to classify organisms such as *Euglena* and *Chlamydomonas* in a separate kingdom, the kingdom Protista (prō·tē′stə). Botanists sometimes classify them as plants, mainly because they have chlorophyll and are able to photosynthesize. However, if the chloroplasts of *Euglena* are bleached out, the chlorophyll becomes ineffective and the organism then lives like an animal by taking in food.*

An organism that seems to be both plant and animal deserves careful attention. For the moment, however, let's regard *Euglena* as a "green organism," not necessarily a plant or an animal. Later you will study about the classification of the plants and organisms such as *Euglena*.

Euglena is often grouped with the algae, a group of plants singularly important to us. As you study these fascinating plants you will see why.

———
* Bleaching out the chlorophyll, without killing the *Euglena*, can be done by using streptomycin.

Algae of the Sea

If you live near the sea, you will find a group of algae with still a different organization, for example, the "sea lettuce," *Ulva* (əl′və). ❷ *Ulva* is a bright green sheet of cells, usually two layers thick. At the base, you would find cells specialized into long thread-like cells. They act to hold the plant to the rocks. These cells are called holdfasts, which we mentioned earlier. The holdfast cells are usually colorless.

Ulva is a multicellular algae, unlike *Protococcus* or *Euglena*. It is also different from *Spirogyra*. How would you describe its differences?

There are thousands of different kinds of multicellular algae. They range from microscopic, filamentous threads, like *Spirogyra*, to the great seaweeds. The giant seaweed, commonly called kelp, rivals the size of a large tree. Often, the green chlorophyll is masked by other pigments contained in the cells. Many seaweeds, the kelp for example, are brown (the brown algae) and some even have a reddish color (the red algae).

Many of the large seaweeds like *Fucus* (fyoō′kəs) have large, multicellular holdfasts to anchor the plants to the sand and rocks of the water. ❸ Sometimes there is a long stem-like structure growing up from the holdfasts and bearing leaflike "blades." Often, these blades have floats or bladders filled with air. The floats function to hold the food manufacturing blades at or near the water's surface, where more light is available.

In the algae, then, we find a progression from the unicellular organism to the multicellular organism. Whichever algae you study, including the large seaweeds with their holdfasts, stemlike structures, and even leaflike blades, you will *not* find a *true stem*—that is, a stem with conducting tissue, with xylem

② *ULVA*

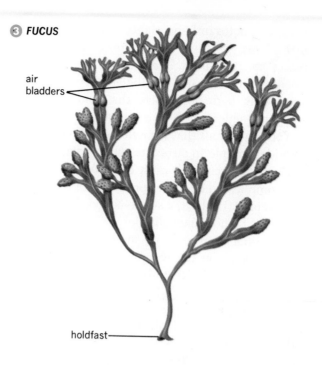

③ *FUCUS*

air bladders

holdfast

and phloem. Neither will you find *true roots*—that is, roots that have absorbing root hairs and conducting tissue. Nor will you find *true leaves*. The algae are all members of the large group of plants called thallophytes (thal′ō·fits), the plants without true stems, roots, and leaves.

Photosynthesis in Single-Celled Plants

You already know how a green plant lives and manufactures food (Chapter 9). A green plant, such as the corn plant that you studied, is complex, with different kinds of cells and tissues specialized in carrying on different functions. A corn plant is comparable to a complex animal in this respect.

In the single-celled algae the individual cell must manufacture food, reproduce, and carry on all the other functions to meet the needs of a living organism. A unicellular alga is comparable, in this respect, to a single-celled animal, except for one important difference—the alga can make its own food.

Some scientists believe the first things that might have been called "living" may have been simple, large molecules that could duplicate themselves. Perhaps these molecules were similar to the viruses. Perhaps they had a make-up like DNA (p. 171). But in time, simple plantlike organisms must have developed—plantlike in their ability to manufacture food. The first plants might have done this with chemical energy (chemosynthetic plants). Or perhaps the first plants used light

223

energy (photosynthetic plants). However the first plants got their energy for food manufacturing, it is most likely that the earliest green plants were simple, single-celled organisms that had developed the remarkable substance chlorophyll or a similar substance.

You may recall that a single-celled animal, although simple in structure when compared with, say, a mammal, must carry on most of the complicated chemical processes of a complex animal. In short, a single-celled, "simple" animal is by no means simple.

The same is true for a single-celled alga. It must carry on the complicated process of photosynthesis. It must absorb water and the substances it needs and in sufficient quantities. It must build up complex proteins, fats, nucleic acids, carbohydrates, enzymes, and other materials, using the energy from the sugar it has made. It must reproduce itself in such a way that the two daughter cells into which it divides both have the same "blueprints" of heredity. True, an alga appears to be simple in structure. Yet a single-celled alga undergoes complex processes biologists still do not completely understand.

REVIEW

1. Why are algae sometimes referred to as the "grass of the waters"?

2. Why is *Euglena* sometimes classed with animals and sometimes classed with plants?

3. What is the function of the chloroplast in algae?

4. Compare the similarities of *Protococcus* and *Spirogyra*. Contrast them.

5. Compare a single-celled alga with a single-celled animal. How are they similar? different?

NEW VIEW

What might happen if all algae disappeared from the earth?

2. VARIETY AND GROUPING

The green algae, as you recall, are representatives of the thallophytes. However, the thallophytes include a great variety of plants besides the algae. The Thallophyta as a great group of plants include all the representatives shown in the following list.

THE PLANT KINGDOM

SUBKINGDOM—Thallophytes: Thallophyta:

PHYLUM—Blue-green algae: Cyanophyta

PHYLUM—Euglenalike algae: Euglenophyta

PHYLUM—Green algae: Chlorophyta

PHYLUM—Golden-brown algae: Chrysophyta

PHYLUM—Brown algae: Phaeophyta

PHYLUM—Red algae: Rhodophyta

PHYLUM—Bacteria: Schizomycophyta

PHYLUM—Slime molds: Myxomycophyta

PHYLUM—True fungi: Eumycophyta

You will find illustrations of each phylum, along with their outstanding characteristics, presented at the end of this chapter. However, not all botanists whose field of study is plant grouping, or, more accurately, plant taxonomy (tak·son′ə·mē), would group all these plants among the thallophytes.

Most taxonomists would agree on placing the green, golden, red, and brown algae in the subkingdom Thallophyta. Others would include the fungi, bacteria, and blue-green algae in a single subphylum. Other taxonomists would place the bacteria and blue-green algae in a separate subphylum, thus separating the bacteria from the fungi.

Still others would place *Euglena*, the bacteria, and the slime molds with the single-celled animals in a new kingdom—the Pro-

red maple   silver maple   sugar maple

tista. But we shall include them in the Thallophyta, as many taxonomists do.

After all, you are at the beginning of your study of the complex field of taxonomy, the grouping of organisms according to similarities in structure. Now you are simply getting a first view of the important groupings. Then, as you proceed in your study of biology—and as more scientific evidence is uncovered by research—the groupings will become clearer and more definite. Let's turn next to an example in higher plants.

The Meaning of Grouping— Naming of Organisms

Probably you are acquainted with various kinds of trees, for example, maples, oaks, or pines. Why are the trees grouped as maples, oaks, or pines? Within maples, for example, there is the sugar maple, the silver maple, and the red maple, among others. Each of these trees is considered a **species** (spē′shēz) of maple. Examine, for instance, the leaves of these three species of maple. ❶ Clearly, each has *different characteristics that identify each species.* Each species has inherited these characteristics. That is, the factors that are responsible for the characteristics are carried in the chromosomes. You may thus recognize a species of maple by its characteristic leaves. Of course, each tree has other specific characteristics; buds, bark, and types of branching, among others.

Keep in mind, however, that although there are sugar, silver, and red maples, among many other kinds, all are maples. We could then really name them as follows:

> Maple, sugar
> Maple, silver
> Maple, red

Thus, we give each species of maple two names. One name, the **genus** (jē′nəs), tells us the tree is a maple. Another name, the species name, tells us the kind of maple: sugar, silver, or red.

Taxonomists use Latin as the official language for naming plants. There are several reasons. First, Carolus Linnaeus (Lin·ā′əs) (1707–1778), who started the system of naming plants, used Latin for the genus and species names. Second, Latin is not now used as a spoken language; thus Latin remains fairly stable and does not change as spoken languages do. Third, the common names for organisms often differ in different parts of the world, while the Latin names are the same everywhere.

225

Unless you like, you need not, for the moment, remember the Latin name for a given genus or species. On the other hand, once you begin to learn them, the task becomes easy and often pleasurable. For example:

Common word	Latin word
maple	*Acer*
sugar	*saccharum*
red	*rubrum*

Thus, the genus and species names of two of the maples are

Acer saccharum (sugar maple)
Acer rubrum (red maple)

Notice that in Latin construction the genus name comes first, followed by the species name. In most cases in this book (as in most introductory books), usually only the Latin genus name is used. Thus, *Spirogyra* is the genus name of a group of algae. There are many species of *Spirogyra,* for instance, *Spirogyra crassa* and *Spirogyra nitida.*

There are also different species of bread mold. You commonly study *Rhizopus nigricans* (rī′zō·pəs nī′grə·kānz)—meaning "bread mold, black." And you, as a member of a great species, have a noble name—*Homo sapiens,* meaning "Man, the wise."

Now let's look into the general, large groupings under which a species is classified. To do this in a way more familiar to you, we shall deal not with plants but with organisms probably more familiar to you—animals. Then we shall return to plant groupings, particularly the thallophytes.

Large Groupings to Small

On the opposite page are photographs of ten animals. ❶ Can you group them in some way? Of course. It's easy. The reason you were able to do so is clear. The animals show certain relationships on the basis of their structure. Surely animals that have feathers have a closer relationship to each other than they do to animals with fur. At least this would seem so for the moment. Similarly, animals with fur seem to have a closer relationship to each other than they do to animals having scales and gills. Then, on the basis of body structures, it is possible to group organisms readily, at least for the large groupings, or **phyla.** For instance, animals such as the insects, crayfish, lobsters, and spiders belong to the phylum Arthropoda (är′throp′ə·də). All the arthropods lack internal skeletons and have jointed legs. All the animals that belong to the phylum Chordata (kôr·da′tə) have a hollow nerve cord on their dorsal (upper) side as adults, as young, or throughout their life. All the animals with backbones belong to the Chordata.

Is it enough to study just one animal to know what a group, say a phylum, is like? A fish and a rabbit are both chordates. A fish has gills, scales, and fins. It lays eggs in the water. A rabbit has lungs, fur, and legs; and it does not lay eggs. It gives birth to live rabbits. So if you studied just a fish, you would not learn very much about a rabbit. For that reason, to understand the grouping, or classification, of a phylum, we must go into its further grouping.

Each phylum is divided further into **subphyla** and then into **classes.** The members of a subphylum are more closely related than are the members of a phylum. The members of a class are even more closely related than the members of a subphylum. All birds, for example, are in one class—Aves (ā′vēz) (from the Latin word *avis,* meaning "bird"). Rabbits are in the class of animals to which dogs, cats, cows, and even human beings belong, a class named Mammalia, or mammals.

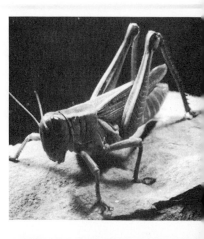

Organism	Species	Genus	Family	Order	Class	Subphylum
MAN	*sapiens*	*Homo*	Hominidae (family of man)	Primates	Mammalia (animals with milk glands)	Vertebrata (animals with backbones)
CRAB–APPLE TREE	*sylvestris*	*Malus* (apple)	Rosaceae (rose family)	Rosales	Angiospermae (flowering plants)	Pteropsida

If you were to study any typical fish carefully, you would really know a great deal about all other fish. For you now recognize that organisms are classified on the basis of similarity of structure. If you were to study a rabbit carefully, you would know quite a lot about mammals. Of course, there would still be many important differences between the animals of each class. Rabbits, for example, are classified within a different **order** than are mammals such as dogs, cats, cows, or human beings. Dogs and cats (and wolves, foxes, and coyotes) are placed in the order Carnivora (kär·niv′or·ə) (meat-eaters).

Even dogs and cats are, as you know, rather different from each other. Dogs, wolves, foxes, and coyotes are placed within a different group under Carnivora than are cats. This group is called a **family.** Dogs are placed in the family Canidae (kan′ə·dē), along with foxes, wolves, and coyotes.

The next grouping, under the family, is then the genus. You have already been introduced to the term. But here you see its use with animals as well. Dogs are placed under the genus *Canis* along with coyotes. Cats are in a different genus, called *Felis,* along with lions and tigers. (In what genus do you think a leopard would belong?)

The final grouping, as you know, is called the species. Thus, the dog belongs to the species *familiaris.* Its name then, based on a system of classification accepted over the world, is *Canis familiaris.* Recall that scientists always use the genus and species name together to name an organism, whether plant or animal. The house cat is *Felis domesticus.*

Classification not only makes it easier to study living things, but, more importantly, it helps us to see relationships. Two house cats are more closely related (same species) than a cat and a leopard (different species). A cat and a leopard are more closely related (same genus) than a cat and a dog (different genera). A cat and a dog (same order) are more closely related than a cat and a cow (different orders). A cat and a cow (same class) are more closely related than a cat and a fish (different classes). A cat and a fish (same phylum) are more closely related than a cat and a fly (different phyla). And a cat and a fly (both in the animal kingdom) are more closely related than a cat and a geranium (different kingdoms).

Living things are classified, then, in order to show their relationships. Occasionally the true relationship is not known, so sometimes an organism must be reclassified. Sometimes

Phylum	Subkingdom	Kingdom
Chordata (animals with hollow nerve cords)	*	Animalia (animal kingdom)
Tracheophyta (vascular plants)	Embryophyta (plants with embryo stage)	Plantae (plant kingdom)

* Zoologists do not use a subkingdom.

major parts of a classification system have to be changed as new knowledge is gained.

Classification is only a means for your study of organisms. By grouping organisms, we can carefully study one organism from each group and know that they are typical of the perhaps thousands or even hundreds of thousands of different organisms within that group.

As you go on in your study of organisms you will learn easily to group

a. a species into its genus
b. genera (plural of genus) into families
c. families into orders
d. orders into classes
e. classes into phyla or subphyla
f. subphyla into phyla
g. phyla into a subkingdom
h. subkingdom into a kingdom.

To help you fix this in mind, in the chart above we have classified man and a crab-apple tree.

Variety Among the Thallophytes

Clearly, the thallophytes are a complex group. At the end of this chapter, you will find an illustrated classification section showing representative plants of all the phyla of thallophytes. What appears to unite the thallophytes is the absence of true roots, stems, and leaves, as well as other characteristics that will be brought out when you study the mosses later. Thallophytes are united in still another way, that is, by the kind of environment forced upon them by the absence of true roots, stems, and leaves. In general, all thallophytes live in a moist environment. Most algae live in what biologists think may have been the environment in which life originated, the sea. We assume the ancient seas to have been warmer than those that bathe three quarters of the globe today.

REVIEW

1. Put these in order of descending complexity: family, phylum, subphylum, order, class, species, genus.

2. What are the characteristics of the Thallophyta? Why would the geranium not be classified as a thallophyte?

3. A common brown alga is known as *Fucus*. Is this the genus or species grouping?

4. The cat belongs to the species *Felis domesticus*. What would you assume is the relationship of the lion (*Felis leo*) and the tiger (*Felis tigris*) to the cat?

5. What could you say about the following organisms: *Pelargonium roseum; Pelargonium argenteum; Amoeba proteus; Amoeba chaos?*

NEW VIEW

1. What makes a fungus a plant, and not an animal? After all, like animals it can't make its own food, and it depends upon photosynthetic or chemosynthetic plants.

2. Do different botanists agree with the *entire* classification given in this book?

Study a few college botany textbooks. How do the botanists who wrote the textbooks agree with the classification given here? How do they not agree?

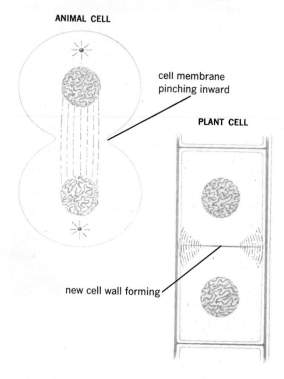

ANIMAL CELL

cell membrane
pinching inward

PLANT CELL

new cell wall forming

3. REPRODUCTION
IN THE THALLOPHYTES

If you watch a filament of *Spirogyra* for a period of time and under favorable conditions (such as plenty of food, proper temperature), you will see cells in the filament divide into two cells. The same kind of asexual reproduction occurs in an onion plant, or any other plant for that matter, when cells divide to form more cells. When cellular division occurs in your body, the cells divide in the same way. There is one important difference, however, between animal and plant cell division. In an animal cell undergoing cell division, the cell membrane pinches inward; while in plants, which have cell walls, a new cell wall is built, dividing the cell in two. ❶

In the single-celled algae, then, each plant divides to make two new cells identical to the parent cell. Actually, no parent organism is left; the parent becomes what we call two daughter cells.

Within the Cell

Your study of *Spirogyra* or any other alga must have convinced you that each daughter cell, or organism, seemed much like its parent organism. Such alikeness must mean that the daughter cells have the same hereditary traits as the parent cell. The same hereditary traits, in turn, must mean that the daughter cells have the same kind of chromosomes as the parent cell.

❷ MITOSIS

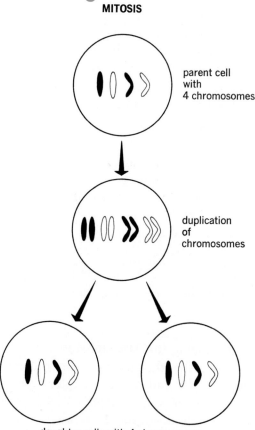

parent cell
with
4 chromosomes

duplication
of
chromosomes

daughter cells with 4 chromosomes
identical to those in parent cell

During asexual cell division (fission, or division of a cell within a filament), the chromosomes in the nucleus duplicate themselves. Each chromosome builds another chromosome exactly like itself. The end result is that each original chromosome has an exact duplicate of itself. The duplicated chromosomes then separate and migrate to each new cell. Thus each daughter cell contains chromosomes identical to each other and to the parent cell. ❷ This process is known as **mitosis** (mī·tō′sis), and this kind of cell division is called *mitotic* (mī·tot′ik) division.

Mitotic division of chromosomes always results in daughter cells with chromosomes identical in both number and kind to each other and to the parent cell. So an alga with 10 chromosomes would produce two daughter cells each with 10 chromosomes. Remember that this is *asexual* reproduction, that is, only one kind of parent is involved. Male and female parents are not involved, nor are sperms and eggs. However, cell division is not the only form of reproduction in the algae. In the algae, and in the fungi as well, are found the beginnings of sexual reproduction among plants. In sexual reproduction two parents and two kinds of cells are involved—one male, the other female.

Beginnings of Sexual Reproduction

Chlamydomonas generally reproduces by fission. During fission, the chromosomes undergo mitosis and each daughter *Chlamydomonas* receives the identical number and kind of chromosomes. However, there are times when certain strains of *Chlamydomonas* act like sex cells, or **gametes** (gam′ēts). Two cells, each of a different strain (usually identified as *plus* and *minus*), draw together and fuse to form a new cell, called a **zygote** (zī′gōt). ❸ When gametes fuse, the result is

❸ **SEXUAL REPRODUCTION IN CHLAMYDOMONAS**

gamete   gamete

gametes fuse

zygote forming

zygote splits, releasing daughter cells

always a zygote. A zygote is always the result of sexual reproduction. The zygote of *Chlamydomonas* then develops a thick wall that can resist unfavorable conditions, particularly drying out. Over a period of time within the zygote, new *Chlamydomonas* daughter cells are formed. When favorable conditions (such as sufficient water) return, the zygote splits open and releases the new *Chlamydomonas*. If you were to explain the importance of a zygote, what might your explanation be?

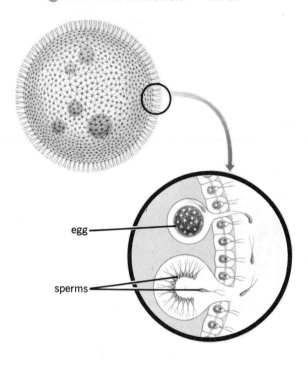

egg

sperms

The *Chlamydomonas* that were acting as gametes were of similar size and shape. But in other algae, the gametes are sometimes a different shape and size. In *Volvox*, a multicellular alga, the gametes are clearly differentiated into sperms and eggs. **1** The sperms are small and swim about by means of flagella. The egg is spherical and nonmobile. The sperm cells then swim to the egg cells.

In many filamentous green algae, *Ulothrix*, for example, one cell or sometimes several cells in a filament may form gametes that look much like *Chlamydomonas* cells. These gametes then fuse to form zygotes. In sexual reproduction in the fungi, such as the bread mold *Rhizopus*, the zygotes that are formed are called zygospores. The zygospores produce filaments with spore cases. The spores reproduce new plants when they fall on food (like bread) and germinate.

In *Oedogonium* (ēd·ə·gō′nē·əm), a filamentous alga, one filament produces mobile sperms, and another produces large oval eggs. The sperms swim to the egg and fertilize it. A thick-walled zygote is then formed which survives unfavorable environmental conditions, like cold and drying out. However, in the algae some zygotes do not have thick walls. In the multicellular marine algae, such as *Fucus* and others, the zygote is thin-walled. But then the ocean doesn't dry out.

Reproduction and the Preservation of a Species

Clearly, the importance of reproduction is to preserve the kind of organism undergoing reproduction, that is, the species. In different species of algae, fission is a common form of reproduction. It involves no union of cells and is, therefore, asexual. The daughter cells are like the parent.

Sometimes, parts of the huge marine kelps and seaweeds simply break off. Each fragment then becomes a new plant. Reproduction by fragmentation, too, is asexual.

But in the algae and, of course, the fungi, we find the beginnings of sexual reproduction by means of gametes. The union of the gametes produces zygotes.

When the gametes are differentiated into male and female, an advantage seems to be offered. The egg is always larger than the sperm, containing amounts of stored food. The zygote formed by this union then has stored food from which to get energy at the time of germination.

The main advantage of sexual reproduction over asexual reproduction, however, is this: A zygote results from the union of two *different* cells and, thus, the daughter cells are different from each other and from the parent cells. Some daughter cells may inherit certain characteristics from the parent cells that will enable them to survive better in the environment. Whereas, in asexual reproduction the new organisms produced are exactly like the original organism and can survive no better.

In the algae just studied, the beginning of sexual reproduction of organisms shows itself. In the brown and red algae, sexual reproduction, as well as asexual reproduction, is also found. In a sense, then, in the algae we begin to see the evolution of sex—that is, we begin to see the development of different kinds of parent organisms, one male, producing male gametes (**sperms**), the other female, producing female gametes (**eggs**).

REVIEW

1. Arrange the following events in the order in which they occur in sexual reproduction of *Chlamydomonas:* zygote forms; gametes fuse; new daughter cells are formed; plus and minus strains draw together; zygote splits.

2. Gametes of a certain alga have a chromosome number of 15. How many chromosomes will the zygote have?

3. The diagram below shows the chromosomes of a cell of an alga. Draw diagrams of the chromosomes found in the daughter cells resulting from asexual reproduction (by means of fission).

4. Explain how sexual reproduction can offer an advantage to a species of organism in its survival. Might it also offer disadvantages?

NEW VIEW

1. Assume that a cell of an alga has 10 chromosomes. Suppose that gametes were produced. These gametes fused to produce a zygote. The zygote in turn produced a new alga cell.

Suppose this happened 5 times, one after the other. What would be the chromosome number after the fifth fusion of the gametes (the fifth generation)?

2. If you can get *plus* and *minus* strains of *Rhizopus,* the bread mold, you can investigate sexual reproduction in a fungus.

Prepare a Petri dish containing a prune agar (prepared as on p. 639 of *Sourcebook for the Biological Sciences,* by Morholt and others, 2nd edition). Wait till the agar cools and jells. Then, with a dissecting needle, place a bit of the plant body of the *plus* strain on one side of the dish, and a bit of the *minus* strain on the other side. Study the growth of the mold daily. In a week or so the mold will grow and fill the dish. What happens when the *plus* and *minus* meet?

You will be able to see small, black bodies form at the point where the strains touch. Examine these black bodies, the zygotes, under the microscope.

Now store some of the zygotes in the refrigerator. Also store some of them in an open jar in a room where they will dry out.

After a few months, sow them in a Petri dish containing glucose and prune agar solution. What do you expect will happen?

Perhaps you cannot get *plus* and *minus* strains of *Rhizopus,* but you can get *Spirogyra* in the ponds around you. Sometimes two *Spirogyra* filaments will undergo union as the cells in adjoining filaments act like gametes. They fuse to form a zygote with a hard, black wall. Allow the water in which *Spirogyra* is forming zygotes to evaporate slowly in a moderately cool part of the room. After a few months, add some fresh pond water. Do the *Spirogyra* zygotes germinate?

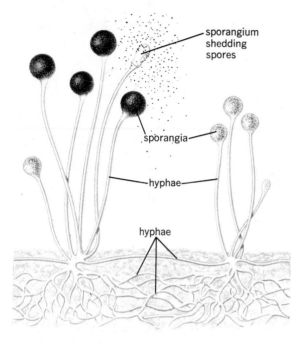

sporangium shedding spores

sporangia

hyphae

hyphae

4. DEPENDENT THALLOPHYTES— THE FUNGI

Fungi are thallophytes that contain no chlorophyll. One of the most familiar is bread mold, *Rhizopus*. We are mainly familiar with three groups of fungi. There are those, such as bread mold, that have bodies made up of threadlike structures called **hyphae** (hī′fē). There also are the yeastlike fungi. And there are the types represented by the mushrooms.

Bread mold is a useful fungus for study. It has a structure common to all filamentous fungi.❶ Its total body is the threadlike **mycelium** (mī·sē′lē·əm). The mycelium might be considered as being made up of threads of hyphae. One hypha is simply part of a mycelium. Thus the rootlike **rhizoids** are simply hyphae. There is also a hypha holding up the **sporangium.** The sporangium carries spores, which can withstand dry conditions and which germinate into a new plant when conditions in the environment are favorable. This is a kind of asexual reproduction.

There are fungi that are single-celled, such as the yeasts. Yeasts can also form spores within a single cell. There are other types of fungi, such as *Penicillium* or *Aspergillus* (as′pər·jil′əs), whose spores are born in long threads or clusters. The left picture below shows *Penicillium* sporangia and their spores.❷ At the right below, is an *Aspergillus* sporangium and its spores.❸

The ways in which the spores are formed (that is, the mode of reproduction), as well as the form of the fungus, are also means used for classifying the fungi.

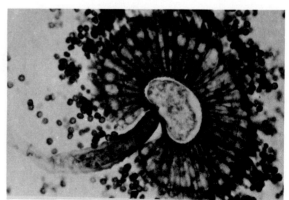

Securing Energy for Living

Fungi of course cannot capture light energy, since chlorophyll is necessary. However, fungi are adapted to securing energy in other ways. Most absorb their food nutrients, their energy, from matter composed of proteins, fats, or carbohydrates. Organisms that absorb their food nutrients from dead organic substances are known as **saprophytes** sap′rō·fīts).

There are some saprophytic fungi that live on organic material in soil, on the decaying leaves, bark, and wood. When you see a mushroom (some people call them toadstools) growing in a yard, you are looking only at the spore-bearing body. The largest portion of the mushroom plant body is actually in the ground beneath the surface. The plant consists of a large network of hyphae in the soil. The hyphae secrete enzymes that break down the organic substances into water-soluble substances that can then be absorbed by the hyphae.

After the fungus has absorbed enough food and has grown sufficiently, it produces a spore-producing organ—what we know as the mushroom—above ground. The spores are released from gills (thin plates arranged like the spokes of a wheel) on the under surface of the umbrella-shaped cap.❹

Other mushrooms and shelf fungi derive their food nutrients from dead wood and even living trees. Their mycelia thread throughout the wood. The spore-bearing body of a shelf fungus protrudes from the tree.❺

The common field mushroom releases almost 2 billion spores, each spore capable of growing into another mushroom plant. The somewhat pear-shaped fungi, the puffball, may release over 7 billion spores!

DANGER: Many mushrooms are good to eat, *but some are deadly.* One mushroom, the *Amanita* (am′ə·nī′tə), looks very much like an edible mushroom, but its poison is almost certain to cause death if it is eaten. There is no known remedy for its poison. *Never pick mushrooms and eat them.* Buy them in the grocery store.

There are also many fungi that are **parasites** (par′ə·sītz), that is, they derive their food nutrients from living organisms. Thus, certain mildews, rusts, and smuts get their food from living plants. Many of these parasites are molds.

■ AN APPRENTICE INVESTIGATION into a Water Mold

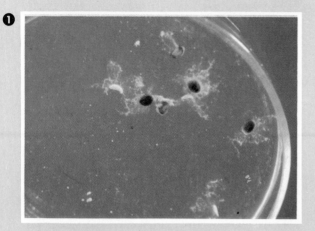

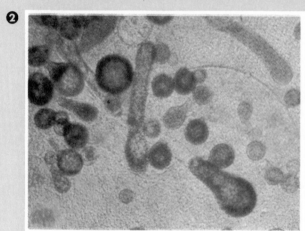

You can use either aquarium water or pond water. Place the water in a shallow Petri dish and drop in 5 wheat grains. If the spores of a common water mold, *Saprolegnia* (sap'rō·leg' nēə), are present, characteristic hyphae will develop on the wheat.❶ Study these hyphae under the microscope. You may be able to observe that the hyphae are of two types. Some hyphae are long, threadlike structures that penetrate the wheat grains; other hyphae, which are blunter, spread out into the water.

Possibly, you will be able to observe spores of *Saprolegnia* being formed.❷ These spores do not have a thick covering. How do you explain this characteristic?

An Investigation On Your Own

Saprolegnia undergoes sexual reproduction. What form does this take? Very careful observation will be needed under the high power of the microscope. A reference book on the fungi will also be helpful.

Perhaps you have found a colorless or gray fungus growing on the gills of a fish in an aquarium. Try to identify the fungus.

Molds

There is a wide variety of molds, sometimes called the filamentous fungi. Molds are filamentous and have a mycelial body. Besides the common bread mold, there are scores of others. There are the mildews that grow on and get their food from leather. There are those fungi living on dead insects and other water animals. These are the common water molds, and their spores may be found in your classroom aquarium or a nearby pond. Try to isolate a water mold for yourself. ■

Smuts and Rusts

The groups of fungi known as smuts and rusts are parasitic. They infect young plants or tissues of plants.

Smuts send their hyphae into such cereal plants as corn, oats, wheat, rice, and rye. The mycelium penetrates throughout the entire plant. Finally, when the plant flowers, the mycelium even penetrates the developing seeds and forms spores within them. The body of the seed finally becomes a mass of sooty black spores.

Rusts are so named because their spores form red, rusty-looking spots on the leaves and stems of the host plants that they parasitize. Many rusts have the peculiar habit of parasitizing two different kinds of plants. They must alternate the plants they parasitize. For example, the black stem rust of wheat plants produces absorbing structures that live in the stems and leaves of wheat plants during the summer. Here they produce orange colored spots on the surfaces of the leaves and stems. These spots are, of course, the spores. These spores can also infect other wheat plants. However, in late summer special winter spores are produced. These remain on the wheat plant throughout the winter and germinate the following spring. The newly germinated fungus plants then produce a new crop of spores. These spores can only develop on the alternate host, the common barberry plant. Once on the barberry, the spores germinate and send their hyphae into the cells of the barberry leaves. Spores finally develop in the barberry plant the following spring, and if these are carried in the air to wheat plants, they germinate and start the wheat infection over again. All of the rusts have alternate hosts. How might you get rid of the wheat rust without getting rid of the wheat?

These are but a few of the thousands of different kinds of rusts, smuts, mildews, and rots that parasitize plants. Animals also are not immune from parasitic fungi.

Parasitic Fungi of Animals

The type of disease in man called ringworm is caused by a fungus. Athlete's foot is also caused by a fungus. The fungus is transferred from person to person by means of the spores that fall from the bare feet of an infected person onto the floors of places such as shower rooms or gymnasiums. When the spores germinate, their absorbing structures grow into the moist skin cells between the toes. Here the plants digest and absorb the cell products. Sometimes their destruction of the cells causes bleeding cracks in the skin. The fungus that causes athlete's foot is difficult to get rid of partly because the plant lives *in* the skin and partly because the spores that are produced are able to survive in socks, shoes, and on floors until a suitable environment presents itself. This is a good example of the ability of spores to tolerate adverse environmental conditions.

There are other parasitic fungal diseases such as *sprue* and *thrush* that affect animals, particularly those in the tropics. You may find it interesting to do a bit of library research to become acquainted with some of the important parasitic fungi infecting animals.

Yeasts and Their Mode of Life

You have perhaps studied the common yeasts in some of your earlier studies in science. Yeasts reproduce asexually by a process called "budding," that is, a small swelling develops on the surface of a parent yeast cell. This swelling, or bud, grows larger and larger and finally a wall is formed between the bud and the parent cell. Sometimes the bud cell then separates from the parent cell. But usually the bud stays attached, enlarges, and starts forming buds of its own. After a period of time, a many-celled chain of cells may result from budding. It will probably not surprise you to learn that some yeasts also reproduce by means of spores. Indeed, there are also yeasts that send out projections toward each other. The contents of the two cell projections fuse, division occurs, and then spores are produced. These spores are known as *ascospores* (as′kō·spôrz)

because they are formed *within* the cell, which was once thought to be shaped somewhat like a sac (Latin, *ascus*). Like the spores of molds, the spores of yeast can survive periods of heat, cold, extreme dryness, and other unfavorable conditions.

The manner in which yeasts derive their energy is most interesting and important. In the presence of sufficient amounts of oxygen, yeasts oxidize sugars, and this oxidation produces water and carbon dioxide. This process is similar to the respiration of all fungi and animals. In producing carbon dioxide, yeasts perform a function that we are able to use. For example, yeasts are used to make bread. The carbon dioxide produced as yeast cells oxidize sugars is released as tiny bubbles. These bubbles, trapped in the bread dough, cause the bread to rise, making it light.

Yeasts can also use another type of respiration in the absence of sufficient oxygen. This type of respiration is known as **anaerobic** (an·âr·ō′bik) **respiration.** The word *anaerobic* means "without air." In anaerobic respiration yeasts produce ethyl alcohol and carbon dioxide. Yeasts also manufacture vitamins. The dried or cake yeast available in stores is a good source of vitamin B.

Lichens—A Case of Mutual Help

Did you ever see a patch of gray-green, crusty-looking material on a tree trunk, a stump, or a rock? If not, look for some, for these are lichens, which are most interesting plants. Some are leaflike, some are cushionlike, some are spongelike, and some are crusty, such as the one shown in the photograph.

A lichen is not a fungus, that is, not entirely a fungus. What we call a lichen is two different kinds of plants living together in close relationship and helping each other. A lichen is made up of a fungus and an alga. The alga manufactures food for itself and for the fungus, which absorbs some of it. But the relationship does not stop here, so the fungus cannot be called a parasite on the alga. The fungus is said to return the favor by absorbing water that the alga then uses to manufacture food. Such a relationship is called **symbiosis** (sim·bē·ō′sis), a condition in which two different organisms live together with benefit to both. Actually, the fungus is getting the best of the bargain, for it has been shown experimentally that the alga can live without the fungus, but the fungus dies without the alga to manufacture its food. For these reasons, biologists hesitate to consider the lichen a *true* case of symbiosis.

We live in relative peace with the fungi we have been studying. Fortunately, the fungi, in general, do not destroy us, except when we are unfortunate enough to eat a poisonous mushroom. However, there are plants often grouped with the fungi against which we must be on constant guard. No doubt you already know these plants as the bacteria. Most people still consider it strange that the organisms most deadly to other organisms, including man, are plants—and plants invisible to the naked eye, at that.

Bacteria—Useful and Harmful

Most bacteria are either parasitic or saprophytic. Only a few are chemosynthetic like those you studied in Chapter 9. All are extremely small, rarely larger than $\frac{1}{25,000}$ of an inch across. Some are as small as $\frac{1}{165,000}$ of an inch across and you would need to place nearly a thousand of them side by side to cover the period at the end of this sentence.

Because bacteria are so small, an individual bacterium is very difficult to see with the microscopes used in most schools. A great amount of magnification by extremely powerful lenses is required to see them clearly.

There are three common shapes of bacterial cells: round, rod-shaped, and spiral-shaped. Those that are round are *cocci* (singular, *coccus*), like these (*Staphylococcus aureus*).❷ Those that are rod-shaped are *bacilli* (singular, *bacillus*) like these (*Bacillus anthrax*).❸ The spiral-shaped bacteria are the *spirilli* (singular, *spirillum*), like these (*Spirillum rubrum*).❹ Sometimes, however, bacteria have flagella that are much like those found on single-celled algae. These flagellated bacteria are named *Salmonella whichita.*❺ Notice that *Salmonella's* basic shape resembles a bacillus.

Bacteria generally reproduce by division. But the neat, clean division of chromosomes found in the cells you have studied is not generally found in the bacteria. In most bacteria the chromosome material is found in granules scattered throughout the cell. Somehow the granules divide fairly equally among the two daughter cells during cell division. There is some recent work to show that under certain conditions, some kinds of bacteria undergo sexual reproduction. That is, two bacterial cells unite, forming a zygote. The zygote cell then forms new individuals.

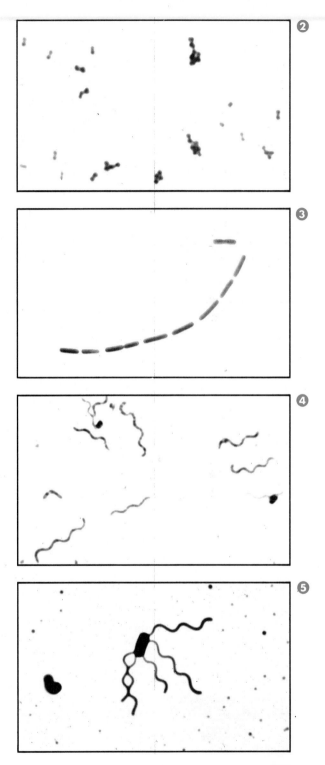

Sometimes bacteria reproduce themselves by dividing in such a way that long threads, or filaments, of cells occur. Sometimes they divide in such a way that masses of cells become clumped together into colonies. The photomicrograph shows the bacteria that cause a severe kind of sore throat. These bacteria are named *Streptococci.* ❶ Streptococci are, as you can see, cocci arranged in a long filament. (What would a streptobacillus look like?) Other streptococci cause scarlet fever. The bacteria that cause boils are shown in the photomicrograph. ❷ These are named *Staphylococci.* Staphylococci are cocci that form colonies, as you can see.

A Problem in Arithmetic

Suppose that a person who had a streptococcic sore throat coughed and *one* individual cell of the streptococci was sucked into your own throat as you breathed. (This would be a rare occurrence, indeed, for sometimes we inhale thousands of bacteria of all kinds in a single breath of air.) With plenty of warmth, food, and moisture in your throat, this single bacterium might divide to form two bacteria in only fifteen to twenty minutes. Each of these, let's assume, would divide after another twenty minutes to form two more. Then, twenty minutes later, these four would divide to produce a total of eight. The eight would make sixteen, the sixteen would make thirty-two, and so it would go, with a new division every twenty minutes.

How many streptococci cells would you have in your throat after twenty-four hours, assuming division occurred every twenty minutes (three divisions every hour)?

The correct answer is 4,700,000,000,000,-000,000,000 bacteria! And, as small as they are, they would form a mass that would weigh nearly 2,000 tons!

Of course, this doesn't happen for many reasons. The numbers of bacteria are controlled by the living things they enter. Most of the bacteria stick to the mucus in your nose and throat and are sneezed out. Others find their way into your stomach and are digested. The white blood cells in your body engulf a great number. The antibodies and antitoxins in your body take care of others. With all the protective mechanisms found in the body, it isn't so very easy for bacteria to overwhelm and disrupt a healthy organism.

However, this little arithmetic problem does illustrate an important truth: disease-causing bacteria are dangerous, even though they are extremely small, because they multiply so rapidly. Although in a human body a single streptococcus would not have produced anything like the number of offspring our arithmetic gave us, since we assumed ideal conditions, it could have produced many millions in twenty-four hours or even less. And the amount of waste products or toxins thrown off as these bacteria live their lives in your throat could make you extremely ill. But as was indicated, the body has its own defenses, and medical science has produced powerful drugs for use against bacteria.

Man, as scientist, has begun to control his environment, sometimes successfully, sometimes with harm to himself and other organisms. One of his successes, not without other problems, resulted from his control of bacteria.

Harmful Bacteria

There are many kinds of bacteria that parasitize man, causing illness and even death. Many other kinds cause diseases in other animals and plants. Some kinds of bacteria seem to be able to parasitize a wide variety of organisms, but most are specialists. Some, for

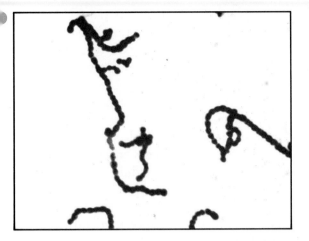

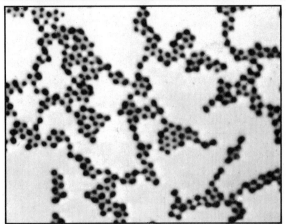

instance, can live only on human blood, and others can live only on nerve tissues.

Bacteria, like all plants (and animals, too, for that matter), manufacture enzymes which are then used to digest foods. Parasitic bacteria secrete these enzymes into the tissues of the organism they parasitize. The enzymes break down the tissues into simpler, water-soluble materials that are then absorbed back into the bacterial cell where they are oxidized to secure energy or used to manufacture new protoplasm for the bacterium.

Remember our arithmetic problem. If, even under ideal and theoretic conditions, a single bacterium weighing far less than a bit of dust can produce nearly 2,000 tons of protoplasm in twenty-four hours, it is clear that bacteria digest, absorb, and change a tremendous amount of tissue from the animals or plants they parasitize.

As you can see, then, bacteria can cause disease or illness in two ways: they produce poisonous or toxic waste materials, and they actually digest and destroy living tissues.

The tuberculosis bacillus actually digests the lung. The tetanus bacillus produces poisonous toxins as it lives and feeds within the body. These bacteria and others are like all other organisms that are adapted to a special environment. Unfortunately, one of their best environments is our bodies.

Helpful Bacteria

Antibiotics are our present best weapon against a wide variety of communicable diseases. Bacterial pneumonia, once a chief killer, took thousands of lives every year. But bacterial pneumonia is much less widespread today because of antibiotics. Scarlet fever, once a chief killer of children, is easily controlled with antibiotics today. Deaths from blood poisoning and other infections by streptococcic and staphylococcic bacteria were once extremely common; now such deaths are quite rare. And so it goes through the entire range of bacterial diseases.

Penicillin, the first antibiotic, was discovered in 1928 by an English scientist named Alexander Fleming. He noticed that a bit of mold that had fallen into a culture of bacteria with which he was working had apparently destroyed the bacteria around it. He transferred some of the mold to another culture of bacteria and found again that the mold produced "something" that destroyed the bacteria. After much experimentation, he discov-

241

Did you know that certain bacteria living in the large intestine help in the digestion of materials and are necessary to normal health? Over one fourth of the dry weight of human feces consists of bacteria. If the intestinal bacteria are destroyed, the body suffers. No one knows exactly why.

Look at the photograph at the left. ❶ You are looking at the roots of a soybean plant. Notice the bumps, or nodules, on them. Each of these nodules contains millions of bacteria. These are among the most important bacteria known to man. They remove nitrogen gas from the air surrounding the roots and manufacture nitrogen compounds from it. They are called the **nitrogen-fixing bacteria.** Green plants must have nitrogen compounds in order to make proteins, but they cannot remove and use gaseous nitrogen from the air. These bacteria do it for them. The plants are then able to use the nitrogen compounds made by the bacteria. In turn, the bacteria secure other food materials that they need from the root tissues of the soybeans. Each helps the other.

A number of beanlike plants (the *legumes*) develop these nodules of nitrogen-fixing bacteria. Plants such as clovers, alfalfa, and soybeans are commonly planted by farmers in order to get nitrogen compounds back into the soil. Such crops are alternated with other crops that take nitrogen compounds from the soil. In this way the fertility of the soil is maintained.

The most important bacteria of all, however, are the ordinary bacteria that are found, literally, almost everywhere and that cause the decay of dead plants and animals.

Suppose there were no decay-producing bacteria or fungi. What would be the result? Convince yourself of this by doing the investigation on the opposite page. ■

ered how to extract the bacteria-destroying substance produced by the mold. He found that this substance, now known as *penicillin,* was extremely effective in stopping the growth of disease bacteria inside the human body.

Although penicillin and most other antibiotics are made from molds, some are made from bacteria. *Streptomycin* and *chloromycetin* are both obtained from bacteria.

Bacteria are also important in many industrial processes. Vinegar, some kinds of cheese, sauerkraut, and other foods require bacterial action. Some bacteria make acetone, which is used to make photographic film, explosives, and other products. One kind of bacteria is used to make methyl alcohol and another kind makes butyl alcohol. Both are used in chemical manufacturing. Other kinds of bacteria make possible still other products of great value to industry. One kind of bacteria is even used to manufacture vitamin B_2.

■ AN APPRENTICE INVESTIGATION into Decay Bacteria

Take ten grains of rice or wheat, and put them in a flask containing about one inch of water. Stopper the flask with cotton. Repeat this procedure with another flask.

Sterilize both flasks in a pressure cooker. (**Caution:** Under no circumstances should you use the pressure cooker without supervision.) Repeat the sterilization 24 hours after the flasks have cooled. The reason for the double sterilization is to kill any bacteria or other fungi that may be in spore form. Be certain to get your teacher's help in this.

Now leave one flask open for 24 hours, and then replace the cotton plug. ❶ Compare the two flasks for at least two weeks or a month. How do you explain the results? ❷ How could you prevent the growth of the organisms in the flask that was opened?

An Investigation On Your Own

Assume now that all decay bacteria and all fungi were killed on the earth just as they were killed in the flasks. What would be the result? What would the earth look like 1,000 years from now? What is your reasoning? What evidence do you have for your prediction?

REVIEW

1. Describe the structure and life of a mushroom. Explain how a mushroom obtains food and how it reproduces.

2. There are many mushrooms that are delicious and perfectly safe. Why, then, is it dangerous for anyone to pick and eat mushrooms found growing outdoors?

3. Describe the structure and life of a mold.

4. Describe the nature and life of yeast plants. How do they reproduce? Why are yeast plants used in making bread?

5. Are molds saprophytic or parasitic? Explain your answer.

6. Define the term *symbiosis* and show how lichens illustrate symbiotic living.

7. How do chemosynthetic bacteria secure the energy with which to manufacture foods?

8. How do parasitic bacteria break down tissues of the organism they parasitize in order to secure food? What is this process called? Where does it take place?

9. Explain the nature and value of nitrogen-fixing bacteria.

NEW VIEW

1. Why is it that fungi and bacteria typically require warm, moist conditions in order to live?

2. What do you think could be done to lessen one's chances of getting athlete's foot? Explain.

3. Fungi and most bacteria secure food from living or dead organisms. How do they take this food into their bodies when they have no mouths, digestive systems, or similar structures? Explain.

5. RELATING THE CONCEPTS

Paleontologists are generally agreed that life did not have its beginnings on land. The evidence points to the waters as the place of the origin of life. But at some time, plants took to the land and conquered it.

Our study of the variety of life, both plant and animal, is intended to give us an understanding of the adaptations of organisms. A study of the adaptations and of the environments in which they took place may reveal clues to the ways in which organisms that were adapted to an aquatic environment were then able to adapt to and gain a foothold on the land. We began our study with the plants that were adapted to the aquatic environment. Certain concepts summarize our understanding of the nature of these plants.

Reviewing the Concepts

▶ *Organisms can be grouped (classified) on the basis of characteristics held in common.* In any study of organisms, we find some characteristics that are also common to others. These characteristics are usually physical structures and are always inherited characteristics. These common structures of organisms give us a basis for classifying them into large groups (kingdoms and phyla) and further enable us to classify them in subgroups (classes, orders, families, and genera).

▶ *The Thallophyta is a large grouping (a subkingdom) of plant organisms without true stems, leaves, or roots.* The algae and fungi fall within this group. Although the variety of thallophytes is large, with the organisms taking many forms, most of them are relatively flat-bodied.

▶ *The thallophytes are adapted to an environment of fresh water, or sea water, or to an environment rich in water vapor.* Organisms generally require water for their metabolism. The thallophytes, however, need either to be immersed in water or, in their active growing stages, to be surrounded by water. Although the fungi and bacteria can survive drying in the spore form, in their active forms the fungi soon die if they are subjected to drying conditions.

▶ *The algae can photosynthesize, whereas the fungi depend on the products of photosynthesis.* Without chlorophyll, photosynthesis does not occur.

Fungi, like animals, depend either directly or indirectly on the food nutrients produced by the process of photosynthesis. Thus, the mycelial threads of the mushroom absorb the food nutrients in soil rich in decaying plants. For example, the filamentous fungi and other fungi absorb their food nutrients from organic materials, such as those found in bread, fruits, meats, and the like.

Testing Yourself

1. What characteristics place an organism within the thallophyte group?

2. *Protococcus*, an alga, lives on the sides of trees on land. Why is it classified with the thallophytes? Has it freed itself of the environment necessary for the life of an alga?

3. Why are the fungi classified with the thallophytes?

4. How is bread mold similar to a filamentous alga? How is it different?

5. Why are the brown, red, and golden algae placed within the thallophytes? Why are they placed in subgroups?

6. What, at present, is your understanding of the concept of *species?*

7. What is the difference between *Spirogyra* and *Spirogyra crassa? Paramecium* and *Paramecium caudatum? Homo* and *Homo sapiens?*

8. What is the importance of classification to the scientist?

9. If you were to describe the variety of organisms classified in the phylum Thallophyta, how would you describe them? Try subphyla first, then classes.

10. How are bacteria harmful? Give several examples.

11. How are bacteria helpful? Give several examples.

12. How is a lichen thought to maintain itself?

13. How useful are the fungi?

14. Compare saprophytes with parasites.

15. Why are chemosynthetic bacteria not considered photosynthetic organisms?

Extending the Concepts

Investigation 1. Here is a chance to use the research facilities of your library. When did man first have conclusive evidence that a given bacterium caused a specific disease?

No doubt men suspected that bacteria caused disease some time before the evidence was clear. Was this in the time of Aristotle? in the time of Leeuwenhoek? in the time of Spallanzani? in the time of Pasteur? in the time of Koch?

Investigation 2. What are the nutritional requirements of various types of fungi?

Place some bread, fruit, a piece of leather, and a piece of wood in different plastic bags. Add five drops of water to each, then close the bags tightly. You will, no doubt, grow a collection of different fungi. Are there any mildews amongst them? Do mildews grow only on leather?

Does bread mold grow only on bread?

You will need to refer to a college textbook on botany to help you identify the different forms. And, of course, you will need a microscope.

Investigation 3. Desmids are found in ponds, lakes, and streams. Can you culture one genus of desmid, say *Closterium?*

You will certainly need pond water or its equivalent. And, of course, you will need to invent a way of isolating a single *Closterium* and of growing a culture of the plants. Or do you know a better way to do it?

Some suggestions for growing algae, such as the desmids, and the make-up of pond water are to be found in *A Sourcebook for the Biological Sciences.*

Suggested Reading

Smith, A. H., *The Mushroom Hunter's Field Guide* (2nd ed.), Ann Arbor, University of Michigan, 1963.

Sterling, Dorothy, *The Story of Mosses, Ferns, and Mushrooms*, New York, Doubleday, 1955.

Prescott, G. W., *How to Know Fresh Water Algae*, Dubuque, W. C. Brown, 1964.

Jaques, H. E., *Plant Families, How to Know Them*, Dubuque, W. C. Brown, 1948.

VARIETY AMONG THE PLANTS

ALGAE TO FUNGI

The algae, the bacteria, the slime molds, and the fungi are all included in the great subkingdom of thallophytes. All are plants without true roots, stems, or leaves, and none produce flowers or seeds. All thallophytes are chained to a moist environment, living either in the water itself or in an environment rich in water vapor. Many contain some kind of colored, organized chloroplasts for photosynthesizing.

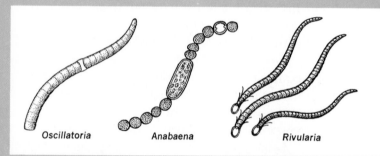

Oscillatoria   Anabaena   Rivularia

BLUE–GREEN ALGAE
(Phylum—Cyanophyta)
These plants have no organized chloroplasts or organized nucleus. A blue pigment in their cytoplasm gives them their color. Food is stored as glycogen.

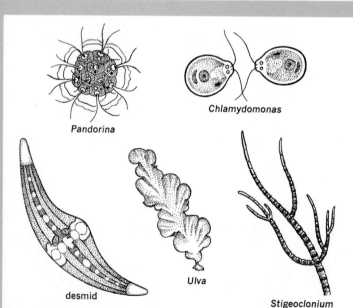

Pandorina

Chlamydomonas

desmid

Ulva

Stigeoclonium

GREEN ALGAE
(Phylum—Chlorophyta)
In these the chloroplasts are green. Plants usually are unicellular, but sometimes colonial or in simple filaments. They store food as starch.

You may find it valuable to refer to the chart, Classifying the Plant Kingdom, on page 256.

BROWN ALGAE

(Phylum—Phaeophyta)
These have chloroplasts that contain a brown pigment as well as chlorophyll. They are always multicellular. They store food as oil or as complex carbohydrates.

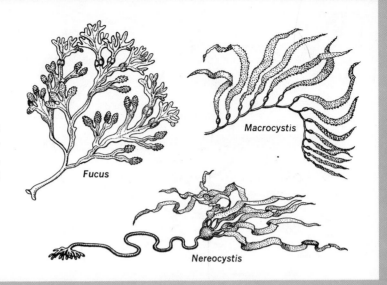

Fucus

Macrocystis

Nereocystis

RED ALGAE

(Phylum—Rhodophyta)
The cells of these algae contain a red pigment in addition to chlorophyll. They store food mainly as starch.

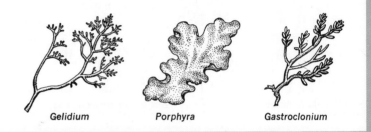

Gelidium

Porphyra

Gastroclonium

GOLDEN–BROWN ALGAE

(Phylum—Chrysophyta)
The diatoms, the chief golden-brown algae, have chloroplasts that contain yellow or brown pigment. Food is stored as oil and carbohydrates, but never as starch. Cell walls containing silica are of two overlapping halves and are ornamented.

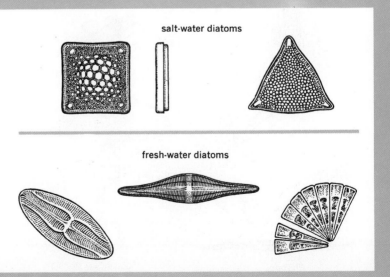

salt-water diatoms

fresh-water diatoms

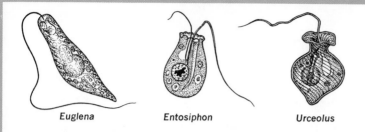

Euglena   Entosiphon   Urceolus

EUGLENALIKE ALGAE

(Phylum—Euglenophyta)

These algae have chloroplasts that are green. Food is stored as a complex carbohydrate. They move by means of one or more flagella.

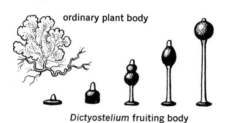

cocci   bacilli   spirilla

BACTERIA

(Phylum—Schizomycophyta)

These are single-celled thallophytes without chloroplasts or colored material. They reproduce by cell division.

ordinary plant body

Stemonitis fruiting body   Dictyostelium fruiting body

SLIME MOLDS

(Phylum—Myxomycophyta)

The plant body is a naked mass of protoplasm. They have no chloroplasts or other pigments. Spores are formed in special fruiting bodies. There are no threads, or filaments.

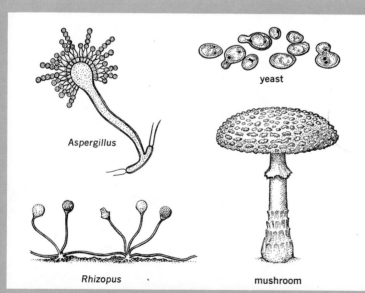

yeast

Aspergillus

Rhizopus   mushroom

TRUE FUNGI

(Phylum—Eumycophyta)

These are thallophytes without chloroplasts or other pigments. The plant body is made up of threadlike structures, the hyphae. This phylum includes molds, yeasts, smuts, rusts, and mushrooms.

11 The Bryophytes and Ferns — A Foothold on the Land

1. PLANTS WITH A TIE TO THE WATER

You may have read stories about persons lost in forests without a compass who found their way out by noticing on which side of tree trunks moss was growing. The idea is that mosses are supposed to grow only on the north sides of tree trunks.

If you have a compass, you might like to check on the story. Where do you find mosses? Be sure that what you find is not a growth of *Protococcus*, a green alga.

You are likely to find mosses just about any place that is usually moist. Mosses do grow heavily on the north side of many tree trunks, but they also grow on the south and other sides of trees in deep, shaded woods.

Because of the earth's tilt on its axis, the winter sun shines from the south. Trees that are spaced far apart get so much sunshine on their south sides that mosses cannot live there. But in dense woods where little sunlight penetrates, you are likely to find just about as much moss on the south side as on the north side of a tree trunk.

You will also find mosses in marshes, on damp rocks and soil, and beside streams and pools—in almost any moist place.

Structure of a Moss Plant

Mosses typically grow in patches. Perhaps you have moss plants growing in a school terrarium. If so, or if you can find green moss outdoors or growing on the soil of a flower pot, carefully remove a single plant and examine it.

In the picture below is one of the largest of mosses, *Polytrichum* (pol·ē·tri′kəm). ❶ Perhaps you have it or a smaller moss growing in your terrarium. *Polytrichum* and other mosses have what look like tiny hairlike "roots" and a "stem" surrounded with green "leaves." The reason we have placed quotation marks around these words is that a moss

❶

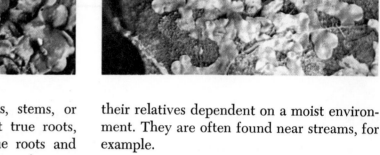

plant does not have true roots, stems, or leaves. You already know what true roots, stems, and leaves are like. True roots and stems have xylem and phloem tissue for conducting water and food substances; the leaves have stomata and guard cells. A moss has none of these things. Instead, the "roots" are actually *rhizoids* much like those of some of the larger algae that you studied in the last chapter. The rhizoids function to anchor the moss plants in the soil or on whatever they are growing. There is no evidence that they absorb water and minerals for the plant. The "leaves" of the moss do contain chlorophyll and manufacture food. They are made up, generally, of several layers of cells, but do not have stomata.

The mosses belong to the class of Bryophytes (brī′ō·fīts) known as Musci (mus′sī). Many of the plants in another class of bryophytes, known as Hepaticae (hə·pat′ə·cī), are flat, hugging the ground. The Hepaticae are commonly called **liverworts**. One liverwort is *Pellea* (pēl′ē·ə). ❶ Another liverwort is *Marchantia* (mär·kan′shē·ə). ❷ If you were to pick up any of the liverworts, you would again find rhizoids like those of the mosses. You would also find *Marchantia, Pellea,* and

their relatives dependent on a moist environment. They are often found near streams, for example.

The Cycle of Reproduction

Study the diagram at the right. ❸ Although it may not be obvious to you at first, the drawing on the left side of the diagram shows two generations of moss plants, one growing out of the other. The lower portion is the familiar leafy moss plant. Growing out of the top of this moss plant is a stalk with a spore case on its end. This stalk and spore case is a totally different generation of moss plant. It is embedded in and lives parasitically on the lower leafy plant. The spore-producing plant, or **sporophyte** (spôr′ō·fīt), meaning "spore plant," is just a long stalk with a spore case, the sporangium, in which the spores are produced. The sporangium does have some chlorophyll during a period of its development and thus manufactures some food. However, it is actually dependent for most of its food on the leafy plant below. (If you have living moss plants, you can probably find some that show this interesting situation.) As you read on, refer back to the diagram as much as necessary.

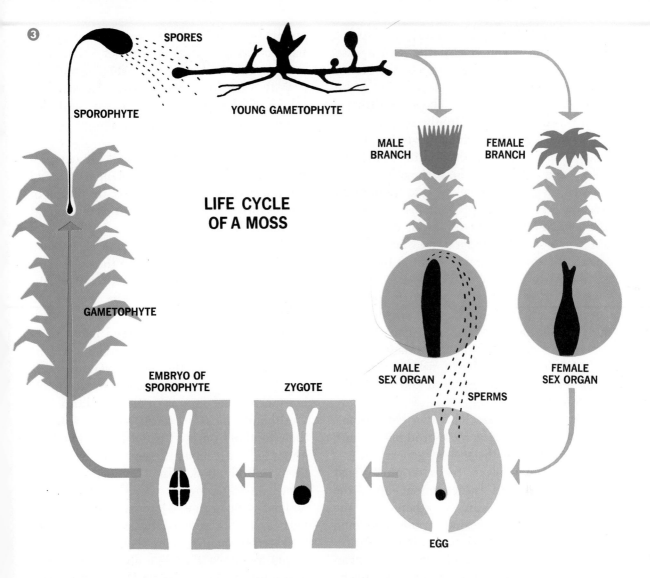

LIFE CYCLE OF A MOSS

③ SPORES

SPOROPHYTE

YOUNG GAMETOPHYTE

MALE BRANCH

FEMALE BRANCH

GAMETOPHYTE

MALE SEX ORGAN

FEMALE SEX ORGAN

SPERMS

EMBRYO OF SPOROPHYTE

ZYGOTE

EGG

The lower, leafy plant is anchored to the soil or is attached to a rock or a tree. The upper, parasitic plant produces spores in the capsule on its end. When the mature spores fall from the capsule into a moist environment, they germinate and grow into leafy plants resembling the lower plant. However, here a difference appears. Some parts of the leafy plants develop sperm-producing branches, and others develop egg-producing branches. The gametes (sperms and eggs) are produced in separate sex organs on separate branches, as shown above. Thus, the leafy plant is called a **gametophyte** (gə·mē′tō·fīt), which means "gamete plant."

The sperms of mosses have long flagella and look and swim much like the swimming algae. Fertilization can occur only when the plant is covered with a film of water (from dew or rain, usually). When environmental

251

conditions are right, the sperms, by whipping their flagella, swim out of the sperm case, down the moss plant, and up another branch containing the egg case, called the **archegonium** (är′kə·gō′nē·əm). They are attracted by a substance released by the egg cases, for they swim down into the archegonium to the egg. One sperm may then unite with (fertilize) the egg within the archegonium. The fertilized egg then develops into an embryo. The moss embryo simply remains attached to the female gametophyte, as it develops a stalk. The stalk lengthens and eventually produces the spore case, which starts the entire reproductive cycle again.

To summarize, the ripe spores are released from the sporangium. Each spore develops into a leafy gametophyte. The male gametes (sperms) swim to the female gametes (eggs) and fertilize them. The fertilized eggs remain *within* the archegonium and finally develop into sporophytes.

Clearly, the mosses have two generations. One generation is a gamete-producing plant, the gametophyte, the second generation is a spore-producing plant, the sporophyte, that grows out of and is dependent upon the gametophyte. You can say, then, that the mosses alternate asexual spore-producing generations with sexual generations that produce sperms and eggs. Study the diagram carefully again to fix this reproductive cycle, called **alternation of generations**, in your mind.

The Dependence on Water

Because the small moss plants have no conducting tissues, they cannot grow very tall above their moist environment. All the cells in the plant body must have moisture near at hand. For the most part, they all grow in moist places. However, there are some that are able to exist in dry places, such as on the bark of trees; but they are not active and cannot reproduce except in wet seasons.

With a friend or two or with your teacher, take a field trip to collect mosses and discover where they grow. You should take a good hand lens with you. ■

Why would most mosses die if the environment dried out? Even if most mosses could survive dryness and make food by means of photosynthesis, the mosses as a group might die out if the sexual plants were kept dry. Remember that there must be a film of water in which the sperms can swim to the eggs. This need for a moist environment also holds true, as you will find out, for the ferns. Mosses and ferns came into existence at a time when great swamps and bogs covered many parts of the earth, and water was abundant. Nevertheless, today, in the inconspicuous moss plant, you see an adventurous organism. It has taken to the land with all its hazards.

Although mosses live on land, in a sense, their foothold on land is not a firm one. For example, the mosses depend on water for their reproduction. When an organism depends on water for its reproduction, its life on land is hazardous. Moreover, the leaves of mosses are not covered by as heavy a layer of waterproof cutin as are those of other land plants, and on land there is always the danger of drying out. Yet it was with the mosses that the invasion of the land by plants began. Soon there were to develop true land plants, that is, plants that did not depend on water for their reproduction, plants with other characteristics that enabled them to survive drying conditions. However, to survive is not enough. A species of organism, if it is to be successful, must reproduce its own kind and spread. In order to reproduce successfully and to spread, the offspring of an organism or of a kind of

■ AN APPRENTICE INVESTIGATION into the Structures of a Moss

It is a good idea to take along on your field trip some newspaper and some jars or plastic bags for holding the mosses. Collect several types of mosses. Wrap some in wet newspaper or place them in a covered jar. Examine one in the field with your hand lens.

With your lens, examine the moss. ❶ How thick are the leaves? Could they withstand the hot sun?

In the laboratory, examine the rhizoids. Don't they remind you of the root hairs of young seedlings? Could the rhizoids anchor a tall plant (say five feet high) to the ground?

Examine a leaf under the microscope. To do so, place the top of the leaf in a drop of water on a slide. Notice the simple cells with their spherical or oval chloroplasts. ❷ How many layers of cells are there? Most leaves of mosses have two or three cell layers. Do you find any stomata?

An Investigation On Your Own
Determine whether the leaves of mosses are protected in the same way as those of trees.

organism must be able to adapt to a variety of environments.

A variety of bryophytes are pictured in the illustrated classification section Variety Among the Plants at the end of this chapter.

REVIEW

1. How do the mosses compare with most of the algae with regard to
    a. their environment?
    b. their reproduction?
    c. their organs of photosynthesis?
    d. their characteristic structures?

2. Compare a moss like *Polytrichum* and a liverwort like *Pellea*. That is, compare the mosses with the liverworts.

3. In a sense, why is the spore-producing generation of the mosses considered to be parasitic on the gamete-producing generation?

4. What is the relationship of the sperms to the gametophyte? What is the relationship of the sporangium to the sporophyte?

5. Which is the asexual generation of the moss plant, sporophyte or gametophyte? What, if any, are the disadvantages of alternation of generations in the mosses?

Harper, 1956, or *The Evolution of Life,* F. H. T. Rhodes, Penguin Books, 1962.

2. Suppose you were designing a plant to survive on land. What kinds of structures or protections might you include?

3. If you can obtain some living moss plants (in the field or from a supply house) with sporophytes attached, you may wish to make a laboratory study of the life cycle of the moss. For instructions for germinating moss spores, use a reference such as *A Sourcebook for the Biological Sciences,* by Morholt and others, Harcourt Brace Jovanovich, 1966 (2nd edition).

4. The alga *Ulva* has alternation of generations. But in *Ulva* the sporophyte and the gametophyte look alike. How, then, do botanists know the generations alternate?

5. *Survival,* in the sense that biologists use the word, means not only survival of an individual organism but also the reproduction and the survival of the species. How are mosses adapted for survival in this sense?

2. EVIDENCE OF A PAST LIFE

At the left you will find a photograph of two pieces of rock, often found around and in beds of coal. ❶ Clearly, the prints in the coal seem to be similar to parts of fern leaves, or **fronds** (frondz), as they are called. What do these imprints mean?

To seek out the meaning of these imprints, we must be concerned with at least two events: first, how the rock was formed, and second, how long ago it was formed.

The Meaning of a Bed of Coal

One useful clue about coal is the knowledge that it is formed in beds. This must mean that large quantities of the material that formed coal must have been deposited at about the same time.

NEW VIEW

1. What does *survival* mean in the evolutionary sense? A good way to approach this question is to do some library research.

A good introductory book to read is *The Earth for Sam,* Maxwell Reed, Harcourt, Brace & World, 1960. Or you might want to read the chapters on evolution in a textbook on biology, such as *Biology: An Inquiry into Life,* BSCS, Harcourt Brace Jovanovich, 1966. You might also like to read *The Story of Our Earth,* Richard Carrington,

Another clue can be found in the imprint of the leaf in the rock that you saw in the photograph. Obviously, the leaf of the plant that made the imprint is no longer alive. We call such an imprint a *fossil* imprint. You probably know that a **fossil** is the remains of an organism that lived in ancient times. The meaning of fossil remains will become clearer to you as you study the formation of coal. (In Unit Seven you will study fossils in greater detail.)

From their study of the fossil imprints, scientists are able to reconstruct the kinds of plants that formed the coal beds lying between and around layers of rocks. To understand how such reconstruction is possible, reconstruct an organism for yourself.

Suppose you found a tooth of the shape shown in the upper drawing. ❷ Suppose you were also a student of anatomy (the study of the structure of organisms) and had studied the anatomy of the skulls of animals. Now study the teeth of the animals now living, which are shown in the lower drawings. What kind of animal has a tooth similar to the one you found? Therefore, from what kind of animal might the tooth have come? (See the answer at the bottom of the page.)

In any event, if you were a skilled anatomist, you might be able to reconstruct the lower jaws of the animals by the size and shape of the teeth. You might even be able to reconstruct the skull. Sizes and shapes of skulls, anatomists know, are good indications of the nature of the animal. Usually, a certain sized skull gives a clue to the size of the body of the animal.

Thus, from actual fossil teeth of an ancient horse and from fossil bones, scientists reconstructed the entire animal shown in the

We would say a mouselike animal. Were we wrong?

COMPARISON OF FOSSIL AND MODERN TEETH

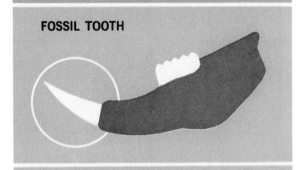

FOSSIL TOOTH

Study the fossil tooth circled in the diagram above. Then compare it with the teeth of three living animals shown below. As similar tooth structure indicates similar adaptation to the environment, predict the type of animal from which the fossil tooth may have come.

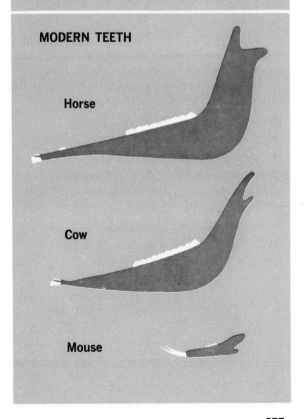

MODERN TEETH

Horse

Cow

Mouse

painting. ❶ Later you will see that by studying the evidence furnished by fossil teeth and jaws, and the front and hind legs of the ancient horses, as well as other fossils, scientists are able to learn much about the past life of the horse.

In much the same way, a student of the anatomy of fossil plants, called a paleobotanist, can reconstruct an entire fossil plant from the imprints of leaves and other fossilized parts of the plant. Put in another way, a paleobotanist is a student of the evolution of plants. Evolution, you may recall from your earlier work in science, refers to the development of organisms over the past ages of the earth. A study of evolution is based on many sciences for example, geology, in addition to paleontology·

From fossil imprints, paleobotanists have reconstructed four major groups of plants that existed in ancient times. However, a brief view of the major groups of plants living today is necessary to understand the past history—the evolution—of plants. The classification chart of the Plant Kingdom shown

CLASSIFYING THE PLANT KINGDOM

SUBKINGDOM—**Thallophytes (Thallophyta)**:
Mainly aquatic plants; single-celled, colonial, or filamentous; no true roots, stems, or leaves

PHYLUM—**Blue-green algae (Cyanophyta)**

PHYLUM—**Euglenalike algae (Euglenophyta)**

PHYLUM—**Green algae (Chlorophyta)**

PHYLUM—**Golden-brown algae (Chrysophyta)**

PHYLUM—**Large brown algae (Phaeophyta)**

PHYLUM—**Red algae (Rhodophyta)**

PHYLUM—**Bacteria (Schizomycophyta)**

PHYLUM—**Slime molds (Myxomycophyta)**

PHYLUM—**True fungi (Eumycophyta)**

SUBKINGDOM—**Embryophytes (Embryophyta)**:
Mainly land plants; more high developed; multicellular

PHYLUM—**Bryophytes (Bryophyta)**: The most primitive land plants; mosses and liverworts living today; no true roots, stems, or leaves

PHYLUM—**Tracheophytes (Tracheophyta)**:
More highly developed; have xylem and phloem

SUBPHYLUM—**Psilopsids (Psilopsida)**: most primitive vascular plants, virtually leafless, rootless; now mainly extinct

SUBPHYLUM—**Club Mosses and Spike Mosses (Lycopsida)**: Roots, leaves, and simple vascular tissue; dominant in Carboniferous period, only a few species left today

SUBPHYLUM—**Horsetails (Sphenopsida)**: Roots, leaves, and some vascular tissue; dominant in Carboniferous period, but almost extinct today

SUBPHYLUM—**Ferns and Seed Plants; Pteridophytes (Pteropsida)**: Conspicuous leaves; true roots; conducting tissue

CLASS—**Ferns (Filicineae)**

CLASS—**Cone-bearing plants; Conifers (Gymnospermae)**: Seed-producing plants with seeds not enclosed in a fruit, but usually in a cone: pines, spruces, cycads, and ginkgo.

CLASS—**Flowering Plants (Angiospermae)**: Seed-producing plants with flowers; maples, cherries, tulips, daisies

here will help. You are already familiar with the large thallophyte subkingdom. Then there is the great subkingdom Embryophyta (em′brē·ō′fī·tə) that contains the phylum Bryophyta, the mosses and liverworts. The next phylum in the embryophytes is known as the Tracheophyta (trā′kē·ō·fī′tə). The tracheophytes contain all plants that have conducting tissues, xylem and phloem. There are four subphyla in the tracheophytes. One, the Psilopsida (sī·läp′·sə·də), includes the most primitive plants. Another, the Lycopsida (lī·cop′si·də), includes the club mosses and spike mosses. The third, the Sphenopsida (sfē′nop′sə·də), includes the horsetails. Most plants in these subphyla are extinct.

Another important subphylum contained in the Tracheophyta is the Pteropsida (tər·op′si·də). The Pteropsida, commonly called pteridophytes (tər·id′ō·fīts), includes all of the well-adapted land plants of today. They are the kinds most familiar to you—trees, grasses, vegetables, fruits, and flowers.

The pteridophytes are divided into three classes: the Filicineae (fil′ə·sin′ē·ē′), the ferns; the Gymnospermae (jim′nō·spûr′mē), the pines and other cone-bearing plants; and the Angiospermae (an′jē·ō·spûr′mē), the flowering plants. The ferns reproduce asexually by means of spores. The last two classes, angiosperms and gymnosperms, are seed plants and reproduce by means of seeds.

The plants that formed coal in ancient times hadn't a flowering plant among them— no roses, apples, or maples. How do we know this? It's simple. There are no fossils of plants with flowers found in coal beds. For the moment, we need to discover the kinds of plants that were common in these ancient times, and to know *when* they existed. Thanks to the methods of modern science, we can date fossils with considerable accuracy.

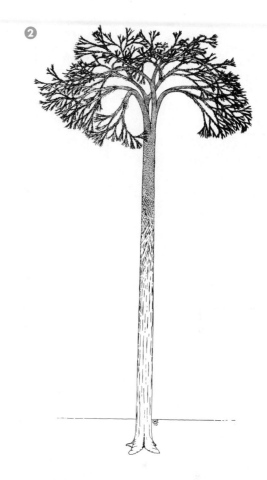

Ancient Forests and Puny Survivors

You probably know that coal is made up mainly of the element carbon. It isn't strange, then, that the ages during which coal was formed are collectively called the *Carboniferous* period. The plants of the Carboniferous period had representatives of two great subphyla of the tracheophytes. The subphylum Lycopsida included the giant club mosses that are now extinct, although they are abundant in the fossil record. One of the giant club mosses, *Lepidodendron* (lep′ə·dō·den′drən), grew over 100 feet or higher and was three or more feet in diameter. *Lepidodendron* and its neighbors, living in the moist forests

great club mosses reproduce by spores. *Lycopodium* bears its spores in clublike structures at the tops of the upright stalks. *Selaginella* bears its spores at the tips of its branches.

A common plant related to the Lycopsida is the horsetail, *Equisetum* (ek′wə·sē′təm). The horsetails are part of the subphylum Sphenopsida. Perhaps you have seen horsetails growing in the dry soil of meadows or along railroad embankments. The strange heads, called **strobili** (strō′bə·lī; sing., *strobilus*), carry the spores. The horsetails are commonly known as "scouring rushes" because in the past they were often used for scouring since they have a large amount of silicon (an element in sand) in their bodies.

Equisetum and its modern, puny relatives are the survivors of the giant horsetails that were neighbors of the giant club mosses in the forests of the Carboniferous period. One form of these giant horsetails, the Calamites, attained heights of 60 to 90 feet.

Our modern forests of today, consisting of seed plants such as pines, sequoias, firs, hemlock, oaks, maples, and beeches, are of fairly recent origin. Long before them were forests of treelike plants, the Lycopsida (club mosses), Sphenopsida (horsetails), and giant ferns, all of which reproduced by spores, not seeds. The spore, not the seed, was the reproductive structure that was first adapted to reproduction on land.

Side by side with the giant club mosses and horsetails were the ancient ferns. But here, too, our modern ferns are puny when compared with the giants of the Carboniferous period. In this period, fernlike plants that reproduced by seedlike structures first appeared. These ferns were called *seed ferns*. The seed ferns no longer exist, and we know about them only from their fossil remains. We shall give the seed ferns more attention later

of the Carboniferous period, helped form our coal beds and left the fossil imprints in the nearby rock layers. Fossil imprints are also found frequently in coal.

The Lycopsida left descendants, the small club mosses living today. One of these is *Lycopodium* (lī′kō·pō′dē·əm). ❶ Another is *Selaginella* (sel′ə·ji·nel′ə). ❷ Like the mosses and ferns, these puny survivors of the once

■ AN APPRENTICE INVESTIGATION into the Structure of Peat

You will need a supply of peat. (Peat can be obtained through a florist or a garden supply center.) It will probably contain a large amount of dead and broken-down mosses. Tease some of it apart and examine it. Perhaps you will also want to examine it under the microscope or with a hand lens.❶

Compare it with some dry, rotting wood that you may be able to collect in the woods. How does peat compare with rotting wood? Do you find any parts that are similar? Do you find any parts similar to those shown in the photograph? Peat is made up of the remains of plants pressed together. If you examine peat through a microscope you may find evidence of the cellular structures of plants—xylem cells or bark cells, for instance.

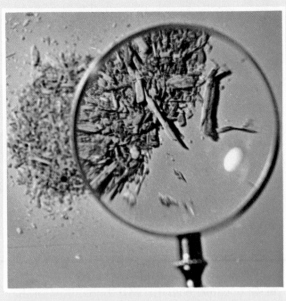

An Investigation On Your Own

Determine the relative water-holding capacity of peat, rich forest soil, garden soil, and sand. In setting up your investigation, try to control other variables such as the amount used, volume, and the initial water content of the peat, soil, and sand.

---

when you study seed plants. The seed ferns, as well as their companions of the Carboniferous period, contributed to the coal beds.

Laying Down Coal Beds

Now imagine for a moment the environment of the Carboniferous forests. From the nature of the plants living at that time and from other evidence, it is possible to reconstruct the environment. In general, the environment was warm and relatively moist and swampy. Imagine a warm, moist tropical forest of giant ferns, horsetails, club mosses, and seed ferns. Imagine, further, the giant plants dying and falling in the swamps and slowly breaking down to form peat. Peat is composed of dead, broken-down plant material

that has been pressed together. Why not examine some peat for yourself in the investigation above. ■

Now back to our story. Imagine one tree falling on another in the water of the quiet swamps. Imagine the pressure built up as the dead trees and plants fall and stack up on each other. And, as you may remember from your earlier work in science, there are processes within the earth that produce heat. The action of pressure and heat in the waters of the Carboniferous period produced peat.

Greater and greater pressure of the constantly accumulating trees and plants never lessened. Flowing water brought sand and silt that accumulated on top of the plant material; this of course caused more pressure

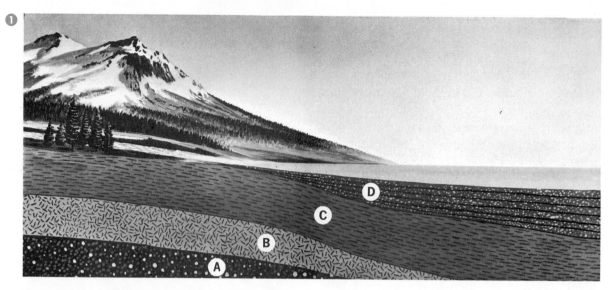

and more heat. Finally, over millions of years, the plant material, first forming a kind of peat, became coal in vast beds. Remember that the basic materials of which plants and other living organisms are built are organic compounds. Remember also that organic compounds contain mainly the element carbon and that coal is largely composed of carbon. Perhaps it is now becoming clear to you why these different ages are called the Carboniferous period.

There are other studies that seem to indicate that the land of the ancient fern forests sank as the coal beds were forming. When this occurred, water flowed in and covered the land. As streams fed into this water, they carried particles of soil and silt, called *sediment*. As this sediment piled up, it became cemented together and formed a kind of rock known as **sedimentary rock.** Often bits of plants became caught in this sedimentary rock, leaving their imprints. The sedimentary rocks also pressed down on the plant material, adding to the pressure and heat. Coal beds are often found between layers of sedimentary rock.

Sedimentary rock layers have great meaning for the scientists who study the fossils. The depths at which the sedimentary rock layers are found often indicate the ages and thus the development of living things over a period of time on this earth. These scientists, as you may already know, are called paleontologists. Their science, paleontology, is a study of the history of the earth based upon rock formations and the fossils they contain. And fossils are found mainly in sedimentary rock.

A Look at Sedimentary Rock Layers

How do paleontologists know when a given organism lived? First, they know that if an organism exists only as a fossil, it lived in ancient times, not in the present. Once this is determined, two important questions to answer are: When did the organism live and flourish? Of two or more organisms all living in ancient times, which lived first?

Some kinds of scientific studies proceed as follows. Suppose that certain fossils are discovered and it is important to know when they lived. Assumptions, or hypotheses, are

■ Making a Model of Rock Layers

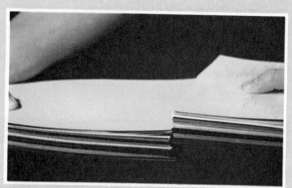

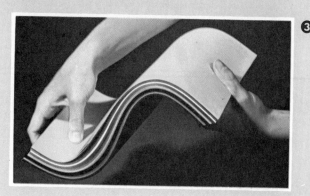

Take several sheets of colored paper of the same size. Also get several pieces of cardboard of the same size. Print the letter A about 20 times on one sheet of paper, scattering the letters over the entire sheet. The letters stand for fossils of type A. Print 20 B's on a piece of cardboard, and so on with C's, D's, and E's, until you have a stack of paper and cardboard of different colors and thicknesses, with different letters (each for a type of fossil) on each sheet. You now have a model of sedimentary rock layers containing fossils. ❶

Suppose the rock layers in your model were broken up in various ways. Perhaps parts of the original layers remained as they were, but other parts sank or were pushed up vertically. ❷ Or perhaps parts of the original layers were curved. ❸ How would you know which fossils came first in the layers that had changed positions?

An Investigation On Your Own

With your model, demonstrate how fossils of type B could appear on top of fossils of type A.

---

developed and evidence is sought to determine whether the hypotheses are correct. The evidence may often be found by studying the sedimentary rock layers. How are these sedimentary rock layers formed?

From your earlier work, you probably know that rivers constantly carry sediment from the land into the oceans. This sediment under great pressures finally hardens into sedimentary rock. Anything—a rock, a shell, a leaf, or the body of a dead plant or animal—might be preserved in the sedimentary rock in fossil form.

Look at the drawing of sedimentary rock layers. ❶ Which rock layer was laid down first? Probably the bottom layer (layer A), layer B next, and so on. Make a model of rock layers for yourself. ■

GEOLOGICAL TIME SCALE (Condensed)*

Era	Period	Approximate Time	Main Forms of Life	Climate
CENOZOIC	Quaternary	2 million years ago	Man dominant.	Climate zones and seasons established as we know them today.
CENOZOIC	Tertiary	63 million years ago	Angiosperms and mammals dominant.	Climate belts developing above and below equator but warm climate still widespread.
MESOZOIC	Cretaceous and other periods	230 million years ago	First angiosperms. First mammals. Gymnosperms and reptiles dominant.	End of era, some variation in climate, but still warm. Beginning of era, worldwide tropical and sub-tropical climate.
PALEOZOIC	Carboniferous and other periods	405 million years ago	Some gymnosperms. Ancient tracheophytes and fish dominant.	Fairly uniform tropical climate throughout the world.
PALEOZOIC	Cambrian and other periods	600 million years ago	First land plants.	Climate becoming warmer.
PROTEROZOIC	PRECAMBRIAN	? ? ?	Thallophytes dominant. First organisms.	Climate cool at end of era. Glaciers earlier.
ARCHEOZOIC	PRECAMBRIAN		No life according to evidence.	

*A more expanded geologic time scale appears on page 397.

The Age of a Fossil

Through careful study over the past centuries, paleontologists have gathered evidence about which fossils preceded others. Furthermore, they have an idea of how old the different layers are.

The age of a sedimentary rock layer can be determined by the kind and amount of the element lead it contains. You probably know something of the nature of an atom. You know, of course, that certain atoms are radioactive. **Radioactive** means that the nucleus of the atom breaks down by giving off some of its nuclear particles, that is, neutrons, protons, or electrons. Atoms that are strongly radioactive, such as uranium, are constantly breaking down. As they break down over a period of time, they change into a special kind of lead atom. This kind of atom of lead weighs more than ordinary lead.

Now uranium takes a long time to break down. Furthermore, within the earth the breakdown of uranium goes on at a constant rate. The period of time it takes half the atoms of a radioactive substance to break down is called the **half-life** of that substance. It is calculated that it takes about $4\frac{1}{2}$ billion years for half the atoms in a piece of uranium to break down into the special kind of lead. By determining the amounts of the special lead contained in a layer of sedimentary rock, paleontologists have a kind of clock to determine the age of a sedimentary rock layer.

The Ancient Ages of the Earth

Through the evidence they have gathered, paleontologists have assigned ages to different kinds of rock layers occurring in ancient times. These ages, called *eras* and *periods*, are known by the names shown in the copy of the Geological Time Scale opposite. The approximate time of the beginning of each era and the periods within an era are also shown. This time span, you recall, is determined by analysis of the radioactive substances in the rock layers of each period.

It would seem, then, that the earth has a long history. It would also seem that paleontologists are apparently certain of several concepts such as these:

a. The era of the algae, the first land plants, and the era of the ferns came long before that of the gymnosperms and angiosperms. The estimate is that the angiosperms first appeared some 100 million to 200 million years ago.

b. The first land plants appeared some 300 million years ago.

REVIEW

1. What is the significance of fossils?
2. How is it possible to reconstruct a skull from a jaw or tooth?
3. How is it possible to reconstruct a tree from an imprint of a leaf and bits of bark?
4. Which classes of plants are not represented in the Carboniferous period?
5. How are the Bryophyta to be distinguished from the Tracheophyta?
6. How do sedimentary layers give evidence of the sequence of fossils?
7. Place these eras in order of their age:
   a. Mesozoic   c. Precambrian
   b. Cenozoic   d. Paleozoic

NEW VIEW

What are the various estimates of the age of the earth? Much evidence indicates it is about 4.6 billion years. Do the estimates in the biology textbooks you have examined agree with each other? Do the estimates change? If so, why?

① RHYNIA

3. EARLY LAND PLANTS

Truly successful land plants have means of reproduction that do not depend upon water. To develop these methods of reproduction was a long evolutionary journey. The journey began, so the evidence indicates, with types of plants like *Rhynia* (rī′nēə) in the subphylum Psilopsida. *Rhynia* is named after the village of Rhynie in northern Scotland. Here fossils of the plant were recently found.

Rhynia seems to be a very simple plant. ① One fossil species was about 10 to 12 inches tall, the other about 20. Both had underground stems, called **rhizomes** (rī′zōmz) and erect stems as well. True roots were absent in *Rhynia*, but rhizoids were present. Each aerial stem branched into two in these psilopsids. Some branches ended in a reproductive organ containing numerous spores. The spores had walls covered by the tough substance

263

cutin, which enabled the spores to survive very dry conditions. The spores also could survive a long resting period during which they might be spread around, or dispersed.

When cross sections of the stem of *Rhynia* were examined, they showed a layer of thick-walled epidermis cells containing stomata, and an outside covering made of cutin. The stem cells also contained chloroplasts, enabling it to carry on photosynthesis. In the center of the stem there was a strand of conducting tissue, made up of xylem and phloem. It was very much like one of the conducting bundles in the corn that you examined in Chapter 6. However, in *Rhynia* there was only one bundle, and it was located in the *center* of the stem.

Thus the evidence showed that *Rhynia* contained the beginnings of the characteristic structures of land plants. Structures such as these enable a plant to live in an environment in which there is danger of drying out. Other fossils of plants, similar to *Rhynia*, have been found in Montana, in central New York, in Canada (near the Gaspé peninsula), as well as those found in Scotland.

If you are ever in Florida, you may come across a little-known plant, *Psilotum* (sī·lō′ təm), commonly called the whisk-fern. Notice its similarity, in a way, to *Rhynia*. Notice the sporangia, bearing spores. The spores are carried by the wind.

When the spore germinates, it forms a small, underground plant body called a **prothallus** (prō·thal′əs). The prothallus of *Psilotum* is the sexual generation, the gametophyte. The sexual generation in all organisms, of course, produces sperms and eggs. When the eggs of *Psilotum* are fertilized by the sperms, a wisk-fern is produced. The whisk-fern produces, as you know, spores. The production of spores (unlike the production of sperms and eggs) is asexual reproduction.

Thus, in *Psilotum*, as in the mosses, there is a true alternation of generations. A sexual generation, which is the gametophyte generation, alternates with an asexual generation, the sporophyte generation.

Why wasn't a prothallus discovered for *Rhynia*? A prothallus is relatively soft and unprotected, depending upon water for the swimming sperms. It would be difficult for a prothallus to be preserved as a fossil, since it would be easily destroyed. Also it is quite small. In view of the fact that the living *Psilotum* is somewhat similar to the fossil *Rhynia*, do you think it is possible that *Rhynia* also had a prothallus?

Adaptation to Drying Out

The success of the land plants is, then, related to the development of structures adapting them to survive in an ecosystem where water is not plentiful. See the meaning of this for yourself. ■

■ AN APPRENTICE INVESTIGATION into Adaptations to Drying Out

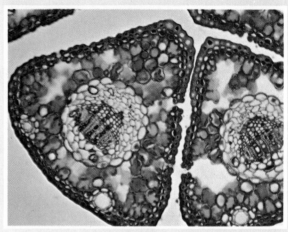

Collect a clump of moss, a mass of algae in pond water, and a twig with a few leaves (needles) of a pine or spruce tree.

Place a bit of the clump of algae, a part of the clump of moss, and a bit of the stem (with a few of the leaves) in three open saucers. Keep other parts of the algae, moss, and leaves in plastic bags.❶ What happens after several days?❷

Which plants survive best in a climate in which they are subject to drying out? Why?

If you examine the leaf of the pine or spruce closely, you cannot help but notice the thick covering, the epidermis, on the needles. If you examined a cross section of a pine leaf, you can see the layers of thick-walled epidermal cells.❸ The twig is covered by a protective bark whose outer cells are cutinized.

An Investigation On Your Own

Compare the spores of several ferns with the spores of several mosses. Is the outer covering of the fern spores thicker or thinner than those of the mosses? Which spores can survive in a drier environment? Why?

The evolution of green plants on land went hand in hand with their adaptation to a cruel environment. They adapted, over millions of years, to an environment in which living tissue, always requiring water, was in constant danger of drying out. To living tissue, drying out is death. And life on land requires special protection against drying out.

In any event, green plants ventured upon land and captured it. In capturing it, they became adapted to it. A study of the ferns will show us at once some of the adaptations of a successful land plant. A study of the ferns will also indicate why the ferns do not still dominate the earth and why they gave way to the seed plants.

② GROWTH HABIT OF A FERN

frond

rhizome

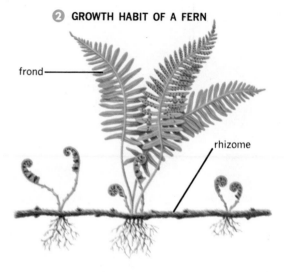

The Ferns—Land Plants with Links to the Water

When you think of a fern plant, you probably think of a plant that looks much like the one (a Boston fern) shown here.❶ What you are observing, however, is only one of the two forms, or *generations*, in a fern's life span.

A fern, such as the one you just saw, develops from a fertilized egg. It has true roots, a stem, and leaves. The typical fern stem, which is a rhizome, grows horizontally and just underneath the surface of the ground.

If you could examine a rhizome in cross section, you would find it has true conducting tissue. Long cells of xylem and phloem are found in continuous strands in the rhizome.

The ferns, like the primitive plants that preceded them—such as *Rhynia* and its relatives and *Psilotum*—are true vascular plants. The conducting cells, the xylem and phloem, transport water and food. Thus they form a vascular system.

Recall that this characteristic of a conducting system binds the ferns together with the cycads, conifers, and flowering plants in a dominant group of plants—the phylum Tracheophyta.

The fronds of the fern grow up from the rhizome, and it is only the fronds of the plant we usually see.❷ They, too, have conducting tissue throughout. As fronds develop, they uncurl from tight, little coils often called fiddleheads. As the rhizome continues to grow and send up more fronds, parts of it die, leaving totally separate fern plants, each with its short rhizome and roots.

As we stated earlier, the portion of the fern that you usually see growing in damp places or in flower pots, is the sporophyte, the asexual generation, containing true roots, stem, and leaves. See for yourself. ■

You are already familiar with the alternation of the sexual generation with the asexual. In the ferns, alternation of generations is strongly developed. The asexual fern plant (the sporophyte), often large, with its rhizomes, roots, and fronds, produces spores. Spores, you recall, are an asexual kind of reproductive cell. Thus a spore does not require fertilization. Yet, given the proper conditions of warmth and moisture, a spore grows into a

■ AN APPRENTICE INVESTIGATION into Fern Spores

Examine the undersurface of a fern frond. Notice the regularly arranged spots. ❶ Look at one of these spots with a magnifying glass or place a very small section of a leaf, with one of the spots, on a microscope slide and look at it under a microscope.

These structures contain the spores and are called **sori** (sôr′ī; singular, *sorus*). ❷ Remove a sorus and open it. Each sorus on the back of the fern frond holds a number of spore cases, or sporangia, each containing numerous spores. What do the spores look like? ❸

Examine the frond again. How many sori are there on one leaf? About how many sporangia are in each sorus? About how many spores are in each sporangium? Roughly, how many spores might a fern plant with five fern fronds produce?

An Investigation On Your Own

If you lay a frond (whose spores are ready to be shed) on a paper for a few days, hundreds of tiny spores should fall out onto the paper. You can dust these spores onto moist sand in a flower pot. (First pour boiling water over the flower pot and sand to kill most of the bacteria.)

Cover the flower pot with a glass plate to keep moisture in, and stand the pot in a plate of water. Place the pot in a light place, but not in direct sunlight. Add water as needed to keep the plate under the pot at least half full. If you are lucky, a few tiny, heart-shaped plants will grow after four or five weeks. Though they may not look like fern plants, they are the sexual generation of the fern.

Keep the plants alive for five or six months. Spray them often with water to furnish water for the swimming sperms. Perhaps you can grow a new sporophyte generation.

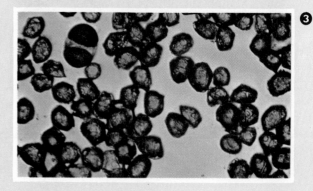

① SEXUAL REPRODUCTION IN THE FERN

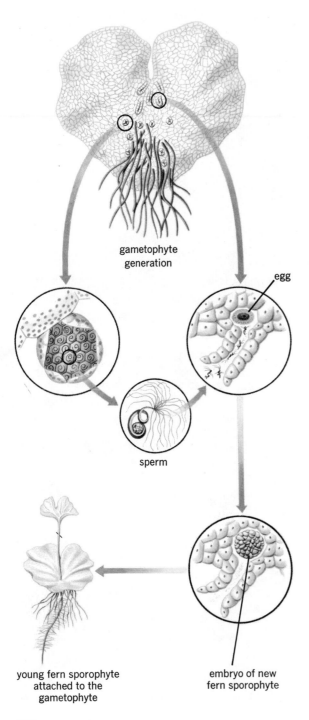

gametophyte
generation

egg

sperm

young fern sporophyte
attached to the
gametophyte

embryo of new
fern sporophyte

new plant—a spore grows into a gametophyte, the sexual generation. Gametophytes are very small, flat, heart-shaped plants that do not look like ferns. Rather, they look somewhat like one of the liverworts in the phylum Bryophyta.

After a few months, each of the very small gametophytes produce sperms and eggs in separate cases. ① The sperms have a tuft of cilia at one end, and they swim through a film of water to the egg cases where they fertilize the eggs. Because water is necessary for sexual reproduction, the fern is not yet fully adapted to a dry land environment. Once fertilized, the egg starts developing by taking food from the plant to which it is still attached, and finally grows into an asexual, spore-producing plant. Let's again stress that alternation of generations alternates a spore-producing generation with a sperm-and-egg-producing generation. In the case of ferns, the spore-producing generation is the dominant plant (it is larger than the gamete-producing generation) and is the plant most people think of when they think of ferns.

Tree Ferns and Fossil Ferns

Not all ferns have underground stems. In the wet jungle of the tropics, tree ferns grow fifty feet or higher. ② The stems of these plants are erect and the leaves grow out like the leaves of a palm tree. Yet they are true ferns. They produce spores, as do all ferns, and the spores develop into an alternate generation of prothalli that produce sperms and eggs.

Fernlike plants were so abundant in the Carboniferous period that this period has often been called the "Age of Ferns." But recall that the giant club mosses and horsetails, as well, were part of the so-called fern forests of the Carboniferous period.

Scientists who have been studying ancient plants think that perhaps most of the fernlike plants of the Carboniferous period were not true ferns but a form of the seed ferns. The ferns, the seed ferns, and the early conifers joined the club mosses and horsetails in forming the coal beds of this period. ❸

Surely these plants had begun to win the land even though the environment was quite moist and warm. But slowly, over millions of years, the environment became drier. And as the land dried out, the ancient forests began slowly, ever so slowly, to also die out. The ancient forests gave way to plants better adapted to withstand the harsher conditions of the new environment. These plants, better adapted to living in a drier environment are the subject of the following chapter.

REVIEW

1. What is the significance of *Rhynia?* of *Psilotum?*

2. What is alternation of generations?

3. Describe the spore-producing generation of a fern plant.

4. Describe the sperm-and-egg-producing generation of the fern. What grows from the fertilized eggs produced by this plant?

5. What is meant by the Age of Ferns?

NEW VIEW

1. Which appeared first on the earth, flowering plants, cycads, or ferns? Give the evidence that supports your answer. In the light of this evidence, which kind of plant do you believe to be the most primitive, and which kind do you believe to be the most advanced?

2. Use encyclopedias and other reference books to learn more about the Carboniferous period of the earth's history and its plants.

3. In a sense, ferns may be considered transitional plants. Transitional from what to what?

4. RELATING THE CONCEPTS

The ancient forests were not at all like those that graced the America of the Indians. The Indians who met the Pilgrims never saw forests of giant club mosses or seed ferns. But settlers of Pennsylvania, Ohio, and West Virginia used these ancient forests as coal.

269

These ancient forests have another significance. They give us evidence of forms of life that no longer exist. They inform the paleontologist of the development and changes in life over the ages.

Reviewing the Concepts

▶ *Plant life had its origin in water.* As far as the present evidence indicates, the early land was inhospitable to plant or animal life. The evidence indicates that plant life and animal life had its origin in an aquatic environment.

▶ *The earliest true land plants that have been recovered as fossils are tracheophytes.* *Rhynia* and its relatives are true land plants, with a vascular system and primitive roots. Their reproductive system, consisting of sporangia with spores that could resist drying out, was an adaptation to life on land. A prothallus of *Rhynia* has not been found, but perhaps the living *Psilotum* is close enough to *Rhynia* to enable us to think that *Rhynia* may have had a similar prothallus.

▶ *Ancient environments supported an ancient plant life.* The evidence indicates that the ancient forests supported a plant life that could survive best in environments that had abundant moisture and high temperatures.

▶ *Modern club mosses and ferns are remnants of ancient dominant plant life.* The ancient club mosses and ferns were giants compared to the puny club mosses and horsetails that survive.

The reproductive and other structures of ancient and modern club mosses, and ancient and modern horsetails, are very close in form. This leads us to the strong hypothesis that the ancient club mosses and horsetails were at least related to the modern plants.

There is mounting evidence that the ancient club mosses were the ancestors of the modern surviving forms.

▶ *Modern plant life as we know it today, particularly the flowering plants, is relatively recent in the time scale of evolution.* Fossils of flowering plants date back to the Mesozoic era, but are not found in the Paleozoic.

▶ *Fossils are preserved in sedimentary rock layers.* Because sedimentary rocks are made up of fine sediment falling slowly and over a long period of time, it is suitable for the preservation of ancient life. In contrast, there are other types of rock formations that are subject to even greater pressure, thus destroying any fossils they might have contained, if there were any.

▶ *Sedimentary rock layers are laid down in sequence, thus indicating a sequence of fossils.* Because sedimentary rocks are laid down one on top of the other, the lowest layers are the oldest. The fossils in the lowest layers are then the oldest, or earliest, fossils. The fossils in the upper layers of a bed of rocks are then considered relatively recent.

▶ *The rate of the breakdown of uranium yields a time scale for the past history of the evolution of organisms.* Because uranium breaks down slowly and at a steady rate, it furnishes a kind of geologic clock. The age of any rock layer containing the lead products of uranium may thus be determined.

▶ *The evidence indicates that the earth is very old, perhaps 4.6 billion years or more.* From evidence of many different kinds, particularly of uranium rock samples, the age of the earth has been estimated at almost 4.6 billion years. Some scientists who have studied the ages of rocks on the moon and meteorites found on earth believe it is even older.

► *There are gaps in the evidence relating to the evolution of plants.* Although it is quite clear that organisms existed and became extinct, it is very difficult to determine the ancestry of modern organisms. For instance, fossils of *Rhynia* cannot be traced back through a steady succession of plants to mosses or algae. Fossils of mosses and algae are difficult to find for several reasons. Mosses and algae are not easily preserved because of their soft tissues. In addition, the sedimentary rocks, in which their fossils might have been preserved, have been twisted and crushed. But, as you shall see for some organisms such as the horse, there is good evidence that links ancient forms to modern forms.

Testing Yourself

1. What is the significance of the Lycopsida in relation to the evolution of plant form?

2. What is the significance of sedimentary rock layers?

3. How is the age of sedimentary rock layers determined?

4. Contrast and compare the structure of the gametophyte and sporophyte of a fern.

5. Why are the Pteropsida classified under the phylum Tracheophyta? Why are the Bryophyta excluded?

Extending the Concepts

Investigation 1. Determine for yourself the growth and succession of fungi in your own microgarden. Three types of microgardens can be grown. They should all be grown in the same kind of container (a glass jar is good) for easy comparison later.

Barely soak three pieces of bread with milk, prune juice, and orange juice, respectively. Barely soak a fourth piece with water.

Expose all to the air for an hour. Then cover all of them as tightly as you can. NEVER OPEN THEM AGAIN. *When your study is finished, put all into the incinerator, or have your mother cover the growths with a strong disinfectant or a cleaning fluid. Some of the forms of fungi or bacteria you have grown could cause disease.*

You can determine whether new fungi or new growths have developed by the differences in color of the growth. Also, the size of the growth will determine, in part, how fast the fungi are growing.

Does one color fungus seem to dominate the growth in each of your jars? Or is there a succession, one fungus giving way to another?

How will you know whether it is the growth medium that is responsible for the growth of one fungus over another? Have you a control?

Investigation 2. Which mosses, ferns, shrubs, or trees dominate the environment in which you live? How will you determine which is the dominant form? How will you identify it?

Join with a few of your classmates to make this a group investigation. You will be able to check each other.

VARIETY AMONG THE PLANTS

MOSSES TO FERNS

The second and final large subkingdom of plants, the embryophytes, includes all the remaining plants—tremendous in number and of great variety in form. For the most part they are multicellular plants. It is true, certainly, that many of the more primitive forms (mosses and liverworts) are closely linked to the water by their need of moisture for reproduction and by their lack of true roots, stems, and leaves. However, even these more primitive plants show the beginnings of the adaptations necessary for functioning successfully on land.

In this chapter you have studied the mosses and liverworts (phylum Bryophyta), some of the extinct forms (phylum Tracheophyta) with a few of their relatives still living today, and the "modern" tracheophytes (ferns) of today. The ferns—at least in structure of the stem, leaves, and roots—are more closely related to the seed plants. However, in their means of reproduction the ferns show a closer relationship to the mosses. Together, these groups of plants illuminate the evolutionary relationships of plants.

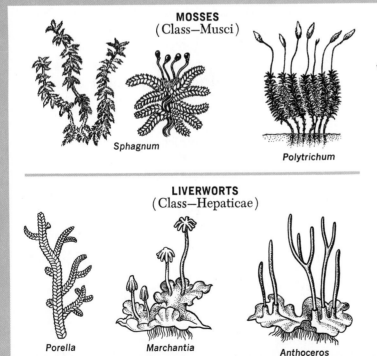

MOSSES
(Class—Musci)

Sphagnum

Polytrichum

LIVERWORTS
(Class—Hepaticae)

Porella

Marchantia

Anthoceros

MOSSES AND LIVERWORTS
(Phylum—Broyophyta)

These are the most primitive land plants living today. They have no true roots, stems, or leaves and are relatively small in size. They show alternation of generations and have swimming sperms.

You may find it valuable to refer to the chart, Classifying the Plant Kingdom, on page 256.

ANCIENT LAND PLANTS AND FERNS
(Phylum—Tracheophyta)

Here we find the beginning of vascular plants with true xylem and phloem. These more ancient plants show an alternation of generations with the sporophyte generation large and dominant and the gametophyte generation small and inconspicuous.

Psilopsids
(Subphylum—Psilopsida)

These are the most ancient tracheophytes, which are now mainly extinct. They are very simple, virtually leafless, rootless plants; and are usually small.

Rhynia (extinct)   *Psilotum*   *Asteroxylon* (extinct)

Club Mosses and Spike Mosses
(Subphylum—Lycopsida)

Only a few species of these once large and abundant plants remain today. They have poor roots and small leaves.

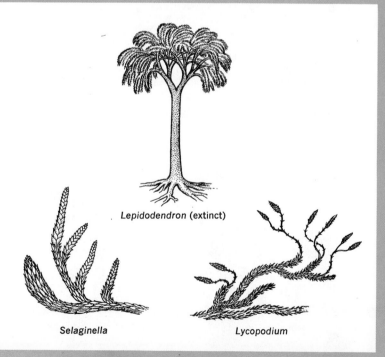

Lepidodendron (extinct)

Selaginella   *Lycopodium*

273

horsetail

calamite (extinct)

Horsetails

(Subphylum—Sphenopsida)
These spore-producing plants are almost extinct today. The few remaining species are usually small herbaceous plants with jointed stems with hollow centers.

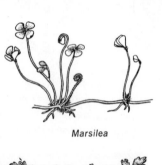

Marsilea

christmas fern

maidenhair fern

staghorn fern

Ferns and Seed Plants

(Subphylum—Pteropsida)
This subphylum includes the largest group of land plants in the Plant Kingdom. They are the most successful land plants. Since this chapter was concerned only with ferns (class Filicineae), only those are pictured here. (The remaining two classes, gymnosperms and angiosperms, are shown in the following chapter.)

Mariopteris (extinct)

Psaronius (extinct)

12 The Seed Plants — Established Land Plants

1. THE GYMNOSPERMS, OR CONE-BEARERS

Plants, like animals, depend on water just as they depend on some form of food. The energy in food cannot be released unless the food is dissolved in water. In other words, the metabolic activities of all protoplasm—breaking down food and releasing energy, building new cells and new cell parts—all depend on water. Protoplasm is composed mainly of mixtures of substances in water.

Most land plants are indeed rooted in soil from which they get their water. When we speak of *established land plants*, then, we do not mean plants independent of water for their metabolic needs. We mean that established land plants have adapted themselves to an environment in which water is less available and in which there is danger of drying out. Moreover, they do not, with a strange exception, depend on water in the external environment to carry sperms to the egg.

This chapter is concerned, then, with the plants that captured the land.

You are probably very familiar with the seed plants if only because you eat so many seeds and fruits yourself. You eat the seeds of wheat in flour and, no doubt, beans and corn are part of your diet. Whenever you bite into a fruit—apple, tomato, watermelon—you come upon seeds. Moreover, you expect that to produce seeds, flowers are needed. You expect apple flowers to produce apple seeds. This is true for the flowering plants.

There is a group of plants, however, that produces seeds without ever producing flowers. This is a relatively small group of plants when compared to the flowering plants.

The flowering seed plants, the **angiosperms,** have many orders. The nonflowering seed plants, the **gymnosperms,** have but three living orders: the cycads, the Cycadales (sī′ kə·dā′lēz); the ginkgoes, the Ginkgoales (gingk′kō′ālēz), with only one living species; and the conifers, Coniferales (kon′if·ər′ālēz), pines, firs, cedars, and spruces. A group of early conifers, the Cordaitales (kôr·dāt′ālēz), are extinct.

All these gymnosperms have xylem and phloem tissues; all have true roots, stems, and leaves; all are woody plants; all produce seeds; and all are fairly large, most being trees. However, none produce flowers. Recall that ferns have all these characteristics, but do not produce flowers or seeds.

The Cycads or Sago Palms

If you live near a botanical garden, you will see cycads. ❶ The cycads are plants that look much like palm trees, but, of course, palm trees are angiosperms, that is, flowering plants. If you live in certain areas of the South or in Hawaii, you will find a number of them growing there. One kind of cycad, a native of Florida, is only about three feet high. Also, many cycads grow in the tropics.

About 150 million years ago, early in the Mesozoic era, cycads grew in most parts of the world. Their fossils are found in such great numbers that scientists think living cycads must once have formed great forests. Cycads were the dominant plants during the period in earth's history when the dinosaurs were the dominant animal. This was the Jurassic period. Cycads were the main source of food for the plant-eating dinosaurs. In fact, this period in time is sometimes called the "Age of Cycads."

Today, cycads have all but disappeared from the earth. They are found only in small areas in tropical and subtropical climates, and in Australia, New Zealand, and Hawaii.

What happened to the cycads to cause this once dominant group of plants to become almost extinct? No one really knows any more than they really know what happened to the once dominant dinosaurs. However, we do know that the climates of the earth underwent great and sudden changes in the past.

Cycads and other tropical plants once lived in Canada and the northern United States. So many cycad fossils have been found in the Black Hills of South Dakota that the U. S. Government has established the Fossil Cycad National Monument there. But the climate changed. North America became very cold. Perhaps this had much to do with the widespread death of many cycads.

Why didn't the cycads continue to grow in those parts of the world that remained tropical? One possible hypothesis is that when other plants developed, that is, the flowering plants, they were even more successful in tropical climates than were the cycads. Flowering plants had barely evolved 150 million years ago when cycads were so plentiful. The oldest fossils of flowering plants are found in rocks that are only about 150 million years old. It is possible, then, that the flowering plants, once they appeared, were better adapted to a wide range of environments than the cycads and crowded them out of even the tropical environments.

Like the dinosaurs, perhaps, the cycads were unable to adapt to changing environments and were not able to compete with other organisms that did adapt. That is, perhaps they could not adapt to their environments as *successfully* as the flowering plants could. So, in competing for the same environment, they could not survive. In a sense, they were like blue grass plants being killed by crab grass in a lawn. The plants that take over are more successful.

Study the photograph of the huge *cones* produced by a cycad. ❶ A cycad produces cones rather than flowers, and the seeds develop, open to the air, fastened to the "shelves" of the cone.

A "Living Fossil"

The ginkgoes are represented by one surviving species, *Ginkgo biloba,* now commonly called the ginkgo. The ginkgo is a "living fossil"; a ginkgo is just like the trees that grew on the earth millions of years ago. The oldest ginkgo fossils (very much like the modern ginkgo tree) are found in rocks that are over 300 million years old (from the late Paleozoic era).

It is thought by some that the ginkgo tree might have become totally extinct except for the fact that ginkgoes were planted in temple gardens in China and Japan for many centuries, and thus the plants were cared for and kept reproducing.

Look at the drawings of ginkgo twigs. ❷ The one at the top has male structures. The one in the middle has unfertilized female structures (which, when fertilized, become seeds). The one at the bottom has seeds.

Pollen grains containing the male reproductive cells, the sperms, are produced in the male structures. When wind blows the pollen grains, some fall on the female structures. Each pollen grain then produces two sperms with cilia. The sperms swim down into the female structure. As in the mosses and ferns, a film of water is necessary for the swimming sperms to reach the eggs.

When the sperm cell fertilizes the egg cell by uniting with it, a seed develops. The seeds are contained within a cherrylike fruit. The ginkgo is indeed a strange tree. It is the only tree with swimming sperms. Do you think it is a successful land plant? Why?

❷ **REPRODUCTIVE STRUCTURES OF THE GINKGO**

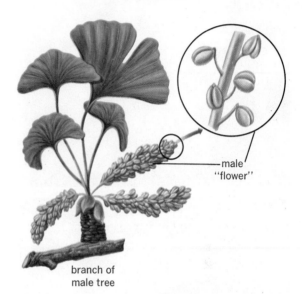

male "flower"

branch of male tree

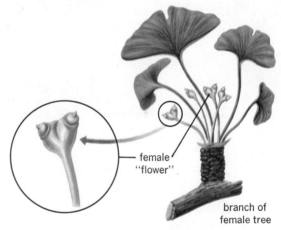

female "flower"

branch of female tree

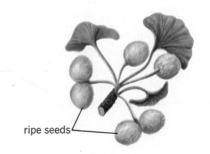

ripe seeds

The Conifers

The conifers (Coniferales) include trees such as firs, redwoods, yews, cypresses, junipers, cedars, pines, and spruces. The name *conifer* comes from the two Latin words that mean "cone bearer."

The cones are the reproductive structures of the conifers just as they are of the cycads. Sperm cells are produced in the pollen grains that develop in male cones. ❶ Egg cells are produced in separate, larger, female cones. ❷ In the photographs of the male and female cones notice that the male cones are produced in clusters, but that the female cones grow separately.

Have you ever stood under pine trees in the spring when the pollen is ripe in the male cones? If so, and if you shake a small pine tree, you can see the "pollen smoke." The pollen grains are tiny and have small, buoyant "wings," or "sails." Wind sometimes carries pine pollen hundreds of miles.

The female cones are sticky at first, and their scales are pressed tightly together. When pollen grains land on this sticky surface, they are held tightly.

Later, as the female cone dries, the scales open. If you look at the lower side of one of these scales, you will find the winged seeds. ❸ A sperm cell from a pollen grain is necessary to fertilize each egg cell for each of these winged seeds.

Most conifers have green leaves the year round, so they are often called evergreens. However, since other plants, the rhododendron and holly, for example, are evergreen, obviously the name is not a good one. But perhaps you didn't know that conifers shed their leaves just as other trees do. The difference, however, is that most conifers shed only a few leaves at a time, all year long; whereas flowering trees usually shed theirs all at one time in the fall.

For a moment, think about the classes of plants you have been studying in order to fix their relationship in mind. The conifers, you will recall, belong to a group of plants known as the gymnosperms. The gymnosperms, you will recall, include the cycads and the ginkgo. However, they also include an important group of early gymnosperms, the so-called seed ferns.  These early gymnosperms bore seedlike structures, but had fernlike leaves. However, the seedlike structures were borne in specialized organs *on the leaves, not in cones.* All of these ancient gymnosperms, except the *Ginkgo,* are extinct.

The early conifers, together with the tree ferns, giant club mosses, and giant horsetails, made up the ancient forests.

Economic Importance of Conifers

Conifers are among our most important trees. The book you are now reading is made of paper that was once the wood of conifer trees. In fact, most of the paper we use is made from the wood of conifers.

Rayon, cellophane, and other cellulose products, such as plastics, lacquers, and photographic films, are made chiefly from conifer wood, as are wood alcohol, turpentine, and acetone. And, of course, softwood (conifer wood) is used for making fences, ship masts, boxes and crates, excelsior, and so on.

As you can see, the nonflowering seed plants—at least the conifers—are extremely important to man. The extinct conifers are also important. We use them, together with the extinct club mosses and horsetails, as coal.

REVIEW

1. How do seeds develop on the ginkgo tree?
2. What is the meaning of the word *conifer?* Describe the male and female cones and explain how seeds develop in conifer trees.

NEW VIEW

1. Why is it thought that cycads were the dominant plants some 150 million years ago when dinosaurs were the dominant animals?

2. What evidence do we have that Canada and the northern United States once had a tropical climate?

3. What is your view of why the cycads and ginkgoes have all but died out since their days of dominance over 100 million years ago?

4. Why are the giant sequoias in danger of extinction?

5. Why would most living gymnosperms be considered successful land plants? Compare modern conifers with their ancient relatives, and with the *Ginkgo,* the seed ferns, and true ferns.

2. ANGIOSPERMS WITH TWO SEED LEAVES

When most people think of plants, they think of one large group—the flowering plants. Flowering plants include bushes, grasses and grains, weeds, vines, most trees, and even a few water plants such as water lilies.

However, not all of the flowering plants have large, obvious flowers. The flowers of an elm or maple tree, for example, are so small that you may never have noticed them.❶ But flowers they have, as do all the plants in this large class. In addition, flowering plants have all of the basic structures you have already learned about—roots, stems, and leaves. And like all vascular plants, they have phloem and xylem tissue.

The angiosperms are the most recent plants to occur in the earth's history. Recall from your study of the geologic time scale chart on page 262 that the angiosperms first appeared in the middle Mesozoic, perhaps over 150 million years ago. Since then they have established themselves throughout the various environments of the earth.

The Seed Leaves

There are two subclasses of flowering plants. These subclasses are given names that describe one big difference between them, that is, the number of "seed leaves" that are found in their seeds. A seed leaf is that part of a seed where food is stored for the embryo plant. The two large parts of a bean or a pea seed are the seed leaves.❷ They are called seed leaves because they are, structurally, modified leaves. They do not look much like leaves, however, because they have been modified to store food and to digest and absorb food from other parts of the seed when the embryo begins to grow. As some plants begin to grow, the seed leaves actually push up above the soil, become green, and start manufacturing food like any ordinary leaves. You can watch these seed leaves, or **cotyledons** (kot′ə·lēd′nz), as they are scientifically called, push through the soil and turn green. See for yourself. ■

A bean is a **dicotyledon.** (*di*– means "two." A bean has two seed leaves, or cotyledons.) Practically all trees except the conifers and palm trees are dicotyledons. Most bushes

■ AN APPRENTICE INVESTIGATION into Cotyledons

Soak several bean seeds in water overnight. Then plant them in moist sand, soil, or vermiculite. Place the pot with the seeds near a window. Keep the seeds moist at all times. In a few days you should begin to see something breaking through the soil. The stem is growing rapidly and pushing the two seed leaves above the soil. They will be thick and whitish. But after a day or two in the light, they turn green.❶ (The seed coat either remains underground or falls off soon after the seed leaves are above the ground.) The seed leaves become thinner, too, as their stored food is used to supply energy for the growing plant.❷ After awhile they wither and drop from the plant; their job completed, they are no longer needed.❸ (If you can get cotton seeds, you will find that the cotyledons turn green and manufacture food for several weeks.)

❷

An Investigation On Your Own

How long do the seed leaves of different plants last? Try bean, squash, tomato, maple, and oak. Be certain to plan careful controls.

❸

❶

DICOT: NET VENATION

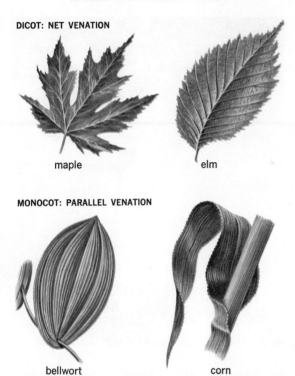

maple   elm

MONOCOT: PARALLEL VENATION

bellwort   corn

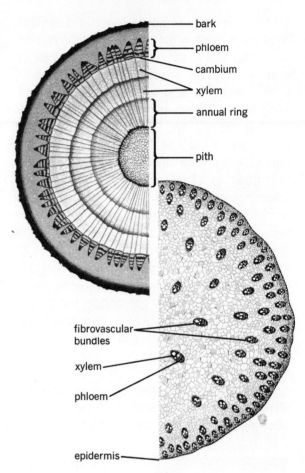

bark
phloem
cambium
xylem
annual ring
pith

fibrovascular bundles
xylem
phloem
epidermis

and vegetables are also dicotyledons. All of these plants have two seed leaves. **Mono-cotyledons** (*mono–* means "one") have but one seed leaf. There is a simple way to tell the difference between dicotyledons and monocotyledons without examining their seeds. Dicotyledons have net-veined leaves, whereas monocotyledons usually have veins that run parallel to each other from the leaf petioles to the tip. Note the netlike branching of the veins, known as *net venation,* in the pictures of the maple and elm leaves (top). ① Note the parallel veins, or *parallel venation,* in the pictures of the bellwort and corn leaves (bottom). ① You can probably think of other examples of each kind of vena-tion—how would you classify a blade of grass? a geranium leaf?

Another important difference between *dicots* and *monocots,* as they are often called, is found in the position of the phloem and xylem tissue in the stems. Remember how these are arranged in a tree stem. Xylem tis-sue forms rings inside the cambium layer. Phloem tissue forms rings outside the cam-bium layer. This arrangement in which a cambium produces xylem on its inside and phloem on its outside is typical of dicots.

There is no cambium layer in monocotyle-dons. Bundles containing both phloem and xylem are scattered throughout the stem. The drawings will help you see the difference between dicotyledon and monocotyledon stems. ❷

Growth Habits in the Dicot Plant

In a sense, most trees are typical dicotyledons. They have all of the *essential* features: net-veined leaves, two seed leaves, and a cambium that separates rings of xylem from phloem. But in another sense, a tree is typical only of other trees. Different types of plants have different habits of growth. Vines, for example, have very different growth habits from trees.

THE TREE HABIT. You are already familiar with this method of growth. A strong, woody stem grows thicker and thicker. It becomes the trunk. Stems branch out from the trunk and these grow thicker, too. Finally, the adult tree stands stiffly erect with green leaves supported by woody trunk, branches, and twigs so that they catch the light.

THE BUSH HABIT. Bushes also have woody stems that grow in thickness. But bushes, or shrubs, send up several main stems from the ground instead of a single main stem or trunk. These stems usually do not become very thick, and the entire plant does not grow very tall. The relatively thin stems do not give the plant enough strength to support high branches.

THE TWINING HABIT. Some kinds of plants have stems that grow very little in thickness, yet grow very long. These plants gain support by winding around other plants for support, or by producing specialized leaves, or **tendrils,** that wind around other plants or objects for support, as does the sweet pea. ❸ Some vines, for example, Virginia creeper, develop tendrils with adhesive discs that attach firmly to brick, wood, or stone. ❸ Other

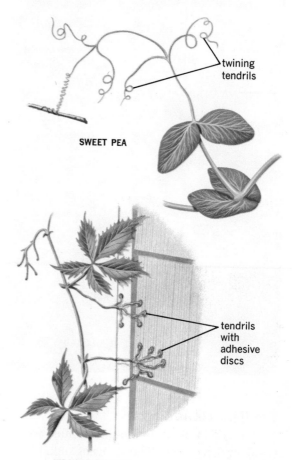

❸ SPECIALIZED STRUCTURES FOR SUPPORT

twining tendrils

SWEET PEA

tendrils with adhesive discs

VIRGINIA CREEPER

vines, for example, English ivy, have specialized roots along the stem by which they attach themselves.

Both herbaceous and woody plants have developed the vining habit. Morning glories, for example, have tender, herbaceous stems; whereas Virginia creeper, Boston ivy, and grapes all are woody plants.

THE CREEPING HABIT. Some plants (watermelons, squash, cantelopes, and cucumbers, for example) are vinelike, but usually spread over the ground rather than climbing into the air on other objects.

The Herbaceous Dicots

Many dicot plants do not have much woody tissue in their stems. The stems of such plants, called **herbaceous** (hûr·bā′shəs) **plants**, are usually soft and green, and they do not grow much in diameter. Most of our vegetables (peas, beans, squash, and tomatoes, for example) are herbaceous plants. So are most of our common flowers (pansies, larkspur, petunias, and chrysanthemums, for example). Herbaceous stems are so soft and weak that they cannot grow very high above the ground without some kind of support.

Some Unusual Food Habits

You have probably seen mistletoe. It is a rather small, compact plant with green leaves and stems but with pale, white berries. It is commonly sold at Christmas time for hanging in one's home.

Mistletoe is a parasite that grows on trees and other plants. It manufactures some of its own food as you would guess from its green color. However, it also sends specialized sucking roots into the branches of the tree it parasitizes and absorbs food from the host tree. This mistletoe is growing out of a tree branch. ❶ No roots are visible; they are inside the branch, drawing up food and water at the expense of the tree. Witchwood, another green yet parasitic plant, grows on corn.

Mushrooms and some other fungi, as you will remember, get their food by absorbing it from the tissues of dead plants and animals in the soil. All plants that meet their food needs in this way are called saprophytes.

A few dicots have developed the saprophytic way of life. The Indian pipe is an example. ❷ The roots of the Indian pipe form an almost solid clump that threads through a fungus in the soil. The fungus absorbs food from decaying organic materials in the soil. The Indian pipe, in turn, absorbs food from the fungus.

The stem of an Indian pipe is pinkish white. There is no chlorophyll whatsoever. The leaves have become tiny, useless scales on the stem. In fact, the only purpose served by the stem at all seems to be to produce and hold a flower at its tip. The Indian pipe is found in moist, woodsy places throughout the United States. It gets its name from the shape of the stems, each with a drooping pipe-bowl-shaped flower at its end.

Recall that *carnivore* means "meat eater." Does it surprise you to learn that over two hundred kinds of flowering plants are carnivores? They do not actually *eat* meat, but they do capture insects and absorb food materials from the insect bodies.

These unusual plants grow mainly in bogs and swamps or in very moist areas. Their adaptations to this way of life are interesting examples of how plants can change over the centuries to complement their environments.

The soil of a bog is usually lacking in certain substances that are necessary for the life and health of plants. Botanists believe that the carnivore habit represents an adaptation to get around this difficulty.

The carnivorous plants are green plants; they manufacture their own sugars. However, they also must have certain substances (especially nitrogen) missing in the bog soil in order to build the necessary proteins from the sugars. The leaves of these plants are specialized in various ways to trap insects and to absorb nutrients from their prey.

The pitcher plants have developed leaves that form a pitcher and hold a liquid containing digestive enzymes. ❸ Insects are attracted by the odor of the leaves and crawl into them. The insides of the leaves are covered with stiff, downward-pointing hairs, or bristles. Thus, when an insect attempts to crawl out, it is unable to get over the bristles. Finally, exhausted, the insect falls into the liquid, drowns, and is digested by the enzymes. The inner cells of the leaf then absorb the digested materials. The materials containing the substances missing in the soil are then combined with the sugars manufactured by the plant to make the various proteins and other substances necessary for maintaining life.

The Venus's flytrap is one of the most interesting plants of this kind, for it has developed leaves that actually move to trap insects. Each of these specialized leaves has a border of bristly "teeth" that may sometimes be a half-inch long. The upper surface of the leaf has several sensitive trigger hairs. When an insect crawls on the leaf and touches one of these hairs, the two halves of the leaf close together swiftly like an open book closing. The two halves of the leaf can close in as little time as a second. Study the photographs showing different stages in the trapping of a fly. ❶ Once the two halves of the leaf have closed, the "teeth" along the leaf edges overlap and the insect is hopelessly trapped. Digestive juices are then secreted that digest the insect's body. The digested materials are absorbed by the cells along the surface of the leaf. The leaf then opens again, allowing the indigestible portions to fall out.

How can the leaf close so rapidly when the sensitive hairs are stimulated? You know that plants have no nerves and no muscles. The rapid movement of the leaf, botanists believe, is a kind of **turgor movement.** In plants, turgor movements are the movements resulting from changes in water pressure in cells. For example, guard cells open stomata as a result of such pressure changes.

The sensitive hairs on the Venus's flytrap are highly sensitive. (Remember that *all* protoplasm is sensitive.) The touch of an insect's body somehow stimulates the sensitive hair cells to lose water, but just how this happens is not known. The base of each sensitive hair is large and each is located on the inner surface along the middle of the leaf, between the two blades. These hair cells quickly "wilt" as water leaves them. Thus the turgor pressure in the adjacent cells on the outer surface of the leaf forces the leaf to close rapidly.

Annuals and Perennials

Some plants, for example sweet peas and marigolds, live but a few months. They die after having lived out their life span in these few months. Plants such as these spend most of their lifetime in growing and in storing food they have manufactured. Then they produce flowers, fruit, and seeds. Death usually results shortly after the seeds have been produced. Plants that have such a pattern are called **annuals,** meaning "yearly."

Other plants live but two years, and are called **biennials** (bī·en′ē·əlz), meaning "two years." Beets and carrots are examples. If you plant a carrot seed, the young plant will grow all season, manufacturing food and storing much of it in the root. However, it will not produce flowers, fruit, or seeds during this first growing year. If you leave the carrot plant in the ground, however, it will start growing again the following spring. Once again it will manufacture food and store it. But then, later in the summer, it will use the stored food to produce flowers from which tiny fruits with seeds will develop. Once this is accomplished, the plant dies. It has reproduced itself, exhausted its stored food supply, and usually will not live another year.

Most plants, however, are **perennials** (pə·ren′ē·əlz), living several to many years. Roses, grapes, delphiniums, and trees, for example, all live for more than two years. Perennial plants must usually grow up, or mature, before they produce flowers and fruits. A walnut tree, for example, will usually not produce flowers and nuts until it is five or six years old. However, after a perennial plant has become mature, it begins to reproduce. Then, unlike annuals and biennials, the perennial plant still has enough stored food to support new growth and reproduction each spring for the rest of its active life.

REVIEW

1. What is a cotyledon? Why is it also called a "seed leaf"?

2. What are three characteristics that distinguish monocotyledons from dicotyledons?

3. What is meant by the term *herbaceous?* Give several examples of herbaceous plants.

4. How are vines adapted to their "vining" life?

5. Give an example of a parasitic green plant and explain how it gets its food.

6. Give an example of a carnivorous plant and explain how it gets its food.

7. Explain what is meant by the terms *annual, biennial,* and *perennial.* Give examples of each.

NEW VIEW

1. Suppose that you wanted to observe the flower of a carrot plant? Would you plant a carrot seed or a carrot root? Explain your answer.

2. Turgor movements account for a number of interesting and rapid plant movements. The speed with which the leaves of a Venus's flytrap close is matched by the speed with which the leaves of the "sensitive plant," *Mimosa,* close. Perhaps you can buy and grow a sensitive plant for study. Or you might investigate the sensitive plant by the use of references.

3. Use library references to learn more about carnivorous plants. What do you think of the theory that these green plants developed the carnivore habit because the soil they live in lacks certain essential elements? How might a scientist study this question?

4. How do you account for the parasitic habit of mistletoe, which is green and manufactures food?

5. Do morning glories and similar vines always twine in the same direction? How about the tendrils of grape vines? Design an investigation by which you may determine the early growth habits of tendrils or stems of different vines.

3. ANGIOSPERMS WITH ONE SEED LEAF

You are already familiar with the characteristics of all monocotyledons: a single seed leaf, parallel-veined leaves, no cambium, and xylem and phloem tubes in bundles scattered throughout the stem.

As was the case with the dicots, there are many interesting variations within the common structural plan of all monocots. Many plants of ponds and streams are monocotyledons. Cattails, pondweeds, and eelgrass are common examples. If you have water plants in your school aquarium, they probably include such monocotyledons as *Elodea*.

Widely different plants such as grasses, pineapples, palm trees, onions, daffodils, and orchids are also variations on the basic monocotyledon plan. So is the banana tree. ❶

Grasses and Grains

All grasses and grains are basically very much alike. In fact, wheat, corn, oats, rye, and other crops that man raises for food were developed from wild grasses.

Wheat was one of the earliest plants cultivated by man. Carbonized wheat grains have been found in the ruins of a town in Iran (Persia). These grains are about 6,700 years old. Even so, these wheat grains are almost identical to wild wheat that still grows in Iran and other places in the Middle East. No one knows exactly where the wild wheat originated. It may have developed over the centuries from wild grasses. Or ancient man may have helped the process along by selecting and planting those wild grasses that had the largest grains. In any event, it is certain that wild wheat did develop from wild grasses.

Modern wheats show thousands of variations, and those commonly planted as crops were developed by man's own efforts. In fact, the ancestry of modern wheat has been traced back to the crossing or mating of a wild wheat called Einkorn with some now unknown wild grass.

Corn is also really just a grass. It is a very important grass, of course, and it has become so much changed that it hardly resembles the common grasses. But upon close examination, you would find it structurally much like any other grass or grain.

There are thousands of different kinds of grasses. Many are considered weeds when they grow in our lawns and gardens because they kill or weaken more desirable grasses or garden crops. This occurs when their roots absorb the moisture and minerals that the other plants need. Also their leaves often keep the sunlight away from crops and cultivated grasses.

Palms, Bananas, and Joshua Trees

Although these trees are all monocotyledons, they are not closely related. However, all grow to tree height.

There are many kinds of palm trees, but the date palm and the coconut palm are the most important to man. These two palms may grow over 100 feet tall. The leaves, which may be several yards in length, grow only at the top of the branchless stem.

Date palms are common plants in the oases of deserts. Scattered over the Arabian, Sahara, and other deserts of North Africa, the Middle East, and Asia are certain areas where underground water or springs make human settlements possible. In these oases date palms provide food and cool shade.

Coconut palms, on the other hand, require a large amount of moisture, either from underground water or a very large yearly rainfall of at least 40 inches a year.

Tropical islands and tropical coastal areas are often bordered with coconut palms. Can you guess why? Of course. There is underground water near the edges of oceans and seas, so coconut palms do well there. The way in which coconut palms spread from one island or one shore to another is interesting. Perhaps you have noticed that the trees often lean out over the water. The fruits (coconuts) are covered with a tough, waterproof coat, and they are light enough to float. From the trees leaning out over the water's edge, coconuts drop into the water and are carried hundreds or even thousands of miles by winds, waves, and ocean currents. Eventually, a coconut may be washed up on the shore of an island far from the tree upon which the coconut developed. When conditions are right, the embryo plant within the coconut produces a root that breaks through the shell and grows down into the sand, using the

stored food in the *single* cotyledon (the coconut "meat") for the necessary materials and energy to produce new plant cells. A tiny stem pushes up into the air, turns green, and starts manufacturing food. ❷ Finally, after many years, another great coconut palm stands at the border of the sea.

Banana "trees" are quite different from palm trees, although they, too, send out leaves only at the top of a single, unbranched stem. Banana plants have no tough, woody outer rind like those of palm trees. They are actually herbaceous plants. However, turgor pressure inside thick-walled cells makes the stem of a banana plant strong and rigid. In addition, the support of the plant is aided by the "trunk," which consists in great part of long leaf-stalks wrapped tightly around the stem.

Another difference between bananas and palms is that bananas grow from football-sized underground bulbs. The banana trees that are grown for their fruit do not produce seeds. The next time you eat a banana look for seeds. You will find tiny dark dots that are only the *vestiges* (ves′tij·iz), or remains, of seeds. The ancestors of modern bananas

veins just as any leaf. A very small, thick stem can be found at the base of the bulb. When a dry onion is planted, roots will start growing from the base of the stem and a green shoot will start growing up from the top of the bulb. There is even a tiny flower bud in the center of the bulb. This is pushed up with the growing shoot and will finally open up to become a flower.

Green leaves higher up on the plant manufacture food that is stored in the bulb leaves. When sufficient food has been stored, the upper leaves dry up and die. The following year, another green shoot, or stem, grows out of the bulb, using the stored food in the bulb for its growth.

Orchids and Spanish Moss

Some monocotyledons have developed an "aerial habit" of life, for example, orchids and Spanish moss. These plants live entirely in the air—roots, stems, and leaves. The plants are supported by other plants or by telephone poles, houses, or other objects. However, aerial plants are not parasites as you might suppose from their habit of growth. The roots of these plants grow down into debris that catches in cracks or in the crotch of trees. Here they absorb rain water and minerals from the matted debris around their roots. Botanists call such plants **epiphytes** (ep′ə·fīts), or aerophytes ("air plants").

Pineapples and Yams

Pineapples and yams are widely different plants that illustrate the great variety of monocotyledons. Pineapple fruits grow from squat plants with spiny-edged, sword-shaped leaves. Yams are not fruits; they are the fleshy, storage roots of the yam plant. Sweet potatoes are much like yams; but they are the storage roots of a dicotyledonous plant.

were capable of reproducing themselves from seeds, but not the modern banana.

Strong ropes are made from the stem fibers of a plant that looks almost exactly like a banana plant—the *Manila hemp* plant.

Joshua trees are cactuslike plants that grow in deserts. But true cactuses are dicotyledons, and Joshua trees are monocotyledons. They sometimes grow to a height of forty feet and grow so thickly that they form a kind of forest in the desert. ❶ Over twenty-five different kinds of desert birds are known to nest in Joshua trees.

Lilies and Onions

Garlic, lilies, onions, tulips, and hyacinths are all very much alike and are grouped in the same order and family. All store food in a thick underground *bulb*.

A bulb is actually no more than a large underground bud. If you cut a dry onion (an onion bulb) lengthwise, you would find the "layers" of the bulb are thick leaves specialized in storing food. If you examined one of these layers closely, you would find that it has

There are over 40,000 different kinds of monocotyledons that are now known to botanists. Because they include the grasses and other small plants, the total number of monocotyledons in the world is far greater than the number of dicotyledons. Entirely herbaceous —remember that they do not have cambium in the stem and that the xylem and phloem are found in bundles scattered throughout the stem—some of them have nevertheless developed erect habits and are even treelike in form. However, they have no actual wood and no bark. A hard outer rind often helps to stiffen the stem, as in bamboo and corn.

Which do you believe is the more primitive group, the monocotyledons or the dicotyledons? Scientists do not always agree on the answer. This question is one of the many thousands not yet answered about plants.

REVIEW

1. Explain why a bulb is said to be a specialized, underground bud. What structures may be found in a bulb?

2. What is meant by an epiphyte, or "air plant"? Name an epiphyte and explain how it is adapted to its way of life.

3. What is meant by the statement that all monocotyledons are herbaceous? What fact about monocotyledons makes the statement true?

NEW VIEW

1. Cactuses are dicotyledons. Joshua trees look like cactuses but are monocotyledons. What would you look for in these plants to demonstrate that these statements are true?

2. You might like to plant a garden of monocotyledons and compare the plants with another garden of dicotyledons. For monocots you may use seeds of corn, wheat, oats, or grass, and bulbs of onions or tulips. For dicots, use peas, beans, radishes, or squash.

❷ STRUCTURES OF A TYPICAL FLOWER

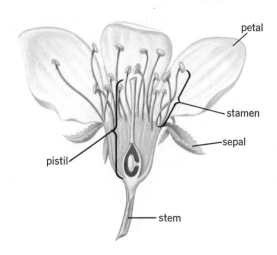

4. REPRODUCTION IN FLOWERING PLANTS

The flowering plants are believed to have evolved from ferns. Flowering plants look quite different from ferns, but what you now know about the reproductive cycle of ferns will help you understand reproduction in flowering plants.

The Structure of a Flower

The diagram above illustrates a typical flower. ❷ At its base are green, leaflike structures called **sepals** (sē′pəlz). The sepals form the outer coat of the flower bud, protecting the flower while it is developing. As the flower opens, the sepals open first and curl back.

The colored, leaflike structures that make flowers so beautiful are called **petals.** Inside the petals are the male structures called **stamens** (stā′mənz), which produce pollen grains at their tips, the **anthers.** At the center of a typical flower is the **pistil,** which contains the female structures of a flower. Examine a flower for yourself. ■

■ AN APPRENTICE INVESTIGATION into Reproduction in Flowering Plants

Almost any flower that you can obtain from a field or garden will do. A gladiola or a tulip is especially good. In each flower, locate the sepals, petals, stamens, and pistil.❶

How many of each are there?

Examine the stamen. Break open its anther. Make a slide of the pollen grains and examine them under the microscope. What shape are the pollen grains?❷

Study the pistil.❸ The top of the pistil, the **stigma,** is sticky. What advantage is there to a sticky stigma?

The ovary is the bulbous lower portion of the pistil. Slice it open with a knife. Notice the tiny **ovules.**❹ The ovules contain the egg cells.

The **style** connects the stigma and the ovary. How long is the style? If the sperm cells of a pollen grain are to reach the ovule, how far must they grow?

An Investigation On Your Own

The flower of a wild rose usually has five petals and a large but varying number of stamens. Determine the number of petals and stamens in as many different *cultivated* varieties of roses as you can. What is the average number of petals? of stamens? What relationship exists between the number of petals and the number of stamens in cultivated roses?

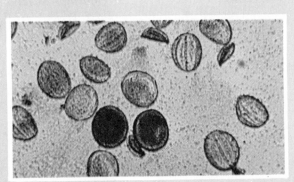

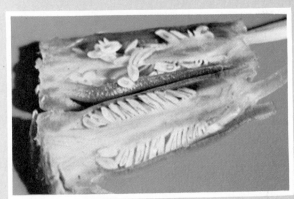

STAMENS AND POLLEN GRAINS. Each pollen grain is actually a single cell with only *half* the number of chromosomes as the other cells in the plant. How does this happen?

A very special kind of cell division takes place as the pollen grains are formed in the anthers. In your earlier courses in science, you may have studied or at least come across the word **meiosis** (mī·ō′sis). Meiosis, or *meiotic* (mī·ot′ik) *division,* is the name given to this particular kind of cell division—the cell division that produces daughter cells with *half the number of chromosomes as the parent cell.* In meiosis, as in mitosis, the chromosomes duplicate themselves before they separate into the new daughter cells. However, in meiosis *four* daughter cells are produced from the original parent cell, each having only *half* the number of chromosomes of the parent.❶ Study the drawing to clarify this in your mind. You will recall that when you studied *mitosis,* you learned that the chromosomes duplicated themselves, that is, doubled in number before the cell divided. But then, only *two* daughter cells were produced. This allowed each of the daughter cells to receive the same number of chromosomes as the original parent cell. In mitosis, then, the daughter cells always have the *same number* of chromosomes as the parent cell, whereas in meiosis the daughter cells have *half the number* of chromosomes as the parent cell. This is the difference to keep in mind.

Now back to the daughter cells, the pollen grains of the anthers. As we said before, each pollen grain is a single cell. The pollen grain is transferred, usually by wind or an insect, to the pistil of the flower. Once on the pistil, the pollen grain absorbs moisture from the pistil and breaks open. Its contents form a **pollen tube** growing down into the pistil of the flower.

❶ MEIOSIS

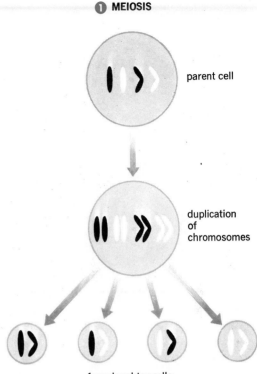

parent cell

duplication of chromosomes

four daughter cells

In the meantime, further divisions of the nucleus in the pollen tube have produced three nuclei. One of these nuclei is the *tube nucleus,* as you can see in the drawing on the next page. The other two nuclei are the sperm cells, or male gametes. At this stage the contents of the pollen tube is actually considered a tiny male plant. Scientists who have studied the evolution of plants have concluded that the pollen tube can be thought of in no other way.

As the pollen tube grows further down the pistil, it reaches an ovule containing an egg cell. At this stage, one of the male gametes unites with the egg cell—the process of fertilization—to form a zygote which develops into a seed. The other male gamete unites with another cell in the ovule which will build the stored food supply of the seed.

❶ REPRODUCTION IN A FLOWER

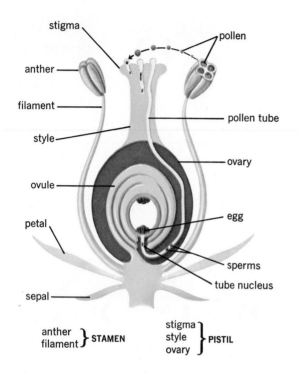

stigma
pollen
anther
filament
style
pollen tube
ovary
ovule
egg
petal
sperms
tube nucleus
sepal

anther ⎫
filament ⎬ STAMEN

stigma ⎫
style ⎬ PISTIL
ovary ⎭

PISTILS AND EGGS. Study the drawing above. ❶ The top of the pistil (the stigma) is usually sticky; this aids in catching and holding pollen grains. Notice, particularly, the egg at the bottom of the pistil. The enlarged part of the pistil is called the ovary. The ovary may contain one or several ovules and each ovule contains an egg. The drawing shows a pollen tube that has grown down to the ovule. Notice the sperm cells toward the end of the pollen tube. One of the sperms will unite with the egg cell in the process of fertilization.

As you can see if you think about it awhile, the pollen tubes and the structures that produce eggs are very much like the tiny sexual plant of the fern. Indeed, as we stated earlier, scientists consider these structures to represent the sexual generation of the flowering plants. ❷ The remainder of the flowering plant—roots, stems, leaves, and most of the flower itself—is considered to be the *asexual* generation upon which the sexual plants live parasitically. Both gymnosperms and angiosperms have alternation of generations, as do the simpler ferns, mosses, and thallophytes.

From Flower to Fruit

Many and varied changes in the flower are set in motion by the union of the sperm and egg cell. A seed containing an embryo plant starts to develop, and, in all flowering plants, a fruit is formed. ∎

❷ EVOLUTIONARY TREND IN ALTERNATION OF GENERATIONS

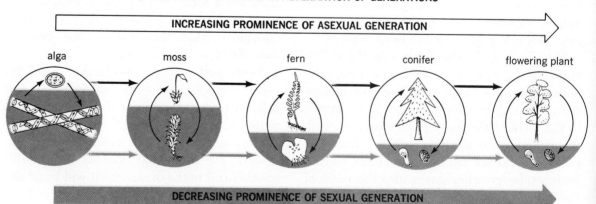

INCREASING PROMINENCE OF ASEXUAL GENERATION

alga   moss   fern   conifer   flowering plant

DECREASING PROMINENCE OF SEXUAL GENERATION

■ AN APPRENTICE INVESTIGATION into Development of a Fruit

It is easy to examine a tomato. Compare it with the photograph shown here.❶ Notice the tiny dried structures at the bottom of the tomato. Do you find dried structures in a circle? It is the remains of the stamens. In the middle of the stamens you may find the single, dried pistil. What, then, is the tomato itself?

A tomato is simply a greatly enlarged ovary of the flower with its surrounding structures. The ovary stores great quantities of food that you eat as the tomato. Inside the tomato, of course, are seeds.❷ The seeds are developed ovules. Inside each seed is a tiny embryo plant that developed from a fertilized egg.

There are many types of flowers. Therefore, there are many types of fruits. Study the photograph of a pea flower.❸ Compare it with the photograph of a pea pod (the developing ovary, or fruit).❹ See if you can discover what has happened to the stigma, ovules, and ovary as the flower developed into a fruit.❺

An Investigation On Your Own

At different times of the year, collect the fruits of some perennials, shrubs, and trees. How does the fruit correspond to the flower?

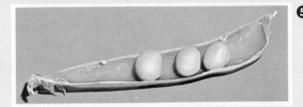

Types of Flowers

Flowers that have all the parts you have studied above are called **complete flowers.** Apple, rose, cherry, and lily flowers are examples of complete flowers.

If any part is missing, the flower is said to be **incomplete.** Many plants produce two kinds of flowers on the same plant, one kind containing only pistils, one kind containing only stamens. This is true of many common trees, of corn, and of other plants. The photograph shows you the stamen-producing, or **staminate** (stam′ə·nāt), flowers and the pistil-producing, or **pistillate** (pis′tə·lāt), flowers of the corn plant. ❶ The common name for a staminate flower of the corn plant is "tassel." The pistillate flowers have "silks" (these are the stigmas), and, of course, the developed ovaries become the grains of corn (the fruits), all arranged around a central stalk, commonly called a "cob."

Corn plants, walnut trees, and birch trees all have staminate and pistillate flowers on the same plants. Other plants, such as willows, cottonwood, and holly trees, have the staminate and pistillate flowers on separate

plants. Pussy willows, the fuzzy pussies that turn yellow in the spring, are the staminate flowers of the pussy willow tree.

COMPOSITE FLOWERS. Sunflowers, dandelions, daisies, zinnias, and many other so-called flowers are really "bouquets" of flowers. Instead of a single flower, these are actually clusters of many flowers on a single stalk.

Pollination

The transfer of pollen grains from stamens to pistils is called **pollination.** Many plants are self-pollinated; that is, pollen may go from the stamen to the pistil on the same flower or the same plant. Many other plants, however, require **cross-pollination** (the transfer of pollen from one plant to the pistil of another plant) in order for the sperm to unite with the egg cell. Can you think of an advantage of cross-pollination?

Bees, moths, butterflies, ants, and other insects also pollinate flowers. Hummingbirds also may pollinate flowers as they search for nectar. Corn plant flowers are among the many that are pollinated by the wind. Usually, the stamens are long and a tremendous amount of pollen is produced. As the pollen is blown into the air and carried for miles, some may fall on the pistillate flowers of the same kind of plant.

The pistils of wind-pollinated flowers are also generally long. Their stigmas are almost always quite sticky, and once a pollen grain falls on the stigma, it is likely to stick there.

Seed Dispersal

Just as important as the formation of seeds is the wide distribution of seeds to ecosystems where they will grow successfully.

What do you suppose would happen if seeds fell to the ground directly under the plant that produced them? If this happened,

the plants that germinated from these seeds would have to compete with one another and with the mother plant for moisture, minerals, and light. Few would live, and those that did would probably be weak and sickly.

Seeds have many interesting adaptations to ensure that they are widely distributed, or *dispersed*. Fruit, such as apples, cherries, and pears taste good to animals. After animals eat them, along with the seeds, the seeds pass through the digestive tract of the animal without being digested. The hard, tough walls of the seeds are not acted upon by the digestive enzymes and then are deposited on the ground in the feces, a long distance from where the fruits were produced. Birds are especially important in dispersing seeds in this way.

Dandelions and milkweeds are examples of seeds having light, fluffy structures that are caught by the wind. ❷ Seeds with structures that are built to be caught by the wind are often blown long distances before they come to rest on the ground. The female cottonwood tree can be quite spectacular as its cottony seeds are caught by the wind.

Ash, elm, and other trees produce seeds with so-called wings, or parachutes. These are maple seeds. ❸ The wind may blow these some distance away from the tree as gravity pulls them toward the ground.

Many seeds have tiny hooks, barbs, and needles that catch onto the fur or hair of animals passing by. They may be carried many miles before they drop or are scratched off.

Many pod fruits, similar to beans, have

297

pods that twist as they ripen and dry. The pods dry unequally, and this produces a strain. They suddenly split open, often throwing the seeds several feet away from the parent plant.

Some plants such as the sedges and coconut palms may drop their seeds into water. Coconuts have been known to float for thousands of miles before being washed up onto beaches where they sprout and grow into new coconut trees.

Vegetative Propagation

As you probably know, we raise most plants by planting seeds. However, if you have ever raised potatoes, you probably cut up potatoes so that each piece had an eye (a tiny bud) and planted the pieces. Potatoes can be grown from seeds, but it is easier and faster to raise them from pieces of potato. Besides, when they are raised in this way, each piece of potato will grow into a plant producing potatoes like the piece you planted.

Each new plant has the same chromosomes as the parent.

The growth of new plants from some part of a plant other than a seed is called **vegetative propagation**. It occurs commonly in nature, and man puts it to good use. See for yourself by carrying out this investigation. ■ Underground storage stems (*tubers*), as in white potatoes, will grow into new plants. Strawberries and other plants send out runners, shoots that grow along the ground. These shoots develop new root systems from which new plants grow. Many grasses spread and form new grass plants from their root systems. Sweet potatoes are storage roots. They, too, will develop new plants.

Lilies, onions, garlic, and many other plants are grown from bulbs (compressed underground stems covered with leaves modified for storage, as you know). And, although it seldom occurs without man's help, a wide variety of plants, from geraniums to some trees, can be grown from cuttings. A twig is cut and put into water or moist sand or soil until it develops roots, just as was done in the investigation. It is then planted and will grow into a complete new plant.

There are even a few leaves that will produce roots and grow into new plants. *Bryophyllum,* for example, has leaves that produce new plants along the notches in the leaves. ❶ These tiny plants loosen and fall to the ground where they may grow into new plants.

Grafting is a process by which a twig or small branch is cut from one plant and made to grow onto the stem of another plant. Buds are also sometimes used for grafts. There are various kinds of grafts, but in each case the important thing is to place the *cambium layer* of the twig to be grafted in touch with the *cambium layer* of the stem to which it is being grafted. Matching up cambium layers, of

■ AN APPRENTICE INVESTIGATION into Vegetative Propagation

Take a carrot and plant it in a pot of soil. The head of the carrot should be just beneath the soil. Do the same with a beet or turnip. Cut a potato in half. Plant each half about an inch below the surface of good garden soil.

Observe them carefully over the next two weeks.❶ Keep notes of your observation.

Cut a three-inch green twig from a geranium.❷ Remove all but the top three leaves.

Plant it in washed sand, with the base of the cutting about an inch and a half below the surface.❸ Observe it carefully over the next two weeks. What happens? Remove it from the pot and examine the end of the twig.❹

An Investigation On Your Own

What factors affect the first appearance of roots on a cutting? Verify your observations.

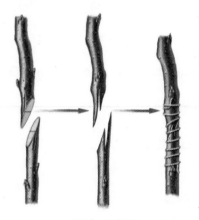

WHIP GRAFTING

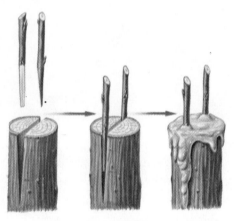

CLEFT GRAFTING

T-BUDDING

course, is necessary so that the rapidly dividing cells of the cambium layer will produce new water-conducting and food-conducting tissues connecting the graft to the mother plant. The drawing shows several kinds of grafting. **1**

Grafting is widely used. The rosebushes that you buy to plant in your yard are almost certain to be grafted roses; that is, a twig from a rosebush that produced especially fine flowers has been grafted to a root stock that is strong and hardy. This is one of the most common uses of grafting. It achieves a double purpose. First, one plant that is especially valuable (because of flower color, or excellence of fruit) can be used for hundreds of twigs. These twigs can then be grafted onto less valuable root stocks. Second, some plants may produce fine flowers or fruit but may have inferior roots. Other plants of the same kind may have roots that are hardy and that will better stand freezing temperatures and other difficult conditions. Therefore, you can take a valuable plant with inferior roots and, by grafting it to hardy roots, achieve a plant that is both beautiful and hardy.

Grafting is used for other purposes, too. Some varieties of plants, such as navel oranges, are seedless. The only way to reproduce such plants is by grafting. Another use of grafting is to reproduce valuable plants that would not breed true, plants whose seeds would not produce plants of the same quality as themselves.

Whatever form it takes, grafting or growing an entirely new plant from a part of another, vegetative propagation is a kind of *asexual* reproduction. The new plant is entirely the result of cell division, not of the union of egg and sperm cells. As you have seen, the ability of plants to reproduce in this way is of great value to man.

REVIEW

1. What is a pollen grain, in terms of alternation of generations? What kind of division in the pollen tube, meiosis or mitosis, produces the sperm cells?

2. What kind of cell division do you believe occurs inside the ovule that results in the production of eggs?

3. Relate each major part of an apple to the part of the flower from which it developed. That is, show what has happened to the ovules, ovary, stigma, stamens, and sepals of the original flower.

4. Define each of the following: complete flower, incomplete flower, staminate flower, pistillate flower.

5. What is meant by vegetative propagation? Is it asexual or sexual? Explain your answer.

NEW VIEW

What part or parts of a flowering plant are considered to be the sexual generation? What part or parts of a flowering plant are considered to be the asexual generation? With this in mind, do you think that it would be correct to speak of the alternation of generations of a flowering plant such as an apple tree? Defend your answer.

5. RELATING THE CONCEPTS

In terms of the long, long development of the plant kingdom, the land plants can be considered newcomers. The angiosperms—the flowering plants—are relatively recent; the earliest angiosperms found as fossils go back perhaps some 150 million years. The gymnosperms—the coniferous plants—are older. The earliest gymnosperms go back to the Carboniferous period, some 300 million years ago. The angiosperms clearly did not exist in the Carboniferous period. They seem to have flourished during a more recent era, the Cenozoic era, although they had their origin in the Mesozoic era (that is, over 150 million years ago, during the Jurassic period).

Nevertheless, the modern gymnosperms (excluding the *Ginkgo*) are established land plants, as are the angiosperms. By established land plants, we mean that their sexual reproduction does not depend on swimming sperms that depend, in turn, upon water in the environment external to the plant. Plants, like animals, do depend on water for their metabolic needs. Nevertheless, many plants can survive periods of drought.

Reviewing the Concepts

▶ *The seed plants are established land plants.* By established land plants, we mean plants that can survive periods of drought, and plants that do not depend on water in the environment for reproduction. On the other hand, algae and mosses generally cannot survive long without water. Ferns are in somewhat an intermediate position because of their underground stems, the rhizomes.

▶ *The seed is adapted for survival and dispersal on land.* Because of a protective coat and a means of dispersal, the seed is adapted for continuing the species on land. The seed can withstand an adverse environment, such as cold, freezing temperatures, and drought. In general, seeds can withstand a period when the conditions are not favorable for growth of the plant, such as winter conditions, dry seasons, and the like.

▶ *The gymnosperms (conifers) trace their ancestry further back than do angiosperms.* Although the evidence is not clear on the origin of gymnosperms, it is clear that they started in an earlier geological period than did the angiosperms. The fossil evidence is fairly clear on this point.

▶ *The angiosperms (flowering plants) are the most recent of land plants.* The fossil evidence indicates that the origin of the angiosperms corresponds to the era in which the early mammals lived, that is, from about 135 million to 180 million years ago. The origin of the angiosperms, like that of the gymnosperms, is not clear.

▶ *Alternation of generations occurs in the seed plants, with the sexual generation represented by the pollen tube and ovule.* The algae, mosses, and ferns had a clearly developed asexual generation as shown in the moss sexual plant and in the prothallus of the fern. In the seed plant, however, the sexual generation is much abbreviated. It does exist, however, in the pollen tube with its sperms and in the ovule with its egg.

Testing Yourself

1. Why is the *Ginkgo* a "living fossil"?

2. There are some groups of gymnosperms that are extinct. True or false? Explain.

3. Place the following groups of plants in order of their earliest existence. In what eras did they flourish?

> angiosperms   thallophytes
> gymnosperms   bryophytes

4. How do the gymnosperms differ from the angiosperms?   .

5. How is the seed-bearing structure of the gymnosperms similar to that of the angiosperms? How is it different?

6. Describe at least three ways in which seeds are dispersed.

7. What is the basis for considering gymnosperms and angiosperms as established land plants?

8. Describe at least four ways in which gymnosperms and angiosperms are economically important.

Extending the Concepts

Investigation 1. Why not become an expert on the seed plants of your area or at least on the trees and shrubs? Of course, it will take a bit of work—mainly field work. Trees and shrubs are fairly easy to identify from their characteristic leaves, buds, twigs, flowers, and fruits.

One beginning book that will help you is *Illustrated Guide to Trees and Shrubs.*

If you wish to learn how to use a *key* to identification, which would be of great value to you, try *Key to Woody Plants.* See the Suggested Reading list.

Investigation 2. What conditions are necessary for the growth of a pollen tube from pollen grains of different species of plants, of different groups of plants (for instance, conifers as compared with those of certain flowering plants)?

You may already know that pollen grains will develop a pollen tube in a 1 percent glucose solution. Do the pollen grains of the pine, for instance, germinate as fast as those of the maple? Can the germination rates be compared even though the pollen grains of the two trees develop at different times of the year?

Do the pollen grains of different species germinate at the same rate?

Suggested Reading

Hutchins, Ross, *The Amazing Seeds,* New York, Dodd, Mead, 1955.

Graves, Arthur Harmount, *Illustrated Guide to Trees and Shrubs* (rev. ed.), New York, Harper & Row, 1956.

Muenscher, W. C., *Keys to Woody Plants* (6th rev. ed.), Ithaca, New York, Comstock, 1950.

VARIETY AMONG THE PLANTS

GYMNOSPERMS AND ANGIOSPERMS

The remaining two classes of Pteropsida, the gymnosperms and angiosperms, represent over 300,000 species of plants living today. These are the seed-bearing plants, most familiar to you. They are the best adapted to land of all the plants. Their vascular tissue is highly developed and they have true roots, stems, and leaves. In their alternation of generations, you find the most highly developed sporophyte generation and the most greatly reduced gametophyte generation. If the seed plants were removed from the surface of the earth, you might, indeed, find the earth unrecognizable to you.

GYMNOSPERMS

(Class—Gymnospermae)

All the conifers and other cone-bearing plants with exposed seeds are gymnosperms. They are the most ancient of seed plants, and among these the cycad is the most primitive. The conifers, with their needlelike leaves, are the most familiar gymnosperms today. Although the *Ginkgo* does not have cones, it does bear exposed seeds.

white pine

white cedar

cycad

Ginkgo

redwood

You may find it valuable to refer to the chart, Classifying the Plant Kingdom, on page 256.

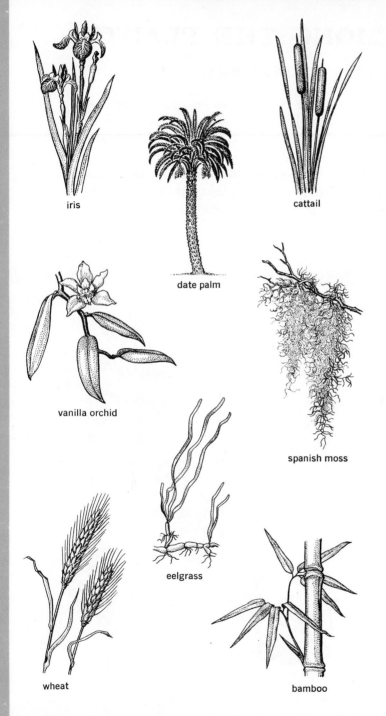

iris

date palm

cattail

vanilla orchid

spanish moss

eelgrass

wheat

bamboo

ANGIOSPERMS

(Class—Angiospermae)

The angiosperms are the great group of flowering plants. The seeds are always enclosed in a fruit. They are further divided into monocotyledons (one seed leaf) and dicotyledons (two seed leaves). The angiosperms are the great food producers on the land for animals and man.

Monocotyledons. This great modern group of plants has leaves with parallel veins, and the vascular bundles are scattered throughout the stem.

Dicotyledons. This is the more ancient of the two groups of angiosperms. Here you will find leaves with netted veins. The vascular tissue is arranged in cylinders in the stem, as in the oak you studied.

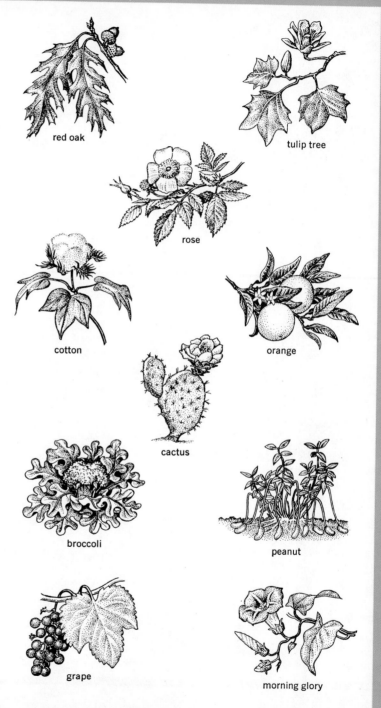

red oak

tulip tree

rose

cotton

orange

cactus

broccoli

peanut

grape

morning glory

ANIMALS

Variety

in

Form

Compare these two organisms.

The Whooping Cranes live in sanctuaries—
and are protected by the government.

On the other hand, the tree frog lives in
its natural environment. It competes with
other organisms; yet it survives.

Why is one protected—and the other not?

13 Animals Without Backbones — Winning the Waters

On the basis of your study of plants, you came to an understanding of the concept that *organisms can be classified on the basis of structures held in common.* How true is this concept for animals? A logical place to begin the study of animal forms is with a group of animals often called the invertebrates. These are the animals without backbones— the single-celled animals, the worms, starfish, and oysters. This group also includes the giant octopus and the tiny organism that causes malaria.

Let's begin our study of invertebrates with an organism whose classification biologists still worry about. Is it really an animal or a plant?

1. SINGLE–CELLED ANIMALS— THE PROTOZOA

There was a time, not so many years ago, when scientists assigned only two kingdoms to living organisms—the Animal Kingdom and the Plant Kingdom. There were, however, some organisms that were troublesome, *Euglena*, for instance. Recall that *Euglena* contains chlorophyll and, therefore, makes its own food, using the energy of light. For this

reason, as well as other reasons, some biologists classified *Euglena* as a plant. You can certainly understand the logic of this. However, *Euglena* moves about by means of a long, whiplike organelle, called a flagellum. Therefore, because it moves about, which is a characteristic of animals, *Euglena* was also classified by some biologists as an animal.

There are many other organisms, such as *Volvox* and slime molds, and even bacteria, that have both animal and plant characteristics. Many bacteria move about by means of hairlike structures similar to flagella.

In an attempt to set the matter straight, a new kingdom, the Protista, was organized. This kingdom usually includes the bacteria, the flagellates, the ciliates, the amoebas, the sporozoans, and the slime molds, among others. You will study certain of these organisms in this chapter. You will determine, at least in part, why it is sometimes *convenient* to group these organisms together (*it is easier to group the other remaining living organisms as either animals or plants*).

As long ago as 1866 the scientist Ernest Haeckel proposed the third kingdom, the Protista. However, only in recent years (almost 70 years later) was the suggestion revived

PHYLUM—**Protozoans (Protozoa):** singe-celled animals

    CLASS—**Flagellates (Mastigophora):** *Euglena*
    CLASS—**Pseudopod animals (Sarcodina):** *Amoeba*
    CLASS—**Ciliates (Ciliophora):** *Paramecium*
    CLASS—**Spore-formers (Sporozoa):** *Plasmodium*

PHYLUM—**Sponges (Porifera):** simple, tubular bodies with pores; bath sponges

PHYLUM—**Cup animals (Coelenterata):** two-layered, cuplike animals with tentacles; *Hydra*

PHYLUM—**Flatworms (Platyhelminthes):** tapeworm

PHYLUM—**Roundworms (Nematoda):** *Ascaris*

PHYLUM—**Spiny-skinned animals (Echinodermata):** usually with five arms or segments; starfish

PHYLUM—**Segmented Worms (Annelida):** earthworm

PHYLUM—**Mollusks (Mollusca):** soft-bodied animals with shells; clam

PHYLUM—**Arthropods (Arthropoda):** segmented animals with jointed legs and an exoskeleton

    CLASS—**Insects (Insecta):** three pairs of legs; three body parts; one pair of antennae
    CLASS—**Arachnids (Arachnida):** four pairs of legs; no antennae
    CLASS—**Crustaceans (Crustacea):** hard exoskeleton; breathe with gills; multiple legs
    CLASS—**Centipedes (Chilopoda):** one pair of legs on each of many segments

    CLASS—**Millipedes (Diplopoda):** two pairs of legs on each of many segments

PHYLUM—**Chordates (Chordata):** dorsal nerve cord; gill slits and notochord in some stage

    SUBPHYLUM—**Acorn worms (Hemichordata):** worm-like animals; notochord in the head only; dorsal nerve cord and gill slits
    SUBPHYLUM—**Tunicates (Urochordata):** saclike, attached animals; gill slits in adult; notochord, gill slits, and dorsal nerve cord in larva
    SUBPHYLUM—**Lancelets (Cephalochordata):** fishlike animal; notochord full length of body; gill slits and dorsal nerve cord
    SUBPHYLUM—**Vertebrates (Vertebrata):** notochord replaced by cartilage or bone, forming vertebral column; brain and spinal cord; gill slits in embryo

        CLASS—**Jawless fish (Cyclostomata):** lamprey
        CLASS—**Cartilaginous fish (Chondrichthyes):** shark, ray
        CLASS—**Bony fish (Osteichthyes):** perch
        CLASS—**Amphibians (Amphibia):** adapted to land and water; gills in larva, lungs in adult; frog
        CLASS—**Reptiles (Reptilia):** scaly skin; eggs with shells; lungs throughout life; snakes
        CLASS—**Birds (Aves):** feathers and wings; four-chambered heart; warm-blooded; robin, ostrich
        CLASS—**Mammals (Mammalia):** fur or hair; feed young on milk; usually bear young alive; cat, man

and accepted to any extent. A number of scientists, though not all, acknowledge the new kingdom, Protista. Others still retain the older classification that places bacteria and slime molds in the subkingdom Thallophyta and the more animal-like of these organisms in the phylum Protozoa. As time and continued study by scientists goes on, these differences will perhaps be settled.

For our study, we shall include these organisms in the phylum Protozoa. But if you come across the terms *protist, protists,* or *Protista,* they will not be strangers to you.

Examine briefly the chart above classifying the Animal Kingdom. Compare it with the chart classifying the Plant Kingdom (p. 256). You will refer to them often. There is no need to memorize them.

The Ciliates

Let's begin the study of Protozoa by collecting and growing some of them. One com-

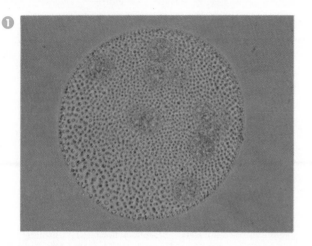

mon group of protozoans, those with cilia, thus called ciliates (sil′ē·əts), are easily found. These single-celled animals are grouped into the class Ciliophora (sil′ē·of′ō·rə). Once you begin to make collections of the Ciliophora found in pond water, you will find many other protozoans accompanying them. ■

You have already studied one ciliate, the single-celled *Paramecium* (pp. 76–82). Now choose one of the following ciliates and make a study of it: *Stentor, Oxytricha, Spirostomum, Euplotes, Vorticella.* You will find drawings of some of these ciliates at the end of this chapter in Variety Among the Animals. Try to answer the following questions. Also compare the activities of the ciliate you select with the activities of *Paramecium.*

a. Which organism are you studying?
b. If the organism is not shown in the drawings on pages 338–40, which one is it most like?
c. How does it move about?
d. How does it get its food?
e. How does it respond to obstacles? to enemies?
f. How does it get rid of wastes?
g. How does it reproduce? (You may not be able to find reproducing animals on

your slide. On the other hand, you may be able to see certain Ciliophora undergoing fission or conjugation.)

If you examine a sufficient number of Ciliophora, it will be obvious that they do indeed belong to a single group.

The Flagellates

In your cultures of the ciliates or the amoebas, you may find some green, single-celled protozoans, the flagellates. These compose the class Mastigophora (mas′ti·gof′ō·rə). *Euglena,* a common flagellate, is spindle-shaped.

If you can find a specimen of *Euglena* to observe, watch its long, whiplike flagellum. Notice its green color, which is due to chlorophyll. Thus, the euglena can photosynthesize. Its red eyespot, it is thought, makes it sensitive to light. Masses of euglenas will congregate where there is light.

Within the flagellates there are also certain "colonial organisms." Each colonial organism is a colony of one-celled organisms living together. It is not a many-celled organism, as you might think. There are flat colonies made up of four individual cells, flat sixteen-celled colonies, and balls of cells, such as *Volvox.* ❶ From your earlier study of the evolution of sexual reproduction in forms like *Volvox* (p. 232), you will remember that *Volvox* even contains different kinds of cells. The majority of the cells in the colony contain chloroplasts and are able to photosynthesize. Some cells form sperms and other cells form eggs. These cells are responsible for the sexual reproduction of the colony. Still other cells enlarge, lose their flagella, and divide several times to form small daughter colonies. The photomicrograph shows eleven of these daughter colonies in the parent. ❶ The daughter colonies are responsible for the *asexual reproduction* of *Volvox.* A few

■ AN APPRENTICE INVESTIGATION into Variety in the Protozoans

One method of collecting certain specimens of the Protozoa is simple. Collect a pint of pond water and some mud. An inch or so of mud in the bottom of the jar will be fine. You can collect the mud from the shallow water near the edge of the pond.

In the classroom, place the jar where it will remain at room temperature (neither too hot, too cold, nor in too bright light). With your fingers, crumble a bit of hard-boiled egg yolk into the water. ❶

The egg yolk will serve as food for the bacteria. In turn, the bacteria will feed the protozoans, particularly two groups. One is the ciliates. ❷ The other is the pseudopod animals [class Sarcodina (sär′kō′dīnə)]. ❸ If the jar is in medium sunlight, still other protozoans called flagellates [class Mastigophora] may also be present in the culture. *Euglena* is one of the more common flagellates. ❹

When you prepare microscope slides, take drops of the culture medium from the top, the sides, and the bottom of the jar. Do you find any of the organisms shown here? Compare the protozoans you find with those shown here.

An Investigation On Your Own

Will the protozoans live and grow equally well if egg yolk is not added? Is egg white as useful as egg yolk? Perhaps cooked beans or meat will do as well. In a sense, you are preparing an artificial ecosystem for protozoans. How will you know which ecosystem is best?

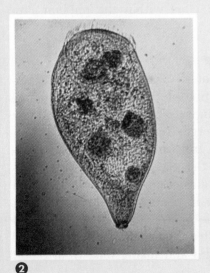

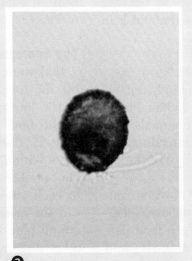

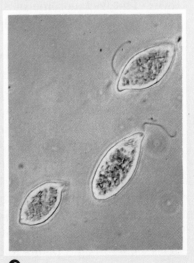

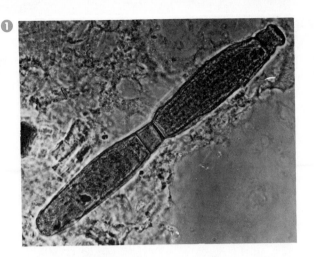

of the cells are not capable of reproduction. These cells toward one end of the colony are particularly sensitive to light. Each of these cells contains a red eyespot that is larger than usual. In *Volvox* you see a protozoan organism in which there is a kind of specialization.

Euglena and its relatives, then, can be classed as protozoans that are able to make their own food. Other flagellates are, on the other hand, colorless. Some, for example, the trypanosomes (trip′an·ə·sōmz′), cause diseases such as sleeping sickness and dum-dum fever. The trypanosome of sleeping sickness is carried by the tsetse fly, whose habitat is in certain regions of Africa.

The Amoebas

Evidently the Ciliophora are closely related animals. Other classes in the phylum Protozoa also contain closely related animals. For instance, let's turn to the class Sarcodina and an animal typical of it—*Amoeba*. Try the investigation opposite. ∎

An amoeba takes in food by flowing completely around the particle. Somehow, amoebas can tell the difference between food particles (microscopic plants and animals) and particles that are not food. Usually two pseudopods completely surround a food particle and then join together over and around the particle. In this way, the food becomes engulfed by the entire body. The food, surrounded by a drop of water, then becomes a food vacuole within the cell. As the food is slowly digested, it is absorbed into the body cell. Any indigestible parts are moved to the cell membrane and pushed through it. As in the paramecium, protein wastes and carbon dioxide diffuse through the cell membrane.

Amoebas reproduce themselves by simple division, or fission, as do the paramecia.

You may find other relatives of *Amoeba*. These organisms, along with the amoeba, form the class Sarcodina.

You have examined representatives of the class Ciliophora, and those of the class Sarcodina. How are they different? Certainly they are different in their form of locomotion. The Ciliophora move about by means of cilia, the Sarcodina by means of pseudopods.

How are they similar? How are all the organisms similar that fall into the phylum Protozoa? Perhaps it would be best to answer this question after you have examined organisms in each class within the phylum Protozoa.

The Sporozoa

If it were at all possible for you to examine the intestine of the common cockroach, or the intestine of certain flour beetles, you might find organisms such as the gregarines. ❶ The gregarines are a kind of protozoan within the class Sporozoa. These single-celled organisms are sometimes connected to each other in chains, as are the two you can see in the photomicrograph. Gregarines are all parasites, living within the bodies of other organisms and taking food from them.

■ AN APPRENTICE INVESTIGATION into the Amoeba

In a jar of pond water, an amoeba is often not as easy to find as a paramecium. Since the amoeba moves along a surface, you may find it on the mud or on the sides of the jar. Should you be lucky enough to have some in your pond-water culture, you cannot fail to recognize the amoeba. Let's look at some amoebas under the microscope.

Compare the amoeba you find with the one in the three photographs. ❶ ❷ ❸ The paramecium has a head end and a tail end, even if it actually has no head or tail. Can you find a head end for the amoeba?

The amoeba is shapeless, or rather, it has an endlessly varying shape. Like all protozoans, the amoeba is but a single cell. However, it has no cilia, no mouth pore, no anal pore. It does have a cell membrane, cytoplasm, and a nucleus. It also has food vacuoles and contractile vacuoles that function as those in the paramecium. Identify as many of the structures as you can.

If you watch an amoeba as it moves about, you see that it moves simply by flowing. First, one part of it extends and then another (usually several at one time). The amoeba then flows into these extensions, or "false feet" as they are called. The technical name of these false feet is **pseudopods** (soo′dō·podz).

An Investigation On Your Own

Devise a procedure to show how an amoeba takes in food, digests it, and gets rid of solid wastes.

Although an amoeba has no definite shape, an amoeba can and does move, eat, digest, excrete, and respond to the environment. It can and does carry on all the basic activities. It meets the same basic requirements of living that a paramecium or any other organism does.

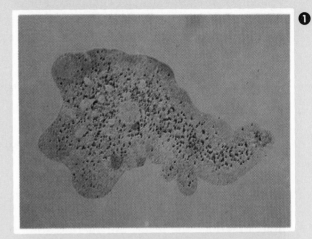

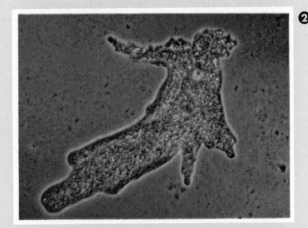

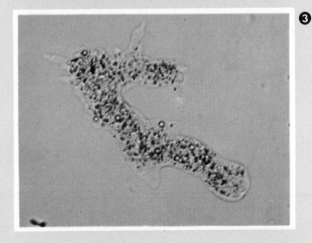

Some of the Sporozoa are among the most virulent of disease-causing organisms. For instance, malaria is caused by the sporozoan *Plasmodium* (plaz·mō′dē·əm). *Plasmodium* spends part of its life cycle within a mosquito. As the infected mosquito takes up blood from man, it injects the protozoans into a person's blood stream. The protozoans then enter the red blood cells, where they feed and reproduce themselves. They burst out of the blood cells at regular intervals of time, causing the chills and fever characteristic of malaria. Recently, certain drugs, particularly atabrine, have been used, as well as the old drug quinine, to reduce the fever. But there is still no cure for malaria. The drugs only control the symptoms. The best control of the disease is achieved by spraying insecticides in the swamps in which the mosquitoes breed.

The Sporozoa, then, are parasitic in nature. In other words, they are not free-living organisms.

REVIEW

1. What characteristics do all the organisms you have just studied have in common?

2. How are the Sarcodina and the Sporozoa alike? How are they different?

3. Make a table or chart that compares the Ciliophora, Sarcodina, Mastigophora, and Sporozoa in the following ways:
   a. manner of movement
   b. way of getting food
   c. structure, external and internal
   d. manner of reproduction
   e. characteristics that place them in the phylum Protozoa

4. How does an amoeba meet the basic requirements of life?

5. Why is *Volvox* called a colonial organism?

6. Name one disease caused by a parasitic protozoan.

NEW VIEW

1. Where might you expect to find protozoans such as the Ciliophora or Sarcodina? Would you look for them on land, in water, or in the air? Would you expect to find them on mountain tops? on deserts?

2. How does the eyespot of *Euglena* adapt it to its environment?

3. Use an encyclopedia to find out more about chalk beds and how they were formed.

4. The Sarcodina and other protozoans often form cysts (sists). The process is called encystment (en·sist′mənt). In the cyst form they can withstand unfavorable environmental conditions. How could you demonstrate that protozoans undergo encystment, or a similar process, which enables them to withstand dry conditions?

Can you find reports and drawings of protozoan cysts?

2. TIED TO THE BOTTOM

If you were to study a sample of the ocean with microscope, hand lens, and searching eyes, you would come upon many strange sights. Some you might pass by as fairly common. For instance, you might think that the animal shown in the drawing was a ciliated protozoan organism.❶ But if you were to follow this ciliated animal throughout its life to its final destination, you would be in for a surprise.

The Pore Animals—Porifera

The tiny ciliated animal would settle down to the bottom and begin to change. Soon you would begin to recognize a sponge. Perhaps it might not become the kind of sponge, the bath sponge, with which you may be familiar. Bath sponges are actually the "skeletons" of sponges. Once the sponge industry was a thriving one, for sponges are excellent for all

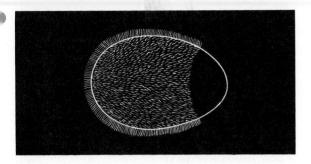

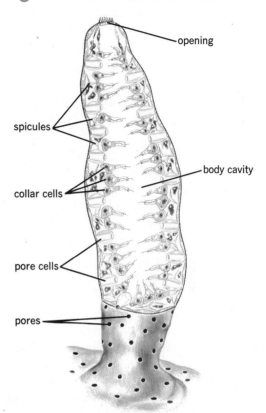

opening

spicules

collar cells

body cavity

pore cells

pores

manner of work that requires a soft porous object. Today the bath sponge has given way to the manufactured porous rubber or plastic sponge. The key word is *porous*, for sponges' "skeletons" contain many pores. For this reason, they are called pore animals, and scientifically named Porifera (pō·rif′ō·rə).

If you were to watch a simple sponge carefully, you would see the function of the pores.❷ Suppose colored particles of a harmless dye (to represent particles of food) were placed in the sea water. You would then see the colored water sweep in through the pores on the body of the animal. The particles of food swept in with the water are caught by the flagellated cells, called *collar cells*, lining the inner body wall. The collar cells also digest the food. The remaining water is carried back to the sea-water environment through the large opening at the top of the animal.

The sponge, then, is a simple animal, taking food and oxygen from the environment through pores and sweeping excess water and wastes into the environment through a single large opening.

The body of most sponges is held together by fibers and *spicules* (spik′yōōlz) which are often a beautiful design. Some sponges, such as the Venus's flower basket, have their "skeletons" made up of substances containing silicon. ❸ Silicon is an important element; sand is composed of the compound silicon dioxide.

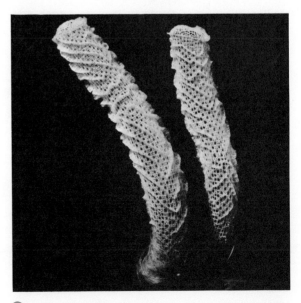

❸

Notice, however, that adult sponges are not free-swimming, as are their ciliated larvae. Sponges are tied to the bottom. That is, they are **sessile** (ses′il) animals, not free-swimming as are most of the protozoans. The sponges sit on the bottom, sweeping the sea environment into their bodies by means of the beating cilia of the collar cells lining their pores.

Now and then a sponge such as *Grantia* sends out a *bud* from its side. The bud develops into a part of the sponge. However, in a sense, it might be considered a separate individual, for if ,it is cut off or breaks off, it easily makes a new, separate sponge. In fact, many sponges can be cut into small pieces, and each piece reorganizes itself (regenerates) into one or more small but living and functioning sponge. In time, the new regenerated sponge grows into an adult.

An adult sponge can reproduce in many ways. It can grow buds from its side. It can also produce special kinds of buds, called *gemmules* (jem′yoōlz). These gemmules

break off and are carried to different parts of the ocean floor where they grow into new sponges. Or one sponge can produce sperms that fertilize the eggs in another sponge. The fertilized egg then develops into a ciliated larva, such as the one shown at the top of page 315.

Sponges are mostly marine organisms, but a few forms live in fresh water. As a phylum, the Porifera are sessile animals. Their adaptations to a life tied to the ocean floor limits them to a quiet life. The water environment envelops them and is circulated throughout their bodies. But they are not the only sessile animals in the waters of this planet.

The Cuplike Animals—Coelenterates

Look at the photograph at the left. ❶ The "plants" you see are not plants. However, they are named after a plant, the Anemone. What you are looking at are actually animals, the sea anemones.

These fascinating animals, along with many others, belong to the phylum Coelenterata (si·len′tər·ā′tə), meaning "hollow gut" or "hollow intestine." We will learn why they have earned this name.

Hydra—a Fresh-Water Coelenterate

Most coelenterates live in the sea. However, there is one that you can find in warm fresh water—*Hydra*. Hydras are tiny animals, about a tenth of an inch long. However, they are quite flexible and may be even half an inch long when they stretch out.

Hydras resemble pieces of short white thread when you see them in the water. But sometimes they are brown or even green. You will discover that when they are disturbed, they contract into tiny knobs. Often, they attach themselves to weeds, sticks, or rocks under the surface. See for yourself. ■

■ AN APPRENTICE INVESTIGATION of the Hydra

The best way to collect hydras is to collect pond plants or twigs from the water. These can be placed in jars along with some pond water and brought to class. Let the water settle and become clear before looking for hydras. Be careful not to disturb the water or you may not find them. If you have been able to collect hydras, observe them carefully in their jars over a period of several days. The series of photographs will help you as you continue with your observations. ❶ ❷ ❸

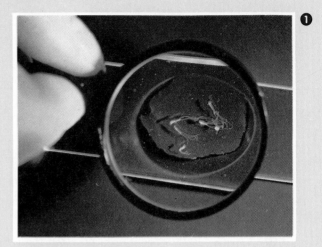

Do the hydras move around? Do they change their sizes? Notice the tentacles that surround the mouth opening. Notice that there is no right or left side to the body, but that the tentacles radiate out from the center in all directions. Scientists say that hydras show **radial symmetry.** What purpose do the tentacles seem to serve? If you use a magnifying glass, you will be able to watch the tiny animals more successfully.

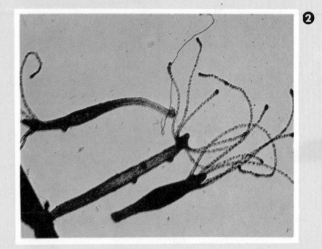

Pour a little of your pond water into a dish or a flat bowl. Locate a hydra and cut off a piece of the plant or twig to which it is attached. Put this in the dish of pond water. Now you can observe the animal more closely with a magnifying glass. But, again, be careful not to disturb the dish or the water. Can you see how the animal uses its tentacles? If you have a little tropical fish food, dust the tiniest pinch of this into the water. Now watch closely. You may be able to see the hydra feeding.

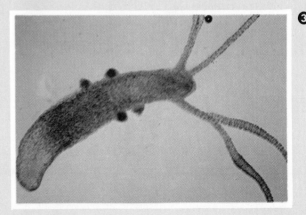

An Investigation On Your Own

How many species of hydra can you collect? Have you found the green hydra?

HYDRA

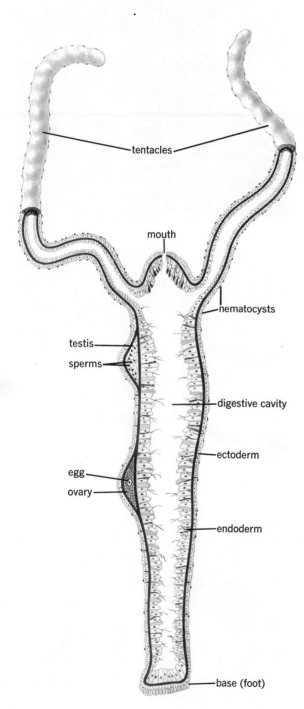

tentacles

mouth

nematocysts

testis

sperms

digestive cavity

ectoderm

egg

ovary

endoderm

base (foot)

If you have not been able to find hydras, wait until next summer when the weather is warm and then try again. Hydras can almost always be found in warm pond water in most parts of North America.

FOOD-GETTING. A hydra does not move around to catch its food. It usually remains attached at its base. The tentacles trail out in the water and are almost motionless. However, when a small animal (or your dried fish food) brushes against one of the tentacles, something very interesting happens. Each tentacle has a large number of stinging cells, the **nematocysts** (nə·ma′tə·sists′), which contain poisonous threads. These threads can be shot out like arrows into the body of any animal unfortunate enough to touch a tentacle. The poison numbs or paralyzes the animal. The tentacle then wraps around the prey and slowly moves the prey toward the hydra's mouth. The tentacle then pushes the food into the mouth. Often you can see through the transparent walls of the hydra's body and observe the animals that have been eaten.

DIGESTION. Digestion in the hydra occurs partly in the saclike cavity of the animal. This is the hollow gut that is the key characteristic of all coelenterates. Digestive enzymes are secreted into this cavity from special cells located in the lining. Small chunks of partially digested food particles are taken into other cells located in the lining. The food is taken into these cells in much the same way as in the amoebas—by pseudopods flowing around the partly digested food particle. Once inside the cell, the particle and the surrounding fluid becomes a food vacuole, as in the amoeba. Digestion of the food is then completed inside the cell.

WASTE REMOVAL. Undigestible particles are excreted by being pushed out of the cells and into the body cavity. Many of the cells lining the body cavity have long whiplike flagella much like the flagella of many protozoans. These flagella circulate digested food and water in the body cavity and throughout the hollow tentacles, and they also whip undigested particles out the mouth opening. So the "mouth" of the hydra serves both as a mouth and an opening for eliminating wastes.

RESPIRATION. The hydra has only two layers of cells, separated by a thin jellylike substance, throughout its body, as you can see in the drawing at the left. ❶ Having only two layers of cells, the **ectoderm** [(ek′tō·dûrm), the outer layer] and the **endoderm** [(en′dō·dûrm), the inner layer], is another characteristic of the coelenterates. Because water (containing dissolved oxygen) bathes the inner cells of the body cavity, as well as the outer cells, would you think that there would be any need for lungs or other organs of respiration? Would you say there is a need for blood or any other means of circulating food and oxygen throughout the body? In hydras, food, oxygen, and wastes can simply diffuse from cell to cell. Diffusion also occurs between the cells and their surrounding water environment. Obviously, there is no respiratory or circulatory system—none is needed.

DETECTING AND RESPONDING TO STIMULI. The hydra has the beginning of a nervous system. As you can see in the drawing above, the animal has a kind of network of special nerve cells. ❷ This "nerve net" is denser near the mouth than elsewhere. Would you suppose, then, that the mouth area is more sensitive than other areas?

If you have living hydras, you might try pushing against one tentacle or one side of the body with a straw from a broom or with a needle. You would discover that the *entire* animal contracts. How do you think the stimulus is transferred or communicated to the

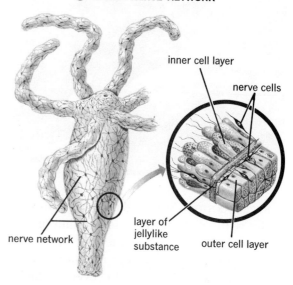

❷ HYDRA NERVE NETWORK

inner cell layer

nerve cells

nerve network

layer of jellylike substance

outer cell layer

other parts of the body? If you applied the same kind of stimulus to a sponge colony, *which has no nervous system,* do you suppose that a similar kind of *entire* reaction would occur?

Hydras also react to chemical stimuli. If you were to place some vinegar (weak acetic acid) beside an animal, you would see a shower of nematocysts from the tentacles shoot into the water.

If you have living hydras, you might investigate their reactions to other stimuli, for example, changes in light and temperature.

MOVEMENT. A hydra moves when the surrounding food supply becomes low. One method of moving is accomplished by *gliding* slowly on its base. This is achieved by an amoebalike, or amoeboid (ə·mē′boid), motion of the cells in its base. Pseudopods are pushed out and then the protoplasm of the cells in the base flow into the pseudopods. This carries the entire animal along. However, a hydra can also move along much more rapidly. It does so by *somersaulting.*

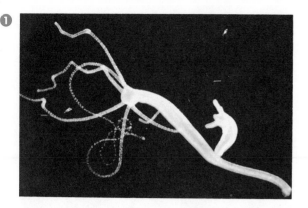

REPRODUCTION. Study the photograph of a hydra with what appears to be a kind of bud or branch. ① Notice that the bud has tentacles. At first, this bud was just a bump on the side of the hydra's body. However, tentacles soon sprouted and in two or three days the "bud" will look just like a small hydra with tentacles and a mouth. In another day or so, the young hydra will simply separate from the parent hydra and glide or somersault off to take up life on its own. Budding is a kind of *asexual* reproduction.

Hydras also reproduce sexually. Swellings appear on the sides of the main body, or stalk. (See the drawing on page 318.) Some of these swellings are testes. The testes produce male sex cells, or sperms. Other swellings called ovaries produce female sex cells, or eggs. Hundreds of tiny sperms break out and swim to the ovaries. One sperm cell will fertilize one egg cell within an ovary. And each ovary on the hydra's body contains but a single large egg. Like a hen's egg, the hydra egg contains stored food that feeds the developing animal.

Coelenterates of the Sea

Now look at the photograph of a Portuguese man-of-war. ② This beautiful blue and purple "animal" is dangerous, and it is *not* an animal. It is actually a *colony* of animals. Its tentacles, with millions of tiny stinging cells, sometimes grow as long as fifty feet. It is these stinging cells that inject the paralyzing poison into an animal or man. Swimmers who brush against the tentacles can be so seriously stung that they become dangerously weakened by the poison. As you might guess from its tentacles and stinging cells, the Portuguese man-of-war is, like the hydra, a coelenterate. And so is the ordinary, small jellyfish, which can raise welts on your skin.

Look at the photograph of two jellyfish swimming along. ③ Although closely related to the hydra, the jellyfish looks altogether different. Why do you think scientists classify jellyfish and hydras together in the same group of animals—the phylum Coelenterata?

You already know the general structure of the hydra. Perhaps you can guess rather accurately about some basic structures of the jellyfish. This shows the real advantage of classifying organisms. Once you know some general characteristics of one phylum or class of animals, you can be fairly confident about the general characteristics of other animals in the same phylum or class, even if you have never seen or studied them.

How many layers of cells would you think a jellyfish has? As you probably supposed, a jellyfish has the same two layers of cells that the hydra has—an ectoderm layer and an endoderm layer. (But in a jellyfish these two are separated by a thick jellylike layer.) Would you expect to find a hollow body cavity? Yes. Would you expect to find both a mouth and an anal opening? No, jellyfish have but one opening that serves for both taking food in and for throwing wastes out, as does *Hydra*. Would you expect to find both a brain and nerves, or no nerves, or only a simple nerve net? You would be correct if you said only a simple nerve net. Would you expect to find tentacles and nematocysts? Yes, of course.

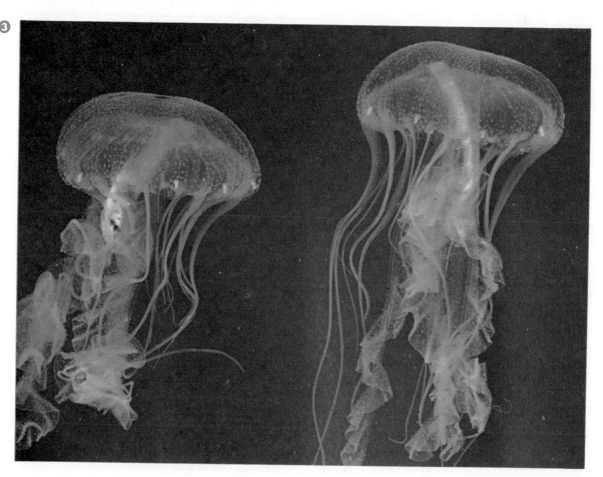

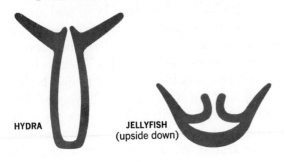

1 BASIC BODY PLAN OF COELENTERATES

HYDRA

JELLYFISH
(upside down)

However, if the coelenterates are so much alike, why are the shapes of these two animals so different? Actually, their shapes are not as different as they may seem at first glance. If you turned a jellyfish upside down and stretched the bowl-like disc upward for a short distance, you would have an animal that greatly resembles a hydra. Study the diagrams here. ❶ At the left is a hydra. A jellyfish, *upside down*, is at the right. They are remarkably alike, wouldn't you say?

REVIEW

1. What is the key characteristic of the phylum Coelenterata?

2. How does a hydra meet the basic requirements of living?

3. List the structural similarities between a jellyfish and a hydra.

NEW VIEW

Over 10,000 different kinds of coelenterates have been classified. Summarize the main characteristics of the phylum Coelenterata by discussing each of the following points:

    a. basic body plan

    b. how food is secured and digested

    c. how coelenterates get rid of wastes

    d. how oxygen gets to the body cells

    e. how coelenterates detect and respond to stimuli in their environments

3. ROUNDWORMS AND FLATWORMS

Perhaps you have a dog or a cat and may have had it "wormed" at one time or another. If so, you were attempting to rid your dog of a *parasite*. As you learned earlier, a parasite is any organism that lives in or on another organism, getting its food from its host and offering nothing in return. Parasites often sicken and sometimes even kill the organism they parasitize.

Many worms are parasites in the bodies of other animals. Several kinds live as parasites in dogs and several kinds parasitize cats. Even man has his share of parasitic worms. There is no warm-blooded animal, in fact, that is not parasitized by several kinds of worms. Different kinds of parasitic worms live in the bodies of cold-blooded animals, and some even live in plants.

Roundworms

The Greek word for thread is *nema*. You would suspect from this that roundworms, phylum Nematoda (nēm·ə·tō′də), are very thin and threadlike. Most are. Perhaps you have already seen roundworms in the pond water you examined with your microscope.

The nematodes seem to be unimportant organisms, yet the world teems with them. They are everywhere. A tumbler of soil may contain a million of them. There are tremendous numbers of nematodes in the waters of the earth. These roundworms live anywhere other animals live. Examine any sample of soil, or the debris from a pond, stream, or lake, and you will find the tiny worms whipping about in the typical movement that betrays them.

Not all roundworms that live freely in the soil and waters are parasitic, but most of the over 20,000 different kinds of nematodes are parasites. Some suck the cell contents of green leaves and cause them to wilt. Others enter roots and stems where they may cause great damage. Every kind of larger animal has its own kind of roundworms that have *specialized* in parasitizing just that one kind of animal. Ten or twelve different kinds of nematodes are *commonly* found in man, and about fifty different kinds are capable of parasitizing him.

Ascaris, a common parasitic roundworm, lives in the intestines of most animals including man.

The hookworm, properly called *Necator americanus*, which translated means "the American killer" is a parasite that enters the body by penetrating the skin of the feet.

Another well-known roundworm, the trichina worm, is a parasite that enters the body via under-cooked pork. It finally invades the muscles of man.

Flatworms

Another phylum of worms, Platyhelminthes (plat·ē′hel′min′thēz), the **flatworms**, also includes troublesome parasites such as tapeworms and liver flukes. However, many of the flatworms are not parasitic. They may be found crawling about on the ground near the edges of ponds or swimming about in the water of ponds, rivers, or oceans. Study the photograph of *Planaria* (plə·nâr′ē·ə), a free-living, nonparasitic flatworm that lives in fresh water. 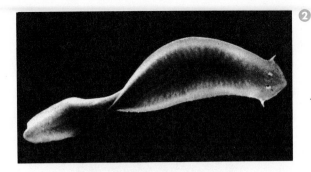 Now look at the photograph of a liver fluke, which is a dangerous parasite of man.

Suppose you were asked to design a parasitic animal that could live in the intestines of another animal. It would have to secure its food from the already digested food of its *host* (the animal it parasitizes), while offering nothing in return. What special structures might this internal parasitic animal need to live there successfully? Would the parasitic animal need digestive glands?

As you know, food passes through the intestines of an animal and the wastes are finally eliminated through the anus. If the parasitic animal passed along with the food and waste materials, it, too, would soon be eliminated and could no longer maintain its parasitic existence. So the animal you are designing must have something to keep it from being passed along and finally eliminated. What sort of structure might be useful in solving this problem?

Will the internal parasite you are inventing have much need of sense organs or a highly developed nervous system? Remember that it will spend its life inside another animal's body, protected by that animal's body. Will it need muscles?

Will the parasite need a reproductive system? While you are answering this question, think about a related question. When the host animal dies, what will happen to the parasitic animal? Should there be some way for the parasite to change hosts?

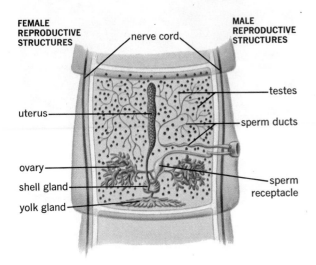

FEMALE REPRODUCTIVE STRUCTURES

nerve cord

MALE REPRODUCTIVE STRUCTURES

testes

uterus

sperm ducts

ovary

shell gland

yolk gland

sperm receptacle

The Tapeworm—An Intestinal Parasite

Let's see now how well you designed an internal parasite. There is, as you know, a parasitic worm, the tapeworm, that actually does spend its life, or most of it, in the intestines of another animal. It secures food in an already digested form from its host.

There are many different kinds of tapeworms. One kind is common in cattle and in man. It is called the beef tapeworm. Like all tapeworms, it is a long, flat, ribbon-shaped worm whose body is made up of sections. Tapeworms, as we mentioned earlier, are grouped in the phylum of *flatworms*.

At one end of the tapeworm is the head, which has four suckers on it. The suckers attach to the wall of the host's intestine to keep the parasite from being passed out of the host's body. Just behind the head are smaller sections. These small sections grow larger and larger as new small sections are formed in the neck region just behind the head. Therefore, the small, narrow sections just behind the head are always the youngest part of the worm. The large, wide sections at the far end

are the oldest. There is an advantage to this arrangement, as you will see later.

Look at the drawing of an old or mature section of the tapeworm. ❶ Study the drawing and the labeled parts. Do you see a *digestive system* or any digestive structures in the mature section? There are none. Did the parasite you invented have one? None is needed because the parasite simply absorbs already digested food through the walls of its cells.

You perhaps noticed something interesting as you studied the picture. The mature sections of a tapeworm contain scarcely more than reproductive organs. When this section becomes completely mature or "ripe," the egg sac expands until it almost completely fills the entire section. At this stage, the egg sac contains many thousands of eggs. The mature section breaks off from the worm and is eliminated from the host's body in the feces.

Now let's see how a man or a cow can become parasitized by the beef tapeworm. It will help you to understand if you look at the diagram of the life cycle of the beef tapeworm, on the facing page. ❷

First, the parasite *must* live part of its life cycle in a human being and part of it in a cow. That is, it could not continue to exist only in a human being *or* only in a cow. It must *alternate* between them.

Second, the parasite has a different form in a human being than it does in a cow. It also lives in a different part of the body in a human being than it does in a cow.

In a human being, the tapeworm lives in the intestine. After a ripe section full of eggs has been eliminated, a cow could possibly eat this section or some of the thousands of developed eggs the section contains. If this should happen, the thick walls of the eggs are digested when the eggs reach the cow's

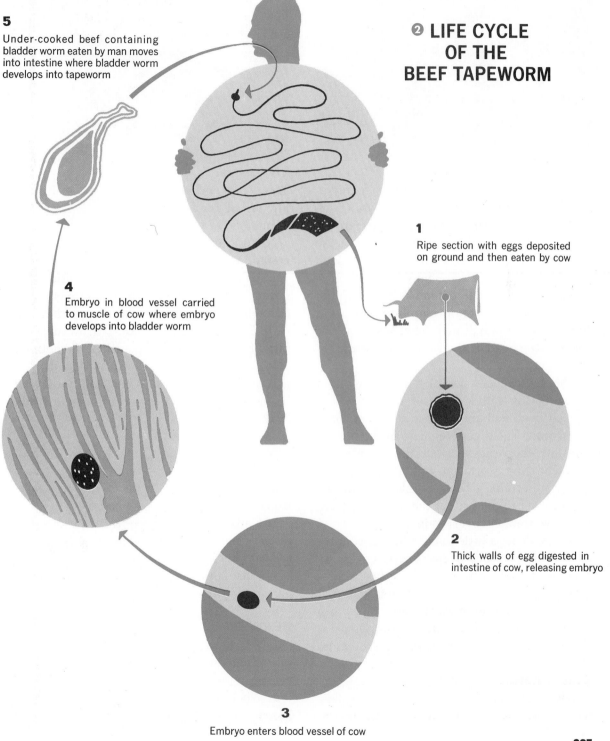

5

Under-cooked beef containing bladder worm eaten by man moves into intestine where bladder worm develops into tapeworm

② LIFE CYCLE OF THE BEEF TAPEWORM

1

Ripe section with eggs deposited on ground and then eaten by cow

4

Embryo in blood vessel carried to muscle of cow where embryo develops into bladder worm

2

Thick walls of egg digested in intestine of cow, releasing embryo

3

Embryo enters blood vessel of cow

325

intestine. Out of each egg comes a microscopic immature worm, or embryo. Each embryo with its six hooks bores through the intestinal wall and into a blood vessel of the cow. The tiny embryo is carried in the blood stream until it reaches a muscle somewhere in the cow's body. Here it hooks itself into the muscle and begins to develop into a sac, or a bladder, about a half-inch long. Inside of this bladder the head of the future tapeworm begins to grow.

The life cycle is completed only when a human being eats a piece of raw or undercooked beef containing these so-called bladder worms. The digestive juices in the human intestine then digest away the bladder, or sac. The tiny worm, at this stage nothing much more than a head, is released and attaches itself to the wall of the intestine. Here the cycle starts all over again.

Today there is little danger in this country of getting beef tapeworm. Years ago, however, beef tapeworm in man was fairly common here. Now, with modern toilets and government inspection of meats, beef tapeworm is rare. But in more primitive countries parasitism by the beef tapeworm is still common.

Other Parasitic Worms

The most common kinds of parasitic flatworms, besides the tapeworms, are the flukes.

There are many parasitic worms in the phylum of roundworms, of which *Ascaris* is a member. ❶

Almost all Annelida (an·ēl′i·də), or segmented worms, such as the earthworm, which you will study later, are nonparasitic. One group of segmented worms, however, lives as a *temporary external* parasite on other animals. These are the leeches. ❷ How are they fitted to live as external parasites? Sometimes in hunting for living organisms in ponds, you may also find leeches. When you do, it will be most interesting for you to make a study of them.

REVIEW

1. Define a parasite.
2. Describe the life cycle of the beef tapeworm. What are its alternate hosts?
3. Explain why a tapeworm has no digestive system (and needs none) although it is a multicellular animal.
4. What is the difference between an internal parasite and an external parasite?

NEW VIEW

1. Which has the more complex body structure, a roundworm or a tapeworm? Explain your answer.
2. Would you say that a tapeworm is more or less *specialized* than a roundworm? Why?

3. Worms are not the only parasites. Can you, for example, think of any insects that are external parasites on animals? Use an encyclopedia to help you in answering this question.

4. We know that man and other organisms are affected by bacteria. Are they similarly affected by single-celled animals? How? Are there any beneficial effects? harmful effects?

4. THE "SPINY–SKINNED" ANIMALS

Starfish are representatives of a phylum of animals the name of which, Echinodermata (i·kī′nō·dûr′mə·tə) means "spiny-skinned." Most of these interesting animals of the sea have a tough, limy, inside skeleton that is very rough and bumpy. The skeleton, which you see clearly in a dried starfish, is just beneath the outer covering, or epidermis, of the body. This internal skeleton is called an **endo-skeleton** (en′dō·skel′ə·ten). Another main characteristic of the echinoderms is that they have no head or tail end, but are shaped much like a wheel. A starfish, for example, has arms, or rays, that stick out like spokes in a wheel or like the points of a star.

A Starfish and Its Ecosystem

Look at the photograph showing some starfish, *Asterias,* in the shallow waters along a seacoast. ❸ Notice that the spokelike arms of the starfish are in different positions.

Now look at the photograph of a starfish opening a mussel. ❹ You can see the tube feet attached to the mussel shell that is lying near the center of the starfish.

Compare these pictures, if possible, with the dried skeleton of a starfish or, better still, with a preserved specimen. You will find that in the dried or preserved specimen the rays are fixed in one position. This is only because the animal is dead. The endoskeleton is made

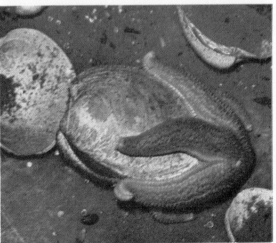

up of a network, or mesh, of hard plates made of lime that the animal takes in from the sea water. These limy plates, imbedded in the soft flesh of the animal, include the spines that stick out. The spines, of course, afford protection. Because the plates are joined together with flexible connective tissue, the animal can bend and twist inside its armor. However, it can move only very slowly.

Perhaps you imagine that a starfish moves by moving its rays one after another. However, this is not so. A starfish *glides* along over the rocks or sand. As long as the surface on which it is moving is fairly smooth, you will not notice any particular change in the position of the rays. However, when gliding over a rock, the rays must bend up to make this possible. Look again at the photograph at the top of the page. You will notice that the bodies of these starfish are bent up and down and sideways to fit the surfaces over which they are gliding.

Study the drawing of the starfish. ❶ Observe that in the endoskeleton of the underside (the *ventral* surface) of this animal, a groove runs down the center of each arm. In each groove you see a large number of tiny tubes. These are called **tube feet.** The end of each tube foot is a suction disc and the top is a bulb. These tube feet, arranged in rows, are connected by canals within the animal's body. The canals also lead to a **sieve plate** located on the upper side (the *dorsal* surface) of the animal, fairly near its center. Sea water enters the canal system through the sieve plate and pours down into the tube feet. Can you think of an advantage of the sievelike structure rather than just a large hole as an opening?

The entire system of tube feet and connecting canals is always filled with sea water in the living animal. It is this "water conducting" system, called a **hydrovascular** (hī′drō·vas′kyə·lar) **system** that enables the animal to glide along.

The rubber bulb of a medicine dropper is something like a tube foot. If you remove the glass part, wet the bottom of the bulb, and touch it to a smooth surface such as the blackboard or a window pane while squeezing the bulb to force the air out, the bulb will stick to the surface.

In your earlier science work you have probably studied what makes such suction cups stick. When air is forced out from inside the rubber bulb, the pressure of air outside forces the bulb tightly against the surface.

An even more dramatic illustration of the strength of a suction cup can be demonstrated with a plumber's plunger. If you wet the rim of the rubber cup and put it flat against the blackboard and then try to pull it off, you will see how strongly a suction cup can stick.

The bulb of a tube foot in the starfish is made of muscle. When the muscle contracts, it forces water, under pressure, into the tube foot. A valve closes and the water expands the tube foot and causes it to extend. The tip of the tube foot is then pressed against a surface. Next, muscles in the tube foot contract, forcing the water to flow back into the bulb and creating a suction in the disc. The disc is thus held tightly against the surface by the pressure of the water outside the disc, just as the medicine dropper bulb was forced against the blackboard because of the outside air pressure. The contraction of the muscle also shortens the tube foot and pulls the animal along.

Although each tube foot is tiny, hundreds of them working at one time draw the entire animal slowly along. If you have a living starfish and an aquarium full of sea water sup-

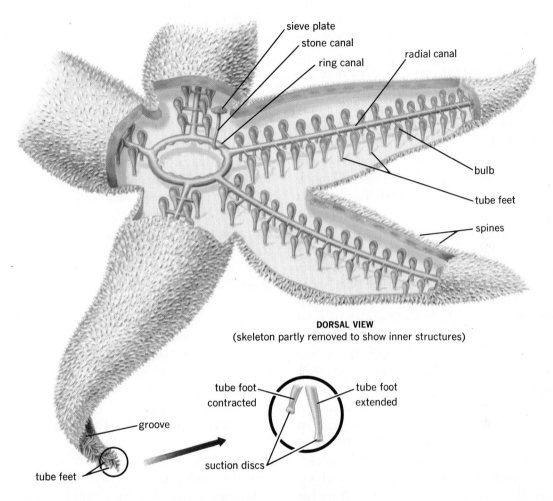

DORSAL VIEW
(skeleton partly removed to show inner structures)

ported so that you can look up through the glass bottom, you can watch the action of the tube feet and the gliding motion of the animal.

FOOD-GETTING. The tube feet also help the starfish get its food, which is chiefly clams and oysters. Have you ever tried to open a clam or an oyster? Two large muscles hold the two shells together, and you probably would not have the strength to pull them apart, even if you could get your fingers in between the tightly fitting shells. How, then, can a starfish open a living clam or oyster?

A starfish glides around a clam and closes its rays around the clam so that the edges of the two shells lie directly under the mouth of the starfish. It attaches its tube feet to both shells and then contracts the tube feet, thereby creating a strong pull on the two shells. However, the total pull of all the tube feet working together is probaby not a hundredth of the strength of the two muscles that hold the clam's two shells tightly closed. If you observed a starfish opening a clam, you would discover that, finally, after several hours, the clam shell would begin to open. But why?

You know that you can lift, and hold at arm's length, a fairly heavy weight. One pound is easy. Perhaps you can even hold ten pounds out at arm's length. However, try this. Take a penny and hold it out horizontally at arm's length. Simple, isn't it? Keep holding it there. Actually, of course, the muscles in your shoulder are holding the entire weight of your arm and the penny does not add much weight. Nonetheless, after a short time you are forced to drop your arm. The muscles become extremely tired, so tired that you simply can no longer hold out your arm.

As we said previously, the clam's muscles are tremendously more powerful than those of all the tiny tube feet working together. However, the starfish does not use all its tube feet at one time. Many will work at one time, creating a small but steady pull. When the muscles in these tube feet become tired, they relax and other tube feet are put into use. In this way, over a period of time a small but constant pull tires the muscles of the clam so that they are forced to relax. Then the shells slowly separate. Just as the powerful muscles of your shoulder and arm cannot hold up the weight of only your arm and a penny for a long period of time, so the clam's muscles cannot hold out too long against the constant pull of the hundreds of tiny muscles in the tube feet.

DIGESTION. You will find no jaws or teeth in the mouth of a starfish. How, then, can a starfish with a tiny mouth eat a clam that may be many times larger than its mouth? If you were to watch a starfish that had just opened a clam, you would see something most unusual.

The starfish really does not *eat* the clam in the usual sense of the word. That is, it does not break up the clam and swallow it. Instead, the starfish forces its own stomach to turn wrongside-out through its mouth so that the inside of the stomach lies against the clam's soft body inside the shell.

You might like to investigate the starfish's digestive system for yourself. ■

Because the starfish takes into its body partially digested materials and then finishes the digestive process in the digestive glands themselves, there is no need for an intestine. Because indigestible materials are rarely taken in, there is really no need for an anus either. The starfish has an anus, however, but it is probably rarely used. If indigestible material happens to be taken in, the material is pushed out through its mouth opening. Many scientists think that the anus of the starfish is only a **vestigial** (ves·tij′ē·əl) **organ,** the useless remains of an organ, that *was* useful at one time in some ancient ancestor from which the starfish developed. Vestigial organs are common in many forms of animal life. You will learn about more of them as you continue your study of animals.

CIRCULATION. The starfish has no blood, blood vessels, or heart. The digestive system and the water circulation (hydrovascular) system are surrounded by a fluid that fills the entire body cavity. The fluid is kept moving by cells with cilia much like those on a paramecium. The circulating fluid moves digested food and oxygen to all the body cells, and it also removes wastes and carbon dioxide.

WASTE REMOVAL. The starfish has no kidneys to remove nitrogenous wastes. However, there are amoebalike cells floating around in the body fluid. These cells flow around, and engulf, the wastes much as an amoeba takes in its food. These amoebalike cells also do an

■ AN APPRENTICE INVESTIGATION into the Digestive System of a Starfish

Examine the ventral side of the starfish. In the central region, locate the mouth (which is circled in the photograph).❶ The lower part of the stomach can be turned inside out and pushed through the mouth so that the lining of the stomach rests against the soft body of the clam or other food. Digestive juices, which are then secreted, partially digest the clam or other food. The semiliquid food is then drawn into the digestive glands that are connected to the stomach by tubes.

To locate these digestive glands, in which digestion is completed, turn the starfish over. With your teacher's help, carefully remove the skin from the central dorsal region and from at least two arms. As you can see, the digestive glands nearly fill the arms of the starfish.❷

An Investigation On Your Own

As you read on about the structure and their functions in the starfish, continue your dissection. See if you can locate the structures, such as the eyespots, skin gills, ovaries or testes, and the anus.

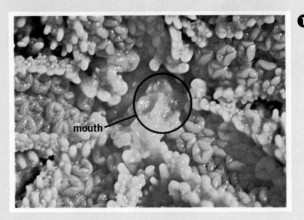
❶

mouth

❷

digestive glands

unusual thing. They make themselves thin enough to flow *through the walls* of the respiratory structures, called **skin-gills,** and out into the surrounding sea water. The nitrogenous wastes are, of course, carried away inside these special cells.

RESPIRATION. The chief function of the skin-gills, however, is respiration. These gills are slender, thin-walled structures that extend out from the body between the hard plates. They look much like the fingers of a rubber glove, with the insides continuous with the body cavity. Oxygen diffuses through their thin walls and into the body fluid with which they are filled. The movement of the cilia of the cells within the body cavity keeps this fluid circulating throughout the body of the starfish. In this manner, all of the body cells are bathed by the fluid. Carbon dioxide diffuses out through the skin-gills and into the sea water.

DETECTING AND RESPONDING TO STIMULI. The nervous system of the starfish is quite simple. A ring of nerve tissue surrounds the mouth. A nerve branches off from this tissue into each of the rays. However, there are sensitive

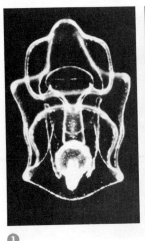

cells all over the surface of the starfish, and at the tip of each ray is an eyespot that is sensitive to light. If you touch a starfish anywhere, the sensitive cells detect the touch and nerves carry a message to other parts of the animal. The tube feet may then begin working to move the animal away.

REPRODUCTION. Each ray of the starfish contains two ovaries or two testes. The eggs and sperms are pushed out from these organs and into the sea water through tiny pores between the rays. The sperms swim to the eggs and fertilize them. The eggs then develop into tiny larvae which do not look at all like adult starfish.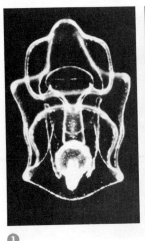

The larvae of the starfish are very important to paleontologists in their attempt to understand how organisms are related to each other. Study the photograph of the larva shown here.  Compare it with the starfish larva. Wouldn't you say that the second larva might be that of a starfish, or of an animal related to the starfish? Many zoologists and embryologists would agree with you. But the second photograph is the larva of an acorn worm, an animal related to the vertebrate animals, that is, animals with backbones. Some students of evolution think that the echinoderms gave rise to animals like the acorn worms.

Viewed in this way, the echinoderms belong to a phylum that might be placed among the *more complex* or *higher* invertebrates. For the purpose of an introduction to the forms of invertebrates, which is the purpose of these chapters, we have placed the phylum of spiney-skinned animals on top of the heap of the *simpler* or *lower* invertebrates. Later, as we discuss the relationship of the various forms of invertebrates, we shall come back to the echinoderms. Especially, we shall come back to the strange but highly important larva of the spiney-skinned animals.

The larvae of the starfish swim about by means of beating cilia. Water currents in the ocean may carry these larvae for many miles. In time the larvae change into small starfish that look like, and grow to become, adults. Do you see any advantage to the sluggish, slow-moving starfish having larvae that swim and are carried for many miles? Starfish are found throughout the oceans of the world. How do you suppose they became so widespread?

ADAPTATION TO THE ENVIRONMENT. A starfish and its environment, the shallow bottoms of seas and oceans, complement each other. Here are the major ways in which the starfish is adapted to this environment.

a. The starfish takes materials directly from the sea water to make its limey endoskeleton. This, in turn, protects the starfish from fish and other sea animals.

b. The tube feet and the entire hydrovascular system are dependent upon a surrounding water environment in order to function.

c. By its structure, the starfish is extremely well adapted to opening and eating shellfish. Tube feet, a stomach that can be turned inside out, and the reduced intestine and vestigial anus represent highly specialized adaptations to a highly specialized diet and way of life.

d. The removal of nitrogenous wastes by amoebalike cells is dependent upon a water environment into which these cells can move.

e. The skin-gills are dependent upon a water environment for the absorption of oxygen and the excretion of carbon dioxide. Such a system would be useless on land, since oxygen must be dissolved in water in order for it to diffuse through the membrane walls of skin-gills.

f. Reproduction depends upon a water environment. Were it not for the water, the sperms could not swim to and fertilize the eggs.

g. The free-swimming larvae serve to distribute the starfish widely. If eggs developed directly into slow-moving starfish, there would soon be too many animals in one spot for the available food. Then all might die of starvation. The larvae with their cilia are adapted to taking advantage of ocean currents in distributing themselves widely.

It is important to keep in mind that the starfish and other echinoderms represent but *one* of many different patterns of life that are complementary to the environment of shallow ocean bottoms. Sea worms, corals, barnacles, crabs, oysters, and fish are widely different in structure and habits, but all are apparently well adapted to the same basic environment.

Variety Among the So-Called Lower Invertebrates

You have now studied several important invertebrate forms in detail and have a good idea of the different kinds of body forms. We have not, of course, studied all of the so-called lower invertebrates. But it would be well to get a bird's-eye view of the different phyla and the major classes of organisms within them. Turn to the section *Variety Among the Animals* at the end of this chapter, showing representatives of the six phyla you have studied.

As you survey each phylum, try to compare the body form with those you have studied more thoroughly—for instance, that of *Hydra,* or the starfish, *Asterias.*

You know that some books place the echinoderms (the starfish) with the higher invertebrates. Why? Recall that the eggs of the echinoderms hatch into a strange kind of young, or larva. This larva looks very much like a larva of the lower vertebrates. It is thought by some scientists, therefore, that the echinoderms may be more highly developed than other animals of the lower invertebrates.

As you go on in your study of biology, you will come to know more of the reasons why animals are classified as they are. You will also come to know why organisms are placed on the lower rungs of the ladder of classification. To be brief, animals such as the sponges and coelenterates are thought to have existed on earth earlier than the echinoderms and worms.

REVIEW

1. Explain how a starfish moves.

2. How does a starfish get, eat, and digest its food? In answering this, explain how a starfish can open an oyster although the oyster's muscles are much more powerful than the muscles in the tube feet of a starfish.

3. Describe, in your own words, the major ways in which a starfish and its particular environment complement each other.

NEW VIEW

1. You now have studied, some in more detail than others, representatives of six phyla of invertebrates: protozoans, sponges, coelenterates, roundworms, flatworms, and echinoderms. Compare typical animals of at least the protozoans, coelenterates, and echinoderms in terms of their structures, the lives they lead, and their adaptations to their environments. Would it be possible to say which, if any, of the phyla is most successful? Or would it be more accurate to say that each seems well adapted to the life it leads and to its environment?

2. A starfish pushes out indigestible materials through its mouth opening, just as a hydra does. It does so, even though, unlike a hydra, a starfish has an anus. Why does the starfish not excrete wastes through the anus? Here is an interesting question. No one can answer it with certainty, but see what you can do with it.

If the starfish came from some ancient ancestor and changed over millions and millions of years to become what it is now, would you say that it developed from some animal like the hydra that passed indigestible materials through its mouth opening? Or would you think that it developed from some animal that had an anus and used it?

This is a difficult question. You cannot check the answer, but you can think about it logically in steps, using certain facts you know.

Fact 1. Hydras have no anuses.

Fact 2. Many other animals have anuses.

Fact 3. Hydras push out indigestible materials through their mouths.

Fact 4. Most animals with anuses eliminate through the anuses.

Fact 5. Although starfish *has* an anus, it eliminates through its mouth.

From these facts, you can reason as follows:

Step A. If starfish developed from an animal that did *not* have an anus, how and why would an anus occur if the starfish *does not need or use*

an anus now? It would seem highly unlikely that the ancestors lacked an anus.

Step B. Therefore, since the starfish *has an anus,* it would appear more likely that it changed from an animal that *also had an anus* and that the starfish just stopped using it.

Does this line of reasoning seem logical and right to you? Or does it seem wrong?

5. RELATING THE CONCEPTS

By studying a vast variety of organisms, we come closer to the identification of the concepts that embrace them. Let's try to get at these embracing concepts that form the foundation for our view of organisms.

Reviewing the Concepts

▶ *All organisms must be able to fulfill certain basic needs or they fail to survive.*

a. It is necessary for body cells to have *food* as a source of energy. Food, in effect, is matter in the ecosystem that can be used as a source of chemical energy. This chemical energy is converted into other forms of energy, for example, energy of movement (mechanical energy) or thermal energy.

For most animals the supply of chemical energy depends upon finding the food, getting it into the body, and transporting the food to all the body cells, if there is more than one cell.

b. Generally, *oxygen* must be supplied to the body cells. Otherwise, most organisms cannot oxidize food nutrients to release energy. This usually requires some means of taking oxygen into the body and transporting it to the cells where it is needed.

c. It is necessary to *get rid of waste products* or poisonous substances produced by the body cells. This is often a quite complicated process in the more complex organisms.

d. Organisms must be able to *react to the environment*. A basic need of animal life seems to be that an animal must eat and avoid being eaten. Therefore, animals must be sensitive and able to respond quickly to their environments in order to live. The environment must *stimulate* an animal to respond. Therefore, the animal must be sensitive to stimuli.

e. All animals must *reproduce* their own kind or else their kind of organism will die out and cease to exist.

▶ *Organisms have structures that adapt them to their environment.* This concept may be stated in another way as *the structures of organisms enable them to meet their life needs.* For example, examine the *Amoeba* from the viewpoint of the structures that enable it to meet its basic needs.

Locomotion—by pseudopods.

Food-getting—by pseudopods.

Oxygen-getting—by diffusion through the cell membrane.

Getting rid of wastes—through the cell membrane. (Excess water also is expelled by means of a contractile vacuole.)

Reproduction—generally by fission, involving especially changes in the nucleus.

Thus an amoeba has structures that are adapted to fulfilling its life needs in the environment in which it lives.

▶ *Similar structures, used in somewhat similar ways, give scientists a basis for classifying or grouping organisms. Difflugia,* like the *Amoeba,* has pseudopods that are flexible and fingerlike. Other protozoans have pseudopods that are slender and needlelike, whereas some are stiff, and still others are branched. Scientists use the presence of pseudopods as a basis for grouping certain protozoans, the Sarcodina.

▶ *Organisms with similar structures are placed in a group.* The Sarcodina have similar structures: pseudopods, contractile vacuoles, food vacuoles, and so forth. Hence we place, or classify, them together in a group, in this case a *class.*

▶ *In classifying organisms, the greater the similarity within a given group, the more limited and precise is the grouping.* For example, the *phylum* Protozoa is a large grouping, the *class* Ciliophora a smaller grouping. *Order* and *family* would be even smaller groupings. In a *family* the organisms would have greater similarities than in the *order.* In the *order* they would have greater similarities than they would in a *class.*

Testing Yourself

1. Why are the Ciliophora, Sarcodina, and Sporozoa classified in one phylum, the Protozoa? What differences place each of them in a different class?

2. What similarities place the seemingly different *Hydra* and jellyfish in the same phylum, the Coelenterata?

3. What characteristics might place all the organisms studied in this chapter into one large group?

4. What different means of taking in food did you find in the organisms you have studied in this chapter?

5. What similarities in taking in oxygen did you find in the organisms studied in this chapter?

6. What similarities in reproduction did you find in the organisms you have studied in this chapter? What differences?

7. What similarities in types of environments to which the organisms are adapted did you find among the organisms you studied in this chapter?

8. What kinds of special adaptations did you find among the lower invertebrates for
   a. parasitic life?
   b. saprophytic life?
   c. free-living life?
   d. marine life?
   e. fresh-water life?
   f. the sedentary life?
   g. the free-swimming life?

9. The flatworms seem to be successful animals. What adaptations make them successful?

10. Why is the starfish considered a more complex animal than a hydra?

Extending the Concepts

Now that you have had some experience in investigations of different kinds, you will have further opportunity in the remaining part of this book to extend your experiences in more demanding investigations. These will include at least three types.
   a. *Library research.* The library is of great importance in scientific investigations.
   b. *Investigations of an observational nature.* These include field trips and work with the microscope.
   c. *Investigations of an experimental nature which emphasize the design or experimental procedure.* Experimental procedures emphasize isolation of a working hypothesis and control of variables.

Where possible, you ought to try at least one of these types of investigations within a period of time suggested by your teacher.

Investigation 1. In this chapter, you studied types of animals without backbones (invertebrates).
   a. the Protozoa—(single-celled animals)
   b. the Porifera—(sponges)

c. the Coelenterata—(coelenterates)
d. the Echinodermata—(spiny-skinned animals)

You also studied the following in less detail:
   e. the Nematoda—(roundworms)
   f. the Platyhelminthes—(flatworms)

You did not examine, among others, animals in the following phyla grouped with the lower invertebrates:
   g. the Trochelminthes—(wheel animals)
   h. the Brachiopoda—(lamp shells)

You will study the Annelida (segmented worms), Mollusca (soft-bodied animals), and Arthropods (joint-footed animals) in the next chapter.

Why not continue your study of invertebrates by reading *Animals Without Backbones?* An extremely well-illustrated, readable book on the invertebrates is *The Lower Animals, Living Invertebrates of the World.* See the Suggested Reading list at the end of this chapter.

Investigation 2. Have you ever fished for and collected planarians (p. 323)? There are several methods of fishing for them. Take a hard-boiled egg yolk and place it in a bag of gauze or cheesecloth. Tie the bag with a long string so that you have a fishing line.

Find a quiet pond with green plants growing in the water. Toss the bag into the water and wait about 5 minutes, then pull it out. Perhaps you will find some flatworms (almost $\frac{1}{2}$ to 1 inch long) clustered around the egg yolk. Shake them into a jar of pond water. Try again at other places on the edge of the pond till you have a dozen or more flatworms. Some types of flatworms prefer raw liver to egg yolk. Try a small piece of raw liver at the end of your string.

Planarians may be kept in the classroom in a plastic covered dish—covered loosely to permit air to enter. Keep the dish in a cool (not cold) place, and away from light. Feed the planarians once a week with a piece of liver or egg yolk. Be sure to remove all pieces of the food after each feeding. Change the pond water (or aquarium water) after each feeding if possible. If you do this gently when the planarians cluster at the bottom or the sides, the planarians will not be disturbed.

Once you have a supply of planarians, you might try various investigations of an experimental nature.

a. *Regeneration Investigation.* Planarians regenerate if cut in half. A sharp knife will do as a surgical instrument.

1. Under what conditions does a planarian regenerate most quickly?
2. What is the smallest piece of planarian that will regenerate?
3. Will the head end or tail end regenerate faster?
4. Can you develop a two-headed planarian?

b. *Can Planarians Learn?* Can you get a planarian to move faster toward a darkened area than to an illuminated one? Will it move faster toward food?

Suggested Reading

Buchsbaum, R., *Animals Without Backbones,* Chicago, University of Chicago, 1948.

Buchsbaum, R., and others, *The Lower Animals, Living Invertebrates of the World,* New York, Doubleday, 1960.

Jahn, T. L., *How to Know the Protozoa,* Dubuque, Iowa, Brown, 1949.

VARIETY AMONG THE ANIMALS

PROTOZOANS TO STARFISH

In studying the tremendous variety of animals, it is logical to start with their ancient home—the waters. The protozoans, sponges, hydra, flat worms, round worms, and starfish—all are bound either to an environment of water or one rich in water.

If, as we suspect, the single-celled protozoans were earliest in origin, what marvelous complexities of adaptations developed in the six phyla pictured below.

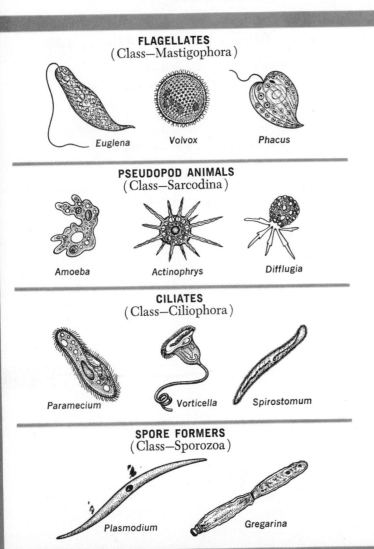

FLAGELLATES
(Class—Mastigophora)

Euglena   Volvox   Phacus

PSEUDOPOD ANIMALS
(Class—Sarcodina)

Amoeba   Actinophrys   Difflugia

CILIATES
(Class—Ciliophora)

Paramecium   Vorticella   Spirostomum

SPORE FORMERS
(Class—Sporozoa)

Plasmodium   Gregarina

SINGLE–CELLED ANIMALS
(Phylum—Protozoa)

These single-celled animals, sometimes living in colonies, represent more individuals than all the remaining animals of the world. They are microscopic, or almost so, and they move about by means of pseudopods, cilia, or flagella.

You may find it valuable to refer to the chart, Classifying the Animal Kingdom, on page 309.

SPONGES
(Phylum—Porifera)

These are the pore animals. Most live attached to the bottom in the shallow waters of the sea. Food and water enter the animal through the many small pores and leave through one large opening. Sponges have no respiratory or excretory systems, and no clearly defined muscle or nerve cells.

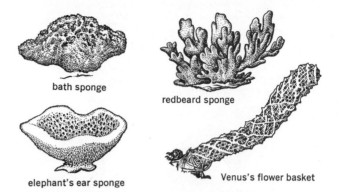

bath sponge

redbeard sponge

elephant's ear sponge

Venus's flower basket

CUP ANIMALS
(Phylum—Coelenterata)

These are hollow, cuplike animals. Water and food enter and leave the body cavity through the mouth. Digestion occurs both in the cavity and in the cells. The body wall has only two layers of cells with a jellylike substance between. All these coelenterates have tentacles and stinging cells.

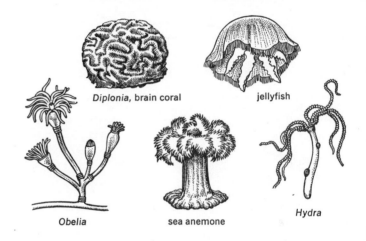

Diplonia, brain coral

jellyfish

Obelia

sea anemone

Hydra

FLATWORMS
(Phylum—Platyhelminthes)

These are long, ribbon-shaped worms that tend to have a definite head and tail region, as well as specialized organs and organ systems. Though some are free-living, many are parasitic, living part of their life cycle in two or even three different organisms.

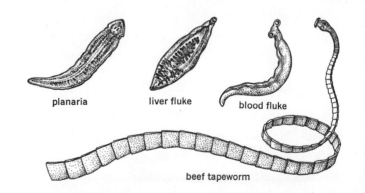

planaria

liver fluke

blood fluke

beef tapeworm

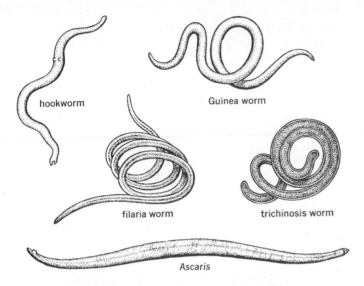

hookworm

Guinea worm

filaria worm

trichinosis worm

Ascaris

ROUNDWORMS

(Phylum—Nematoda)

These microscopic or semimicroscopic roundworms have smooth bodies and are unsegmented. They have a mouth and anus, but no definite respiratory or circulatory organs. Many live in the soil and many are parasitic.

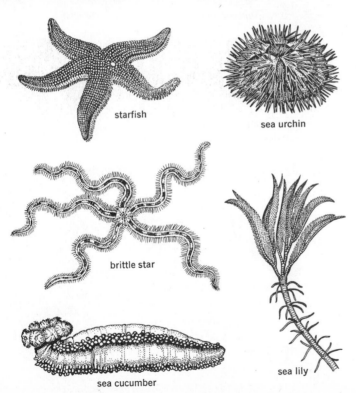

starfish

sea urchin

brittle star

sea lily

sea cucumber

SPINY–SKINNED ANIMALS

(Phylum—Echinodermata)

These animals have a body plan entirely different from that of any other animal. They move by tube feet and have a unique hydrovascular system that is found in no other organisms. Their body plan is based upon five sections or a multiple of five. All are marine organisms.

14

Animals Without Backbones — Toward Wider Adaptations

To most people, the invertebrates you have been studying make up a mysterious, little-known world. But the world of the invertebrates has begun to open for you. You have seen their numerous adaptations to an aquatic world—whether fresh water or salt water. Everywhere, the supply of water determines their success.

In this chapter you will study the higher invertebrates that are far more familiar: the annelids, or segmented worms (earthworms), the mollusks (clams and snails), and the arthropods (lobsters, insects, and spiders). Let's begin with the earthworm, a common and certainly an important invertebrate.

1. SEGMENTED WORMS—THE ANNELIDS

Earthworms can usually be found by digging in moist, rich soil, where they remain in the daytime, coming out only at night to feed. Even then they usually come only part way out of their burrows to feed on dead leaves and other plant materials.

Have you ever examined an earthworm closely? If so, you may have noticed that it seems to be made up of rings, or segments, fastened together. In fact, the earthworm belongs to the phylum of *segmented worms*. The phylum name is Annelida.

There are over 6,000 different kinds, or species, of segmented worms. If you live near the sea, you may have seen a close relative of the earthworm. This worm lives under stones or in burrows in the sand or in the mud between low and high tides. It has paddlelike feet and, along the New England coast, may grow to be a foot long. Look at the photograph of *Nereis*, or clam worm. ❶ Can you tell why it is classified in the same phylum as the earthworm?

❶

Habits of the Earthworm in Its Environment

You can collect earthworms by digging for them, or you can find them at night with a flashlight. Earthworms are fun to study, and if you can find large worms, such as the "night crawler," it makes your study easier. Unlike most animals you have already studied, the earthworm is large enough for you to easily see the arrangement of its body structures.❶

What can you learn about the anatomy of an earthworm by examining it from the outside? Does it have a head end and a tail end or are both ends the same? Does it have a mouth opening and an anus?

Think a moment. How would you tell if a living earthworm had a head end? Suppose you placed a living worm on a moist paper towel and let it crawl around. When an earthworm crawls, the same end is always at the front of the direction of movement. Does this help you decide if the worm has a head end and a tail end, or at least whether both ends are the same?

Does the earthworm have a *top* side and a *bottom* side? Suppose you turned an earthworm on its back. You would notice that it very quickly turns itself over again. You can conclude from this that it does have a top (dorsal) side and a bottom (ventral) side.

If you now examine the surface of an earthworm more closely, you would notice that its body is covered with a slick, slimy substance. This substance is called *mucus*. How do you suppose that mucus helps the animal? Remember where the earthworm lives. If you rub some of the mucus between your thumb and finger, your thumb and finger slip over each other easily. This should help you arrive at at least one use of mucus to the worm. How does an earthworm move around? The mucus would make it slippery, would it not? If you placed the worm on a moist paper

towel, you would find that it crawls easily.

When the head end of an earthworm stretches out, the tail remains stationary. Then the head end thickens, pulling the tail forward. What structures enable the worm to move in this way?

If you have a living worm, run your finger lightly and slowly over the top. It feels smooth and slick, but if you turn the worm over on its back and stroke the underneath surface lightly and slowly, it feels as if you are rubbing your finger over tiny bristles.

Each segment (ring) of the worm, except the first and the last, has four pairs of tiny bristles on the bottom and side surfaces of the skin. In the drawing of the earthworm you can see two pairs.❶ The worm can push these bristles out or pull them in by means of tiny muscles.

As the worm, in moving, stretches out the front part of its body, it sticks out its bristles on the front end. These catch onto the surface the worm is crawling on. Then the worm pulls in the bristles at the rear and pulls the rear end forward. The bristles in the rear end are then stuck out and those in the front end are pulled in. The front end stretches out again and the entire process is repeated.

Did you ever try to pull a worm out of its burrow? If not, dig up a spadeful of garden soil and locate a worm part way out of the broken soil. Try to pull it out. How can so slick a worm hold on to its burrow so well? You have probably guessed the answer. It sticks out its bristles and it thickens that part of the body still in the burrow. In this way it wedges itself in. Sometimes a worm will break in half if you pull hard enough and if it has braced its bristles well enough into the walls of its burrow.

You must realize by now that the mucus helps the worm slide through its burrow in

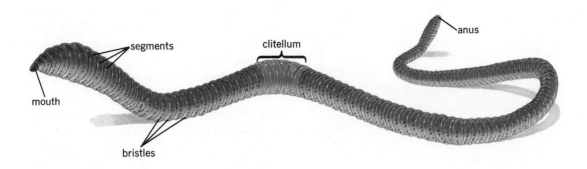

the soil. It helps, too, in "cementing" the walls of the burrow, for some of the mucus rubs off and makes a smooth surface along the burrow wall. However, these functions only partially account for the value of the mucus to the worm. Perhaps a most important function of the mucus lies in the manner in which the worm gets its oxygen.

Moisture and the Exchange of Gases

An earthworm has no lungs. It does not even have gills as a fish does. An earthworm gets its oxygen by diffusion through the membranes of its skin cells. You know that oxygen dissolves in water, and that oxygen diffuses from the water through the cell membranes of many organisms. This same process occurs in the earthworm. With its coating of mucus and in its normal environment of moist soil, there is sufficient moisture on its skin to dissolve oxygen from the air. From here, the oxygen diffuses into the cells of the worm. If the skin becomes dry, there is no moisture to dissolve oxygen and thus, in time, the worm dies of suffocation, that is, a lack of oxygen.

As well as secreting mucus from mucous glands in their skin, earthworms also secrete another fluid through tiny pores from inside their bodies. This fluid keeps the skin moist for a while if the earthworm remains above ground, and thus the animal has no difficulty getting oxygen. However, in time, in dry air, the moisture evaporates faster than the worm can secrete new fluid and finally the worm dies of suffocation.

Food-Getting

Earthworms make their burrows in a most interesting way. They actually *eat* their way through the ground. From time to time they come to the surface and push bits of the earth out of their bodies. These bits of earth can often be seen as small piles of "castings" around the openings of the burrows. You can easily find these castings if you look for them.

The purpose of digging the burrows is not only to make tunnels, but also to get food. Rich soil has food material in it, as you know —decayed bits of leaves and seeds, and even living plants and animals of very small size. These are the chief foods of the earthworm. There are also times when the earthworm feeds on the surface of the ground, usually at night and usually with only a part of its body out of the burrow. It picks up bits of leaves which it drags back into its burrow to eat.

You may wish to dissect an earthworm to study its internal parts. ■

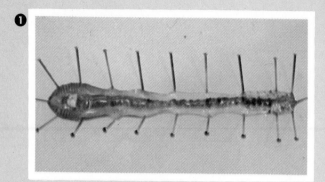

Large earthworms are best for your dissection, although you should be able to locate and identify the chief internal organs even in a smaller earthworm.

Earthworms can be killed easily by placing them in a jar of water and adding chloroform, a little at a time. You can then stretch your worm out in a dissecting pan containing wax, or on a corkboard, a piece of pine, or other soft wood. Be certain the top surface of the earthworm is up before you pin the first segment of the head end down firmly. Next, run another pin through the tail end so that it, too, is firmly fixed.

With a sharp knife, a razor blade, or a scalpel, cut carefully through the body wall starting at the *tail end.* Do not cut too deeply or you will cut into the internal organs. After you have made a cut about an inch long, try to force the skin open with the points of pins or dissecting needles. You will find that there are internal partitions at most segments. Cut these away from the body wall. Now you can pin back the body wall as shown in the photograph. ❶

Continue cutting, pinning the body wall back every five segments, until you reach the head end. ❷ Now all the internal organs should be exposed. Observe that the right and left sides are mirror images of each other. Biologists say that the earthworm has **bilateral** (bī·lat′er·al) **symmetry.**

Using the photographs and drawings as a guide, see how many of the various organs you can locate in your worm. Counting the segments from the head end will help you locate the different organs.

Digestive system. This system is a long tube that runs from the mouth to the anus. ❸ The mouth opens into the *pharynx* (segment three). This area contains glands that secrete fluids to lubricate the food. The pharynx is muscular, so that the food is mixed with the fluids. Food then goes through the *esophagus* into the thin-walled *crop.* The crop stores the food temporarily, and releases it slowly to the thick, muscular *gizzard.*

An earthworm has no teeth or jaws. The food is chewed in the gizzard. Grains of sand in the gizzard tear food particles apart as the muscular walls of the gizzard work the food back and forth. (Do you know of another kind of animal that grinds its food in a gizzard?)

From the thick, muscular gizzard, the food now ground up passes into the long intestine. Digestive enzymes are secreted from glands that line the intestinal tube. These digest fats, proteins, and carbohydrates. In addition, an enzyme called cellulase (sel′yə·lāz) digests cellulose (woody walls of plant cells). The human body has no such enzyme. However, the ability to digest cellulose is essential for the earthworm. Digested foods are absorbed into the blood stream from the intestine, and the remaining indigestible materials are excreted through the anus.

Circulatory system. The circulatory system consists of five pairs of hearts (segments seven through eleven) and blood vessels that run lengthwise in the body. The hearts are really just muscular tubes that connect the large dorsal blood vessel with a similar large ventral blood vessel. If you have a freshly killed earthworm, you may be able to observe one or more of these hearts expanding and contracting as it forces blood along.

The hearts force blood from the large dorsal blood vessel to the large ventral blood vessel. The blood moves through the ventral blood vessel and goes out through many branching vessels to the digestive organs and other body parts. After going through thin-walled capillaries, the blood moves into larger vessels and finally enters the large dorsal blood vessel where it moves forward to the hearts again.

Respiratory system. You already know that the earthworm has no real respiratory system. However, a large number of capillaries carry blood to the moist skin where the blood gives up carbon dioxide and takes up oxygen. The oxygen combines chemically with the hemoglobin in the blood. The same reaction occurs in your body. The hemoglobin, which is dissolved in the liquid part of the blood stream, carries oxygen to all parts of the body.

Excretory system. Every segment of the body except the first three and the last few segments has a pair of kidneylike organs that excrete

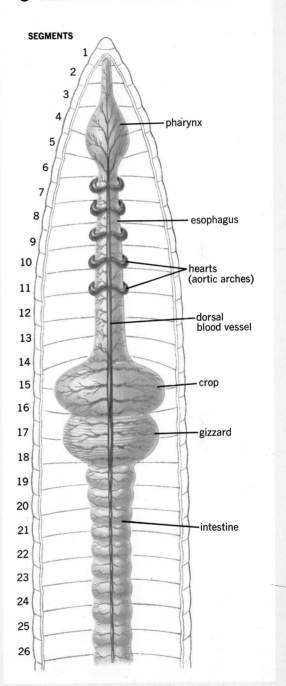

❸ DIGESTIVE AND CIRCULATORY SYSTEMS

SEGMENTS

pharynx

esophagus

hearts
(aortic arches)

dorsal
blood vessel

crop

gizzard

intestine

❶ REPRODUCTIVE AND EXCRETORY SYSTEMS

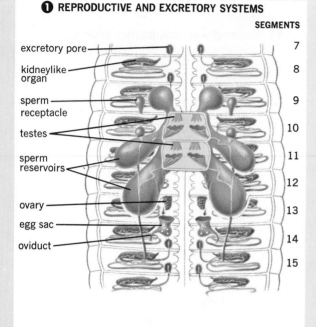

SEGMENTS

- excretory pore — 7
- kidneylike organ — 8
- sperm receptacle — 9
- testes — 10
- sperm reservoirs — 11
- — 12
- ovary — 13
- egg sac — 14
- oviduct — 15

❷ NERVOUS SYSTEM

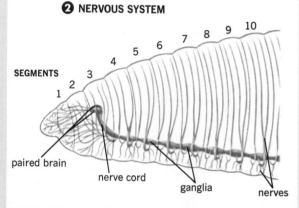

SEGMENTS
1 2 3 4 5 6 7 8 9 10

- paired brain
- nerve cord
- ganglia
- nerves

the nitrogenous wastes. All liquid wastes are excreted by these coiled-tube kidneys through the excretory pores.

Reproductive system. Each earthworm is both male and female. That is, each earthworm produces both sperms and eggs. In reproduction, two earthworms exchange sperms. They never fertilize themselves.

The male reproductive system includes two pairs of tiny *testes* (segments ten and eleven). These can be found in the lower part of the

segments. They are difficult to find, so you may wish to use a hand lens to locate them. Much easier to see are the large *sperm reservoirs* in which the sperms develop further and are stored in a fluid until needed. The three pairs of sperm reservoirs extend up and around the esophagus in segments nine to twelve.

The female reproductive system consists of tiny *ovaries* on the underneath surface in segment thirteen. Eggs develop in the ovaries and then pass to the *egg sacs*. From here they leave the body through tiny tubes opening through the body wall (segment fourteen). You will need a hand lens to locate the ovaries.

You may have noticed the band around the outside of an earthworm (p. 343). It has a Latin name, *clitellum* (klī·tel′əm). The clitellum secretes a kind of slime that forms a sheath that picks up both the eggs and the sperms as it slips forward over the body of the worm. This sheath then changes into a kind of cocoon that is deposited in the moist earth where the eggs hatch out into tiny worms.

Nervous system. Above the pharynx (in segment three) is a tiny, paired brain. Two nerve cords run from here down to the bottom, where they connect, becoming a nerve cord. This nerve cord runs along the lower part of the worm and on to the last segment. In each segment you will find the nerve cord swelled into a collection of nerve cells, called *ganglia.* (The brains are really just large ganglia.) Nerves branch off from these ganglia and the nerve cord to all parts of the body. Some of these nerves end in structures that are sensitive to light. These light-sensitive structures are most numerous at the head and tail ends.

An Investigation On Your Own

You might find it interesting to devise investigations to determine what parts of the worm's body are most sensitive to vibrations.

The Earthworm and Specialization

On page 313 you will find photomicrographs of *Amoeba*, and on page 317, *Hydra*. Look at these two animals again and compare them with the earthworm. It is clear that the amoeba is the simplest of the three and that the earthworm is the most complex.

In the following table you will find these three animals compared in their functions and structures for meeting the basic problems of living. Study the table carefully.

It is interesting that the amoeba, which has no specialized structures at all, is quite as successful in meeting the problems of living as is the earthworm. After all, amoebas and similar protozoans probably lived on the earth for millions upon millions of years before the first earthworm or other segmented worm appeared.

Why do you suppose the earthworm needs specialized structures and organs whereas the amoeba apparently does not? Why do you suppose the hydra has more specialized structures than the amoeba, but fewer than the earthworm?

For one thing, the amoeba, being but a single cell, does not need specialized organs and tissues such as heart and blood. There are no other cells to which food, or oxygen, or wastes must be transported. The amoeba

FUNCTION	STRUCTURE		
	Amoeba	*Hydra*	*Earthworm*
food-getting	no true structure, pseudopods part of cell	tentacles, stinging cells, mouth	mouth
digestion	no true structure, occurs in an organelle, the food vacuole	saclike cavity with amoebalike cells	food tube including crop, gizzard, intestine, and digestive glands
circulation (food and oxygen)	none	none	heart tubes and blood vessels
respiration	none	none	none (except glands that secrete mucus)
waste removal	none	amoebalike cells and flagellated cells	kidney tubes, excretory pores, and anus
sensory stimulation	no true structure, only basic sensitivity of protoplasm	nerve net	brainlike ganglia, nerves and nerve endings (sensitive to light, touch, odors, temperature, and vibrations)
reproduction	none	testes and ovaries	testes, ovaries, sperm reservoirs, egg sacs, and clitellum

simply takes food from the water into its single cell and all processes are carried on there. The hydra, being multicellular, uses its mouth and other structures in order to take food inside its body. However, since its body is made up of only two layers of cells, it is not necessary for it to have a circulatory system. However, the earthworm needs not only a mouth to take food into its body, but also must have a means of circulating the digested food to the many cells throughout its body. Therefore, a circulatory system is necessary.

Compare the nervous systems of the earthworm and the hydra with the absence of such a system in the amoeba. The single-celled amoeba is sensitive to light, heat, chemicals, and so forth, just as the hydra and the earthworm are. You recall that all protoplasm shows *sensitivity*. If you were to jab an amoeba with a thin needle, the amoeba would respond by moving away. However, suppose that the earthworm or hydra were jabbed with a needle and that they did not have nerves. The cell touched would be sensitive, but the cell might not be capable of moving away since it is held in place by many other cells. However, a system of nerves would *communicate* the stimulus of the needle to all the other cells and the entire animal could react by moving away. This is, of course, exactly what happens.

In short, multicellular animals *must* have specialized structures simply because they are multicellular, and because each cell individually cannot meet all the basic needs of life. Some cells have become specialized for receiving or communicating stimuli (nerve cells of many kinds). Some cells have become specialized for digesting food (digestive gland cells) or for contracting (muscle cells). Some cells have become specialized for reproducing (sperm and egg cells). In true multicellular animals, such as the hydra and the earthworm, the specialized cells and organs *require* the cooperation of other specialized cells and organs in order to exist.

At the end of this chapter you will find a section called *Variety Among the Animals*. There you will find drawings of many other animals. Examine the drawings of other annelids and read the explanatory text so that you will understand why the animals shown there are grouped together in one phylum.

REVIEW

1. The hydra and the earthworm are both multicellular animals, but the earthworm has a circulatory system while the hydra does not. Why?

2. Of what advantage to an earthworm is the mucus it secretes?

3. Explain how the four pairs of bristles on each segment help the worm in crawling and in anchoring itself in its burrow.

4. Why must an earthworm have a moist environment?

5. Describe the food-getting habits of an earthworm.

6. Aside from protection, why does an earthworm dig burrows in the soil?

7. Describe the digestive system of an earthworm. Explain the purpose of the following organs: pharynx, esophagus, crop, and gizzard.

8. Why can an earthworm digest woody materials (cellulose) while a human being cannot?

9. Describe the flow of blood through the circulatory system of an earthworm.

10. How does an earthworm get rid of nitrogenous (protein) wastes?

11. Describe, in general terms, how earthworms reproduce themselves.

12. Would you say that an earthworm has a brain, several brains, or no brain at all? Explain your answer.

NEW VIEW

1. As you know, an earthworm's skin must be moist so that dissolved oxygen can be taken into its body. Do you suppose that other animals must have moist membranes for the absorption of dissolved oxygen into their bodies? What about your lungs? Must their linings be moist? Answer this question in terms of your present judgment and the evidence you have at this time.

2. Suppose you wanted to keep some earthworms for future experiments or for fishing. What kind of environment must you provide in terms of food, moisture, and temperature? You might wish to keep an earthworm farm for a while. How would you go about this project?

3. What is the advantage to an earthworm of having light-sensitive nerve endings concentrated at both the head end and tail end of the body?

4. Did you ever notice after a heavy night of rainfall that a large number of earthworms are lying on the sidewalks? Some people say that earthworms must have been "drowned out." They think that so much rain fell that the worms were about to drown and thus came out of their burrows to keep from drowning. Do you believe this? Why or why not?

5. Write a one- or two-page paper explaining why multicellular animals require specialized parts and body systems whereas single-celled animals do not need such specialized structures.

2. SOFT–BODIED ANIMALS— THE MOLLUSKS

Think of a clam, an oyster, or a snail out of its shell, and you will recognize why the phylum has been named Mollusca (mol′ əsk·ə), meaning "soft." The squid and the octopus also belong to this phylum. Perhaps you know the phylum by the beautiful shells, often called sea shells. Sea shells is not always a correct term for many mollusks. Some, such as the fresh-water snails and fresh-water clams, do not live in the sea, and some snails live on land.

The shells of mollusks fall into four main groups. Mollusks with *hinged* shells include oysters, clams, scallops—this is perhaps the most familiar group of mollusks. Those with *coiled* shells are also well-known—they include snails, conches, and periwinkles. The *tusk*-shelled mollusks and those with *cross-plated* shells are probably less familiar to you, but examples of these groups (the *tusk* and the *chiton*) are illustrated on page 372.

Partly because of their protective shells, the phylum of mollusks is one of the most successful. It ranks next to the arthropods (which you will study next) as one of the most successful groups of animals. It contains some 70,000 different species. A further reason why they are successful may be found in the adaptation of the mollusk body to the environment. Mollusks have the main organ systems of man—circulatory, digestive, respiratory, nervous, muscular, excretory, and reproductive systems. The octopus and squid have a sort of internal supporting skeleton, although you may not want to dignify it with that name. It is actually cartilage, not bone.

If you have an aquarium in the classroom, carefully watch the snails. Notice how they move about on a broad muscular foot. Most mollusks travel on such a foot. The foot, which protrudes from the front of the clam, is a tough plough-shaped organ with which the clam digs its way along. However, the squid and octopus move in a different way. They squirt water out of a tube, which moves them in the opposite direction.

The soft body structures of a mollusk can best be studied by examining a clam or mussel, insofar as it is possible to do so. ■

■ AN APPRENTICE STUDY IN ANATOMY: The Clam

❶

Let your teacher open the clam or mussel for you. A sharp knife is needed to cut the two strong muscles that control the opening and closing of the two half shells. Can you find where each of the muscles was attached? Find the front muscle attachment. Which is stronger,

❷

esophagus, intestine, mouth, shell muscle, digestive gland, stomach, heart, kidney, shell muscle, anus, siphons, gills, mantle, shell, ovary, foot

the front muscle or the hind muscle? How did you decide which is stronger?

Now examine the body. Notice the fine tissue covering it.❶ This is the *mantle*. In the living clam it lines the inside of the shell, and its cells produce (actually secrete) the shell. In the oyster, the mantle secretes the pearl layer. Sometimes this pearly substance is secreted around a foreign body, a sand grain perhaps, within the shell, and a pearl is formed. Examine your clam shell. As the mantle secretes the substance that forms the shell, lines of growth are formed on the outside of each half shell. How many lines of growth are on your specimen?

Study the diagram of the internal anatomy of the clam.❷ Try to find the various organs, particularly the heart, the stomach, and the ovaries.

See if you can find the *siphons* at the rear of the clam. One siphon brings in fresh oxygenated water. Another siphon sends the deoxygenated water out again.

Once the water is taken into the body chamber, or mantle chamber, of the clam it passes over the gills. There the oxygen is removed. Then the water flows out through the upper siphon. Food particles carried by the water enter the mouth.

An Investigation On Your Own

Trace the intestine from the stomach to the anus. In the heart cavity, the intestine appears to pass through the heart. Does it, or is the heart wrapped around the intestine?

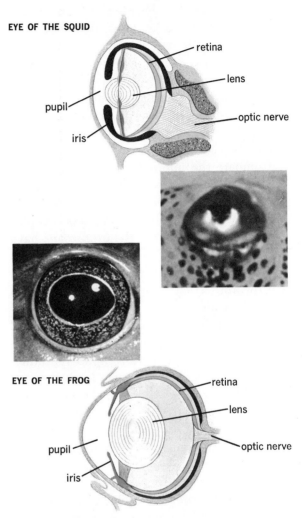

EYE OF THE SQUID

retina
lens
optic nerve
pupil
iris

EYE OF THE FROG

retina
lens
optic nerve
pupil
iris

Your brief observation of the body of the clam should enable you to reflect on these two questions.

  a. How is the mollusk more advanced in its body structure than a worm?
  b. Are the Mollusca more successful than the Annelida?

A study of another characteristic of certain mollusks will help you in your answers.

A Molluscan Eye:
An Organ of Higher Complexity

If you were able to study the scallop, *Pecten,* you would find a strange characteristic—the beginnings of a true eye or eyes. The eyes of *Pecten* are located along the rims of the mantle. ❶ Actually, this mollusk views the world with many eyes. Probably, the eyes of *Pecten* permit it to see differences in light and dark, but they are certainly not as effective as the human eye.

On the other hand, compare the eye of the squid with that of a frog, a member of a higher phylum. ❷ Now you can begin to see why the mollusks are placed high in the group of invertebrates. The mollusks have structures that are more effective adaptations to the environment than have the lower animals. They

also have the same body systems as we do, and they are beginning to show specialized *sense organs,* such as the eye. Of course, some of the lower invertebrates had developed sense organs. *Planaria,* for example, has two eye spots which enable it to sense different intensities of light. *Euglena* has an eye spot. But the eye of the Mollusca shows the beginning of a complex structure similar to the well-developed eyes of higher animals.

Increasing Complexity—
Hydra to Earthworm to Clam

Whereas the last chapter was concerned with the lower invertebrates, this chapter is concerned with the higher invertebrates. Having studied numerous invertebrates and having dissected several typical forms, you have a concept of the *increasing complexity* of the invertebrates as you go from the hydra, to the earthworm, to the clam. But what does "increasing complexity" mean?

Compare the internal structures you have studied of at least two of the lower invertebrates with the higher invertebrate, the clam. Certainly the protozoans seem less complex than the clam, although the protozoans have adapted successfully to their environment.

Compare, for instance, a hydra with an earthworm. Then compare the earthworm with the clam.

a. Which has the more complex structure? Why do you say so?
b. Which has the more complex reproductive system? How do you know?
c. Which of the three phyla (to which these animals belong) includes more species?

"Increasing complexity," then, must mean that the organism is adapted by means of more complex organs to living in a greater variety of environments. Thus, the Mollusca are found in a variety of environments (even on land), whereas the coelenterates are limited to an aquatic environment. Increasing complexity of organs usually puts an organism into a so-called higher group. Thus the eye, the muscles, and the means of food-getting all place the Mollusca on a higher plane than *Hydra* or the earthworms. There is still another meaning of higher and lower invertebrates or vertebrates; it has to do with the *fossil record.*

The Fossil Record

From your earlier work, you know that organisms that no longer exist were living in past ages of the earth. You know, for instance, of organisms such as *Rhynia* and the seed ferns among the plants. A common example of animal forms existing as fossils, with which you are no doubt familiar, is a group of reptiles known as the dinosaurs. You will study the dinosaurs later, as you study more about the fossil record. You know that many of the extinct plants and animals left their remains preserved in the rocks. Remember that it is these preserved remains, whether preserved in pitch or in sedimentary rock, that are called fossils. Usually an organism was preserved only in part; hard parts such as bones or shells of the Mollusca were preserved in rock.

Remember that sedimentary rock is formed from sediment carried by rivers down into the ocean. Sand, clay, and lime all form sediment that settles in layers to form the sedimentary rock. The layer laid down first is the oldest layer; the newest one is usually the top layer. Certainly, then, the top layers would hold the fossil record of the more complex organisms, since those organisms lived at a later time.

Thus, no reptiles would be found in the earliest rocks because reptiles appeared later in the life history of the earth. Similarly, mammals, such as the elephant or the horse, would not be found in the same early layers as the early mollusks, or early amphibians. Generally, the more complex forms of life are found in the rocks laid down recently, that is, recently in terms of the age of the earth.

Fossils of the horse are found in the more recent layers when compared with the fossils of early fish, amphibians, and reptiles. Thus the fossil record is also evidence of the rise of organisms.

The higher invertebrates (animals without backbones) and the vertebrates (animals with backbones) are found only in the more recent sedimentary rock.

An organism that is commonly assigned the title of "higher organism" or "higher invertebrate" is thought to be more recent in animal development and more complex in its structure than the so-called lower organisms.

You would expect, then, that fossils of the earliest Mollusca would be found in the sedimentary rocks of more recent origin than fossil remains of the first lower invertebrates. The evidence to support this hypothesis is not as easy to find as you might suspect. Why?

Which would you expect to be more easily preserved in sedimentary rock, an earthworm or a clam? Clearly, a clam would because of its hard outer shell. The soft body might not be preserved, but the shell might. The fossil record is, therefore, richer in fossils of the Mollusca than it is in fossils of the worms.

On the basis of the evidence, it seems fairly clear that by the end of the Cambrian period, in the Paleozoic era, representatives of almost all the major phyla of animals were already on earth. Notice the words *almost all*. The chordates, the phylum of animals which embraces the vertebrates, were still to come into existence. The seas swarmed with invertebrates. ❶ Among the animals that can be recognized as mollusks were many extinct forms. Clams and oysters were not abundant in the Paleozoic seas. The most conspicuous types were ancestors of the octopus and squid. The beaches of ancient times certainly had strange shells that the modern collector no longer finds. Nevertheless, had you visited a Cambrian sea you would have recognized the mollusk forms.

It also happens that certain of the worms form outer cases of protective shells from materials in the environment. These cases or shells are occasionally preserved in the fossil record. ❶ Also, the phylum Brachiopoda (brā·kē·op′ə·də) (the lamp shells) contains lower invertebrates that form outer shells. Many of these were also preserved.

From the fossil records available, paleontologists, particularly paleozoologists, who study the evolution of animals, have reconstructed the past history of the lower and higher invertebrates.

REVIEW

1. What are the characteristics that place a squid, a clam, and a snail in the phylum Mollusca?

2. What are the organ systems that enable a mollusk, such as the clam, to carry on the following life functions?

    a. respiration

    b. digestion

    c. reproduction

3. How does the molluscan eye compare with that of *Planaria?*

4. Why are the mollusks considered to be more complex than a flatworm or an earthworm?

NEW VIEW

As you know, fossils are preserved in sedimentary rock. Other than the fact that most lower invertebrates had soft bodies, what reason might you give for the relative lack of fossils of lower invertebrates in older rock layers?

3. ANIMALS WITH JOINTED LEGS— THE ARTHROPODS

Insects and their relatives are members of the phylum Arthropoda (är·throp′ə·də). The word *Arthropoda* means "joint foot." Vertebrates have jointed legs, but arthropods are the only *invertebrates* with jointed legs.

Arthropods are the most varied, the most complex, and the most highly developed of all the invertebrates. Arthropods make up the only major invertebrate phylum with a large number of animals fully adapted to life on the land. Most land arthropods have no need of a moist environment. Also, arthropods are the only invertebrates that fly.

Arthropods live almost everywhere. They can be found in salt water and in fresh water, in soil, on land, and in the air. Some parasitize plants; others parasitize animals. They range in size from tiny mites about $\frac{1}{50}$ of an inch long, hardly visible to the naked eye, to the size of giant Japanese crabs sometimes 12 feet across from leg tip to leg tip.

The arthropods are the largest phylum in the animal kingdom. About 85 percent of all the animals in the world are arthropods! The insects (class Insecta) alone contain over 900,000 different kinds, or species, of animals. (That is to say that 900,000 have been identified and classified by scientists thus far. No one knows how many kinds actually exist.) The insect *class* contains over eighteen times as many different species as the entire vertebrate *phylum.*

Outside Skeletons

There is another characteristic, other than jointed legs, that distinguishes the arthropods from other invertebrates. All arthropods have a kind of skeleton, but it is an outside skeleton, or exoskeleton. An arthropod's exoskeleton forms a tough, jointed suit of armor. Although it is rather thin and flexible in some animals such as flies or spiders, in other animals such as beetles or lobsters it is thick and rigid. The exoskeleton obviously protects the soft body underneath from injury. It also serves to keep the animal from drying out, and provides a support, as do bones in your body, for the attachment of muscles.

Your bones grow as your body grows. Bone is living tissue and more bone tissue is formed as needed. An arthropod's exoskeleton, on the other hand, is not living tissue and contains no cells. It is a substance secreted as a liquid that quickly hardens. As you may suspect, this hard armor creates a problem for a growing arthropod. How is it possible for a small young arthropod to grow up into a large, adult arthropod when its body is covered by a tough, unstretchable armor? The difficulty is solved, for most arthropods, by splitting their protective armor and crawling out of it.

Most arthropods shed their exoskeletons, a process called **molting**, from four to seven times as they grow and mature. Just before an arthropod molts, it secrets a new, thin, flexible exoskeleton inside the old one. The old exoskeleton then splits along the top surface and the animal slowly crawls out of the old armor. ❷ It then swallows air or water to make itself as large as possible and waits until the new armor has hardened. A chemical change similar to that which causes house paint to dry hardens the new exoskeleton. (It combines with oxygen from the air.) Until

the new armor has hardened, the arthropod can move about only slowly and is nearly defenseless.

The Grasshopper, a Common Arthropod

Let's now look into the life of a common insect, the grasshopper. In the spring, when the weather has become warm, small grasshoppers hatch out of the eggs that were laid in a hole the previous fall. If you look around in the grass or in fields in the spring, you should be able to find these miniature grasshoppers. They look exactly like the adult grasshoppers, but they are stubbier and have no wings. Not all newly hatched insects look like the adults. Most, in fact, look altogether different. The young, or larvae, of butterflies, for example, are caterpillars that look nothing at all like their parents.

The young grasshopper feeds on plants for a few days and then molts. As the exoskeleton splits, the young grasshopper crawls out and is, for a while, quite soft. It hides in the grass until its new exoskeleton has hardened. Then it becomes active and eats again. Molting occurs five or six times as the grasshopper grows to maturity. Wings start to appear after the first or second molt. You can find this stage, too, in the early summer. The wings look like small pads.

Grasshoppers generally feed locally, hopping from one plant to another, but if food is scarce nearby they will fly fairly long distances to find nourishment. Because of this, they can become serious pests and ruin crops. Acres of corn plants can be stripped until they look as though a giant machine had cut and shredded them. If grasshoppers cannot find their usual green plant food, they will attack even cotton and wool clothing. They have also been known to eat the wood of fences and houses.

On the other hand, grasshoppers serve as food for many other animals. Mice, moles, skunks, and other insects eat their eggs. The young grasshoppers are a tasty tidbit for certain flies and wasps, and for frogs, snakes, and many kinds of birds. One reason birds are so valuable to man is that they eat many harmful insects, including grasshoppers.

There are insects that lay their eggs specifically on grasshoppers. As the young worm-like larva hatches out, it burrows into the grasshopper's body. Here the young parasite eats its fill. It may sicken or even kill the grasshopper.

Of course, man himself poisons grasshoppers by the millions in order to save his crops. Another way in which man cuts down on the numbers of grasshoppers is by plowing under his fields, particularly weed fields, in the fall. Plowing tears up the egg holes of the grasshoppers and thus exposes the eggs to the winter cold, which kills them.

The grasshopper, like all arthropods, is distinguished from other lower animals by its possession of an exoskeleton and jointed legs. Let's examine these distinguishing characteristics as well as other structures and their functions in the common grasshopper. ■

356

■ AN APPRENTICE STUDY IN ANATOMY

External Anatomy

Compare your grasshopper or other insect with the body chart of the grasshopper. ❶ The labels will tell you the names of the external body parts. Also study the descriptions below as you examine the insect.

Head. The grasshopper, like most insects, has three simple eyes. These do not form clear images as your eyes do. The grasshopper, like most insects, also has a pair of compound eyes. They are like many simple eyes grouped together. Compound eyes form true images much as your eyes do, but the image is made of many small parts, like a mosaic.

The grasshopper has upper and lower lips, but its two jaws bite sideways instead of up-and-down as do yours. (Use a needle to lift the upper lip so you can see the jaws.) Notice that the jaws have toothed edges that are very hard and jointed, and tubelike structures used for touching or tasting. (Some insects have sucking mouth parts.)

The grasshopper has a pair of *antennae* (singular, *antenna*). The antennae have tiny sensory hairs sensitive to smell and touch.

Thorax. Three pairs of jointed legs are fastened to the thorax. The first two pairs are used for walking, the third pair for jumping.

Two pairs of wings are also attached to the thorax. (Pull the wings out sideways.) Notice that each of the first pair of wings is narrow. Each wing of the hind pair, used for flying, is wide and is folded up under a front wing.

Abdomen. The breathing pores, or *spiracles,* are tiny holes on each side of the abdomen. Some are on the sides of the thorax as well. These spiracles open into tubes inside the body. These tubes, called *trachea,* branch again and again until they reach all the body cells. Their function is to carry oxygen.

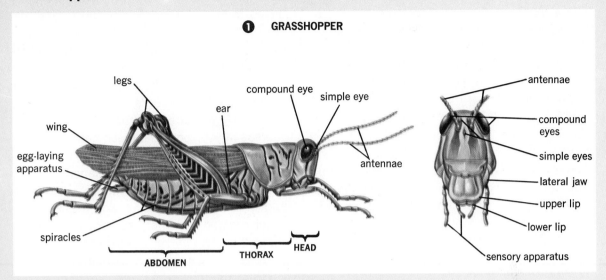

❶ GRASSHOPPER

legs
wing
egg-laying apparatus
spiracles
ear
compound eye
simple eye
antennae
ABDOMEN
THORAX
HEAD

antennae
compound eyes
simple eyes
lateral jaw
upper lip
lower lip
sensory apparatus

A grasshopper has an ear on each side at the front of the abdomen. The ears are only membranes much like your eardrums.

Female grasshoppers have a structure at the tip of the body that is used to dig a hole in the ground. In this hole, the female lays eggs that have been fertilized within her body by the male. During the proper season of the year, young grasshoppers, called **nymphs** (nimfs), hatch out of the eggs. Male grasshoppers, of course, do not have an egg-laying apparatus.

Internal Anatomy

Insects are the most complicated of all animals without backbones. In their own way they are as complicated as a vertebrate animal, such as a dog or a man.

Study each diagram carefully to help you in locating the different structures. Pin out the insect as shown in the photograph. ❷ Then follow carefully the directions your teacher gives you for opening the body wall. Use a fine pointed forceps to chip away the exoskeleton.

Nervous system. First chip away the exoskeleton of the head. The *brain* is in the upper part of the head (see p. 359). The largest part of the brain is connected with and receives messages from the eyes. Two nerve cords pass around the food tube, or esophagus, and join together underneath to form another brainlike structure, or ganglion. Then a *ventral nerve cord* goes along the ventral part of the body to

❷

the tail end. Notice that there are several *ganglia* along the nerve cord. The largest of these ventral ganglia sends nerves to the large jumping legs. Many other nerves branch out from the nerve cord to all the body structures.

Muscular system. The muscles are attached to the exoskeleton of the leg. For every muscle that bends a body part in one direction (bending a leg joint, for example), there is another muscle that bends it in the other direction (stretching out a leg at its joint, for example). The muscles work as your muscles do by shortening, or contracting. One muscle will pull a leg up while another muscle will stretch it out. One muscle opposes the other, just as the muscles in your body do. But instead of being fastened to bones inside the body of the grasshopper, they are fastened to the exoskeleton.

Digestive system. Have you ever watched a grasshopper eating green leaves? It uses its legs to put the food between its jaws. Its jaws work sideways and the toothed edges cut the leaf into pieces that are then swallowed. A tonguelike structure helps to guide the food into the mouth much as your tongue does. As the food is chewed, it is mixed with saliva and then swallowed. The food is stored in the *crop* and is then passed slowly into the *gizzard*. The gizzard grinds up the food and then passes it slowly into the *stomach*. Large glands secrete digestive juices into the stomach, where the food is digested. The digested food is absorbed into the blood stream through the stomach and intestinal walls. Indigestible food materials pass into the *rectum,* where water is reabsorbed into the blood stream. Then the unused materials are eliminated through the *anus.*

Respiratory system. Notice the *spiracles* in the body wall. The spiracles, or breathing pores, open into *air tubes,* or trachea, that branch to all parts of the body. The diagram shows only the main air tubes. Some of these are connected to large *air sacs* in the thorax and abdomen. Muscles cause the body to contract and expand. This constant movement pumps air in and out of the air sacs. Not all insects have air sacs, but all insects have spiracles and air tubes. The body cells of the grasshopper absorb oxygen directly from the air tubes, whereas in your body the blood carries oxygen to the body cells. In insects, oxygen in the blood stream is of minor importance.

Recall that in all the animals you have studied, a film of moisture was necessary to dissolve oxygen. In the grasshopper, even the tiniest branches of the air tubes have a film of moisture lining their walls. Once oxygen dissolves in the moisture, it diffuses through the membranes of the tubes and into the body cells. The grasshopper is not in danger of drying out. The exoskeleton prevents evaporation from the outside of the body and the air tubes are so deep inside the body that the film of moisture cannot dry out easily.

Excretory system. Kidneylike tubes remove the cell wastes from the blood stream and pass these wastes into the *intestine* where they are eliminated with the food wastes. Find the kidneylike tubes if you can. This will be difficult, but the body charts will guide you.

Reproductive system. The male and female sexes are separate in the grasshopper, as they are in all insects. The male has testes which produce sperms.

The female has *ovaries* which produce eggs. Find the ovaries. The sperms are introduced by the male into the female's body. The fertilized eggs are then passed out of the body and deposited in the ground.

An Investigation On Your Own

How is the grasshopper adapted to its environment? Analyze your observations.

NERVOUS, DIGESTIVE, AND CIRCULATORY SYSTEMS

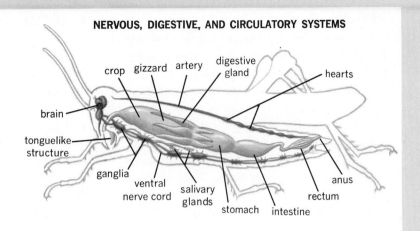

crop · gizzard · artery · digestive gland · hearts

brain

tonguelike structure

ganglia · ventral nerve cord · salivary glands · stomach · intestine · rectum · anus

RESPIRATORY SYSTEM

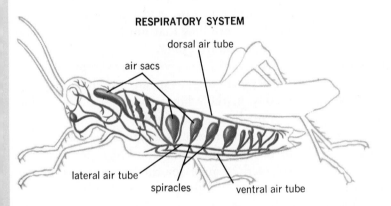

dorsal air tube

air sacs

lateral air tube · spiracles · ventral air tube

ANATOMY OF THE GRASSHOPPER

EXCRETORY AND REPRODUCTIVE SYSTEMS

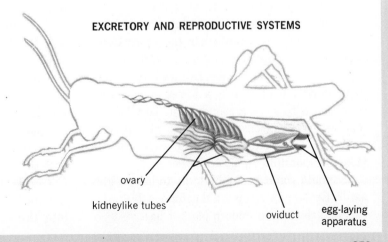

ovary

kidneylike tubes · oviduct · egg-laying apparatus

1. Would you say that a grasshopper has a brain? Would it be better to say that it has several brains or, even better, ganglia?

2. Why do muscles work in pairs, with one muscle of a pair opposing the action of the other?

3. Describe the digestive system of a grasshopper and explain the function of each part.

4. Why is it unnecessary for blood to carry a large amount of oxygen to the body cells in an insect?

5. What are the functions of an exoskeleton?

6. How is it possible for a young grasshopper, covered with armor, to grow into an adult?

NEW VIEW

1. You now know the major parts of a grasshopper's body. Examine other insects and compare them to the grasshopper. Do they all have two pairs of wings? (What about a fly?) Do all insects have eardrums on the front part of the abdomen? (Look up *katydid* in an encyclopedia or other reference book and locate its ears.

Compare the wings of a grasshopper with those of a beetle. Beetles are classified in the order Coleoptera (kō′lē·op′ter·ə), which means "sheath wing"; grasshoppers are classified in the order Orthoptera (ôr·thop′ter·ə), which means "straight wing." Can you discover why?

Examine a butterfly's wing under a microscope. Why is a butterfly classified in the order Lepidoptera (lep′ə·dop′tər·ə), meaning "scale wing"?

2. An insect is far more active and responsive to its environment than is a lower invertebrate such as a jellyfish or a roundworm. To what extent are the nervous system and the possession of an exoskeleton to which muscles are attached responsible for this difference?

3. Would you expect a butterfly to have a gizzard? Explain in terms of the food a butterfly eats and the kind of mouth parts it has.

4. SOCIAL INSECTS

Most animals live solitary lives. They may be found in the same environments as others of their kind, but usually they pay little or no attention to each other. Earthworms, hydras, and grasshoppers are examples of such *solitary* animals. However, some animals band together for protection or for getting food more successfully. Wolves hunt in packs, and deer live in herds. These animals are more social than the solitary animals.

Ants, bees, some wasps, and certain other insects show the most highly developed kinds of social life. These *social insects* not only live together, but also specialize in particular kinds of activities that must be done to keep the community going.

Honeybees are a common example of social insects. If you were to watch honeybees closely in their home, or hive, here is what you might see and learn.

The hive might be located in a hollow tree, or it might be found in a box especially constructed by man for this purpose. Whatever the location of the hive, you would find sheets of wax hanging from the top and sides. (In man-made hives, special wooden frames are constructed to hold the wax.) You would find bees busy at work making the sheets of wax and turning them into combs. You probably have already seen these combs. They are built of hundreds of six-sided cells. Bees use the cells to store honey for their own use.

If you watched the bees that were making the honeycomb, you would find that they scraped the wax off the surfaces of their abdomens with their hind legs. The wax is secreted by glands on the abdomen.

You would also observe other bees streaming into the hive and then releasing a fluid into the completed cells of the comb. ❶ If you tasted this fluid, you would find that it was sweet and that it had a flowerlike odor. This fluid is flower nectar. The bees suck it up through their tubelike mouth parts from the bases of flower petals. The nectar is then swallowed, but it passes only into the first section of the stomach, the honey stomach. Here digestive juices change the sugars of the nectar into a simpler kind of sugar and other substances are added. It is then deposited into the cells of the comb and is now what we know and eat as honey.

By glancing around at the many cells, you would notice that not all cells were being filled with honey. Many cells would contain what might look like a short, fat, white worm, called a grub. This grub is the larva, or infant stage, of the bee. You will recall that an infant grasshopper resembles an adult grasshopper. However, the infant bees do not look at all like adult bees.

Some bees function as nurses to tend and feed the larvae. For the first few days after an egg hatches into one of the eyeless, legless larvae, it is fed a kind of milk that the nurse bees secrete from glands in their heads. After the period of milk feeding, most of the larvae are fed a combination of honey and pollen, which the bees also collect from flowers.

A few of the larvae are fed solely on what is called "royal jelly." This feeding difference makes an amazing difference in ways in which the larvae develop. Those larvae fed on honey and pollen develop into *worker bees* (always females) or into males which are called *drones.*  Although the worker bees are females, they cannot produce eggs. Their egg-laying structures become modified into stingers. Those female larvae fed nothing but royal jelly develop into females called *queen bees.* The queens have both egg-laying structures and slender stingers.

About six days after the larvae first appear, they have grown so large that each almost fills its entire cell. The nurse bees now build a wax cap over each cell. At this time important changes take place as the larva lies quietly in its cell. This stage is called the **pupa** (pyo͞o′pə) stage. Then, after twelve days to two weeks (depending upon whether the pupa will become a worker, a drone, or

worker

drone

queen

a queen), the adult bee breaks out of the cell. During this short time an amazing change has taken place. The wormlike larva has changed into a bee with wings, chewing and sucking mouth parts, two large complex eyes, three simple eyes, two pairs of delicate wings, and six legs.

If you kept track of the adults breaking out of their cells, you would find interesting differences in the jobs of the workers, drones, and queens. The workers (remember, these are modified females) do all of the work of the hive. They collect pollen and nectar, they make the combs, they take care of the larvae, they clean out the hive, they swarm out to attack enemies with their stingers, and do everything but lay the eggs. Laying the eggs is the job of the queen.

Workers are produced constantly during warm weather. Queens are produced only when the hive begins to be overcrowded. When that occurs, nurse bees feed only royal jelly to some of the larvae in order to produce queens.

The first queen that breaks out of its cell flies out into the air, mates with one of the drones (males), and then returns to the hive to become the new queen. In the meantime, the workers destroy the surplus queens.

However, about a week before the new queen breaks out of her cell, the old queen leaves the hive with about half of the workers. They fly off in a cloud in what is called *swarming*. They establish a new hive in a suitable place, such as a hollow tree or a large crack in a rock, and start a new community.

The new queen devotes her life to one job alone—egg laying. She may live from three to five years, and during that time she may lay over a million eggs. Workers tend her carefully. They feed her, stroke her, and build special cells in which she deposits her eggs.

Drones do almost nothing. However, the drones are necessary, of course, to mate with the queen. Only one drone mates with the queen, and her body stores throughout her lifetime the many millions of sperms that he deposits. The sperms fertilize the eggs laid during the long life of the queen. The *fertilized* eggs produce both workers and queens. Occasionally the queen lays *unfertilized* eggs; these develop into drones. After the mating flight and toward the middle of summer, the workers chase out of the hive, or kill, most of the drones. The drones have done the one job they are capable of doing; they are no longer needed.

How do bees learn to do all the things they do? How do the workers learn to locate flowers, sip nectar, collect pollen, make honeycombs, take care of the larvae, and sting enemies? The answer is that they do *not* learn to do these things. A bee is *born* with these abilities. Its behavior is said to be *instinctive*, or inborn, *behavior*. The behavior of all insects, and most animals without backbones for that matter, is thought to be largely instinctive.

However, bees can be taught a few simple things. So can other insects and other invertebrates. Bees, for example, have been taught to go to a blue cardboard rather than a yellow one to get food.

What Is an Insect?

From your study of insects thus far, what characteristic would you say they seem to have in common? Use the bee or the grasshopper as a "typical" insect.

Count the number of legs. You will find that all insects have six legs. The number of legs is the most definite characteristic that distinguishes insects from other arthropods, for insects vary tremendously in body form.

They also vary tremendously in the kinds of environments in which they live, and in the kinds of young they produce.

There are, however, a number of basic characteristics that *most* insects have in common besides the number of legs. Exceptions to these characteristics are unusual. Such exceptions are found mainly in highly specialized insects that have become parasites, or in insects that have become highly adapted to a very special environment. Listed below are characteristics common to most insects.

a. Three pairs of jointed legs. This is the key characteristic of *all* insects.

b. Body divided into three parts: head, thorax, and abdomen. Legs are attached to thorax.

c. Heart, a long tube.

d. Long, branching tubes for breathing.

e. Blood carrying food but little or no oxygen.

f. Usually two pairs of wings. (However, not all adult insects have wings. Do worker ants have wings?)

g. One pair of antennae.

REVIEW

1. Describe in general terms the life of honeybees.

2. Why are honeybees called social insects?

3. Where does beeswax come from?

4. Explain how a bee makes honey.

5. Describe each of the following stages in the life cycle of a honeybee: egg, larva, pupa, adult.

6. What determines whether a bee will be a drone or a worker?

7. What determines whether a female larva will become a worker bee or a queen bee?

8. What is meant by instinctive behavior?

9. What is the key characteristic that distinguishes insects from other classes of arthropods?

NEW VIEW

1. You may wish to learn more about honeybees and other social insects such as ants and termites. Use encyclopedias or other references and report your findings to the class.

2. Would you consider insects *as a class* to be successful members of the animal kingdom?

5. A VIEW OF OTHER ARTHROPODS

Did you ever see a web that looked like the one shown in the photograph? ❶ Notice particularly the zigzag mark. This web is the trademark of the garden spider, or orb weaver. If you can find a web that looks like the one in the picture, try touching the silken strands of the web. You will find that the strands that radiate out like the spokes of a wheel are not sticky, but the strands that are circling around in a spiral fashion are extremely sticky.

❶ HEAD OF A SPIDER

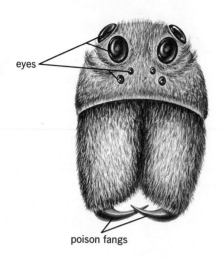

eyes

poison fangs

The Spiders

A spider's web is a kind of net for catching food. If an insect should fly or blunder onto one of the sticky threads, the insect becomes caught. It might eventually free itself, but usually the spider is waiting nearby. If the insect is small, the spider will grasp it and inject a poison that paralyzes the insect. The mouth of the spider is too small to take in solid food. Instead, it injects digestive juices into its prey and then sucks up the liquified insides. If the insect is large—a grasshopper, for example—the spider does not grasp it and eat it immediately. Instead, it winds around the insect a mass of sticky threads secreted from its silk glands located at the tip of its abdomen. These threads (the same kind used for spinning its web) harden into silk on contact with the air. The spider turns the insect over and over while spinning out more and more silk until the insect is helplessly bound.

Study the drawing of the head of a spider. ❶ Notice the long poison fangs. Notice, too, the eight simple eyes of the spider.

All spiders have eight legs. This is an easy way to distinguish spiders from insects. Another difference between spiders and insects is that spiders do not have a separate head and thorax. The head and thorax are combined, as you can see if you will look carefully at a live spider or at the photographs above. Spiders do not have wings, nor do they have compound eyes as insects do. Instead they have from one to six pairs (usually four pairs) of simple eyes.

Not all spiders build webs. One, called a wolf spider does not need a web. It pounces on its prey, which usually consists of very small insects.

Most spiders are useful to man because they destroy many insect pests. There is only one spider in our country that is really dangerous, the black widow spider. ② This spider is common in the southern and western parts of the United States, but occasionally it is found elsewhere in this country. The poison of the female black widow spider can make a person seriously ill and can even cause death. This spider is about half an inch long, is shiny black, and has an unusual orange-red mark shaped like an hourglass. The red hourglass makes it easy to distinguish a black widow spider. However, the marking is located on the underside of its abdomen. Take care not to be too familiar with a black, shiny spider until you see its underside.

The tarantula is the largest of the spiders. ③ Like all wolf spiders, it builds no web, but instead pounces on its prey—usually an insect. The bite of a tarantula can be painful and make a person very ill, but it is usually not fatal. Tarantulas in the United States are found in the South and Southwest, the warmer parts of the country. They are often up to two or three inches across. Tarantulas that live in some tropical countries may reach six or seven inches in size. These larger specimens can even catch and kill small birds by pouncing on them.

Crabs and Other Crustaceans

The most certain way to tell a crab or one of its relatives from an insect or a spider or another arthropod is to count the antennae. Insects have one pair of antennae, spiders and other arachnids have none, and crabs and other crustaceans [(krus·tā′shənz) the class to which the crabs and their relatives belong] all have two pair of antennae. Crustaceans also differ from insects by having gills for breathing. Most spiders have a simple pair of

lungs and air tubes, and you recall that insects have only a highly branched network of tiny air tubes.

Lobsters and crabs, such as this blue crab, are giants among crustaceans. ④ There are also many kinds of small crustaceans in the oceans. For every lobster or crab, there are millions of these small crustaceans.

Fresh-water ponds, lakes, and streams also contain several forms of tiny crustaceans, in addition to the small lobsterlike crayfish. Fairy shrimps and *Daphnia* (daf′nē·ə) are two common crustaceans. Both are often collected from ponds and raised to provide food for tropical fish. If you raise tropical fish and buy packaged food for them, the food will probably contain dried *Daphnia*.

Daphnia is fairly easy to obtain and is useful for a study of a microscopic crustacean. Nevertheless, it shows increasing complexity over the lower invertebrates and even the

■ AN APPRENTICE INVESTIGATION into the Structure of Daphnia

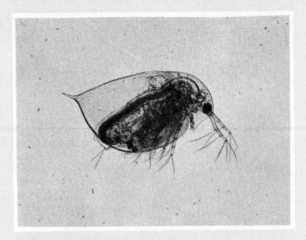

Get a supply of live **Daphnia** from a store that carries tropical fish. If you cannot find a supply of **Daphnia**, try finding **Daphnia** in some pond water. In what kind of ecosystem does **Daphnia** survive and multiply?

Daphnia will live in the same egg-yolk culture you used for **Paramecium** (see p. 311). The food chain is somewhat as follows: bacteria feed on the egg yolk, paramecia feed on the bacteria and smaller protozoans, **Daphnia** feeds on the protozoans and other organisms and bits of egg yolk as well.

Place some **Daphnia** in a small dish containing an inch of water. Also place some **Daphnia** in a narrow test tube. You may now be able to study **Daphnia,** which grows to about an eighth of an inch long, with the naked eye, with a hand lens, and with a microscope.

Compare your **Daphnia** with the photograph here. ❶ Does **Daphnia** have a mouth? a heart? What is the function of the branched antennae? Does **Daphnia** have other specialized organs?

An Investigation On Your Own

Daphnia sometimes reproduces by parthenogenesis (pär′thə·nō·jen′ə·sis), which means that its young are sometimes produced by the female from eggs with no fertilization by sperms. Can you find such a female? How could you demonstrate that the young of **Daphnia** are sometimes produced parthenogenetically?

Design an experimental procedure and carry it out with the assistance of several of your classmates. Of course, the investigation may not be easy to do.

Mollusca. If you are able to find some *Daphnia*, it will make an interesting study. ■

As a result of your study of *Daphnia*, see if you can answer the following questions.

 a. Why is *Daphnia* considered more complex than an earthworm? (Your answer to this question should be based on your study of the specialized organs of *Daphnia*.)

 b. Would you say that the larger an organism is, the more complex it is? (Compare *Hydra* with *Daphnia*.)

Centipedes and Millipedes

The insects, arachnids (spiders and their relatives), and crustaceans form the three main classes of the phylum Arthropoda.

Centipedes (hundred-legger) and millipedes (thousand-legger) are two different and smaller classes of arthropods that look like worms with legs. You have probably seen the common "hundred-legged worm," or house centipede. ● These tiny arthropods, grouped within the class Chilopoda (kī·lop′ə·də), are often found running swiftly on their long, jointed legs, in basements, near sinks, or in other damp places.

You may have seen millipedes, or "thousand-legged worms," in gardens, fields, or under decaying logs. These millipedes, class Diplopoda (dip·lop′ə·də), curl up into a tight spiral when disturbed. Count the legs of a garden millipede. Do millipedes really have a thousand legs?

A Look at the So-Called Higher Invertebrates

You may not have thought that a mollusk, such as a clam, was a higher invertebrate. However, if you had studied a large octopus or squid, you might have assumed more readily that mollusks are higher invertebrates. Size is not necessarily an indication of complexity of development. With the study of the arthropods, the concept of increasing complexity as the basis for classifying arthropods as higher invertebrates is easier to understand.

Read and consider carefully the following facts about the arthropods. See whether or not you believe these facts support the statement that the arthropods are the most highly developed invertebrates.

a. Arthropods make up the largest and most varied phylum in the animal kingdom.

b. The largest *class* of arthropods is the class Insecta. There are more than eighteen times as many different species of insects as there are species in the entire vertebrate phylum (to which man belongs).

c. Insects vary tremendously in body form. The distinguishing characteristic of the class, however, is that all adults have six legs. And the bodies of all adult insects are divided into three parts: head, thorax, and abdomen.

A grasshopper is fairly typical of many insects. The young of such insects look much like the adults. The young of other insects—

bees, flies, and butterflies, for example—look more like tiny worms. The grasshopper, like most insects, has both simple eyes and a pair of compound eyes. A grasshopper has biting and chewing mouth parts. Other insects have sucking mouth parts. An insect's antennae are sensitive to smell and to touch. Their ears are comparable to the human eardrum.

d. Insects have well-developed nervous systems. The brain, in the upper part of the head, attaches to a nerve cord that runs through the ventral part of the body to the tip of the abdomen. A number of ganglia, or smaller brains, are found along this cord, and nerves branch off from it to all parts of the body. Muscular, digestive, respiratory, excretory, and reproductive systems are all well developed. Body cells absorb oxygen directly from the air tubes of the respiratory system.

e. There are *social organizations* among the insects. Bees, ants, some kinds of wasps, and other insects are, as you remember, called *social insects:* they live together in communities and specialize in the work of the community. Even the body parts of such insects are specialized for the tasks they perform.

f. Aside from the insects with their wide adaptation to all environments, water as well as land, the arthropods as a phylum have a wide variety of forms and a wide distribution.

For instance, the spiders, ticks, scorpions, and mites (all arachnids) have eight legs, not six. Further, the head and thorax are not separate as in the insects. The arachnids are widely distributed over the world.

The crustaceans, such as crabs, shrimps, lobsters, and water fleas, are adapted to their environment by other structures. Except for the sow bugs, which live on land, the crustaceans live in water; they breathe by means of gills.

Wide distribution of a phylum, then, means a great variety of adaptations to a great variety of environments. The arthropods are found in almost all environments of the earth. This wide adaptation indicates that the organisms are biologically successful. Further, a vast population indicates success of the organism. Recall that about 85 percent of all the different animal species in the world are arthropods. This indicates successful reproduction and a high survival rate. The class Insecta is, then, the most successful class of organisms by this standard. The majority of organisms—by species—on this planet are insects. In fact, it has been said that if man were to stop his warfare on insects for only two weeks during their reproductive season, he might find it hard to survive on this earth.

A Long History

Recall, too, that by the Cambrian period in the Paleozoic era the seas swarmed with invertebrates. The largest and most common organisms of the Cambrian period were the arthropods. They were ancient forms, of course, and do not belong to the modern classes of arthropods.

The Cambrian arthropods that left the most fossils were the trilobites (trī′lō·bīts). Most of the trilobites were one or two inches long, but a few were more than 20 inches long. They had segmented bodies, a characteristic of the arthropods (also characteristic of the annelids), as well as large eyes. The trilobites were the dominant animal form throughout most of the Paleozoic era before they became extinct.

In the Silurian and Devonian seas we find other extinct forms, known as the eurypterids (yōō·rip′tər·idz). ❶ Similar to the arachnids, some were more than 6 to 8 feet long, the largest arthropods known. But it was in the late Devonian forests that familiar arthropods, the first insects, were to be found.

Dragonflies, very similar to modern dragonflies, were common during the Carboniferous period. One kind was probably the largest insect known, with a wing spread of almost a yard. Imagine such an insect that was larger than most birds. Cockroaches were also abundant, and although some were almost 4 inches long, they would be recognized as similar to modern cockroaches. The cockroach, then, has a long ancestry. Beetles, moths and butterflies, bees, and flies did not come till the late Paleozoic era.

Scorpions, spiders, and centipedes were present in the forests of the Coal Age. And roaming among them were the largest land animals of the coal forest, huge amphibians. The amphibians will be studied in the next

chapter. It should now be clear that the arthropods have a long history—back to the Cambrian. In the late Devonian and early Carboniferous they were the dominant invertebrates adapted to land, although a few land snails are found in the fossils of the Carboniferous.

Finally, among the invertebrates, the insects are the most recent class of organisms to develop along the evolutionary time scale.

This is not to say, however, that the arthropods, standing on top of the heap of invertebrates, were then ancestors of the vertebrates.

The story of the succession of animals in the earth's history is a fascinating story that we will turn to next in the study of the lower vertebrates. But before you go on, you will want to fix in mind the great variety that exists among the arthropods that you will find on pages 372–73.

REVIEW

1. Spiders belong to a different class of arthropods than the insects. What are two characteristics that distinguish these classes?

2. How do spiders make their webs? What is the purpose of a spider web? Do all spiders make webs?

3. How do crustaceans differ from insects and spiders?

4. What are the basic characteristics of the phylum Arthropoda?

5. Why is the Arthropoda considered a successful phylum?

NEW VIEW

1. Are spiders as a group useful or harmful to man? Explain your answer.

2. Explain how you believe it is possible for a sow bug, which breathes with gills, to live out of the water.

3. The first unit of this book dealt with living communities. You may recall that fairy shrimps, copepods, and other crustaceans are often second links in both fresh-water and marine food chains. What is the basic food supply (the energy supply) of the smaller crustaceans?

4. At this point in your study, spend a moment thinking about this question: How did the variety of organisms develop their vast variety of adaptations?

6. RELATING THE CONCEPTS

Consider all you have learned up to now in an attempt to view the populations of organisms on this earth. There seems, indeed, to be some semblance of order.

Perhaps these concepts embrace the significant aspects of what you have observed.

Reviewing the Concepts

▶ *There is great variety among the organisms populating the earth.* Algae, fungi, mosses, ferns, conifers, flowering plants, protozoans, sponges, coelenterates, annelids, echinoderms, nematodes, mollusks, and arthropods—to mention very general groupings —all show vast variation in body shape and in structure.

▶ *All organisms have basic needs of matter and energy.* Whether it is *Euglena*, *Rhizopus* (the bread mold), *Lumbricus* (the earthworm), *Homarus* (the lobster), or *Homo* (man), the needs of organisms have many likenesses.

By some means, organisms must get their energy from the environment. Green plants use the sun's energy; animals get their chemical energy from food nutrients.

Organisms also use matter from the environment for growth and repair of their bodies. Plants and animals need elements such as magnesium, iron, calcium, phosphorus, nitrogen, and, of course, require oxygen for respiration.

▶ *Organisms are interdependent with the environment and with each other.* Not only do animals and plants depend upon the environment for their source of energy and matter, but also they interchange energy and matter with each other. How long could animals live without plants as a source of food? How long could plants live without the carbon dioxide that animals produce and the minerals they return to the soil?

▶ *Organisms are specially adapted to the environment in which they live.* How is *Paramecium* adapted to its water environment? A moss to a moist environment? A cactus to a dry environment? An earthworm to a moist environment? A starfish to feeding on an oyster? An insect for flight?

▶ *Organisms can be grouped, that is, classified or categorized, because of their possession of structures in common.* Certain animals have external skeletons and jointed legs; we classify them in one phylum and name them arthropods. Others have ringed bodies (segmented bodies); we group them in one phylum and name them annelids.

Other organisms produce flowers and seeds. We classify them as flowering plants (angiosperms), and further group them with other seed bearers having complex vascular tissues into the subphylum Pteropsida.

▶ *Once organisms are classified in phyla, the phyla may then be placed in order of ascending complexity of organization.* When we examine the thallophytes (flat-bodied plants), bryophytes (mosses), Filicinae (ferns), angiosperms (flowering plants), we detect an ascending complexity. The seed plants are considered more complex in structure than the algae, fungi, mosses, or ferns. When we study certain fossil ferns and certain fossil seed plants (the seed ferns), the differences are not so clear.

Similarly, from the protozoans to the arthropods we can see an ascending order of complexity. The insect (on top in order of complexity) seems clearly more complex in structure than an earthworm, an earthworm more complex in structure than a coelenterate, a coelenterate more complex than a protozoan.

▶ *The most successful groups of organisms are adapted to a variety of environments.* The arthropods constitute 85 percent of the animal population. Why? Reexamine once again their great variety in body structure. Because of this variety, they are adapted to a wide variety of environments, and are widely distributed. Why, for example, do you find insects in environments such as the desert? Why do you not find earthworms there?

Testing Yourself

1. Is this statement true? Animals depend upon green plants that photosynthesize. But how do green plants depend upon animals, or do they?

2. How can a protozoan, a sponge, and a lobster live in the same environment?

3. How are such different organisms as *Euglena*, an earthworm, a starfish, and a tarantula able to supply their same basic needs of matter and energy?

4. Why is special adaptation to an environment sometimes dangerous to the organism? Give an example.

5. Arrange the following phyla in order of their *descending* complexity.

    Annelida   Arthropoda
    Nematoda   Echinodermata

Where would you place the Coelenterata in such a list? Justify your answer.

6. Select a so-called higher invertebrate and a so-called lower invertebrate and show how they fulfill their basic needs.

7. Compare and contrast an insect and an earthworm with regard to their structures for:

    a. locomotion   c. circulation
    b. respiration   d. reproduction

8. Why are fossils of insects, mollusks, and brachiopods more readily available than those of worms? of protozoa?

9. Why are the insects considered a successful class of organisms?

Extending the Concepts

Investigation 1. Library Research. You might be interested in doing some research on these questions.

1. Are there any insect parasites? If so, are they present in all orders of insects or are they limited to certain orders?

2. What is the economic loss as a result of the activity of insects in the United States? What order of insects is mainly involved? Are there any economic benefits from insects? How would you calculate these benefits?

Investigation 2. Dissect a crayfish or a lobster, or both. Previously, you have been given directions for dissecting type forms such as the earthworm or grasshopper. Now find these directions for yourself. One source would be a laboratory manual in biology. Where might you get one?

VARIETY AMONG THE ANIMALS

EARTHWORMS TO INSECTS

All the invertebrates did not remain in the sea; some soon found their way to the land. There they adapted—as you see in the phyla below—to all environments. Find a plot of land and there you will find an invertebrate. This is true of the waters as well.

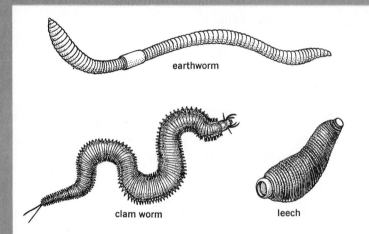

earthworm

clam worm

leech

SEGMENTED WORMS
(Phylum—Annelida)

This is the phylum of segmented worms, of which the familiar earthworm is a member. All have well-developed digestive, circulatory, and nervous systems. Each segment (except the first few and the last) contain kidneylike organs, but respiration takes place through the skin. Although many lack appendages, short bristles are often present on each segment except the first and last.

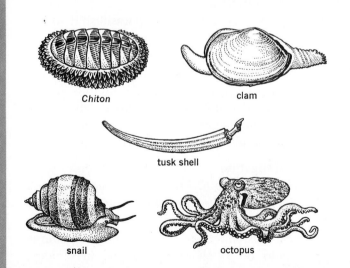

Chiton

clam

tusk shell

snail

octopus

MOLLUSKS
(Phylum—Mollusca)

Many of these soft-bodied animals secrete protective shells around themselves. They may have either a muscular foot or tentacles. All have a mantle, which usually (but not always, as in the squid and octopus) secretes a shell. All mollusks have a true circulatory system.

You may find it valuable to refer to the chart, Classifying the Animal Kingdom, on page 309.

ARTHROPODS
(Phylum—Arthropoda)

All arthropods have an exoskeleton and jointed legs. All have segmented bodies, usually with three body regions—head, thorax, and abdomen. With the exception of the spiders, all have antennae and compound eyes. The classes of arthropods differ in several ways, including number of legs and method of breathing.

INSECTS
(Class—Insecta)

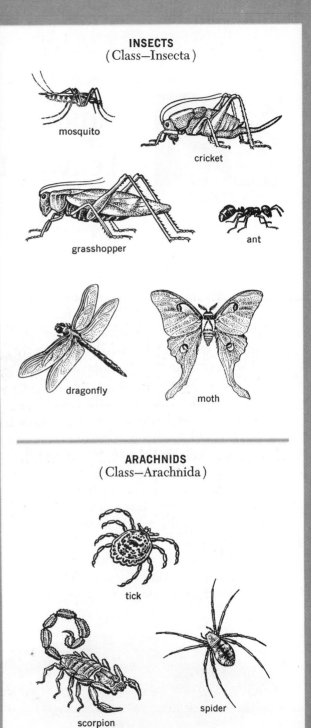

mosquito

cricket

grasshopper

ant

dragonfly

moth

CRUSTACEANS
(Class—Crustacea)

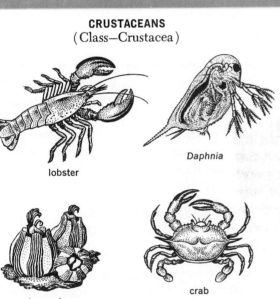

lobster

Daphnia

barnacles

crab

ARACHNIDS
(Class—Arachnida)

tick

scorpion

spider

CENTIPEDES
(Class—Chilopoda)

MILLIPEDES
(Class—Diplopoda)

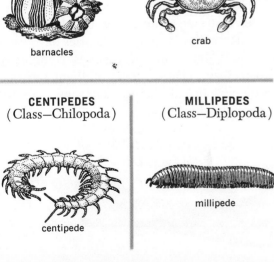

centipede

millipede

15 | Animals with Backbones— Leaving the Waters

The surviving giants of the animal kingdom are animals with backbones. Most are of weights and sizes that would be impossible for animals without internal skeletons to attain. Elephants, for example, may weigh more than six tons. They are the largest land animals living today. The giant dinosaur *Brontosaurus* (bron·tə·sôr′əs) (which means "thunder lizard"), living some 180 million years ago, was nearly 70 feet long and weighed about 30 tons. The great blue whale living today reaches a length of over 100 feet and a weight of over 150 tons. Backbones and skeletal frameworks make such great size possible.

Of course, not all vertebrates are giants. Man is a rather middle-sized vertebrate, although even he is a giant if you compare him with most invertebrates. The smallest of the vertebrates is a tiny fish, the *Goby*. It is only a half inch long. Even so, the *Goby* weighs millions of times more than the smallest invertebrate, the protozoa *Plasmodium vivax*, which causes malaria. Plasmodium is only $\frac{1}{8,000}$ of an inch long.

1. FROM EARLY CHORDATE TO THE FIRST VERTEBRATE

No one knows just how or when the vertebrates first came into being, or what animal was their ancestor. Several theories have been proposed, but none of them is completely satisfactory. That is, none of them satisfactorily explains all of the facts as a useful theory should.

The first vertebrates for which there is a very good fossil record were armor-plated primitive fish, or ostracoderms (os·trak′ŏ·dûrmz). ❶ These fish, some of which were only a few inches long, were relatively complex, and had a primitive backbone although they were jawless. Other primitive fish also found in the Silurian seas had a strange pattern of scales, while a few apparently had no scales. These primitive fish could not have been the first vertebrates to appear on the earth. They must have appeared millions of years after the first vertebrates; at least, that is what paleontologists believe. But of these first vertebrates, or the ancestors of the vertebrates, there are no good fossil records. The earliest fossil thought to be part of a vertebrate is from early Ordovician times, perhaps 500 million years ago. It is a single, small jaw containing sharp, pointed teeth. Other than this fossil, only some fragments of bone and tiny teeth have been found.

Chordates Without "Backbones"

Though there is no good fossil record of the first vertebrates, there are animals alive today that scientists believe may be something like the ancestors of the first vertebrates. If you were to see these animals, you almost certainly would classify them as invertebrates, not vertebrates. One of these early chordates, the acorn worm, or tongue worm, was actually first classified as an echinoderm, or starfishlike animal. ❷ Another, the sea squirt, or tunicate, looks more like a sponge than anything else.

Is there any relationship between the acorn worm, which we classify as a chordate, and the starfish, which, as you will recall, is classified as an echinoderm? Do they have characteristics in common? If you studied their development from the egg, you would find

that the larvae of both these animals do *not* look like the adults. On the other hand, as you may recall from page 332, the larvae of both these animals show a distinct similarity. Because of this similarity, they are thought to be related. However, the adult starfish and the adult acorn worm look nothing alike. You will find many times that the evidence from a study of embryos, or immature forms, reveals the relationship of organisms. Recall from your study of the invertebrates that some zoologists consider the echinoderms to be ancestors of the chordates because of the similarity of these larvae. Further study is necessary, however, in order to establish the theory that the echinoderms were the ancestors of the chordates.

From a study of the *adult* acorn worm, it becomes necessary to classify it as a chordate, not an invertebrate, for the following reasons. It has a small, thick, but flexible cord of cartilage extending for a short distance along the back side. All chordates have such a cord of cartilage, although in vertebrates it is found only in the early embryos. By now you must have guessed that the name of the phylum Chordata comes from the existence of this cord of cartilage. The word *chordata* itself comes from a word meaning "cord."

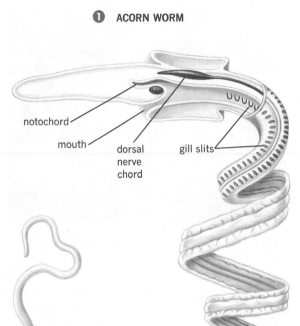

❶ ACORN WORM

notochord

mouth

dorsal nerve chord

gill slits

This cartilaginous cord of the acorn worm is known by the technical name, **notochord**. ❶

As well as a notochord, the acorn worm, like all chordates, has a nerve cord. Furthermore, the acorn worm also has gill slits. Does this remind you of a fish? All of these structures—the notochord, the nerve cord, and the gill slits—are important identifying characteristics of the animals that are classified as chordates.

At low tide along the Atlantic coast, it is possible to find small, baglike organisms attached to the rocks or wharf pilings. These are adult tunicates, whose only chordate characteristic is gill slits. The larva of the tunicate is a free-swimming organism, something like a tadpole. If you dissected the larva, you would find a notochord, a nerve cord, and gill slits. Clearly, then, the tunicate is a chordate.

Thus far you have learned that the phylum Chordata includes the acorn worm (subphylum Hemichordata), the tunicates (subphylum Urochordata), and the subphylum Vertebrata (fishes, amphibians, reptiles, birds, and mammals). Study the chart classifying the Animal Kingdom on page 309 to fix this in your mind.

What structural characteristics would you expect the embryos of the animals in these subphyla to have? Would you automatically expect the adult animals to have each of these structural characteristics?

Which Subphylum?

In the shallow waters of almost any warm or tropical sea, you would be likely to find a slender, fishlike animal about two inches long (sometimes longer) swimming about or sometimes buried in the sand with only its head sticking out. It would be a lancelet, or *Amphioxus* (am'fē·ok'səs). Study the drawing and photograph of this animal. ❷ ❸ How would you classify it?

These would be the questions to ask.

a. Does it have a dorsal nerve cord?

b. Does it have a notochord?

c. Does it have gill slits?

Amphioxus shows all three characteristics. Thus, you would classify it as a chordate.

Study the classification chart again (p. 309). How is *Amphioxus* classified further into its subphylum? Could it not also be a vertebrate? No, it has no bones. It has no spinal column of cartilage or bone enclosing a spinal cord, so it could not be in the subphylum Vertebrata. It cannot be classified in the subphyla Hemichordata or Urochordata. It must, therefore, be classified correctly in the subphylum Cephalochordata (sef'ə·lō·kôr·dāt'ə) which includes the fishlike animals with the same structures.

AMPHIOXUS (LANCELET)

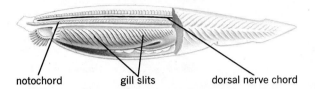

notochord   gill slits   dorsal nerve chord

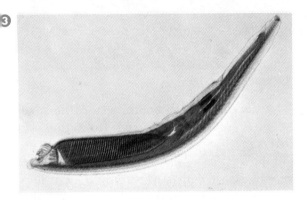

The remainder of the animals you will study in this and the next chapter are true vertebrates—animals with true backbones. Nevertheless, they all have the three characteristics of chordates *at some stage in their history*. But the notochord, in animals with backbones, exists only *before* the animals are born, that is, in the embryo stage. In vertebrates, by the time of birth, the notochord has changed into a backbone of cartilage or bone. The backbone is made up of many short *vertebrae* fastened together with connective tissue so that the back can bend. The vertebrate backbone gives great strength to an animal, and allows for greater size in animals. In most vertebrates the backbone also surrounds and protects the spinal cord, or dorsal nerve cord.

We will begin the study of the vertebrates with the cartilaginous fish, including such animals as this shark. Also in this class are the rays.

Cartilaginous Fish—True Vertebrates

Sharks and rays are found in largest numbers in the warm seas of the tropics. However, some kinds are found in the cold northern and polar seas. All are *carnivores* (flesh eaters). The entire skeleton of a shark or ray, unlike the skeleton of a trout or salmon, is made of cartilage. This characteristic accounts for their name, *cartilaginous* fish. They are in the class Chondrichthyes (kon·drik'thē·ēz').

Sharks are swift swimmers and they spend most of their time hunting fish that they then attack and eat. Rays live on or near the bottom of shallow waters where they feed mainly on many kinds of invertebrates. A few kinds of sharks and rays live in rivers, but only in the river mouths where they empty into the oceans.

A shark is marvelously adapted for the life it lives. It is shaped so that it slips through

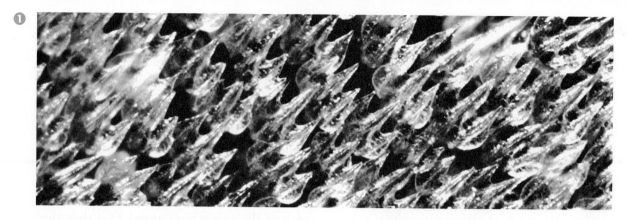

the water with very little friction. Its body bends and swings sideways; its streamlined body enables the shark to shoot forward rapidly in the water. The shark's sense of smell, its *olfactory sense,* is very good. Water currents carry particles of blood or other substances to its nostrils. The shark literally follows its nose to the source of the blood. This ability makes the shark a nuisance to ocean fishermen because sharks often steal bait off hooks, or even a fish itself after it is hooked and the fisherman is trying to bring it in. Sharks also use their jaws and fins to tear nets if they are caught in them. A few kinds of sharks will attack swimmers at a beach or in the ocean, but this is relatively rare. Generally, sharks stay away from human beings or simply observe them and then swim away.

Sharks do not have the same kind of scales as most fish. Their skins are covered with what feels like rough sandpaper. If you examined the skin through a magnifying glass, you would find it covered with a regular pattern of tiny, backward-pointing spines. Each spine is like a tiny tooth with both dentine and enamel just like those substances in your teeth.

The mouths of sharks contain row upon row of teeth. The teeth are actually formed from the skin in the mouth, just as the small spinelike scales are formed from the skin covering the body. Actually, the teeth are simply very large, sharp, spinelike scales. Embryologists, scientists who study the development of structures in the embryo, believe that these teeth are simply modified scales.

Both sharks and rays lay eggs. Sometimes the eggs are laid in the water, but most generally their eggs hatch inside their bodies. In the development of the embryo, the yolk in the egg supplies the food whether it develops inside or outside its mother's body. Of course, inside the mother's body, the egg is more protected. When the eggs hatch, the young are immediately able to swim around, find food, and take care of themselves.

Bony Fish

If you do not have an aquarium with fish in it, now is a good time to start one either at home or at school. The simplest fish to keep is a small goldfish. Unlike a tropical fish, it does not need a fairly constant temperature.

To closely study a bony fish, class Osteichthyes (os'tē·ik'thē·ēz'), you should have a living fish to observe as well as a dead fish to dissect. Examine the living fish and the fish you are dissecting, as it is called for. ■

■ AN APPRENTICE STUDY IN ANATOMY: A Bony Fish

External Anatomy

Compare your fish with the photographs to find all of the structures.❶❷❸ The gills are under a *gill cover*. Lift up the edge of the gill cover of your dead fish and cut it away, so that the gills underneath are exposed.

Fish breathe by taking water into their mouths. Once inside, a valve to the esophagus and stomach closes so that the water will not run into the stomach. As the fish swallows, the water passes over the gills and goes out of the fish's body through the gill slits under the gill cover. Notice that you can place your finger or a pencil in the fish's mouth and push it outside from under the gill cover.❷ Whenever a fish eats food, there is a chance that the food, like water, might pass out again under the gill covers. Or particles of food might become tangled in the gills. The *gill rakers* prevent this from happening.

Notice too, that the bony fish has jaws. The shark also has jaws; however, its mouth is located on the underside of its body. The fish were the first vertebrates with jaws.

Can you locate ears on a fish? A fish has internal ears lying inside the skull. However, they have no openings to the outside of the body, nor do they have eardrums. Because fish have no eardrums and no openings to the outside, they probably cannot hear sounds as well as you. But it has been shown that fish do respond to sound vibrations. Parts of the ears are probably also used as balancing organs (as are parts of your ears).

Can you locate the small openings that are the nostrils?❸ How many are there? Of what use to a fish might nostrils be? Your nostrils are connected by a passageway to your throat. If you were to experiment by temporarily taping shut the mouth of a fish so it would have to

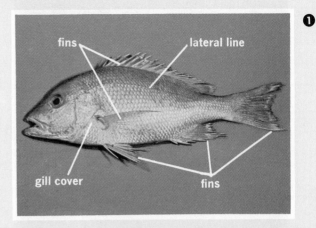

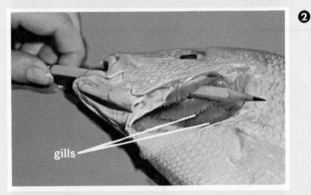

fins   lateral line

gill cover   fins

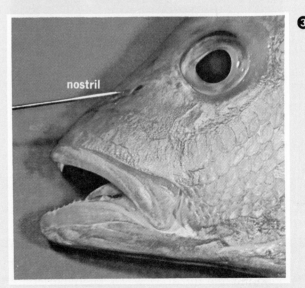

gills

nostril

sensitive to substances dissolved in water, so a fish has a good sense of smell. Numerous taste buds are located in and around the mouth of a fish.

Notice the thin colored line that passes from the head to the tail along the skin on each side of the fish. These are the *lateral lines*. They mark the position of hundreds of tiny holes, or pores, leading to a canal in the skin. In the canal are nerve endings that detect disturbances of the surrounding water or water movements. Thus the fish would be aware of nearby moving objects, or even perhaps obstructions in the water.

Notice that a fish has no eyelids. Its eyes are covered with a tough, transparent membrane. The eye has a lens that focuses light on a sensitive retina, just as your eyes do. Thus a fish sees objects clearly. Recall that the invertebrates, except for a few of the mollusks, could not see objects sharply.

Notice the locations of the fins. Although they are used mainly for swimming, they are also used in keeping a fish right side up. Most fish are top heavy; that is why when they die, they float upside down. If you can observe a fish in an aquarium over a period of time, you should be able to discover just how the fins are used. How many fins does the fish have? How many of these fins occur in pairs? Which fins are used in turning? Which does the fish use to back up? Carefully observe the tail fin as the fish swims forward. Does the fish move forward in a straight line or in a slight side to side motion?

Can you find the *anus* in your fish? You will notice that there are two tiny openings on the ventral surface of the body just in front of the anal fin. The anus is the opening nearest the head end. The other opening allows liquid wastes to be eliminated and allows eggs or sperms to pass out of the body. The eggs of

breathe through its nostrils, you would discover that the nostrils are not used for breathing. You can certainly see why not, since they do not open into the throat. However, the nostrils are

most fish are usually fertilized outside of the body. The male empties a mass of sperms, called *milt,* over the eggs in the act of *spawning.* Some kinds of male fish, however, fertilize the eggs within the female's body. When this occurs, the eggs are then hatched within the female and the young are born ready to swim about.

If you have a tank of tropical fish in the classroom, you may have some live bearers (as they are called). The guppy is one kind of fish that hatches its young inside the female, as are the swordfish and platy.

Before you dissect your fish to study the internal anatomy, let's investigate the function of the *swim bladder* of the fish. The swim bladder adjusts the fish's buoyancy to water pressures at different depths. By contracting certain muscles, a fish can adjust the swim bladder to a smaller size. The contraction compresses the air in the bladder and decreases the size of the fish while its weight stays the same. This causes the fish to sink. The fish will rise when its body muscles relax and the swim bladder expands again to its original size. This is similar to the way a gas-filled balloon rises in air.

It is simple to make a model that will show how the swim bladder works. ❶ The amount of water in the pill bottle must be carefully adjusted. The pill bottle should float upside down in the water of the large jar so that the bottom of the pill bottle is level with the water surface of the large jar. When you press down on the rubber sheet, the pill bottle will sink in the water. ❷ The air trapped between the rubber sheet and the water contracts and pushes against the water in the jar. This forces more water into the pill bottle and squeezes its trapped air into a smaller volume. When the pressure on the rubber sheet is relieved, the pill bottle rises. By means of its swim bladder,

❸

the fish is able to remain stationary in the water at any depth without moving any of its muscles. Explain why the air trapped in the pill bottle is like the air in the swim bladder.

Internal Anatomy

To study internal structures of a fish, it is necessary to dissect a fish, or your teacher may do it for you. It must be done carefully. Start your cut on the underside (the ventral side) just in front of the anus. Because the scales are tough and slippery, you should scrape them off the ventral surface before you make your cut. This is a good opportunity to examine some of the scales with a hand lens. How are they adapted for protecting the fish?

Cut carefully just through the body wall so that you do not destroy any of the organs. Cut all the way to the head. Now using heavy scissors, cut up the side just in back of the head and again just in front of the anus. ❸ This last cut should extend about half way to the top (to the lateral line is about right). Now lay back this flap of body wall and muscle so that the internal organs can be seen. Compare your fish with the drawings that follow. Locate as many of the structures shown in the drawings.

To find the swim bladder, located high up in the body cavity, you will need to remove most of the other organs.

Circulatory system. Locate the *heart* in your fish. The heart of a fish has only two chambers: one *auricle* and one *ventricle.* (Your heart, as you already know, has four chambers: two auricles and two ventricles.) Blood from all over the body, including the gills, is carried to the auricle of the fish's heart. The auricle is a sort of collecting chamber. The auricle contracts, or squeezes, and pushes the blood through a valve and into the ventricle. The ventricle is composed of powerful muscles. When it contracts, the valve leading from the auricle closes, keeping the blood from flowing back into the auricle.

As the strong muscles of the ventricle contract, the blood is forced into a large artery. (Recall that arteries are blood vessels carrying blood away from the heart.) The artery divides into smaller and smaller branches until the branches are of capillary size. Many capillaries are embedded in the gills, where carbon dioxide is given off into the water and oxygen is taken from the water. The blood is carried in blood vessels to all the organs and tissues of the body. Oxygen and dissolved food diffuse into the body cells, and carbon dioxide and nitrogenous wastes are picked up.

When the blood reaches the *kidneys,* the nitrogenous wastes are removed by the kidneys. From the kidneys, these wastes pass to the outside of the body through tubes and a *urinary bladder.*

The blood is carried back to the heart through *veins;* thus the circulation goes on.

Digestive system. Do fish have teeth? Look into the fish's mouth or run your finger inside it. The answer depends upon the kind of fish you have. Some fish, such as pickerel and barracuda, have long, sharp teeth. But in many fish, perch for example, the teeth are tiny, knobby things, incapable of tearing food apart or of chewing. About their only use is to hold slippery food. Other fish have mouths so smooth that it is difficult to find any teeth.

As in most vertebrates, the *stomach* of the fish is chiefly a storage organ. Some digestion takes place there, but the *intestine* is the main organ of digestion. From the intestine, most food is absorbed into the blood stream.

You will probably find some white or yellowish structures partially surrounding the organs. This is simply stored fat. All vertebrates change food that is not immediately needed by the body into fat for storage or into a kind of animal starch called glycogen. Glycogen is stored in the liver. The *liver,* as well as being a storage gland, is also a digestive gland. It secretes a substance called bile that flows into the intestine where it helps to digest fats.

Nervous system. As you recall, many invertebrates that have nervous systems have only a number of ganglia instead of a single large brain. In the more active mollusks, these ganglia are concentrated in the head region; while in the squid and octopus, the ganglia are massed together to form a distinct brain.

This concentration of ganglia into a single, distinct brain is typical of all vertebrates. The brain is surrounded and protected by the bones of the skull. The brain of a fish is rather small. It is difficult to reach it through the bony case of the head without destroying it. However, you may wish to try. If so, you will need the diagram of the brain (and nervous system) of a fish.

Notice the large *olfactory lobes,* the *optic lobes,* the *cerebrum,* the *cerebellum,* the *medulla.* You need not try to remember these names, but it is interesting to know their functions. Each part is chiefly responsible for specific functions, as they are in your brain.

The *olfactory lobes* receive messages from the nostrils. They are large because a fish depends upon its sense of smell to locate food. This sense is highly developed in fish.

CIRCULATORY SYSTEM

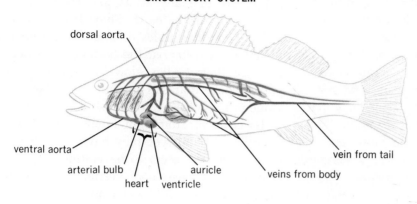

dorsal aorta

ventral aorta

arterial bulb

heart

ventricle

auricle

veins from body

vein from tail

ANATOMY OF THE FISH

DIGESTIVE AND EXCRETORY SYSTEMS

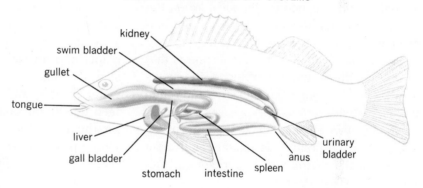

kidney

swim bladder

gullet

tongue

liver

gall bladder

stomach

intestine

spleen

anus

urinary bladder

NERVOUS SYSTEM

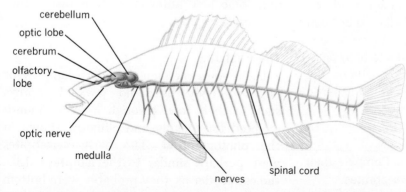

cerebellum

optic lobe

cerebrum

olfactory lobe

optic nerve

medulla

nerves

spinal cord

The *optic lobes* receive messages from the eyes, which are important, of course, in locating food and in avoiding danger. So these, too, must be highly developed.

The *cerebrum* is the region of the brain where messages are relayed from one area to another. Here decisions are made and messages are sent out to all parts of the body that are under the voluntary control of the fish. The cerebrum is the seat of consciousness and of voluntary activity. Here is where messages from the sense organs are sorted out and sent out to muscles. The cerebrum is not large in the fish, but in man, with his high level of consciousness, thought, imagination, and decision making, it is the largest part of the brain.

The *cerebellum* is chiefly concerned with coordination and balance of the body. When the cerebellum of an animal is damaged, the animal has difficulty in controlling its movements.

The *medulla* contains the nerve centers that control heartbeat, the flow of blood, the movement of food through the digestive tube, and the other basic, automatic processes that keep an animal alive. The medulla is the most primitive part of the brain. It is roughly equivalent to the ganglia distributed in various parts of the bodies of invertebrates.

The brain is connected, by *spinal nerves* and the *spinal cord* (dorsal nerve cord) to all parts of the body. The spinal cord extends down the back, inside the vertebrae which surround and protect it. Nerves leave the spinal cord through tiny gaps between the vertebrae. Some nerves, the motor nerves, carry messages to body parts from the brain and spinal cord. Others, the sensory nerves, carry messages from the sense organs to the spinal cord and brain.

An Investigation On Your Own

Locate several cranial nerves. Compare their function with those in other vertebrates.

The Lives of Fish

Fish are of many kinds, and they live in waters over all the earth. Some kinds live at a depth of three miles or more in the completely dark waters at the bottom of the sea. Parts of their bodies glow like fireflies. Do you suppose that this luminescence has any value to these fish? Certain fish live in underwater caves far from light. Some cave fish are completely blind, yet they have eyes. However, their eyes seem to be vestigial organs. Recall our discussion of vestigial organs on page 330. How would you acount for the eyes of cave fish?

As you know, some fish live in fresh water and some live only in the seas. Only a few are able to live in either fresh or salt water. Some fish are carnivorous, some are herbivorous, and some eat both flesh and plant tissues. Tiny fish and young fish eat single-celled plants and animals and bits of plant tissue, as well as small crustaceans, worms, mollusks, water insects, and insect larvae. Larger fish feed chiefly on smaller fish. In the water, as on the land, there are always food chains. Green plants make the food, various animals, including a few fish, eat the green plants, small fish eat the plant-eating animals, and larger fish eat the smaller fish.

Fish are eaten not only by other fish, but also by seals, sea birds, water snakes and turtles, some land animals, such as bears, and, of course, by man.

The First Jaw

Have you ever seen a modern lamprey or hagfish? They have no jaws. Lampreys suck in their food through a round mouth adapted for sucking and clinging, shown in the photograph. ❶ The early vertebrates were perhaps similar to the lampreys. Like the ostracoderms, they probably were bottom feeders, sucking in food through a mouth that was like a vacuum cleaner. Their mouths were located on the underside of a curiously shaped head. These early jawless vertebrates, class Cyclostomata (sī′klə·stō′mə·tə), could not bite or clamp their prey with jaws.

In the late Silurian and early Devonian periods, the jaw, a tremendously important structure, appeared among fishlike vertebrates. These were the placoderms (plak′ō·dûrmz). In appearance they were like the fish and were covered with scales. Some were small; others were giants. Almost 10 to 15 feet long, they had a fierce appearance, powerful jaws, and a bony shield that protected the head. These early placoderms are considered to be ancestors of the sharklike fish and the true bony fish. Strangely enough, the first fossils of the bony fish are found in the sedimentary rocks deposited in fresh waters.

By the Devonian period, the groups of fish that were to give rise to modern ones were already present. One line was to lead to the modern bony fish, which you may have eaten (bass, salmon, tuna, trout). Others led to the lungfish and the lobe-finned fish. For many years scientists thought that the lobe-finned fish were extinct. But since 1938, several strange looking coelacanths (sē′lə·kanths), living representatives of the lobe-finned fish, have been found off the coast of Africa.  You will consider the lungfish and the lobe-finned fish later as you study the amphibians, the animals that have bridged the two environments of the water and the land.

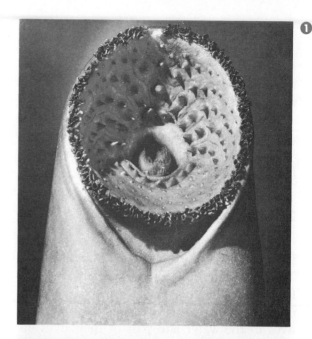

REVIEW

1. What are the three distinguishing characteristics of the phylum Chordata?
2. Why are fish classified as chordates as well as vertebrates?
3. Explain why you are classified as a chordate even though you have a backbone rather than a notochord in your back?
4. Shark and ray eggs can be hatched in two different ways. Explain any advantage that you think one way has over the other.
5. Can a fish hear?
6. What is the probable function of the lateral lines of a fish?
7. Explain how the swim bladder adjusts the buoyancy of a fish.
8. Describe the circulation of blood in a fish.
9. Describe the brain of a fish and explain the function or functions of each part.

NEW VIEW

1. A dog is a vertebrate animal, hence it is a chordate. How do you explain the fact that an adult dog does not have the gill slits that are characteristic of the phylum Chordata?

2. Why do you think vertebrate animals, as a group, are so much larger than invertebrates? What problems would an invertebrate encounter if it weighed as much as an elephant?

2. FROM WATER TO LAND

The word **amphibian** (am·fib′ē·ən) comes from two Greek words meaning "both lives." The vertebrates in the class Amphibia include frogs, toads, and salamanders. Because most of these animals usually spend part of their lives in the water and part of their lives on land, Amphibia is an appropriate name for this class. A frog, for example, breathes through gills and swims about like a small fish during its larval stage. Later, it develops lungs and legs, and lives as a land animal, but one that swims freely in ponds and streams during its adult life. Amphibians actually do live both the life of a water animal and the life of a land animal. In a sense, amphibians

represent a bridge between life in the water and life on the land, and, as you will see later, they are considered to be the descendants of the first vertebrates to take up life on land.

Problems of Moving to the Land

Some 400 million years ago the first animals left the seas and took up life on the land. These first land animals were arthropods—spiders and scorpions. The seas of the Cambrian and Devonian eras swarmed with arthropods—trilobites and arachnids, or scorpionlike animals, known as eurypterids. It was not long after, as geological time goes, until vertebrates followed them to the land. These vertebrates are thought, by some scientists, to be related to the ancient lungfish. After all, present-day lungfish are able to carry on respiration when they are stranded on the muddy bottoms of dried-up marshes and ponds.

Most scientists, however, believe that some ancient relatives of the lobe-finned fish, which also had lunglike structures, crawled from pool to pool plodding along on heavy fins some 350 million years ago. Notice the heavy fin of the lobe-finned fish shown in the photograph on page 385. It is obvious how it could support the animal on land.

Some Problems of Living on Land

The sea provides a rather constant temperature and, above all, constant moisture. As you know, water contains dissolved oxygen, so oxygen is available to diffuse through wet membranes such as those covering gills.

When animals left the water, they had to have a way of getting oxygen from the air. They also needed a means for keeping their respiratory membranes moist. The scorpions and spiders developed gill-like structures called **book lungs.** This term comes from the appearance of these breathing structures. Book lungs have "leaves" that increase the amount of surface of the membrane exposed to the air. This is exactly what the gills of fish do. The important difference between gills and the book lungs of scorpions and spiders is that the book lungs are deep *inside* the body and can be kept moist by body fluids, while gills are near the body surface and must be kept moist by a constant flow of water around them. The oxygen in the air, of course, dissolves in the moisture on the book lungs.

The first vertebrates to take to the land, the ancient lobe-finned fish, developed a still different adaptation. Recall the swim bladder that enables the fish to rise and sink in the water. In most fish the swim bladder is a membranous sac, completely closed to keep the air in. Being buried deep inside the fish's body, the membranous sac is, of course, moist. In lungfish and lobe-finned fish, however, the swim bladder has become changed so that there is an opening from it into the throat. A modern lungfish, when it is in water, breathes through gills, as does any fish. But when a lungfish climbs up on land, it swallows air into its swim bladder, and oxygen from the air dissolves on its moist membranes. Thus the swim bladder becomes a simple kind of lung.

This is probably what occurred when the ancient lungfish and lobe-finned fish climbed onto land. They probably began to breathe through their swim bladders, which you might call the forerunner of modern lungs.

Why do we discuss lungfish and lobe-finned fish in this section of amphibians? We do so because there is some (although not final) evidence that amphibians evolved from ancient lobe-finned fish. The amphibians were the first class of vertebrates, except for the lobe-finned fish, to live on the land. Rocks so old that they contain no fossils of reptiles, birds, or mammals do contain fossils of amphibians. The early amphibians had fishlike tails and were, in many ways, remarkably like the lobe-finned fish from which they almost certainly evolved. ❶ Many of these amphibians were among the large vertebrates of the Carboniferous forests.

One group of modern amphibians, the salamanders, looks somewhat like those ancient amphibians, but they do not have fishlike tails. You may have seen salamanders. They have a lizardlike shape, but they are totally different from lizards.

Look at the photographs below. ❷ A salamander larva is shown at the top and the adult beneath it. This is the common spotted salamander. Notice that the larva has external gills (the feathery structures at the top that

❷

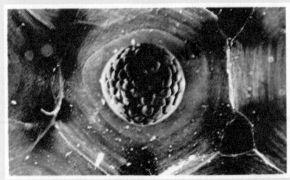

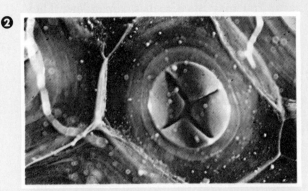

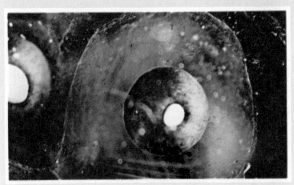

Courtesy Carolina Biological Supply Company

Use a hand lens to examine different eggs. Notice that the eggs have a dark upper surface and a creamy lower surface, where the egg yolk is concentrated. Follow the development of the egg and compare it with the different stages shown in the series of photographs. Notice that the early division of cells is unequal. The top layer divides much faster than do the cells that must divide through the lower yolk layer.

After fertilization, the egg divides into two cells.❶ And then into four cells.❷ Soon the original egg becomes a ball of cells. This is the **blastula** (blas′chŏŏ·lə) stage.❸ Then the ball seems to push in one side and this is the **gastrula** (gas′trŏŏ·lə) stage.❹ Slowly the young embryo develops into a small, wriggling tadpole.❺ How is the tadpole like a fish? Notice

its gills used for taking oxygen from an aquatic environment. Notice its tail, useful in locomotion in an aquatic environment.

Watch the tadpole develop. How long does it take? This depends upon temperature, and food, and, of course, the kind of frog. The common leopard frog becomes a tadpole within 10 to 12 days after the egg is fertilized. The tadpole develops legs and lungs, and eventually loses its gills and tail.❻ This is called undergoing **metamorphosis** (met′ə·môr′fō·sis). After metamorphosis, it is a land animal, but it still has the ability to return to water, swim beautifully, and remain under the water for long periods of time. Complete metamorphosis takes about 75 to 90 days in most frogs. Do you remember an invertebrate that undergoes complete metamorphosis?

388

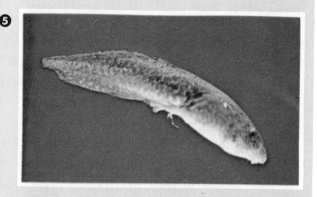

An Investigation On Your Own

How does the development of a frog depend upon the kind of food the tadpoles are fed? Feed tadpoles on plants, lettuce, for example. Feed others on pieces of cooked liver. Feed still others on both plant and animal food. Can you control the variables such as temperature, light, and amount of food? On the basis of your experimental procedure, are valid conclusions easy to reach?

Do you see how the development of an amphibian gives us clues about its relationship to water animals and to land animals? What are these clues? Reason along the lines of these questions. How is the amphibian, young or adult, adapted to an aquatic life? How is the young or adult amphibian adapted to a terrestrial life?

look somewhat like wings) but that the adult does not. The adult salamander breathes through internal lungs. Its lungs are simple saclike structures into which air is swallowed.

Some kinds of salamanders, for example, mud puppies, keep their gills when they become adults. However, these adults that retain their gills live in water throughout their lives.

Many amphibians have still another way of breathing. Their skins, which are always kept moist, contain many blood capillaries. They simply breathe through their skins, since the many capillaries are able to remove the oxygen dissolved on their moist skin.

The Early Stages of an Amphibian

In the early spring, frogs gather in ponds. As the female lays her eggs in the water, the male floods the eggs with the sperms. The sperms fertilize the eggs, and development of the eggs begin.

If it is at all possible, try to collect some frog eggs in early spring. If you can do this, place the eggs and the pond water in which you collected them in the refrigerator. Divide them up into at least four portions for examination by different members of your class. What are the stages of early development? That is, what is the *embryology* of the frog? ■

The Lives of Amphibians

Most amphibians live in or near water. However, there are some toads that are able to live in hot, desert areas. They stay in burrows during the day. At night, when it is cooler and the air is more moist, they come out and catch insects.

There are very small frogs that spend most of their time on plants, shrubs, or trees. Notice the disclike pads on the toes of the

"spring peeper," or tree frog. ❶ These pads enable the frog to stick to the branches and twigs as it climbs about looking for insects.

Have you ever watched a frog or a toad catch an insect? If so, you have noticed that its tongue is fastened to the front of its mouth. By flipping its tongue out when a fly or other insect comes near, a frog or toad is able to catch the insect on the tongue's sticky tip.

Frogs and toads eat insects, worms, small crustaceans, and small mollusks. Like other animals, amphibians not only eat but are eaten as well. Herons, large fish, and snakes use them for food. Most amphibians can defend themselves only by jumping or swimming away. But toads have bumps, or "warts," on their bodies which secrete a bad-tasting material, so most animals leave toads alone.

Amphibians take on the same temperature as their surroundings. Such animals are called "cold-blooded"—not a very logical term. If the air temperature is 100°F, the temperature of a cold-blooded animal sitting on the ground will also be about 100°F, which is not very cold. All vertebrate animals except birds and mammals are cold-blooded.

In cold climates, frogs and salamanders become dormant. During this period, they burrow into the mud at the bottom of lakes or rivers that do not freeze solidly to the bottom. Toads and land salamanders burrow deep into the ground to spend the cold winter. During this dormant period, the activity of the body cells of the amphibian slows down tremendously. The heart barely beats, and the blood barely flows. The lungs (or gills in water amphibians) usually stop working entirely. The animals seem to be dead. Just enough oxidation in the body cells takes place to keep them alive, and the animals live off the food stored in their livers and in other parts of their bodies as fat. Their skin absorbs the small amount of oxygen needed. When spring comes, their body activities return to normal, and they become active again.

Would it be true to say that an amphibian has two kinds of adaptations to the environment? Would it also be true to say that an amphibian lives in two ecosystems? Why?

Another View of the Amphibians

While studying the vertebrates, the opportunity arises for examining the science of classification more closely. Recall that the classification of organisms depends in great part upon their structural relationships. By now you have begun to understand the nature of a phylum. For example, all chordates have the following structures in common:

a. a notochord at some stage in their development
b. a dorsal nerve cord
c. gill slits at some stage in their development

The nature of the subphylum also rests upon organisms having certain characteristics in common. The subphylum in which animals such as *Amphioxus* (subphylum Cephalochordata) are placed is different from the subphylum of the fish or frog (subphylum Vertebrata). What characteristics determine that

Amphioxus, a fish, and a frog be placed in the same *phylum?* The answer to that is easy. A notochord, a dorsal nerve cord, and gill slits are present at some stage in each animal. What places *Amphioxus* and the fish in different *subphyla?* For one thing, there is a bony skeleton present in the fish, but not in *Amphioxus.* This shows us that the fish is a vertebrate (subphylum Vertebrata).

Both the fish and the frog have bony skeletons, so both are in the subphylum Vertebrata. However, they are placed in different classes under this subphylum. Why is this so? The fish has fins, gill slits in the adult stage, scales, and a heart with two chambers, among other characteristics. The frog has no scales, fins and gills only in the tadpole stage, and a three-chambered heart (as you will remember from your dissection of a frog). These are the structural characteristics that place the fish and the frog in different classes.

Now what determines the different *orders* within the same class of organism. You can probably guess—other differences in structural characteristics. For example, the class Amphibia, of which the frog is a member, has at least three orders as follows:

a. order Stegocephalia (steg·ō′sə·fā′lē·ə) (extinct amphibians)

b. order Urodela (yŏor′ō·del′ə) (salamanders)

c. order Anura (ə·nyŏor′ə) (frogs and toads)

If you live in an environment in which frogs, toads, and salamanders are easy to find, you can collect specimens and discover the differences that place them in different orders.

The final classification of genus and species is also determined by certain characteristics held in common. For example, frogs are all in the same *genus,* the genus *Rana* (rā′nə). The grass frog is *Rana pipiens,* the green frog is *Rana clamitans,* the bull frog is *Rana catesbeiana.* From your dissection of a frog, you have a fair knowledge of the anatomy of the frog. Perhaps you can use this knowledge to discover differences in species characteristics. Or perhaps there are only obvious external characteristics that determine the species. Maybe the different species of frogs differ in their development from eggs to adults. You can determine this if you can find several species of frogs to study.

Thus organisms are classified—both plants and animals—into many, many groups, all based on characteristics held in common. From the single-celled organisms to the most complex, all that have been discovered have been classified and assigned names from the kingdom down to a genus and species.

REVIEW

1. What problems do land animals face that water animals do not?

2. How did the adaptation of the swim bladder into simple lungs help the lobe-finned fish to take to the land?

3. What evidence supports the theory that amphibians evolved from lobe-finned fish? What evidence indicates that lungfish, lobe-finned fish, and amphibians existed on the earth before reptiles, birds, and mammals?

4. Explain what is meant by the term *cold-blooded animal.*

5. In what way do a fish and an amphibian have similar methods of securing oxygen?

6. Describe the embryology of the frog.

NEW VIEW

1. Explain what is meant by hibernation, and describe how amphibians hibernate.

2. Bears and other animals are also said to hibernate. Use library references to determine in what sense such animals hibernate.

3. RELATING THE CONCEPTS

The experimental evidence continues to mount in support of the major concepts that have threaded their way through this book.

There is great variation among organisms.

Organisms are adapted to their environments.

Organisms are interdependent with each other and with their environment.

Organisms are related through structure.

You should now be able to make your own statements in support of these concepts.

Reviewing the Concepts

▶ *The vertebrates have a long history.* The fish trace their history to the Ordovician, Silurian, and Devonian periods, over 425 million years ago. During these periods, the oceans were swarming with invertebrates; the cartilaginous fish, as well as the hagfish (jawless chordates) already existed.

▶ *The origin of the amphibians points to the fish, probably the lobe-finned fish.* The lobe-finned fish seem to have at least two adaptations that favor survival and success on land —a swim bladder adapted for terrestrial respiration, and fleshy pads on the fins which aid in moving about on land.

▶ *The early amphibian environment is thought to have been the coal-age forests.* Recall from your study in Unit Four that Coal-Age forests are thought to have been warm, moist forests dominated by ancient club mosses, horsetails, and seed ferns. Early amphibians (the Stegocephalia) probably shared the forest with smaller animals, but particularly insects, such as huge dragonflies and cockroaches. Many small insects of the period are fossilized in amber.

▶ *The anatomy of organisms discloses the relationships of structures.* All chordates have a dorsal nerve cord, a dorsal notochord, and gill slits at some time in their development.

The closer the anatomical relationships among organisms, the closer their taxonomic placement. Thus *Rana pipiens* (the grass frog) and *Rana catesbeiana* (the bull frog) are so close in their relationships, that an external study and a dissection of one is a guide to the external and internal anatomy of the other. Therefore, they are placed in the same *genus;* relatively minor characteristics (such as color, size, and spotting) place them in different species. So, too, with the taxonomic groupings of *order, class,* and *subphylum.*

As the organisms proceed upward in order, class, and subphylum, their structural characteristics contain greater variations. The order Anura, for example, includes frogs and toads, whose anatomy has greater similarity than the other animals in the class Amphibia to which both frogs and toads also belong. Whereas the class Amphibia includes only amphibians (salamanders, frogs, and the extinct, huge, lumbering Stegocephalia), the subphylum Vertebrata includes the fish as well as the frog.

▶ *The embryology of organisms indicates relationships.* A study of the early embryology of the amphibians indicates their relationships. All develop from eggs laden with yolk; all develop into tadpoles.

Testing Yourself

1. Imagine a huge chordate (much like *Amphioxus*) in the Devonian sea. What characteristics would the animal have that would classify it as a chordate?

2. Imagine finding the eggs of a Stegocephalian. Describe the early development of the eggs.

3. Why are the hagfish considered the most primitive living vertebrates?

4. How does a shark differ from a salmon? From a lamprey?

5. Classify both the frog and the salamander into the following groupings: phylum, subphylum, class, order.

The next six questions refer to the chart at the right. The questions are meant to guide you in a review of certain aspects of the paleontology of the invertebrates and lower invertebrates.

6. In which era would you place major development of the higher invertebrates?

7. In which period would you place the ancient cockroach?

8. In which period would you place the greatest development of the early fish?

9. In which period would you place the greatest development of the Stegocephalia?

10. How old, at least, are the earliest vertebrates? In which period would you place their origins?

11. How old are the earliest invertebrates? In which era would you place their origins? What evidence would you use?

Extending the Concepts

Investigation 1. Of what economic importance are the hagfish and lampreys? the bony fish? How would you estimate this in dollars?

Investigation 2. What species of amphibia are in an environment easily accessible to you?

Investigation 3. The grass frog and the spring peeper among other amphibians have an unusual response to changes in the environment. Their skin seems to alter its coloration.

Era	Period	Approximate Time	Animals
PALEOZOIC	Permian	230 million years ago	Expansion of primitive reptiles.
	Carboniferous	280 million years ago	First reptiles. Amphibians dominant on land. Expansion of insects.
	Devonian	345 million years ago	First amphibians. First insects. Age of Fish.
	Silurian	405 million years ago	Extensive spread of invertebrates.
	Ordovician	425 million years ago	Earliest known fish.
	Cambrian	500 million years ago	Appearance of many marine invertebrates.
PROTEROZOIC		600 million years ago	First known fossils. Primitive Invertebrates
ARCHEOZOIC		???	Evidence of life, but no recognizable fossils.

Determine whether the amphibians you can collect in your region also respond to a change in the color of the environment.

How do you explain the change? A reference in the area of animal physiology will be useful. One textbook is *Animal Physiology* by K. Schmidt-Nielsen.

Suggested Reading

Herald, *Living Fishes of the World*, New York, Doubleday, 1961.

Ommanney, and the Editors of LIFE, *The Fishes* (Life Nature Library), New York, Time, Inc., 1963.

Cochran, *Living Amphibians of the World*, New York, Doubleday, 1961.

VARIETY AMONG THE ANIMALS

EARLY CHORDATES, FISH, AND AMPHIBIANS

A paleontologist was once asked when the most exciting time in evolution was. His answer was, "When the first amphibian, or was it a fish, stepped on land."

Whereas the lower invertebrate phyla are vast in their complexity and seem unrelated, there seems to be a steady procession of evolution in the fish and amphibians.

NOTOCHORD ANIMALS
(Phylum—Chordata)

The great variety of animals following are all chordates—members of the phylum Chordata. All have notochords at some stage in their lifetimes—some in their adult lives, some only in their embryo stages. It is in the fish (subphylum, Vertebrata) that the first true backbone appears. The animals shown below give a view from the early chordates to the first vertebrates.

Hemichordates
(Subphlylum—Hemichordata)
These are wormlike animals with the notochord only in the head.

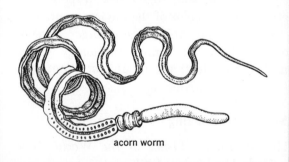
acorn worm

Tunicates
(Subphylum—Urochordata)
These animals are saclike and attached. The notochord appears only in the larva.

tunicate

lancelet

Cephalochordates
(Subphylum—Cephalochordata)
These somewhat fishlike animals contain a notochord running the entire length of the body.

You may find it valuable to refer to the chart, Classifying the Animal Kingdom, on page 309.

Vertebrates
(Subpyhlum—Vertebrata)
There is a notochord in the embryo but none in the adult.

JAWLESS FISH
  (Class—Cyclostomata)
The skeleton is of cartilage, and there are no jaws.

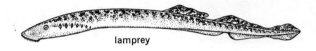

lamprey

CARTILAGINOUS FISH
  (Class—Chondrichthyes)
These fish have a skeleton of cartilage, visible gill slits, and a mouth on the underside.

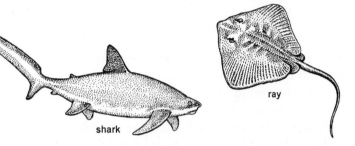

ray

shark

BONY FISH
  (Class—Osteichthyes)
The skeleton is of bone, and the gill slits have a covering.

bass

perch

AMPHIBIANS
  (Class—Amphibia)
These animals are adapted to life in water and on land. They usually breathe with gills as larvae and with lungs as adults.

salamander

toad

newt

frog

16 | Animals with Backbones — Conquest of the Land

Picture a scene such as this. ❶ The time is some 200 million years ago, the Mesozoic era, the Triassic period. Suppose we could re-create this scene with living organisms. The ponds would be full of fish—lobe-finned fish and lungfish, cartilaginous fish and bony fish. These may have fed on each other. Certainly

the fish had plenty of aquatic insects to serve as food.

At the edges of the ponds would be several large reptiles, looking somewhat like modern crocodiles. But the fossil evidence indicates they are only distantly related. Between the ponds you could find the descendants of the

GEOLOGIC TIME SCALE

Era	Period	Epoch	Approximate Time	Plants	Animals	Climates
CENOZOIC	Quaternary	Recent	2 million years ago	Herbaceous plants dominant. Decrease of trees.	Man dominant. Insects abundant. Many large mammals extinct.	Changes of seasons and climate zones as we know them today.
CENOZOIC	Quaternary	Pleistocene	2 million years ago	Herbaceous plants dominant. Decrease of trees.	Man dominant. Insects abundant. Many large mammals extinct.	Changes of seasons and climate zones as we know them today.
CENOZOIC	Tertiary	Pliocene	13 million years ago	Herbaceous plants numerous. Grasslands on increase.	Mammals abundant.	Cooler climates well-established away from equator.
CENOZOIC	Tertiary	Miocene	25 million years ago	Forests shrinking. Beginnings of grasslands.	Increase of mammals.	Climates cooling and becoming less humid.
CENOZOIC	Tertiary	Oligocene	36 million years ago	Tropical forests throughout world.	Appearance of modern mammals.	Warm and humid climates still prevalent.
CENOZOIC	Tertiary	Eocene	58 million years ago	Spread of angiosperms.	Archaic mammals.	Climate zones established.
CENOZOIC	Tertiary	Paleocene	63 million years ago	Rise of modern angiosperms.	Expansion of mammals.	Climate zones first appear.
MESOZOIC	Cretaceous		135 million years ago	Spread of flowering plants. Decrease of gymnosperms.	Decrease of reptiles. Climax of dinosaurs, later extinct. First modern bony fish.	Generally warm and humid climates, but some variation.
MESOZOIC	Jurassic		180 million years ago	First flowering plants. Gymnosperms and cycads dominant.	First birds and mammals. Giant dinosaurs abundant.	Worldwide warm and humid climates.
MESOZOIC	Triassic		230 million years ago	Increase of gymnosperms. First cycads.	First dinosaurs. Appearance of mammal-like reptiles.	Worldwide tropical and subtropical climates.
PALEOZOIC	Permian		280 million years ago	Decrease of ancient plants. Seed ferns disappear.	Expansion of primitive reptiles.	Variable climates. Glaciers in southern hemisphere.
PALEOZOIC	Carboniferous		345 million years ago	Primitive gymnosperms. Tropical fern forests. Club mosses, horsetails, and seed ferns.	First reptiles. Amphibians dominant on land. Expansion of insects.	Climate warm and humid throughout world.
PALEOZOIC	Devonian		405 million years ago	First extensive vascular land plants, mainly Psilopsida and Lycopsida.	First amphibians. First insects. Age of Fish.	Quite warm uniform climate, but some drying out.
PALEOZOIC	Silurian		425 million years ago	First known land plants, mainly Psilodpsida.	Extensive spread of invertebrates.	Slight cooling and extensive drying toward end of period.
PALEOZOIC	Ordovician		500 million years ago	No known land plants. Marine algae widespread.	Earliest known fish.	Uniformly warm climate.
PALEOZOIC	Cambrian		600 million years ago	Marine algae, fungi, and bacteria.	Appearance of many marine invertebrates.	Climate becoming warmer.
PROTEROZOIC			???	Earliest fossil algae.	First known fossils. Primitive Invertebrates	Cool climate with glaciers earlier.
ARCHEOZOIC				No known plant fossils.	Evidence of life, but no recognizable fossils.	? ? ?

ancient forests of club mosses and horsetails —much smaller than their ancestors of the Coal Age forests. The environment had begun to dry out. The cycads, ancient conifers, and ginkgoes were becoming the dominant forms in the nearby forests.

Among the horsetails you might find some fast-moving, lizardlike reptiles with small, sharp teeth indicating adaptation to an insect diet. Slender dinosaurs (reptiles), not very large—about 3 to 6 feet long—might also be found scurrying around, fleeing from a predator or pursuing their prey.

Later in the Triassic, the forests were to be full of insects. But the huge lumbering amphibians had begun to disappear. Would you care to offer an explanation? In the Jurassic and Cretaceous, the dinosaurs (dī′nō·sôrz) became abundant, among them the huge animals we usually associate with the term *dinosaur*. Now study the geologic time scale on the preceding page and refer to it as you read on. In time, as you make constant reference to the time scale, it will become more and more a part of your knowledge.

But the Mesozoic era was not only the Age of Reptiles. The forms of life we see about us today had also begun to develop—turtles in the Triassic, lizards in the Jurassic, and snakes in the Cretaceous. Also in the Jurassic we begin to find the first fossils of the true mammals—small and seemingly insignificant in that era, but nevertheless mammals. But let's go back to the reptiles of the Mesozoic.

The fossils of some of the first reptiles are so much like the fossils of amphibians that it is difficult to be sure which they are. Just as scientists have some evidence from the fossil record that amphibians evolved from fish, so they believe that reptiles evolved from amphibians. In both cases the fossil record supports the hypothesis.

For 100 million years after the first reptiles appeared, their number and variety increased. Finally, about 165 million years ago, there were so many reptiles of all sizes and sorts that some scientists have termed the Mesozoic era of geological history the Age of Reptiles. Remember also that in the Mesozoic modern forms of life had their beginnings. Perhaps the Mesozoic era should be called "The Age of the Great Beginning" because the mammals were to become the dominant vertebrates on land.

1. REPTILIA—THE REPTILES

Some of the ancient reptiles, such as *Brontosaurus*, were herbivorous. Others, like the *Tyranosaurus* (ti·ran′ō·sôr′əs) *rex*, were carnivorous.❶ *Tyranosaurus* (meaning "tyrant lizard") was nearly fifty feet long and almost twenty feet high. It must have been a terrifying reptile, particularly to the other animals

it attacked. No wonder they were named dinosaurs (meaning "terrible lizards").

But not all dinosaurs were large and terrible. Some were as small as puppies. Also, the dinosaurs lived in many different kinds of environments. Some of the plesiosaurs (plē′ sē·ō·sôrz′), for example, returned to the sea and developed flippers with which to swim.❷

One group of reptiles, closely related to the dinosaurs, even took to the air. These pterosaurs (ter′ō·sôrz) ("wing lizards") had thin membranes stretched between their bodies and their arms, which included a very long finger bone. They flew much as bats do today. Although some of these flying reptiles were as small as bats, some were over twenty-four feet from wing tip to wing tip—the largest animals that ever flew.

Later in the Mesozoic

Naturally, an animal like *Tyranosaurus rex* would capture anyone's attention. Because

of the fantastic variation of the dinosaurs, we often think only of them when we think of the Age of Reptiles. Yet the Mesozoic was much more than an age of reptiles. In the Mesozoic, many groups of animals we know today began their development. Recall that the first lizards, turtles, and snakes (class Reptilia) are found in the Mesozoic. And in the Jurassic, animals that must be called true mammals (class Mammalia) first appeared.

By the end of the Triassic, animals that might have been considered mammal-like reptiles had disappeared. Up to that period, reptiles had developed which had the following characteristics:

a. Specialized teeth were present. The teeth resembled those in the jaws of mammals. One could recognize incisors, canines, and molars.

b. The legs were positioned beneath the body, similar to those of a dog. Those of a lizard are usually joined at the sides of the body.

c. There were fewer bones in the skull of the mammal-like reptile than in the more ancient reptile. In the mammalian skull, there are fewer bones.

Paleontologists do not think of these animals as true mammals, but as mammal-like reptiles.

The Jurassic holds still another surprise. In this period, there appeared the first animals that might be considered to be birds. They had feathers. Apparently one group of reptiles had developed into birds.

See if you can imagine a primitive bird. It would have teeth, as reptiles do. It would have a long, bony tail with joints, as reptiles do. But it would also have feathers. Such a fossil bird is the famous *Archaeopteryx* (är′ kē·op′ter·iks).❶ *Archaeopteryx* had feathers on its wings, and imprints of these feathers were left in ancient mud that later became sedimentary rock. *Archaeopteryx* was clearly about halfway between a reptile and a bird. Scientists are fairly certain that this creature shows that birds had reptiles as ancestors—as did the mammals.

Modern Reptiles

Perhaps you have noticed that crocodiles, alligators, and lizards look more like ancient dinosaurs than do other modern reptiles. They are also the largest reptiles living today. Alligators sometimes reach sixteen feet in length, and the Indian muggar (a narrow-snouted crocodile) may reach thirty feet in length. These animals are covered (as are all reptiles) with thick, dry scales that offer protection and keep their bodies from drying out. Underneath the scales, crocodiles and alligators also have a thick, tough, leathery skin. They also have bony plates on their backs, something like those of the great dinosaurs. Like most reptiles, alligators lay eggs with shells.

The shells are leathery, not brittle like those of a bird. After the young hatch, they are fully formed, and they rush for the water as fast as they can.

Lizards vary greatly in appearance. Some, such as the horned toad (which is a lizard, not a toad), look something like the small dinosaurs might have looked.  ❷ Other lizards have scales so small that the animals seem smooth and glossy. One, the chameleon, changes its color according to its background; on green plants it is green, on brown logs it is brown. ❸ The chameleon catches insects much as a frog does. Its tongue flicks out to several inches in length when it catches them. Some lizards, such as the glass snake, have no legs but move along like a snake or burrow through the soil like a worm. ❹

Turtles are encased in armorlike shells made of bone and covered with a substance similar to that of your fingernails. The backbone and ribs are fused to the bony back part of the shell. In most turtles, the head, tail, and legs can be drawn into the shell for safety when the animal is attacked.

Although a turtle does not have teeth, its jaws form a kind of strong beak. A large snapping turtle can even be dangerous, since it is possible for its beak to cut through a person's finger, even breaking the bone.

Many turtles are carnivorous. They live in rivers, ponds, and lakes where crustaceans and fish are available. Some turtles are herbivorous, but most are **omnivorous** (om·niv′ ôr·əs), eating both animals and plants.

Some sea turtles, such as the loggerhead, grow to four feet in length and weigh over 500 pounds. On the other hand, you can buy tiny turtles that fit on a half dollar. In nature, turtles (and all other reptiles) hibernate just as amphibians do, usually for five or six months.

Snakes are highly specialized reptiles. They perform a good service for man by eating insects, field mice, and other pests.

With very few exceptions, snakes and other reptiles in the United States are not poisonous. The only poisonous lizard in the United States is the Gila monster.  Fortunately, the Gila monster is not widespread. It is found only in the southwestern parts of the United States.

Among the few poisonous snakes in the United States are the *coral snakes* such as this one.  Coral snakes live chiefly in the southern and southeastern parts of the United States. They are small, beautiful, and deadly. Their bodies are covered with rings of red, black, and yellow. Each black ring has a yellow border on both edges. Although small, these snakes produce a venom, or poison, more dangerous than that of any other North American poisonous snake.

The rattlesnakes, the copperheads, and the water moccasins are the only other poisonous snakes in the United States. All are members of the pit viper group—so called because of a depression, or pit, between each eye and the nostrils. These pits are sensitive to heat. Pit vipers have wide, triangular-shaped heads, and their eyes have vertical pupils.

Rattlesnakes are the most widespread of the pit vipers. About twelve different kinds live in the southwest United States. The timber rattlesnake is found throughout most of the eastern half of the United States.

Copperheads and water moccasins (also called cottonmouths because the mouth is white inside) are closely related. They are more dangerous than rattlesnakes because they have no rattles for warning before they strike.

The heads of all pit vipers are very much alike, triangular and distinct. All have two

long, curved, hollow teeth, or fangs. These are not found in nonpoisonous snakes nor in the coral snakes. The fangs are attached to a bone that is hinged to the upper jaw. When a pit viper's mouth is closed, the fangs are folded neatly against the roof of the mouth. When the snake opens its mouth to strike, muscles erect the fangs. Tubes or ducts connect the fangs to large poison glands on each side of the head.

Pit vipers use their fangs and venom to paralyze animals they use as food. They will also, of course, use these weapons for defense if something alarms them. Pit vipers strike from a coiled or partly coiled position. They can strike a distance of one third or more of their own length.

REVIEW

1. What is the evidence that reptiles evolved from amphibians?

2. What is meant by the term "Age of Reptiles"?

3. What two classes of animals first appeared during the period that the giant dinosaurs became abundant?

4. Explain how the head of a pit viper is designed to permit the erection of the fangs and the injection of poison.

NEW VIEW

1. The Age of Reptiles is clearly an age in which reptiles were dominant. Why did they not remain dominant? There are different points of view on their sudden extinction. The library will help. You might also consult high school and college textbooks, as well.

2. Some persons are afraid of snakes and other reptiles. To what extent do you believe this fear to be justified? What could you say to a person to help them understand the value of reptiles in nature?

2. AVES—THE BIRDS

Perhaps you have a canary or a parakeet. Look carefully at its legs. What do you see? Scales. Perhaps you have noticed the legs and feet of chickens. They are covered with scales very much like those of a snake. Even modern birds are not completely removed from their reptile ancestors.

However, birds, which are in class Aves (ā′vēz), are different from reptiles, of course. Perhaps you can figure out what the most important difference is. Below is a list of some differences between reptiles and birds. Think about these differences and what they mean.

DIFFERENCES BETWEEN REPTILES AND BIRDS

Reptiles	Birds
scales, no feathers	feathers, scales on legs and feet
four legs or no legs	two legs and two wings
teeth	no teeth, but a beak
cold-blooded (body temperature changes with air temperature)	warm-blooded (body temperature always about the same)
bones heavy, solid	bones light, hollow, and filled with air

The Importance of Being Warm-Blooded

Perhaps you said that the feathers of birds, or their wings, were the most important difference. If so, you were doubtless thinking that flight was the most important thing. Flight is certainly a great difference between modern birds and modern reptiles.

Consider for a moment the importance of being warm-blooded. Only birds and mammals are warm-blooded. A warm-blooded animal has a constant body temperature that varies only slightly regardless of how hot or how cold the environment becomes. This enables such animals to stay warm, and their body tissues to keep working efficiently even when it is very cold.

Think for a while about the kinds of animals you see on a cold, winter day (if, of course, you live where it gets cold in winter). Perhaps it is cold outside now. If so, spend some time looking out of the window. Or, better yet, take a count between now and tomorrow at the same hour of all the different kinds of animals that you can find.

Now, can you remember anything about the different animals you saw last summer? Last fall? In the warm months of the year you can find all sorts of insects and other invertebrates. And, if you go to the right places, you can find amphibians, fish, and reptiles.

During the winter, you can probably find only birds and mammals (such as dogs, cats, human beings, mice, horses, cows, rabbits). You might find a few insects inside your house or inside the school building where it is warm. You might find some spiders there, too. But outside, all the animals seem to have disappeared except birds and mammals. Underneath the ice of rivers and ponds, you would find fish still swimming around, but that is because the water temperature there is above freezing.

Cold-blooded animals would freeze to death in winter if they did not hibernate or have some other way to spend the winter. Warm-blooded animals can be just as active in freezing weather as in warm weather. Birds have a thick coat of warm feathers. This holds a blanket of still air next to the bird's body and keeps the heat of the body from escaping.

The advantage of being warm-blooded is more than just being able to avoid freezing.

Have you ever seen anyone trying to start an automobile in cold weather? The engine usually is slow starting. Finally, when it does start, it "misses" and sputters and may even stop again until it is "warmed up."

Living things are much the same. They work better when they are warm. Suppose you have a glass of cold water and a glass of hot water and put a lump or a teaspoon of sugar in each one. In which glass does the sugar dissolve more rapidly? It is generally true that warm water dissolves things more rapidly than cold water.

Your body, and those of all living things, is largely water, as you know, in which many substances are dissolved, such as sugar, minerals, salts, and many other things. Chemical reactions occur much faster when solutions are warm than when they are cold. Therefore, foods digest faster and are absorbed faster. Oxidation occurs faster. In fact, all living processes happen faster when an animal's body is warm.

Have you ever watched flies on a very cool day in the fall? Flies sit and are easier to catch or to swat at such times. When the sunshine warms them enough, they become more active. But in the cool evening they become quieter again. Or they may zoom around crazily, bumping into things. What is occurring is that their body chemistry is working too slowly for them to be very active.

The Importance of Feathers

Have you ever seen a parakeet or a canary asleep on its perch. It fluffs up its feathers until it looks like a fluffy ball. Feathers are marvelous insulation. There are tiny *down feathers* that form a kind of undercoat beneath the larger feathers. These down feathers trap air so that air currents cannot carry away the heat of the bird's body. You may have seen sparrows or other birds on a cold winter morning. They, too, look like fluffed up balls. They thicken the layer of insulation this way in order to keep warm. It is much the same as your putting on several sweaters, or putting on a sweater under your heavy coat, to keep warm on a cold winter day.

Examine a feather with a magnifying glass. Birds usually shed their feathers a few at a time and grow new ones. Use the drawing to help you discover how a flying feather is made. ❶ Notice particularly how the barbs are fastened together with little hooks. This keeps the flying feathers stiff when they are used in flight. Down feathers are made differently, as you can see.

Did you ever see a bird preening its feathers? By using its beak, it works over its flying feathers. This locks together the branches of the feathers again when they become unhooked, as they sometimes do.

Adaptations for Flight

Feathers are but one of a bird's adaptations for flight. The body is streamlined so that there is little air resistance. The bones are light and most are hollow and filled with air. The wings are moved by large muscles attached to the breastbone. These flying muscles are the "white meat" or breast of a chicken or turkey. The next time you have chicken to eat, notice how these muscles are fastened to the breastbone. Notice how the breastbone sticks out like a keel of a boat.

Have you ever watched a bird alight on the ground or in a tree? It is interesting. The tail feathers act like a rudder to help guide the bird, and they also act as a brake. Both the tail and the wings are stretched out so that they catch the air and bring the bird to a stop just before it hits its landing spot. The long, stiff wing feathers are tilted by muscles

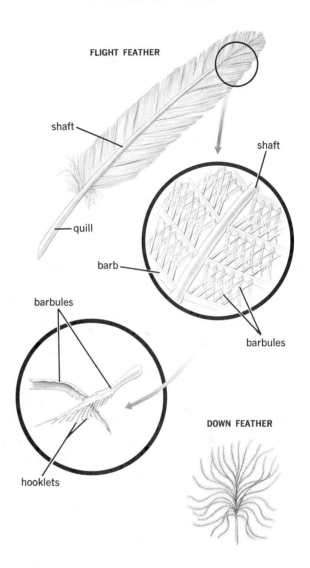

❶ STRUCTURE OF A FEATHER

FLIGHT FEATHER

shaft

quill

shaft

barb

barbules

barbules

hooklets

DOWN FEATHER

so that they guide the bird exactly. It took man a long, long time to learn how to build airplanes that would fly. But, even now, airplanes are clumsy compared with birds.

Feathers, wings and keel muscles, and warm-bloodedness are not the only adaptations of birds. One good way to look further into the matter is to dissect a bird. ■

Most chickens that are sold to be eaten these days are already cleaned. But if your mother ever buys a bird with its internal organs still present, ask her to let you study them before she cleans the bird. The drawings will help you identify the parts of a bird's body.

Digestive system. A bird has no teeth for grinding up food. The food is pecked or torn off by the beak and swallowed. It goes down the *esophagus* to the *crop,* where it is stored and moistened. Sometimes a chicken stores so much food in its crop that the crop bulges far out. It looks and feels as if the chicken has a round bean bag at the base of its neck.

From the crop, food passes, a little at a time, into the *gizzard.* Here, digestion occurs as the thick muscular walls of the gizzard contract, grinding up the food. The grinding of the food is helped along by bits of gravel that the bird eats from time to time. It is necessary to feed pet canaries or parakeets gravel so that they can grind up their food. The gravel acts like teeth. From the gizzard, the food goes into the *intestine* where further digestion occurs and where it is absorbed into the blood stream. The *liver* and the *pancreas* secrete digestive juices that pass into the intestines. Any undigested food leaves the body through the *cloaca.*

Respiratory system. In a bird, this system is unusual in that the *lungs* are connected to *air sacs.* These air sacs are found in almost every part of the body. There are air sacs even in the long bones. Although little absorption of oxygen occurs within the air sacs themselves, they can hold large amounts of air. The air sacs also help regulate body temperature.

Because a bird is typically very active, the body cells oxidize food at an extremely rapid rate. This process requires a large amount of oxygen. Air is pumped into and out of the lungs and air sacs by slight motions of the ribs to which the upper surface of the lungs are attached. Thus when the bird is flying, a rapid expansion and contraction of the lungs occurs. Birds, unlike mammals, have no diaphragms.

The rapid oxidation of food produces a considerable amount of heat in the bird's body. When you become too warm your sweat glands pour out sweat which evaporates, thus cooling your body. A bird, however, does not have sweat glands. Its body is cooled mainly by means of the air in the air sacs. As the bird exhales, the warm air in the air sacs is removed and is replaced with cooler inhaled air.

Notice the position of the *syrinx* (sir'ingks), or song box. You can just see its outline under one of the air sacs. When you speak or sing, the sound is made by vibrating cords in your voice box, or larynx. The song box of a bird also contains cords that vibrate as the air is forced over them. But the syrinx is located at the base of the *trachea,* or windpipe, rather than at the top as your larynx is.

Circulatory system. This system is much like yours; the *heart* is almost identical. The heart has four chambers. It is really two pumps in one. Blood from the lungs flows into the *left auricle,* a thin-walled collecting chamber. This contracts and forces the blood into the *left ventricle,* a powerful, thick-walled, muscular pump. The left ventricle contracts and forces blood through the arteries to the cells of the entire body. Through the thin-walled capillaries, oxygen is given to the cells and carbon dioxide is taken up from them. The blood now returns through the veins to the *right auricle* and from there to the *right ventricle,* a muscular pump somewhat smaller than the left ventricle. The right ventricle contracts and forces the blood out to the lungs

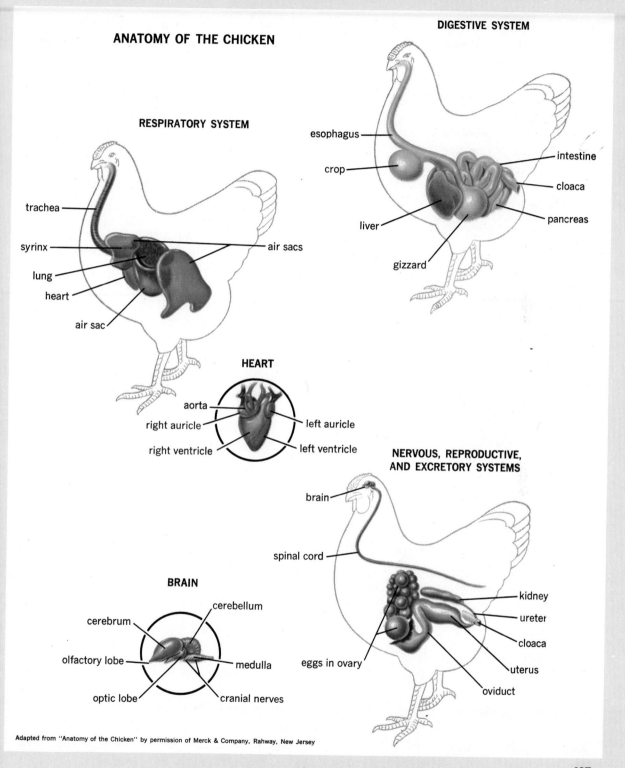

ANATOMY OF THE CHICKEN

DIGESTIVE SYSTEM

RESPIRATORY SYSTEM

esophagus
crop
intestine
cloaca
liver
pancreas
gizzard

trachea
syrinx
lung
heart
air sac
air sacs

HEART

aorta
right auricle
left auricle
right ventricle
left ventricle

NERVOUS, REPRODUCTIVE,
AND EXCRETORY SYSTEMS

brain

spinal cord

BRAIN

cerebrum
cerebellum
olfactory lobe
medulla
optic lobe
cranial nerves

kidney
ureter
cloaca
uterus
eggs in ovary
oviduct

Adapted from "Anatomy of the Chicken" by permission of Merck & Company, Rahway, New Jersey

where carbon dioxide is given off and oxygen is taken up. The blood then returns to the left auricle of the heart, ready to be pumped throughout the body again.

As you can see, the heart of a bird forces the blood through two distinct paths. The four-chambered heart prevents blood from which oxygen has been removed from mixing with oxygen-rich blood just returned from the lungs.

Birds have an extremely fast rate of heart beat. The heart of a bird at rest may beat several hundred times a minute. In flight this may rise to a thousand beats a minute. Take your own pulse at rest and after exercise. Compare the rate of your heart beat with that of birds.

Nervous system. The brain of a bird is proportionately larger than the brains of fish, amphibians, and reptiles. However, the *olfactory lobes* (the portions dealing with interpretation of odors) are proportionately smaller. Therefore, as you might guess, a bird has a poor sense of smell. The *optic lobes* (the centers of sight) are large and, as you might expect, birds have keen eyesight.

The *cerebellum* is quite large, too. Recall that the cerebellum is the portion of the brain where coordination is centered. It is easy to understand why the cerebellum of a bird is so large when you think of the swift and complicated patterns of flight of a bird. Perhaps most interesting of all is the size of the *cerebrum.* It is much larger, proportionately, than that of any animal except the mammals. Would you think it likely that a bird is more intelligent than a fish or a frog or a snake? Remember the cerebrum is the center of thought and memory.

Reproductive system. The male bird produces sperms in testes that lie in the back of the bird. Tubes connect the testes to the *cloaca,* the opening to the outside. Sperms flow down these tubes and out the cloaca.

The drawing shows the reproductive organs of a hen. The *kidneys* and their tubes, or *ureters,* that carry urine to the cloaca are also shown in the drawing.

The way birds' eggs are formed and laid is quite interesting. Most female birds have but one *ovary* in adult life. Tiny eggs develop within the ovary and then push out from its surface into the body. Each small egg has a large mass of stored food attached to it. This food is the yellow-colored yolk of the egg. As the eggs leave the ovary, they are picked up by a funnel-shaped opening of the *oviduct.* After it reaches the oviduct, the egg can then be fertilized by a sperm. Contractions of the oviduct and the sweeping motion of a lining of cilia (recall how these worked in the protozoa) move the egg down the oviduct. Albumen (egg white) is secreted around the egg by glands in the middle portion of the oviduct. The shell is secreted by other glands in the lower part of the oviduct. Now the completed egg is passed out of the body through the cloaca. The egg is "laid."

An Investigation On Your Own

How is the bird adapted to its environment? Analyze your observations.

Special Adaptations of Birds

If there is a concept that your study of living organisms has shown again and again, it is this: Organisms are adapted to their environments. A survey of birds will reveal strong support for this concept.

If you possibly can, undertake a study of the adaptations of birds. Examine the drawings of certain adaptations of the beaks and feet of birds shown here. ❶ With these adaptations well in mind, make a survey with a pair of binoculars of the birds in your area.

A STUDY IN ADAPTATIONS OF BIRDS

◄ EVENING GROSBEAK
A thick, short beak is adapted for cracking seeds. What birds do you know with this adaptation?

PINTAIL GADWELL DUCK ►
You can see how a duck's feet are adapted for swimming. What other animals have this adaptation?

◄ TRI–COLORED HERON
This long beak is used like a pair of tweezers in snatching fish out of water.

BLUE HERON ►
How is this bird adapted for wading? Of what use is wading to a heron?

◄ RED–HEADED WOODPECKER
The woodpecker uses its beak like a pickaxe in digging out wood-boring insects.

BARN OWL ►
The strong curved claws of the owl are adapted for grasping. Could a duck grasp its prey?

◄ BROWN THRASHER
A probe beak is useful in seeking out insects in the ground.

YELLOW–BREASTED CHAT ►
Perching feet have three toes pointing forward and one pointing backward. Could a wading bird perch easily on a limb?

◄ SPOONBILL
The spoonbill is useful in gathering water insects and crustaceans.

ARIZONA WOODPECKER ►
Feet with two toes pointing forward and two pointing backward are adapted for climbing. Could a woodpecker survive if it had to live like a heron?

◄ RED–TAILED HAWK
A sharp, hooked beak is adapted for tearing flesh of larger animals.

What adaptations do you find in beaks and in feet? Which birds are the winter residents in your area? Which are the first to visit your area in the spring? Is there any relationship between feet or beak adaptations and the time birds first visit your area?

REVIEW

1. What are the advantages of a warm-blooded animal over a cold-blooded animal?

2. Explain how a typical bird is adapted for flying.

3. Describe a bird's digestive system and discuss the functions of its main structures.

4. What special adaptations are found in a bird's respiratory system?

NEW VIEW

1. Why is a bird's heart more efficient than that of a fish or an amphibian? Is it more efficient than the heart of a reptile? Explain.

2. Do you think that the unusually large cerebellum of a bird is of any special help in flying?

3. MAMMALIA—THE MAMMALS

Although birds and mammals are both warm-blooded, you would hardly mistake a mammal for a bird. Mammals are warm-blooded animals with fur or hair. They also are the only animals with **mammary glands** which secrete milk for feeding the young. Mammals also differ from other animals in having a flat, sheetlike muscle separating the chest cavity from the abdominal cavity. This muscle, called the **diaphragm**, helps pump air into and out of the lungs.

Mammals probably first appeared on the earth about 180 million years ago, long after the first vertebrates, the fish, which appeared about 425 million years ago. Recall that the fossil record seems to point to the evolution of mammal's from certain ancient mammal-like reptiles. However, the evidence is not yet definite. More study is needed to determine from which group of reptiles the mammals descended.

Like other successful groups of organisms, the mammals show wide variation in their adaptations to different environments. A survey of the different groups within the class Mammalia will emphasize the variety of organisms.

Egg-Laying Mammals

Perhaps the strangest modern mammal is the duck-billed platypus. ❶ It has a ducklike bill, webbed feet, and lays eggs in the same way that a reptile or a bird does. Thus, you can see that this animal kept one of the characteristics of its reptile ancestors—that of egg laying. Almost all other mammals bear their young alive. In spite of its egg-laying characteristic, the platypus has mammary glands, although they are not as highly developed as those of more familiar mammals, such as the rat, cow, or horse. The platypus has all other characteristics of mammals. It is warm-blooded, has fur, and has a diaphragm. It is clearly a mammal. The platypus is found only in Australia and on the island of Tasmania, off the coast of Australia. Another mammal, the spiny anteater of Australia, also lays eggs. The egg-laying mammals are often not considered by some to be *true mammals.*

Animals with Pouches

Australia is the home of many interesting and strange animals. The kangaroo, as well as the egg-laying mammals, are found there. The kangaroo and other odd mammals of Australia do give birth to their young, however, *before they are ready to be born.* The female then keeps them in a pouch while they are growing and developing. The mammary glands are located inside the pouch. At the time of birth, the incompletely developed young crawl out from their mother's body and into the pouch. There they attach their mouths to the mother's mammary glands, remaining there sucking milk and never letting go until they are much older and much better developed. Notice how the baby kangaroo rides around in its mother's pouch even after it is large enough to hop around on its own legs. ❷

America also has one of these interesting pouched animals, the opossum.

Mammals of the Sea

Several kinds of mammals spend their lives in the sea. Among these are the seals and walruses. ❸ They are carnivores and are quick and intelligent. They have large fangs or canine teeth that are used in tearing flesh. Their bodies are streamlined like a fish and their legs have become flippers, adapting them for a life in the sea. Being mammals,

❷

they breathe by means of lungs and have all other basic mammal characteristics.

The largest animals in the world today are mammals, the whales. Recall that one kind of whale, the blue whale, grows more than 100 feet in length and may weigh 150 or more tons. This giant has no teeth, and despite its size eats nothing but tiny algae and shrimplike crustaceans.

Other whales, much smaller in size, have teeth and eat fish and squids. Killer whales even hunt in packs as wolves do. Porpoises are closely related to whales.

All of these sea mammals breathe by means of lungs. However, they can hold their breath

❸

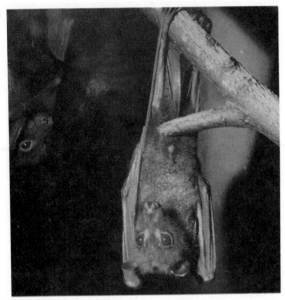

for long periods of time. Some of the large whales can stay under the water for as long as an hour. When they come up, they blow out their breath through their nostrils, called *blow holes*, at the top of their heads.

You have certainly heard of blubber. When old whaling ships of the northeastern United States set out to sea to harpoon whales, getting the blubber was the purpose. Blubber is the thick layer of fat stored underneath the skin of the whale. All warm-blooded animals (birds and mammals) have fat under their skins for insulation. However, the whales have far more fat than other animals for insulating their bodies against the cold water.

Flying Mammals

Have you ever seen a bat flitting around at dusk? A bat is a small mammal that looks something like a flying mouse. The wings are thin, leathery membranes extending from the arms and long fingers in front to the small hind feet and tail. Hanging by their hind feet from trees, roofs, and sides of caves, from

rafters or in barns, bats sleep during the day. But at dusk they come out and spend the night catching flying insects.

How does a bat catch a flying insect, particularly at night? By experimenting with bats, biologists have discovered that bats accomplish this by a kind of "animal *sonar*." (Sonar is a method ships use to determine their distances from objects by sending out soundwaves and catching the echoes bouncing back.) Bats make high, shrill cries in short bursts, or pulses, constantly while in flight. You cannot hear these sounds because they are pitched too high for most human ears to hear. When the sound waves hit an object—even a tiny insect—the waves bounce back to the bat's sensitive ears. The bat apparently can determine from the returning echoes exactly where the insect is located, and how far away.

Fruit bats, or "flying foxes," are much larger than insect-eating bats. Fruit bats live in Africa, parts of Asia, and Australia. One kind of fruit bat has a body a foot long and a wingspread of about five feet. These bats live on fruits, as their name suggests. The fruit bats in the photograph are Asian.

Mammals with Hoofs

Most mammals have claws or nails at the ends of their fingers and toes. However, in some mammals the claws have changed into hoofs. For example, cows, horses, deer, rhinoceroses, camels, sheep, pigs, and llamas have hoofs. All of the hoofed mammals are herbivores. They are particularly important to man because he has domesticated many of them and raised them for work and for food.

The Primates

This group of mammals is of particular interest because it includes the monkeys, apes, and even man, himself. Primates as a group have the largest brains (compared to body size) and the greatest intelligence of all animals. They have flattened nails, and they can grasp objects and carry them between their thumbs and fingers. Among the smaller primates are the tarsiers. ❷ Baboons are medium-sized primates. ❸ A particularly large primate is the gorilla. ❹

A Comparison of the Organs and Their Functions in Mammals

The purpose of your study of the structure of organisms has been to give you a basis for comparison of body structures and their functions. And on the basis of this knowledge, you will be able to understand better the relationship among organisms.

Having studied in detail the anatomy of a vertebrate, the bird, you have a basis for understanding more fully the body organization and functions of a warm-blooded vertebrate. The internal organs of a man, a cat, a cow, a rabbit, and a rat are a little different. However, all have the same organs, and the differences in the structures and functions of the organs are really very slight. It would be well, however, to review your understanding of the internal structure of a mammal.

At the right are several drawings of the internal anatomy of the rat. You have studied enough different animals by now to know the functions of most of the organs. You have studied especially the anatomy of man. As you study the drawings of the anatomy of the rat, it would be well to review the anatomy of man (pp. 102–125).

Certain structures are worth special mention from the viewpoint of the classification of mammals. Note especially the *diaphragm* that separates the chest cavity from the abdominal cavity. As you know now, this is a specifically mammalian characteristic. When a mammal exhales, the diaphragm relaxes and the liver, stomach, and other abdominal organs push the diaphragm against the lungs. The ribs also push in on the chest cavity. This creates greater air pressure inside the lungs than the air pressure outside the animal's body. Therefore, air flows out, and the lungs become smaller. When the animal inhales, the muscular diaphragm tightens and pushes the abdominal organs down and away from the lungs. Muscles between the ribs contract and the ribs push out. These two movements make the chest cavity larger. As a result, the air pressure inside the lungs is less than the outside air pressure, so the outside air flows into the lungs, which become larger.

Now notice the *size* of the brain in comparison with the other organs. The rat's brain is much larger, compared with the size of its entire body, than the brain of any other animal you have studied. However, man's brain is much larger than the rat's and it practically fills the entire skull except for the jaws. Notice, particularly, the size of the cerebrum in the rat and in man. Both are much larger than any other part of the brain, and both have a surface that is creased and folded. Mammals are by far the most intelligent of animals.

Does the relatively large cerebrum (compared with the cerebrum of organisms that have preceded the mammals in evolution) indicate why this may be so?

From your study of the brains of the fish (p. 383), the frog (p. 100), the bird (p. 407), and man (p. 111), see if you can answer the following questions.

a. In relation to the other parts of the brain, which is the largest: the medulla, the cerebellum, or the cerebrum?
b. How do the cerebrums of the different vertebrates compare with each other?
c. How do the cerebellums of the different vertebrates compare with each other?
d. Now consider the brains of all the animals. When, in terms of the various large groups of organisms, does the brain seem to have developed its three distinct parts?
e. Which, of all the classes of organisms you have been studying, have the most complex brains? What is the basis for your conclusion?
f. On the basis of your study, would you support or deny this statement: Mammals, as a group, have the most intelligence of all animals?

The Rise of the Mammals

Picture, once again, an ancient scene. Time: the Mesozoic era, the Cretaceous period, about 135 million years ago. You could not fail to recognize the organisms—reptiles, dinosaurs.

Can you, now, guess at a scene early in the next following era, the Cenozoic era? Time: about 63 million years ago.

The dinosaurs are now gone. Yet the modern reptiles are present—turtles, crocodiles, lizards, snakes, but no dinosaurs. What is the

ANATOMY OF THE RAT

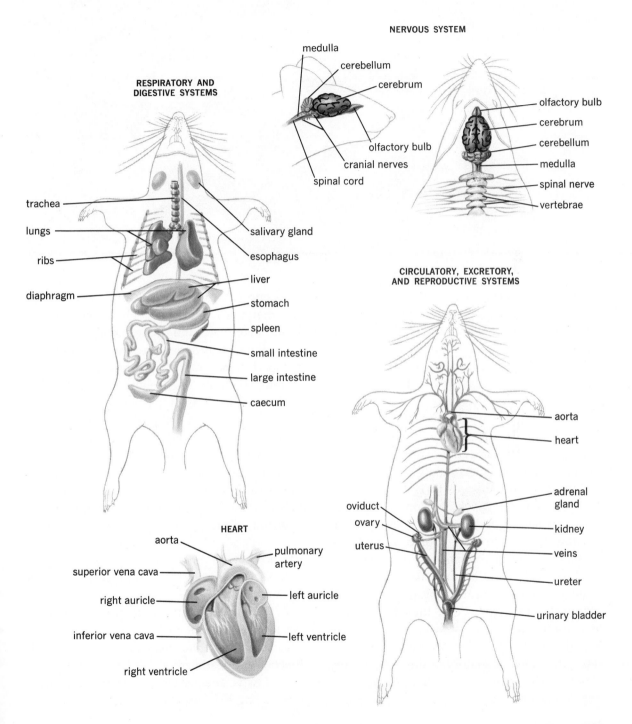

NERVOUS SYSTEM

medulla
cerebellum
cerebrum
olfactory bulb
cranial nerves
spinal cord

olfactory bulb
cerebrum
cerebellum
medulla
spinal nerve
vertebrae

RESPIRATORY AND DIGESTIVE SYSTEMS

trachea
lungs
ribs
diaphragm
salivary gland
esophagus
liver
stomach
spleen
small intestine
large intestine
caecum

CIRCULATORY, EXCRETORY, AND REPRODUCTIVE SYSTEMS

aorta
heart
adrenal gland
kidney
veins
ureter
urinary bladder
oviduct
ovary
uterus

HEART

aorta
superior vena cava
right auricle
inferior vena cava
right ventricle
pulmonary artery
left auricle
left ventricle

explanation? Surely some close relatives of the ancient dinosaurs should have survived. The mystery is still with us, and paleontologists are still at work trying to solve it.

Nevertheless, as you know, the early mammals began to flourish in the forests of the middle and late Mesozoic era. True, they were no larger than the modern rat. Some were like the shrew and some were like the opossum. As the Cenozoic era opens, we find the expansion of the mammals, the order that embraces warm-blooded, furry animals.

In the Eocene epoch, beginning some 58 million years ago, the fossil record of the mammals is ample. The hoofed animals are present; so are the whales. Bats appear. So do the first elephantlike animals.

Imagine a scene in the middle Cenozoic. Mammals are everywhere; they have taken over the environment as the reptiles did before them. Do you recognize horses? Do you recognize any predatory animals? In any event, in the middle Cenozoic, perhaps during the epochs known as the Oligocene and Miocene (36 million to 13 million years ago) the mammals flourished. There were swimming mammals and flying mammals—some were hunters, others were grazers. Some developed hoofs, some developed fins, some developed claws. The Cenozoic era is the Age of Mammals. It is of particular interest, for toward the end of this era, man appears.

By now, your study of forms among the animals and plants should have given you a grasp of the rich and beautiful variety of life on earth. You have, in a way, a capsule history of the organisms—both plant and animal —on this earth.

REVIEW

1. What characteristics distinguish mammals from other animals?

2. Why is the platypus considered by some not to be a true mammal?

3. How does the diaphragm in mammals function in breathing?

4. How is intelligence related to brain structure among the classes of vertebrates?

NEW VIEW

Next time you have chicken for dinner, persuade your family to let you have all the bones.

Can you find any relationships between the wing bones and leg bones? How are they adapted for their functions?

If you have a manikin or skeleton of a monkey, or a skeleton of a cat or rat, compare the leg bones of the chicken with the leg bones of the monkey, cat, or rat. What similarities do you find? What differences?

How do you account for the similarities? for the differences?

4. RELATING THE CONCEPTS

Richness in variety is common in the world of organisms. Your studies of the forms of reptiles, birds, and mammals surely do not deny these concepts:

Organisms have structures that adapt them to their environment.

Similar structures and their similar functions give scientists a basis for classifying, or grouping, organisms.

Organisms with similar structures are placed in a group.

In classifying organisms, the greater the similarity of the structures within a given group, the more limited and precise is the grouping.

These concepts were stated in Chapter 13 with reference to the *lower* invertebrates.

Do these concepts support what you know of the *higher* invertebrates, the mollusks and arthropods, for instance? Do these concepts embrace what you know of the *lower* vertebrates, the fish and amphibians? Do your past studies of organisms force you to doubt any of these concepts?

Reviewing the Concepts

▶ *Living things have a long past history.* Clearly, plants and animals have existed in the past. Many organisms are no longer in what we might call a "catalogue of living things." Many organisms—dinosaurs, trilobites, seed ferns, and others—are extinct.

▶ *Present groups of organisms can, at times, be traced to organisms of the past.* Thus, present evidence indicates that reptiles seem to have given rise to the early birds. Fossils of *Archaeopteryx* support this line of reasoning. Present evidence also indicates that mammal-like reptiles gave rise to the early mammals.

▶ *Organisms may be grouped in ascending phyla of increasing complexity.* Certain structures of the mammals are more complex than those of reptiles. And structures of the reptiles, in turn, are generally more complex than those of amphibians and fish. Throughout the history of vertebrates, the heart progresses from two chambers to four. The brain becomes larger and more complex. Body functions progress from those of cold-blooded organisms, restricted to special environments, to those of warm-blooded organisms able to function in many environments.

▶ *As organisms ascend in complexity, their young need increasing care.* Generally, the young of fish and frog are able to fend for themselves. Reptile and bird eggs are protected by shells. Mammalian young develop inside the mother. Among all the mammals, whose young receives most care?

▶ *An increase in intelligence becomes apparent in proceeding from fish to mammals.* By intelligence we mean an ability to respond to a variety of stimuli, and to modify the environment. Which order of mammals is the most intelligent?

Testing Yourself

Judge each statement to be *true* or *false* and support your judgment with evidence.

1. One group of flying reptiles developed feathers on its wings. This and other facts, such as the scales on the legs of modern birds, make it highly likely that birds evolved from reptiles.

2. Birds and mammals are the only warm-blooded animals. These animals maintain a constant body temperature regardless of the temperature of the air around them. Thus these animals have a body efficiency throughout the year much higher than the body efficiency of cold-blooded animals.

3. All animals are adapted to the lives they lead. For example, birds are adapted in many ways for flight: light, hollow bones, large flying muscles attached to a keel-like breast bone, stiff flight feathers, and air sacs connected to the lungs.

4. The four-chambered hearts of birds and mammals are more efficient than the hearts of fish, amphibians, and reptiles. In effect, four-chambered hearts are two pumps in one. The right side of the four-chambered heart pumps blood into the lungs. The left side pumps blood throughout the body. Hence, oxygenated blood pumped throughout the body is not mixed with blood that is poor in oxygen and rich in carbon dioxide.

5. Mammals secrete milk from milk glands, or mammary glands, have hair or fur on their bodies, and have a diaphragm that separates the chest cavity from the abdominal cavity. Mammals have the most highly developed brains of all animals and are, as a group, much the most intelligent of all animals.

6. Mammals probably evolved from some ancient reptile about 180 million years ago. One group of modern mammals lays eggs much like those of reptiles.

7. Although fossils are available, the evidence secured from them is not to be trusted. There is no way of knowing that extinct animal or plant life really existed.

8. The most intelligent group of mammals is the primates. This group, which includes man, has the largest brains, proportional to their sizes and weights, of all animals. They have flattened nails rather than claws on their fingers, and most of them can grasp and carry things between their fingers and thumbs.

9. A greater variety of organisms exists today than existed in the Eocene.

10. The mammals are the dominant vertebrates of the earth today.

11. The insects are the dominant invertebrates of the earth.

12. The dinosaurs disappeared because they could not compete with the mammals.

Extending the Concepts

Investigation. Perhaps you and several of your classmates wish to dissect a small mammal, such as a rat, to study the circulatory and nervous systems. It is best to purchase a preserved, injected rat.

You should get a biology laboratory manual to help you trace the circulatory system and the nervous system.

Suggested Reading

Carr and the Editors of LIFE, *The Reptiles* (Life Nature Library), New York, Time, Inc., 1963.

Carrington and the Editors of LIFE, *The Mammals* (Life Nature Library), New York, Time, Inc., 1963.

National Geographic Society, *Wild Animals of North America,* Washington, D.C., National Geographic Society, 1963.

VARIETY AMONG THE ANIMALS

REPTILES, BIRDS, AND MAMMALS

Just as seed plants conquered the land, so did the animals in the classes pictured below. The evolution of these animals is closely knit—and once again the relationships through common ancestry can be seen clearly.

Presented here is an overview of the last three classes of vertebrates—reptiles, birds, and mammals.

REPTILES
(Class—Reptilia)

The reptiles are cold-blooded animals with thick, dry scales. They have lungs throughout life. They reproduce by means of eggs with leathery coverings, although a few bear their young alive. Usually there are two pairs of limbs, but these may be vestigial or absent.

box turtle

king snake

leopard lizard

crocodile

You may find it valuable to refer to the chart, Classifying the Animal Kingdom, on page 309.

BIRDS
(Class—Aves)

These are warm-blooded animals with feathers. Birds lay hard-shelled eggs. They have beaks but no teeth; forelimbs are modified into wings, and hindlimbs are adapted for perching, running, or swimming. Air sacs extend from the lungs into the bones and spaces between organs.

heron

albatross

ostrich

hawk

pheasant

robin

gull

penguin

Canada goose

MAMMALS
(Class—Mammalia)

These warm-blooded animals have fur or hair. The young develop internally in true mammals, and are then fed on milk from mammary glands. A diaphragm separates the chest and abdominal cavities. All mammals have four-chambered hearts. Typical mammals have four limbs, each containing one to five claws, hoofs, or toes with nails.

platypus

kangaroo

armadillo

mole

bat

seal

rabbit

lion

rat

cow

elephant

horse

tarsier

whale

baboon

monkey

chimpanzee

THE
CONTINUITY
OF
THE
ORGANISM

Compare these two organisms.

Which one can survive in the wild?
How?

Which one must have the care of man?
Why?

What is the difference between the two
organisms? How do you account for
the difference?

17 | Continuity Through Genes

1. MENDEL—AND HIS ANALYSIS

This work had its origin more than a hundred years ago, in the years 1857 to 1866 to be specific. It began in the mind of a stoutish monk, Gregor Mendel, working in a monastery garden in what was then Brünn, Austria, now Brno, Czechoslovakia. Mendel was, in fact, a teacher with an interest in mathematics and science—and a burning curiosity to find out how organisms inherit their traits. For instance, how do you inherit the color of your eyes, the texture and color of your hair, your height, your shape? Whom do you resemble? Your mother? Your father? Neither? Why is this so?

It was in questions such as these that Mendel was interested. But he didn't choose animals to experiment with. He chose peas. Can you guess why?

The Usefulness of Peas

Many times experiments fail because the experimenter does not choose, or happen upon, an organism that is suitable for the kind of experiment the scientist wants to do. As you shall see, if Mendel had chosen the four o'clock rather than the garden pea plant, he

might have come to different conclusions, at least at the beginning. But we're getting ahead of our story.

The pea is a remarkable experimental plant. It's almost as if the flower were made for experimental work in heredity. See for yourself. ■

Mendel's Observations and Experiments

Mendel observed that some pea plants were tall, that is, they had long stems, whereas others had short stems. Some of the plants produced yellow seeds (yellow peas) and some produced green seeds. Some of the seeds produced were wrinkled and some were smooth. Mendel was able to develop what we call **purebred** strains of the pea plant—strains that always produced the same characteristics, yellow seeds, for example, generation after generation. He produced purebred tall plants and purebred dwarf plants. How did he know they were purebred for tallness? He made certain. He kept self-pollinating the plants until seeds from tall plants produced only tall plants. His plants were purebred.

He decided to "cross" some of these purebred plants. He used as parents purebred plants which differed in some characteristic

■ AN APPRENTICE INVESTIGATION into the Structure of a Flower

You will want to dissect a pea flower. Because of the very small size of the garden pea, you may prefer to dissect a sweet pea, which is quite similar. Use the photographs to help you. Examine the structure of the flower, particularly the stamens and the pistil. To locate these structures, you will have to open the keel of the flower. The photograph shows the keel opened and pushed to one side to expose the reproductive structures. ❶ How many stamens are there? ❷ How many ovules in the ovary? ❸ (You can use your fingernail to break open the ovary.) Examine the keel further. Would you expect the plant to be self-pollinated, or cross-pollinated? Clearly, the pea plant is self-pollinating. To cross one pea plant with another, you would have to open the fused petals of the keel.

It is important to understand that the garden pea plant (the type Mendel used) is self-pollinating. If it were cross-pollinating, of course, one plant would receive its pollen from another plant. But in the pea plant self-pollination is assured. You can assure self-pollination for almost any plant by placing a bag over each flower. Then only the pollen of the same flower can fall on the stigma. In this way you can be certain of the traits passed on.

An Investigation On Your Own

In the spring, grow some red-flowered petunias and some white-flowered petunias from seed. (Grow only plants from purebred seeds.) As soon as the plants begin to flower, determine whether the seeds produce only the color of the flower named on the packet.

What color offspring would be produced if you crossed the red-flowering plant with the white-flowering plant? How would you do it? How would you gather your results?

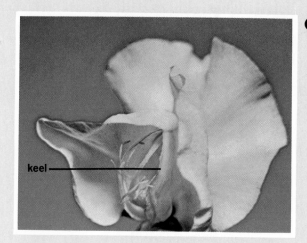

❶

keel

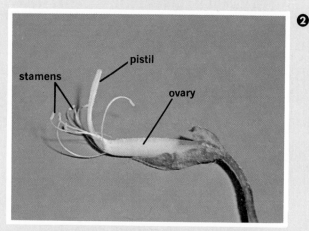

❷

stamens   pistil   ovary

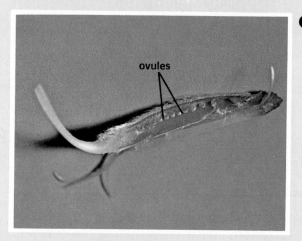

❸

ovules

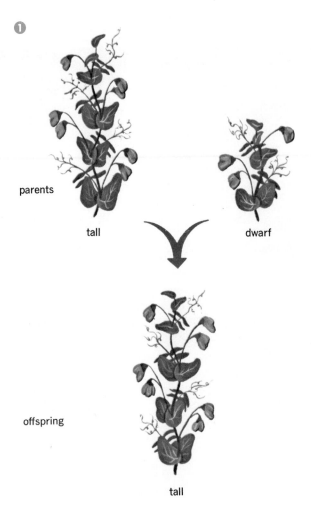

parents

tall   dwarf

offspring

tall

such as flower color or height. For instance, he took the pollen (which contains male sperm nuclei) from a purebred tall plant and used it to fertilize the eggs of a purebred drawf plant. He then planted the seeds that were produced and waited until these seeds had grown into new plants. What type of offspring do you think he obtained? Tall? Dwarf? In between?

All the plants were tall.❶

Mendel then crossed these tall plants with each other and planted the seeds that were produced. What do you think the plants in the next generation were? All tall? Dwarf? In between? Mendel found that the plants of this second generation had both tall and dwarf plants in the proportion, or ratio, of three tall plants to one dwarf plant.❷

When Mendel used purebred plants that produced smooth seeds and crossed them with those that produced wrinkled seeds, he again got the same ratios. The first generation *all* had smooth seeds. The second generation, on the other hand, had smooth and wrinkled seeds in the ratio of three smooth-seeded plants to one wrinkled-seeded plant.❸

Mendel carried out other crosses of purebred plants and always got the same kinds of ratios. Clearly, these results were not accidental. Something very definite was causing these ratios to occur.

Mendel's Reasoning

Let's consider the cross between purebred parents with yellow seeds and purebred parents with green seeds and follow Mendel's reasoning. All the offspring of the cross had yellow seeds in the first generation. Mendel hypothesized that somehow the trait for yellow seeds was more powerful than the trait

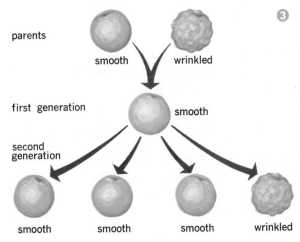

parents

smooth   wrinkled

first generation   smooth

second generation

smooth   smooth   smooth   wrinkled

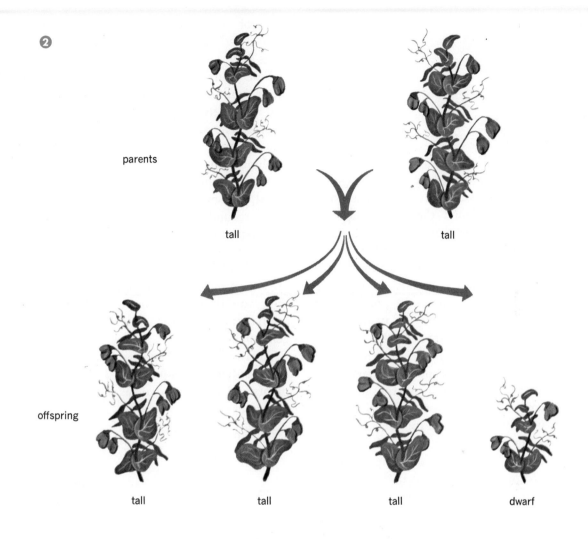

parents

tall

tall

offspring

tall

tall

tall

dwarf

for green seeds, and thus covered up the expression of green-seededness. In other words, yellow seeds were somehow **dominant** over green seeds.

Surely, the offspring had determiners for both yellow seeds and for green seeds. Such an offspring is known as a **hybrid.** A hybrid has two different determiners (later called **genes**) for a trait.

Mendel had to assume that the hybrid inherited genes from both its parents. Further, he had to explain why the hybrid that re-

suited from crossing a plant with yellow seeds and a plant with green seeds, produced yellow seeds and not seeds that were in between in color—that is, yellowish-green. He hypothesized, you recall, that one determiner, or gene(in this case, for yellow seeds), must be *dominant.* The other, the gene that was not expressed, must be **recessive** (in this case, for green seeds). Thus, the dominant trait seems to "hide" the recessive one.

Mendel further hypothesized that when two organisms are mated, the genes within

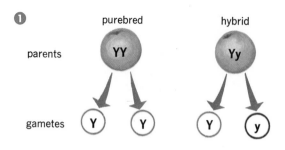

❶ purebred   hybrid

parents   YY   Yy

gametes   Y   Y   Y   y

one organism can join freely with the genes in the other organism. How do genes combine? Mendel assumed that the genes for any trait within an organism separated or became *segregated* from each other when sperms or eggs (the gametes) are produced.

Mendel had to find a method for showing (on paper) how the genes in a purebred or hybrid organism separated, or were segregated, into different gametes, that is, into different sperm or egg nuclei. In the figure for the production of gametes, we have used the customary way of showing the genes for each inherited characteristic. ❶ The dominant gene is usually represented by the capital letter of the name of the characteristic, and the recessive gene by the corresponding small letter. According to this procedure, the capital Y stands for the dominant gene for yellow seeds, the small y stands for the recessive gene for green seeds.

Since *two* parents pass on their heredity (their genes) to their offspring, Mendel *assumed* that each parent gives the offspring one gene for each trait. Study the chart at the right to fix in your mind how we show the mating between a purebred yellow-seeded plant and a purebred green-seeded plant. ❷

Would you question any of Mendel's assumptions as shown in the drawing? It seems that the diagram explains how two parents, one pure for yellow seeds (YY) and the other

pure for green seeds (yy), produce only yellow-seeded offspring, all of which are hybrids (Yy).

Test yourself for a moment or so. Using letter symbols for the genes, mate a pure tall and a pure dwarf pea plant. Dwarfness is recessive. The answer is given at the bottom of this column.*

Mendel also assumed that when two organisms are mated, the genes that had segregated, or separated, into different gametes could recombine freely. Consider now what the offspring would be in a cross between two plants that are hybrid for producing yellow seeds. ❸ Only the combinations YY, Yy, and yy can occur in the offspring. Notice that there are three offspring that show the recessive trait for green seeds. What is their gene make-up?

The result is a ratio of 3 to 1, usually written 3:1. That is, Mendel found 3 yellow-seeded plants to 1 green-seeded plant, or 3 dominant to 1 recessive.

* All the plants are hybrid tall (Tt).

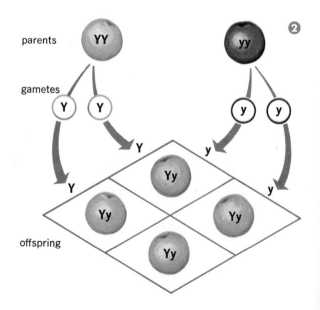

❷

parents   YY   yy

gametes   Y   Y   y   y

         Y   y
            Yy

   Y   y

      Yy   Yy

offspring   Yy

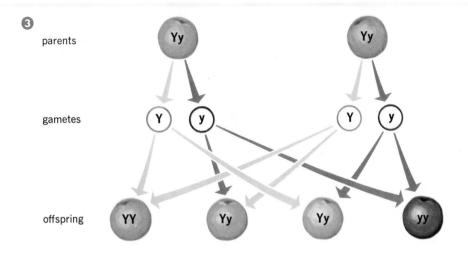

❸

parents

gametes

offspring

Mendel's Results and His Conclusions

Mendel was a very careful experimenter. The charts below and on the following page show the results of some of his many experiments with the garden pea plant. Scientists today can follow the results of Mendel's work because he kept such accurate and excellent records.

After studying his findings, you can see that when parents that are pure for different traits (yellow or green, tall or dwarf) are crossed, only one of the two traits shows in the offspring. The other trait remains hidden. Mendel called this the dominance or recessiveness of traits.

In his cross of hybrid plants, why didn't Mendel get an exact 3:1 ratio? What explanations are possible?

To convince yourself that a 3:1 ratio among the offspring of hybrids can result from the

CROSS OF PUREBRED PLANTS

Traits of parents	*First generation offspring (hybrids)*	*Which trait is dominant?*
yellow seeds × green seeds (YY × yy)	All yellow seeds (Yy)	
smooth seeds × wrinkled seeds (SS × ss)	All smooth seeds (Ss)	
green pods × yellow pods (GG × gg)	All green pods (Gg)	
tall × dwarf (long stem × short stem) (TT × tt)	All tall (long stem) (Tt)	

429

Traits of parents	Offspring	Ratio	
		Actual	Assumed
yellow seeds × yellow seeds (Yy × Yy)	6,022 yellow 2,001 green 8,023 total	3.01:1	3:1
smooth seeds × smooth seeds (Ss × Ss)	5,474 smooth 1,850 wrinkled 7,324 total	2.96:1	3:1
green pods × green pods (Gg × Gg)	428 green 152 yellow 580 total	2.82:1	3:1
tall plants × tall plants (Tt × Tt)	787 tall 277 short 1,064 total	2.84:1	3:1

chance combination of eggs and sperms, you might try this investigation. ■

On the basis of his experiments, Mendel arrived at a general rule for the way the genes are segregated into the gametes. The rule for the segregation of genes into gametes, or the *Law of Segregation,* as it is often called, states: When gametes are formed, the *two members of each pair of genes must separate, and only one of each pair of genes can go to one gamete.* Remember that when you selected beads from each unmarked container, you selected either a "gene" for blue color or a "gene" for yellow color from each parent.

The meaning of the Law of Segregation is simple. If, in the case of yellow and green peas, the parent is purebred yellow (YY), its gametes will carry one gene for yellow (Y), not two. If the parent is purebred green (yy), its gametes will carry a single gene for green (y). If the parent is hybrid yellow (Yy), half its gametes will carry the gene for yellow (Y) while the other half will carry the gene for green (y). Why?

Mendel was able, then, to come to these conclusions about the way organisms inherit their traits:

a. Determiners, or genes, are responsible for the inheritance of traits.

b. For any single hereditary trait, a plant has at least two genes. These may be alike (in purebred plants) or different (in hybrids).

c. When a purebred dominant is crossed with a recessive (which, of course, must be purebred), the dominant trait is expressed in the offspring while the recessive trait remains hidden.

d. When the genes are segregated into gametes, each gamete has only one gene for the particular trait. (The Law of Segregation.)

■ AN APPRENTICE INVESTIGATION of Genetic Ratios

You will need 100 blue beads and 100 yellow beads (or beads of any two colors). You will also need two containers (paper cups or boxes). Place 50 blue beads and 50 yellow beads into one of the containers and mix them thoroughly. Place another 50 blue beads and 50 yellow beads into the second container, mixing them thoroughly.

Now without looking into the two containers, remove one bead from each container at the same time.  You can, of course, pick up two blue beads at the same time, a blue bead and a yellow bead, or two yellow beads. ❷

Work with a partner who will tally the number of pairs of blue beads, number of pairs of yellow beads, and the number of pairs of one blue and one yellow bead. Repeat the procedure at least twenty times, but each time be sure to *return each bead to the container from which it came before picking up another pair of beads* (Why?)

Let the original containers represent hybrid parents that can produce gametes that contain either a gene for blue color (dominant trait) or a gene for yellow color (recessive trait). Then two blue beads represent a purebred blue offspring, one blue bead and one yellow bead represent a hybrid blue offspring, and two yellow beads represent a yellow offspring.

From your tally, how many offspring were produced carrying the dominant trait (purebred blue and hybrid blue)? How many offspring were produced showing the recessive trait (yellow)? Do you find a ratio of approximately 3:1? Now combine your results with those of your classmates. Does the ratio now become closer to 3:1? Why?

An Investigation On Your Own

You have probably realized by now that the pairing of genes occurs by *chance*. What is the ratio you might get of heads to tails (two heads, one head and one tail, or two tails), if you tossed two pennies several hundred times? How does this ratio help explain Mendel's results?

e. When the gametes of hybrid parents unite (in fertilization), the ratio of the inherited traits can be predicted. Thus the mating of two hybrid yellow plants, Yy × Yy, results in a ratio of 3 yellow to 1 green offspring. That is: 1 YY plus 2 Yy gives 3 yellow (dominant) to 1 yy green (recessive).

Mendel had done an amazing piece of work. He had begun to look—with the eyes of a scientist—into the behavior of gametes during reproduction of the organism. Not knowing the real nature of a gene, he still tried to explain how it worked. Was he correct? We shall see.

REVIEW

1. If a purebred tall pea plant is crossed with a purebred dwarf pea plant, what kind of plants will be produced in the first generation? How did Mendel explain the result?

2. If these first-generation plants (see question **1** above) are then crossed, what kind of plants will be produced in the second generation?

3. Explain how Mendel's Law of Segregation accounts for the first generation of plants resulting from the cross indicated in question **1** above.

4. Explain how Mendel's Law of Segregation accounts for the second generation of plants (see question **2** above).

5. When purebred black-furred guinea pigs are mated with white-furred guinea pigs, all the offspring are black furred.

a. Which trait is dominant?

b. Using letters as symbols for traits and the type of diagram shown on page 428, draw the make-up of a purebred black-furred parent, a white-furred parent, and the offspring of the cross.

6. Mate two hybrid black-furred guinea pigs. Use the same type of diagram as in **5b** above. What ratio do you get? Explain your results.

NEW VIEW

Brown eyes in human beings are dominant over blue eyes.

a. Would you expect two blue-eyed parents to have any brown-eyed children?

b. Can two brown-eyed parents have blue-eyed children? Explain.

2. A THEORY

If Mendel were right, shouldn't we be able to *see* the genes on which he based the explanation of his results? How very important it would be if we might look into a cell and determine whether the cell carries genes, say, for wrinkled seeds or red color in flowers, for blue or hazel eyes, or for high intelligence. The concept is fascinating—let's set out to find the location of the gene.

A Line of Reasoning

Detectives arrive at the solution to a crime by examining either the clues or the facts. The scientist is somewhat like a detective in that he must also rely on the facts to lead him to the proper solution to his problems. What, then, are the facts that led to the discovery of the location of the genes in the cell?

Recall that in flowering plants, a pollen grain falls on the stigma of the pistil. The pollen grain (whether of the pea, a tulip, or an oak) contains a sperm nucleus that unites with an egg nucleus in the ovule (p. 293). Thus, the beginning of a new plant, with specific traits, arises from the union of egg and sperm.

Multicellular animals have a similar beginning. Sea urchins or starfish growing in a laboratory can be studied while reproducing. If we look through a microscope, we can observe that a sperm head fuses with the nucleus of an egg cell. From then on the zygote

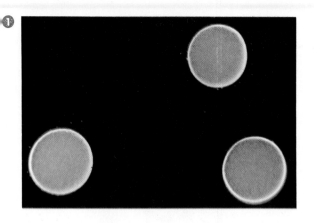

(fertilized egg) divides, forming a larva. Then in time, the adult develops.

Since reproduction begins with the fusion of egg and sperm, it appears that the nuclei or the cytoplasm of these cells is in some way responsible for the passing on of traits from the parents to the offspring. ❶ Perhaps the nucleus is the home of the genes.

But could the genes of a cell be located in its cytoplasm? After all, the cytoplasm of an egg is the largest part of the cell?

An early scientist decided to investigate whether the nucleus or the cytoplasm was responsible for the offspring's heredity. He found that by shaking sea urchin eggs vigorously, he could get them to lose their nuclei. However, not all the eggs lost their nuclei and he set out to separate the eggs into two groups—those with and those without a nucleus. Then he added sperm from a different species of sea urchin to each group of eggs. Those eggs with only a sperm nucleus developed into sea urchins that resembled the species from which the sperm was taken. Those eggs that contained their own nuclei and the sperm's nucleus had traits of both species.

Clearly, then, it must be the nucleus that is in some way involved in heredity. Indeed,

Walter S. Sutton, working early in this century, centered his thoughts about the nucleus, specifically on the chromosomes. From your earlier studies you learned that chromosomes are tiny bodies located within the nucleus.

Sutton's Reasoning

Sutton reasoned that if he could show that Mendel's observations of the way peas inherited their characteristics were related to the way chromosomes behaved, some clue could be found to the location of the genes. For our purpose, we need to look once again at the behavior of chromosomes. In our study we shall use an animal with which Mendel and Sutton were not well acquainted, in fact, may not have investigated. Then we shall return to Sutton's reasoning.

The animal we shall study is the famous fruit fly, *Drosophila* (drə·sof′ə·lə). ❷ Biologists have experimented with and know more about the inheritance of *Drosophila* than any other organism in the world. *Drosophila's* chromosomes are very convenient to study. They are easy to recognize, and they are only 8 in number. That is, a *body cell* (say, a nerve cell or a salivary gland cell) of the adult fly has 8 chromosomes.

❷

MALE   FEMALE

433

❶ MITOSIS

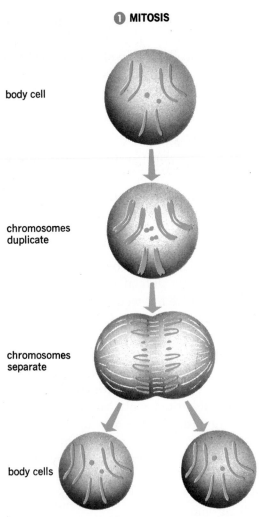

body cell

chromosomes
duplicate

chromosomes
separate

body cells

❷ MEIOSIS

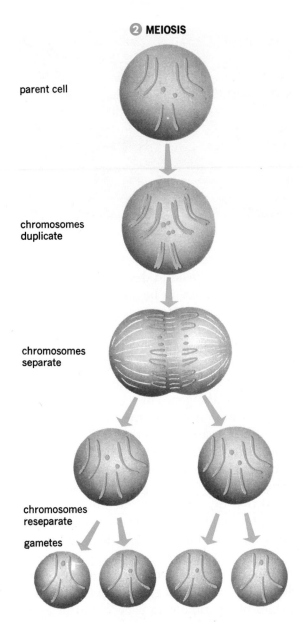

parent cell

chromosomes
duplicate

chromosomes
separate

chromosomes
reseparate

gametes

When a body cell divides, its chromosomes duplicate lengthwise. You remember that we call this process *mitosis*. Study carefully the diagrams of mitosis in a *Drosophila* body cell. ❶ The process is simplified to focus on the end-result. Notice that each of the eight chromosomes duplicates lengthwise so that at one time each body cell undergoing mitosis has 16 chromosomes. Finally, as the cell pinches in and forms two cells, each body cell has 8 chromosomes, the normal number. *Mitosis*, then, results in the normal body chromosome number. In man, the body cell

chromosome number is 46. Each of your body cells has 46 chromosomes. Cell division of any one of your body cells produces two cells, each with 46 chromosomes.

Examine once again the chromosomes in a body cell of *Drosophila*. The term "body cell" refers to any cell that is not a gamete (a sperm or egg cell). Suppose you were to examine the egg cells of *Drosophila*. How many chromosomes are there? Four—not eight! And how many chromosomes would you observe in each sperm cell? Four, of course.

From your earlier studies of the formation of gametes, you might have expected this reduced number. Unlike body cells, gametes are formed by *meiosis*, not *mitosis*. What is the difference between meiosis and mitosis as far as the chromosomes are concerned? Here is a diagram of *meiosis* (simplified to focus on the end result). ❷ A comparison with the diagram for *mitosis* (at the left) highlights the difference.

Notice that as a result of mitosis, each body cell has the same chromosome number as the original dividing cell, the parent cell. In meiosis, on the other hand, each gamete has *one half* the chromosome number of the parent cell. But the chromosomes of one gamete are mates of the other, are they not?

The result of meiosis then, is a reduction of the chromosome number *by one half*. If the sperm nucleus has one half the chromosome number, and the egg has one half the chromosome number, what happens in fertilization? The body chromosome number is restored through fertilization. *Meiosis reduces* the chromosome number by half. *Fertilization restores* the chromosome number. ❸

Sutton's Analysis

Sutton knew the behavior of chromosomes during meiosis from his study of the behavior of chromosomes in a number of plants and animals. First he carefully analyzed the behavior of chromosomes during meiosis and fertilization. Then, as a result of his analysis, Sutton hypothesized somewhat as follows:

a. Assume that the chromosomes contain the genes.

b. Assume further that each chromosome of a pair carries one of the genes for a specific trait. One chromosome, for example, might carry the dominant gene for color (for yellow seeds); the paired chromosome of a hybrid would carry the recessive gene (for green seeds). The genes would follow Mendel's Law of Segregation—each gene of a pair segregating into a different gamete.

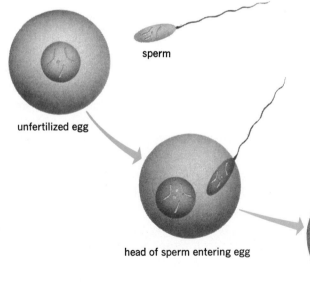

sperm

unfertilized egg

head of sperm entering egg

❸ **FERTILIZATION**

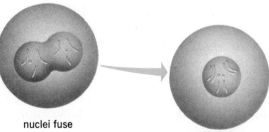

nuclei fuse

fertilized egg

435

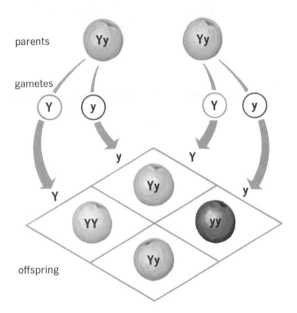

❶ ASSUMED BEHAVIOR OF GENES

Mendel's analysis
of a hybrid cross

parents

gametes

offspring

Assumed Ratio: 3 Yellow: 1 Green

Y = yellow (dominant)

y = green (recessive)

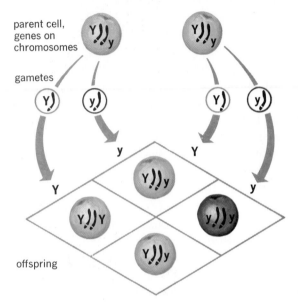

❷ ASSUMED BEHAVIOR OF CHROMOSOMES

Sutton's analysis
of a hybrid cross

parent cell,
genes on
chromosomes

gametes

offspring

Assumed Ratio: 3 Yellow: 1 Green

Y = gene for yellow on one chromosome

y = gene for green on the mate of
the chromosome containing
gene for yellow

c. When the genes of a hybrid segregate and recombine in the offspring, a large number of offspring show a 3:1 ratio that can be explained by the behavior of chromosomes during meiosis and fertilization.

Sutton hypothesized, therefore, that the genes, the determiners of heredity, are in the chromosomes.

Sutton undoubtedly compared his analysis with Mendel's results. We have simplified the comparison in the diagrams above.❶ ❷ Study both of the diagrams carefully. Sutton's hypothesis sounds reasonable, doesn't it? But is his hypothesis correct?

Soon there were other observations in support of Sutton's hypothesis that the chromosomes are the carriers of hereditary traits.

Now that you have advanced your understanding of the way traits are inherited, perhaps you will want to analyze certain traits of man. There are several traits whose inheritance you can analyze. One of them, strangely enough, is the ability to roll the tongue. Can you roll your tongue? Some people can, others can't. Is tongue-rolling a dominant trait or a recessive trait? How would you go about determining whether the tongue-rolling trait is dominant or recessive? One way is to study your classmates. ■

■ AN APPRENTICE INVESTIGATION of Hereditary Traits

How many of your classmates can roll their tongues?  How many cannot? Now ask representatives from other classes to determine the numbers in their classes that can roll or cannot roll their tongues. (Perhaps you might use all the classes in your school.)

Tally the total number of those who can and those who cannot roll their tongues in all the other classes observed. Compare the total with the number in your class. How does the data from the other classes agree with the data you obtained from your class? Which figure is most reliable? Why? In three schools where this investigation was done, the following data was obtained.

	Tongue rollers	Non tongue rollers
school 1 (South)	292	86
school 2 (Northeast)	172	59
school 3 (West)	460	167

The students in all three schools concluded that the tongue-rolling trait was dominant. From the results in your school, do you agree with them?

An Investigation On Your Own

Ear lobes can be free or attached. With a mirror, study your own ear lobes. Are they free, as in the photograph at the left? 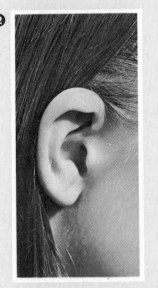 Or are they attached, as in the photograph at the right? 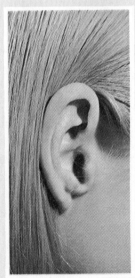 Look around you. Which trait is dominant? Which trait is recessive?

Here is something else for you to investigate on your own. Are you a tongue roller or a nonroller? If you cannot roll your tongue, you know your genetic make-up. What is it? If you can roll your tongue, is your possible genetic make-up RR or Rr? Find out. (*Clue:* Check your parents and any brothers or sisters for the tongue-rolling trait.)

You are, of course, not surprised that many human hereditary traits have been studied. Three other traits that you might find very interesting to study are eye color, hair color, and shape of head. But it is far more difficult to study traits of man than traits of *Drosophila*. Why?

Labeled Chromosomes

If only we could label the chromosomes to know which genes they carry. *Drosophila* is indeed a useful animal, for it was soon discovered that one of its chromosomes carries its own label. In the diagram below at the left are the chromosomes of a cell of a female *Drosophila*.  At the right are those of a male *Drosophila*. Do you see any difference?

female   male

The male *Drosophila* cell has eight chromosomes; so does the female. But the chromosomes of the male show one peculiarity. One chromosome has a hook on it. Examination of the cells of the male *Drosophila* shows that each cell has a chromosome with a hook on it. The hooked chromosome is named the "Y" chromosome. Its mate, the rod-shaped chromosome, is named the "X" chromosome. Does the possession of a Y chromosome make the animal that possesses it a male? So it would seem.

Suppose we observe the behavior of the X and Y chromosomes during meiosis. If they are indeed chromosome mates, then we should find them separating during meiosis.

Below, you will find a simplified diagram of meiosis in the male fruit fly.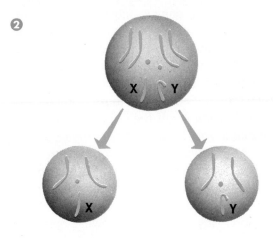

Does the diagram support the idea of segregation of chromosomes? It does, for it is clear that the Y chromosome separates from the X chromosome into a different gamete.

In actuality, the chromosomes of *Drosophila* are very much like those shown in the diagrams. Compare the diagram of chromosomes of a male *Drosophila* at the left with a microscopic view of the chromosomes of a male *Drosophila*.

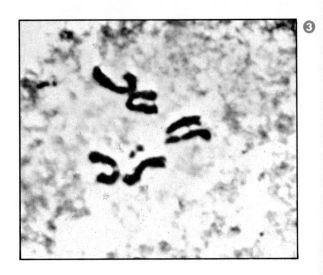

Note again the make-up of the chromosome content of a female body cell, and that of the male. We have labeled the X and Y chromosomes and included the traditional symbols for female and male. **4**

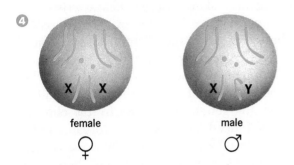

A female seems to have the XX chromosomes; a male, the XY chromosome pattern. Is this pattern supported by breeding experiments? Suppose we mate a male and female. What gametes are produced? (We have noted only the letters XX and XY representing the XX and XY chromosomes, since we are paying attention only to these. Of course, the other chromosomes are there as well.) Don't all eggs carry an X chromosome, while sperms carry either an X chromosome or a Y chromosome? **5**

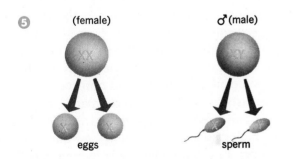

If we now place the letter representing these gametes on our square, we can determine the chromosome make-up of the zygotes produced. **6**

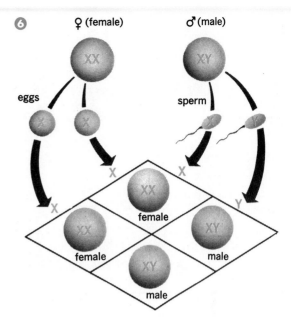

We find (as geneticists have found in many experiments) that whenever there are two X chromosomes (XX), the offspring is a female. Whenever the X and Y chromosomes are paired (XY), the offspring develops into a male. Clearly, whether the egg is fertilized by a sperm carrying an X or a Y chromosome determines the sex of the individual.

Later experiments have led to the conclusion that the Y chromosome has no direct effect in determining sex. It is the X chromosome that determines the sex of the individual fruit fly. (Further in your studies you will find that the Y chromosome actually contains very few genes.)

Apparently *two* X chromosomes (XX) make the fruit fly a female. The presence of only *one* X chromosome (XY) makes it a male. In fact, if for some reason the Y chromosome is lost, the animal is still a male. Clearly then, here is evidence that an inherited trait such as sex involves the chromosomes and thus lends support to Sutton's hypothesis.

439

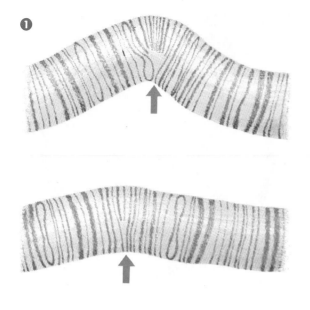

Further Evidence

Many studies soon confirmed Sutton's hypothesis. Evidence began to come from all directions. Geneticists have concluded that *Drosophila* must have hundreds of genes, since they have observed hundreds of traits in this animal that has been so important to the study of heredity. If *Drosophila* has hundreds of genes, where are they? It has only eight chromosomes; the genes must be in the chromosomes.

Scientists soon found, for example, that part of a chromosome can be lost. In *Drosophila* particularly, the changed chromosome can be identified and followed as it is passed on to the offspring. These offspring may show a certain abnormal characteristic, such as notches on the edges of their wings, or totally lack a certain characteristic. Undoubtedly, the gene for the normal characteristic is in the lost part of the chromosome. If the genes for the same characteristic are absent in both chromosomes, the offspring usually dies. The figure above illustrates portions of two chro-

mosomes of *Drosophila* showing a loss in ten and two bands, respectively. ❶

Others have shown that one part of a chromosome can, by accident, become attached to another chromosome. Then the offspring may show unusual characteristics or an unusual combination of characteristics. These changes in the offspring can be traced to the transferred part of the chromosome.

Through evidence of this kind, it has become clearer and clearer that the hereditary traits, the genes, are carried by the chromosomes. Indeed Thomas Hunt Morgan, and the scientists who assisted him in working with *Drosophila*, strengthened Sutton's hypothesis and developed the *Chromosome Theory of Heredity*. Stated simply, the theory says that the *chromosomes are the carriers of hereditary traits*. The Chromosome Theory of Heredity soon came to mean that the chromosomes were the carriers of the genes.

The Meaning of a Theory

The word "theory" is too often used to mean any kind of explanation. Thus someone will say, "My theory concerning flying saucers is that they are sent from a planet in outer space." The word *theory* as used by the scientist is a different matter. A theory, to have respectability in science, is an explanation of the facts known at the time. A fact, as we understand the word in science, is an observation confirmed by trained observers.

Scientists patiently observe many, many objects and events. Thus cytologists (sī·tol′ə·jists), biologists who study cells, saw chromosomes before these bodies were hypothesized to be carriers of hereditary traits. The presence of chromosomes in the cell nucleus was observed by many different biologists. The presence of chromosomes was a fact. Mendel first reported his work in 1866. It was really not before 1900 that other scientists confirmed his findings. As you will see later, the scientists Karl Correns, Hugo DeVries, and Eric von Tschermak—a German, a Dutchman, and an Austrian, respectively—added to Mendel's findings. Sutton, as you know, proposed that the genes are actual physical units in the chromosome. Next, Morgan and his students (in studying the inheritance of sex and other characteristics in *Drosophila*) actually associated certain hereditary traits with certain chromosomes. The only satisfactory explanation of all these facts is the Chromosome Theory of Heredity.

A theory, then, is a *satisfactory explanation* of the facts. It is a pattern that puts all the observations together into a sensible, satisfying explanation. What makes a theory satisfactory? A theory remains satisfactory as long as it explains the facts available. As soon as observations are made and confirmed that are not explained by the theory, scientists begin developing a *new* theory. The new theory must explain the facts available.

For the person who is not a scientist, a theory does more than explain the available facts. Since it is a pattern that brings together the observations of scientists, it helps us to view the world in an orderly way. That is, the theory helps us put many facts together in a pattern. Otherwise the world, as we see it, might seem to be in a jumble.

REVIEW

What is the evidence that leads to the following lines of reasoning? Use the historical and experimental facts you know in answering.

1. The hereditary material is in the nuclei of the gametes.

2. The hereditary material is in the chromosomes of the nuclei of the gametes.

3. In the zygote, one set of chromosomes (half the body chromosome number) from the male gamete and a similar set of chromosomes from the female gamete are sufficient to pass on the hereditary traits of the species.

4. Meiosis reduces the chromosome number by one half. Fertilization restores the body chromosome number. Mitosis maintains the body chromosome number.

5. The main difference in the behavior of chromosomes during mitosis and meiosis is the reduction in chromosome number during meiosis.

6. In *Drosophila*, the X chromosome determines (to a large extent) the sex of the individual.

NEW VIEW

1. In your earlier work, a theory was considered to be an "explanation of the available facts." What other function does a theory serve?

2. Man has a pattern of sex determination similar to that of *Drosophila*: XY signifies maleness, XX femaleness. In later work, you will find that this is not the entire story; other chromosomes also affect sex determination. Are there other patterns of sex determination? (*Clue:* Investigate this question for birds first.)

3. Find the contributions of each of these geneticists to the development of the Chromosome Theory of Heredity:

> Calvin B. Bridges
> Alfred H. Sturtevant
> Theophilus S. Painter

3. A CLUE TO THE MAKE–UP OF THE GENE

Recall the great host of animals and plants that make up the phyla you have studied: owls, oaks, elephants, eels, roses, rats, wheat, whales, dogs, dahlias, fruit, flies, corn, mosses, ferns, starfish, lobsters, bees, man—truly a great variety.

WHITE EYES

BROWN EYES

BAR EYES

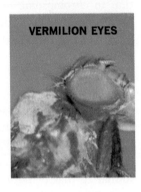

VERMILION EYES

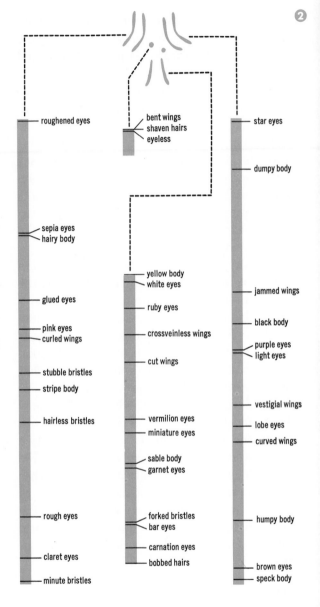

Focus on any one organism you have studied, say the fruit fly. Note the variety of its hereditary traits. It can have, and does have, either red eyes, white eyes, brown eyes, vermilion eyes, or eyes of several other colors. ❶ It can have, and does have, either long wings, short wings, or curly wings. By tracing the different chromosomes in *Drosophila*, and by tracing damaged chromosomes, various genes in *Drosophila* have been associated with various chromosomes. By tracing specific chromosomes (such as the X or Y chromosomes), and by various other ways, genes in *Drosophila* have actually been located in the different chromosomes. The result of this work over 35 years has been the development of chromosome maps. ❷ Geneticists are reasonably sure the "genes" (or *whatever genes are*) are located in the chromosomes at the places indicated. What kind of evidence confirms the location, or *locus* (lō′kəs), of each gene on a chromosome?

To find a clue to the nature of the gene, we need to do a simple investigation to get some idea of the size of the gene. Perhaps it is not so simple, but try it. ■

■ AN APPRENTICE INVESTIGATION into the Size of Genes

Measure the size of the nucleus of one of your cheek cells. First make a stained slide of your cheek cells. If you have not already done so, see the **On Your Own** section (p. 525). Stain it with iodine. Then examine the slide under the microscope.

This time use a micrometer disc, which your teacher will place inside the eyepiece of the microscope for you. In the illustration of the micrometer disc, notice the marks. ❶ Each space between the smallest mark is equal to 50 *microns*. If you are not already familiar with the metric system, you should know that

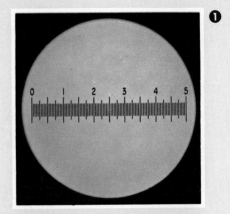

1,000 microns = 1 millimeter
25 millimeters = 1 inch

As the apparent size of the space between the marks on a micrometer varies with the power of your microscope, your teacher will tell you the number of microns in each small division of the micrometer disc you are using.

Sight the cell so that it falls under the micrometer disc. ❷ Using the high-power objective of your microscope, determine the number of small divisions on the micrometer scale that the cell covers. Then multiply the number of divisions the cell covers by the value your teacher will give you.* Your answer is the measurement of the cell in microns. (The value for each small division shown is 1.7 microns. Isn't the cell about 99 microns in diameter?) Now try to measure the nucleus.

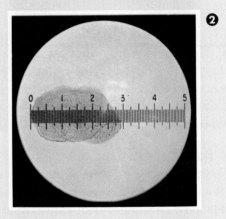

The average measurement of cells in one class showed the cheek cell to be an average of about 97 microns in diameter. The nucleus was about 7 microns.

What is your measurement? Your measurement will be very rough, of course, with an

* The numerals on the micrometer have to do with determining the value for each microscope, and they should be disregarded.

error perhaps of 20 to 30 percent. Nevertheless, we may assume that a nucleus of a human cell is roughly 5 to 7 microns. In that nucleus are packed 46 chromosomes. In these 46 chromosomes are all the genes that, at this moment, we consider responsible for the hereditary traits. What would be your hypothesis on the size of the gene?

An Investigation On Your Own

What is thought to be the size of the gene? Will your investigation show that a gene is actually a *recognizable* body?

What references will you use? Are they reliable?

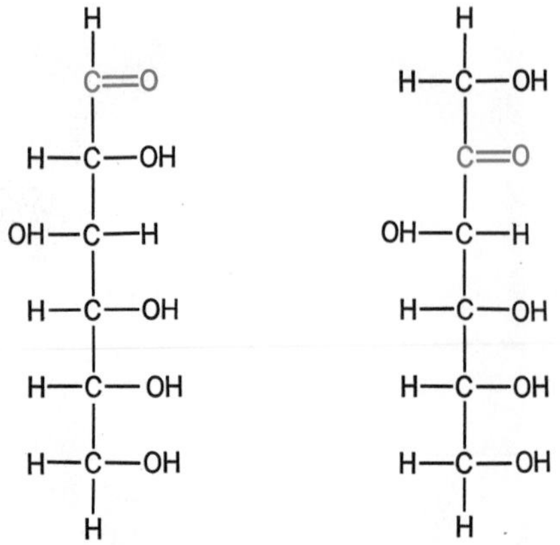

GLUCOSE   FRUCTOSE

In any event, a gene must be extremely tiny. How could a gene, such a tiny structure, be responsible for a hereditary trait? Perhaps the action of the gene is chemical in nature. Let's follow this line of reasoning to see where it leads us.

The Nature of the Gene

First, a gene must surely be made up of matter, and all matter is made up of atoms. So atoms must be smaller than genes. Atoms are very tiny indeed. For instance, it would take about two million atoms of hydrogen to span the diameter of the period at the end of this sentence. It is possible then that the gene could be made up of atoms combined in a molecule or molecules. Could there be enough space in a chromosome for all the molecules that make up the different genes?

Suppose the genes were made up of different combinations of certain molecules. Suppose these molecules could be arranged in the chromosomes in a manner that might account for the make-up of the various genes. Then, knowing how tiny atoms and molecules are, we might be able to account for the variety of traits in an organism. We might then be

partly satisfied that the eight chromosomes of *Drosophila* are responsible for its many hereditary traits. So, too, are the 46 chromosomes of man.

We do know that protoplasm is made up mainly of atoms of the elements carbon, hydrogen, oxygen, and nitrogen. Phosphorus and sulfur, among other elements, are also present—especially in proteins. Can a gene, perhaps, be a small particle made up of atoms, of carbon, hydrogen, oxygen, and nitrogen, and other atoms such as phosphorus?

We know further that a molecule made up of relatively few atoms can change its character and action simply by a rearrangement of its atoms, or by adding new ones. You already suspect this from your study of the compounds in protoplasm. For example, examine once again a diagram of a molecule of the common sugar, glucose. ❶ Earlier (p. 164) you studied this molecule written as a "ring" formula. But chemists frequently write the formula as a "straight chain," as shown here. Now count the number of atoms of carbon, hydrogen, and oxygen each formula contains. Aren't they the same? Do the same for the molecule of another sugar, fructose. What is the difference between glucose and fructose? The diagram above clearly indicates the difference in structure between the two molecules. A different placement of one carbon and one oxygen atom results in a new kind of sugar. The structure of the molecule plays an important part in its action.

Recall, too, that similar molecules can combine to form polymers (p. 165). Thus, amino acids added to each other can form complex proteins. The complex proteins have different properties from the simple amino acids, the parts that make them up. What has this to do with chromosomes and genes?

444

Investigation has shown that the chromosome is composed of substances that have arranged themselves to form a long and complex molecule. Although your knowledge of chemistry is insufficient to fully understand it, let's take a first glimpse at the structure of a chromosome. This is done with the clear understanding that the chemistry of the chromosome is very complex. Certainly it is difficult for a beginning student to understand all the details. But at least you will be aware that research is going on that has lifted part of the curtain of mystery. Mendel would have been delighted to know the little bit of information you are about to study. Knowing even this, he would have felt that his work had a more secure basis—indeed, a solid basis.

100 Years and More After Mendel

When Thomas Hunt Morgan and his students proposed the Chromosome Theory of Heredity, they clearly meant that the chromosomes are the basis of heredity. That is, the chromosomes carry the hereditary units called genes. But the chemical make-up of the chromosomes was just beginning to be studied. Morgan and his students had only glimpses of forthcoming events.

Chemical analyses of the nuclei of a great number of different cells in a variety of organisms were made by a number of scientists. Whether the organism was a protozoan, a yeast, an insect, or a mammal, the nucleus of each cell was invariably found to contain nucleic acids. When the heads of various sperm, which contain very little else but chromosomes, were analyzed, scientists found mainly nucleic acid molecules. Chromosomes were then suspected of being made up of nucleic acid molecules. Many different kinds of experiments were soon performed to determine the *kind* of nucleic acid molecule found in

chromosomes. One of the most important experiments was designed by O. T. Avery, C. M. MacLeod, and M. McCarty working at the Rockefeller Institute for Medical Research in New York City. Much of their work involved numerous experiments with pneumococci.

To begin with, you ought to know that there are several kinds of pneumococci. You recall that the pneumococcus is a bacterium that causes pneumonia. One kind of pneumococcus has a capsule on it. Another kind is without a capsule. The trait, ability to form a capsule or not form a capsule, is inherited. That is, both kinds of bacteria produce offspring like themselves by binary fission.

The experimenters reasoned perhaps somewhat as follows. If we can find the substance that is responsible for the formation of a capsule in some pneumococci, perhaps we can produce this trait in the bacteria that are normally without capsules. After much careful work, they isolated this substance from the bacteria with capsules. This substance was *deoxyribonucleic acid,* commonly called **DNA.** No doubt you are already familiar with DNA as a word. What would happen if this DNA, from the bacteria with capsules, were to enter the bacteria without capsules? What is your hypothesis? Before you go on reading, form a reasonable hypothesis.

When the DNA from the bacteria with capsules is placed in contact with the bacteria without capsules, the DNA enters them. How exciting it must have been for the experimenters to wait for the outcome of their experiment.

Clearly, the DNA from the bacteria with capsules entered the bacteria without capsules, and enabled them to form capsules. In other words, a hereditary trait had been changed by DNA.

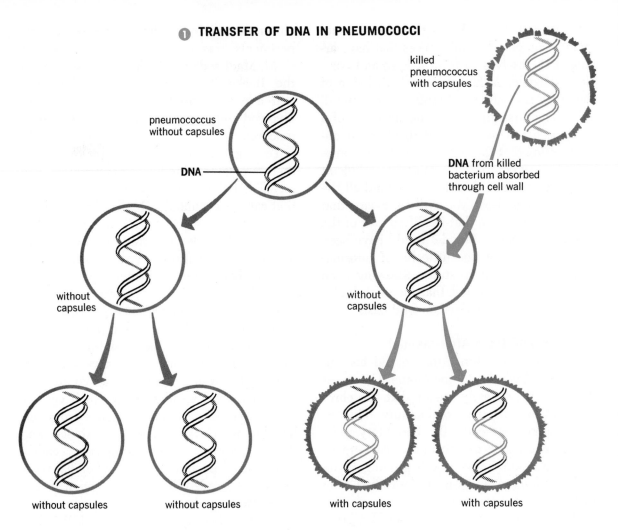

killed
pneumococcus
with capsules

pneumococcus
without capsules

DNA —

DNA from killed
bacterium absorbed
through cell wall

without
capsules

without
capsules

without capsules

without capsules

with capsules

with capsules

The results of their experiment are shown above. ❶ Was your hypothesis correct?

Avery, MacLeod, and McCarty had shown for the first time that a *substance* that controls heredity can be extracted from one organism and transferred to another organism in which the trait is normally absent. (Bacteria without capsules produced capsules.) Thus, they showed that the substance DNA acts like a gene and is, truly, the hereditary material of the cell.

Since this experiment in 1944, many related ones have been performed. Experiments with viruses, other bacteria, and complex plants and animals show that the hereditary material of the chromosome is indeed DNA, or a substance closely related.

Is DNA the gene? Is the chromosome made up of DNA in such a way that its structure might explain the variety of traits in a single organism? We shall see; but first we need further information on the way genes act. Then we shall return to a closer examination of DNA, this most important of all substances as far as the heredity of organisms is concerned. We leave this to the next chapter.

1. What is a chromosome map?
2. What evidence do we have that genes exist?
3. What is the significance of the work of Avery, MacLeod, and McCarty?

NEW VIEW

Suppose that the DNA of the bacteria with capsules had been placed in contact with the bacteria lacking capsules. Suppose further that the bacteria without capsules were unaffected, that is, they did not form capsules.

a. What would the experimenters have done?
b. What conclusions might they have drawn?
c. How could they have changed their hypothesis?

4. RELATING THE CONCEPTS

You may know the old maxim, "Blood will tell." The maxim was based on the erroneous concept that it was the blood that carried hereditary traits. Of course, we now might say "Chromosomes will tell." But even this is not the entire story, as you shall see when you have completed the work of this unit.

As is our custom, however, it is useful to see where we are.

Reviewing the Concepts

We have emphasized two major concepts.

▶ *Chromosomes carry hereditary traits.* If we had made a statement about the function of the chromosomes some 40 years ago, we might have said more definitely, *Chromosomes are the carriers of the hereditary traits, the genes.* As you shall see, we say chromosomes carry hereditary traits.

The two statements seem to be alike, but closer study will indicate that one statement indicates the *probability* that the chromosomes are the *only* carriers of hereditary traits. The other statement indicates that the chromosomes carry hereditary traits, but there is a *possibility* that hereditary traits are also carried elsewhere. Which statement of the concept indicates the possibility that hereditary traits are also carried elsewhere? The next chapter will carry the concept forward.

In any event, there is no doubt that the chromosomes carry what we have called *genes.* That is what the Chromosome Theory of Heredity indicates. Are genes the hereditary traits? Mendel thought so.

Is DNA the gene?

At this point in your study, you may be convinced of this. Remain skeptical for a little while at least.

▶ *When gametes are formed, the two members of each pair of chromosomes separate into different gametes.* If we now focus on the genes in the chromosomes, we may state this concept another way: When gametes are formed, the two members of each pair of genes *must separate*, and only *one* of each pair can go to a gamete. This statement is known as Mendel's *Law of Segregation.*

The meaning of this law is clear. If a parent has a gene make-up of RR, each gamete will carry one gene for R, not two. If the parent is rr, each of its gametes will carry a single gene for r. If the parent is Rr, half its gametes will carry a gene for R, the other half will carry a gene for r.

Testing Yourself

On the basis of your understanding of the concepts (and your study of organisms) found in this chapter, try to determine whether each of the following statements is true or false. Explain the reason for your choice in a few sentences.

1. In the mating of two yellow-seeded pea plants containing the genes YY, only green-seeded offspring were produced. Yellow (Y) is dominant.

2. In the mating of two green-seeded pea plants containing the genes yy, only yellow-seeded offspring were produced.

3. The mating of a tall plant (dominant) with a dwarf plant (recessive) (TT × tt) results only in plants with a gene make-up of Tt.

4. The mating of two hybrids (Rr × Rr) generally results in the production of 3 red-flowering plants to 1 white-flowering plant. Red (R) is dominant.

5. The mating of two hybrids (Rr × Rr) *could* result in the production of all red-flowering plants.

6. A fruit fly with a chromosome make-up of XX is a male.

7. Meiosis reduces the body chromosome number by one half.

8. Mitosis reduces the chromosome number by one half.

9. Theory and fact are identical.

Extending the Concepts

Investigation 1. Let's try crossing a plant that is hybrid for two traits. You have been working with one set of genes in an organism. That is, there is a pair of genes for each trait, seed color (yellow or green), seed shape (smooth or wrinkled), or height (tall or dwarf). We have been able to pose certain types of problems to you. Do you recall what happens when hybrid yellow-seeded peas are mated (p. 429)?

1 YY = yellow (dominant)
2 Yy = yellow (hybrid dominant)
1 yy = green (recessive)
3:1 = ratio of yellow seeds to green seeds

Suppose, however, that the yellow-seeded hybrid (Yy) also has smooth seeds. Furthermore, it is hybrid for smooth seeds (Ss). Both green and wrinkled are recessive traits. Thus its genetic make-up is YySs (yellow, smooth seeds). Notice that there are as usual two genes for color (Y and y) and two genes for shape (S and s). Here they are shown combined into one cell. ❶

Yy Ss

What are the possible types of gametes that this parent cell can produce? Apply the Law of Segregation. Notice we are assuming that each of these genes is on a *different* chromosome. Further, we know that for each trait there must be a *pair* of genes. Therefore, there are two pairs of chromosomes involved; one pair containing the gene for seed color, the other pair containing the gene for seed shape.

During meiosis, each gene segregates from its mate into a different gamete. That is, the genes for color segregate independently of the genes for shape. Therefore, the gene for either color can combine with the gene for either shape. In other words, how the chromosomes line up during the formation of gametes (meiosis) determines the possible types of gametes. Thus, *four* types of gametes are possible: Ys, ys, YS, yS. ❷

    ❷

YS   Ys   yS   ys

Now as you mate the plants, remember that the sperm nuclei can be of four types. So can the egg nuclei. Study the diagram of

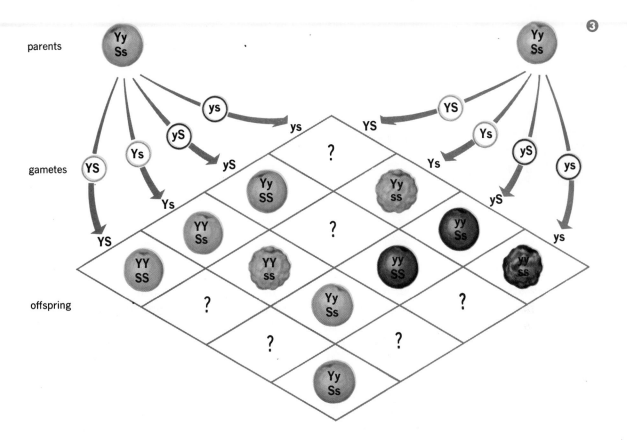

parents

gametes

offspring

the mating. ❸ Can you give the gene make-up for the offspring in the empty boxes? (*Do not write in this book.*)

We predict that when you complete the matings you will find the following ratio.

9 yellow, smooth-seeded plants
3 yellow, wrinkled-seeded plants
3 green, smooth-seeded plants
1 green, wrinkled-seeded plant

The ratio of offspring resulting from the mating of plants that are hybrid for two traits (called a *di*hybrid) is 9:3:3:1. Compare this ratio with the ratio of offspring resulting from the mating of plants hybrid for a single trait.

Try This: A purebred rough, black-furred guinea pig is mated to a smooth, white-furred guinea pig. Only rough, black-furred hybrids are produced. What is the result of the mating of two rough, black-furred hybrids? What is the ratio?

Investigation 2. Is a given organism purebred or hybrid for a given trait?

Suppose you had a black-furred guinea pig. (Black is dominant over white.) What might be its genetic make-up—BB or Bb? It could be either. If it were BB it would be a purebred dominant. If it were Bb it would be hybrid. How can you tell?

If you were to mate this black-furred guinea pig with a white one, would the results (the offspring in the litter) enable you to determine whether the black-furred parent was BB or Bb? Explain your answer.

18 | Genes in a Code

The danger of simplifying any subject is that it may appear too simple. For this reason we urged you to remain skeptical until more of the story came to light. We repeat, you are really *at the very beginning* in your study of the way in which organisms inherit traits.

We now dig deeper into the geneticist's examination of the gene. But for the moment we leave the gene itself to examine the environment in which it acts. Then we shall return to focus on the gene.

1. GENES AND ENVIRONMENT

You may have noticed that an oak seedling or a magnolia seedling or an apple seedling does not flower the first year of its growth. In fact, it may take several years before it flowers. Why is this so? Surely, the oak, the magnolia, or the apple have the genes for flowering. When the sperm nucleus fused with the egg nucleus in fertilization to form the zygote nucleus, the genes were there. What caused the delay? To discover an important aspect in the action of genes, however, we turn our attention to the study of a rabbit.

A Rabbit's Fur

The Himalayan rabbit has a white coat except for its nose, feet, tail, and ears. They are black. Obviously, both the white and black colors result from the action of genes. But, suppose you were to shave the fur off the back of a Himalayan rabbit and were to place an ice pack over the spot while the fur grew out again. What would happen? The fur, which had been white before you shaved it, would grow out black. ❶ Were the genes under the ice pack for white fur or for black fur?

Obviously, the genes were capable of producing either a black coat or a white coat. A change in the environment made the difference. In this case, the change in environment was a change in temperature. The ears, nose, tail, and feet are just a bit colder than the rest of the body. It is thought that this temperature difference is responsible for the difference in color; that is, genes, under different conditions, produce different results.

Clearly, then, the gene for "black" acted only at a certain temperature. In other words, *the gene acted in a certain way only in a special environment.* This may not surprise you. In fact, your work with "pieces" of an organism placed in different environments showed that they developed differently. Do you recall that pieces of the same potato, each piece having the same genes, developed differently in different environments (p. 205)? How true is this generally for genes and their behavior? We look for further information in the study of a salamander.

Genes and the Internal Environment

Near Mexico City, Mexico, and in several other places, there lives a salamander that breathes with external gills, even as an adult. The Mexicans gave it the name Axolotl (ak′sə·lot′l). 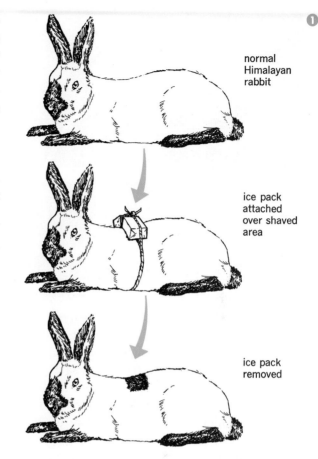 In many places in America there lives a salamander that breathes, as an adult, with internal lungs instead of external gills. It is called a Tiger salamander, or Ambystoma (am·bis′tə·mə).

normal Himalayan rabbit

ice pack attached over shaved area

ice pack removed

Notice how different Axolotl and Ambystoma look. Zoologists once thought that they belonged to different species. However, it was found that young Axolotls changed into Ambystomas when they were fed an extract of the thyroid gland. The two animals are the same species. Axolotl is an immature form of Ambystoma. Apparently, the larva does not change its gills into lungs in some regions because of a thyroid deficiency. Add thyroid extract to the larva's diet and the genes are capable of completing the transition, or metamorphosis, from the larva to the adult Ambystoma.

Evidently, the gene or genes responsible for the metamorphosis of Axolotl act best in an environment with available thyroxin. The genes that act to change the larval salamander to the adult do so only when sufficient thyroid extract is present. The evidence that the environment affects the action of the genes is overwhelming. The gene carries a potential; the environment determines its expression.

Now, examine two purebred rats from the same litter. ❶ Purebred, in this case, refers to the fact that they are not hybrid for the traits affecting growth. Purebred animals or plants are said to be **homozygous** (hō′mŏ·zī′gōs) for the trait being considered. Thus, a purebred yellow-seeded pea plant (YY) is homozygous. On the other hand, a hybrid organism is **heterozygous** (het′ər·ō·zī′gōs), so a hybrid yellow-seeded pea plant (Yy) is heterozygous.

The rats shown are homozygous for the genes affecting growth. The rat at the top has merely been fed a diet deficient in one substance—the vitamin thiamin. To repeat, both animals have the same genes for the growth factor; only the environment has changed. Do you know of any similar effects in other organisms—in man, for example?

Do you recall the effects of an increase or decrease in growth hormones (p. 193)? And perhaps you know that identical twins—twins with the identical gene pattern—have occasionally been separated when they were very young. Studies show that if these twins are raised in distinctly different environments, they may differ not only in weight but also in height. Once again, we are forced to conclude that genes produce certain effects in certain environments. That is, genes and environment together produce certain results.

Interaction of Genes

Mendel chose well when he chose the garden pea as an experimental plant in which to study traits that were either dominant or recessive. But for almost 40 years Mendel's work was unknown. This may surprise you, but in 1866, when Mendel published his work, communication was not as efficient nor as fast as it is today. However, at the beginning of this century, three scientists, at almost the same time, discovered Mendel's work. Each had been reading the reports of other scientists in an attempt to find some explanation of the results of their work with hybrids. They were DeVries, von Tschermak, and Correns. They confirmed Mendel's observations, and each, as is the habit of scientists, carried his research further. It is Corren's work that we will investigate.

Correns worked with a common flower, the four o'clock. When white four o'clocks are mated, all the offspring are white. When red four o'clocks are mated, all the offspring are red. Surely, one trait must be dominant over the other. Or is it?

❷

Correns found that when he mated red four o'clocks with white four o'clocks, the off-spring were neither red nor white—but *pink*. **❷** It seemed as if the pink hybrids were formed by a *blending* of the color red with white. In fact, this kind of inheritance was first called "blending inheritance." However, this was not an accurate description. If the genes for red and white actually blended,

❸

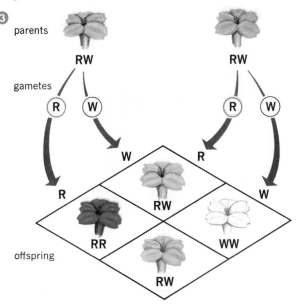

parents

gametes

offspring

pure red color and pure white could not come out in the offspring when pink hybrids are crossed. But Correns found that when the pink hybrids are crossed, both red and white four o'clocks do appear again. Therefore, we can conclude that the two genes somehow modify each other.

Suppose we mate two pink hybrids (RW). What kind of offspring do we get? **❸** Red flowers (RR), white flowers (WW), and pink flowers (RW). Notice that we have used two different letters, both capitals, to represent a pair of contrasting genes. This procedure is usually used when neither one of the genes is dominant.

Evidently, the gene for red and the gene for white have not blended. Otherwise, how could pink hybrids produce red or white off-spring? Instead of blending, the genes have simply *interacted*. That is, the DNA produc-ing red color has somehow interacted with the DNA producing white to produce pink. Perhaps the DNA for red color doesn't inter-act with the DNA for white. Perhaps it is the substances they produce that interact or blend. We shall examine this idea more deeply as we study more evidence of how the genes act.

Development of a Chick

Results that provide more evidence on the action of DNA is to be found in the develop-ment of a chick. The eggs we eat are usually unfertilized eggs, so they would not develop into chicks. A fertilized egg, however, needs only to be kept at the proper temperature and humidity, and turned over occasionally to develop into a chick. Hens sit on their eggs to keep them warm and humid; and they turn the eggs over once in a while with their feet.

You can observe the development of a chick for yourself. ■

To observe the stages in the development of a chick embryo, you will need a half-dozen fertilized eggs. You will also need a small incubator. Set and maintain the temperature of the eggs at 100°F (about 38°C). Be sure there is a dish of water to maintain the humidity. Turn the eggs over every day.

Examine one egg at the beginning. Crack the egg open and examine it with a hand lens. A shell covers and protects a chicken egg. Underneath the shell are two rather tough membranes. Usually, these are separated at one end of the egg by a small air chamber. The main mass of the egg is made up of a yellowish yolk surrounded by albumen (the "white" of the egg). ❶ Yolk contains fat, proteins, carbohydrates, salts, and vitamins. The albumen is chiefly protein. Together, the yolk and albumen make up the stored food that the developing chick embryo will live on until it pecks its way out of the shell.

Attached to the surface of the yolk is a small disc containing living protoplasm. This is where the embryo will develop. In a fertilized egg, the original cell (formed by the union of the sperm cell and the egg cell) has already begun dividing by the time the egg is laid by the hen. Nevertheless, the dividing cells will be impossible to see with a hand lens.

If the egg is incubated (either by the hen or in an incubator), the small disc of living protoplasm grows larger and changes shape. The original cell divides to make two cells. Each of these cells divides to make four; the four divide to make eight; the eight divide to make sixteen; and so on. Soon, different cells begin to divide at different rates to produce a mass of cells.

After only 24 hours the chick embryo is clearly visible. Very carefully crack another

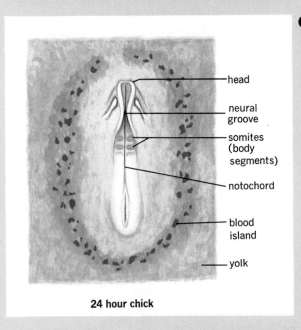

head

neural groove

somites (body segments)

notochord

blood island

yolk

24 hour chick

egg and place its contents in a dish containing a small amount of a 1 percent salt solution that is slightly warm. Compare your observations with the diagram of a 24-hour-old chick embryo. ❷ The *head* is clearly indicated. Down the center of the back is a tiny cord, the *notochord*. It is important to our study of genes to remember the presence of the notochord.

Next, examine a chick at about the 48-hour stage. ❸ Notice how fast the embryo has grown. The original cell has become many thousands of cells. Moreover, the body has begun to have a definite shape and the body parts are carrying on their specialized work. You can easily see the heart beat in a live 48-

hour chick embryo. The *heart* pumps blood out to the yolk, which is now contained within a **yolk sac.** From the yolk, food is transported to the active and rapidly dividing cells. Other blood vessels carry waste materials out of the embryo's body and deposit them in a special sac called the **allantois.** Respiration is through the shell. Oxygen diffuses through the shell into the fluid in the allantois, and blood vessels carry it into the embryo's body. Carbon dioxide diffuses out from the allantois into the air surrounding the porous egg shell.

At the 72-hour stage, the blood vessels extend out through the yolk sac and the allantois. ❹ Notice, too, the heart, eye, wing buds,

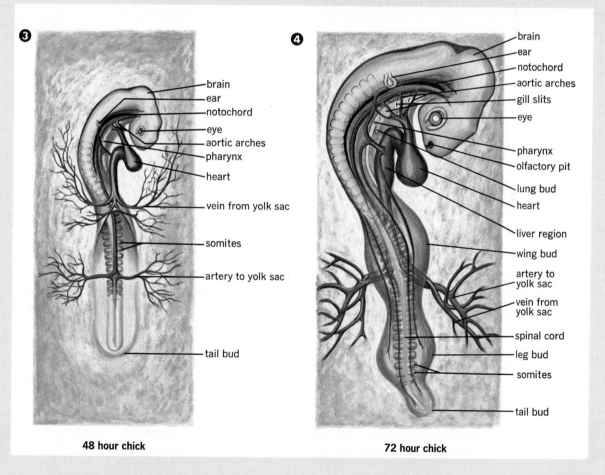

❸
brain
ear
notochord
eye
aortic arches
pharynx
heart
vein from yolk sac
somites
artery to yolk sac
tail bud

48 hour chick

❹
brain
ear
notochord
aortic arches
gill slits
eye
pharynx
olfactory pit
lung bud
heart
liver region
wing bud
artery to yolk sac
vein from yolk sac
spinal cord
leg bud
somites
tail bud

72 hour chick

and leg buds. The wing buds and leg buds will, of course, develop into the wings and legs a little later on. Notice, finally, the *gill slits*. These, like the notochord, are evidence that the chicken is a chordate. What happens to the gill slits in later stages? Does a newly hatched chick have gill slits? Does a fish have gill slits? Does a frog have gill slits at any stage in its life history?

Permit the two remaining eggs to develop fully into chicks. It will take 21 days from the beginning of incubation. What characteristics will the newly hatched chick have?

If you are fortunate enough to observe the chick breaking out of its shell, you may also notice another interesting structure. A tiny bump called an **egg tooth** develops on the tip of the chick's beak by about the 14th day. The chick uses this egg tooth to crack the shell.

An Investigation On Your Own

You have two chicks left. Feed them very carefully and maintain the best environmental conditions possible. Where will you find out how to do this?

When do the chicks develop their first secondary sex characteristics? (What are secondary sex characteristics?) Why did they not develop these characteristics at hatching?

What color are the chickens when they are hatched? When do their feathers begin to change color? When is the change complete?

A study of the developing chick indicates certain aspects of the action of DNA. Long before the 21 days are up, the chick has all of its body parts, down to the tiniest details, including scales on its legs, claws on its feet, and feathers over its body. The remarkable fact is that in only 21 days a single fertilized egg cell has developed into a complete chicken. It has done so by converting the stored food inside the shell into living tissues and energy—all under the direction of its DNA.

Under the Direction of DNA

While a chick has DNA for a *notochord* and for *gill slits*, these structures do not continue to develop in the embryo. The mammalian embryo also has a notochord and gill slits. Study the diagrams of the different embryos—fish, amphibian, reptile, bird, and mammal. ❶ Each of these embryos contains a notochord, gill slits, and tail. Yet in none of these does the notochord develop. In the reptile, bird, and mammal, gill slits are not developed in the young or the adult. The human embryo, an example of a mammal, also has a notochord, gill slits, and a tail, but none of these traits is present at birth.

What are we to conclude from these observations? The DNA, that is, the gene, for certain traits is present in the embryo, but is not *expressed* in the adult. The full action of the gene for notochord and gill slits is *suppressed*. This, then, is another example of an important concept. In other words, a gene in a chromosome does not act independently of other genes in the chromosomes. The DNA of the chromosomes act together. Otherwise the parts of an embryo would not develop in *sequence* (one after the other) nor in a *relationship of position* (one next to the other).

You could not help but notice the orderly development when you examined the incubated 24-, 48-, and 72-hour chicks. Did not the traits seem to develop in sequence and in relation to each other? For example, did the heart develop *without* blood vessels?

Note too, that the brain developed in the head, not in the foot. In normal development the genes of an organism interact with each other. That is, the DNA seems to function as a code that "tells" the embryo how to develop. For example, at a certain time the chick embryo develops an egg tooth, which is useful to the chick for getting out of the shell and apparently has no other purpose.

How do we use the term *code?* Below is a sample of the international Morse code and its translation. A code is, of course, a system of symbols that may be used for communicating instructions.

Translation: Duplicate this DNA

Below is a code used in a computer. The code is both abbreviated and compact. It can be crowded into a smaller space than what it stands for. The code instructs the computer to do complex tasks.

A
B A 1
● ● ● ○ ○ ○

It is useful to think of the chromosomes as carrying a code of heredity. From this point of view we can consider the DNA in the chromosomes as a *code of heredity that "tells" the organism how to develop.* As we continue our study, we may discard or we may reconfirm this view.

REVIEW

1. What evidence can you give to support *or* disprove each of the following statements?

 a. The environment of the gene includes not only the external environment of the organism, but also its internal environment.

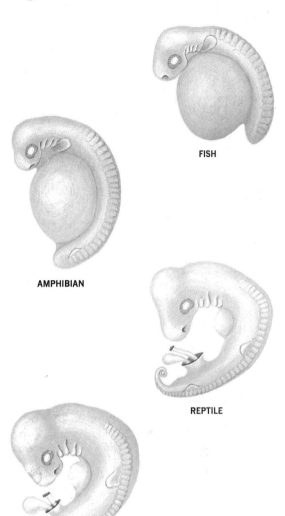

① COMPARISON OF VERTEBRATE EMBRYOS

FISH

AMPHIBIAN

REPTILE

BIRD

MAMMAL

b. A gene seems to act only in a special environment.

c. Genes interact.

d. In the development of an embryo, genes seem to act in sequence.

e. The action of genes may be *expressed* or *suppressed,* depending on the environment.

2. What is the reasoning behind the designation of DNA as a "code" of heredity?

3. Purebred round squash plants (RR) crossed with purebred long squash (LL) produce oval squash plants (RL). What type of offspring could two oval squash plants (RL × RL) produce? Work this out as you did with four o'clocks.

NEW VIEW

Look carefully at the diagrams of an embryo of a fish and an embryo of a mammal (pig) on page 457. Note the gill slits and tail in both.

a. In which is there full expression of the genes for gill slits?

b. In which is there suppression of full development of the action of the genes for gill slits?

c. Is there full expression or suppression of the tail in both animals?

2. GENES AND THE CELL

Have you ever wondered why birds and mammals grow eyes in their heads, not, for instance, on their feet; or why nails grow on the ends of the toes and not, for instance, on the head. Why, if every body cell has a full set of chromosomes, should this be so?

Since the nuclei of every cell (except the sex cells) are identical, the chromosomes are also identical. If the chromosomes are identical, then the genes must be identical. If the genes are identical, then each cell nuclei must have the same DNA code. Why, then,

does a cell in the region of the head produce substances to form eyes while a cell in the region of the toe produces substances that form nails? What about the cytoplasm? Is it identical?

Recall your study of the structure of the cell. The nucleus is bathed in cytoplasm. Earlier we were content to label these structures in the cell—nucleus (with its chromosomes), cytoplasm, and cell membrane. Now, as we examine the cytoplasm more closely, we find that it is made up of various structures. ❶ Examine the cell for a few moments, and note particularly the structures called **ribosomes.** We shall return to them shortly.

In any event, observe that the cytoplasm has a complex structure. Perhaps it is the cytoplasm that holds the answer to the question: How do different parts of an organism have *different* structures if all of its cells have the *same* chromosomes and genes? We may get some interesting clues by studying the cytoplasm further.

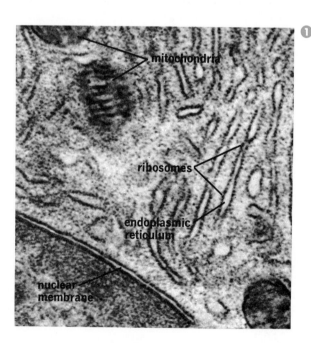

❶

mitochondria

ribosomes

endoplasmic reticulum

nuclear membrane

Genes and Cytoplasm

Sometimes organisms seem particularly well suited for certain investigations. For instance, *Drosophila*, with its small number of chromosomes and its easy breeding habits, seems to be "made" for the study of heredity just as Mendel's garden peas, with their traits of self-pollination, seemed ready-made for his experiments. To find the answer to our question of why and how different parts of the same organism have different structures, we shall investigate another organism that is relatively simple—an alga, the capped *Acetabularia*.

There are two species of *single-celled* capped algae that we are interested in. One species has a cap shaped like an umbrella; the other species has a berry-type cap. Both types are two to three inches long. Both have their *single nucleus* embedded in the base of the cell.

If we wish, we can cut away part of the cytoplasm very easily. Furthermore, we can graft the cytoplasmic "stem" of one species, say the umbrella-capped one, onto the base of the other alga. This has been done, as shown in the illustration. ❷ Study the drawing carefully as you read the description of the experimental procedure.

Remember that we started out to determine what effect cytoplasm has on the development of a trait. In this case, the trait is the *shape* of the cap—umbrella cap or berry cap. We cut off the cytoplasmic top of the berry-cap alga. We do the same for the umbrella-cap alga—and we throw away both caps. Then we graft the cytoplasmic stem from the berry-cap alga onto the base of the umbrella-cap alga. Remember that the base contains the nucleus. Which cap will the new alga develop—umbrella cap or berry cap? *It develops an umbrella cap.*

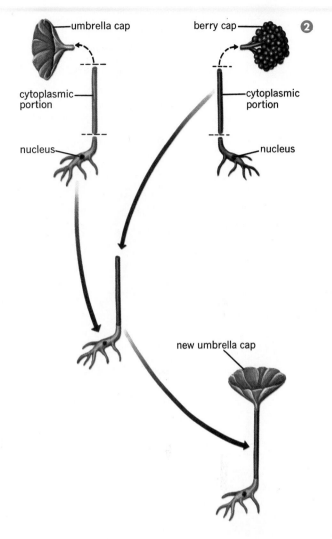

Apparently the nucleus has a very strong influence on the cytoplasm. The genes (in the nucleus of the umbrella-cap alga) dictated to the cytoplasm of the berry-cap alga what kind of cap to form.

Suppose we now graft the cytoplasmic stem from the umbrella-cap alga onto the base of the berry-cap alga. What kind of cap will develop in this organism? If the nucleus (that is, the genes) influences the foreign cytoplasm, then what should the cap be? Develop a hypothesis. Then read the note at

459

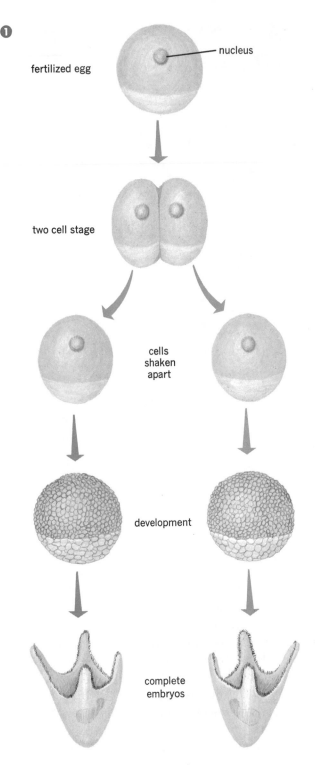

①

fertilized egg — nucleus

two cell stage

cells shaken apart

development

complete embryos

the bottom of this page to find out what kind of cap actually developed.* Was your hypothesis correct? From such experiments, we conclude that the genes exert their effect through the cytoplasm.

Another Experiment

Suppose we now study an experiment using a different organism—a sea urchin. Sea urchins are marine organisms (echinoderms) that produce eggs and sperms in large numbers. The eggs can easily be fertilized in pans of sea water in a laboratory; then the developing young embryos can be studied.

In fertilized sea urchin eggs, we find that each egg divides into two cells, then four, and so on; but, by removing the element calcium from the sea water, we can shake the fertilized egg cells apart at the two-cell stage. Each cell forms a complete embryo. **①** That is, two sea urchins (twins) result from one fertilized egg. If we do this at the four-cell stage, four embryos develop (quadruplets). What are we to conclude from experiments such as this? Apparently, if the cytoplasm divides equally (as it does in mitosis), then the gene and cytoplasm develop normally.

As further evidence of the importance of the cytoplasm, scientists have pricked sea urchin eggs that have *not* been fertilized. The eggs develop normally. These eggs, not having been fertilized, have only half the chromosome number. Apparently in some organisms, if the cytoplasm of the egg is complete, the embryo will develop with only half the chromosome number.

By using a centrifuge (a device that whirls the eggs about), we can extract the nucleus of the egg without damaging its cytoplasm. Then we have an egg without a nucleus,

* The organism developed a berry cap.

which, when fertilized by a sperm cell, proceeds to develop.

Consider again how the egg cell normally divides when it undergoes the first cell division. The egg cell divides in a *vertical plane,* much like the planes between the sections of an orange. But suppose we were to cut an egg in a *horizontal plane.* 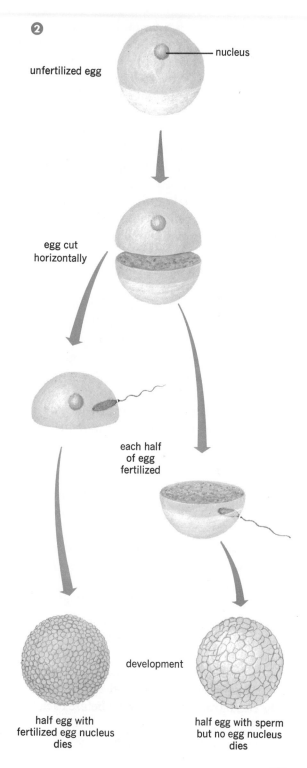 One half of the egg might have an egg nucleus; the other half would not. Both halves heal. We would then have eggs with half the cytoplasm, but the cytoplasm comes from different parts of the egg—upper part and lower. If each half is fertilized by a sperm, the half-eggs begin to divide. Should they develop normally? They don't. Both soon die.

The half-egg with the fertilized nucleus has a normal fertilized nucleus and, perhaps, the upper half of the cytoplasm. To all appearances, it had everything the cells that developed into twins had. Yet it dies.

After many such experiments, biologists have concluded that the two halves of eggs divided in the vertical plane received similar cytoplasm. Therefore, development was normal. The two halves divided on the horizontal plane did not receive similar cytoplasm; therefore, development was abnormal. In other words, the lower part of the egg has *some* of the cytoplasmic material needed for normal development, but *not all.* The upper half has *some* cytoplasmic materials needed for normal development, but *not all.* Only when the egg divides in a vertical plane does the egg get all the cytoplasmic material needed for normal development.

From this experiment and others, it seems that the cytoplasm has a great deal of influence on the development of the embryo. In other words, the cytoplasm is needed for full action of the genes. Genes alone are not enough. Genes and cytoplasm act together.

unfertilized egg

nucleus

egg cut
horizontally

each half
of egg
fertilized

development

half egg with
fertilized egg nucleus
dies

half egg with sperm
but no egg nucleus
dies

461

In Summary: The Gene and Its Environment

As of now, the great amount of experimental work that has been done seems to support what we have uncovered in these two accounts of experiments with two different organisms. In the experiment with the umbrella- and the berry-cap algae, the materials in the nucleus (the genes) seemed to have an overwhelming effect on the cytoplasm. In the experiment with the sea urchin eggs, the materials in the cytoplasm had an effect on the genes. In experiments with four o'clocks, we also found that genes interact to produce certain effects.

At this point we may conclude that *genes and cytoplasm interact to produce their effects.* In other words, it is not the gene alone, but the gene in its environment that produces a given trait. Genes interact with genes; genes interact with cytoplasm. In short, genes are affected by their environment. With this knowledge, we have begun to gain further insight into the vast concept that *an organism is the product of its heredity and environment.*

REVIEW

1. What evidence is there that in the development of a trait (at least of certain traits) that genes and cytoplasm act together?

2. Is there any evidence, up to now, that an organism is *not* the product of its heredity and environment? Explain your answer.

3. Explain how each of the following procedures can contribute to our understanding of the influence of cytoplasm on the development of an embryo.

a. separating the two cells that result from the first division of a fertilized egg

b. cutting an egg horizontally before each half is fertilized

c. pricking unfertilized eggs

NEW VIEW

What is the significance of the following observations?

a. Certain kernels of some varieties of corn are red in color. The red color does not develop in strong light.

b. Some barberries have rich red leaves. If you push aside the outer leaves, those hidden from the sun are pale red or greenish.

3. CRACKING THE CODE

Chromosomes are remarkable structures. The genes in the chromosome somehow act at the proper time and seem to do so by interacting with each other and with the environment in which they do their work. The *environment* for any gene consists of:

a. *other genes.* For example, Correns found that in four o'clocks the genes for red color interacted with genes for white color to produce pink flowers.

b. the *cytoplasm* (a kind of environment) outside the nucleus. For example, in sea urchin eggs the genes interact with certain parts of the cytoplasm in the development of the organism.

c. the *environment within the organism.* For example, certain organs, such as gill slits and a notochord, will develop only at a certain time in the development of the body of the chick.

d. the *environment outside the organism.* For example, in the potato, the development of chlorophyll depends on the amount of light in the environment.

"Direction" from the Chromosomes

In our study of the umbrella-cap alga (*Acetabularia*, p. 459), we began to understand that the nucleus *directs* the development of certain traits. Moreover, it directs this development even through strange cytoplasm. Thus an umbrella-cap nucleus directed berry-cap cytoplasm to produce an umbrella cap. How does the nucleus do this?

It took more than a century of biological work to come to the chromosome theory of heredity. Today, when almost 90 percent of all scientists that have ever lived are at work, knowledge in science is developing at an astounding rate, doubling about every 15 years. With so important a goal as understanding the way genes act, many biologists have become involved in this work.

The important question is this: How does the hereditary substance DNA, located within the chromosome, direct the production of traits by the cytoplasm? Could the DNA of the nucleus send a message of some kind to the cytoplasm? Could this message be in the form of a substance released by the nucleus into the cytoplasm? For our umbrella-cap alga, the sequence may be something like this:

DNA OF NUCLEUS
located specifically within the chromosomes
produces

↓

SUBSTANCE A
which migrates into the cytoplasm where it
influences the production of

↓

SUBSTANCE B
which in turn influences the production by
the cytoplasm of the trait

↓

UMBRELLA CAP

Is such a scheme purely imaginary or does it exist? Such a scheme would need to be supported by a structure that helps explain how DNA affects the cytoplasm in the umbrella-cap alga. Does such a structure exist?

Introducing the Hereditary Code

To describe what is presently known about the structure of chromosomes and genes would take several very large volumes. Why, then, begin its study during these years in school? There are at least two reasons. The term "DNA" is being mentioned in newspapers and on TV with increasing frequency. But more important, the concept is exceedingly important in your understanding of the way living things develop. And you are, first of all, a living thing.

A *complete* understanding of DNA and its work requires a thorough knowledge of certain fields of chemistry, biology, physics, and mathematics, so it is necessary for us to simplify a complex concept. But always there is a beginning. At this stage of your study, it may be enough to know that the heredity of organisms is being studied, something of the way it is being studied, and the direction of the study. In short, the purpose of being a student is to be informed—as best you can—at every stage of your life.

A Model of DNA

You have viewed the chromosomes under the microscope—and in photographs. ❶ Most

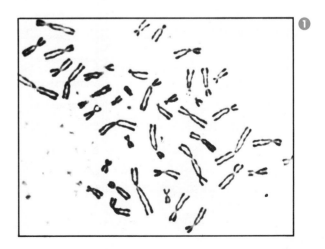

chromosomes, as you can see in the photographs of human chromosomes, appear to be rod-shaped bodies made up mainly of deoxyribonucleic acid—DNA. (Chromosomes also have a protein coat, but this need not concern us here).

If we could make a model of DNA, what would it look like? The model that appears on page 171 is based on the study of many biochemists, chemists who specialize in the study of living things. As early as 1900, the chemical make-up of DNA was known. But it wasn't until the period 1953 to 1962 that J. D. Watson and F. H. C. Crick, working in Cambridge, England, with M. H. F. Wilkins, used X-ray methods to determine its structure. In 1962, the three scientists were awarded the Nobel Prize for their tremendous contribution.

Study the model once again. Each small sphere represents an atom. In turn, the atoms are arranged in a definite pattern. What you see is a twisted ladder, or double spiral of atoms making up DNA. When we untwist the spiral, we find a basic shape somewhat like this.❶ What is the ladder made of?

The sides of the ladder are made up of two kinds of smaller molecules.

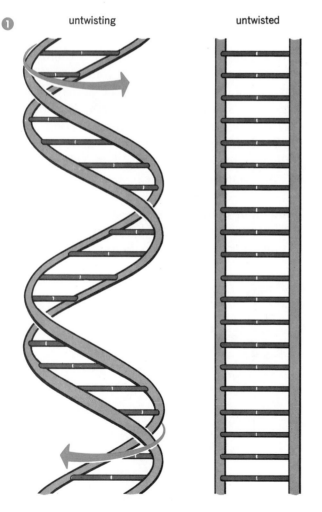

❶ untwisting   untwisted

Phosphate   (or phosphoric acid) made up of phosphorus, oxygen, and hydrogen atoms.

Deoxyribose   a sugar containing 5 carbon, 10 hydrogen, and 4 oxygen atoms per molecule; ribose, a related sugar, contains one more oxygen atom per molecule than deoxyribose. The prefix *deoxy*– means less oxygen.

The sides of the ladder are therefore made up of deoxyribose molecules alternating with phosphate molecules.❷

The rungs of the ladder are made up of four closely related compounds containing nitrogen in addition to carbon, hydrogen, and oxygen.

Adenine
Thymine
Cytosine
Guanine

If you wish to undertake a further study of these special compounds, turn to page 475. There the "skeleton structures" of each of

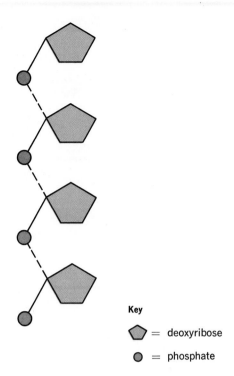

Key

⬠ = deoxyribose

● = phosphate

Using a piece of cardboard, copy and cut out the design of A, G, T, and C. ❸ Then trace and cut out three copies of each design on pieces of different colored paper—one color for each substance as indicated below. (Be sure to mark each design with the appropriate letter, representing adenine, thymine, cytosine, and guanine, respectively.)

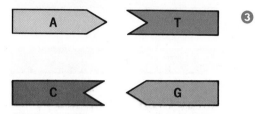

Now take the shapes you have cut out to represent the four substances that make up DNA (we are omitting the sugar and phosphate) and try to duplicate this arrangement of pairs. ❹

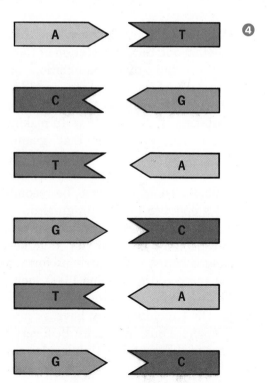

these substances is given—if only to assure you that these compounds are not as "imaginary" as you might think.

The rungs of the ladder consist of pairs of these four substances. It has been found that adenine is always paired with thymine, and cytosine is always paired with guanine. As the pairs are not joined very strongly, there is a weak area between them. Let's call this weak area where they are joined a bond. Thus, the two strands (sides) of the ladder are joined together their entire length by weak bonds.

In studying the DNA molecules, scientists discovered that there may be as many as 20,000 adenine–thymine (A–T) and cytosine–guanine (C–G) pairs. These many pairs can be arranged differently to produce many different DNA molecules. Why not try the following to see how this is possible.

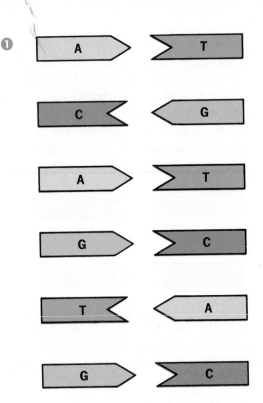

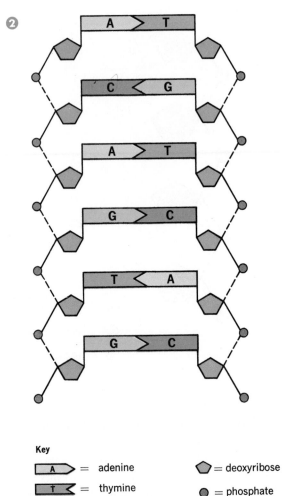

Key

A ⟩ = adenine		⬠ = deoxyribose
T ⟨ = thymine		⬤ = phosphate
C ⟨ = cytosine		
G ⟩ = guanine		

DNA molecules can be very long, but let's assume that one tiny, tiny section of the DNA molecule contains these combinations of substances (joined to phosphate and deoxyribose). Can you make the new combination of substances shown above? ❶ In making the recombination, remember that guanine is always paired with cytosine, and that adenine is always paired with thymine. (The thymine and adenine could, of course, be recombined on sides opposite to their original ones.)

Even a few minutes spent in shifting the colored paper reveals that you could keep on working 8 hours a day, perhaps for a week, before you could recombine 1,000 such pairs in all their different patterns. Recall that a single DNA molecule may have as many as 20,000 pairs. Thus, there must be a very large number of different DNA molecules each of which has a different effect on the organism.

DNA Duplicates Itself

The chromosome is mainly a long, long molecule of DNA. The DNA molecule is composed of units of adenine–thymine or guanine–cytosine combined with phosphate and deoxyribose. These units are strung together, one after the other, in many different sequences. Thus, genes may be thought of as specific sequences of these units controlling the characteristics of an organism. As recently as 1970, Gobind Khorana succeeded in the

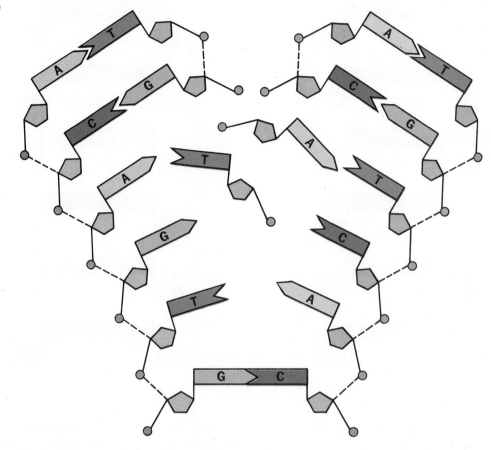

first complete synthesis of a gene. Khorana described the gene, consisting of 77 units, as a relatively simple gene of a yeast cell. It is estimated that the genetic material in a human cell has 6 billion units.

DNA of chromosomes is encased inside the nucleus, surrounded by the cytoplasm of the cell. How does DNA direct the cytoplasm to produce different substances that seem to affect traits of the organism? Perhaps we can get a clue from the way the chromosomes divide in mitosis. Examine the model of part of a chromosome, that is, the model of DNA at the left. ❷ Notice how the A-T and C-G units arrange themselves.

To duplicate itself, each chromosome, made up of huge numbers of specific units, would have to split down the middle. Then each part would have to build a new "partner." The process is thought to happen like this. ❸ The weak bonds somehow break and each unit starts to "unzip" itself, almost as if it were two parts of a zipper. Then each part "attracts" to itself the substances that complete the pattern. By this action each original "face" of the DNA molecule replaces its lost partner. This new partner is identical with the original partner. As the result of this process of duplication, or *replication* as it is called by biologists, two new, yet identical

467

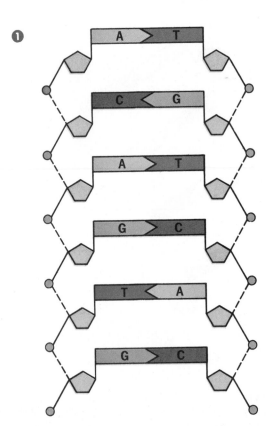

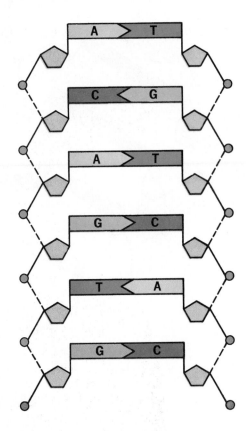

chromosomes—each like the original chromosome—are produced. ❶

As you study these drawings, keep in mind that they are only *models,* and models are often used to explain something that is more difficult to put into words. This model of DNA attempts to explain what we think we know at this stage of investigation into the replication of DNA. The chromosome *does duplicate itself.* There is no question about that. The "zipper" theory is one useful explanation of the way in which it is done.

DNA and Its Messengers

The zipper theory helps us to understand how DNA duplicates itself. But how does DNA direct the development of the various substances in the cell?

Study once again the cell on page 458. Note the ribosomes. The ribosomes contain a nucleic acid somewhat like DNA. This nucleic acid is shown as **RNA,** ribonucleic acid.* At present, scientists believe the ribosomes, with their RNA, play an important part in synthesizing different proteins in the cell. These proteins play a great part in determining how cells do their work. The DNA in the chromosome somehow affects the RNA in the ribosome. The ribosome, in turn, affects the kinds of proteins produced in the cell.

But how does the DNA in the chromosome affect the RNA in the ribosome? After all, these substances are in different parts in the

* RNA differs in the kind of sugar (ribose) it contains, and also in other ways, an understanding of which we leave to your further study.

■ AN APPRENTICE INVESTIGATION into Messenger RNA

❷

Get some string, the kind of white string used to tie packages. Cut the string into lengths of about 8 inches. Tie a bolt, a nut, and a screw along one string. On another string, vary the sequence; tie the nut first, then the screw, then the bolt. On the third string, vary the sequence once again. These are "models" of different sequences in DNA molecules.

Now prepare a solution of table sugar (sucrose). A liter will do. Heat the water to boiling. Dissolve the sucrose in the boiling water until no more sucrose dissolves. (Since this takes a great deal of sugar, perhaps one model can serve for the entire class.) Pour the syrup—for that is what it is—into three tall jars or cylinders. Then suspend the three DNA models in the sugar solution.❶ What happens?

In one trial, the molecules of sugar were "attracted" to the models as shown.❷ Each "DNA model" had a different pattern of sugar molecules—a different messenger RNA.

Of course, what you have seen is known as crystallization. The crystals of sugar formed different crystal patterns around different "units" in the DNA model. In any case, *different sequences of DNA somehow form different messenger RNA*. The oversimplified model is meant merely to fix this concept in mind. How it actually happens is the aim of research now going on all over the world.

An Investigation On Your Own

Analyze the role of template RNA. Summarize the result of your library research.

cell. After much experimentation, a *messenger* was found. What happens is something like this.

The DNA molecule, with its different units, attracts substances to itself. Sometimes instead of making more DNA, the DNA makes a new kind of molecule, known as **messenger RNA**. It is this messenger RNA that is released through the nuclear membrane and attaches itself to the ribosomes. What kind of model would help us understand this interaction? Try this one. ■

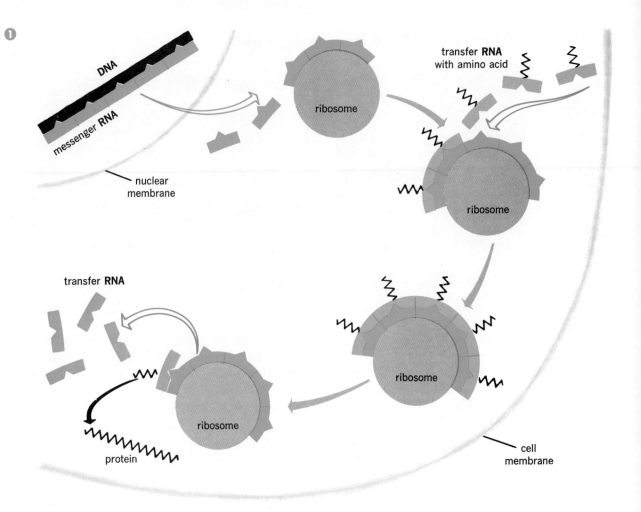

DNA

messenger RNA

nuclear
membrane

ribosome

transfer RNA
with amino acid

ribosome

ribosome

transfer RNA

ribosome

protein

ribosome

cell
membrane

But the story is not yet complete. In order to form proteins, the individual amino acids in the cytoplasm must be transferred to the ribosomes, where they are joined together. How is this done? Further experimentation has shown that there is another kind of RNA molecule, **transfer RNA,** already free in the cytoplasm. This transfer RNA picks up individual amino acids and carries them to the ribosomes. ❶ At the ribosomes, the transfer RNA molecules, along with the attached amino acids, arrange themselves in a definite order under the direction of messenger RNA.

That is, somehow the amino acids in the cytoplasm of the cell join with one another to form a protein. Once this is accomplished the protein and transfer RNA move away from the ribosome. Then transfer RNA is free once again to pick up more amino acids and bring them to the ribosome.

Is the concept of DNA action we have been describing without support in the laboratory? No, many laboratory investigations support it. For example, certain atoms of a molecule can be made radioactive and thus tagged. These tagged molecules can then be readily traced.

Messenger RNA and transfer RNA have been made radioactive and, therefore, it has been possible to trace their movements in a cell.

Results of these and related experiments indicate that the *sequence* of the units in the DNA molecule determines the nature of the protein produced. (Were you not asked to vary the order of the "units" in your investigation on p. 469?) And even more exciting, the evidence points strongly to the fact that the sequence represents a code consisting of a triplet (three units) in the DNA molecule. The code is believed to be responsible for directing the order of particular amino acids in a particular protein. For example, while in the process of development the human needs the amino acids, histidine (his′tə·dēn), arginine (är′jə·nēn), and glycine (glī′sēn). These amino acids are properly arranged in specific proteins through the action of the DNA code.

The DNA Code

To understand how triplets (only three units) can act as a code for many traits, try this word game. How many three-letter words can you make out of the four letters ATCG? Perhaps ACT, CAT, TAG, GAT; at least these. How many strange words can you make up—words that do not exist? Perhaps AGT, TGA, CTA, ATG, and on and on. Four letters can be put together in many triplet combinations. How many triplets could you make? Could you make 64? Yes, you could.

Now, let's compare this language code with the DNA code. If we let the four letters ATCG stand for adenine, thymine, cytosine, and guanine, and the three-letter words for all the possible arrangements of these compounds into various triplets, we have 64 possible triplets—many more than we need to arrange all the known amino acids into pro-

teins. (Perhaps some of these give other "directions" to the cells.) Suppose, for example, the units containing adenine, thymine, and guanine were in a triplet:

Then this particular code word ATG gives "directions" about the amino acid histidine. If the units in this triplet were

the code word AGC would give "directions" about arginine. And if the units were

then the amino acid "directed" would be glycine.

When we say that the code gives "directions," we mean that somehow it determines the position an amino acid shall occupy in a long series of amino acids.

Thus, DNA controls the hereditary traits of an organism through its genetic code (triplets).

However, the code could not "direct" the kinds of proteins assembled at the ribosome were it not for such substances as messenger RNA and transfer RNA. Indeed, our scheme presented on page 463 to explain how the nucleus of an algal cell controls its type of cap can now be summarized as follows:

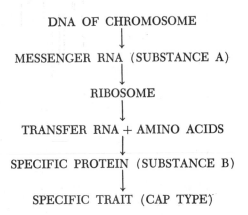

DNA OF CHROMOSOME
↓
MESSENGER RNA (SUBSTANCE A)
↓
RIBOSOME
↓
TRANSFER RNA + AMINO ACIDS
↓
SPECIFIC PROTEIN (SUBSTANCE B)
↓
SPECIFIC TRAIT (CAP TYPE)

The DNA code is thus at the center of an explanation of the inheritance of traits in all organisms.

The wrinkled seed, the red four o'clock, red hair, blue eyes—these all begin with the DNA molecule. The DNA code passes on its traits from generation to generation. Mendel reported this transfer of traits in his study of garden peas, Correns in his study of four o'clocks. The DNA in the chromosomes and genes seems fairly stable. Otherwise, how could the colors of flowers be predicted from their seeds?

The industry of farming depends in good part on the fact that heredity is fairly stable. We plant a potato, and we expect similar potatoes. A Baldwin apple tree should give us Baldwin apples.

How do we account then for organisms with their different traits? Look about you. Notice that all your classmates are similar to you in having the physical traits you have. They have eyes, hair, nose, mouth, arms, legs, and other traits. Yet the eyes may be quite different—blue, brown, gray, hazel, even violet. The hair may be black, brown, blond, or red.

Sometimes individuals inherit new traits. How traits sometimes change from one generation to the next, is left to the next unit.

REVIEW

1. Give evidence from at least one study to indicate how each of the following acts as the environment of a gene.
   a. the other genes in the nucleus
   b. the cytoplasm
   c. the internal environment of the organism
   d. the external environment of the organism

2. Why is DNA sometimes called the "boss" in the development of the organism?

3. Use the evidence derived from experiments on the umbrella-cap alga to show how DNA directs, or "bosses," the development of the umbrella cap.

4. What is the significance of the work of Watson, Crick, and Wilkins?

5. How does DNA duplicate (replicate) itself?

6. What is the significance of the sequence of units in a DNA molecule?

7. In what order would you place the following actions?
   a. the action of messenger RNA
   b. the action of DNA
   c. the action of ribosomes

NEW VIEW

1. A specific trait in mammals is the presence of hair. To produce hair, the amino acid *myosin* must be present. In what order would you place the following to indicate the steps followed for the development of the trait *hair?*
   a. specific protein in hair
   b. specific trait (hair)
   c. messenger RNA
   d. chromosome DNA
   e. ribosomes
   f. transfer RNA + amino acids

2. Have we found out all we need to know about the action of DNA? If not, propose what you think is lacking.

4. RELATING THE CONCEPTS

How does a living thing, say a bacterium, differ from a pebble? Both apparently are made of molecules. To be sure, the bacterium is made up of more complex molecules, especially the complex proteins. Both are affected by the environment. Heat may destroy the bacterium; it may also help crack the pebble.

The similarity seems to end when we ask: *How is the continuity of that particular species of bacterium carried on? How is the continuity of the pebble carried on?* For the bacterium, we come upon that remarkable substance DNA. For the pebble, we find that the continuity of the individual pebble is not assured. Only its molecules seem to go on. Of course, when a given bacterium dies, its molecules also go on. But for a species, DNA seems to be the guide to continuing the species. Our concepts about the nature of living things seem to be coming together.

Reviewing the Concept

Cast your mind's eye back over your work this year. More and more the living things, the organisms, you have observed have certain similarities among them. That is to say, the following concepts apply to them. A concept, after all, is a statement of similarities.

▶ *Organisms are adapted to their environment.*

▶ *Organisms are interdependent with their environment; they take matter and energy from the environment, and return matter and energy to the environment.*

▶ *Organisms have changed over the ages.*

Now we begin to find that DNA is part and parcel of the organism's existence. DNA, working within its immediate environment, affects the way the organism adapts to its environment. In this unit, then, we have dwelt on *these* significant concepts.

▶ *An organism is the product of its heredity and environment.* A green plant seems to develop its chlorophyll in light. Without proper food, an organism doesn't develop its full size. In other words, DNA exerts its full effect in an environment that furnishes the optimum conditions of matter and energy. The term *optimum* refers to the best environment for the particular DNA. Thus, the action of the gene (DNA) that controls the production of chlorophyll in leaves depends upon an optimum condition in the environment—light. Light is not an optimum condition for a fungus, which is adapted to the dark or deep shade.

Moreover, the other genes in the nucleus are also part of the environment for any specific gene. The gene for red color in four o'clocks is affected by the gene for white. The result is gene interaction—to produce pink.

Finally, DNA does not act alone. It depends upon substances in its environment such as RNA in the nucleus and cytoplasm. Surely it depends for its action on the ribosomes in the cytoplasm.

Clearly, DNA interacts with the environment. The organism is the product of:

a. its heredity (its total DNA).

b. the immediate environment of DNA (nuclear RNA, and ribosomes in the cytoplasm).

c. the environment of matter and energy which surrounds the organism.

▶ *The code of heredity is found in deoxyribonucleic acid.* At this time, the evidence points to units joined together in a long molecule of DNA as the basis of heredity. Present

473

explanations look upon the units of the DNA molecule as parts of a code. This code sends its "messages" (through messenger RNA) out into the cytoplasm. There the ribosomes, with the help of transfer RNA, act as factories for the manufacture of proteins. Proteins are, in turn, the characteristic substances of protoplasm within the cell. An organism, in turn, may be said to be the result of the interaction of all its cells, constantly interacting in a constantly changing environment. This is, of course, a greatly oversimplified statement.

Testing Yourself

1. Without referring to the text, sketch out a model of DNA.

2. How does the concept of DNA as a code for heredity explain the variety of traits in an organism such as the garden pea?

3. Does the concept of DNA as a code for heredity explain the variety of traits in an organism such as Drosophila?

4. DNA, ribosomes, transfer RNA, messenger RNA, amino acids, and proteins seem to act in a step-by-step process. Describe the sequence.

5. What is the significance of the experiment on the change of capsuleless bacteria into capsuled bacteria?

6. What is the significance of the experiments on the umbrella-cap alga?

7. What is the significance of the study of developing sea urchin eggs?

8. How has the concept of the gene changed over the past 100 years?

9. Show how a theory (perhaps the chromosome theory) is changed as new observations are made.

10. Were Mendel's ideas on inheritance of traits wrong? Explain your answer using examples from more recent experiments.

Extending the Concepts

Investigation 1. At New York University Medical School, Dr. Severo Ochoa and his co-workers are engaged in an experiment to determine if in duplicating itself the DNA molecule does indeed take substances from the cell and make an "image" of itself.

A microorganism whose DNA is a simple, long strand is used. One portion of the microorganism, call this portion A, is grown in a medium in which the atoms of nitrogen and hydrogen are composed of *heavier isotopes* * than the average atoms of nitrogen and hydrogen. Moreover, the heavy nitrogen and hydrogen are radioactive. Call this the "heavy atom" culture medium. One portion of the same species of microorganism, call it portion B, is grown in a medium whose atoms of nitrogen and hydrogen are *lighter* than those of A. Call this the "light atom" culture medium.

The microorganisms divide by fission about every half hour. At this time each DNA strand duplicates. In doing so, it makes an "image" of itself as it "unzips."

Eventually, the A group has its DNA made up of *heavy* atoms of nitrogen and hydrogen. Let's call this *heavy* DNA. ❶

The B group has its DNA made up of *light* atoms of nitrogen and hydrogen. Let's call this *light* DNA. ❷

* What is an isotope? What is heavy nitrogen? What is heavy hydrogen? Search these out. If the isotope is radioactive, how can its presence be detected?

After many, many days of growth, the DNA could be analyzed by Ochoa and his co-workers. By using methods of detecting radioactivity, they could determine the make-up of the DNA. They indeed had two kinds of microorganisms.

a. The microorganisms of portion A growing in the "heavy" medium had "heavy" DNA.

b. The microorganisms of portion B growing in the "light" medium had "light" DNA.

Now Ochoa *switched* the organisms. He placed "heavy DNA" organisms in the "light" culture medium. He placed "light DNA" organisms in the "heavy" culture medium. The organisms were permitted to grow and divide in these culture media. What is your hypothesis concerning the kind of "image" each DNA formed? Specifically:

a. What "image," or duplicate, will "heavy" DNA form in the "light" medium? Draw a model of this kind of DNA. Perhaps it would be like one strand from each model at the left.

b. What "image" will "light" DNA form in the "heavy" medium? Draw a model of this DNA.

c. What experimental technique would you devise to determine the answer to a and b above? Did you include a control experiment?

Models similar to those Ochoa made (which were based on his findings) are at the top of the next column. ❸ Draw your models before you look there. How close are you?

Dr. Ochoa is a Nobel Prize winner. For what work did he receive the prize? Search this out in the library.

❸ "heavy" **DNA** in "light" medium

"light" **DNA** in "heavy" medium

Investigation 2. Below are diagrams of the four related compounds that form the rungs of the ladder of a DNA molecule. ❹ As you know, the enormous variety in pattern in DNA of these four units makes possible the enormous variety of organisms.

Although you have not had sufficient chemistry to analyze these compounds fully, you can probably answer these questions:

a. What similarity of structure exists among these four compounds? What differences?

b. Which compounds are most closely related? On what basis did you relate the compounds?

c. What relationship exists between the structure of the compounds and the arrangement in the rungs of the DNA ladder?

❹

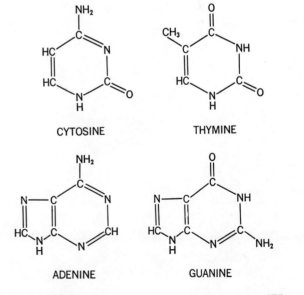

CYTOSINE

THYMINE

ADENINE

GUANINE

THE CONTINUITY OF LIFE

Compare these two organisms.

Examine carefully the traits of the fruitflies—all of one species. How are the fruitflies different?

Did you know that all the varieties of the fruitfly have been "made"—as it were—in the laboratory?

And what of the huge deep-sea fish? It has remained—according to evidence—in much the same form over the ages.

How do you account for the changes in the fruitfly? How do you account for the slow change—if any—in the fish?

19 | Continuity and Change in Organisms

1. THE SUDDEN CHANGE

A breeder of dogs such as Great Danes pretty much knows his business. He breeds a male and female whose heredity he knows. In other words, he counts on the DNA code in each dog to express itself. Given the proper environment, the dogs will develop into the beautiful, strong, vigorous Great Danes that he expects.

The breeder does not expect Great Danes to produce spaniels, poodles, bloodhounds, or terriers. He counts on the DNA to be stable. Yet, if DNA is stable, how can you account for the great variety of dogs? How do you account for the variation that exists within a single variety of dog, for instance the poodle?

To answer this question, you need to go back more than one hundred years to 1866, when Gregor Mendel published his work. You would think that the world would have acclaimed his work—but not so. In the 1860's, there was no radio, no TV, no system of world reporting, and few scientific journals.

Today, generally speaking, a scientist can communicate rather quickly the results of his work to other scientists. Furthermore, his work is summarized, in short forms called "abstracts," and published in special journals. Today, a truly significant discovery such as Mendel's would be circulated around the world quickly. Mendel would probably have been awarded the Nobel prize.

It wasn't until 1900 that DeVries, Correns, and von Tschermak rediscovered Mendel's paper in a small journal. They confirmed his work, and carried out further investigations on their own. Correns discovered "blending inheritance" (p. 452). In studying the evening primrose, DeVries discovered that certain varieties of evening primrose *changed* over several generations, and changed suddenly. Dwarf primroses became tall; tall primroses became dwarf. He was convinced that this was the result of changes in the genes.* He called these changes **mutations** (myōō·tā′shənz).

Soon other observers noticed that characteristics in a species could suddenly change for no observable reason. They produced varieties of themselves. For example, Morgan and his co-workers observed a *Drosophila* with small and imperfectly formed wings (called

---

* Later research showed that the changes in the evening primrose resulted from the unusual formation of a ring of chromosomes at meiosis.

vestigial wings) in a culture of *Drosophila* with normal wings. This fly was a **mutant,** an organism that shows a changed hereditary trait, a mutation. How did Morgan know that the vestigial wings of the fly resulted from a change in a gene? How could you make certain? Of course, you would mate the vestigial-winged fly with a normal-winged fly.

Suppose all the offspring of their mating, which are hybrids, showed normal wings. Would you conclude then that the change was not a mutation—that it was not a change in the gene? Of course not. The gene for vestigial wings might be recessive, as indeed it is. The trait for vestigial wings would show up when the hybrids were mated.

To determine whether a mutation has occurred, geneticists and plant and animal breeders mate the organism having the new trait again and again. They must be certain that the change is a change in the gene, that is, in the DNA.

From Muller to Beadle and Tatum

Further experimental evidence soon became available that genes do indeed change. The foremost experimenter in this area was Herman J. Muller.

In 1927, Muller asked whether or not mutations could be produced artificially. There were already some clues that this might be possible. Muller used X rays on *Drosophila,* and he did produce mutant flys. For instance,

he produced a fruit fly with white eyes, as well as other mutants—including some very bizarre forms. As a result of many years of work, Muller developed several important concepts. First, *mutations can be produced artificially.* Second, *mutations are changes in the gene.* Third, *most mutations are harmful and often result in the death of the mutant.*

You might have suspected the last concept. After all, the pattern of the DNA molecule in an organism is passed on by organisms that are adapted to their environments. These organisms have survived to reproduce generation after generation. If we change the DNA molecule, we change the organism.

However, beneficial mutations do occur, as you shall soon see. At present it is important to know that an organism with a mutation may find it difficult to compete successfully.

VESTIGIAL WINGS

WING OUT

CURLED WINGS

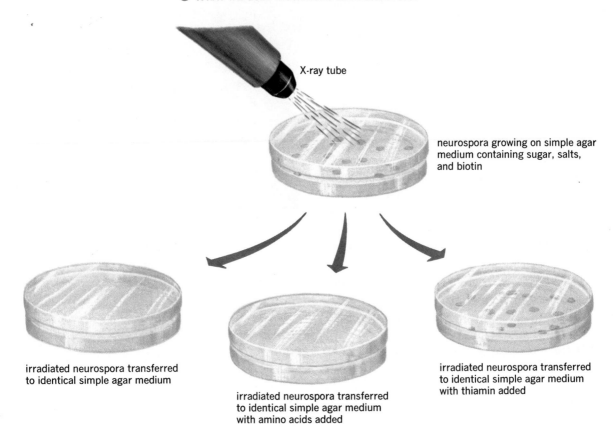

X-ray tube

neurospora growing on simple agar medium containing sugar, salts, and biotin

irradiated neurospora transferred to identical simple agar medium

irradiated neurospora transferred to identical simple agar medium with amino acids added

irradiated neurospora transferred to identical simple agar medium with thiamin added

After all, the mutation is part of an organism that is adapted to a special environment. When is a mutation beneficial? Formulate your own hypothesis. You will have an opportunity to ask this question again and again.

What happens when a gene mutates? The work of George W. Beadle and Edward L. Tatum gives us further indications. Like Muller, these experimenters were awarded the Nobel prize. Beadle and Tatum, in the early 1940's, brought about mutations in the pink mold *Neurospora* by using X rays.

Molds, as you know, do not contain chlorophyll. They absorb their nutrients, such as sugar, minerals, and certain vitamins (for example, biotin) from living organisms. Once

they absorb these nutrients, they can make, that is synthesize, the amino acids and proteins they need. A mold, like any cell, is a chemical factory.

Using X rays, Beadle and Tatum produced mutants that could *not* synthesize certain compounds. One irradiated strain of the mold, for example, had lost its ability to synthesize thiamin, a vitamin essential to the growth of *Neurospora*. In other words, for these mutant molds to be able to grow, thiamin had to be *supplied* in the medium in which they were grown. ❶ Otherwise they died from a lack of this vitamin.

Beadle and Tatum demonstrated that the mold's failure to synthesize thiamin actually resulted from a mutation in the gene (or genes) that controlled an enzyme. This enzyme was necessary for synthesizing thiamin from certain amino acids. When the amino acids from which thiamin is synthesized were added to the medium, the molds still did not grow. But when thiamin was added to the medium, the molds grew normally. This experiment demonstrated that the genes that were necessary for the synthesis of thiamin were changed. By now, some forty strains of *Neurospora,* each deficient in the ability to synthesize one substance, have been produced.

These famous experiments yielded two important clues to the nature of mutations.

First, a change in the DNA molecule changes the chemistry of the cell. For example, if there is a change in the part of the DNA molecule responsible for synthesizing thiamin, the *Neurospora* mold cannot produce thiamin.

Second, since the substances in the cell produce the different traits, a change in the substances produces different traits. Didn't a change in the cell substance result in a change from normal wings to vestigial wings in *Drosophila?*

We may assume, then, that if the change in DNA is not too damaging a change, the offspring will inherit the new trait. If the new trait adapts the organism to the environment, or has no effect at all, the new trait will pass on to following generations. If the new trait does not adapt the organism to the environment, the organism may die. Then the mutation dies with it. For instance, suppose a mutation in *Drosophila* produces a wingless *Drosophila.* There is such a mutant and, of course, it can survive in the bottles in which it is kept. But could it survive in the natural environment?

REVIEW

1. What is the meaning of *mutation,* as DeVries thought of it?

2. What is the meaning of *mutation,* as Morgan thought of it?

3. What is the meaning of *mutation,* as Muller thought of it?

4. What is the meaning of *mutation,* as Beadle and Tatum thought of it?

NEW VIEW

1. How would you determine whether a change in a trait is a mutation? Describe the kind of experiment you would do.

2. What effect does gamma radiation have on growing plants? You might investigate the *gamma garden* at Brookhaven National Laboratories, Upton, New York.

2. CASE STUDIES IN CHANGE— FLIES AND HORSES

Clearly, change occurs in organisms. DeVries observed a naturally occurring change in the evening primrose. Morgan observed a naturally occurring change in the fruit fly— the vestigial wings. In your study of plants and animals in Units Four and Five, you could not fail to observe that organisms have changed over the ages of the earth. Trilobites, dinosaurs, and seed ferns no longer exist as living organisms—they exist as fossils.

The geologic time scale of changing organisms, with which you are already familiar (p. 397), virtually shouts "change." You now have begun to understand how change occurs. You have begun to see that *the only permanent thing is change.* How true is this?

Man can also change organisms. In Beadle and Tatum's work, you have seen that *change* can result in the inability of the organism to produce certain substances needed for growth—thus death occurs. Similarly, Muller used X rays to produce many mutations in the fruit fly. He found, for example, that a change in the genes resulted in white eyes rather than red eyes. Since Muller's first experiments, eleven different mutant genes for eye color have been produced. What might have caused the variations, these heritable differences in structure or function, in *Neurospora* and *Drosophila*?

We may reason from these experiments that mutations induced by X rays altered DNA—indeed, any mutation means an altered DNA molecule. The altered DNA code then sends "different messages," through messenger RNA, to the ribosomes to produce different substances. These different substances result in the expression of different traits. The altered DNA is inherited and the variation is passed on to the offspring.

While many of these changed traits result in a less well-adapted organism, some changes better adapt the organism to its environment. Moreover, while some series of mutations can be brought about quickly—the changes in the traits of eye color in *Drosophila* were observed in the laboratory within a period of 50 years—others occur slowly over the periods of written and fossil history.

Let's examine the results of change in an organism that has been studied intensively and extensively over the period of fossil history as well as the period of written history. There is an organism whose fossils are preserved in fairly large numbers. The organism is the horse. How fruitful it would be if you could have a complete fossil collection of the horse. Then you could investigate the horses of the past at first hand—but this is impossible. However, in another way you can investigate how the horse has changed since its earliest fossil records. ■

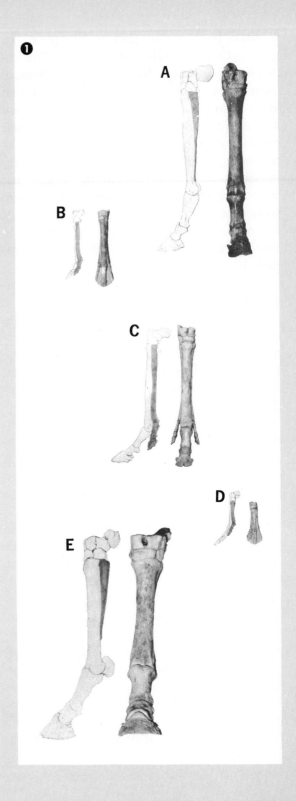

■ AN APPRENTICE INVESTIGATION into Change and the Horse

The "evidence" is presented to you here in an artificial way, through drawings and photographs of actual specimens. In this way you will do a kind of apprentice investigation in response to this question: How would you say the horse changed over the period of geologic history?

What would you say may have been the sequence of the development of the horse's leg since the Eocene Epoch? ❶ What may have been the sequence of development of the horse's skull? ❷ On a piece of paper, write down the letters in the order that you think they may have developed.

Check your hypothesis with the chart on the following page.

An Investigation On Your Own

During its long history, the horse has changed from a browsing to a grazing animal. Study the changes in the horse's teeth. How do they indicate a change in food habits?

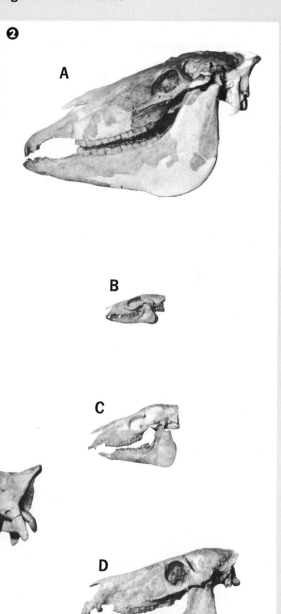

❷

A

B

C

E

D

HISTORY OF THE DEVELOPMENT OF THE HORSE

Genus	Epoch	Legs	Skulls	Probable Appearance
Equus (modern horse)	Pleistocene — 2 million years ago	E	E	
Pliohippus	Pliocene — 13 million years ago	A	A	
Merychippus	Miocene — 25 million years ago	C	D	
Mesohippus	Oligocene — 36 million years ago	B	C	
Eohippus	Eocene — 58 million years ago	D	B	

Did you arrange the sequence of change in the horse properly? Perhaps you did so mainly on the basis of increase in size and complexity of the horse's skull. The first horse, *Eohippus*, was only about the size of a fox terrier. *Eohippus*, with its four toes, evolved to a three-toed horse called *Mesohippus*. The next horse, called *Merychippus*, still had three toes, although the two smaller toes did not quite reach the ground. *Pliohippus*, the next development of the horse, ran on only one toe, while vestiges of the other two toes remained well up its leg. The modern horse, *Equus*, also runs on only one strong toe, or hoof—

actually his toenail. Yet vestiges of two toes still remain. Would you say that the modern horse has changed much in appearance over the past two million years?

A Tentative Statement

From your studies thus far, you have a basis for considering the nature of inherited change in organisms. In a given species, such as the fruit fly, an inherited change ordinarily takes place in the hereditary code, the DNA. In duplicating itself, the DNA molecule is passed on to other cells, including the gametes. The gametes pass the changed DNA code to the offspring. Thus an inherited change is passed on to the offspring, generation after generation.

What happens in a group of apparently *related organisms*, like horses? Are we to assume that heritable changes, mutations, occurred in *Eohippus*, the Eocene horse? Are we to assume that these heritable changes were passed on to the offspring of *Eohippus*? Are we to assume that *Eohippus* itself was changed because of the change in DNA? Is there another reasonable assumption you can make?

What might be a tentative hypothesis for the changes in a long line of horses that seem to have resulted in the modern horse, *Equus*? Might it be like this: Several times during a period of almost 60 million years, changes in the genes of one species of horse were passed on to the offspring, resulting in a new species. Perhaps you could state the hypothesis in this way: *Over the ages, new species seem to arise from preceding organisms through mutation.*

Suppose that you could somehow take a quick journey through the last 3 billion years on earth and view the evolution of its organisms.

The Long and Magnificent Journey

The evidence is clear. At one time earth turned on its axis and revolved around the sun—but man was not on earth. Fossil evidence tells us that the seas were first populated by hosts of invertebrates.

From single-celled to multicellular animals, the invertebrates reigned—at least up through the Cambrian. Then the early fish made their appearance—great sharklike creatures and heavy-armored ones, the ostracoderms. Perhaps these ostracoderms produced the adventurous line of fish that found the land and gained a foothold. These land-probing fish, perhaps somewhat like our modern fish in appearance, won the land, and from them came the early amphibians. And the amphibians somehow mutated—mutation upon mutation—to produce the early reptiles. These huge creatures lumbered through the Carboniferous forests of fern, seed-fern, and giant lycopods.

The environment kept changing even as did the animals and plants. Slowly the warm, moist lands that favored the forests of giant club mosses and ferns began to dry out, but many of the smaller reptiles somehow survived.

From these reptiles, two great lines developed—the birds and the mammals. With the rise of these warm-blooded animals, the conquest of the land became a certainty. Meanwhile the grasses, the shrubs, the trees—all cone-bearing or flowering—conquered the land as well. The ferns and mosses were relegated to the shade of the great land plants of today.

The mammals at first were small, insignificant creatures, but their ability to maintain a more constant body temperature and their better brains enabled them to survive in environments that the reptiles could not conquer. And conquer they did in the Cenozoic—duckbills, marsupials, mastodons, elephants, rodents, horses, great cats, giant sloths, deer, giraffes, monkeys, and apes. And somewhere in the last years a line of great mammals began to stand upright, walk upright, and look straight ahead with eyes in an upright head. Their hands could fashion tools, and their vocal cords and lips, could fashion speech.

Thus man came to be and developed his culture—farms, factories, cities, and schools. He developed art, music, and books—even bombs. This was man.

485

All this took about 3 billion years. We know this much now, and we are constantly searching to learn still more.

REVIEW

1. Describe how a mutation in the DNA molecule might result in a change that would better adapt an organism to its environment. Over a long period of time, with many mutations occurring, describe in detail how a new species might develop.

2. What is a geologic time scale?

3. What is the importance of the horse in the study of change over the ages?

4. How do we know that *Equus* developed from *Eohippus*?

5. In which periods were the invertebrates dominant?

6. In which periods were the reptiles dominant?

7. In which periods were the seed ferns dominant?

8. In what epoch did the mammals assume dominance?

9. In what period did early man appear on the scene?

NEW VIEW

1. What is the meaning of the term *evolution*?

2. Study the evolution of an organism such as the elephant or the camel. Compare it with that of the horse. A reference that may be useful is *The Fossil Book: A Record of Prehistoric Life.* See the Suggested Reading list at the end of this chapter.

3. Suppose you could combine all geologic history into a period of 24 hours. On such a 24-hour time scale, how long in hours, minutes, or seconds would each era and period have lasted? For instance, you might assume man's stay on earth (over 1 million years) to be equal to one second.

3. THEORY TO ACCOUNT FOR THE EVIDENCE

How does one account for the evidence? Men try to account for what they know—and organisms are related in a variety of ways and have had a long history. For example:

a. DNA is basic to the inheritance of organisms.

b. Organisms are composed of cells.

c. The chemistry of certain cells is similar in a variety of organisms. Thus the hormones (for example, insulin) of certain animals can be interchanged; and the enzymes, for example, pepsin, of one organism act in other organisms.

d. The embryos of related groups of organisms, such as the vertebrates, show a close similarity (p. 457). We can explain this similarity only through their possession of certain genes in common. This suggests a common ancestor.

e. The anatomy (for instance, the skeleton) of related groups also shows a similarity in structure and function. This similarity again suggests the possession of certain genes in common. This, in turn, suggests a common ancestor.

f. The fossil evidence indicates that organisms have had a long ancestry. The major groups we know today, for example, echinoderms, have a long history. Echinoderms go back 550 million years; insects go back some 400 million years. Amphibians go back over 350 million years, and mammals some 180 million years. The evidence suggests that man goes back some 1 million years.

The fossil evidence also indicates that about 2 billion to 3 billion years ago the algae, fungi, bacteria, and the simplest invertebrates were widely prevalent.

g. The earth appears to be at least 5 billion to 6 billion years old. Mountain ranges and rivers have come and gone. Environments have changed from worldwide tropical and subtropical climates to the environments of the present.

How do we account for the development of this great variety of organisms over millions upon millions of years? The custom of science, as you know by now, is to fashion theories to explain evidence. Theories are useful as long as they explain the evidence available. For instance, before the mass of evidence we have just been examining was available, Thales (thā′lēz), who lived in Greece about 2,600 years ago, tried to account for the origin of organisms. He thought that the "four elements" (as they were called then) of Earth, Air, Fire, and Water joined to form the first organisms. Over the years, many different thinkers and scientists have tried to account for the fossil evidence. Slowly over hundreds of years the evidence has been gathered and been recorded. Most of the evidence has been unearthed, however, in the past 200 years, as science came of age.

The Growth of a Theory

The concept of change is not new. The earth has changed since its origin. Organisms have changed throughout the earth's history. Continents have changed. Mountains have changed. Oceans have changed. The earth has changed. Stars have changed.

Certainly you have come upon the experience of change. You yourself have changed over the years. How? Why? Your town or city has changed. How? Why?

Organisms have been changed by men. Domestic animals have changed. How do you explain the appearance of Hereford cattle, the white-feathered turkey, the new varieties of corn, wheat, apples, oranges? How were they produced?

It is fairly easy to explain how these organisms were produced. (Indeed, much of Chapter 20 is given over to a study of this kind of change.) Man can explain these changes; their history is, in large part, recorded by man.

But how does one explain changes in the earth *before* recorded history? Surely one must speculate, one uses the evidence one has, one subjects one's explanation to criticism. Can there be error? Of course. But science can correct itself—with new evidence and better thinking. New theories replace those the evidence does not support.

To explain the change in organisms over the ages required putting together many concepts. They were put together in the person of Charles Darwin more than 100 years ago. Notice we say *in* Charles Darwin, because a theory is born *in* thought. It is born in a careful synthesis, or putting together, of many facts, many concepts.

Charles Darwin was a young naturalist whose imagination and thinking were fired by his observation of the life about him. In the early 1830's, he was influenced by the work of Charles Lyell, an English geologist. Lyell had shown that the changes in mountains can be explained; mountains are worn down slowly by water, wind, and the action of alternate heating and cooling. In the same way, too, a valley could be explained; it is carved out by the eroding force of a river.

In 1831, Darwin was 22 years old. At this age he set out on a now famous voyage to study the living things along the coast of South America and on the islands of the Pacific. The ship on which he sailed was the *Beagle*. He observed first-hand what you already know: the great variety of organisms,

and the special adaptations of organisms to special environments. For instance, on the Galápagos Islands off the west coast of South America, Darwin observed several members of a species of huge tortoises found nowhere else. ❶ They were especially adapted to life on these islands.

By 1858, after more than 25 years of work, the general outlines of a theory had formed in his mind. He had even written a description of the theory, which he showed to fellow scientists. But he did not publish it. He carefully collected some observations, more facts in support of his theory. Soon, however, he was forced to publish his theory. A young naturalist, Alfred R. Wallace, sent Darwin an essay that formulated the theory Darwin had been working on for the past years. Darwin, a humble man and a decent one, wanted to give Wallace the honor of publishing his theory first. But friends intervened, and Darwin and Wallace presented their theory jointly in 1858. In November 1859, Darwin published his theory *On the Origin of Species by Means of Natural Selection.* Darwin's theory is known as the *Theory of Natural Selection.* What did it say?

Darwin's Theory of Evolution—Then

Darwin brought certain concepts to the theory he stated. We might summarize these concepts as follows.

a. *The number of organisms that a favorable environment can support is limited.* Thus, if all the eggs laid by a codfish developed into adult codfish, the oceans would soon have no room for them or any other life. If all the eggs of a fly became adults and reproduced, the entire earth would literally be covered with flies in a few years. In his work, Darwin was especially influenced by the work of Thomas Malthus (1776–1834), whose thesis was that the human population increased faster than the food supply.

b. *Organisms vary widely. They vary also in the traits that adapt them to the environment.* For example, some horses can run faster and longer than others. If getting food depends on speed, then the horses that can run faster and longer will get food sooner than the slower ones. If escaping from an enemy, say a mountain lion, depends upon speed, then those horses that can run faster might escape.

c. *Those organisms whose variations best adapt them to the environment tend to survive.* For example, among horses, those that could run fastest survived to reproduce. As the environment changed, a horse with a single, well-protected hoof could run faster on a rocky, dry surface than could horses with less well-protected hoofs.

In any event, Darwin's theory proposed that *the environment selected for survival those organisms that were best adapted to it.* That is, *the organisms best fitted to the environment survived.*

The organisms that survive make possible their evolution in other forms. Obviously, the organisms that do not survive will not become a part of evolution. An example from modern times will illustrate Darwin's theory. When DDT was first used to kill insects, it was most successful against houseflies. But not all houseflies died. Now, some 20 years since the widespread use of DDT began, there are houseflies with great resistance to DDT. Experimental evidence obtained from breeding these houseflies shows that many have a resistance to DDT. Scientists offer this explanation for the survival of the houseflies.

Houseflies *vary* somewhat genetically. Most had genes that caused them to be *susceptible* to DDT. A few had genes that caused them to be *resistant* to DDT. Both survived in the absence of DDT. That is, both kinds of flies were adapted to an environment in which there was no DDT.

The environment changed when DDT was introduced. *Those houseflies not adapted to the new environment did not survive.* They did not reproduce; they did not pass on their genes. Those houseflies that were adapted to the new environment (through possession of a resistance to DDT) survived. They passed on their genes to their offspring. Presently, a population of houseflies resistant to DDT exists. The present variety of houseflies is adapted to the present environment.

Be certain that you are completely clear on a major point. The environment does *not* produce the organism that is adapted to it. The organism, with the genes that adapt it, *exists* before the environmental change occurs. If the environment does change, then those organisms with the adaptation survive.

Darwin's Theory of Evolution—Now

Darwin's Theory of Natural Selection has remained much as he developed it. Our understanding of it has improved, however. For instance, Darwin did not know of Mendel's work, although his work and Mendel's were published within a few years of each other. Since then, we have learned something of the way organisms change through change in DNA, that is, through mutation. No doubt, if Darwin were living today he would be overjoyed by the amount of supporting evidence for his theory that attempts to explain the nature of evolution. Today he might reason somewhat as follows.

a. Organisms are adapted to their environment. Certainly their genetic make-up is the "blueprint" that determines their traits. However, the traits expressed by an organism are the product of both its heredity *and* its environment—that is, an organism develops best in a favorable environment.

b. Again and again, DNA changes; genes mutate. If the mutation is not too severe, the DNA will have the mutation built into it. So organisms begin to vary. They show variations in color, size, shape, speed, and the like.

c. Usually the environment can feed and shelter most variants (organisms with variations). When food is plentiful, the different variants can survive. If the environment changes greatly, those variants best adapted to the new environment survive. Then they pass on their DNA to their offspring. As a result, the organism has an opportunity to evolve into other organisms.

In essence, Darwin's theory states that *the environment selects those organisms best adapted to it.* This selection by the environment of the organisms most fit to survive is known as **natural selection.** Natural selection, then, is the manner in which organisms that are best fitted or adapted to survive in the changing environment naturally *survive* and in time *evolve* into other organisms.

Let's assume, for example, that there is a certain windswept island off the coast of a large body of wind-calm land. On the windswept island and on the mainland a certain species of insect is found. However, the variety of insect on the island is *wingless*. The variety of insect on the mainland *has wings*. Otherwise, the insects are identical. Does the theory of natural selection explain the existence of these two varieties of insects?

Does the theory of natural selection explain the existence of protective coloration in the photographs of the two ermines? ① The same species is shown in both photographs; the ermines were merely photographed at different times of the year. Now find the Anaea butterfly in the photograph. ②

Does the theory of natural selection explain these three cases? If it does not, what theory would be more useful? Recall that a theory is useful only if it explain the facts. Recall that a fact is an observation confirmed by different scientists. If a theory does not explain the existing facts, then the theory is discarded.

REVIEW

1. Explain in your own words the meaning of *natural selection*.

2. In your own words, apply the theory of natural selection to the resistance of flies to DDT.

3. How does the environment "select" the organisms best adapted to it?

4. Why didn't Darwin use Mendel's work in fashioning his theory?

5. What contribution did Alfred R. Wallace make to the theory of evolution?

NEW VIEW

Jean Baptiste Lamarck proposed a theory of evolution. Search it out. How did it differ from Darwin's theory?

4. RELATING THE CONCEPTS

There is continuity of organisms. The organism may reproduce itself by fission, as do certain microorganisms. A bacterium divides, reproducing its own kind. So does a paramecium. The genetic code of an organism, the DNA, in this way is duplicated and passed on. The organism maintains its continuity. Or it reproduces sexually; two gametes unite and a zygote is produced. Each gamete brings to the zygote a set of chromosomes, a set of DNA molecules. The offspring that develops from the zygote maintains the continuity of the organism. It becomes adult, it produces gametes, and so on and on—in continuity.

Not only is the organism continuous, but all of life is continuous as well. You have come a long way. You began your work this year with an examination of the organism in its environment. Your study, your investigations, and the explanations led to the concept that *an organism is adapted to its environment.* That is, organisms interchange matter and energy with the environment.

As you studied organisms in the environment, you began to see how the environment affects them. Organisms are dependent on the environment for the matter and energy they need for survival. They also depend on the environment for their development. Thus, *an organism is the product of heredity and environment.* Once an organism begins its development, the presence or absence of light, heat, pressure, air, or other physical features of the environment help determine the expression of its traits.

Reviewing the Concepts

We have unraveled a thread that seems to go back in time, back to the first organisms. You have now become aware of these concepts.

▶ *There is a biological relationship among all organisms.* When the DNA that is basic to life in all organisms is analyzed, the DNA molecule is found to have a structure that is very similar no matter what the organism. Furthermore, except for viruses, most organisms have a cellular organization. And again, organisms have similar life activities.

▶ *Organisms classified in a group have similarity in structure and function.* When you studied plants (Unit Four) and animals (Unit Five), you grouped them according to common structures. You can see that what was "common sense" grouping now has a much

deeper meaning. For example, members of the five classes of vertebrates show close relationships in their embryology. They also have relationships in their body chemistry. Thus, the functions of a red blood cell in a bird are very similar to the functions of a red blood cell in a mammal.

▶ *Closely related organisms have a common ancestry.* You can trace the horse, or the elephant, or the camel and seem to find a common ancestry. For instance, the horses we know about, past and present, seem to come from *Eohippus.* The evidence seems to pile up. So we begin to suspect that life has been continuous over the ages. That is, organisms gave rise to each other.

▶ *The hereditary code of organisms can change.* You have begun to see that a trait is not necessarily permanent. Through mutation, the DNA code can change. Muller's work, confirmed by others, showed that genes change. What actually changes when a gene mutates? Perhaps an atom of carbon, hydrogen, oxygen, or nitrogen exchanges its place with another. Perhaps part of the DNA code is rearranged. In any event, mutation results in the change of a gene.

We know that a mutation is a change in the gene because the change is passed on to the offspring—over a number of generations. Thus, within a species, variation results at least from mutation and recombination of genes.

▶ *Organisms best fitted to survive in the environment give rise to other organisms.* Over the ages those organisms best suited to the environment were able to reproduce themselves—and to mutate. Those mutants best fitted to survive produced other mutants in turn. Over millions upon millions of years, the chain of life developed. What we see on earth today are the survivors of a long line of ancestors. Those species of plants and animals that did not survive are sometimes found as fossils.

▶ *Organisms have evolved from each other.* Through the studies of the fossil evidence, the evidence from the development of the embryo, the evidence from anatomy, and the evidence from the chemistry of the cell, we have come to understand how the Theory of Natural Selection was evolved. We have come to understand that the history of the earth is a long history. We have come to understand that in mutating, the DNA in organisms produced new varieties of organisms. Those varieties and species that were adapted to the environment survived and evolved into other species.

Testing Yourself

1. What was Muller's hypothesis? What was Muller's conclusion?

2. What was the hypothesis of Beadle and Tatum? What were their conclusions?

3. As a result of the evidence of variation in the eye color of *Drosophila,* how do you explain the cause of variation in a species?

4. How do you explain the change of *Eohippus* successively into other genera of horses, and finally into *Equus?*

5. What can happen to the DNA molecule to produce the effect known as a mutation?

6. A *Drosophila* is irradiated. One of the offspring has violet eyes. How would you determine whether the "new" trait is inherited?

7. How would you determine whether a mutation in *Drosophila* eye color is a dominant or recessive trait?

8. What evidence can you give for the statement: Organisms in a given phylum are related in structure.

9. What is the importance of studies on the relationships of fossils and living horses over approximately 60 million years?

10. Why is the evidence for the relationships among the chordates (Chordata) more satisfactory then the evidence for the relationships among the members of a phylum such as the annelid worms (Annelida)?

11. Why has Darwin's theory survived?

12. Why didn't Darwin base his theory on the evidence from a study of mutation?

13. What is the importance of a theory?

Extending the Concepts

Investigation 1. You may be interested in studying the appearance of mutant organisms within very recent times. Search out the history of a sheep mutant—the ancon sheep. Search out the history of a cattle mutant—the polled cattle.

Investigation 2. Have any theories of evolution besides the one discussed in this chapter been developed?

Begin your study by referring to a history of biology, such as *A History of Biology* by C. Singer. See the Suggested Reading list at the end of this chapter. Select one of these theories of evolution and analyze it. Why was it satisfactory? Why was it unsatisfactory?

Perhaps now you would like to begin a more thorough study of fossils. A book such as *Fossils*, by E. Laurence Palmer will be a very good beginning. Also see the Suggested Reading list at the end of this chapter. Share your knowledge and collection of fossils with your classmates.

Investigation 3. What is the effect of irradiation (X rays and gamma radiation) on plants?

Biological supply houses across the country * have available supplies of seeds (of a variety of plants) that have been subjected to irradiation by X rays. If your school can make them available to you, plant them. How would you determine whether mutations have occurred?

---

* Addresses of two biological supply houses are:
Carolina Biological Supply Company, Burlington, North Carolina.
General Biological Supply House, Inc. (Turtox), 8200 S. Hoyne Avenue, Chicago 20, Illinois.

Investigation 4. You have dissected the common grass frog, *Rana pipiens*. Are the characteristics of the species the same for specimens across the country?

Perhaps your teacher will order several frogs from each of several supply houses. Study their external markings. How do they compare? (Be certain you compare males with males, and females with females.) Then compare your observations with those of Dr. John Moore in *Ward's Natural Science Bulletin*. Also see the Suggested Reading list below.

Suggested Reading

Fenton, Carroll L., and Mildred A., *The Fossil Book: A Record of Prehistoric Life*, New York, Doubleday, 1958.

Singer, Charles, *A History of Biology*, New York, Abelard, 1959.

Matthews, W. H., *Fossils: An Introduction to Prehistoric Life*, New York, Barnes and Noble, 1962.

This frieze of horses (and bulls) was painted by Cro-Magnon man on the walls of the Lascaux Cave in France some 25,000 years ago.

"Yellow Horses" was painted by Franz Marc in Germany in 1911.

20 | Changing Man and the Changing Environment

What would you assume from a study of the two paintings shown on the opposite page? Were the people who painted them intelligent, and knowledgeable? One was painted some 25,000 years ago by men who lived in what is now France. The other was painted by the famous German painter Franz Marc. His paintings hang in the finest museums of Europe and the United States. Both paintings are clearly the work of man.

If we could dress a man of about 25,000 years ago in a modern suit, shirt, and tie, and give him a modern haircut, he might pass in the streets as modern man. If he could speak the language, if he could stop staring at the ways modern man lives and remain stalwart in the face of speeding automobiles and zooming planes, he might even wonder how man had changed the environment.

Neither man nor the environment were, you see, always as they are now.

1. BEFORE THE TRIBE AND TOWN

There is very little doubt that most men now live in groups—in tribes, compounds, villages, towns, cities, counties, states, nations. A modern town is amazing. Think about it for a moment. Do you live in a town or city? What do you do for yourself? What does your family do for itself? Does it grow its own food? Does it spin the yarn or fiber for its clothing? Does it build its own shelter? Does it gather its own fuel for heat? Does it make its own light?

To make a long story short, most men no longer wrest their livelihood directly from the environment. All over the world, men specialize in doing some of the things early man did for himself. Some men, such as farmers and ranchers, grow food. Some men, as truckers or railroad men, transport the food to where it is used. Some men regulate the spinning machines, while others, as tailors, make the clothing. Some men, as miners and oilmen, secure the fuel. Still others, engineers, get electricity to us. And so it goes.

Early Man

The first men did not have the problems of the town. They had more fundamental problems—those of survival. Man himself changed over more than a million years, and during these years he struggled to survive in an environment that also fed his enemies. So the evidence indicates.

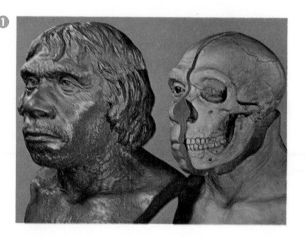

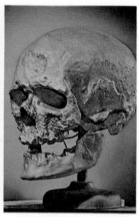

What characteristics would you assign to an organism to place him in the genus *Homo* (man)? Examine closely the fossil skulls and heads above. They were reconstructed by paleontologists, the scientists who study extinct men. How different are they from modern man? Yet both men are placed in the genus *Homo*.

Neanderthal man appeared on the scene in the late Pleistocene, perhaps some 100,000 years ago. ❶ From the fossils of his skeletons, a short, heavy-boned, very strong man has been reconstructed. Notice the heavy face, the prominent ridges above the eyes, the sloping forehead. Notice the heavy jaws—but the small chin.

Neanderthal man had a large head. The capacity (volume) of his cranium was about 1,450 cubic centimeters. The average capacity of the cranium of modern man is about 1,450 cubic centimeters. From his flint tools and from the way he buried his dead, it would seem that Neanderthal man was intelligent and had some social organization. After all, he was able to survive in an environment full of large and hostile animals.

However, he is not classified as *Homo sapiens* (man, the wise)—the species of which you are a member. Rather, he is *Homo neanderthalensis* (nē·an′dər·thäl·en′sis), a different species. But he is man, is he not? He seems to have lived most of his life in Northern Africa, Asia, and Western Europe. The first fossil came from a limestone cave in the Neander Valley (Neanderthal, *thal* being the older German word for valley), near Dusseldorf, Germany. Other fossils indicate that the cold, damp climate forced him to seek refuge in natural caves.

Perhaps some 50,000 years ago, Neanderthal man disappeared. That is, there seems to be no fossil evidence of his existence during the past 50,000 years. Perhaps Neanderthal man could not compete with the men—probably very much like ourselves—who came out of the east. Whatever the reason, *Homo neanderthalensis* ceased to be the dominant species of man some 50,000 years ago.

What kind of man succeeded Neanderthal man? We know him as **Cro-Magnon man,** clearly a *Homo sapiens.* ❷ He could pass as one of us if his large size and large skull did not give him away. Many fossil skeletons indicate that he was often larger than most of us living today. But he was *Homo sapiens.*

Cro-Magnon man was an intelligent, active man, tall and vigorous. He was also, from what we know, an artist. The pictures he drew on the ceilings and walls of the caves of northern Spain and southern France tell us of the animals he hunted, of the animals that gave him food and clothing. His world was one of wild horses, reindeer, wolves, bisons, and woolly mammoths. ❸ He hunted these animals with spear and arrow; finely chipped stone spear points and arrow heads are found where he lived. He had the leisure, apparently, to paint and to carve decorations on his tools and ornaments. ❹

Whenever men have leisure to paint and to make ornaments, they must have mastered their environment enough to rest, to think, and, perhaps, to play. To be able to paint means to have time away from food gathering or food growing, for one needs leisure to paint. In Cro-Magnon man we have, then, the beginnings of civilization. He hunted in groups. He also seems to have lived in groups. He lived perhaps some 40,000 to 20,000 years ago. The time of Cro-Magnon man was the peak of the Stone Age, the age of stone tools.

About 10,000 to 8,000 years ago, the large mammals that Cro-Magnon man had shared the earth with began to disappear. The reason

for their disappearance is as yet uncertain. However, with their extinction some 10,000 years ago, we come to the end of the Pleistocene era. Then, what we know as modern times began.

We have, then, some indication that man, *Homo,* lived and flourished some 100,000 years ago, in Northern Africa, parts of Asia, and Western Europe. We know that *Homo sapiens* now flourishes throughout the world. But what of the time before Neanderthal man and Cro-Magnon man?

The Java Man and His "Ancestors"

If we wanted to search for fossils of man, we would have to search for fossil skeletons that show the possibility of *erect posture.* For man is the primate that walks erect. We would also need to find a skull capable of holding a fair-sized brain. Such was the find of Eugene Dubois (dōō·boys′), a Dutch anatomist, in a layer of volcanic ash on the bank of the Trinil River in Java. He found a jawbone, teeth, part of a skull, and a thighbone. The thighbone showed that the individual stood erect; the cranium portion of the head showed a capacity for a good-sized brain. Dubois named the fossil *Pithecanthropus erectus* (pith′ə·kan′thrō·pəs ē·rek′təs), but it is

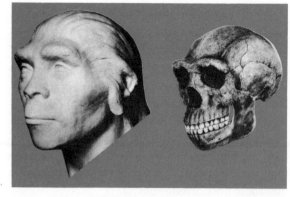

usually known by the name **Java man.** ❶ Later somewhat more complete skeletons were found.

Other fossils followed. In the late 1920's several teeth, parts of two lower jaws, and several skull fragments were unearthed in a cave at Choukoutien near Peking by the paleontologist Davidson Black. This fossil find, which he named *Sinanthropus* (sin·an'thrō·pəs) *pekinensis,* is known as **Peking man.** ❷ Bones of some forty specimens have since been found. With these fossil specimens were so-called stone "chopping stones." The chopping stones show considerable improvements over the poor flint tools found near Java man. Can we call the Java fossils "man"? Can we call the Peking fossils "man"? Were they "pre-man"? Study the reconstructions once again. How do they compare with those of Neanderthal man?

The Java and Peking fossils go back over half a million years. In 1924, Raymond Dart was studying a piece of limestone from a quarry at Taung, South Africa. He found, embedded in rock determined to be over a million years old, a skull unlike any he had ever seen before. It was the skull of a young "child," and several teeth were still in place. ❸ Dart named the fossil *Australopithecus* (ô·strā'lō·pi·thē'kəs) *africanus.* Since then

numerous australopithecine fossils have been found with the characteristic heavy jaw, low forehead, and small brain capacity. The australopithecines probably had an erect posture and used bones and teeth as tools. Though they could *use* tools, it is doubtful that they could *make* tools—except, perhaps, simple "pebble tools."

Today there is general agreement that the Java, Peking, and Taung fossils show human features. In fact, most paleontologists and anthropologists (scientists who study the physical characteristics and cultural history of man) prefer to classify both Java and Peking man as *Homo erectus,* possibly the earliest species of man. Cro-Magnon man is really *Homo sapiens,* whereas Neanderthal man is placed in a different species. But the various australopithecine fossils are *not* classified as *Homo.*

Are they pre-man? In recent years, numerous fossil finds in widely scattered parts of the world indicate that man has slowly evolved over more than a million years. The search is also on for earlier primates who might show evidence of pre-human traits. Much more evidence is needed before scientists can shed a clear light on man and his relatives.

Why do scientists who study man stress the importance of tools? The making of tools must

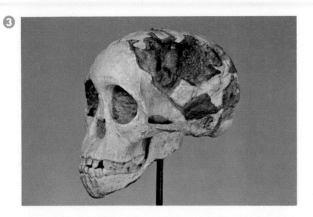

mean an attempt to control the environment. The hand is fit for many things, but it cannot split wood or break rock. Such activities require something harder. A hand ax, primitive as it is, can scrape away meat, break a bone, wedge apart wood, or even crack the skull of an attacking animal.

Moreover, once a tool is made, how does the tool-maker show others, say his children, how to make similar tools? Must not the tool-maker use signs or sounds to show his offspring how to make a similar tool? In other words, once Peking man learned how to make tools, he may have also found a way to communicate the ways of making tools to others. To live in groups requires a way to communicate many things by some means, however primitive. How true is this statement? If true,

then the pre-humans had in them the beginnings of cooperation. All this is speculation, of course. We will probably never know how accurate our speculation is.

REVIEW

1. Compare and contrast Neanderthal man with Cro-Magnon man with respect to physical traits and at least these cultural traits: tool-making, art, food-getting.

2. Compare Neanderthal man with modern man with respect to physical and cultural traits.

3. Compare the australopithecines with Neanderthal man with respect to physical traits. What is your hypothesis concerning the possible cultural traits of the australopithecines?

NEW VIEW

1. What primitive societies still flourish in North America? Study one primitive society sufficiently to enable you to give a report on its food-getting, art, music, clothing, and shelter.

2. What is your speculation as to why Neanderthal man disappeared some 50,000 years ago?

2. MAN—THE BEGINNINGS OF TRIBE, TOWN, AND CITY

Nowadays, you gather food in a most convenient way. The "gathering" occurs in a store of some sort. There you can generally rely on finding the food you want; it has only to be prepared or cooked for eating. Today, whole dinners are cooked and frozen; they need only be heated.

You and your family are so completely interdependent with other families in other towns and cities over the country that you rely on them to grow your food and to bring it to you. You rely on men on farms or ranches or cities everywhere in the country to supply your food by truck, train, or plane. It was not always so. Man was not always so fortunate. Man was once at the mercy of his environment as far as his food supply was concerned.

We get our knowledge of the way men lived in the past in at least two ways. The archeologist studies the sites where men lived, by digging out their villages and cities. So he learns how men lived. The anthropologist studies living communities; and in studying them tries to determine how customs arose and to discover the origin of cultures. By *culture,* an anthropologist means the sum total of all the ways men live. By combining what archeologists and anthropologists find, and by studying their interpretations of their findings, we come to some knowledge of how early men may have lived.

For instance, we learn that to live a life in one place—*a settled life*—requires different ways than does a roving life—*a nomadic life.* In a settled life, people may live in towns or cities. In a nomadic life, the people are usually organized into a tribe with its chief. Whenever man lives in a tribe, a town, or a city, he has learned to collaborate with other men to get his food and shelter.

Man as a Food Gatherer

No doubt, you have seen movies about the early colonial times. You have seen a group of colonists head west—on horses, in wagons, or even on foot. Most carried many supplies with them. Most of them lived "off the land," at least in part. Their guns and knives were used to hunt animals for meat. Other tools, their hatchets, were used to cut wood for fires and for shelter. Some used skins for making clothing, and tools (such as knives, needles, scissors) to sew the clothes. They were relatively fortunate; they had tools that allowed them to dominate the environment. Nevertheless, they lived off the environment.

On the other hand, consider an Indian village of the past. Their food, clothing, and shelter were taken directly from the land. Do you recall how certain Indians depended on the buffalo for meat, clothing, and shelter? They needed to understand their environment in order to survive.

Just as certain Indians used the buffalo, so the nomadic Australian aborigines use the kangaroo. They use the kangaroo as meat; its tendons are used to bind their spears; its teeth and claws serve as ornaments. The bones of the kangaroo are used for tools and pins.

And what of the Eskimo? Although many of them now live in wooden buildings in villages, we have evidence that they too lived close to their environment. Snow and ice gave them huts; the seal, walrus, whale, fish, and furred animals gave them food and clothing, as well as oil for their lamps.

In any event, a study of peoples now living gives us further understanding of an important concept: *organisms are interdependent with their environment.* Early man was surely interdependent with his environment—as hunter or as settler. As a food gatherer, he harvested his food from the environment. Usually the environment was rich enough to support him. Occasionally it failed him.

Soon man, gathering in tribes, began to search for ways in which he could assure his food supply. He did not want to be at the mercy of the environment. He did not want to fluctuate between plenty and famine. He began, in short, to grow his food.

Man as an Inventor

How did man change from a nomad to a settler in the first place? One good hypothesis, based on observation, shows that many settlements were near rivers, lakes, seashores. Per-

haps early man began with fishing settlements. Fish hooks are found in the remains of many settlements that existed before "farming" settlements. Men could live on shellfish and fish.

Some early lake dwellers are known to have raised domesticated cattle, pigs, sheep, goats—and even dogs. Perhaps wild dogs and pigs visited the settlements to feed on scraps of food. Perhaps these and other animals stayed around and reproduced. Perhaps this is the way the early "settlers" learned to breed animals for food and clothing. The photograph shows a model of an actual Swiss lake dwelling in which remains of all these animals as well as fish spears and fish nets have been found. ❶

Or imagine an early community in the tropics, where fish and fruit were plentiful. Perhaps early man threw the seeds of the fruits into a heap. Perhaps the seeds gave rise to the fruits they ordinarily spent their days searching for. Perhaps certain men or women found that these seeds could be planted to yield the fruit. It may have been like this; it may have been in some other way—but early man discovered farming. Yet man didn't stop with the cultivation of plants or the domestication of animals. He began to remake his environment—to control it.

Man as a Maker of Tools

It would be fascinating to take a trip to sites of settlements of some 10,000 years ago, 7,000 years ago, 5,000 years ago, 3,000 years ago, and 1,000 years ago. There you could observe vividly the differences between the cultures of various peoples. Instead we offer you two full pages of tools and suggest the following investigation. ■

■ AN APPRENTICE INVESTIGATION into Prehistoric and Recent Tools

The tools illustrated here are tools from about 8,000 years ago to the present. See if you can arrange them in order of their age. Also try to determine the use of each tool.

You can check your findings with those on page 505, where the age and use of the tools are given. How close were you?

Now arrange the tools into groups according to their use and study their differences according to their age.

An Investigation On Your Own

Make a tool from a seashell, or from a twig or branch. Or try to duplicate a stone hand ax shown on page 499 by chipping a rock that you find outdoors. Did you succeed? Was man of 8,000 years ago a good tool maker?

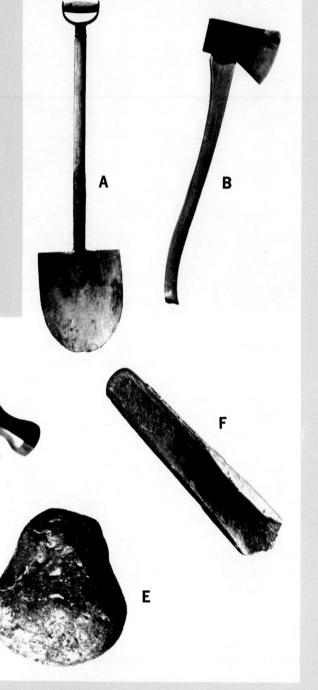

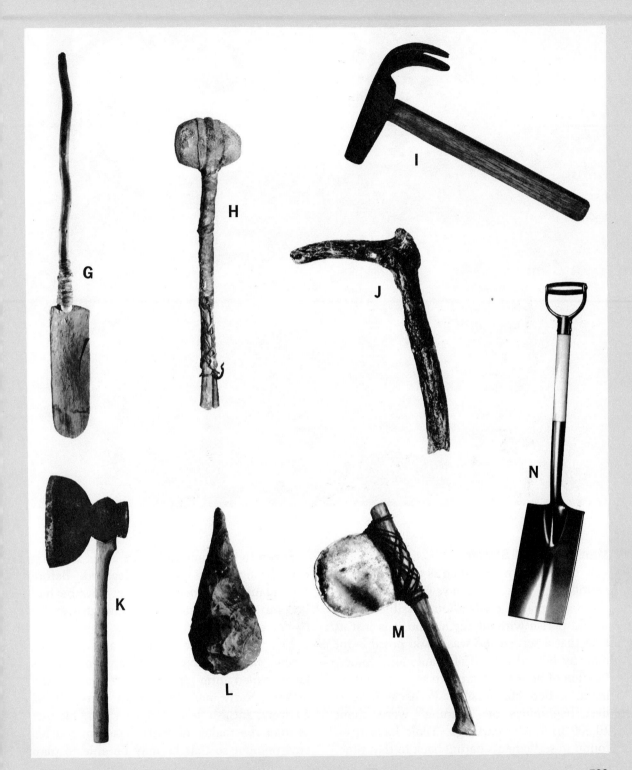

Man as a Food Grower

A modern farm or ranch is a beautiful invention. ❶ It is not always understood that the farm makes civilization possible. Cities would perish without them. And it is just as true that a settled life was made possible for man by his cultivation of plants and domestication of animals. That is to say, agriculture made settled life possible. Perhaps the earliest beginnings of "farming" were about 10,000 to 7,000 years ago. Tools have been found in settlements dating back to that time.

Seven to ten thousand years is not too long considering what we have learned. Before this, man was a *food gatherer;* now he had become a *food grower.* As a food grower, he could remain settled.

The species name for man, as you know, means *man, the wise.* Some anthropologists have called him *Homo faber* (man, the maker). Early man lived at the mercy of his environment. Modern man, accepting his role as man the maker of tools, has changed his environment so that he may be able to plan

TOOLS FROM 8,000 YEARS AGO TO THE PRESENT

Tool	Approximate number of years old	Use
L	7,000–8,000	chopping
J	7,000	digging
E	6,000	pounding
F	3,000–5,000	gouging
H	4,000	pounding
M	4,000	chopping
C	1,800	chopping
G	1,000	digging
A	100–150	digging
I	100–150	pounding
K	100–150	chopping
B	modern	chopping
D	modern	pounding
N	modern	digging

his future. If you are at the mercy of famine, or flood, or fear of constant death, you cannot plan for the future. Man thus began to change his environment. It took a long, long time. Slowly man began to live with his fellows in a community, a village, a town, a city. Many times the changes he produced were wise ones—at other times he paid a penalty for his lack of wisdom.

REVIEW

1. Compare a food-gathering society with a food-growing society.

2. Growing food seems easy. Why did it take so long for the food-growing culture to develop?

3. How do tools give us information about the culture of early man?

4. Make a list of some inventions of man and how they may have affected his way of life.

NEW VIEW

Compare your town with a "settlement" of early man with regard to the following:

    a. sources of food, clothing, shelter.

    b. ways of passing on information.

    c. ways of transportation.

    d. ways of getting heat and light.

3. MAN AND ARTIFICIAL SELECTION

Go to a modern market. Oranges, apples, cabbage, poultry, beef, beans, cultivated strawberries and blueberries, ice cream, cereal, canned foods of all kinds—food in plenty greets you. In all probability, not many of these foods existed 100 years ago in the form found today. Certainly, they did not exist in these forms 500,000 years ago. Although wild cattle, wild boars, and wild fowl did exist, the modern cattle, pigs, and chickens did not. Although wild grasses and wild cereal grains of different kinds did exist, rice, wheat, oats, and corn as we know them did not. Neither did cotton, flax, nor the sheep bred for wool. How did they come to be? We can only guess, but the guesses are *educated guesses.* That is, they are guesses based on some information; they are *hypotheses.* Of course, there can be good hypotheses and bad hypotheses.

As man passed on his knowledge of the environment to his offspring, man passed on the methods of **artificial selection** of organisms. Recall that *natural selection* is the way the environment operates to select those organisms *best adapted* to survive in the environment. Thus the mutations best fitted to the environment have the best chance for survival. When man selects the organisms *he* wants to survive, he has introduced *artificial selection.* Thus, man, not the natural environment, selects the organism for survival.

505

Artificial Selection at Work

Assume that you own a magnificent pair of gray German shepherd dogs. Assume also that in the first litter, all of the dogs are gray, replicas of the parents. This is logical, since the dogs are purebred and they have at least the same DNA for the trait of gray color.

The second litter of pups are also gray. In the third, however, a completely black, male puppy is born, magnificent in every way. You and your parents decide to develop a variety of black German shepherds and you select this male for breeding. This, in effect, is the nature of artificial selection.

Perhaps in the natural environment a *black* puppy born to *gray* wolves (which, like dogs, are in the genus *Canis*) might not have survived for various reasons. Black might be more easily seen among gray tree trunks; the puppy might, therefore, be easier prey.

Selected and protected by man, varieties that might not survive in the natural environment *do survive in the artificial, man-made environment*. For example, there are polled (hornless) cattle, particularly the famous polled Hereford (her′ fərd). ❷ Compare the polled Hereford with horned cattle, particularly with the longhorn that is now almost extinct. ❸ What particular characteristic would enable the longhorn to have a better chance of survival in the natural environment? The polled cattle *selected* by man (artificial selection) then survive in an *artificial environment perfected by man*.

Breeding—Then and Now

There is a distinct and important difference between the way man selected the polled Hereford and the way he may have selected (domesticated) the early varieties of wild plants and animals he desired. Early man was not a geneticist. Probably his selections were based on *trial and error*. The method of trial and error is a way of learning, but a time-consuming one.

Assume that early man learned that certain seeds, say, of a melon, could be planted. Assume that somehow he had learned that the strange bodies in the fruit, which he ordinarily spat out on the earth, grew into melons. He then learned to collect the seeds. Assume further that a mutant appeared, a melon twice the size of the wild variety. Man's brain was good. He reasoned that seeds of this giant melon might produce giant melons. Good reasoning but bad science, *perhaps*.

Suppose that the trait for the *giant* melon were recessive. Since the flower of the melon is open, the pollen of a *dwarf* melon could be transferred (by insects or wind) from the stamen of a dwarf plant to the stigma of the giant mutant flower. The seeds of the giant mutant flower might then produce, in the second generation, all dwarf melons. Only if early man saved these seeds and planted them, might he find the dominant (the dwarf) and the recessive (the giant) forms.

In other words, man used trial and error methods in breeding the form he desired. If the trial were successful, a "new" form might be found. If the trial were a failure, a "new" form might not be found. Over a long period of time, trial-and-error methods may work. Over a short period of time, trial and error may result in failure.

Scientific knowledge of the way genes are inherited, however, permits the breeder to partly set aside trial and error. He can, instead, make a prediction of the results with a limited error. That is, *if* the trait the breeder desires is inherited, then the breeder has the insight to plan a way of reaching his goal.

How long did it take man to advance from trial-and-error learning in breeding desired plants and animals to learning on the basis of data gained through scientific work?

Suppose we accept that man began growing food, as opposed to gathering it, about 7,000 to 8,000 years ago. Then scientific breeding based on the knowledge of genes can be assumed to have originated around Mendel's time. However, it is known that plant and animal breeding is an art that was practiced at least 2,000 to 1,000 years before Mendel—so much knowledge of breeding had been gained through trial and error.

Modern Breeders at Work

Since man as a food gatherer lived as part of the environment, his food supply depended on how rich in food, that is how productive of food, his environment was. Early man, both as food gatherer and as food grower, would have very much liked to have been assured of:

a. *a steady or increasing yield of food.* That is, he would have liked his environment to yield him more food—fish, beef, eggs, grain, fruit.

b. *food of better quality.* Even now we prefer sweeter and meatier fruits, tender rather than tough meat, seeds that produce flour with more protein or more starch, seedless fruits.

c. *animals and plants with special characteristics.* He wanted stronger animals to bear his burdens (oxen, mules, horses), swifter animals, flowers that were larger and lasted longer, disease-resistant plants (for example, wheat and oats that withstood rust, smut, and other fungi).

Now that plant and animal breeders base their work on an understanding of genetics, their aims are still somewhat the same. They breed for the following traits:

507

a. steady or increased yield.

b. improved quality.

c. special characteristics.

To develop these qualities they use the following procedures.

First, they *select* the organisms for their desirable traits—increased quantity, improved quality, or some other special characteristics.

Second, they *hybridize,* or cross two organisms with the desired traits. They continue crossing individuals until an organism that combines the desired traits is produced.

Finally, they *inbreed* the hybrid offspring until they have a pure breed of organisms with the desirable traits. The inbreeding is, of course, highly selective. Any offspring that does not meet the standards set by the breeder is not used for breeding.

In achieving his purpose, the breeder assures the offspring the best environment for the development of the trait. For example, the genes in a breed of cattle may be for increased yield of beef or milk, but if the feed, or pasture, or other environmental factors are not at their best, the genes may not express themselves.

In this way, man acts as an agent of evolution through artificial selection. Many of his selected organisms might not survive in the wild. That is, they could not survive natural selection. For instance, compare the huge hog bred for bacon and ham with the swift, vicious wild hog, or boar, as it is sometimes called. The domesticated hog is clever but slow, and no match for the speedy predators in the wild. The wild boar, any hunter will tell you, is one of the toughest animals in the field—clever, vicious, and wily.

REVIEW

1. Compare and contrast artificial selection with natural selection.

2. Compare and contrast the "natural" environment of 50,000 years ago with man's "natural" environment today.

3. Assume a rancher wants to develop cattle with thicker hides than those that now exist. How would he go about it?

4. Compare breeding by means of trial and error with breeding by means of modern scientific methods.

NEW VIEW

1. Can man with his knowledge today produce a new species or organism? Why or why not?

2. Selecting, hybridizing, and inbreeding are three major steps in breeding new varieties. Would new varieties be developed this same way if man were not present to act as the selector? Why or why not?

4. MAN—CHANGING THE ENVIRONMENT

Imagine a South American native ill with a fever in the year 1,000. Imagine the attempt to cure him—the witch doctor dressed in his awe-inspiring costume, doing his magic dance, uttering his magic words, giving the sick man a magic powder. Suppose this treatment continues every day for a week. A few days after the week's treatment, the patient recovers. What was responsible? The magic rites? The magic drug? The passage of a week's time in which the body's natural immunity overcame the illness?

We cannot know what was responsible for the cure; and because we cannot know, we cannot say which *cause* was responsible for the *effect*, the "cure." But suppose we know that the magic drug was prepared from the bark of the cinchona (sin·kō′nə) tree. The bark of the cinchona tree contains the drug *quinine* (kwī′nīn), which acts to depress many fevers, especially those of malaria. Therefore we might conclude that the drug was responsible for the recovery. To confirm this hypothesis we would have to have been there and insisted that the drug be given without the magic dance, or the magic words.

Almost 2,000 years ago men were still finding answers to their questions by the trial-and-error method; in the year 1,000 this was still generally true. Here and there some Greek and Arabian philosophers and Italian physicians and investigators had begun to invent a method by which they could invent new ways of doing things. This is sometimes known as the scientific method, or as the experimental method. Percy Bridgman, a Nobel Prize winner in physics, calls it "the methods of intelligence." Whichever term you prefer, science is a way of exploring the objects and events around us, and of seeking orderly explanations of these objects and events. But these orderly explanations must be tested—through investigation and through experiment. In short, do these explanations work? For example, what evidence through investigation have you for the explanation (theory) that the inheritance of physical traits is the result of the action of DNA (of genes)?

Science is a way, in short, of understanding ourselves and the environment. Once we understand the environment, we can modify it. In modifying or changing it, unfortunately, we may either improve it or destroy it.

Some Results of Understanding the Environment

The phrase "understanding the environment" is a powerful phrase even though it may not seem so. The environment around us consists of matter, energy, and life. In understanding the environment of matter, the environment of particles, atoms, and molecules, scientists and engineers have almost completely changed your life. Drugs such as those used in developing the vaccines of smallpox and polio have lengthened your life; gasoline enables you to go long distances; oil heats your houses; paints preserve homes and bridges; aspirin makes slight pain bearable. New metals and plastics, new medicines, new fibers—these and many other inventions—are changes resulting from understanding the environment of matter.

The understanding of the environment of energy has resulted in magnificent achievements. The entire space program is the result of the work of scientists in past centuries; Galileo (1564–1642) and Newton (1642–1727) first gave us understanding of the motion of objects. The automobile, airplane, heating systems, cooling systems, refrigerator, light bulb, radio, TV, radar, sonar, and most

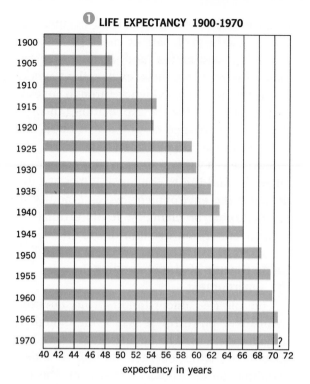

❶ LIFE EXPECTANCY 1900-1970

Year	
1900	
1905	
1910	
1915	
1920	
1925	
1930	
1935	
1940	
1945	
1950	
1955	
1960	
1965	
1970	?

40 42 44 46 48 50 52 54 56 58 60 62 64 66 68 70 72
expectancy in years

recently lasers have resulted from scientists understanding energy.

Understanding life in the environment has resulted in vast achievements. An understanding of the variety of food organisms, their breeding, their genetics has resulted in a tremendous increase in our food supply. Knowledge of disease organisms has added about 23 years of life to every infant born in this decade, compared with an infant born in 1900. ❶ However, knowledge of the environment has resulted not only in benefits but also in destruction. This last aspect of man's work we shall deal with later.

Understanding begins with understanding how the world works. The concepts in this book are but an introduction to the understandings that have come out of man's use of the methods of intelligence, the methods of the scientists.

The Methods of Intelligence

The methods of intelligence we are to examine took about a million years to develop. That is, man as a scientist began with *man;* no other organism uses the methods of intelligence as man does. A pig, a dog, a chimpanzee, and a gorilla can learn by trial and error; only man *designs* an investigation. You have been designing investigations throughout your work this year. Now let's analyze what is at the center of an investigation.

In the investigation there are observations to be made and there may be an experiment. However, the essential feature of the scientist's pursuit is knowing whether he is accurate in his predictions; he always tries to test what he thinks will work. *Testability* is the essence of science. Perhaps you like the term *verification* rather than testability. What does testing, or verifying, predictions involve? Two examples from the field of biology may help us to understand.

Early in the days before scientists understood the nature of disease, it was not understood that bacteria caused disease. The work of Louis Pasteur (1822–1895) and Robert Koch (1843–1910), among others, was truly pioneer work, done amid great misunderstanding. These scientists designed investigations, with control experiments, in order to test the accuracy of their predictions. Thus, Koch discovered the cause of tuberculosis, the tubercle bacillus. He injected a number of animals (say 20) with the bacillus he predicted would cause the disease. He tested his prediction by not injecting 10 other animals; this was his control experiment. None (or practically none) of his control animals should develop the disease, if his prediction was correct. All (or practically all) of Koch's injected animals should develop the disease. ("Practically none" or "practically all" allow

510

for errors.) The injected animals developed tuberculosis; the uninjected animals did not. Koch's predictions were verified.

Pasteur worked on the problems of immunity against bacteria, among other things. For example, he developed antibodies against a disease of sheep, anthrax. In one of the experiments he designed, he injected 20 sheep with an antibody against the anthrax bacillus, and shortly thereafter injected them with the anthrax bacillus. He also injected 20 other sheep with just the anthrax bacillus. The 20 sheep injected with the antibody lived; the 20 controls died of the disease. Pasteur tested his predictions through the control experiment.

There are other ways of testing one's predictions, or hypotheses. How did Mendel test his? He predicted, you recall, that if two hybrids are mated, the offspring should be in a ratio of 3:1 (3 with the dominant trait, 1 with the recessive). His test was one of mathematical reasoning based on the way he thought genes worked.

How did Muller test his prediction (hypothesis)?

How did Beadle and Tatum test their hypothesis?

How did Darwin test his theory?

How do plant and animal breeders test their hypotheses?

A definition of science would then emphasize testing one's beliefs, one's theories, one's predictions, one's hypothesis. A definition of science might be:

*Science is the exploration of the objects and events in the material universe, in order to develop orderly explanations (concepts) of these objects and events; and these explanations must be testable.**

* Based on a definition by George Gaylord Simpson, a leading paleontologist, now at Harvard.

The methods of intelligence the scientist uses enable him to do at least three things.

First, *to explore the objects and events around him.* For this he uses many kinds of tools to aid his senses: microscopes, telescopes, sonar, radar, and X rays, among many others.

Second, *to develop orderly explanations.* These are the hypotheses and theories of science, that is, the concepts of science.

Third, *to test his concepts.* For this he sets up investigations and experiments of all kinds. His investigations may be observations in the laboratory or the field, mathematical solutions, or control experiments. The variety of investigations is great.

Is there a way in which we might summarize the scientists methods of intelligence? Perhaps this way.

A scientist, having spent his life in learning, begins his days with understanding and knowledge. Knowledge and understanding are always incomplete or even, at times, incorrect. Nevertheless, a scientist begins with an understanding—a concept. Assume that a scientist (many years ago) was working in the field of prevention of disease; specifically working on the disease pellagra (pə·lā′grə). The concept he brought to his work was: Diseases are caused by bacteria. However, he was not able to isolate a bacterium for pellagra. Instead he isolated a problem: What causes pellagra? He had read that a lack of vitamins causes certain diseases. Perhaps, he hypothesized, pellagra is caused by lack of a vitamin. Follow the diagram to trace one way of work in which the scientist attempts to verify his hypothesis—and in so doing, not only finds new knowledge but also new problems.

If you study the diagram carefully, you will come to understand that the scientist

❶ A DIAGRAM OF A SCIENTIST'S WAY: his methods of intelligence

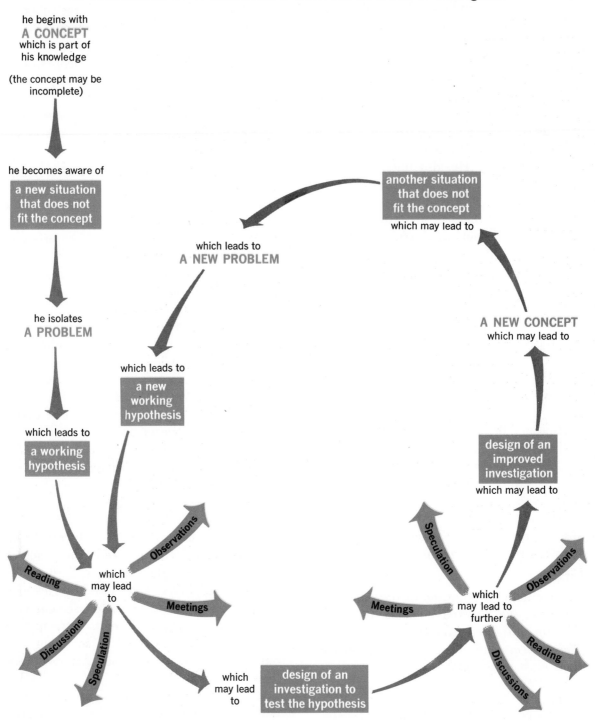

he begins with
A CONCEPT
which is part of
his knowledge

(the concept may be
incomplete)

he becomes aware of

a new situation that does not fit the concept

he isolates
A PROBLEM

which leads to
a working hypothesis

which may lead to

Reading

Observations

Meetings

Discussions

Speculation

which may lead to
design of an investigation to test the hypothesis

which leads to
a new working hypothesis

which leads to
A NEW PROBLEM

another situation that does not fit the concept
which may lead to

A NEW CONCEPT
which may lead to

design of an improved investigation
which may lead to

which may lead to further

Speculation

Observations

Meetings

Reading

Discussions

does not begin with a problem. ❶ He begins with long study and training; he learns what others before him came to know and *how they came to know it*. In other words, he learns of the orderly explanations developed by other scientists; and he learns, through investigation, how they tested their explanations. On this base of knowledge, won by others, the scientist begins his own investigation. He stands, as the great scientist Isaac Newton said, "on the shoulders of giants." On the base of the known, the scientist investigates the unknown.

In science, we have, then, a vast amount of knowledge; and we know, in most cases, how we came to know what we know. And what of you? Is science your field of work—your life work? If so, you will contribute to the body of knowledge. You will find your life well spent.

REVIEW

1. Do you prefer the phrase "scientific methods" to "methods of intelligence"? If so, why? If not, why not?

2. What part does the hypothesis play in the work of the scientists?

3. Why does a scientist generally not begin with a "problem" but with "knowledge" of the field in which he is working?

4. Are the methods diagrammed on page 512 superior to trial-and-error methods?

NEW VIEW

Science is thought by many people to be without values. A value is something we prize—whether it is an object, an event, or a behavior. Thus we prize an object (our mother's, father's, or friend's picture), an event (the signing of the Declaration of Independence), a behavior (a handshake or an act of kindness).

Truth is a value. Openmindedness is a value. Humility is a value. So, too, these are values: accuracy, honesty, happiness, acknowledging the contributions of others, kindness, good sportsmanship, and the like. What other values can you name?

Which values would you expect scientists to prize? Make a list of these values. Discuss them. If your teacher wishes, discuss them in class.

5. RELATING THE CONCEPTS

Look back to the beginning of the year's work. You began with a study of the environment. You found that organisms were adapted to their environment. Throughout your study, you became increasingly aware of man's interdependence with his environment. Indeed, each introduction to a new unit of work focussed on this aspect of the concept of *environment*: man modifies the environment. Perhaps you questioned man's use of his environment: was it altogether wise? For better or worse, man is the only organism who can change the physical environment by his own inventions. To do this he invented "methods of invention." These are the ways of the scientist, the methods of intelligence.

Reviewing the Concepts

▶ *Like the other organisms inhabiting this planet, man has evolved from ancestral organisms.* The evidence is not as clear as we should like, but the evidence available indicates that *Homo sapiens*, the present species of man, is not the only species of man ever to inhabit the earth. He was preceded by such species as *Homo neanderthalensis* (Neanderthal man). It is not known which species of man was the ancestor of modern man. The study of the evolution of man is complex.

513

▶ *Early man learned to adapt to his environment first as food gatherer, then as food grower.* Man first gathered his food from the plants in his environment, and got his meat and fish by hunting or fishing. As he learned, first by trial and error and later through careful observation, he began to plant his own crops and domesticate his own animals.

Man learned fast. But just as important, he passed on his knowledge to his offspring, who, in turn, added to the fund of knowledge. Over the million or so years of his existence, man stored his knowledge and learned to become independent of food shortages. He stored knowledge, and he stored food.

▶ *Man invented a "method of intelligence": science.* Science is a way of exploring the objects and events in the world about us; it uses all the methods of intelligence. In exploring the world of matter, energy, and life, man, as scientist, develops orderly explanations of what he observes; then he tests these orderly explanations, or concepts. A concept that is faulty when tested is dicarded. For example, once man believed that the disease organisms arose spontaneously from mud or decaying organisms. When the microscope was invented, man could see that microorganisms came from other microorganisms. He then discarded the theory of spontaneous generation. A theory that does not stand the tests of science must be discarded. Thus far, the theory of evolution has stood up against the test of time.

▶ *Man has modified the early environment.* Science and engineering have combined to build the concepts and tools that changed the environment. With his submarines and aqua lungs, man competes with the fish; with his airplanes, he competes with the birds. His automobiles outrun the fastest animals. By controlling the temperature with his heating and cooling devices, man can live anywhere on earth. And now he reaches into space.

Man has at his disposal the concepts and tools to change the environment. Will he be wise enough to conserve it in health and in beauty? You will play a part in the conservation of the environment.

Testing Yourself

1. How did Neanderthal man differ from modern man? How was he similar?

2. How did Cro-Magnon man's life differ from that of modern man?

3. Describe early man as food gatherer.

4. Describe early man as food grower.

5. Describe early man as tool maker.

6. Is learning to make a rock into a tool similar to learning to drive a car? What are the differences in the two acts of learning?

7. Give an example of plant or animal breeding that demonstrates the application of genetics.

8. What is the difference between *natural selection* and *artificial selection?* Give an example of each.

9. Life expectancy has increased from about 47 years in 1900 to just over 70 years in 1970. Give several reasons for this increase.

10. How did Gregor Mendel use the "methods of intelligence" to determine the way organisms inherit traits? How did other scientists build on his work?

Extending the Concepts

Investigation 1. Perhaps a scientist lives near you. Or perhaps you live near a university. With your teacher's permission, arrange an interview with a scientist. Try to find out what the scientist thinks of the way scientists work. Would he or she agree with the "model" on page 512?

Investigation 2. Biological evolution is based on changes in the genes (DNA). Cultural evolution is a name given to changes in ways of life or ways of behaving. If you accept this concept of cultural evolution, perhaps you would like to investigate the following:

    a. Describe at least two ways in which man's behavior has changed since the time of Neanderthal man.

    b. In what ways do you see man changing culturally to adapt to life in crowded cities?

Suggested Reading

Howell and the Editors of LIFE, *Early Man* (Life Nature Library), New York, Time, Inc., 1965.

Carrington, Richard, *A Million Years of Man*, Cleveland, World Publishing Co., 1963.

Coon, Carleton S., *The Story of Man*, Second Edition Revised, New York, Knopf, 1962.

Moore and the Editors of LIFE, *Evolution* (Life Nature Library), New York, Time Inc., 1962.

21 | Life — What of the Future Environment?

Observe living things anywhere in their environment—in a forest, the sea, a pond, or a cave. Wherever we go, we find living things adapted to the environment in which they live, that is, *if the environment will support life.*

The living things in a forest are different from the living things in a pond or river. A deer is adapted to life in the forest, to living on land.❶ A minnow is adapted to life in the water—its gills, its fins adapt it to an aquatic environment. Whatever organism we study, we find adaptations in structure that fit the organism to the environment. The structure of a robin's wings adapts it to flight. A frog's webbed feet adapt it to swimming. From such observations is fashioned a major concept:

Organisms are adapted to their environment.

We observe more. We find organisms, in the forest or in the stream, in movement, searching for food. We find the source of their food in one type of organism—the green plant, the basic source of energy for all organisms. The green plant, through photosynthesis, captures the sun's energy and converts it into carbohydrates. Then the green plant combines the carbohydrates with minerals from the soil into proteins, and sometimes rearranges the carbohydrates into fats. The green plant thus serves its own growth needs, but in so doing it furnishes food for the plant consumers, animals.

Animals, in turn, furnish food for each other, and return carbon dioxide to the air, to be used by green plants in photosynthesis. Thus one basic chemical reaction underlies the capture of energy:

$$\text{energy} + 6\ CO_2 + 6\ H_2O \longrightarrow C_6H_{12}O_6 + 6\ O_2$$

Organisms are not only adapted to their environment, then, but are interdependent with

it. Thus we come to understand another major concept describing the activities of organisms.

Organisms are interdependent with each other and with their environment; they exchange matter and energy with each other and with their environment.

We study the internal structure of organisms, and almost at once come to see a unity among all organisms. The cell is the unit of structure that we observe: all organisms are made of cells, with the exception of the viruses. The cell is also the unit of function: it manufactures enzymes and hormones, it secretes substances to make bone and cartilage. In multicellular organisms the cells are interdependent, working with each other to maintain the health of the internal environment—the tissues, organs, and organ systems of the organism. Thus we come to a major concept that emphasizes the unity of living things:

Organisms are composed of cells; the cell is the unit of structure and function.

Now we begin to see likenesses in organisms. We begin to understand how it is that organisms have similar life functions: food-getting, responsiveness, growth, reproduction. We see, too, that organisms can be grouped on the basis of similarity in structures. We seek out similarities in organisms, and find that organisms fall into large groups: kingdoms. In turn, kingdoms have useful subdivisions: phyla, classes, orders, families, genera, and species. Groups overlap—lions and whales, for example, are mammals. And they are also chordates, having a dorsal nerve cord and dorsal rod of cartilage (a notochord) like amphibians, reptiles, and fish.

We also have to account for differences as well as similarities in organisms. A whale and a sequoia are similar in that both are made of cells, but they are also different. We find an explanation of differences in a remarkable substance: deoxyribonucleic acid, DNA.

The hunt for DNA began years ago. The scent was detected by a great and humble man, Gregor Mendel, who searched over 100 years ago for determiners of heredity. Since his work, the determiners of heredity have been identified as the genes within the chromosomes. The chromosome is the home of this magnificent molecule, DNA. And DNA in turn has been found to be a code of heredity. It is a code made up of substances that can recombine to form patterns, like letters in an alphabet. Each pattern controls the formation of substances in the cell through the messengers we call RNA, ribonucleic acid.

Thus the cell performs its functions, from DNA in the nucleus to RNA in the cytoplasm to protein substances that form the cell and the traits of the organism. And even DNA doesn't act alone. If a substance to produce a certain trait is not present in the environment, DNA cannot produce the trait.

The trait to make chlorophyll, for example, is inherited; but without light, which is part of the environment, the green color of chlorophyll is not produced. So we bring the base of heredity, DNA, and the environment together in still another major concept:

An organism is the product of its heredity and environment.

DNA can vary greatly since the substances it is made of can recombine in many different combinations. Thus we can begin to understand the great variety of organisms—but only those organisms that are fitted to the environment survive. An eagle born without wings does not survive because it is at the mercy of its environment—which includes those who feed on helpless eagles.

We come, then, to understand that it isn't just that organisms are adapted to the environment, but that organisms *not adapted* to the environment do not survive. Darwin called this process *natural selection.* He was striving to account for the variety of living organisms and for the fossils of organisms that had not survived. He accounted for them with his *theory of natural selection.*

Darwin proposed that the environment selected those organisms fittest to survive. Since food supply is limited, since shelter is limited, since enemies in the environment catch and kill those that are slow, diseased, or otherwise unfit, the environment naturally selects those fit to survive. This theory of *natural selection* helps us to understand how organisms die out. The environment changes. The organisms that do not change fast enough to adapt to changes in the environment do not survive. Thus, seed ferns died out, as did the dinosaurs and trilobites.  Their fossils remain to tell us of a world long past and of environments that no longer exist.

Yet, in a sense organisms do not die out completely, for their DNA is passed on, generation after generation, even though it changes through mutation. We are then able to form another great concept, one that unites all organisms:

Organisms are continuous over the ages past.

We trace present organisms back in time through their fossils. The modern horse we trace back 60 million years, to a small animal the size of a fox. Mammals and birds are traced back to reptiles; reptiles show their unity with the past, for we trace their ancestry to the Coal Age and before. As we do, we come upon a wondrous understanding. It isn't really strange that organisms have simi-larities, for the organisms of the present developed from those that survived in the past. We begin to understand the differences and the variety as well, for DNA has the potential for great variety in its make-up. Which organisms survived out of this variety, through the ages of the earth, the environment determined by natural selection. All organisms now alive, man included, survive because of their fitness to the environment.

At least, this is true up to now. Now man has added another kind of selection to natural selection. Man, with a new degree of adaptiveness permitted by his brain, has brought about *artificial selection.* Because of his brain, man can adapt to many environments—by taking his environment with him. He puts his environment into a submarine, and competes with fish. In an airplane, he rivals the birds in flight. He takes his environment into a capsule and invades space. Because he invades other environments, he controls other organisms. In a sense, **man** can now determine which organisms are to survive.

Man—let's say *we,* for we are talking about ourselves—we change organisms by selecting those mutants that fit our needs. The cattle, fowl, plants on our farms and ranches could not survive in the natural environments of the world today. They survive only in the artificial environments made by us. We substitute artificial selection for natural selection.

We not only change the organisms about us, we change the environment. We pollute rivers and the air. We cause soil erosion and our rivers turn brown.

On the other hand, we can, and sometimes do, build beautiful homes, towns, and cities. We can, and sometimes do, cleanse the rivers. We can, and do, stop erosion. We can keep forests and fields in beauty. We can use our knowledge wisely to conserve our world in beauty, fit for all organisms.

But has man done so? Let's probe the question: Has man conserved the environment?

1. ON THE DESIRE TO CONSERVE

The scientist values accuracy; he values truth. To value something is to prize it.

This year you had some experience with the art of investigation. You not only investigated with the help of your teacher and the authors of this book, but also on your own. In fact, in almost each apprentice investigation there were suggestions titled "An Investigation On Your Own." If anything, you must have learned that to investigate *on your own* meant not only giving up time and energy, but giving considerable thought as well. To investigate on your own is to value knowledge. The investigator values accuracy and truth.

To value plants and animals—and man—is to conserve them. To conserve means to use wisely. Conservation is then a value. To conserve sequoias is to value sequoias. To conserve the eagle is to value the eagle.

To conserve means to make choices. To make choices means to value one thing above another. For example, to conserve soil may

mean *not* to plow it to plant crops (wheat, corn, apples, grapes, or pecans.) To conserve a forest may mean *not* to cut down part of it to free the land in order to build homes.

Choices *to build* or *not to build, to plow land* or *not to plow* are choices in which values play a large part. Choices like these are not given to science, but to the scientist acting as a citizen. They are choices given to any citizen. They are choices given to you.

Of course, many choices to conserve are based on the knowledge gained by scientists. For example, scientists have investigated the results of polluting a lake or river with DDT. They have investigated the effects of **biological magnification** on the killing of algae, fish, and birds. What is meant by biological magnification? Simply, the term means that an effect on living things, a biological effect, is magnified by organisms which feed on each other. The diagram shows the effect of a pesticide such as DDT. ❷ Notice that a trace of

❷

DDT found in algae is magnified many times in the tiny water fleas. Why? The tiny water fleas feed on the algae. The DDT from each alga is absorbed in the stored oil or fat of the water flea. The many water fleas taken in by the small fish leave their DDT in the fat of the small fish. Why does the level of DDT increase in the fat of the larger fish? Why may DDT kill a bird that feeds on the larger fish?

If these algae, fish, and birds are to be conserved, a *choice* must be made by the citizens who live in the area of the lake or river. In other words, the citizens use the concepts and facts discovered by scientists, *but they, as citizens, act on their own values.* In the past, citizens (or their elected representatives) have made unwise choices. For example, they have not used the concepts underlying conservation to save their lakes; Lake Erie was almost destroyed. ❶ They have not always valued their cities; they have polluted the air. They have made the cities ugly.

Let us probe several problems in conservation of the environment. Perhaps you will be able to make firmer your own choices, based on your values. You can do so in the way to which you have become somewhat accustomed—*by investigating.* But first some cases of wise use and misuse.

Cases of Use and Misuse

CASE 1. Man has learned to use fuels for heating and for transportation. He has learned to live in cities.

The total effect of great numbers of people living together in a large city means that the waste gases from the use of oil, gasoline, incinerators, furnaces, industrial plants, and the like are released into the air. Thus, in one area alone it is estimated that the organic compounds released in the atmosphere are about 2,900 tons a day. In this area it is estimated that some 790 tons of the gas nitrogen dioxide (NO_2) are released into the air daily.

Where winds are normal, these harmful and poisonous substances are carried away and diluted by the air. But in certain areas, particularly where the average daily tempera-

ture is high, a layer of warm air may keep the gases and wastes from escaping. The result is smog. If the smog content is high, the results may be eye irritation and actual physical harm to the people. The effects of smog on health are not yet completely known, and it is still a matter of much discussion.

Smog is the evidence of pollution of air. We can control air pollution as we have begun to control water pollution. True, it will be expensive. It may mean using sources of fuel that do not produce pollutants, perhaps nuclear power plants and electric heating. No doubt it will mean controlling automobile exhaust fumes and industrial smoke. It may mean a different automobile engine.

Is your area affected by smog? What are the sources of the smog? What is being done to correct the condition?

CASE 2. Now let's look back about 8,000 years to another unwise use of knowledge. Some agricultural scientists think that the ancient Sumerians invented irrigation. They built a network of canals that brought water

to the plains of Mesopotamia, a country in ancient Asia. The canals, still the wonder of modern engineers, did their work. The valley flourished. People flocked to the cities. In order to house them, the trees near the upper Euphrates and Tigris Rivers had to be cut down. The inevitable followed. After the trees were cut, the rainfall was not broken by the trees, nor could the forest floor absorb sudden or savage downpours. The result was floods. The floods washed the soil into the irrigation canals and ditches and clogged them. The Sumerian farmers and their slaves labored to remove the silt. At times, the removed silt stood almost 50 feet high along the banks of the canals. Finally, it became impossible to keep the canals clear.

Historians say that from that point the irrigation system failed. The land could no longer support the population that had flocked to the cities. The Sumerian civilization began to die out.

Of course, it is not possible to know whether the Sumerians knew that cutting down the

forests might result in floods, which in turn would fill the canals with silt. Canals and lakes are often clogged by silt, and so are small rivers. Moreover, silting kills the fish.

CASE 3. In contrast, let's look at a wise use of the environment.

The Ohio River was once called an "open sewer"; the industrial wastes made the river foul in many places. The photograph of the Ohio River shows fish that died as a result of industrial wastes being dumped into the river. ❶ Now it is again becoming a haven for swimming, fishing, and other uses fit for life. The Ohio is on its way to becoming a clean, clear river once again. Why?

The Ohio River Valley Sanitation Commission has developed a series of agreements to which industrial plants, cities, and towns along the river are now adhering. For instance, before water from towns and cities is released into the river, the water is passed through sewage or chemical disposal plants. In these plants the impurities, the poisons,

and the bacteria are reduced. Then the water can be used again and again. Some industrial plants use the same water as many as 30 to 50 times.

Do you know any place where the rivers are silting? Do you know any place near you where the rivers or lakes are being used to receive garbage or refuse? Do you know any place near you where the river is used to receive the waste of an industrial plant?

There are many associations like the Ohio River Valley Sanitation Commission springing up over the country. Is there one in your area?

CASE 4. In a certain town, a tract of land, some 240 acres in size, was sold to a builder. This builder did not use his bulldozer to uproot trees and tear up the topsoil, unlike the situation shown in the photograph. ❷ He had seen how rain and wind eroded the soil, leaving gullies—and ugliness. Consequently, the owners of the new homes did not have to undo any damage. They did not have to fill gullies or plant new trees and grass.

Rather, this builder designed his homes using the trees as shade. He used plastic coverings to keep the soil from eroding until the new grass could grow. Moreover, he set aside eight and a half acres for a park. He had learned that man needs to live in serenity. He needs not only pure food, pure water, pure air, but space as well. He needs an area where his children can play in safety and in health. Is there a park in your area?

MORE CASES? We could multiply the cases wherein man, having learned how to harness fuels, electricity, and machines to produce the things he wanted, also changed his environment. He has not always used his knowledge wisely. It is possible to list example after example. Man knows that the plants and animals in an area are interdependent. Over the years the environment can support certain kinds of animals and plants in numbers that seem almost to control themselves. Yet, knowing better, man introduced the rabbit into Australia. And with no natural enemies of the rabbit on that continent, they multiplied and became an expensive pest.

Modifying the Environment

Man knows well how to build cities; how to control pollution; how to control erosion. Yet have you passed roads with garbage and junkyards along the sides? Have you passed areas where the stench of wastes from industrial plants hangs in the air? Have you traveled along the highway in the "fresh" air only to find the air filled with the exhaust gases of automobiles?

These questions lead to an investigation on your own—an investigation that will require your taking several long walks around your own town or city.

Is a river being polluted? Why?

Is soil eroding? Why?

Are organisms—large trees, shrubs, birds, insects, fish—being destroyed? Why?

Are the roadsides being used as garbage dumps; are they full of litter? Why?

It may be that there are good and sufficient reasons why some of these events are happening. It is important to at least know why.

Clearly, man—after a million years—has learned to modify his environment. He has built hospitals; he has developed medicines; he has eliminated many diseases; he has prolonged life. He has learned how to make his environment yield him food, lumber, wool, cotton; he has built homes and fashioned clothing to protect him against the weather. He has developed new combinations of metals, new fibers, new building materials; the chemists' magic is everywhere. He has built engines to transport him on the ground, in the air, and out into space. Man has walked on the moon.

The men who travel to the moon go in space ships and wear space suits. In a sense they take the earth's environment (purified, of course) with them. Men who can invent ways of going to the moon can invent ways of conserving the environment of the earth. Conserving, of course, means wise use. Conservation means the recognition by man that he is not only interdependent with his environment, he is also responsible for it. Should not man, if he values a healthy and healing environment, keep it in health and beauty? Should he not keep his environment fit for all life and for living?

Now to your independent study.

REVIEW

1. Give an example of a change in the environment that demonstrates the application of science as a method of intelligence. How does your example demonstrate man's ability to test his findings?

2. Give an example to demonstrate man's poor use of his environment. Use an example in your community perhaps. How should this misuse be corrected?

3. Give an example to demonstrate man's wise use of his environment. Again use an example in your community. How may these examples be multiplied?

NEW VIEW

1. The suggestion has been made that man might save the plants and animals of the world if he were to build his houses underground. What do you think of this suggestion?

2. Another suggestion has been made that man might live in huge mile-high buildings. Each building might house 5,000 people. The mile-high house would have hospitals, banks, movie houses, shops, supermarkets—everything people in a "town" of 5,000 might need. Not only would this save space, but also among the apartment cities would be forests, fields, streams, and lakes. What do you think of this suggestion?

2. ON THE WISE USE OF ECOSYSTEMS: AN INDEPENDENT STUDY

You have seen a pond. Possibly you have observed life in it. But it isn't always easy to get to a pond. It isn't always convenient to study a pond in winter time. But, you can study the life in a micropond. *Micro,* of course, means tiny, or small. A micropond, therefore, is a tiny pond. As the term is used here, it means a pond developed *in a jar.*

One such micropond has been studied by two students for more than a year. The organisms, including the algae, protozoans, and other microscopic invertebrates the students found during one year, are shown on page 526. You may find these photomicrographs, as well as the references at the ends of chapters dealing with these organisms, useful in identifying the organisms in your microponds. ■

■ AN INTRODUCTORY INVESTIGATION into Succession in Microponds

NOTE: Each investigation lettered A, B, C, D, or E may take more than a month. Some will take more than a year.

Quart jars are fine as the containers, or "walls," of your micropond. Be certain that they are all alike and that each has a cover. A screw cap is best, since it can be left on loosely to permit air to enter.

To make your microponds, prepare four jars as follows: Fill each jar three-quarters full with pond or aquarium water. To one jar, add a lima bean-size bit of hard-boiled egg yolk.❶ Crumble the piece between your fingers. To the second jar, add 10 rice grains.❷ To the third, add 10 wheat or oat grains. To the fourth, add 2 sprigs of *Elodea.*❸ Keep all jars in medium light and away from heat. Would it be better to have two jars for each? Why?

At least every three days, examine about five drops from the top, sides, and bottom of each culture. Be sure to use a separate medicine dropper for each jar.

Compare the organisms that develop in the egg-yolk culture with those that develop in the other cultures.

The following questions may guide you in your study. Undoubtedly, you will also have questions of your own.

A. Do similar organisms succeed each other in the different cultures? For instance, when and where does an organism such as *Paramecium* appear? What organism precedes it? What organism follows it? Or is there no succession?

B. In which type of culture does succession occur the fastest? the slowest? How do you explain your observations?

C. In which types of culture do organisms reach the peak of their population fastest? slowest? How do you explain this?

D. Do the cultures ever die out? If so, why? If not, why not?

E. Is there a cycle of succession? That is, do organisms seem to die out, or decrease greatly in population, only to reappear, or increase, again later?

Microscopic Organisms in a Micropond

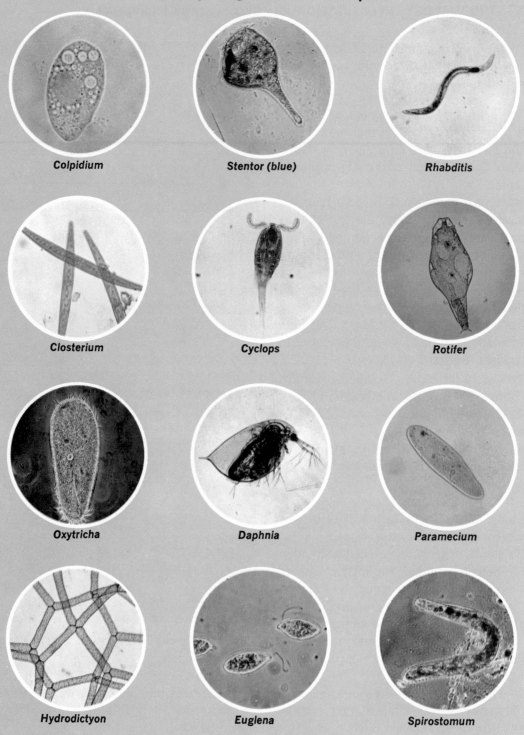

Colpidium

Stentor (blue)

Rhabditis

Closterium

Cyclops

Rotifer

Oxytricha

Daphnia

Paramecium

Hydrodictyon

Euglena

Spirostomum

A Newer View of Succession— and Interdependence

How can you use what you have learned about succession in your investigation of microponds? Let's probe the concepts underlying your observations.

In Unit I, you studied:

Life in a Pond
Life in a Swiftly Flowing Stream
Life in a Deep Lake
Food Chains and Their Links

Review once again the underlying concepts in these sections (pages 4–22 and 35–40). Is there anything you uncovered in your investigation that does not fit these concepts?

Plants and animals within a given environment are interdependent.

Interdependent living things are joined in a community.

In any living community there are food chains typical of that community.

Continuing Your Investigation into Ecosystems

Surely, the word "overfeeding" is too simple a word. Yet try this for yourself and determine whether "overfeeding" might be useful—up to the point where a more accurate term can be substituted.

Analyze once again your experience with the microponds and the growing of a culture of protozoans (page 311). What must have happened to the egg yolk? How could it serve as food for the protozoans? They could, of course, feed on it directly. And, no doubt, protozoans sweep some of the finer particles of egg yolk into their gullets. So too with tiny particles of other foodstuff. However, if you examine the culture carefully—and with a powerful (oil immersion) microscope—you will find the story is different. You will find the culture swarming with bacteria. These are the bacteria of decay (page 243). You will also find organisms, such as colpidium (page 526), that feed on the bacteria. In turn, the larger protozoans feed on the smaller ones, and on the bacteria as well.

Suppose you were to add too much egg yolk, or rice, or wheat. That is, you "overfeed." One possibility is that the bacteria will multiply very rapidly, and so will the smaller organisms. As these organisms move about and use energy, they use up oxygen. As you learned, they use up oxygen in their cells as they use the food for growth, for repair, and for energy. Soon the limited oxygen supply in the jar is used up. Then the organisms die.

We observe then: overfeeding is dangerous to the life in the culture.

Overfeeding in One Ecosystem

Suppose we consider a lake near a city. A lake is an ecosystem; it is an environment to which living things are specially adapted. The city discharges *treated* sewage into the lake. By treated sewage we mean that bacteria in sewage-treating plants have "fed" on the sewage. In feeding on the sewage, the bacteria break it down into harmless products, carbon dioxide, and water.

Suppose now the sewage of the city increases due to an increase in population in the city. Suppose the city cannot now *treat* (use enough bacteria to break down) all the sewage. Untreated sewage now flows into the lake. The lake is *polluted*—by sewage.

Suppose, too, the water from rains and rivers flows into the lake. Suppose the rain and river water carries with it fertilizer used on the farms and fields.

Now both the sewage and the fertilizer may act as *nutrients* for algae. The algae will multiply very rapidly, as will the bacteria.

Further, the algae may form masses on the lake. ❶ The bottom layers of the algae which are not now reached by sunlight die. The bacteria multiply greatly and use up the oxygen. The net result—the oxygen supply of the lake is used up. Fish and other aquatic animals die. The lake may die.

This is perhaps oversimplified, but it is a model of what happens in a lake when it is "fed" with too much nutrient—sewage and fertilizer. Scientists call this type of pollution **eutrophication** (yōō′trä·fə′kā·shan). The term means, in a sense, overfeeding. In the next few years, you will hear more and more of eutrophication.

Investigating Pollution—and the Possible Misuse of Ecosystems

Now to some questions which may serve as guides to your investigation:

1. Is there any pollution of rivers, ponds, or lakes in your area?
2. What is the kind of pollution taking place?
   a. Is it eutrophication?
   b. Is it dumping of garbage?
3. What is being done to avoid changing the ecosystem?

You may not care for these possibly restrictive questions. You may want to investigate the effect of eutrophication on specific organisms of your own choice.

a. What is the effect of eutrophication in a pond or lake on a specific protozoan of your choice (say, *Paramecium*)?
b. What is the effect of eutrophication on a green alga of your choice?

You may not care to study eutrophication. Perhaps you would prefer to study the effects of biological magnification (see page 519).

1. Is there any destruction of living things in your area?
2. Is it due to biological magnification?
3. If so, which pesticides are being used?
4. Are you certain that your investigation is carefully designed? Perhaps the destruction of life is not due to biological magnification. Factories may be discharging chemical wastes into the stream or lake.

Perhaps your tastes run to another type of investigation, such as research in the history of science.

Pollution is not new in history. For example, before the compulsory treatment of sewage was introduced, our water supply was polluted. Then cholera and typhoid epidemics raged.

1. When was this?
2. How was this pollution controlled?
3. In your investigations, can you uncover a clue for control of modern pollution?

3. WISE USE OR MISUSE OF ECOSYSTEMS: A CONTINUING PROBE

At the right are certain observations made by ecologists. You may wish to select any of these (or similar ones) as subjects for investigation:

Bald Eagle (*Haliaeetus leucocephalus*)

These two species of organisms are two among a number of *endangered species.* ❷ ❸

The Wildlife Federation (Washington, D.C.) lists almost 70 endangered species.

What is an endangered species? Endangered by what?

Are there endangered species in your region? If so, which? What is being done to remove the danger?

Pasqueflower (*Anemone pulsatilla*)

These sequoias are part of the Sequoia National Park in California. ❹

They are part of a natural park preserved by Congress as one of the forest preservation areas throughout the United States.

Is there a "wild" area near you which is the subject of controversy? Is it to be preserved?

(By the way, is there any difference in meaning of the terms conservation and preservation? If so, what is it?)

Sequoia (*Sequoia gigantea*)

529

Farmland in the Tennessee Valley was once facing destruction. Certain of the areas were flooded. Land was eroded. ❶

Then the Tennessee Valley Authority (TVA) was instituted. ❷

What is the function of the TVA?
What are its advantages?
What are its disadvantages?

Is there a plan to conserve a flooded area in your environment? What is the plan?

There are not only problems in conserving the land, water, and air, but there is the problem of conserving people—and their living areas.

This scene was photographed during the famine in India in 1966. ❸

What is the cause of famine? Can it be prevented? How?

This is an example of housing in certain cities. How can this area be conserved? ❹

Not all problems of conservation are like those just pictured. Here are five observations captured by camera.

Take a camera in hand. Are there problems in conservation in your area? Where are your data? How would you act to conserve the area you explored with your camera?

We have the knowledge to make our environment fit for life. Conservation, after all, takes place when we recognize that we are interdependent with our environment.

Then it is very clear that all of us are responsible for our environment.

Then we realize that *all of us must work to make the environment fit for life—and fit for all children who are yet to be born.*

Extending the Concepts

Investigation 1. Try to do these investigations to see for yourself how man through his actions, well intended or not, may alter the environment or cause the extinction of organisms.

    a. Investigate the history of the passenger pigeon. They no longer exist. Is this to be repeated for other species?

    b. Investigate the history of the buffalo. What saves the buffalo from extinction?

    c. Investigate the history of our virgin forests. Do any exist now?

    d. Investigate further the history of the sequoia trees. Will the sequoia survive?

Investigation 2. In one large city, a task force reported that there were many sources of air pollution, for example, incinerators, automobiles, industrial plants, and coal-burning electrical plants. All these, and others, were produced in a year:

    298,000 tons of nitrogen dioxide.
    597,000 tons of sulphur dioxide.
    567,000 tons of hydrocarbons.
    230,000 tons of soot and ashes.
    1,536,000 tons of carbon monoxide.

The task force calculated that for each inhabitant of this city, 730 pounds of pollutants were produced.

    a. If the average person weighs 140 pounds, how many times his weight was produced in pollutants?

    b. What are the major sources of air pollution in your town or city?

Suggested Reading

Parson, Ruben L., *Conserving American Resources*, Englewood Cliffs, Prentice-Hall, 1964.

Sollers, Allan A., *Ours Is the Earth*, New York, Holt, Rinehart and Winston, 1963.

McClung, Robert M., *Lost Wild America;* New York, Morrow, 1969.

McCoy, J. J., *Shadows Over the Land*, New York, Seabury, 1970.

Nickelsburg, Janet, *Ecology; Habitats, Niches, and Food Chains*, Philadelphia, Lippincott, 1969.

Roosevelt, Nicholas, *Conservation: Now or Never*, New York, Dodd, 1970.

Yearbooks of the U. S. Department of Agriculture, *Food for Us All*, 1969; *Outdoors U.S.A.*, 1967; *A Place to Live*, 1963; *After a Hundred Years*, 1962; *Soil*, 1957; *Water*, 1955.

The Microscope:
An Aid to Observation

1. EXAMINING THE MICROSCOPE

The compound microscope is a rugged instrument, but it *is* an optical instrument and its use and care must be thoroughly understood to avoid damaging it. Your teacher will probably show you how to use the microscope and take care of it. The following instructions are, however, basic and should be studied with care. In reading them, refer to the picture and its labeled parts on page 535.

The Parts of a Microscope

The microscope is mounted on a weighted **base** that gives it stability. The upper part of the microscope is attached to the base in such a way that the upper part can be tilted. Some students and their teachers prefer to tilt the microscope toward them for more comfortable viewing through the **eyepiece;** others do not. When you are observing *wet-mount* specimens, which you will learn to prepare later in this section, you should not tilt the microscope. Why? Some modern microscopes are so constructed that only the eyepiece is permanently tilted at an angle.

The microscope should always be kept under a cover, to keep dust from the optical system. Always carry a microscope in an upright position with one hand grasping the **arm** and with the other hand resting under the **base.**

The optical system of a microscope includes the **ocular lens system,** or **eyepiece** (several lenses mounted in a tube). The eyepiece can be removed from the **tube** in which it fits, but this must not be done unless the teacher directs you to do so. The other part of the optical system is the **objective lens system.** Some microscopes have but one objective, yours probably has two (one low power, and one high power), and some have a third objective of very high power.

The magnification of a microscope is the result of the magnification powers of the eyepiece and the objective in use. Both magnification powers are marked. Your eyepiece is probably marked 10X (meaning that it magnifies ten times). Other common eyepiece magnifications are 5X and 7.5X. The most common low-power objective has a magnification of 10X. (Examine the markings on the objectives. If one is marked 10X, this will be the low-power objective.) The total magnification of a microscope with an eyepiece of. 10X and a low-power objective of 10X is 10×10, or 100. A common high-power objective has a magnification of 44X. If it is being used with a 10X eyepiece, the magnification of the microscope is 440 (44×10). Determine the magnification of your microscope when each objective is being used.

A slight pressure by your fingers at the side of the base of one of the objectives will cause it to turn on the revolving **nosepiece.** This is the way objectives are changed from low power to high power. When an objective is in proper position for viewing, there will be a slight click, and it takes additional pressure to move the revolving nosepiece further.

The two adjustments (the **coarse adjustment** and the **fine adjustment**) are used to focus the microscope. It is particularly important that you follow the instructions below on focusing or you may break the objective lens and also destroy the specimen.

Your specimen is placed on a microscope slide (or may already be mounted on a prepared slide). The slide is placed on the **stage** and held in place by the flexible **clips** on the stage. Light enters the microscope through a hole in the stage (the specimen is centered above the hole). The **mirror** under the stage is used to reflect light through this hole and into the barrel of the microscope. One side of the mirror may be a plane-surfaced mirror and the other side may be concave. The concave mirror will reflect more light into the microscope than will the plane mirror. Too much light is as bad as too little light in viewing specimens. The **diaphragm** controls the amount of light that goes through the stage and into the objective lens. Turning it one way opens the diaphragm iris and admits more light. Turning it the other way cuts down on the amount of light admitted.

Using the Microscope

1. Place the microscope on the table, with the arm toward you.

2. You may, if you and your teacher prefer, tilt the microscope so you can look through the eyepiece more comfortably.

3. Place the low-power objective in position so that it lines up with the hole in the stage. Be certain that the objective clicks securely into place.

4. While watching the objective lens from the side, lower the objective slowly by using the coarse adjustment. Lower the objective until it *almost* touches the stage. Be certain the objective does not go too low or you may break the lens and also crack a slide. (NOTE: Some microscopes have an automatic stop that prevents lowering the objective until it hits the slide. Yours may not have such a stop, however, so always proceed with caution.) Notice the direction in which you turned the coarse adjustment to lower the objective. Now turn it in the other direction to raise the objective. When you are sure that you know the directions that lower and raise the objective, you are ready to place a slide on the stage.

5. Place a prepared microscope slide, which your teacher will give you, on the stage (or you can prepare a simple slide to practice on by cutting a letter "e" from the smallest print you can find in a newspaper or magazine and then mounting it as described for wet mounts, page 536).

6. Open the diaphragm until the maximum light comes through as you watch through the eyepiece.

7. Watching from the side, lower the objective until it *almost* touches the slide. Now, while looking through the eyepiece, focus slowly by turning the coarse adjustment in the direction that raises the objective. Continue slowly until the specimen seems fairly clear.

8. Using the fine adjustment, turn it a little one way, then the other, until you have found the exact focus at which your specimen is the clearest. It is not necessary to turn the fine adjustment more than a few degrees in either direction—never more than half a turn.

9. Now try closing the diaphragm. Find the position where the amount of light coming through gives you the greatest clarity.

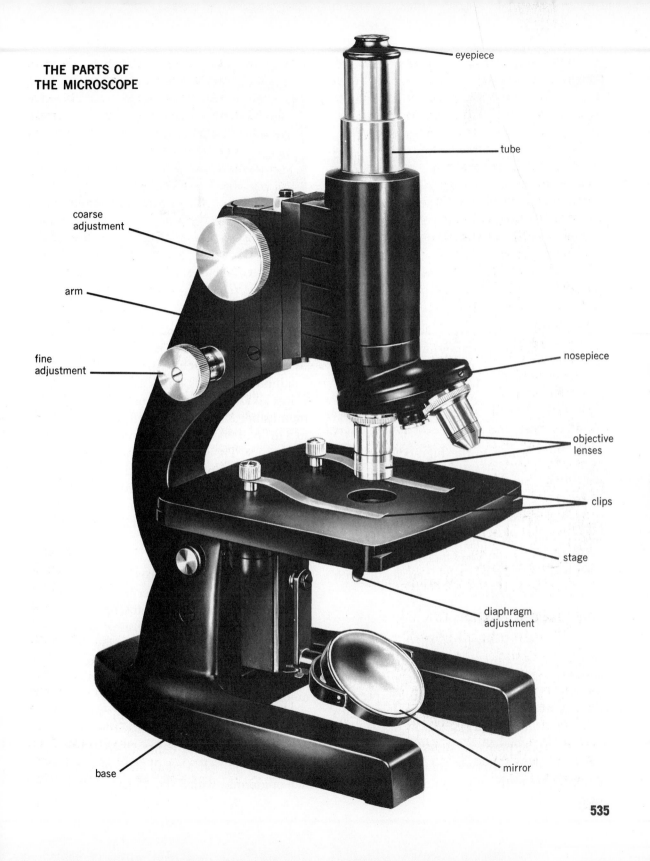

**THE PARTS OF
THE MICROSCOPE**

eyepiece

tube

coarse
adjustment

arm

fine
adjustment

nosepiece

objective
lenses

clips

stage

diaphragm
adjustment

base

mirror

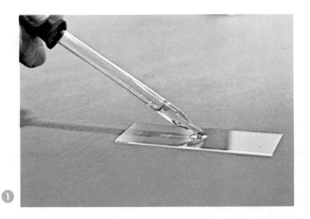

Also experiment with the mirror position. Move it slightly and observe the results.

10. Move the slide very slightly. Notice that the specimen appears to move in the opposite direction. Try moving the slide until you can place and move your specimen as you wish without mistakes. With a little experience you will be able to move your slide to view any part you wish.

11. Now change to the high-power objective. First get a perfect focus with the low-power, then change the objective. Look through the eyepiece again. The specimen should be visible but somewhat out of focus. Correct the focus using *only the fine adjustment.* Always center your specimen and focus first with low power. Only then should you change to high power.

2. PREPARING SLIDES

Because of its great magnification, only very small and thin materials can be examined with a compound microscope. A wide variety of techniques are used to prepare slides. For most work it is best to purchase slides from supply houses. Your school probably has sets of prepared slides.

It is possible, however, for you to prepare simple slides with only a limited amount of

equipment and materials. If you work carefully, you should have good results.

There are three general methods of preparing slides. The first is used for examining living materials such as protozoa, algae, and small bits of tissues (such as the epidermis of a leaf). These slides are usually called **wet mounts** because the specimen is simply placed in a drop of water. Wet mounts are, of course, temporary. The second method is designed to produce **permanent mounts** that can be used for months or years. The third method is designed to produce slides of fluids such as blood. They are called **smears.**

Wet Mounts

SINGLE-CELLED ORGANISMS. Place a small drop of pond water or water from a culture of organisms on a clean microscope slide. (A medicine dropper or a matchstick can be used to transfer the drop.) ❶ Gently lower a cover slip (sometimes called a cover glass) on top of the drop. ❷ Your slide is now ready to examine under the microscope.

TISSUE MOUNTS. Take a fresh lettuce leaf, or any convenient leaf. Tear it toward the main vein, or midrib. Using a pair of tweezers (forceps), pull off a small strip of the tissue-like epidermis, which should have become ex-

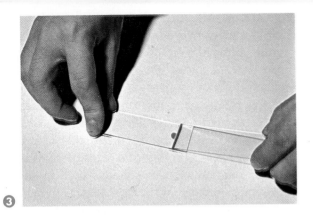

posed by tearing. (It will be a very thin membrane.) Place this in a small drop of water on a microscope slide, and cover it with a cover slip. As you examine it under the microscope, look for stomata and the guard cells surrounding them. The cells may be seen more clearly if you stain the tissue with methylene blue, Lugol's solution, or a very dilute iodine solution. Your teacher may have these stains available for you. To use the stains, place a drop on a clean slide and let it dry. Then, when you later place a drop of water on the slide and add your specimen, the stain slowly dissolves and stains the specimen.

Smears

All smears are prepared basically in the same way. A liquid or semi-liquid specimen (such as blood or crushed tissue) can be spread out on a slide and left to dry without a cover slip. It can then be examined under a microscope. The idea in making a smear is to spread out the cells into a very thin layer. The most important thing is to have completely clean microscope slides. Either use new slides or slides that have been soaked in 95 percent alcohol, dried with clean cleansing tissues or paper towels, and then passed through the flame of a Bunsen burner or alcohol lamp.

BLOOD SMEARS. If a freshly cut piece of beef is pounded, it is simple to collect a drop of the juice (containing blood) that comes out. A freshly killed chicken or a fish are other possible sources of a drop of blood.

In making the smear, place the drop of blood on *one end* of a new or very clean slide. Hold another new or clean slide by one end and place the other end on the drop of blood. Wait until the drop spreads completely along the edge of the slide you are holding. Now slant the slide you are holding until it forms an angle of about 20 or 30 degrees with the horizontal slide. ❸ Now *push* the slide smoothly but rapidly to the opposite end of the horizontal slide. This should form a smooth, thin film of the blood. ❹

After the smear dries, examine it with the microscope. Move the slide around until you find a very thin part of the smear. The red blood cells should be clearly visible.

OTHER SMEARS. You can grind and mash other tissues with a mortar and pestle. Pound and mash them until you have a kind of "soup." Smears can be made of this "soup." It is easy to investigate different plant tissues such as leaves, or you can examine bits of meat. You can stain the smears with dilute iodine, Lugol's solution, or methylene blue.

Permanent Mounts

One primary problem in preparing permanent slides is that the water in living cells tends to discolor the resinous Canada balsam in which the specimen is mounted. Techniques of removing the water (dehydration) are rather complicated. It is perhaps easier to prepare your slides in clear syrup (such as Karo) instead of the more commonly used Canada balsam. The syrup method is described below. The Canada balsam method is also described. It should be used, however, only for relatively dry specimens such as legs and wings of small insects, scales from a butterfly wing, mouth parts of a mosquito, pollen, or a piece of the compound eye of an insect.

SYRUP TECHNIQUE. Slides of small ants, fleas, chiggers, mosquitoes, insect larvae, gnats, and such insects should be prepared first with the syrup technique. Place a fairly large drop of Karo on a clean microscope slide. Use a forceps to place your specimen in the position you want it in the drop of syrup. Now place a small, thin piece of broomstraw at the side of your specimen but still in the drop of syrup to keep the cover slip from crushing your specimen. Carefully place a cover slip on edge at one side of the drop and release it so it sinks slowly over the drop of syrup. This should prevent air bubbles from being trapped in the syrup. Let the cover slip settle and gently arrange it over the specimen. Use wet cleansing tissue to remove any Karo that has spread outside the cover slip. Label the slide and set it aside for at least 24 hours.

CANADA BALSAM TECHNIQUE. This method is best for relatively *dry* specimens such as insect wings, mouth parts, and legs. You can experiment, however, with mosquitoes, and other specimens that you have permitted to dry for several days or weeks. Bits of feathers, scales of butterfly wings, and similar relatively dry specimens work admirably.

If you wish to investigate further, try drying other specimens by placing them in a series of alcohol baths (first in 30 percent alcohol, then in 50 percent alcohol, then in 70 percent alcohol, an hour or two in each). Finally, place the specimen in *absolute* (100 percent) alcohol and leave for an additional hour. After this, place the specimen in xylol (to remove the alcohol) for two hours. Now your specimen should be completely dehydrated and you can proceed with the Canada balsam method of permanent mounting.

Place a small drop of Canada balsam in the center of a clean slide and place your specimen in the drop of balsam. Hold a cover slip on edge and touch it to the side of the drop of balsam as you did with the syrup. Now tilt the slide and gently push it down at an angle on the balsam. Release the cover slip and let it settle slowly over the balsam drop and your specimen. You will probably need to adjust it horizontally by using a toothpick to press on its surface. The important thing is to avoid trapping air bubbles. Wipe off the excess balsam by using a rag dipped in xylol. Label the slide and let the balsam harden for 24 hours.

GLOSSARY

The definitions of the words below apply mainly to their use in this textbook. Many of the words have other or additional meanings in advanced work in science. The page reference next to an entry generally indicates the place in the text where a major discussion of the subject occurs or the subject is illustrated. A few words whose meanings you probably know from earlier work in science do not have page references.

Words are pronounced as they occur within the textbook, according to the following pronunciation key.

PRONUNCIATION KEY

SYMBOL	KEY WORDS	SYMBOL	KEY WORDS	SYMBOL	KEY WORDS
a	add, map	ī	ice, write	th	thin, both
ā	ace, rate	o	odd, hot	u	up, done
â(r)	care, air	ō	open, so	û(r)	urn, term
ä	palm, father	ô	order, jaw	y	yet, yearn
e	end, pet	oi	oil, boy	ə	an unstressed vowel
ē	even, tree	o͞o	pool, food		as in the words focus,
i	it, give	o͝o	took, full		sicken, clarity, above

adaptation, a structure or behavior that enables a plant or animal to live successfully in its environment

ADP (adenosine diphosphate), the substance formed in cells when ATP is broken down and energy is released, and which, with energy from glucose, is then changed back into ATP, 173

air sacs, in man, the sac-shaped extensions of the tiniest breathing tubes in the lungs, through which oxygen and carbon dioxide are exchanged in the blood stream, 119; air-filled structures at the ends of the trachea in insects, and connected to the lungs in birds, 358, 406

albumen, a white, gelatinlike substance, containing protein, surrounding the yolk of a hen's egg, 70

algae, simple plants, both single-celled and many-celled, containing chlorophyll

allantois, one of the membranes that develops around a vertebrate embryo; lets oxygen enter, and forms a sac for storing wastes from the embryo, 455

alternation of generations, the reproductive cycle, mainly in plants, in which one generation reproduces sexually (sperms and eggs) and the next generation reproduces asexually (spores) in a regular rotation, 252

amino acids, the nitrogen-containing molecules that plants and animals combine in great variety in building their particular cell proteins, 169

amphibians, cold-blooded vertebrates, such as the frog; the young breathe by means of gills and the adults usually breathe by means of lungs, thus capable of living both in water and on land, 386

anaerobic respiration, the process by which an organism is capable of releasing energy without the use of oxygen, 238

anal pore, a tiny opening in the paramecium's cell membrane, through which undigested material is discharged, 78

anatomy, the scientific study of the structures of plants and animals

angiosperms, seed plants that develop flowers, 280

annelids, the segmented worms, 341

annual rings, the pattern of rings of xylem tissue seen in the cross-section of woody stems, each ring representing a year's growth and formed by differences in xylem-cell size in different seasons, 141

annuals, flowering plants that complete their life cycle, including the production of seeds, in one year, 287

antennae, projecting sense organs on the heads of insects and related invertebrates, 356

anther, the pollen-containing structures at the tip of the stamen of a flower, 291

anthropologist, a scientist who studies man's past and present life, including the physical and cultural patterns of man's societies, 500

antibiotics, substances, produced by bacteria or fungi,

used in medicine to stop the growth of disease micro-organisms in the body, 241

arachnids, arthropods with four pairs of legs, mainly the spiders, 309

archaeologist, a scientist who studies man's past history through manmade objects and other remains found in the earth

archegonium, the egg-producing organ in mosses and ferns, 252

arteries, blood vessels that carry blood away from the heart, 117

arthropods, major land-adapted invertebrates with jointed legs, including insects, spiders, and crabs, 354

artificial selection, the selection and breeding of particular plants and animals to produce offspring with desired traits, 505

ascospore, a type of fungal spore formed by sexual rather than asexual reproduction, 237

asexual reproduction, a form of reproduction in which a single parent produces offspring; fission, budding, and spore formation are common forms, 80

ATP (adenosine triphosphate), a cell substance that stores the energy from oxidation of glucose, and which releases the energy by releasing a phosphate group, thus making energy available to the cell, 173

auricle, in vertebrates, the chamber of the heart that receives blood from the veins and sends it to a ventricle, 98

auxin, a plant hormone that regulates growth, 198

bacteria, very small single-celled plants without chlorophyll, 239

biennial, a flowering plant that completes its life cycle in two years, producing flowers and seeds the second year, 287

bilateral symmetry, the arrangement of the body form of an organism in which the right and left sides are alike, 344

bile, a liquid substance secreted by the liver, stored in the gall bladder, and which flows into the small intestine where it aids in the digestion of fat, 116

biological magnification, effect of a foreign substance is magnified by organisms that feed on each other, 519

biome, a natural association of plant and animal life in a given climate, usually extending over a large region of the earth, 44

blastula, an early stage in the development of an animal embryo, in which repeated cell division has formed a hollow ball of cells, 388

bone tissue, the hard supporting tissue giving shape to the vertebrate body and protecting soft organs, 83

bryophytes, many-celled green plants whose primitive roots, stems, and leaves are without true conducting tissues; the mosses and liverworts, 249

budding, a method of asexual reproduction in which a small outgrowth from a single parent develops into a new, identical organism, 237

cambium tissue, a layer of actively dividing cells, in certain seed plants, which increases the thickness of stems and roots and forms the conducting tissues, 128

capillaries, the smallest blood vessels through whose thin walls the blood and body cells exchange materials, 118

Carboniferous period, the period in geologic history during which the huge deposits of coal were formed in the earth, 257

cartilage, tough, flexible supporting tissue in animals, which helps maintain the shape of certain organs such as the ear, 85

cell, the basic structural unit of living organisms, usually microscopic and consisting basically of a nucleus, cytoplasm, and cell membrane, 70

cell membrane, the thin, outer layer of cytoplasm of a cell, 74

cellular respiration, 58; see also **respiration**

cellulose, a carbohydrate, the chief substance contained in the cell walls of plants, 71

cell wall, the tough, nonliving outside layer of a plant cell, consisting mainly of cellulose secreted by the cytoplasm of the cell, 71

cerebellum, that part of the vertebrate brain controlling balance and coordinating the movements of the voluntary muscles, 111

cerebrum, that part of the vertebrate brain producing thought, sensation, and voluntary movement, 110

chemosynthetic bacteria, nongreen plants that derive their energy for living from oxidizing inorganic compounds, 211

chlorophyll, the green substance in plants that is able to capture and transform light energy into the chemical energy that can be used by the living organisms, 130

chloroplasts, the chlorophyll-containing structures of varying shapes in plants, 130

chordates, animals that at some stage of their lives have a notochord, gill slits, and a nerve cord, 309, 374

chromosomes, structures carrying the hereditary traits and contained in the nucleus of a cell, visible during cell division, 73

cilia, hairlike structures on the surface of some cells; the beating motion of which enables some single-celled organisms to move, 77

ciliates, single-celled organisms with cilia, 309

circulatory system, the series of organs, consisting of the heart and blood vessels in vertebrates, that enables the blood to be moved throughout the body, 98

class, in a classification system, one of the major groupings under a phylum or subphylum, 226

clitellum, a thick outer ring of tissue, around the earthworm's body, used in reproduction, 346

cloaca, a cavity opening to the outside of the body at the end of the intestines in the frog and many other vertebrates, serving as a common passageway through which wastes, eggs, and sperms leave the body, 98

cold-blooded animals, animals whose body temperatures vary depending upon the temperature of their surroundings; all animals except birds and mammals, 390

colonial organisms, single-celled organisms that form distinctive groups of cells, living and moving together, 310

community, in biology, a group of interdependent organisms in a particular environment, 11

concentrated solution, one that contains a large proportion of dissolved materials, 189

condensation, the changing of a substance from a gas to a liquid, 52

conducting tissue, the tissue that carries fluid substances throughout a plant, 129

conjugation, a method of sexual reproduction among lower organisms, in which two cells exchange nuclear material and often their cytoplasm, 80

connective tissue, tissue which joins, or connects, certain body parts together, 85

conservation, the wise use of all our resources, 519

consumer, in a food chain, a plant or animal that cannot derive its energy from inorganic matter but must depend upon other plants or animals, 8

contractile vacuole, a structure whose function is to expel the excess water in a simple organism, thus maintaining the water balance, 78

contraction, the shrinking in size of a substance as its molecules move closer together, 19

cork cambium, the thin layer of actively dividing cells that produces the bark of woody stems, 139

cotyledon, the food-storing portion of a seed; also known as the "seed leaf," 280

crop, the food-storing organ in the digestive system of the earthworm, bird, and certain other animals, 344

cross, a genetic term meaning the mating of two genetically different organisms

cross-pollination, the transfer of pollen from the stamen of one plant to the pistil of another plant, 296

cutin, a waxy substance secreted by cells of the epidermis of plants, forming a waterproof coating, 130

cytoplasm, all the living material of the cell, other than the nucleus, 70

dark reaction, the chemical reactions in photosynthesis that occur only after the light reaction, 208

decay, the breakdown of dead plant or animal organic matter into inorganic substances by the action of bac-

teria or fungi, 15

decay bacteria, bacteria which, in obtaining their energy, cause the decay of the organic substances in dead plants and animals, 38

deoxyribonucleic acid, see **DNA**

dermis, the thick, living layer of the skin underneath the thinner epidermis, 91

diaphragm, the thick sheet of muscle separating the chest from the abdomen in mammals, and which assists breathing, 124

diastase, an enzyme controlling digestion of starch, 163

dicotyledons, flowering plants whose seeds have two cotyledons, or seed leaves, 280

diffusion, the spreading of one substance in another substance; if left undisturbed, two substances diffuse evenly throughout each other, 187

digestion, a process that changes large molecules into smaller ones that can diffuse through cell membranes and be used by cells, 112

digestive system, the series of organs taking part in the digestion and absorption of food, 98

DNA (deoxyribonucleic acid), the nucleic acid in chromosomes that contains, in the arrangement of its units, the master code for the hereditary traits, 171

dominant trait, an hereditary trait that always dominates a recessive trait in an organism, 427

duct gland, a body organ that delivers its products to another part of the body through tubes, such as a digestive gland, 194

ductless gland (endocrine gland), a body organ (or tissue) that delivers its products, known as hormones, directly into the blood stream, 194

ecology, the study of the interdependence of organisms and their environment, 13

ecosystem, all living and nonliving things that supply organisms their needs for life in a selected area, 61

ectoderm, in the hydra and related animals, the outer layer of body cells, 319

egg, the female reproductive cell of a plant or animal, 233; also, the egg with its protective covering, as laid by birds and other animals

embryo, a developing organism in its earliest stages, from the time the egg is fertilized to the time of birth, hatching, or germination

endocrine gland, see **ductless gland**

endoderm, in the hydra and related animals, the inner layer of body cells, 319

endoskeleton, the internal skeleton of an animal, 326

energy, the ability to do work; when applied to a cell or organism, the ability to carry on its life processes, 214

environment, all the surrounding physical conditions in which an organism or cell lives, including available energy, and living and nonliving materials

enzymes, a group of proteins produced by cells, affecting the rates of particular chemical reactions, 77

epidermis, the outer, protective cell layers of an organism, 90, 128

epithelial tissue, the layers of cells covering inside or outside surfaces of an animal's body, 83

esophagus, in the digestive system, the tube connecting the mouth with the stomach, 107

eutrophication, changes resulting from an oversupply of dissolved nutrients in a body of water, 528

excretory system, a series of organs adapted to removing wastes from an organism

exoskeleton, the stiff, tough outer covering on the body of certain invertebrates, providing support and protection for the softer inner parts, 105

expansion, the increasing in size of a substance as the distances between its molecules increases, 19

extensor, a muscle connecting the bones of a limb (or other body part) such that when contracted, it straightens the limb, 106

fatty acid, one of the soluble products into which fats are broken down in the body by digestion, 120

femur, the upper leg bone of vertebrates, 103

fertilization, the union of sperm and egg in sexual reproduction

fibrovascular bundles, conducting tissues arranged in bundles, running lengthwise throughout some plants, 130

fission, a method of asexual reproduction in single-celled organisms, in which the cell divides in half and each half develops into a new organism exactly like the original organism, 80

flagellum, a long, whiplike projection of protoplasm, used in movement by some protozoans, 308

flexor, a muscle connecting the bones of a limb (or other body part) such that when contracted, it bends the limb, 106

food chain, a series of organisms, starting with a green plant, in which each organism serves as a source of energy for the next one in the series, 16

food vacuole, an area within the cytoplasm of a simple organism where food collects and is digested, 77

food web, the many connected food chains by which the organisms of a particular community obtain their sources of energy, 47

fossil, preserved remains in the earth's rock of a plant or animal of an earlier age, 255

fronds, the large, spore-bearing leaves of ferns, 254

fructose, a sugar whose molecules contain the same number and kind of atoms as the glucose molecule, but in different arrangement ($C_6H_{12}O_6$), 164

fungi, plants without chlorophyll, such as mushrooms, molds, and yeasts, 234

gall bladder, the sac that stores bile from the liver and releases it into the intestine as needed, 98

gamete, the two cells that unite in sexual reproduction, 231

gametophyte, the sexual generation (or stage) in the reproductive cycle of a plant, in which sperms and eggs are produced, 251; see also **alternation of generations**

ganglia, a mass of nerve cells, 346

gastric juice, digestive juice in the stomach, produced by glands in the stomach wall, 115

gastrula, a stage in the development of an animal embryo, in which the mass of cells takes on a cup shape, 388

gemmule, a portion of a sponge which breaks off and is capable of reproducing the sponge asexually, 316

gene, that part of a chromosome determining the inheritance of a particular trait, 427

genetics, the scientific study of how traits are inherited, 431; a scientist working on such problems is a geneticist

genus, in a classification system, a subgrouping of plants or animals that consists of related species, 225

geotropism, the growth of a plant in response to gravity, 198

germination, the beginning of growth, or sprouting, of a seed, spore, or other reproductive plant body, 55

gills, thin-walled tissues in fish and other water animals, permitting absorption of dissolved oxygen from the surrounding water, 379

girdling, removing a ring of outer tissues, including food-conducting tissue, from around a woody stem, 139

gizzard, an organ in the digestive system of the earthworm and other animals; it grinds food by muscular action and friction from swallowed sand or gravel, 344

gland, an organ in animals, secreting a particular substance or substances

glucose, a simple sugar ($C_6H_{12}O_6$); the product of photosynthesis in green plants, 160

glycerol, one of the soluble products into which fats are broken down in the body by digestion, 168

glycogen, a starchlike compound formed by animals and stored until needed, 120

grafting, in plants, a method of reproducing a plant asexually, by growing a portion of one plant upon another plant, 298

guard cells, the two cells that surround and form the stomata in plants and regulate the opening and closing of stomata, 131

gullet, see **esophagus**

gymnosperms, the nonflowering seed plants, such as the conifers, 275

half-life, the time it takes for half the atoms of a particular radioactive element to break down into a new kind of element, 262

heart muscle tissue, the special type of contracting tissue producing the movements of the heart; shows up as striped tissue under the microscope, but is not under the control of the conscious mind, 87

heartwood, the darker, older wood toward the center of a tree trunk; made up of dead xylem cells no longer acting as conducting tissue, 138

hemoglobin, a compound in red blood cells that combines temporarily with oxygen, and thus enables oxygen to be carried to the cells, 122

herbaceous plants, seed plants that do not develop bark or other woody tissues in their stems, 141, 284

heterozygous, an organism carrying unlike genes for a particular trait or traits, 452

hibernation, the inactive state, by which some animals live through the winter, in which all body processes are greatly slowed, 21

high-energy bond, a type of linking of atoms that releases great amounts of energy when broken, 174

holdfast, a structure found at the base of certain lower plants, which attaches them to rocks or the sea bottom, 220

homozygous, an organism carrying matching genes for a particular trait or traits, 452

hormone, a substance made by an organism and which controls important processes of that organism, such as growth, 85, 196

humerus, the upper arm bone in vertebrates, 103

humus, soil containing large amounts of decayed plant and animal material, 144

hybrid, an organism carrying unlike genes for the same trait, 427

hybridizing, crossing organisms with different traits to get offspring with the most desirable traits of both parents, 508

hydrogen bacteria, bacteria that obtain their energy by oxidizing hydrogen compounds, 212

hydrolysis, a chemical reaction in which complex molecules are broken down into simpler molecules by combining with water, 168

hydrovascular system, the water-conducting vessels in the starfish, connecting with the tube feet and affecting their movements, 328

hypha, one of the threadlike structures of the basic body of a fungus, 234

hypothesis, a possible explanation of scientific evidence

imbibition, a process in which water is absorbed by a relatively porous solid substance, 150

impulse, a nerve message triggered by a stimulus or a response and carried by nerve cells, 88

inbreeding, crossing closely related organisms to produce offspring with the same traits, 508

inorganic compounds, in general, compounds that do not contain carbon, 160

insects, invertebrates with six legs, three main body segments, and often, when adult, wings; the largest class in the phylum Arthropoda, 354

insulin, a hormone produced by the pancreas, controlling the oxidation of sugar in the body, 194

invertebrates, animals without backbones, 92

involuntary muscle tissue; see **smooth muscle tissue**

iron bacteria, those bacteria able to obtain the energy for living by oxidizing iron compounds, 211

Islets of Langerhans, ductless tissues that produce insulin, scattered throughout the pancreas

kidneys, the organs that remove waste substances from the blood and change them into urine, 84

kinetic energy, the energy of an object in motion; the kinetic energy of moving molecules results in the diffusion of gases and liquids, 187

lacteals, the ends of lymph vessels within each villus of the small intestine; they absorb digested fats, 120

large intestine, the organ of the digestive system in higher animals that receives undigested matter from the small intestine, 98, 115

larva, the immature form in the development of some animals, which differs from its adult form, 11

lateral lines, a series of minute pores forming a line running along each side of a fish; the pores contain nerve endings that sense disturbances in the surrounding water, 380

lenticels, the openings on the surface of young, woody stems, through which gases enter and leave, 137

lichen, a symbiotic relationship of a fungus and alga, 44, 238

ligament, tissue that connects bone to bone, 85

light reaction, an important series of reactions in photosynthesis that take place only in the presence of light; during this reaction, light energy is absorbed by chlorophyll and changed into the chemical energy of ATP, 208

liver, in vertebrates, large gland that produces bile, stores extra sugar in the form of glycogen, and has other vital functions in metabolism, 115

lymph, basically blood plasma that carries necessary materials to the cells and removes waste materials from the cells, 83

mammals, warm-blooded vertebrates having hair, a diaphragm, and milk glands by which they feed their young, 410

mammary glands, milk-secreting glands in mammals, 410

mantle, the sheet of tissue enclosing a mollusk's soft body and secreting the substance that becomes the shell, 350

medulla, that part of the brain controlling certain reflexes and automatic life processes, such as the movement of food through the digestive tract, 111

meiosis, cell division that results in half the number of chromosomes as the parent cell, 293

meristematic tissue, plant tissue that actively carries on cell division, producing growth and the different tissues of the plant, 128

messenger RNA, the RNA, produced by the DNA in the nucleus, and which functions as a template for protein building in the cytoplasm of the cell, 469

metabolism, all the processes of a cell or organism by which it changes matter and energy from the environment into usable forms, 178

metamorphosis, change from the larval form of an organism to a very different adult form, occurring in insects and some other animals, 388

mitosis, cell division from which two identical cells result, each containing the same number and kind of chromosomes as the parent cell, 231, 434

molecule, the smallest whole unit of a substance that is made up of two or more atoms, 76

molting, the shedding of the exoskeleton and secreting a new exoskeleton during periods of growth, 355

monocotyledons, flowering plants whose seeds have only one cotyledon, or seed leaf, 282

motor nerve, a nerve that carries an impulse from the brain or spinal cord to a body structure, causing it to respond, 110

mucous membrane, thin layer of protective tissue, secreting mucus, which lines the digestive tract and other organs in man, 90

mucus, a slimy substance produced by mucous glands of animals

multicellular organisms, plants and animals made up of many interdependent cells having specialized functions, 83

mutant, an organism that contains a trait not inherited but resulting from a change in its genes, 478

mutation, a sudden change in a gene, resulting in a new trait inheritable by offspring, 478

mycelium, the main body of a fungus; a mass of thread-like structures (hyphae) that absorbs nutrients, 234

natural selection, Darwin's theory that those plants and animals with traits best adapted to the environment survive and produce offspring, and that the plants and animals alive today arose by this natural process throughout the ages, 489

nematocysts, stinging cells in the tentacles of the hydra and related animals; used to paralyze living prey, 318

nerve, a bundle of nerve fibers bound together by connective tissue, 89

nerve net, a network of nerve cells that functions as a simple nervous system in the hydra and related animals, 319

nervous system, the entire network of nerve cells that enables an animal to be aware of its environment and react to it

neuron, the nerve-cell body and its branches, along which nerve impulses travel, 88

nitrogen-fixing bacteria, bacteria that are able to use free nitrogen from the air for making complex nitrogen compounds; often found associated with green plants, 242

notochord, a cartilaginous cord on the dorsal side of all animals in the chordate phylum at some stage in their development, 376

nucleic acids, extremely complex and the largest of all molecules found in living organisms; direct all cellular functions, 171; see also **RNA** and **DNA**

nucleus, the dense mass of living material enclosed within a membrane in the cell, controlling all cell processes, 73

nymph, the young form of an insect that has incomplete metamorphosis, such as the grasshopper, 357

oral groove, the sunken area, in the cell membrane of a paramecium, through which food enters the cell, 77

organ, a part of the body of an organism made up of a group of tissues with related functions, 93

organelle, a structure, in a single-celled organism, adapted for a particular function, similar to an organ in a more complex organism, 82

organic compounds, compounds whose basic structure is made of carbon, once thought to be formed only by living things, 160

organ system, a series of organs adapted to carry out particular functions for the body, 93

ovary, the female reproductive organ of plants and animals in which egg cells are formed

ovules, egg-containing structures, in the ovary of a flower, that develop into seeds, 292

oxidation, a chemical reaction in which oxygen is combined with another substance, giving off energy, 406

pancreas, a gland, near the stomach in vertebrates, that secretes digestive juices and insulin, 98

parasite, an organism that lives in or on another organism from whose body it takes nutrients, thus harming it to some extent, 235

pepsin, an enzyme, in the digestive juice of the stomach, that aids in the digestion of proteins, 116

perennials, flowering plants that have a life cycle of more than two years and which, when mature, continue to produce flowers and seeds season after season, 287

permeability, a property of plant and animal membranes, allowing substances to pass through them, 191

petal, one of the leaflike, often brightly colored, parts surrounding the reproductive organs of a flower, 291

petiole, the stalk attaching a leaf to the stem, 131

phloem tissue, the food-conducting tissue in green plants, 129

photosynthesis, the process by which plants with chlorophyll use light energy to manufacture carbohydrates, 206

phototaxis, an automatic response of an animal to the stimulus of light, 79

phototropism, the growth response of a plant to the stimulus of light 198

phylum, one of the major groupings in a system of classification of plants or animals, 226

pistil, the organ of a flower, containing the female reproductive structures, 291

pistillate flower, a flower containing only the female reproductive structures, 296

pith, the storage tissue that lies in the interior of the stem of certain plants, 142

pituitary gland, a ductless gland, lying underneath the brain, that secretes hormones controlling growth and the secretions of other ductless glands, 194

plankton, the 'floating animal and plant life, usually microscopic, in a body of water, 28

plasma, the fluid portion of the blood, which carries necessary nutrients to the cells and removes waste materials, 83

platelets, tiny bodies in the blood, essential to blood clotting, 84

pollen grains, tiny structures produced in the male portion (stamen) of the flower, containing the sperm cells, 277

pollen tube, the tube that grows downward from a pollen grain after it falls on a pistil of a flower, and through which sperm cells travel to the egg in the ovary, 293

pollination, the transfer of pollen from stamens to pistils of flowers by wind, insects, or other agents, 296

polymerization, a chemical reaction in which two or more molecules of the same kind are linked, forming a larger molecule and releasing water, 165

polypeptides, long-chain molecules built up from amino acids and combined to form proteins, 170

producer, in a food chain, the organism able to make its food from inorganic substances, and upon whom the other plants and animals in the chain depend, 4

proteins, complex, nitrogen-containing compounds made by living organisms from amino acids; essential to protoplasm, 168

prothallus, the tiny plant that is the sexual stage, bearing the eggs and sperms, in the life cycle of ferns, 264

protoplasm, the living matter making up the cells of living organisms, 71

protozoans, single-celled animals, 76

pseudopod, a projection of protoplasm in some single-celled animal, such as the amoeba, 313

pupa, a stage in some insect's development, during which the larva within a case changes into the adult form of the insect, 361

purebred, a plant or animal with genes exactly alike for a particular trait or traits, 424

radial symmetry, the arrangement of the body form in which like parts are arranged like the spokes of a wheel, as in the starfish, 317

radioactivity, the natural decomposition of an element, releasing particles and energy from the nuclei, and thus changing it into another element, 262

recessive trait, an hereditary trait that shows itself only when an organism has two identical genes for the trait, 427

red blood cells, the cells in the blood that contain hemoglobin and carry oxygen to the tissues, 83

reflex act, an automatic response of an animal with a nervous system, in which the impulse reaches the brain after the initial response, 110

rennin, an enzyme, in the digestive juice of the stomach, that aids in the digestion of milk protein, 116

reproduction, the life process by which organisms reproduce themselves, 101

reproductive system, the structures in a plant or animal that function to produce offspring

respiration, the release of useful energy for living from the chemical substances in cells, 123

respiratory system, the organs that take in oxygen from the air and release carbon dioxide to the air, 123

rhizoid, a rootlike structure, in simple plants, that serves to anchor the plant and absorb substances, 234

rhizome, a plant stem growing horizontally, usually underground, 263

ribosomes, submicroscopic structures, within the cytoplasm of a cell, where proteins are synthesized, 458

RNA (ribonucleic acid), the nucleic acid, found in both the nucleus and cytoplasm, that subsequently directs the cell's synthesis of proteins, 171

root cap, thick-walled, dead cells forming a protective cap over the growing tip of a root, 148

root hairs, threadlike projections of the epidermal cells of the root, through which soil water and dissolved minerals are absorbed, 144

root pressure, pressure resulting from absorbed soil water within the roots of plants; helps push water upward through the stems, 149

salivary gland, one of the glands that secretes saliva into the mouth, 107

saprophyte, an organism that secures its nutrients from dead or decaying matter, 235

sapwood, the young, living xylem of a stem, 138

science, the exploration of the objects and events in the material universe, in order to develop orderly explanations of these objects and events; and these explanations must be testable, 511

sedimentary rock, the rock layers formed by pressure from the accumulation of sand and soil at the bottoms of lakes and oceans, 260

self-pollination, the transfer of pollen to pistils of flowers on the same plant, 425

semipermeable membrane, a membrane through which some kinds of molecules diffuse easily, but through which other kinds diffuse slightly or not at all; cell membranes are all semipermeable, 191

sepals, green, leaflike structures surrounding a flower bud, opening as the flower blooms, 291

sessile animals, animals not free to move about but living attached to some solid surface, 316

sexual reproduction, the union of two cells from two parents that results in offspring, 80

skin-gills, respiratory structures of the starfish, through which oxygen enters and carbon dioxide and other wastes leave the body, 331

small intestine, in vertebrates, the chief organ of digestion and the one from which most of the digested food is absorbed into the body, 98

smooth muscle tissue, the contracting tissue producing the movements of all the inner organs other than the heart, and not under the control of the conscious mind, 87, 107

sori, small clusters of spore cases, located on the underside of fern fronds, 267

species, one of the smaller subgroupings in a classification system of plants or animals, consisting of interbreeding organisms of a single kind, 225

sperm, male reproductive cell, 233

spicules, needlelike, solid structures that make up the framework of certain sponges, 315

spinal column, that portion of the internal skeleton composed of a series of small bones running along the back, surrounding and protecting the nerve cord, and giving support to the vertebrate body

spinal cord, the large bundle of nerve tissue running inside the length of the spinal column of vertebrates, 102

spiracles, the external openings of the air tubes in an insect's body, 356

spleen, an organ, near the stomach, that functions as a reservoir for red blood cells, and destroys worn-out red blood cells, 85

sporangium, the spore-bearing case of some plants, 234

spore, an asexual reproductive structure of some plants, 234

sporophyte, the asexual spore-producing generation in the reproductive cycle of the higher plants, 250; see also alternation of generations

stamen, the pollen-bearing male reproductive structure of a flowering plant, 291

staminate flower, a flower that has only the male reproductive structures, 296

stigma, the top portion of the pistil of a flower, 292

stoma, one of the microscopic openings formed and controlled by guard cells in the epidermis of a leaf or stem, and through which carbon dioxide, water vapor, and oxygen enter and leave the plant, 131

style, the elongated portion of the pistil of a flower, 292

sucrose, a sugar from sugar cane or sugar beets, commonly called table sugar ($C_{12}H_{22}O_{11}$); glucose and fructose are simpler sugars ($C_6H_{12}O_6$), 162

sulfur bacteria, bacteria able to oxidize sulfur compounds for energy, 212

supportive tissue, any type of tissue that aids in the support of an organism, 85

symbiosis, a close physical relationship of two organisms, to the advantage of both, 238

syrinx, the "song box" of birds; a structure at the base of the trachea, containing the vocal cords, 406

taxis, a fixed, automatic response of a simple organism to some stimulus, 79

taxonomy, the science of classifying, or grouping, organisms according to structural and other similarities, 225

tendon, tissue that connects muscle to bone, 85

testes, the male reproductive organs, in which sperms are formed, 101

thallophytes, members of the subkingdom containing the simplest plants, including bacteria, algae, and fungi, 224

theory, an explanation of an object or event based upon all the observations that have been gathered, 72

thermotaxis, an automatic response of a simple organism to the stimulus of heat, 79

thyroxin, a hormone produced by the thyroid gland, controlling the rate of metabolism and influencing physical and mental growth, 184

tissue, a group of cells having the same or related functions, 83

trachea, in mammals, the air tube connecting nasal passages and lungs, 124; in insects, one of the tubes carrying air into the body, 358

transfer RNA, a kind of RNA, found only in the cytoplasm, that, under direction of messenger RNA, carries to the ribosomes the amino acids needed to build proteins, 470

transpiration, the process by which green plants lose water by evaporation through their stomata, 150

trichocysts, in the paramecium, threadlike protective structures that shoot out when the paramecium is in danger, 81

tropism, an automatic growth response of a plant to a stimulus, 198

tuber, an enlarged, underground storage stem, such as the white potato, 181

turgor movement, plant movement resulting from differences in water pressure between neighboring cells, 286

vascular rays, conducting tissue in woody plants, carrying materials horizontally through the roots and stems, 146

vegetative propagation, a method of reproducing a plant asexually from one of its parts, other than a seed, 298

veins, blood vessels that carry blood toward the heart, 118; in plants, fibrovascular bundles, 129

ventricle, in vertebrates, a muscular chamber of the heart that pumps blood through the arteries, 98

vertebra, one of the many bones making up the spinal column of a vertebrate animal, 102

vertebrates, animals with an internal skeleton organized around a spinal column, 92

villi, fingerlike projections along the inner wall of the small intestine, through which digested food is absorbed, 120

viruses, submicroscopic particles having properties of both living and nonliving matter, 75

voluntary muscle tissue, the contracting tissue connected chiefly to the parts of the skeleton and permitting movement under control of the conscious mind, 87

white blood cells, various types of colorless cells, in the blood, that engulf and digest foreign bacteria, 82

X chromosome, the sex-determining chromosome, producing a female if inherited in a pair, producing a male if inherited singly, 438

xylem tissue, the water-conducting tissue in green plants, 129

Y chromosome, a sex-determining chromosome, found only in males, 438

yolk, the yellow portion of the egg of a hen and of certain other animals, and which serves as food for the developing embryo, 70

zygote, the cell formed by the union of two sex cells (gametes) in sexual reproduction, 231

INDEX

A page reference in **boldface** type indicates an illustration.

A

Acer rubrum, **225**, 226
Acer saccharinum, **225**
Acer saccharum, **225**, 226
Acetabularia, **459**, 462
acorn worm, 309, **375**, 376
adaptation: to environment, 13, 14, 65, 96, 265, 332–33, 488–89, 490, 491, 505; of organs, 96, 409
Addison's disease, 196
adenine, 464, 465, 466, 471, **475**
adenosine diphosphate, *see* ADP
adenosine triphosphate, *see* ATP
adjustment, microscope: coarse, 526, **527**; fine, 526, **527**, 528
ADP (adenosine diphosphate), 173, 174, 181, 191, 194–95, 215
adrenal glands, 196; rat, **415**
adrenalin, 196
aerial plants, **48**, 49
agave, 55
ages of the earth, 262, 393, 397
air: composition, 203; condensation of water vapor, 52, 53; pollution, **520–21**; pressure, 38, 51, 53; temperature in relation to air pressure, 51–53
air sacs: bird, 406, **407**; grasshopper, 358, **359**; human, 118–20, 124
air tubes, grasshopper, 356, **359**
alanine, **170**
albumen, **70**, 162, 454
alfalfa, 242
algae, 220–24, 229, 263; blue-green, 224, 256; brown, 28, **29**, 222, **223**–24, 233, 256; carotene in, 185; filamentous, **221**, 232; and food chains, 16; fresh-water, 4, **6**, **7**, 12, 14–15, 21, 28; golden-brown, 224, **247**, 256; marine, 28, **29**, 30, 222–23; microscopic, 28, **29**, 30, 35, 36; multicellular, **221**, 222, **223**, **232**; photosynthesis, 223–24; plankton, 30; with pyrenoids, **221**; red, 28, **29**, 222, 224,

233, 256; reproduction, 220–21, **230**, **231**, **232**–33; single-celled, **220**, **221**, **222**–24, 230, **459**
allantois, 455
Allee, W. C., 48
alligator, 400
alternation of generations, 250, 251–52, 264, 266, **268**, 294
altitude of land mass related to climate, 42, 44
Amanita, 235
Amaryllis, **134**
Ambystoma, **451**
amino acids, 125, 169, **170**–71, 182–83, 188, 444, **470**–71, 481; *see also* proteins
ammonia, 78, 163
Amoeba, 83, **158**, 159, 311–12, **313**, 347–48
amphibians, 309, 368, 385, **386**, **387**, **388**, **389**, 390–91, 397; early stages, 389; embryo, **457**; evolution, 387, 397; fossils, 387, 397; reproduction, 388–89
Amphioxus (lancelet), 309, 376, 377, 390–91
anaerobic respiration, 238
anal pore, *Paramecium*, 77, 78
angiosperms (flowering plants), 136, 154–55, 256–57, 263, 275–76, **280**, **281**–300, 432; dicotyledons, **280**, **281**, **282**, **283**, **284**, **285**, **286**, 287; monocotyledons, **288**, **289**, **290**, 291; reproduction in, 291–300
animal classification chart, 309, 326, **341**, 368, **372**; *see also* earthworm
annual rings, **141**, **282**
annuals, 55, 287
anteater, 49, 411
antennae, grasshopper, 356, **357**
anthers, **291**, **292**, **294**
anthrax, 511
antibiotics, 201, 241–42
antibodies, 240, 511

antitoxins, 240
antlers, 92
ants, 360, 368
Anura, 391
anus, clam, **350**; earthworm, **343**, 345; fish, 380, **383**; frog, 98, 101; grasshopper, 358, **359**; human, 115
aorta, **117**, **122**
apes, 412, 413
apprentice investigation into: algae, 221; *Amoeba*, 313; breaking apart water molecules, 213; carbon dioxide used by plants, 207; chick embryo, development of, 454–57; circulation of blood, 119; cotyledons, 281; *Daphnia*, structure of, 366; decay bacteria, 243; diffusion, simple, 187; diffusion, 133; diffusion through membrane, effect of concentration on, 189; drying out, adaptations to, 265; electrolysis, 213; enzyme action, 163; fern spores, 267; flowering plants, reproduction in, 292; flowers, structure of, 425; frog, development of, 388; fruit, development of, 295; genes, size of, 443; genetic ratios, 431; growth of green plant, 204; hereditary traits, 437; horse, evolution of, 483; *Hydra*, 317; making blueprint of water-plant leaves, 9; making micro-pond, 12; messenger RNA, 469; minerals in body, 183; moss, structure of, 253; muscle cells, structure of, 87; paramecium's response to danger, 81; peat, structure of, 259; plant hormones and phototropism, 197; protozoans, variety in, 311; reactions of plants to light, 34; RNA, messenger, 469; root hairs, 147; root system, 143; salt-water effects on fresh-water life, 25; simple diffusion, 187; soil composition, 145; starch digestion, 113–

14; starfish, digestive system of, 331; system, of *Elodea,* 60; tools, prehistoric and recent, 503; variation of light intensity with latitude, 43; vegetative propagation, 299; water, contraction and expansion of, 19; water mold, 236; water movement and temperature, 17; water in protoplasm, 161; xylem tissue, 140

apprentice study in anatomy: bird, 406–08; clam, 350; corn plant, 151–52; earthworm, 344–46; fish, bony, 379–84; frog, 97–102; grasshopper, 356–58; human circulatory system, 122; human muscular system, 108; human nervous system, 111; human skeletal system, 103

aquanauts, 37, 39

aquarium (micro-pond), 11, 12, 220, 378, **525–26**

arachnids, 309, **363, 364–66,** 368, 372, 386

Archaeopteryx, **400**

archegonium, 252

arctic biome, 44–46, 54

arctic food chain, **45**

argenine, 471

arm, microscope, 533, 534, **535**

arteries: frog, 99; grasshopper, **359;** human, **117–20, 122**

arthropods, 226, 309, 354, **355–56, 357–58, 359–60, 361, 362, 363, 364, 365, 366, 367–68, 369, 373,** 386; exoskeletons of, **355;** as largest phylum, 354, 367

artificial selection, 505–06, **507–08,** 518

Ascaris, 323, 326

ascorbic acid, 184–86

ascospores, 237–38

asexual reproduction, **80,** 220, **230–34,** 237, 264, 266, 300, 310, 320; *see also* fission

Aspergillus, **234**

Asterias (starfish), 28, 31, **327–28, 329–30, 331, 332–33,** 375, 432

atabrine, 314

athlete's foot, 237

atoms, 262; arrangement of, in molecule, 164; combining, 61–63; recombinations of, in plants and animals, 61–63

ATP (adenosine triphosphate), **173–74,** 178, 181, 191, 194–95, 215

ATP–ADP cycle, 174, **175**

auricles of heart, 98, **117–18,** 120, 382, 406; *see also* heart

Australopithecus africanus, 498, **499**

auxins, 198

Avery, O. T., 445–46

Aves, *see* birds

axolotl, **451–52**

B

baboon, **413**

bacilli, **239**

Bacillus anthrax, 239, 511

backbone, 102, **103,** 377

bacteria, 77, 84, 224, **239–43,** 256, 445; antibiotics made from, 242; decay, 15, 38, 62, 79, 242, **243;** destroyed by white blood cells, 84, 240; flagellated, **239,** 308; harmful, 240–41; helpful, 241–42; hydrogen, 212; intestinal, 242; iron, 211, 214; nitrogen-fixing, **242;** reproduction, 239–40; rod-shaped, **239,** round, **239;** spiral-shaped, **239;** sulfur, 212, 214

badger, 57, 58

banana tree, **288–90**

Banting, F. G., 194

barberry plant, 237

bark, 128–29, 137, **138, 139,** 282

base, microscope, 533, **535**

bass, pond, **10**

bat, **412**

bathyscaph, 37

bathysphere, 37

Beadle, George W., 480–81

beak, bird, **409**

beans, **280, 281**

bear, 15, 45, 50

beaver, 8

Beebe, William, 37

beef tapeworm, 324, **325–26**

bees, 360, **361–62,** 368

beetles, **11,** 368

behavior, instinctive, 362

bellwort, **282**

beriberi, 185

Bernard, Claude, 194

Best, C. H., 194

biceps, **106, 108**

biennial plants, 287

Bikini Atoll, 27

bilateral symmetry, **344**

bile, 116, 195, 382

biological effect, 519

biological magnification, 519

biome: arctic, 44–46, 54; desert, 55–58; fir, 46, 47, 54; spruce, 46, **47,** 54; temperate hardwood forest, 47; tropical rain forest, 48–50

birch tree, 45, 46

birds, 47, 309, 403–10; adapted for flight, 405; apprentice study in anatomy, 406, **407–08;** class Aves, 226, 309, 403; desert, 57; eggs laid by, 74; embryo, **457;** feathers, 92, 404, 405; fossils, **400;** and reptiles, differences between, 403; seed-eating, 47; special adaptations, 408, **409–10;** tropical, 49; warm-bloodedness, 403; water, 45, 46

Black, Davidson, 498

black widow spider, **364–65**

blackbird, redwing, 10

bladder, urinary: fish, 382, **383;** frog, **101;** human, **125;** rat, **415**

blade of leaf, 130, **131**

blastula, **388**

blood: circulation, 117–21, **122;** deoxygenated, 122; *see also* red blood cells, white blood cells

blood poisoning, 241

blood tissue, 83, **84,** 85

blood vessels, 86, 88, 90, 91, 117, **118–19, 120, 121, 122–23**

blow holes, whale, 412

blubber, 412

boar, wild, **508**

bobcat (lynx), 47, 58

bonds, high-energy, 174

bone tissue, 83, **85,** 86; *see also* skeletal system

book lungs, 386–87

brace roots, **151**

Brachiopoda, 354

brain: bird, **407–08,** 414; earthworm, **346;** fish, 382, 384, 414; frog, **100,** 414; grasshopper, 357, **359;** human, 109–10, **111,** 414; rat, 414, **415**

bread mold, 226, 232, **234**

breathing, 120, 123

breeding, selective, 506–08

Bridgman, Percy, 509

brittle-bush, 55

bromeliads, 49

Brontosaurus, 374, 399

Bryophyllum, **298**

bryophytes, **249, 250, 253,** 256, 268, **272**

bud: flower, 136, 291; stem, **136**

bud scales, 135, **136**

bud scars, **136**

budding, 237, 320

buffalo, 500

bulbs, **134,** 290, 298

bush habit, dicot, 283

butterfly, 368, 490, **491;** larvae, **11**

butyl alcohol, 242

C

cactus, **55, 56,** 58, 290
caddis fly, larva, 13
Calamites, 258
calcium phosphate, in bone, 85
cambium tissue, 128, **129,** 135, **138–** 39, 139, 141, **146, 282,** 298, 300
Cambrian period, 353, 368–69, 386, 485
camouflage, **490, 491**
Canada, arctic biome, 46
Canidae, 228
Canis familiaris, 228
capillaries, 91, **118–19, 120–21,** 123, 195
carbohydrate balance, 181
carbohydrates, 161–62, 164–65, 179, 182, 198, 202, 210–11; in food, 180
carbon, 260; in protoplasm, 159
carbon dioxide, 61, 63, 78, 84, 118, 137, 163, 214; and breathing, 120, 123; in green plants, 131–32, 203, 206–08, 210; produced by yeast, 238
Carboniferous period, 256–60, 268–69, 368–69, 387, 485
cardiac muscle, 92, **117**
caribou, 45, 46
Carnivora, 228
carnivorous plants, **285, 286**
carotene, 185
carp, 10
Carpenter, Scott, 37
carrot: as biennial, 287; cross section, **146**
cartilage, 85, **86**
cartilaginous fish, 309, **377, 378,** 395, 396
caterpillar, 11
catfish, 10, 14
cattle, 506, **507**
cell(s), **70–94,** 109, 348; in balance, 186–93, 198; cheek, **71,** 81, 82, 90; chemical activity, 158–77; cytoplasm, **70, 71–74,** 158, 433, **458–59, 460,** 461–62, 470; difference between animal and plant, **71,** 230; egg, **70,** 73, 74, **232–33, 268,** 293, **294, 388, 407–08, 433, 439, 460, 461** (*see also* egg); energy process, 172–74, **175,** 195, 215; "free-living," **76–83;** frog skin, **71;** and genes, 458–62; of multicellular organisms, **71,** 83–94, 348; muscle, **86, 87,** 171, 178, 191 (*see also* muscle tissue); nerve, **88, 89,** 90, 171; nucleus, **70, 71–74,** 158, **433,** 445, **458,**

460, 461; plant, *see* plant cells; red blood, 83, **84,** 85, 184, 187, 192; regulation of body, 193–99; size, 74; skin, **71;** sperm, 73, **232–33, 268,** 293–94, **433, 439, 461;** as unit of structure and function, 93, 94; white blood, **84,** 240
cell division, 230, 231, 239, **293, 434–35, 436, 438, 460, 461**
cell membrane, **71,** 73, 74, 158, 230, **458;** diffusion through, 74, 114, 118, 133, 149, 187–89, 191–92; selectivity, 112, 191–93
cell theory, 72, 174
cell wall, **71,** 73, 74, 230
cellular oxidation, **214**
cellulase, 345
cellulose, 61, **71,** 74, 162, 165, 168, 345
Cenozoic era, 414, **416,** 485
centipede, 309, 366, **367,** 368, **373**
central cylinder, of corn root, **152**
centrifuge, 460
Cephalochordata, 309, 376, **377, 390**
cerebellum: bird, **407–08;** fish, 382, **383–84;** human, **111;** rat, **415**
cerebrum: bird, **407–08;** fish, 382, **383–84;** frog, **100;** human, **111,** 414; rat, 414, **415**
chameleon, **401**
Chara (stonewort), **5,** 220
chat, yellow-breasted, **409**
cheek cell, **71, 443**
chemical change, 60–61, 64, 65
chemosynthesis, **211–12, 214,** 223
chick, development, 453, **454, 455–** 57
chicken, anatomy, 406, **407–08**
Chilopoda, 309, 366, **367–68**
chiton, 349
Chlamydomonas, 220, **222,** 231–32
Chlorella, 217
chloromycetin, 242
chlorophyll, 33, 129, 133, **184,** 204–06, 208, 210, **214–15,** 222
Chlorophyta (green algae), 28, 217, **223–24, 232,** 256
chloroplast, **130, 131,** 204–05, **221–** 22
Chondrichthyes, 309, **377, 378**
chordates, 226, 309, 353, **375, 376, 390**
chromatin, **73**
chromosomes, 73, 74, 171–72, 230, 239, **293,** 344, 433, 435, 436, 438, **439,** 440, 445, 458, 462, 463–64, 466; as carriers of hereditary traits, **436, 439, 440–41,** 445, 457–58, 462–63; chemistry, 445; of *Drosophila,* 433, 434, 435, 438,

439, 440, 442, 444, 459; duplication, **434,** 467–68; genes carried by, 435, 436, 438, 440, 442, 445, 462; meiotic division, **293, 434–** 35, 438; mitotic division, **230–31, 293, 434–35,** 435, 467; X, **438, 439,** 442; XX, **439;** XY, **439;** Y, **438, 439,** 442; *see also* DNA; genes
Chrysophyta (golden-brown algae), 224, 256
cilia, **77, 78, 79,** 310, **311**
ciliates, 309–10, **311–12**
cinchona tree, 509
circulatory system: bird, 406, **407–** 08; clam, **350;** earthworm, 345, 347–48; fish, 382, **383;** frog, 98, **99;** grasshopper, 356, **359;** human, 117–21, **122–23, 124;** rat, **415**
clam, 28, 30, 31, 328, 330, 349; apprentice study in anatomy, **350;** *see also* mussel
class, defined, 226
classification: Animal Kingdom, 226, 228–29, **309,** 376, 390–91; Plant Kingdom, 224–26, 228–29, **256–** 57
clay soil, 144
climate of land mass, and life, 42, 44–50
clips, microscope, 534, **535**
clitellum, 343, 346–47
cloaca: bird, 406, **407–08;** frog, **98, 100, 101**
Closterium, 245
clover, 242
club moss, 256, **257, 258,** 269, 279, 397
coal, formation, 254–55, 257–60, 269
cocci, **239,** 241
cockroach, 368
coconut palm, **289,** 298
cod-liver oil, 185
coelacanth, **385, 476–77**
coelenterates, 309, 316, **317, 318, 319, 320, 321, 322,** 333; freshwater, 316–20; marine, 320–22
coiled shells, 349
cold, common, 75
Coleoptera, 360
collar cells, sponge, **315**
common cold, 75
communities: defined, 11; fresh-water, 4–24, 26; interdependence, 15; land, 42, 44–50, 54–58; marine, 24–41
complete flower, **292, 294,** 296
composite flower, 296

Ingenhousz, Jan, 202–03
inhalation, 120, 123–24
inorganic compounds, 160–61
insects, 104, 309, 362–63, 367–69, 372, 397; exoskeleton, 105; larvae, **11, 13, 15, 16,** 361–62; nervous systems, 367; number of species, 354, 367; pond, 10, 11; social, 360–63, 368; tropical, 49; *see also* arthropods
instinctive behavior, 362
insulin, 194–96, 198
intelligence, methods of (Bridgman), 509–13, 514
intestinal glands, 92
intestines: bird, 406, **407;** clam, **350;** fish, 382–83; earthworm, **344, 345;** frog, 98; grasshopper, 358, **359;** human, 88, 107, **115–16, 120,** 182, 194, 242; parasites in, 323–26; rat, **415**
invertebrates: defined, 92, 308; higher, 333, 352–53, 367–68; lower, variety among, 333
investigation, art of, 8; introductory into microponds, **525–26**
involuntary (smooth) muscle, 86–88, 90, 92, 107
iodine, 184, 187
iron, in hemoglobin, 184, 192
iron bacteria, 211, 214
iron carbonate, 211
irrigation, 514
islets of Langerhans, 195

J

jack rabbit, 57, 58
jaguar, 49
Java man, 497, **498**
jellyfish, 26, 27, 320, **321, 322**
Joshua tree, **290**
juniper tree, 54
Jurassic period, 276, 397, 400

K

kangaroo, 411, 500
kangaroo rat, **57, 58**
kelp, 30, 222, 232
kidneys: bird, **407–08;** clam, **350;** fish, 382, **383;** frog, 99, 100, **101;** human, 84, 85, 123–24, **125,** 182; rat, **415**
kinetic energy, 187
Koch, Robert, 510–11

L

lacteal, **120**
lake, deep: amount of oxygen dissolved in, 20, 21; autumn in, 18; climates in, 16; life in, 16, 18, 20, 21; spring in, 21; summer in, 20, 21; temperatures of, 16, 18, 20, 21; winter in, 18, 20, 21
Lake Erie, 520
Lamarck, Jean Baptiste, 490
lamprey, 309, 384, **385**
lancelet (*Amphioxus*), 309, 376, **377,** 390–91
land communities, 42, 44–50, 54–58
land mass, climate and life, 42, 44–50
large intestine: frog, 98; human, **115,** 116; rat, **415**
larvae: *Ambystoma,* 387, **451;** insects, **11, 13, 15, 16,** 361, 362; salamander, **387;** sponge, **315, 316;** starfish, **332,** 333; tunicates, 376
larynx: frog, 99; human, **124**
lateral lines of fish, 379–80
latitude of land mass, and climate, 42, 44
leaf, 204–05; anatomy, **130, 131–34, 152, 253, 265;** turgor movement, 286; veins, **130, 152, 282, 283, 288**
leaf scars, **136,** 137
leech, 11, 326
left auricle, **117, 120,** 406, 408
left ventricle, **117, 120,** 406
legumes, 242
lemmings, 46
lens system, microscope: objective, 525; ocular, 525
lenticels, **136–37**
leopard moth, 49
Lepidodendron, **257**
Lepidoptera, 360
lichens, 44–46, 54, **238**
ligaments, 85, 86
light: and chlorophyll, 33; intensity, 33, 43; ocean penetrated by, **32,** 33; required by plants, 204–06, 211; response to by *Paramecium,* 79
light reaction, in photosynthesis, 208
lilies, 290
link, in food chain, 16
Linnaeus, Carolus, 225
lips, 90, 107
liver: bird, 406, **407;** fish, 382, **383;** frog, 97, **98, 99;** human, **115–16, 120,** 165, 181, 183, 190–91,

195; rat, **415**
liver fluke, **323**
liverworts (Hepaticae), **250,** 256
lizard, 49, 57, 387, 397, 400, **401, 402,** 414
lobe-finned fish, **385,** 396
lobster, 11, 104, 309, 365, 368; exoskeleton, 105
longhorn cattle, 506, **507**
lungfish, 385–87, 396
lungs: bird, 406, **407;** frog, 99; human, 119–20, 123, **124;** rat, **415;** salamander, 389
Lycopodium, **258**
Lycopsida, 256, **257, 258, 264**
Lyell, Charles, 487
lymph, 83, 121
lymphatic system, 120–21
lynx (bobcat), 47, 58

M

McCarty, M., 445–46
MacLeod, C. M., 194, 445–46
macronucleus, *Paramecium,* 77, 80, 81
magnesium, 184
malaria, 314, 509
Malthus, Thomas, 488
mammals, 226, 228, 309, **410, 411, 412, 413–14, 415, 416;** Age of, 416; comparison of organs and functions, 413–14; egg-laying, **410–11;** embryo, **457;** evolution, 410; first appearance, 400, 410; flying, **412;** fossil record, 352, **416;** hoofed, 412; intelligence, 414; with pouches, 411; rise of, 414–16; in sea, **411–12;** warm-bloodedness, 403, 410
mammary glands, 195, 410–11
man: and artificial selection, 505–08; classification, 228–29; Cro-Magnon, **496–98;** environment changed by, 509–13; as food gatherer, 500–01; as food grower, 501; fossil record, **496, 497, 498;** as inventor, 501–02; Java, 497–98; as middle-sized vertebrate, 374; Neanderthal, **496,** 498, 513; Peking, 498–99; as toolmaker, 496–98, **499, 502, 503–04**
Manila hemp, 290
mantle, clam, **350**
maple, **225–26, 297**
Marchantia, **250**
Marianas Trench, 32
marine communities, 24–41
Mariposa lily, 55

555

marrow, 85, 86

marten, 8

Mastigophora (flagellates), 309, **310**, 311–12

matter, conservation of, and interdependence, 59, 60–63, 65

medulla: bird, **407**–08; fish, 382, **383**–84; human, **111**; rat, **415**

meiosis, **293**, 434–36, 438

melon, tsama, 500–01

membrane(s): Goldbeater's, 114, 118, 133, 192; selectivity, 112, 191–93; semipermeable, 191

Mendel, Gregor, 424, 426–33, 436, 440–41, 445, 452, 459, 472, 478, 489, 514

meristematic tissue, 128, **129**, 148, 154

Merychippus, **484**

Mesohippus, **484**

Mesopotamia, 521

Mesozoic era, 276, **396**, 398–400, 414, 416

mesquite, 55

messenger RNA, 469, **470**–72, 482

metabolism, defined, 178

metamorphosis: defined, 388; incomplete, 201

methyl alcohol, 242

metric system, 443

micrometer, **443**

micron, defined, 443

micronucleus, *Paramecium*, **77**, **80**

micro-pond (aquarium), 11, 12, 220, 378, **525–26**, 527

microscope, use of, 533–36, **535**; in apprentice investigation, 25, 81, 87, **119**, 145, 189, 221, 236, 253, 267, 292, 311, 313, 366, 443; in apprentice study in anatomy, 152; *see also* arm, base, clip, diaphragm, eyepiece, mirror, nosepiece, stage, tube

mildew, 235, 237

millimeter, defined, 443

millipede, 309, **367**, **373**

milt, 381

mimicry, **490**, **491**

mineral balance, 183–84

minerals: defined, 160; diffused into plants, **190**; in food, 179–80

mink, 8

minnow, 12

Miocene epoch, 416

mirror, microscope, 534, **535**, 536

mistletoe, **284**

mites, 368

mitochondria, **458**

mitosis, **230**–31, **293**, 434–35, 467

moccasin, water, 402

molds, 235, **236**, 480; antibiotics

made from, 241–42; bread, 226, 232, **234**; mutant, 480–81; slime, 224, 256, 308; water, **236**

molecule(s), 188; kinetic energy of, 187; large, synthesis of, 165–68; protein, 75, 76, 168, **169**, **170**, 188; *see also* DNA

mollusks, 309, 349, **350**, **351**–52, **353**, 367, **372**; eyes, 351; fossils, 352, **353**; number of species of, 349; shells, 349

molting, in arthropods, **355**

monkeys, 49, 412

monocotyledons, **282**–83, **288**, **289**, **290**–91; and dicots, differences between, **282**; number of, 291

moose, 47

Morgan, Thomas Hunt, 440–41, 445, 478, 481

mosquitoes: larvae, **11**; malaria, 314

moss, 15, 44–46, 54, **249**, 256; dependent on water, 252; reproductive cycle, 250, **251**–52, 294; structure, **249**–50, **253**

moss animals, 28

moth, 368; leopard, **49**

motor nerve, **89**, 110

mountain goat, 54

mountain stream, life in, 13–15

mountains: condensation of water vapor, 52, 53; cooling and heating, 51, 52, 54; life on, 54

mouse, 47; pocket, 57; white-footed, 57

mouth, 115

mouth pore, *Paramecium*, **77**

mucous membrane, 90

mucus, 92, 115, 342

Muller, Herman J., **479**–80, 482

multicellular organisms, cells of, **71**, 83–94, 348

Musci, 250; *see also* moss

muscle tissue, 83, **86**, **87**, 88, 93; *see also* cell(s), muscle

muscular system: grasshopper, 358; human, **93**, **106**–07, **108**

mushrooms, 234, **235**, 284

muskox, 46

muskrat, 8, **21**, 47

mussel, 10, 349; *see also* clam

mutations, 478, **479**, **480**–82, 485, 489

mycelium, **234**–36

myosin, 168

Myxomycophyta (slime molds), 224, 256, 308

N

natural selection, 488–90, 518

Neanderthal man, **496**, **498**

Necator americanus, 323

nectar, flower, 361

nematocyst, **318**, 321

Nematoda (roundworms), 309, 322–23, 326

Nereis, **341**

nerve cord, 376; acorn worm, **376**; amphioxus, 376, **377**; earthworm, **346**; grasshopper, 357, **359**

nerve impulse, 88, 89, 93, 109–10; pathway, **89**

nerve net, **319**, 321

nerve tissue, 83, **88**, **89**, 90, 93

nervous system: bird, **407**–08; earthworm, 346–48; fish, 382, **383**–84; frog, **100**; grasshopper, 357–58; human, 109, 110, **111**; hydra, **319**, 321; rat, **415**

net venation, **282**

neurons (nerve cells), **88**, **89**, 90, 171

Neurospora, **480**–82

neutrons, 262

Newton, Isaac, 509, 513

niacin, 185

niche, in food chain, 16

night blindness, 185

nitrogen: heavy, **474**; in protein, 168, 179, 182–83; in protoplasm, 159

nitrogen dioxide (NO_2), 520

nitrogen-fixing bacteria, **242**

node, of heart, 93

nodules, of nitrogen-fixing bacteria, **242**

nosepiece, microscope, 533, **535**

Nostoc, **6**, 220

notochord, 376, **377**, 390–91, **454**, **455**, 456

nucleic acids, 161, 171–72, 445, 468

nucleus of cell, 70, **71**, 72, **73**, **74**, 158, **433**, 445, **458**; DNA of, **458**, **459**, **460**, **461**–62, **463**; in pollen tube, 293, **294**

nutrients, 527; needed in diet, 179–80, 182

nymph: dragonfly, **11**; grasshopper, 357

O

oak tree, 47

Obelia, 27

objective, microscope: high-power, 526, **527**, 528; low-power, 525–26, **527**, 528

ocean, 26; blue color, 31, 32; depth, 31; elements in, 24; food chains, 35–39; life, 26, 28, 30–33, 35–

frog, **97, 98**; grasshopper, 358, **359**; human, 92, **115**–16; rat, **415**
stomata, **130, 131**–32, 134, 137, 150, **152**, 206
Stone Age, 497
stonewort, **5**, 220
stream, mountain, life in, 13–15
streptococci, 240, **241**
Streptococcus, 240, **241**
streptomycin, 242
striated (voluntary) muscle, **87**, 106–07
strobili, 258
style of flower, **292, 294**
subphylum, defined, 226
sucrose, 162, 165
sugar, 165, 182; composition, 61, **164**; digestion, 115; test, 114, 163
sulfur bacteria, 212, 214
Sumerians, irrigation by, 514
sunfish, 12
supportive tissue, 85; plants, 129
survival, and theory of evolution, 488–89
Sutton, Walter S., 433, 435–36, 439–41
swarming, 362
sweat glands, **91**, 123, 125
swim bladder, 381, 387
symbiosis, 238
symmetry: bilateral, **344**; radial, **317**
syrinx, 406, **407**

T

tactic response, 79
tadpole, 10, 14, 388, **389**
tapeworm, 323, **324, 325**–26
tapir, **49**
tarantula, **364**–65
tarsier, **413**
Tatum, Edward L., 480–81
Taung fossil, 498, **499**
taxonomy, *see* classification
Teddy Bear cholla cactus, **56**
teeth, 92; fossil, **255**
tendons, 85, 86, **106, 108**
tendrils, **283**
testability in science, 510–11
testes, 195–96; bird, 408; earthworm, **346**–47; frog, 101; grasshopper, 358
testosterone, 196
tetanus bacillus, 241
Thales, 487
thallophytes, 220–24, 256, 309; dependent, *see* fungi; photosynthesis, 223–24; phyla, 224, 229, 256; reproduction, **230, 231, 232**–33;

294; variety among, 229
theory, 72, 440–41, 487, 490
thermal energy, 64, 65
thermotaxis, 79
thiamin (vitamin B_1), 185, 452, 480–81
Thimann, Kenneth, 198
thorax, grasshopper, 356, **357**
thrasher (bird), 57, **409**
thrush (disease), 237
thymine, 464, **465, 466**, 471, **475**
thyroid gland, 187, 195–96
thyroxin, 184, 196, 452
ticks, 368
tidal pool, life in, 26–28
tips, roots and stems, 128
tissue, defined, 83
toad, 10, 386, 389–91
toadstool, **235**
tomato, **295**
tongue, 107, 436–37
tools, early man, 496–98, **499, 502, 503**–05
tortoise, 57, **488**
toucan, **49**
trachea, **124**; chicken, **407**; grasshopper, 356, **359**
Tracheophyta, 256, **257, 266**
traits, 427–30, 436–38, 440, 489; and DNA, 445, 471–72; dominant, 429, 436; and mutations, 481–82; recessive, 429, 436; *see also* chromosomes; genes
transfer RNA, 470–72
transpiration, 135, 150
tree ferns, 268, **269**, 279
tree frog, **390**
tree habit, dicot, 283
tree stem: inner structure, 137, **138**–40, **141**; outer structure, 135, **136**–37
Triassic period, **396**–97, 400
triceps, **106**
trichina worm, 323
trichocysts, **81**
trilobites, 368, 386, 481
tropical rain forest, **48**–50
tropism, 198
trout, **14, 15**, 377
trypanosome, 312
tsetse fly, 312
Tschermak, Eric von, 441, 452, 478
tsama melon, 500–01
tube, microscope, 533, **535**
tube feet, starfish, 328, **329**–30, 332
tube nucleus in pollen tube, 293, **294**
tuber, 298; defined, 181
tuberculosis bacillus, 241, 510
tundra, 46

tunicates, 309, 375–76
turgor pressure, 286, 289
turtle, 8, 10, 16, 397, 400–01, 414
tusk-shelled mollusks, 349
twining habit, dicot, **283**
Tyrannosaurus, 399

U

Ulothrix, **5**–6, 220, 232
Ulva, 222, **223**
uranium, 262
urea, 123, 125, 163, 182–83
urease, 163
ureter, **125**, 408; bird, **407**–08; frog, **100**; rat, **415**
urinary bladder: fish, 382–83; frog, **101**; human, **125**; rat, **415**
urine, 123, 125, 182–83
Urochordata, 309, 376
Uroedela, 391
uterus: bird, **407**–08; frog, **101**; rat, **415**

V

Vallisneria, 7, 533
valves, heart, 93, 121
van Helmont, 202–03
vascular rays, **146**
vegetative propagation, **298, 299**–300
veins: fish, 382; frog, 99; human, **117**–18, **121, 122**; leaves, **282**–83, 288
ventral nerve cord, grasshopper, 357, **358**
ventricles, heart, 98, **117**, 119–20, 382
Venus's flytrap, **286**
Venus's flower basket, **315**
verification, in science, 510–11
vertebrae, **103**, 377
vertebrates, 92, 309, 376; backbone, 377; embryos, **457**; first, 374–75
vestigial organ, defined, 330
vestigial wings, in *Drosophila*, **479**, 481
villi, **120**
vining habit, dicot, **283**
viruses, **75, 76**
vitamin A, 184–85
vitamin B complex, 184–85, 238, 452
vitamin B_1 (thiamin), 185, 452, 480–81
vitamin C (ascorbic acid), 184–86
vitamin D, 184, 186

PICTURE CREDITS

Illustrators: John Ballantine, BMA Associates, Inc., Diamond Art Studio, Howard Friedman, Harbrace Art Staff, Gordon Irving, Cliff Line.

For permission to adapt from original artwork or photographs, grateful acknowledgment is made to the following:

BIOLOGICAL SCIENCES CURRICULUM STUDY: pp. 89, 129, 466, adapted from *Biological Science: An Inquiry into Life* by the Biological Sciences Curriculum Study, © 1963 by the American Institute of Biological Sciences, Washington, D.C. By permission of the Biological Sciences Curriculum Study.

HARCOURT BRACE JOVANOVICH, INC.: pp. 93, 121, adapted from artwork of "The Human Body" by Caru Studios, Inc., New York City. Research by the editors of Harcourt Brace Jovanovich, Inc., copyright © 1957 by Harcourt Brace Jovanovich, Inc.

HARPER & ROW, PUBLISHERS, INCORPORATED: p. 231, adapted from Figure 31.2, p. 469, "Chlamydomonas" from *Principles of Biology*, Third Edition, by W. Gordon Whaley, copyright © by Harper & Row, 1964.

HOLT, RINEHART & WINSTON, INC.: pp. 94, 118, adapted from Figure 6.2, p. 226, and Figure 2.18, p. 38, from *The Living Body*, Fourth Edition, by Best and Taylor, copyright 1938, 1944, 1952, © 1958 by Holt, Rinehart & Winston, Inc.

McGRAW-HILL BOOK COMPANY: pp. 130, 136, adapted from *Botany: Principles and Problems* by Sinnott and Wilson, copyright © 1966 by McGraw-Hill Book Company. Used by permission.

STANLEY G. JEWETT, JR.: p. 13, adapted from an original color transparency of the net of a water-net caddis fly.

ELLA THEA SMITH: pp. 99, 100, 151, adapted from "The Leopard Frog" and "Seed Plants," copyright © 1959, 1960 by Harcourt Brace Jovanovich, Inc., in *Exploring Biology*, Sixth Edition, by Ella Thea Smith.

JOHN WILEY & SONS, INC.: p. 131, adapted from *A Textbook of General Botany For Colleges and Universities*, Fourth Edition, by Richard M. Holman and Wilfred W. Robbins, copyright 1939 by John Wiley & Sons, Inc.

The photomicrographs on page 6, three top photos; 7, second photo from top; 25, all photos; 71, bottom photo; 81; 119, left; 138, both; 142, left; 189, all photos; 220; 221; 222; 311, right, were made in the Microscope Applications Laboratory by Renate Gieseler of E. Leitz, Inc.

COVER: Harbrace

FRONTISPIECE: Brett Weston from Rapho-Guillumette

UNIT ONE: p. 2: top, Woodrow Goodpaster from National Audubon Society; bottom, Grant Heilman; p. 4, Hal H. Harrison from National Audubon Society; p. 5, all Harbrace; p. 6: two top photos, Harbrace; two bottom photos, Winton Patnode from Photo Researchers; p. 7: top, Harbrace; bottom, Evelyne Appel; p. 9, all photos, Harbrace; p. 10, Treat Davidson from National Audubon Society; p. 11, all by Alexander B. Klots; p. 12, Harbrace; p. 15, Willis Peterson; pp. 17, 19, all Harbrace; p. 21, Wallace Kirkland from Rapho Guillumette; right, Miami Seaquarium; p. 25, all Harbrace; p. 27: left, Verne Peckham from National Audubon Society; right, Miami Photo Features; p. 28, Annan Photo Features; p. 29: top, John Kaufman; bottom left, RUNK/SCHOENBERGER from Grant Heilman; bottom center, Winton Patnode; center right, Harbrace; bottom right, courtesy Carolina Biological Supply Company; p. 30: top, Russ Kinne from Photo Researchers; bottom, Dennis Brokaw from National Audubon Society; p. 31, G. R. Roberts; pp. 34, 35, 36, all Harbrace; p. 37, Les Requins Associés; p. 42, R. L. Young; p. 43, both Harbrace; p. 44: top, from film, "Where Mountains Float," courtesy Danish Information Agency; bottom, U.S. Department of Agriculture; p. 46, Annan Photo Features; p. 47: left, Ed Cesar; right, Grant Heilman; p. 48: left, Karl Weidman from National Audubon Society; middle, Walter H. Hodge; right, Harbrace; p. 49: left, top right, and center right, Karl Rettenmeyer; bottom right, John Kaufmann; p. 54, Ray Atkeson; p. 55: left, Mervin Larsen; right and p. 56, Willis Peterson;

p. 57: top, Willis Peterson; bottom, photo by Charles Bogert, courtesy of The American Museum of Natural History; p. 58, Kenneth W. Fink from National Audubon Society; p. 60, all Harbrace.

UNIT TWO: p. 68: top, Hoppock Associates; bottom, photo courtesy Pfizer, Inc.; pp. 70, 71, all Harbrace; p. 72, New York Photo Library—Rare Books Division; p. 73, The Electron Microscope Laboratory, The University of Texas; p. 75: left, C. A. Knight and R. C. Williams, Virus Laboratory, University of California, Berkeley, California; right, The National Foundation—March of Dimes; pp. 77, 81, Harbrace; p. 84, courtesy Richard T. Silver, M.D., New York Hospital, Cornell Medical Center; p. 85, Harbrace; p. 86: top, Edward J. Reith, Ph.D., and Michael H. Ross, Ph.D.; center, Harbrace; bottom, Dr. Arthur W. Ham, Chief, Department of Medical Biophysics, University of Toronto; p. 87, Edward J. Reith, Ph.D., and Michael H. Ross, Ph.D.; p. 88, courtesy Clay-Adams, Inc., New York City; p. 90, Eric V. Grave; pp. 97, 105, 113, 114, 119, 129, 131, 132, 133, 134, 138, all Harbrace; p. 139, G. R. Roberts; p. 140, all Harbrace; p. 141, Ed Cesar; pp. 142, 143, 145, 146, 147, 148, 150, all Harbrace; p. 152: top and middle, Harbrace; bottom, courtesy Carolina Biological Supply Company.

UNIT THREE: p. 156: top, Tom Hollyman from Photo Researchers; bottom, Harbrace; pp. 158, 161, 163, all Harbrace; p. 171, The National Foundation; p. 179, both, U. S. Department of Agriculture; p. 181, courtesy of Clay-Adams, Inc., New York City; pp. 183, 187, 189, all Harbrace; p. 193, Wide World Photo; pp. 197, 204, 205, 207, 213, all Harbrace.

UNIT FOUR: p. 218: top photo and insert, Grant Heilman; bottom photo, Grant Heilman; bottom insert, Harbrace; pp. 220, 221, 222, all Harbrace; p. 227: left column, Arthur W. Ambler, John H. Gerard, Treat Davidson, all from National Audubon Society; Russ Kinne from Photo Researchers; middle column, Australian News and Information Bureau, John H. Gerard from National Audubon Society, Allan D. Cruickshank from National Audubon Society; right column, Gordon S. Smith from National Audubon Society, Otto Angermayer from Photo Researchers, S.A.T.O.U.R.; p. 234, both Harbrace; p. 235: left, Harbrace; right, Ken Brate from National Audubon Society; pp. 236, 238, all Harbrace; pp. 239, 241, left, Einar Leifson; right, S. S. Schneirson, M.D.; p. 242, The Nitragin Co., Inc.; p. 243, Harbrace; p. 249, photo by H. Schiller, courtesy of The American Museum of Natural History; p. 250: left, Hugh Spencer; right, Harbrace; p. 253, both Harbrace; p. 254, courtesy of The American Museum of Natural History; p. 256, painting by Charles R. Knight, courtesy of The American Museum of Natural History; p. 257, Dr. Donald Eggart; p. 258, both, Hugh Spencer; p. 259, 261, all Harbrace; pp. 264, 265, 266, 267, all Harbrace; p. 269, Ruth Smiley from National Audubon Society; p. 276, Harbrace; p. 278, all William M. Harlow; p. 279, courtesy of Dr. Henry N. Andrews, Jr. from the *Annals of the Missouri Botanical Garden*; p. 280: left, W. V. Crich from National Audubon Society; right, Harbrace; p. 281, all Harbrace; p. 284: left, Raymond L. Nelson from National Audubon Society; right, photo by T. L. Keith, courtesy of The American Museum of Natural History; p. 285, Charles E. Mohr from National Audubon Society; p. 286: top, Hugh Spencer from National Audubon Society; middle and bottom, Walter H. Hodge; p. 288, Felix Saunders from National Audubon Society; p. 289, Taylor R. Alexander; p. 290, William Belknap from Rapho Guillumette; pp. 292, 295, all Harbrace; p. 296, Jane Lotta; p. 297, both from Roche; pp. 298, 299, all Harbrace.

UNIT FIVE: p. 306: top, Fred Lahrman from National Audubon Society; bottom, Edward S. Ross; p. 310, Harbrace; p. 311: top, bottom left, and bottom right, Harbrace; bottom center, Triarch Incorporated, Ripon, Wis.; pp. 312, 313, all Harbrace; p. 315, courtesy of The American Museum of Natural History; p. 316, Douglas Faulkner; p. 317, Harbrace; p. 320: top, N. J. Berrill; right, George Lower from National Audubon Society; p. 321, Robert C. Hermes from National Audubon Society; p. 323: top, Dr. James V. McConnell; bottom, courtesy George H. Conant, Triarch Incorporated, Ripon, Wis.; p. 326: left, John R. Clawson; right, Allan Roberts; p. 327: top, D. P. Wilson; bottom, Dr. E. R. Degginger; p. 331, both Harbrace; p. 332, both from D. P. Wilson; p. 341, Dr. J. A. L. Cooke from The American Museum of Natural History; pp. 344, 350, all Harbrace; p. 351: left column, Constance P. Warner; right column, left side, Gordon Smith; right side, Robert Hermes, both from National Audubon Society; p. 353, Field Museum of Natural History; p. 354, Grant Heilman, photographed from North Museum, Franklin and Marshall College; p. 355, H. Vannoy Davis; p. 357, Harbrace; p. 361, Treat Davidson from National Audubon Society; p. 363, courtesy of The American Museum of Natural History; p. 364: top, H. A. Thornhill; bottom, Bucky Reeves, both from National Audubon Society; p. 365, John H. Gerard from National Audubon Society; p. 366, Harbrace; p. 367, both Allan Roberts; pp. 369, 374, Field Museum of Natural History; p. 375, Russ Kinne from Photo Researchers; p. 377: left column, Harbrace; right column, both from Marineland of Florida; p. 378, Ernest Libby; pp. 379, 380, 381, all Harbrace; pp. 385, 386, all courtesy of The American Museum of Natural History; p. 387: top, J. L. Stone; bottom, Stephen Collins, both from National Audubon Society; p. 388, all photos courtesy Carolina Biological Supply Company; p. 389, both from Grant Heilman; p. 390, George Porter from National Audubon Society; p. 396, Field Museum of Natural History; p. 398, Yale Peabody Museum; p. 399, Field Museum of Natural History; p. 400, courtesy of The American Museum of Natural History; p. 401: top, John H. Gerard; middle, Anthony Mercieca, both from National Audubon Society; bottom and p. 402, top, Willis Peterson; p. 402: bottom left, Kirtley-Perkins; bottom right, Dade Thornton; p. 409: left column, Allan D. Cruickshank, Helen Cruickshank, and John H. Gerard, John H. Gerard from National Audubon Society, John H. Gerard from Monkmeyer, Bucky Reeves, H. A. Thornhill; right column, Anthony Mercieca from National Audubon Society, Ron Austing and Karl Maslowski, both from Photo Researchers, Allan D. Cruickshank from National Audubon Society; p. 410, Australian News and Information Bureau; p. 411: top, Willis Peterson; bottom, Zoological Society of San Diego; p. 412, Eric Ambler from National Audubon Society; p. 413: bottom left, New York Zoological Society; top right, Eric Ambler; bottom right, R. Van Nostrand, both from National Audubon Society; p. 416, Charles R. Knight, Field Museum of Natural History.

UNIT SIX: p. 422: top, Mary Eleanor Browning from DPI; bottom, Anthony Mercieca from National Audubon Society; pp. 425, 431, all Harbrace; p. 433: top, D. P. Wilson; bottom, both Richard F. Carter; p. 437, all Harbrace; pp. 438, 442, Richard F. Carter; p. 443, Harbrace; p. 451: left, G. R. Roberts; right, Constance P. Warner; p. 452, U. S. Department of Agriculture; p. 453,

courtesy NORTHRUP–KING Co.; p. 454, Harbrace; p. 458, courtesy of Don W. Fawcett, Harvard University Medical School; p. 463, Margery W. Shaw, M.D.; p. 469, Harbrace.

UNIT SEVEN: p. 476: top, all Richard F. Carter; bottom, Jacques A. Stevens; p. 479: top, Indiana University News Bureau; bottom, all Richard F. Carter; pp. 482, 483, 484, all Harbrace, photographed at The American Museum of Natural History; p. 487, courtesy of The American Museum of Natural History; p. 488, R. Van Nostrand from National Audubon Society; p. 490: left, Ed Cesar; right, John H. Gerard from National Audubon Society; p. 491, Edward S. Ross; p. 494: top, French Press and Information Office; bottom, Staatsgalerie Stuttgart; p. 496, all courtesy of The American Museum of Natural History; p. 497: top, courtesy of The American Museum of Natural History; bottom, Field Museum of Natural History; pp. 498, 499: top, courtesy of The American Museum of Natural History; bottom, Harbrace, photographed at The Museum of the University of Pennsylvania; p. 501, courtesy of The American Museum of Natural History; pp. 502, 503: A, New York State Historical Association; B, Grant Heilman; C, courtesy of The American Museum of Natural History; D, Grant Heilman; E, The Metropolitan Museum of Art; F, G, H, courtesy of The American Museum of Natural History; I, Grant Heilman; J, Brown Brothers; K, Grant Heilman; L, courtesy of The American Museum of Natural History; M, The Metropolitan Museum of Art; N, Union Fork and Hoe Co.; p. 504, U. S. Department of Agriculture; p. 506, Harbrace, courtesy of the Fleisherheim Shepherds; p. 507: top, Grant Heilman; bottom, U. S. Department of Agriculture; p. 508: left, Grant Heilman; right, New York Zoological Society; p. 516, Dr. E. R. Degginger; p. 518, courtesy of The American Museum of Natural History; p. 520, Federal Water Quality Control Administration; p. 521, Neal Boenzi, "The New York Times;" p. 522, U. S. Department of Agriculture; p. 523, Rhoda Galyn; p. 525, all Harbrace; p. 526: left column, Harbrace, RUNK/SCHOENBERGER from Grant Heilman, Eric Grave, Harbrace; middle column, all Harbrace; right column, Harbrace, Eric Grave; p. 528, Walter Chandoha; p. 529: top, Karl H. Maslowski from National Audubon Society; middle, Dr. E. R. Degginger; bottom, Ewing Galloway; p. 530: top two photos courtesy Tennessee Valley Authority; third photo from top, Marilyn Silverstone from Magnum; bottom, Henry Monroe from DPI; p. 531: left column, top, Walter Chandoha; bottom, Harbrace; right column, Laurence Lowry from Rapho Guillumette, Mrs. Edward Finnegan from National Audubon Society, Robert W. Young from DPI.

THE MICROSCOPE: p. 535, American Optical Instrument Company; pp. 536, 537, 538, all Harbrace.

$$130$$
$$\times 18$$
$$1000$$
$$0150$$
$$500$$
$$1500$$